FIFTH EDITION

Educational Psychology

N. L. Gage
Stanford University

David C. Berliner
Arizona State University

HOUGHTON MIFFLIN COMPANY   Boston   Toronto

Dallas   Geneva, Illinois   Palo Alto   Princeton, New Jersey

To our children and their partners and our grandchildren:

Elizabeth

Tom, Jenni, Julia

Sarah, Shelley

Anne, Barbara

BethAnn, Todd

Lisa, Bob, Kevin

Brett, Sharon, Zoe

Carlos, Anne

Leticia, Mark, Sasha

Figure 4.4 adapted from *Introduction to Psychology,* Fifth Edition by Ernest R. Hilgard, Richard C. Atkinson, and Rita L. Atkinson, copyright © 1971 by Harcourt Brace Jovanovich, Inc., reprinted by permission of the publisher.

Part opening photo credits: Part I: © 1991 Michael Weisbrot; Part II: © 1991 Michael Weisbrot; Part III: © 1991 Susan Lapides; Part IV: © 1991 Michael Weisbrot; Part V: © 1991 Paul S. Conklin

Senior Sponsoring Editor:	Loretta Wolozin
Project Editor:	Carla Tishler
Assistant Design Manager:	Karen Rappaport
Production Coordinator:	Frances Sharperson
Senior Manufacturing Coordinator:	Marie Barnes
Marketing Manager:	Diane McOscar

Cover credit: Philip Baldwin and Monica Guggisberg, "The Search," 1990. Free blown, assembled glass. (45 cm × 7 cm) Photo by Dan Kramer.

Library of Congress Catalog Card Number: 91–71992

ISBN: 0–395–54556–0

FGHIJ-D-99876

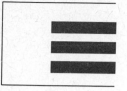

Contents

I

Educational Psychology: Some Background

1

2

The Tasks and Objectives of Teaching   31

II

Student Characteristics

3

Intelligence   50

4

The Development of Cognition, Language, and Personality 104

5

Human Diversity and the Schools: Culture, Gender, and Exceptionality   166

III

Learning and Motivation: Theories and Applications

Operant and Social Learning   224

7

Memory, Cognitive Processing, and the Transfer of Learning   271

8

Motivation and Learning 326

IV

Teaching Methods and Practices

9

Lecturing, Explaining, and Small-Group Methods   385

11

Classroom Teaching   494

V

Assessment

14

The Teacher's Assessments and Grades   619

 # Preface

Purpose

The excellent reception given our first four editions by instructors and students, as reflected in their abundant use and approval of those editions, has encouraged us to prepare this fifth edition. The basic purpose of our book remains the same: to give prospective and practicing educators—primarily teachers, but also administrators, counselors, and specialists of all kinds—an introduction to what educational psychology can provide by way of facts, concepts, principles, and research methods that will be both theoretically enlightening and practically useful. We want our students to take what we present as theory and put it into use in their classrooms.

Organization

This book is organized around a model of the teaching process. Beginning with objectives and student characteristics, the model then presents ideas about learning and motivation, the choice and use of teaching methods, practices, and styles, and concludes with a consideration of the assessment process. Although the sequence of this book's sections and chapters reflects this logical model, we have not assumed that the actual sequence of any teaching performance or episode follows such a logical order.

To make *Educational Psychology* more accessible and useful we've streamlined and reorganized coverage, reducing the chapter total from 24 to 14. In addition, we've restructured the text into five parts focusing on background, student characteristics, learning and motivation, teaching methods and practices, and assessment. We feel that this new organization condenses content into a more useful form for most instructors and their students.

Features of the Revision

This new edition incorporates many of the exciting and useful results of research and development that have emerged since the fourth edition. The text has been revised and updated throughout to keep up with advances in research, theory, and practice.

Part I, "Educational Psychology: Some Background."   In Chapter 1, "Educational Psychology's Purposes and Methods," we expand our explanation of levels of correlation and create new examples of "obvious" research results. In Chapter 2, "The Tasks and Objectives of Teaching," we address the debate on knowledge versus higher-order objectives and its resolution: the dependence of thinking on knowledge.

Part II, "Student Characteristics."   We've added coverage of research on the heritability and changeability of intelligence and its relationship to job success in Chapter 3, "Intelligence." In Chapter 4, "The Development of Cognition, Language, and Personality," we cover revisions of Piaget's theory and the role of bilingualism in developing cognitive competence. Findings revealing fewer differences in ability associated with gender and the latest estimates of students with exceptionalities across the categories have been added to Chapter 5, "Human Diversity and the Schools."

Part III, "Learning and Motivation: Theories and Applications."   In Chapter 6, "Operant and Social Learning," we expand our discussion on the role of punishment in education and explore the form of social learning that takes place in mentoring. Chapter 7, "Memory, Cognitive Processing, and the Transfer of Learning," contains new material on the use of semantic maps, elaboration on the generative theory of learning, and increased attention to the role of cognitive strategies and conceptual maps in learning. In Chapter 8, "Motivation and Learning," we've expanded our section on attribution and its role in motivation.

Part IV, "Teaching Methods and Practices."   We believe that our three-chapter section on teaching methods is unique to texts in this field, providing concrete advice on putting theory into practice. Additions in Chapter 9, "Lecturing, Explaining, and Small-Group Methods," include expanded coverage of the nature, values, and pitfalls of low-inference variables in thinking about teaching, more on rhetorical devices in lecturing and explaining and the value of note-taking, more research on guided peer-questioning in small-group teaching, and expanded discussion of the effectiveness of cooperative learning. Chapter 10, "Individual Instruction and Humanistic Education," highlights new information on learning strategies, intelligent tutoring systems, and an evaluation of the current status of humanistic education. In Chapter 11, "Classroom Teaching," we focus on planning for the use of pedagogical content knowledge, teaching scaffolds (instructional supports), the flexibility of classroom recitation, the instructional conversation, and cross-cultural differences in academic learning time.

Part V, "Assessment."   Chapter 12, "Basic Concepts in Assessment," Chapter 13, "Assessment and Standardized Tests," and Chapter 14, "The Teacher's Assessments and Grades," provide new information applicable to real classroom situations. These chapters expand their coverage of the importance of construct validity, offer further information on interpreting standardized tests, and discuss the possible effects of "high-stakes" standardized testing on the educational system. We also discuss the role of informal assessment—in particular the place of performance tests and portfolios in student assessment.

Features of the Text

The text includes the following features to help students fully understand content and make the best use of material in each chapter:

Chapter Outlines

Each chapter opens with an outline of major content headings. These outlines serve as advance organizers that preview chapter content. Students can use these as a brief structuring of material to come and as a study aid in reviewing chapters.

Chapter Overviews

The chapter overviews provide a concise introduction to the most important topics in each chapter. The authors pose questions about the material to be covered and encourage students to start thinking about what they already know in each area and what they can expect to learn from each chapter.

Recaps

These in-text summaries gather, condense, and clarify research and findings in relevant areas of educational psychology. They provide pauses in which students can briefly review important portions of a chapter.

Marginal Notes

Notes highlighting important points appear in color in the margins of each page. Students can use the marginal notes as quick guides to key ideas and issues in each chapter.

Chapter Summaries

Each chapter closes with a condensed restatement of the most important ideas in that chapter.

Glossary

A glossary providing brief definitions of key terms appears at the end of the text.

Author/Reference Index

This index lists and describes the sources used in preparation of this text. It provides an excellent list of resources for further study in every area of educational psychology.

Instructional Components That Accompany the Text

Study Guide.   This edition, like its predecessors, is supported by a *Study Guide* designed to direct students to the most important points of each chapter. Each *Study Guide* chapter provides chapter objectives, chapter overviews, definitions of key concepts, projects and activities that call for application of key concepts, multiple-choice tests for students to use in monitoring their understanding of each chapter, and suggestions for term papers. All these *Study Guide* features call on students to make active use of the material they have learned in each chapter. Students can use the *Study Guide* as an ongoing aid to understanding text and lecture material and as a review of the whole course.

Instructor's Resource Manual.   The *Instructor's Resource Manual* has been developed as a separate resource to accompany the fifth edition of *Educational Psychology*. It begins with a discussion of the field of educational psychology and of the introductory course. Next, it provides a checklist of things to think about and do in managing an educational psychology course, and provides suggestions on how to use textbooks to define and teach the course. The authors also provide a sample syllabus to be adapted for classroom use and a list of films and readings addressing selected topics in educational psychology.

Test Bank.   Multiple-choice questions and essay questions are provided for each text chapter and are keyed to important topic areas within each chapter. Answers and feedback for each answer, as well as cross-references to text pages, are provided for each correct answer.

Computerized Ancillaries.   A test bank data disk is available in Apple and

Transparencies.   New to this edition is a set of 80 colorful overhead transparencies reproducing text figures, as well as selected tables, and new graphics designed for the transparency package.

Acknowledgments

Helpful reviews of the manuscript were provided by the following:

William M. Bart	*University of Minnesota*
Theodore Coladarci	*University of Maine*
Richard Craig	*Towson State University*
Howard Epstein	*Miami University*
John A. Flanagan	*Colorado State University*
Andrew Garrod	*Dartmouth College*
Venu G. Gupta	*Kutztown University of Pennsylvania*
Dean Meinke	*University of Toledo*
Glen I. Nicholson	*University of Arizona*
Ann Pratt	*Capital University*
Joy Rogers	*Loyola University of Chicago*
Norma Stevens	*Belmont College*
William Stillwell	*University of Kentucky*
Dan W. Stuempfig	*California State University at Chico*
Mack Wedel	*Central State University*

We are grateful for the unstinting attention to detail, schedule, and much else provided by Carla Tishler of Houghton Mifflin Company and for the editorial work of Peggy Gordon of P. M. Gordon Associates. And once again, our wives, Maggie and Ursula, gave us indispensable moral support.

N.L.G. and D.C.B.

Educational Psychology: Some Background

Psychology is the study of the thoughts and actions of individuals and groups. Educational psychology is the study of those thoughts and actions that are related to how we teach and learn. From that study, we have identified principles and methods that can improve teaching and learning. In Chapter 1, we examine some of the broad ways in which educational psychology can help educators in general and teachers in particular. We also look at how researchers go about gathering the scientific knowledge on which the principles and methods of educational psychology are based. In Chapter 2, we talk about creating educational objectives, the first step in teaching, and examine both the need for clear objectives and the techniques for writing them that have been developed by psychologists and other educational researchers.

1

Educational Psychology's Purposes and Methods

OVERVIEW

Psychology is the study of the thoughts and actions of individuals and groups. Educational psychology is the study of those thoughts and actions that are related to how we teach and learn, particularly in school settings. This chapter first presents an introduction to educational psychology and a look at the nature of the research on which the field of educational psychology is based. We examine the basic concepts and the relationships among concepts that educational psychology, like other sciences, uses to interpret and relate significant events. These concepts and relationships help us explain, predict, and control phenomena related to teaching and learning.

Then we discuss the empirical methods (methods relying on experience) used by educational psychologists to determine how important variables are related. Throughout this book we refer to the empirical underpinnings of the concepts and relationships within educational psychology.

But there are those who insist that educational psychology has only the weakest empirical base. They argue that educational psychology tells us only what we already know—common sense generalizations about teaching and learning. We think we will convince you that the evidence shows otherwise. In this chapter we look at several of these common sense generalizations and see how they can be misunderstood.

The Purpose of Educational Psychology in the Preparation of Teachers

Let us start this journey through educational psychology by asking you some questions. How many teachers have you had so far in your life? Just count your "official" teachers, in school, at camp, at the recreation center, and in church, mosque, synagogue, or temple. Don't include your parents, brothers and sisters, or other "unofficial" teachers, although they no doubt have taught you much. Stop for a moment, and decide on a number.

What number did you get? Some of our students have been exposed to well over a hundred people who were expected to teach them something. Even at the low end of the range, most of our students have come across more than thirty teachers—still a reasonably large group.

Now think about those teachers. How many of them were really good teachers?

What number did you choose—four, six, eleven, fifteen? Many of our students tell us that only about 10 percent of their teachers were really good. Thus if they thought they had had ninety-six teachers, they usually remember between seven and twelve as being outstanding.

Now stop again and think about the qualities you had in mind when you sorted teachers into the "good" and "less good" categories. What makes a "good" teacher?

Our students often tell us that their good teachers were those who

- put things in ways they could understand.
- pushed them to get the best from them.
- really spent time trying to understand them as people.
- were well organized.
- had a sense of humor.
- made them feel good about themselves.
- were enthusiastic about what they taught.
- were fair.
- made them feel responsible.

These characteristics of "good" teachers are what we talk about in this text. We discuss ways of teaching to promote understanding in the chapter that describes lecturing and explaining. The idea of teachers' pushing to get the best from students is the expectancy effect we describe in the chapters on intelligence and classroom teaching. We discuss understanding students as people in the chapters on students' cognitive and personality development and in the chapter on individual instruction and open education. We look at ways of building students' self-esteem in our chapters on learning and teaching. We examine the effects that organization, humor, and enthusiasm have on learning in the chapters on teaching methods and practices. Fairness is a topic in the chapters on

*• Teachers evaluate
students' learning
and their
achievement of
educational
objectives.
(© Paul Conklin)*

testing and measurement. We talk about making students feel responsible for
their learning in the chapters on learning and motivation, particularly in discussions of how positive reinforcement can be used by teachers.

We expect the concepts and ideas in this book to help you understand the
tasks teachers face whenever they enter a classroom. And we expect these
concepts and ideas to help you become more like the teachers you think of as
good teachers. That is the purpose of including educational psychology in programs that prepare teachers.

Educational Psychology and the Tasks of Teaching

The challenge of teaching begins on the very first day of school. You walk into a
classroom, put your books and things on the desk, probably print your name on
the chalkboard, and turn around to face the class. Whether this is your first class
or your thirtieth, the moment is exciting and challenging. Your students may be
second-graders or high-schoolers. They may be with you for the whole day or
just for fifty minutes. You may be teaching a variety of subjects or only one.

Whatever your situation, the tasks you must accomplish raise problems that teachers have always had to face. And these problems arise in some form the first day and every day you teach.

Educational psychology serves teachers, in fact all educators, by helping them deal with these problems. Sometimes educational psychology leads directly to a solution. More often it is only part of the solution, a basis for it. In other words, educational psychology serves as a foundational discipline in education just as the physical sciences serve engineering. Engineers designing a bridge or a refinery must have a knowledge of physics and chemistry, of course, but they also must have aesthetic, economic, and political understanding. Similarly, teachers must combine insights from educational psychology with ethical thinking about what is good for their students and for society—with sociological awareness of community dynamics, economic analyses of costs, and political insights into the probable effects of their work on coming elections. In an auto mechanics course, for example, ideas from educational psychology would be combined with

- philosophical ideas about the nature of equality.
- sociological understanding of the community's opinions about female mechanics.
- economic information about job markets for women and the costs of training mechanics.
- political insights into problems of obtaining financial support from the school board for school shop facilities.

Educational psychology can provide insight into many aspects of educational practice. It offers important ideas about learning and about influences on learning exerted by families, business, industry, and the community. It also bears on educational administration, curriculum development, counseling, and other educational activities. But educational psychology, and hence this book, is most concerned with the teaching and learning processes in classrooms. More precisely, we deal primarily with the problems that arise in carrying out the tasks of teaching.

Passion and Educational Psychology

Like most textbooks, this one is written in something of a neutral, dispassionate style. That style should not deceive you. This book deals with the hopes and fears, the joys and sorrows, the loves and hates, the successes and failures, the glorious clarities and desperate confusions of human beings. Beneath what is described in the cold abstractions and analyses of these chapters, there lie the emotional depths and peaks of real life:

- The confusion of an 8-year-old girl caught up in a conflict between her teacher and her best friend.

- The depression of a tenth-grade boy who is convinced that he will never amount to anything.
- The embarrassment of a 15-year-old girl who cannot keep her mind on her geometry lesson.
- The confusion of a third-grade class of Mexican-American children trying to understand a unit on given names and surnames.
- The anxiety of a high-school senior as he goes off to take the Scholastic Aptitude Test.
- The bitterness of an African–American eleventh-grader with a trigonometry class whose relevance to his impending unemployment he cannot see.

Educational psychology also deals with the brighter side of life:

- The change from failure to mastery by half of a fifth-grade class in its achievement in reading and mathematics.
- The switch from disruptive student behavior to concentration on tasks in a ninth-grade general science class.
- An increase of average scores on reading tests to a level previously unknown for classes in the poorest district of a city.
- The winning of a college scholarship by a girl who had appeared, in the sixth grade, to be an early dropout.

Educational Psychology in Action

Let's look at an example of how research in educational psychology combined with a concern for practice can help teachers meet the challenge of teaching. Consider the problems of classroom management faced by all teachers—especially novice teachers. Novices realize that some reasonable level of classroom order is necessary for learning, but they worry about creating that order.

This problem has been attacked by many researchers. One successful approach was developed by L. M. Anderson, Evertson, and Brophy (1979). They were interested in improving reading achievement in first-grade classes serving middle-class children in a small city in Texas. They focused on how to run a reading group in an effective way. They became familiar with the objectives of reading instruction at that grade level in that community. They studied the characteristics of the students in the schools. They observed the way in which the students went about their learning and how they were given appropriate motivation. They also observed the teaching practices and styles of the teachers in the community's first-grade classes, especially during reading-instruction periods. Finally they became familiar with the tests and other ways in which evaluation of the pupils' reading achievement was obtained.

On the basis of what they knew about previous research findings and the schools with which they were working, the researchers devised a special

• *This book and educational psychology deal with the hopes and fears of human beings. (© 1987 Susan Lapides)*

training program to help teachers learn about some successful teaching practices. The classes whose teachers used the research-based teaching practices scored, on the average, about 30 percentile ranks higher on an achievement test of reading than did the classes of teachers who did not use the research-based recommendations. The research informed teachers about more effective ways to manage reading groups, and the teachers were influenced by that research to change their practices. Their new ways of teaching led to much higher levels of achievement. This is, of course, a major purpose of research in education. Research in educational psychology should provide teachers with information about the tasks they must face so that they can make informed decisions. Research cannot tell teachers exactly what to do with their class in their setting, but at its best, it helps teachers make wiser decisions in the settings they are in. We now look more closely at the research and the methods upon which educational psychology depends.

The Research Results of Educational Psychology: Obvious or Not?

Some people question the results that have emerged from psychological studies of teaching and learning. Phillips (1985), for example, regarded research on the importance of students' spending time engaged with their subject matter as revealing only a truism: "One gets the sense that these findings [about instructional time] are almost necessarily (and perhaps even trivially) true" (p. 311). "Indeed, it suddenly seems strange to dress up these truisms as 'findings' " (p. 312). Similarly, a newspaper article on a government document entitled *What Works,* which discussed research findings considered potentially helpful to schools and teachers, was headlined "Researching the Obvious" (*Arizona Daily Star,* March 8, 1988). And in the June 1990 issue of *The Atlantic Monthly,* Murphy (1990) said, "A recent survey (by me) of recent social-science findings . . . turned up no ideas or conclusions that can't be found in Bartlett's or any other encyclopedia of quotations" (p. 22).

Let's look at a few "obvious" generalizations from research on teaching:

Some "obvious" propositions

1. When first-grade teachers work on reading with a small group of children, some attend closely to just those children in the small group, whereas others monitor children's activities throughout the classroom. The class's reading achievement is higher *when teachers monitor just the children in the small group.*
2. When teaching reading, some third-grade teachers make greater use of paper-and-pencil activities, such as textbooks and workbooks, whereas others rely more on manipulatives, such as games and toys. Reading achievement is higher *when teachers use more manipulatives and fewer paper-and-pencil activities.*
3. In grades 1–9, students were found to get better scores on achievement tests in classes with *less teacher control and more student freedom to select activities.*
4. Some teachers work hard to create a warm, positive emotional climate in their classes, showing a lot of concern for children's feelings *and* giving praise frequently. Others maintain a friendly but more businesslike climate. For third- to sixth-grade children from middle-class families, achievement is higher *when teachers maintain a warm and not so businesslike emotional climate.*

People with varying degrees of closeness to teaching (engineering students, psychology students, teacher trainees, and teachers) in both the United States and Singapore were asked to rate these research findings on a four-point scale: (1) extremely obvious, (2) obvious, (3) unobvious, (4) extremely unobvious. "Obvious" was defined as "self-evident . . . the researchers were almost certain to find what they did." Before you read further, you might try to rate these four propositions, just as the subjects did in this research study.

The four groups of people in each country (1,215 in all) did indeed rate each of these "findings" (and several others not given here) as obvious. But what is interesting is that they rated the "finding" as obvious both when it was the actual finding and when it was the *opposite* of the actual finding. Half the people in this study got the actual finding to rate and half got the opposite of the actual finding. The opposites of the actual findings were stated in the preceding list. Did you rate these as obvious findings, as did many of the raters of this study?

The actual findings from educational research are these:

1. When first-grade teachers work on reading with a small group of children, some attend closely to just those children in the small group, whereas others monitor children's activities throughout the classroom. The class's reading achievement is higher *when teachers monitor the whole class.*

2. When teaching reading, some third-grade teachers make greater use of paper-and-pencil activities, such as textbooks and work-books, whereas others rely more on manipulatives, such as games and toys. Reading achievement is higher *when teachers use more paper-and-pencil activities and fewer manipulatives.*

3. In grades 1–9, students were found to get better scores on achievement tests in classes with *more teacher control and less student freedom to select learning experiences.*

4. Some teachers work hard to create a warm, positive emotional climate in their classes, showing a lot of concern for children's feelings *and* giving praise frequently. Others maintain a friendly but more businesslike climate. For third- to sixth-grade children of relatively high economic status, achievement is higher *when teachers maintain a more business-like climate.*

BUT!

In short, this study by L. Wong (1987) showed that people tend to consider research findings obvious regardless of whether the "finding" is what was actually found or the opposite of what was actually found. The same result was obtained by Baratz (1983) for social research findings in areas other than teaching. The idea that research in educational psychology yields only the obvious is stronger than people realized, because *intelligent judges regard findings as obvious even when they are the opposite of what was actually found!* As Baratz stated, "No matter which result was presented, the majority of the subjects thought they could have predicted it" (pp. 25–26).

As Lazarsfeld (1949) commented after a similar discussion: "Obviously something is wrong with the entire argument of 'obviousness.'" Many of the generalizations about human behavior that nonresearchers are ready to endorse turn out to be simply untrue or insufficiently qualified. Almost any flat statement, delivered with conviction—without ifs, ands, or buts—strikes us as not only unquestionable but also obvious. This effect occurs especially in areas like human behavior and education, with which everyone is very familiar. What

Inappropriateness of obviousness argument

we need is research evidence to back up even the most "obvious" generalizations. "The feeling that a research result is obvious is untrustworthy" (Gage, 1991, p. 15).

The Concepts and Principles of Educational Psychology

Like any science, educational psychology uses concepts, principles, and methods. Here we focus on the concepts and principles; we discuss the methods later in this chapter.

   Concepts in educational psychology refer to aspects of our behavior, mental processes, and the environment as we become involved in educational activity. For example, concepts about behavior and educational environments include intelligence, engaged time with the curriculum, aggression, anxiety, cooperative learning, teacher fairness, and lecture methods. Concepts about mental processes are attention, encoding, and memory. A concept is the organized information we have about an entity. Everything we know about intelligence or memory constitutes our concept of intelligence or our concept of memory. Concepts have boundaries and relationships. Thus, when we think about intelligence, we do not usually think about the concept of honesty, but we might very well think about school achievement, another concept. The meaning, boundaries, and relationships connected with a concept are derived from everything we know about that concept.

The *principles* of educational psychology describe relationships between concepts. For example, "Intelligence is positively related to school achievement," "Cooperative learning environments influence student attention," and "Students tend to remember best what is taught at the beginning and end of lectures, not what is taught in the middle" are all principles. When we link concepts by stating some kind of relationship, we are developing a principle.

Concepts and Variables

Concepts may take the form of *variables*—attributes that vary among individuals or events. The concept of human intelligence, for example, is a variable because human beings vary in intelligence.

What we mean by a *concept* is partly a matter of definition and partly a matter of the methods of studying the concept or measuring the corresponding variable. For example, the meaning of the concept of intelligence depends in part on how we define *intelligence*. Generally our definition rules out moral considerations. Highly intelligent people may or may not be kind or honest. The definition also distinguishes intelligence from wisdom. Highly intelligent people may or may not handle practical or personal matters wisely. The psychologist's concept of intelligence usually emphasizes speed and ability in solving problems expressed in verbal, mathematical, or spatial (that is, geometric or diagrammatic) symbols.

Psychology deals with many unique concepts and variables. Much of this book is concerned with the concepts that have been developed by educational psychology—broad concepts such as intelligence, learning, attitude, and motive, and more specific concepts such as stimulus control (which refers to how behavior is elicited in one situation and not another), content validity (whether subject-matter items on an achievement test are those that a student has been taught), and teacher warmth.

Example of a concept: Intelligence

Qualitative and Quantitative Variables.   How do we identify and define variables? Typically they come from our own experience—either informal or arranged. The qualitative researcher, describing events, and the quantitative researcher, measuring characteristics of events, both contribute variables from their experience for us to consider. What is important is to analyze both the inner thoughts and the outer behavior of people under study in ways that are valuable to observers and participants. The observer tries to find out how the people—say, students and teachers—perceive, feel about, and understand what is going on in a given situation—say, the classroom. Therefore, instead of leaping immediately to make up a set of predefined variables, the qualitative researcher tries to get deeply involved in the world of the people being studied. Research of this kind has been called *interpretive research* (Erickson, 1986). Interpretive research is concerned with the meaning of events for the people involved in them.

Interpretive research

An example of what qualitative research can yield is Rist's (1973) study of an urban school. He described in great detail how a kindergarten teacher, on the eighth day of school, divided her students into three "ability" groups based only on nonacademic criteria: appearance, demeanor, her beliefs about their family's income, and the like. The teacher expected and got different performances from the three groups of students, and these differences were fostered and helped to persist in later grades by the teachers of these students. None of this would have been revealed without the sensitive and thorough observations of the qualitative researcher.

Possibility vs. probability

Studying a single classroom or school could demonstrate the *possibility* of a social-class bias on the part of a teacher or school. But what about its *probability?* Here we need evidence from more situations and quantitative treatment of the variables. Haller and Davis (1980) questioned whether reading achievement or socioeconomic status had more to do with assignment to reading groups in thirty-seven classes in grades 4 through 6 in four school districts. They found "little support" for any high probability of what Rist had shown to be a possibility. That is, student social class did not play a major role in teachers' assignments of students to reading groups. What qualitative research revealed to be possible was shown by quantitative research to be improbable in the four districts studied. Both kinds of research, then, contribute to our understanding of educational variables.

Alterable and Unalterable Variables.   Because education is aimed at *causing* wanted changes in people—in their knowledge, skills, and attitudes—the discovery of ways to cause these changes has great practical importance. So, as B. S. Bloom (1980) pointed out, educational psychologists should be more interested in *alterable variables* and less interested in those that seem unchangeable or static. For example, "available time" for a school subject—say, the number of days of instruction in algebra—is usually determined by school law. It is not nearly as easy to change as "time on task," which the teacher can increase through certain teaching practices. "Intelligence" is less alterable than "entering ability," the specific knowledge needed for learning a particular subject. "Parent status" or "student's socioeconomic background" is less alterable than a "home environment process" like parents' encouraging their child to do well in school. Alterable variables have greater promise, almost by definition, for improving education. In later chapters we look at examples of many of them in use.

Relatively unalterable variables, however, are also worth studying. Even if these variables cannot be manipulated to control or improve education, they can help us understand education. And sometimes we can adapt educational practices to unchangeable student characteristics, such as ethnic background, socioeconomic status, or gender, as we see in Chapter 5. In making these kinds of adaptations, we need to learn how relatively unalterable variables are related to the connections between educational processes and outcomes. So we study student gender, for example, and discover that girls tend to do less well than boys after instruction on certain spatial tasks and that boys tend to do less well

• *We need to learn how variables unalterable by the home teacher, such as home environment, are related to educational processes. (© Ellis Herwig/The Picture Cube)*

than girls after instruction on certain verbal tasks (see Chapter 5). Knowing these tendencies from studies of the unalterable variable "student gender," we have a better understanding of some educational problems.

Principles

In addition to dealing with concepts, educational psychology is concerned with descriptive principles, or statements that describe the relationships between variables. For example, individuals who have higher intelligence tend to achieve more scholastically. This is a principle. It describes a relationship between two variables (intelligence and scholastic achievement). If a principle is firmly established, it is called a *law*. Scientific principles and laws serve as guidelines for practice. For example, we have learned that students with high need for social acceptance (a concept or variable) tend to achieve more (a relationship) with teachers who show a lot of warmth (a concept or variable). So we might suggest that a teacher display more warmth with certain students to see to it that the students' needs are met.

Laws

Scientific principles, including the relationships between the variables of educational psychology, are not simply matters of definition, as they are in logic or mathematics. They must be derived empirically; that is, they must be based on experience. Educational psychology is an empirical science: It accepts a relationship as a principle or law only if that relationship agrees with the facts of experience as determined by systematically collected data.

Using Concepts and Principles in Explanation, Prediction, and Control

Objectives of science

The objectives of educational psychology, like those of any science, are to explain, predict, and control the phenomena with which it is concerned. To *explain* is to account for relationships between variables in ways that are reasonable, logical, and justifiable. That is, the relationships make sense in terms of everything we know at that time. To *predict* is to foretell, with better-than-chance accuracy, the value of one variable given knowledge of the value of another variable. Predictions are educated guesses, or *hypotheses*. To *control* is to manipulate (to administer in varying amounts) one variable in such a way as to change the value of another variable. When we try to improve our students' level of learning, concentration, or memory, we are trying to control these variables. Let's look at examples of how all three of these goals have been attained in educational psychology.

An Example of Explanation

As an example of explanation, we can use the work of educational psychologists (summarized by Berliner, 1990) who set out to discover why some classes achieve much more than others in reading, mathematics, and other subjects. The researchers observed in the classrooms and gradually developed a tentative explanation of what made the difference between the high-achievement and low-achievement classes. They got the impression from their observations and other sources that class time was being used differently in the various classes. Some teachers allocated more time to, say, reading and mathematics than other teachers did. Also some teachers appeared to use allocated time more efficiently, so that their students were "engaged" with the subject matter for a much higher percentage of the allocated time. The researchers developed theories that used instructional time as a key concept and made well-substantiated arguments about the importance of time in learning. They identified logical relationships between the variables.

Logical relationships

An Example of Prediction

This explanation based on instructional time seemed plausible. But educational psychologists realized the idea would be on firmer ground if it was found to have predictive power, that is, if instructional time turned out to predict achievement.

So the researchers measured allocated time and engaged time in several dozen classrooms at the same grade level. Later in the school year they measured reading achievement. They found that the earlier-in-the-year measures of allocated and, especially, engaged time in the classrooms actually predicted end-of-year gains in reading achievement. They had found a temporal relationship between the variables. The predictions held up even when other factors, such as the ability level and average income level of the classes' families, were held constant. The predictive power of the use-of-time measures supported the attempt to use this concept to explain differences in class achievement.

Temporal relationships

An Example of Control

For an example of control, we turn to the work of educational psychologists who wanted to see whether changing teaching practices would change (that is, exert control over) class achievement. Gage and Needels (1989) reviewed thirteen experiments of this kind conducted by different teams of researchers. Each team picked teaching practices that had turned out in earlier studies to predict class achievement. Then they educated one group of teachers (the experimental group) in the use of those practices. Another group of teachers, much the same as the experimental group in important ways, received no instruction in the teaching practices until the study was over; this was the control group. The two groups of teachers were carefully observed as they went about their classroom work. It turned out that, in twelve of the thirteen studies, the experimental group used many of the recommended teaching practices much more than did the control (untreated) group. And most important, in those twelve studies the classes of the experimental-group teachers did much better on achievement tests. So the use of the teaching practices that predicted achievement also had value for controlling, or changing, achievement. A causal relationship had been found.

Causal relationships

Later, when the effective teaching practices were examined to discover why they might have improved achievement, it seemed that they improved the use of time in the classroom. The effective practices worked because they reduced disruptive behavior, captured and maintained student attention, induced students to participate in learning activities, reduced the time students had to wait to have their written work checked, and so on. This explanation, then, provided us with logical understandings about why some variable predicts achievement or can control (cause a change in the level of) achievement.

Explanation, Prediction, and Control: Their Interaction

Explanation, prediction, and control are different, yet largely interdependent, goals of research and science. Sometimes we can at least partially explain but not predict or control very well, as in the case of earthquakes and volcanoes. Sometimes we can predict or control without explaining ourselves very well, as in the case of taking aspirin to relieve a headache—a practice that worked successfully for decades before anyone explained why. Sometimes we can explain and predict very well, without having any control, as in the case of the motion of the planets in our solar system. But as much as possible scientists, including educational psychologists, want to reach all three goals when they study the phenomena they are concerned about.

RECAP

The three goals of scientific effort—explanation, prediction, and control—depend on certain kinds of relationships between variables. Explanation depends on rational, sensible, and logical relationships; prediction depends on temporal (time) relationships; and control depends on causal, or functional, relationships. The three kinds of relationships are not at all the same; we can have one without the others, at least to some degree. As we study teaching and learning, we use all three kinds of relationships—logical, temporal, and causal. Each has value for specific purposes.

Methods for Relating Variables

As we have said, scientific effort is aimed at explanation, prediction, and control. All three of these objectives require the discovery of relationships between variables. We have already classified these relationships according to whether they are logical, temporal, or causal. Here we classify relationships according to the three main ways of studying them: correlation, experimentation, and interpretation.

Correlational and Causal Relationships: The Differences

A *correlational relationship* indicates that certain values of one variable tend to be found together with certain values of another variable. For example:

More high-scoring students on a scholastic aptitude test tend to become honor students.
Fewer middle-class than economically poor students tend to drop out of school.

Correlations may or may not reflect a cause and effect. If variable A correlates with variable B, it may be because, among many other possibilities,

- A causes B: $A \longrightarrow B$
- B causes A: $A \longleftarrow B$
- A and B cause each other: $A \longleftrightarrow B$
- C causes A and B: $C \underset{B}{\overset{A}{\diagdown}}$
- E causes C and D; and C causes A; D causes B: $E \underset{D \longrightarrow B}{\overset{C \longrightarrow A}{\diagdown}}$

FIGURE 1.1

Cause or Correlation?

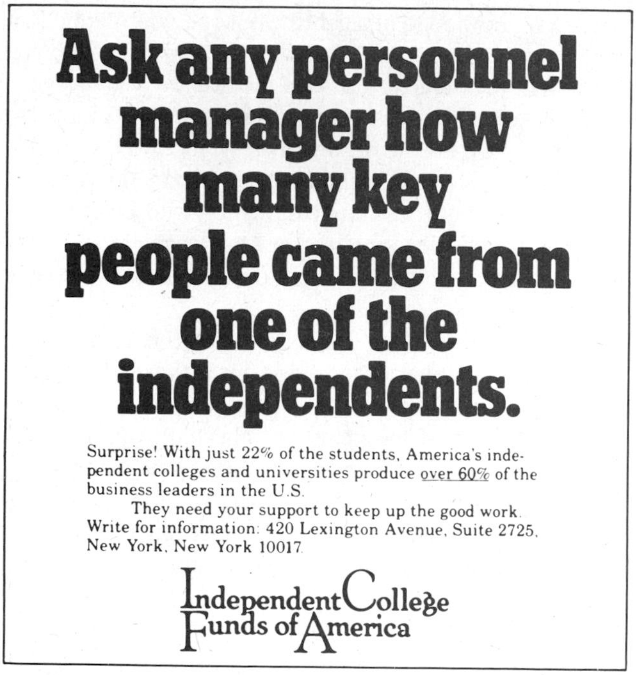

Source: *Time,* January 5, 1981, p. 8. Reprinted with permission of the Foundation for Independent Higher Education.

The correlational method is good for determining only whether temporal (concurrent or predictive) relationships exist. A concurrent relationship is one between variables measured at the same time; the number of hours since your last meal and the strength of your hunger pangs would have a concurrent relationship. A predictive relationship is one between a variable measured at time 1 and another variable measured later, at time 2; the relationship between scholastic aptitude measured in the fall of one year and grades obtained by the same students in the spring two years later would be a predictive relationship.

Figure 1.1 shows an ad that could be interpreted to suggest a causal relationship between going to an independent college and becoming a business leader. Why is it wrong to say that going to an independent college *causes* one to have a better chance of becoming a business leader?

A *causal relationship* exists where change in one variable brings about (results in, influences, effects, determines, produces, causes) change in the other. The best, but not the only, way to determine whether two variables are causally related is to perform an experiment. In doing an experiment, we manipulate one of the variables (the independent variable), then measure the other (the dependent variable). If the second variable is found to have changed as a result of the deliberate manipulation of the first, the change is said to be an effect of the first variable.

Suppose you teach algebra to one group of students but not to another. Teaching or not teaching algebra would be your independent variable, the one you manipulate. Your students' knowledge of algebra would be your dependent variable. If the group you've taught has greater knowledge than the group you did not teach, we would say that your teaching *caused* the greater knowledge.

Whether a relationship is causal or just correlational can have immense practical importance. One dramatic example of controversy about the nature of a relationship between variables centers on cigarette smoking and lung cancer (Eysenck, 1980). No one argues about the empirical relationship: Lung cancer does occur more often among people who smoke cigarettes than among those who do not. And the more cigarettes people smoke, the more likely they are to develop lung cancer.

Does smoking cause cancer?

But does cigarette smoking *cause* lung cancer? Or is the relationship simply correlational, with both variables determined by a third? This third variable might produce both the variations in cigarette smoking and the corresponding variations in the incidence of lung cancer. The identity of a third variable has been the subject of much conjecture. It might, for example, be an innate tendency toward tension, which produces both a greater craving for the relaxing effect of cigarette smoking and a predisposition toward lung cancer. Or it might be greater air pollution in cities, where cigarette smokers more often live.

Suppose it were possible to carry out an experiment on cigarette smoking. To do so, we would choose a large sample of people. Then we would put the names of the people in a hat and draw half of them. We would ask this *randomly assigned* group to smoke cigarettes, making sure that the other group did not smoke cigarettes. After ten to thirty years, we would measure the incidence of lung cancer in each group. If the incidence in the two groups differed more than chance would allow and all other variables were constant (as would be likely if the two groups had been randomly assigned to the two treatments), we would have conclusive evidence that cigarette smoking causes lung cancer. This kind of experiment is, of course, ethically impossible.

An ethically impossible experiment

Education and Relationships

The nature of relationships—causal or just correlational—is also important in education. The relationship between IQ and vocabulary is a case in point. Psychologists demonstrated long ago that people of higher intelligence, with higher IQ scores, tend to know the meanings of more words. Intelligence can be measured with verbal, spatial, or mathematical problems—it does not matter. If the people have grown up in a middle-class American environment, those with higher IQ scores tend to have larger vocabularies.

People with higher IQ scores also usually do better in school and have higher-paying and higher-status jobs. So higher IQ is recognized as a good thing. If it goes along with a larger vocabulary, then the obvious thing to do is to build your vocabulary. Learn the meaning of more words, and your IQ will go up. You will get higher marks and eventually an executive position in business. This is the reasoning that underlies the flourishing "build your word power" business.

But as Flesch (1954) pointed out, the reasoning is false. Higher intelligence does lead (cause) people to acquire larger vocabularies. But it does not follow that the reverse is true—that a larger vocabulary causes higher intelligence. A larger vocabulary is just a symptom of what is really important, higher intelligence. Strengthening a weak vocabulary does not improve the low intelligence that caused it. Whether or not a relationship is causal can make a serious difference in the practical consequences of a relationship.

Can "word power" improve intelligence?

Determining Correlational Relationships

How do we determine whether a correlational relationship exists? First, we need some basis for pairing the values of one variable with those of the other. For example, in determining whether IQ and scholastic achievement are correlated, individual students are the basis for pairing; that is, we pair some numerical indicator of each student's IQ with a numerical indicator of his or her achievement. We would need to obtain measures of the two variables—say, IQ and achievement—by testing a number of students with an IQ test and determining for those students their grade-point average. If the two variables are, say, class size and achievement, our basis for pairing them would be the classroom. We would pair the number of students in the class with the class's average achievement, for a number of classrooms.

Basis for pairing

Second, we would treat the numerical values of the two variables for the group of students by a statistical method that yields a correlation coefficient, a statistic that tells us whether a relationship exists. *Coefficients of correlation* are numbers that vary from −1.00 through zero to +1.00; they tell the direction and closeness, or tightness, of the relationship between two variables. The closer the correlation coefficient is to −1.00 or +1.00, the tighter the association between two variables. The closer a correlation is to zero, the looser the association between two variables. At zero, two variables are said to be uncorrelated—they are independent of each other. Body weight and intelligence, for example, show little relationship to each other. Statistically they have a correlation of around zero. But high school grade-point average and college grade-point average show substantial relationship to each other, usually yielding correlations of between .40 and .60. Body weight (as measured with a spring scale) on the moon and on earth, although different because of different gravity, would be perfectly correlated; that is, the correlation would be +1.00. Knowing one weight, we could easily and exactly predict the other by a simple translation. Because the two variables are perfectly correlated, we could go from one weight system to the other without any errors. Another example of perfect positive correlation (+1.00) is that between temperature in Fahrenheit degrees and temperature in Celsius degrees.

Coefficients of correlation

Coefficients of correlation give us very useful information. Figure 1.2 shows contrived *scatterplots* for various levels of correlation. Notice how the correlation coefficient (in the corner) gets lower as the dots become less closely clustered along the straight line. This line shows where the average for each vertical column of dots would be if we divided the scatterplot into vertical columns for

FIGURE 1.2

Scatterplots Illustrate Higher and Lower Correlations, and Positive and Negative Correlations

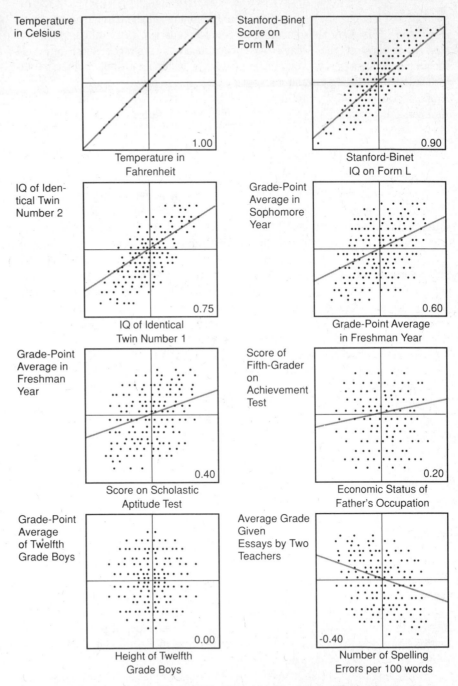

Source: Adapted from L. J. Cronbach (1984), *Essentials of Psychological Testing,* fourth edition (New York: Harper & Row), p. 138. Used by permission of HarperCollins Publishers.

each value on the horizontal axis; it is called the regression line. The labels for the two axes of each scatterplot name the variables being correlated. We have chosen these labels as plausible examples of each level and direction of correlation. Notice that the scatterplot in the lower right-hand corner illustrates a *negative* correlation: The higher the rate of spelling errors is, the lower the teachers' grades for the essays tend to be.

The following list gives several examples of information that correlations can give us:

- The correlations between an adolescent's reputation for a kind of behavior, as reported by peers, and objective observation of that kind of behavior often range as high as .70 (Newman & Jones, 1946). Asking for peer judgments about a student's behavior of a certain kind is almost as good as observing that kind of student behavior because the two are highly correlated. If a student is judged by his or her peers to be a leader, we might not want to make time-consuming, expensive observations of the student in various activities. We know that sometimes our observations will be different from the peer ratings because the two variables are not perfectly correlated. But the relationship between the two variables might be high enough for our purposes.

- In general the correlation between a person's scholastic achievement and a rating of the person's home on material possessions, spaciousness, cleanliness, and so forth, is about .40 (Anastasi, 1958). The physical condition of children's homes has a substantial, but far from perfect, association with the children's achievements. Common sense tells us that other variables are at work, for example, parents' intelligence, educational level, and financial status. But knowing this consistent finding helps us think about the relationships among these variables. Perhaps (a) higher parental intelligence causes both (b) better physical conditions in the home and (c) higher achievement in their children. If *a* influences both *b* and *c,* then *b* and *c* should be correlated. And they are.

- The correlation between the personality trait of tidiness and knowledge of biology is zero for twelfth-grade boys (Flanagan et al., 1964, p. 8–6). Neatness is not associated with any form of scientific knowledge, although many believe it is a part of good scientific work.

- The interest of twelfth-grade boys in working in the skilled trades correlates about –.34 with their information about theater and ballet (Flanagan et al., 1964, p. 8–7). Boys with "blue-collar" interests tend not to be "culturally" oriented. The negative correlation tells us that the higher one's interest in going into skilled trades is, the lower one's knowledge of ballet and theater tends to be.

Negative correlations

Negative correlations are interpreted in much the same way as positive correlations. That is, the closer to –1.00, the stronger the relationship between the paired variables, and the closer to 0.00, the weaker the relationship. The negative sign only means that high values of one variable tend to go with low values of the other variable. For example, high rates of spelling errors per 100 words written are associated with low grades on essays. A positive sign means that higher values of one variable are associated with higher values of the other variable, say, average reading speed and number of reading assignments completed.

In short, coefficients of correlation are used to describe the relationships between pairs of variables. They are one of the most important tools of the social sciences. Correlations, said E. L. Thorndike (1939, p. 42), "are destined to play somewhat the part in the social sciences that equations do in physics, chemistry and engineering." But remember that *correlation* does not necessarily mean "causation." To determine whether the relationship between two variables is due to some cause-and-effect connection between them requires other ways of working with variables.

Determining Causal Relationships

Experimentation: Manipulation and measurement

As we noted above, to determine whether changes in one variable *cause* changes in another, we should, if possible, conduct an experiment. The term *experiment* has a specific meaning here: It is not synonymous with research, investigation, study, and the like; it refers to situations in which the researcher manipulates one variable (the independent variable), then measures the values of another variable (the dependent variable). For example, suppose we expose four groups of students to four different explanations, each covering the same subject matter—say, the addition of simple fractions. And suppose we measure understanding on an examination for the four groups of students. We would be conducting an experiment. We have manipulated one variable (the type of explanation) and have measured the values of another variable (amount of understanding). If the test scores have different average values corresponding to changes in the type of explanation, we can infer that the differences in the independent variable (type of explanation) caused the average differences in the dependent variable (score). We would then conclude that the explanation differences caused the differences in the scores.

Random assignment

In an educational experiment we usually try to assign students randomly to the different treatments we are studying. We do this to balance out the groups so that no one of them is likely to have an advantage over the others. Random assignment usually balances out, from one group to another, all the variables (such as age, sex, intelligence, social class, and anxiety level) that could affect our experiment. Unless we balance things out, we may infer a causal relationship that does not really exist; the differences in score might be due to differences in one of the variables that we failed to balance out.

Experimental design

We also try to design our groups so that we have experimental groups and control groups (groups that do not receive experimental treatment). We try to make sure, perhaps through observation, that the independent variable is actually used ("implemented") as it should be. We try to observe pupils before and after we manipulate variables. With proper design we try to control all the factors that might mislead us in our search for causal relationships.

Finally, in most experiments we use statistical analysis to obtain estimates of whether our findings—one or more differences on the dependent variable— are only so small as to be due to chance or so large as to reflect a causal relationship between the independent and dependent variables. When statistics tell us the findings are *significant* (that something besides chance is at work), we can say that a causal relationship is operating. We say this with more or less confidence depending on the size of the groups we studied as well as the size of the difference between the groups on the dependent variable.

Statistical analysis

Experimental methods in educational psychology, like those in any other science, require technical ability and artistry. Good experiments, those that allow for clear causal interpretations, are less common than we would like. Nevertheless, when random assignment is used with good experimental design and appropriate statistical analysis, the findings are likely to be trustworthy.

Qualitative Research

Qualitative research, the field-based rich description of events, may use correlational and experimental methods, but this kind of research almost always looks for something more. It tries to clarify relationships, to describe the many interacting forces at work, to invest relationships with meaning, and to interpret them from the perspective of the participants themselves.

Imagine you're a researcher observing a class in the Southwest. The teacher asks the students—a group of American Indian children—several questions and gets no answers. If you're a qualitative researcher, it's not enough to report these facts. You want to understand the relationships at work here. Does the teacher feel he is a failure? Does he feel frustrated? Does he think the students are rude or ignorant? What about the students? Are they confused by a person who asks questions to which he already has the answers (something no one in the students' community would do)? Are they confused by a situation that asks them to violate their cultural norms by showing off (if they give the correct answer) or by shaming themselves (if they give the wrong answer)?

Understanding personal meanings

A qualitative inquiry generally goes further than a quantitative one in trying to understand the personal meanings of an event for the people involved. This interpretive approach to data collection is most useful when it is more important to understand local conditions than state or national trends (see Erickson, 1986). The method would be helpful for studying the meaning of teacher dissatisfaction in a particular school, for example, but not the problems of teacher dissatisfaction throughout the profession. The interpretive approach is also useful for understanding a one-time event, say a teachers' strike in Jackson, Mississippi. The interpretive approach is particularly useful for understanding a complex situation, such as how a change in the attendance boundaries of a school affects

Interpretive approach

• *Teaching is an opportunity for shared learning experiences and discoveries. One goal of qualitative research is to understand the personal meanings of an event. (© 1991 Susan Lapides)*

student achievement, teachers' expectations, parents' views of the school, resale values of homes in the area, and administrators' roles.

The quantitative and qualitative styles of research both try to make sense of some phenomenon. But their users approach their goal with different questions, different ways of collecting data, and even different beliefs about what it means to make sense of a phenomenon. The two approaches should be regarded as complementary, not competitive. Each has advantages and disadvantages.

Replication

In most fields of science, we are not convinced by the results of a single study. Even if the results are statistically significant—that is, even if they probably are not due to chance fluctuations in random sampling—we remain skeptical. Our skepticism may be hard to explain, even irrational, but it exists. We want to see whether another study yields the same results. And a third study. And a fourth. And so on . . .

This *replication,* or repetition, of studies of the same or roughly similar phenomena is common in the natural and social sciences. Hundreds of studies of the cigarette smoking–lung cancer relationship have been performed (U.S. Surgeon General, 1979). Scores of studies of open versus conventional education and their effect on student achievement have been performed (Giaconia & Hedges, 1982). Their results have made the findings on these relationships much more convincing than those of a single study.

But how do we synthesize the findings of many different studies of the same relationship? Yes, we must read each study and summarize its results. With many studies of the same phenomenon, however, it is difficult to keep all the results straight and then to form a valid impression of what they mean. It is like trying to remember the exam scores of thirty students; the numbers begin to blur. For this reason, Glass (1976) invented what he called *meta-analysis,* the quantitative synthesis of results (usually by averaging) across many studies of the same relationship—either correlational or causal. We describe the results of meta-analyses of various sets of replications throughout this text. For example, we discuss the meta-analysis by Giaconia and Hedges (1982) on open education in Chapter 10. These meta-analyses often give us a better way of estimating the relationship between two variables because they summarize results across many different studies. They make more intelligible the results of a number of replications.

Meta-analysis

Using Research to Guide Practice

How should you use what educational psychology offers? We will be telling you about relationships between variables—between teaching practices and learning outcomes, between intelligence and achievement, between gender and interests, between age and personal concerns, between social class and hopes. What should you do with this information?

The relationships we describe are never perfect. There are always exceptions to the trends that correlations equal to less than +1.00 or –1.00 describe. For example, in the area of health, the relationships between smoking and lung cancer, and between cholesterol level and heart disease, are far from perfect. The same is true of relationships between teaching practices and student achievement. What the teacher and the physician can do with their knowledge about relationships is fairly similar. They can use this knowledge "artistically"— think about it, take other factors into account, weigh the costs and benefits of any course of action, try to estimate the likelihood of exceptions to the trend, and keep in mind the usefulness and the inadequacies of the knowledge that scientific method has yielded (Gage & Berliner, 1989).

Use knowledge artistically

Some people react to the imperfections of scientific knowledge in the social sciences, including educational psychology, by rejecting outright the whole idea that teaching can benefit from this kind of knowledge. Our own position is the same as that of philosopher Josiah Royce (1891):

> It is vain that the inadequacy of science is made a sufficient excuse for knowing nothing of it. The more inadequate science is when [used] alone, the more need of using it as a beginning when we set about our task. . . . Instinct needs science, not as a substitute but as a partial support. . . . [W]hen you teach, you must know when to forget formulas, but you must have learned them in order to be able to forget them. (Royce, p. 124)

By *instinct* Royce meant our natural impulses and common sense. By *forget* he meant knowing when to make exceptions to what is implied by statistical trends. Sometimes we should make exceptions; sometimes we shouldn't. The art of teaching resides in knowing, with the scientific knowledge that educational psychology provides, when to make exceptions.

The research in the social and behavioral sciences, including educational psychology, is of high quality. Despite popular belief to the contrary, the consistency of results compares favorably with that of the physical sciences (Hedges, 1987). The relationships between variables often are even stronger than those on which some medical practice is based (Gage, 1985).

But unlike the systems studied in the natural sciences, classrooms and other social systems are not consistently uniform. Thus findings about human behavior cannot be applied with as much certainty as can findings in the natural sciences. When A causes B in a physics experiment in Switzerland, it also does so in Kansas City. We cannot be sure, however, that the relationship between C and D in suburban classrooms outside San Francisco holds in urban Houston. It might. It is probably a good bet. Certainly the research finding is worth taking seriously. But it does not provide us with as much confidence as a physicist or a chemist has in applying findings from one setting to another.

Teachers need to monitor and reconsider ideas because schools and classrooms differ from place to place, from time to time, from one set of circumstances to another. The weight-bearing strength of concrete or the lubricating efficacy of oil is much more stable over place and time than is the effect of thought-provoking questions on achievement in a classroom. So the findings of educational research should never be turned into rules that teachers should always follow. For example, the frequency of a teacher's higher-order (i.e., thought-requiring) questions (see Chapter 11) is associated with higher levels of class achievement (Redfield & Rousseau, 1981). But this relationship does not mean that you should ask eight or fourteen or twenty higher-order questions each classroom period. There are many reasons why, with a particular class on a particular day, you should not be asking lots of higher-order questions. You may be working toward curriculum goals that require rote learning, such as remembering atomic weights or the rhyming pattern of a sonnet. Or you may want to see to it that students share basic knowledge about some phenomena, and so you may ask many lower-order questions before moving the class to higher-order questions. Or you may be working with students who need

● *You may want to see that students share basic knowledge about some phenomena.*
(© Susan Lapides)

memory-level questions to gain confidence in answering questions. Or your students may be a bit restless, and if you use many open-ended questions, you may lose control. Or you may be trying to foster a discussion, in which case, surprisingly (see Chapter 11), it may be better to avoid questions. Or . . .

The research findings presented throughout this book should be taken seriously. But those who evaluate teachers sometimes become overzealous about these findings. They may try to turn findings worth thinking about into rules that must be obeyed. We don't agree. Research findings should guide your thinking about teaching. They should not be used to dictate action. Sometimes the simple, straightforward implication of an association between teaching practice A and wanted outcome B should be followed. But often it should not. Knowing the difference is what distinguishes the wise and effective teacher.

Research findings are guidelines, not rules

SUMMARY

Educational psychology is a science. But it is not often the basis for valid prescriptions or rules. Its major purpose is to provide information to help teachers make wiser decisions.

The concepts, or variables, that we study are aspects of our behavior and mental processes as we teach and learn. Their meaning, boundaries, and relationships are defined by our experience and knowledge. Some are alterable; some are not. But all have a relationship to how we teach and how our students learn.

The principles derived from the study of educational psychology depend on the application of scientific methods to determine relationships between concepts. Principles help us explain, predict, and control the phenomena of teaching and learning. Explanation depends on a logical relationship between variables; prediction, a temporal relationship; control, a causal relationship. To move toward these goals, to uncover the relationships between variables, we use three methods—correlation, experimentation, and interpretive inquiry.

Correlation tells us that certain values of one variable tend to be found with certain values of another variable. It does not tell us whether the values of the first variable produce the values of the second—that is, it does not show cause and effect. Correlation, then, helps us to predict relationships between variables, not necessarily to explain or control them.

Experimentation allows us to determine logical, temporal, and, most important, causal relationships. In an experiment, we manipulate an independent variable, then measure the values of a dependent variable. If those values have changed, we can, under the right conditions, assume that the independent variable caused the change. The right conditions include random assignment (which balances out many other characteristics of the subjects), sound experimental design, and valid statistical analysis.

Interpretive inquiry, the third method we use to determine relationships between variables, rests on qualitative research. It is not enough to simply observe and record an event. In interpretive work the researcher must look deeper, must attempt to describe the many relationships at work and the feelings of the people involved.

The development of educational principles does not stop with one correlation, one experiment, or one interpretation. The skepticism inherent in science demands replication (another trial with the same results, then another) and meta-analysis (a synthesis of the findings of the various similar studies). What we end up with is information—the best information available about teaching and learning. But it is important to realize that the principles of educational psychology are just that, principles. They are guidelines with which to work, not hard-and-fast rules. It is critically important to understand them; it is just as important to know when—and when not—to follow their implications.

Educational psychology, like the other social sciences, is often criticized for dealing with the obvious. But close examination reveals that intelligent judges tend to regard as obvious even the opposite of actual results.

2 ≡ The Tasks and Objectives of Teaching

OVERVIEW

What does a teacher do? One fairly standard answer lists five tasks: (a) choose objectives (b) in the light of an understanding of your students and (c) with an understanding of the nature of their development and learning processes, then (d) select and use appropriate ways of teaching, and finally (e) evaluate your students' learning, as a basis for beginning the process all over again, either with the same students or a new group. In this chapter we show how later chapters will help you prepare for these tasks.

Then this chapter goes into the following questions: What do you want your students to learn? How should they behave (think, feel, move) differently after you've taught your unit or course? Have you ever wished a teacher had told you more clearly what you should have been learning and why?

These questions deal with educational objectives. *Objective* means the same as wanted outcome, goal, aim, purpose, terminal behavior, intention. We use *objective* because of its wide acceptance as a technical term in education. Logically, a statement of objectives is the first step in the instructional process. Whatever the scope of the undertaking—a nation's educational system, a school's curriculum, a course, a class session, a day's assignment, or a one-minute explanation—it makes sense to decide where you want to go before you start to move. Even this book—its discussions of student characteristics, of learning, of motivation, of teaching, of methods of evaluation—must be related to the objectives of instruction. In the background of every kind of teaching is the question "What do you want students to learn?"

In this chapter our goal is to help you understand the tasks of teaching and then define educational objectives in ways that will be most useful to you and your students. We talk about the tasks of choosing objectives, understanding student characteristics and the learning and development of students, selecting and using appropriate ways of teaching, and evaluating student learning. Then we talk about the ways in which you should state objectives and about a framework—the behavior-content matrix—for organizing your ideas about what your students should learn from what you assign and teach them. We discuss the pros and cons of stating objectives. We also discuss the ways in which objectives are classified. And we end with a look at how objectives are developed in the cognitive domain.

Using Educational Psychology to Make Decisions

The instructional process involves five primary tasks:

1. Choosing objectives
2. Understanding student characteristics
3. Understanding and using ideas about the nature of learning and motivation
4. Selecting and using ways of teaching (methods and practices)
5. Evaluating student learning

Five tasks of teaching

Each of these tasks creates problems for both teachers and their students. Educational psychology can help teachers make wiser decisions as they try to solve these problems.

Figure 2.1 shows the relationship of tasks (and problems) to *Educational Psychology*. The model applies equally well to short-term instruction and to instruction that lasts a semester or more.

Objectives

The model shows that a teacher begins with some idea of purpose—the *objectives* that students should be helped to achieve. The problem for the teacher is to choose objectives that are important. The problem for the students is often stated as "I don't know what she wants! Why doesn't she tell us what she wants us to learn?"

Student characteristics

While choosing objectives, the teacher uses information about the important *characteristics of the students*. As the figure shows, the two activities occur simultaneously, and each influences the other. The teacher's challenge is to understand the students—how they differ in abilities, strengths and weaknesses, and stages of development. In the students' words, "My teacher doesn't really know me!" "Why does he treat us as if we're stupid?" "Why doesn't he realize how much we do (or don't) know?" The teacher develops objectives and thinks about the characteristics of students before instruction begins.

Learning process

Next the teacher must use ideas about the *nature of learning and motivation* to design teaching procedures that incorporate what we know about how students learn and how they are motivated. From the students' viewpoint, the

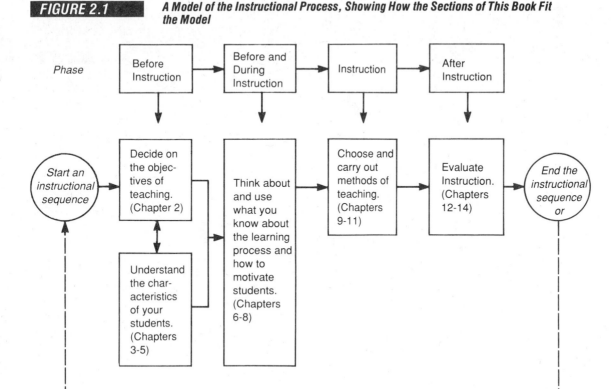

FIGURE 2.1   *A Model of the Instructional Process, Showing How the Sections of This Book Fit the Model*

problem is to make learning easier and more useful. They want to be told what is important, and they want instruction to be interesting. Students need to be told clearly that they are doing a good job or to be given guidance on how to improve (for example, "Try to check your comprehension by asking yourself to put it in your own words"). Some planning can be done ahead of time, but *applications* of learning theory also take place during instruction.

On the basis of all the preinstructional thinking and activity, the teacher selects and uses one or more *teaching methods and practices*. The teacher's dilemma here is deciding whether to lecture, discuss, show movies, tutor, read aloud, provide programmed instruction, leave students alone, or try some combination of these activities. The problem from the students' side: "How come we never do anything in class but hear the teacher talk, talk, talk?"

Teaching methods

Finally the teacher *evaluates* the students' learning, their achievement of educational objectives. Evaluation means designing and using procedures to find out how well the students have learned. The students' problems are learning the required material and demonstrating their learning by taking tests and getting good grades. Their demands are for fairness in testing and grading.

Evaluation

• *The teacher's objectives, the goals of student learning, can be suggested by a teacher's enthusiasm. (© 1991 David E. Kennedy/ Texas Stock)*

If evaluation shows that students have learned what they should, instruction can move forward. But if evaluation reveals that some or all students have not acquired the knowledge, understanding, and skills that were taught, remedial instruction is necessary. It may even be necessary to start the entire instructional sequence over again—rethinking objectives, student characteristics, the learning process, and teaching strategies.

Why State Objectives?

People involved in all kinds of educational tasks insist that statements of objectives are helpful, even essential. They claim that formulating objectives is the necessary first step in developing tests and in designing training to fit the requirements of jobs. The clearer the objectives, the better trained the individuals who receive instruction (Gagné, 1964).

In planning classroom teaching, unless they think about a sequence of objectives, teachers tend to focus on the daily content of instruction and to ignore what students should learn to *do* with that content. And without the "what to do," students usually assume that they just need to memorize content (R. W. Tyler, 1964). A history teacher, for example, may want students to be able to draw on historical sources to explain present-day events. But if the teacher doesn't explain this intention to the students, they may assume that they should simply memorize what they read. They may not realize that they should look at contemporary problems in historical perspective. "When objectives are identified and defined only casually, if at all, the students are likely to get the wrong image of what the teacher is trying to teach and what the student is expected to be able to do" (R. W. Tyler, 1964, p. 78).

Objectives can apply to education as a whole or only to teaching. Many educational objectives are broader than any single teacher can hope to achieve. In this chapter we focus on the teacher's objectives—what you as a teacher want your students to achieve as a result of your efforts.

Criteria for Formulating Objectives

Objectives must be stated clearly. It is too easy to indulge in what has been called "word magic," or statements of educational goals in language that is vague, unhelpful, and basically empty, even though it expresses lofty ideals. To avoid word magic, educators and especially educational psychologists have increasingly adopted the principle that objectives should be stated in terms of observable behaviors—what we can see students do with what they've learned.

Word magic

Observable behavior

An objective is a wanted outcome of some activity. If we state that the wanted outcome for students who read this book is an understanding of educational psychology, we have stated an objective. But is it a clear, explicit objective? Is it stated in terms of observable behaviors? What do we mean by "understanding"? We could try to clarify our objective by stating that students should be able to grasp the significance of educational psychology or of empirical methods in education. Or we might say that students should know and appreciate the concepts and principles of educational psychology. But all of these objectives are still examples of word magic. Unless we spell out what students *do* when they "understand," "grasp significance," "know," or "appreciate," we are offering an ambiguous description.

Evidence of Achievement

The kind of description we need is one that states the terminal behavior of students in ways that specify the evidence that the objective has been achieved. Thus we can state that among the many objectives for this book is that the students should be able to

Terminal behavior

- differentiate between the correlational, experimental, and interpretive methods in educational psychology.
- describe advantages and disadvantages of stating objectives in behavioral terms.
- contrast the views of psychologists who disagree about how heredity and environment affect intelligence.
- solve a problem in classroom management using principles of learning.

- make up an original example of a situation that would justify using the lecture method.
- identify teaching behaviors associated with humanistic approaches to teaching.

Each of these objectives is more precise than those that use words like *understand* or *appreciate. Differentiating, describing,* and *identifying* are relatively well-defined terms, telling us what to look for. They allow us to describe goal behaviors clearly and explicitly.

Conditions of Performance

Simple statements of wanted behavior are not enough. We must also specify the important conditions under which the behavior is expected to occur. For example, suppose our objective is that "Students should be able to contrast the hereditarian and environmentalist arguments about determiners of intelligence." We might want to add to it the conditions under which the students must work, such as with or without class notes or the text, at home or in class, in oral or written form, on the basis of this text only or on this and other sources.

Phrases that inform students about conditions are easy to recognize. They look like this:

- Given a problem in factoring . . .
- Given a list of well-known American novelists . . .
- Given any reference of the learner's choice . . .
- Using a ruler and a triangle . . .
- Within five minutes, the student should . . .
- Using an outline map of California . . . (see Mager, 1962, p. 26).

Acceptable Levels of Performance

Our objectives are still not in their clearest form. We must also state the minimum acceptable level of performance. Should the students be able to solve one type of problem? Three? Four out of six? Questions in only one form? In several forms? We need to make clear to the learners the criterion for success. Phrases that inform students about levels of performance are easy to recognize. They look like this:

- . . . must list four steps . . .
- . . . answer all ten multiple-choice items correctly . . .
- . . . distinguish three main ideas . . .
- . . . write (spell) accurately 90% of the 10 words presented . . . (Kibler, Barker, & Miles, 1970)

It is not enough, then, to say that students should be able to add. We might also want to specify how many digits the numbers to be added contain, how many rows of numbers will be in each column, how quickly the addition should be done, and what the criterion for success is. It is not enough to say "Students should understand the writing style of Phillip Roth." It might be better to say, "Given ten pairs of short prose passages—each pair having one selection by Phillip Roth and one by a different author—students should be able to choose at least nine of the ten selections written by Roth." In science, rather than simply understanding the concept of titration, the objective could be the ability to

1. construct a definition of the word "titration."
2. identify a situation involving the process of titration from a written list of similar situations.
3. describe in writing how the process of titration is involved in a particular experiment.

Table 2.1 lists examples of different objectives (wanted behaviors) in different subject areas. Use it as a guide and try formulating some of your own objectives, keeping these criteria in mind:

Criteria for judging objectives

1. Does the statement describe how learners act when they have achieved the objective?
2. Does the statement describe what learners are given or not given when they will be expected to act competently?
3. Does the statement indicate at least the lower limit of what you will consider acceptable performance?

TABLE 2.1

Examples of Teaching Objectives

Government. When given a series of instances of government activities, the student should be able to identify the instance as the proper interest of the legislative, judicial, or executive branch of government. (8 out of 10 correct)

Economics. Using no references, the student should be able to write five ways in which socialist and capitalist countries are alike and five ways in which they differ.

Statistics. Without notes, the student should be able to recall, without error, the formula for computing the rank-difference correlation coefficient.

Music. Given the name of a note and the scale, a member of the chorus should be able to sing the note accurately 9 out of 10 times.

Physical Education. On a level surface, the student should be able to do 30 push-ups in three minutes.

Arithmetic. Given an electronic calculator, the student should be able to call out the answers to 100 percent of the multiplication and division items containing numbers up to seven digits.

Art. When presented with pairs of paintings, the student should be able to choose the painting of the impressionist period 7 out of 10 times.

Algebra. The student should be able to solve 8 out of 10 quadratic equations of the type $AX^2 + BX + C = 0$, in class without any aids.

It has been our objective that, given this introduction and one hour's time, you should be able to construct ten behavioral objectives in any subject matter area of your choice, eight of which meet the criteria listed above.

The Behavior-Content Matrix

Our examples of learning objectives show that objectives refer both to kinds of behavior and to kinds of subject matter or content. The subject matter or content can be stated in highly general terms (American history, general science) or more specific ones (economic interpretation of the Constitution, the laws of the lever). You can see behavior-content combinations in a *matrix,* a gridlike table with rows and columns. The rows are labeled with types of behavior, such as the ability to recall, apply, interpret, or evaluate. The columns are labeled with categories of content, such as periods of American history, categories of national life (political, economic, social), or topics in general science (sound, light, heat). The cells of the matrix, where the rows and columns intersect, specify combinations of behavior and content. For example, the students should be able to recall (behavior) the approximate beginning and end years of the precolonial period (content). Or they should be able to interpret (behavior) tables containing statistical data on the growth of the American economy during Reconstruction (content).

Table 2.2 shows a behavior-content matrix for different behaviors and content areas. The behaviors—listed in the rows—refer to six kinds of cognitive processes: knowledge, comprehension, application, analysis, synthesis, and evaluation. (We come back to these later in this chapter.) The columns define content areas—here, Chapter 1 of this text, a novel, and a legislative process. The cells of the matrix have been filled in with sample (but incomplete) objectives. By specifying the behavior you want from your students and outlining the subject matter you plan to teach, you can develop your own behavior-content matrix. The matrix can guide your teaching and the learning of your students throughout the course.

Tests that match teaching to learning

Notice that the behavior-content matrix also allows you to construct achievement tests that match what you have taught and what you have asked students to learn. After you have created a behavior-content matrix, with one or more objectives in each cell of the matrix, you can specify how many items of each type to use in a comprehensive examination. To make up a test for Chapter 1, you would review the matrix and decide, for example, to write two test items requiring knowledge, one item requiring comprehension, three items requiring application, and so on. If you did this for each intersection of a wanted behavior

Representative tests

and a content area, you could be sure that the test was representative—that it tapped a fair sample of the content you covered in the instructional unit. The test would be fair because the test items are linked to your instructional objectives. And you can be sure that you have included the right proportion of items that require simple knowledge, deeper understanding, and the ability to apply ideas.

TABLE 2.2   *A Behavior-Content Matrix with Three Examples*

Behavior	Content		
	Chapter 1 in *Educational Psychology*	Hemingway's *The Sun Also Rises*	Legislative Powers of the Federal Government
Knowledge (to recall, recognize, acquire, identify, define)	Students should be able to define *correlation* and define *negative* and *positive correlation*.	Students should be able to recognize a passage that uses *irony*.	Students should be able to draw a chart of or describe how a bill is voted on in Congress.
Comprehension (to translate, transform, put in own words, rephrase, restate)	Students should be able to interpret the statement that the correlation between high school and freshman college grade-point averages is between .40 and .60.	Students should be able to describe the main idea of the story.	Students should be able to describe the roles of the two houses of Congress.
Application (to generalize, choose, develop, organize, use, transfer, restructure, classify)	Students should be able to use the concept of correlation in interpreting a news item about age differences in science achievement.	Students should be able to write one or two paragraphs about the Vietnam War in Hemingway's style.	Students should be able to write a letter to their congressman about a current bill, arguing a position in a persuasive manner.
Analysis (to distinguish, detect, classify, disseminate, categorize, deduce, contrast, compare)	Students should be able to distinguish between correlation and causation.	Students should be able to describe the personality flaws in the character of Brett Ashley.	Students should be able to distinguish between Democratic and Republican positions on a bill.
Synthesis (to write, tell, produce, constitute, transmit, originate, design, formulate)	Students should be able to design an experiment identifying the independent and dependent variables.	Students should be able to provide other plausible endings, given the major themes in the story.	Students should be able to describe the arguments of Democrats and Republicans for and against a bill and predict its final form.
Evaluation (to judge, argue, validate, assess, appraise, decide)	Students should be able to describe the weaknesses and advantages of correlational, experimental, and interpretive inquiries.	Students should be able to evaluate the novel, given the author's goal.	Students should be able to evaluate the wisdom of Congress's action on a particular bill.

Source: Adapted from N. Metfessel, W. B. Michael, and D. A. Kirsner, "Instrumentation of Bloom's and Krathwohl's Taxonomies for the Writing of Educational Objectives," *Psychology in the Schools, 6,* 227–231. Copyright 1969 by Clinical Psychology Publishing Co., Inc. Used by permission.

Creating a well-constructed behavior-content matrix can be a challenge. It demands skill, practice, and time. But once developed, a matrix can guide your instructional activities and your students' learning activities, and it can tie instruction to evaluation. In a sense, a matrix is a road map that shows you where you're heading and how to tell when you've arrived.

Justifying an Objectives Development Effort

Not everybody thinks that the effort to develop objectives and behavior-content matrices is important. Many have criticized this approach to instruction, claiming that it limits students' learning and that it is too time-consuming, among other things. But many others believe that behavioral objectives are a defense against the fuzzy thinking that can make teaching less good than it ought to be. Let's look at five common arguments (A) against behavioral objectives and five replies (R):

A. Many good teachers do not use behavioral objectives.
R. Many good teachers might be even better if they did.
A. Only trivial objectives can be put into behavioral terms.
R. With ingenuity, most important objectives can be stated clearly in behavioral terms.
A. Certain subject matters do not lend themselves to behavioral objectives.
R. If there are any criteria for student performance in any subject matter area, then objectives can be stated for that performance.
A. Behavioral objectives are antithetical to human dignity; they pin down goals of human learning in ways that demean those goals.
R. It is more respectful of human dignity to let students know what they should be learning than to hide it from them.
A. The unanticipated outcomes of instruction may be the most important outcomes of instruction.
R. Terrific. Let them happen. But we can also plan for certain outcomes in advance.

The first advocates of behavioral objectives stressed the need to specify what we want our students to achieve—in unambiguous language that focuses on observable behavior. They insisted that conditions of performance be noted and that levels of acceptable performance be defined. But in defending the use of behavioral objectives, some of those advocates have become more moderate. Some educators no longer emphasize precision; they claim that vague objectives allow students to pursue their own means to the ends chosen by society. And many educators value such freedom. They would accept as an objective "The student should have an awareness of, concern for, and sense of responsibility about contemporary events, issues, and problems" (Dressel, 1977, p. 13). In

• *It is more respectful to let students know what they should be learning.*
(© Suzanne Szasz)

our opinion such an objective becomes useful only if it is elaborated and spelled out. We would want to define key words in the statement, give examples of relevant learning experiences, and add some ideas about evaluating achievement of the objective.

No teacher should be required to base instruction on the hundreds of objectives and subobjectives that could be specified for a unit, term, or year of instruction (Gronlund, 1985). But a teacher should develop some reasonable number—say, two to six—of general objectives for each major unit of instruction. Of course, the teacher will have help in formulating objectives—help from national and state, governmental and professional, local district and school resources. And these objectives should be statements of the major goals to guide the teacher and the student through the curriculum. As we said earlier, objectives can act like a road map. A road map, to be useful, need not specify every town and creek. So objectives for a unit of instruction need not specify every change in student behavior.

Arguments for sensible objectives

Some writers argue that behavioral objectives, by telling students what they should learn, help students achieve those objectives. Others insist that behavioral objectives, by defining what students should learn, restrict students' interests and learning.

What does research show? Klauer (1984) analyzed twenty-three studies involving fifty-two comparisons between (a) students given behavioral objectives, learning directions, or questions before reading an instructional text and (b) students who did not receive these guides. He found that students who received objectives tended to learn more of the relevant material—that is, material related to the stated objectives—but they learned less of the material **Relevant and** that was not relevant to the objectives. So giving students specific information **incidental learning** about what you want them to learn is likely to improve their learning of it, but it may detract from their learning about things you have not defined. Apparently giving students instructional goals and objectives influences their intentions; it directs their attention to those parts of the material that are most related to achieving the stated goals and objectives. Students do pick up a considerable amount of incidental information, even when guided by specific objectives. But if you want them to pick up more general information, use a general objective, not a specific one.

Another reviewer independently reached the same conclusion (Hamilton, 1985). Both analyses suggest that in the classroom it is a good idea to provide students, in advance, with instructional objectives or statements about the goals of learning when they are using a text as a means to learn. And there is every reason to believe that behavioral objectives and statements of goals work equally well with lectures, discussions, and other oral forms of instruction.

Classifying Objectives

Educators and psychologists have developed a number of schemes for classifying objectives. These schemes make distinctions that help us organize the job of defining objectives. They also help us teach and evaluate our students.

Cognitive, One major set of distinctions draws from the distinctions among cognitive, **affective, and** affective, and psychomotor behaviors. *Cognitive* objectives deal with intellectual **psychomotor** processes like knowing, perceiving, recognizing, thinking, conceiving, judging, **objectives** and reasoning. When a teacher is concerned about Joe's inability to spell words correctly, she is referring to an objective in the cognitive domain. *Affective* objectives deal with feeling, emotion, attitude, appreciation, valuing, and the like. When the teacher worries about Joe's boredom with reading, she is dealing with the affective domain. *Psychomotor* objectives deal with skilled ways of moving, such as handwriting, typewriting, throwing a ball, dancing, and playing a musical instrument.

None of these kinds of behavior is isolated from the others. While we are thinking, we also experience emotions and display certain movements. When we are lost in feeling, swept away by a movie, symphony, or poem, we are still thinking and posturing. And whenever we perform a high dive or play the piano, we also think about how we are moving and have feelings about our performance.

Although the three types of objectives are intertwined, it often is useful to focus on one at a time. A group of educational measurement experts attempted some years ago to classify educational objectives. They divided the whole field of objectives into the three "domains" we've just described: cognitive, affective, and psychomotor. Eventually they published *taxonomies*—classification schemes—for the cognitive domain (B. S. Bloom, Engelhart, Furst, Hill, & Krathwohl, 1956) and the affective domain (Krathwohl, Bloom, & Masia, 1964). Later, similar taxonomies in the psychomotor domain appeared (for example, Harrow, 1972). In each of these taxonomies, objectives are arranged in sequence, moving up from lower (less complex) to higher (more complex) levels of behavior (or thinking, feeling, or moving).

Taxonomies

Because the cognitive-domain taxonomy has been widely used and cited, it is the only one we deal with here. But you should look up the taxonomies in the affective and psychomotor domains, particularly if you plan to teach poetry, music appreciation, art, sewing, cooking, typewriting, physical education, dance, playing a musical instrument, or other subjects where these taxonomies have the most obvious relevance. These subjects also have cognitive objectives, of course, and all three kinds of objectives often interact in important and stimulating ways.

The developers of the cognitive taxonomy identified six major areas within which cognitive objectives can be classified:

1.00 Knowledge: The ability to remember—recall or recognize— ideas, facts, and the like in a situation in which certain cues, signals, and clues are given to bring out effectively whatever knowledge has been stored. *Examples:* Students should be able to provide the dates of the last three American wars. Students should be able to list the three components of a behavioral objective.

Strangely enough, knowledge in this sense is often a controversial objective. Both educators and students sometimes question the value of "mere" knowledge, the ability to remember facts, dates, ideas, formulas—things that can always be "looked up." Yet, a professor of mathematics (Effros, 1989) objected to a National Research Council report that said "educators should deemphasize rote learning." He argued, "One cannot master the applications of mathematics unless one can handle addition, multiplication and fractions completely automatically and by hand" (rather than by calculator). One can acquire "an intimate and instinctive knowledge of numbers" only by rote.

And, as Hastings (1977) pointed out, memorization gets to be important for actors (to know their lines), for football players (to know their signals), and for typists (to know their spelling and alphabetization). The same is true of vocabulary for writers, common integrals for mathematicians, rules of style for editors, atomic weights for chemists, and much more. You should be able to think of the kinds of knowledge—the things to be remembered—that are worth having in your own fields of interest. Knowledge is not harmful to creativity or self-expression. In fact a large knowledge base may be necessary for creativity.

2.00 Comprehension: The ability to receive what is being communicated and make use of it, without necessarily relating it to other materials or seeing its implications. This is generally what we mean when we say we "understand" something, although it is a minimal kind of understanding. *Examples:* Students should be able to explain the causes of the Civil War . . . translate a paragraph from Spanish to English . . . give examples of protein-rich and protein-poor foods.

3.00 Application: The ability to use abstractions, rules, principles, ideas, and methods in particular and concrete situations. *Examples:* Students should be able to use barometers to predict weather . . . find unknowns in equations . . . determine an adequate diet for themselves . . . pronounce correctly words of the type consonant-vowel-consonant (*D-O-G*) after certain instructions in phonics.

4.00 Analysis: The ability to break down some communication into its constituent elements or parts. *Examples:* Students should be able to distinguish between the different parts of a research article . . . compare and contrast the capitalist and communist economic systems . . . deduce the central theme of a short story . . . distinguish statements of fact from statements of opinion.

5.00 Synthesis: The ability to work with pieces, parts, and elements, combining or putting them together in some way to form a whole or constitute a new pattern or structure. *Examples:* Students should be able to do something unique, such as propose a plan for the governance of the class, write a story on their summer vacations, combine what they know about adding one-digit numbers with what they know about place value in order to develop skill in the addition of two-digit numbers.

6.00 Evaluation: The ability to make quantitative and qualitative judgments about the extent to which materials and methods satisfy criteria. According to the builders of the taxonomy, this is the highest level of cognitive ability. *Examples:* Students should be able to judge the merits of a story or play . . . argue the case for or against welfare programs . . . appraise how well a voter turnout campaign works . . . decide whether physical violence is ever justified.

Knowledge vs. higher-order skills

The debate about what we want students to learn is still going on (e.g., N. Cole, 1990). At one end some educators want more emphasis on basic skills and facts. When was the U.S. Civil War? Where is Egypt? What is valence? How much is 9×27? Who wrote *Moby Dick?* At the other end, we find educators arguing for higher-order skills and advanced knowledge. We want, they say, critical thinking skills, problem-solving abilities, understanding and expertise, an increase in the student's "web of associations," the ability to translate ideas into a new context, self-guiding and self-monitoring strategies.

In our opinion, this is not an either-or issue. As many others have said, we cannot do critical thinking, problem solving, or self-monitoring in a vacuum. We need lots of knowledge—of facts, ideas, definitions, principles, examples, chess moves, dates, names, and so on—to use in our critical thinking and problem solving. That is why experts in one field are nonexperts in others. The chess champion can solve problems and think critically in chess, but he is a duffer in politics. The brilliant computer scientist is just average in human relations. The star sportswriter becomes a bore when he writes about concerts instead of baseball. In short, we see no good alternative to giving our students the best of both worlds: lots of knowledge of all sorts and plenty of skill in using that knowledge in critical thinking, problem solving, and the enjoyment of life.

The greatest value of the taxonomy and related materials has been their influence on making objectives and test items deal with more kinds of cognitive activities (Metfessel, Michael, & Kirsner, 1969). This influence is important because many teachers tend to concentrate on knowledge objectives, seldom moving higher in the taxonomy.

To appreciate the widespread emphasis on lower-level objectives, consider an analysis of *all* study questions, exercises, suggested activities, and test items in nine sets of world history textbooks and their accompanying workbooks, test booklets, and teachers' manuals (Trachtenberg, 1974). More than 61,000 items were identified, then classified according to the definitions provided in the taxonomy. Over 95 percent of them required knowledge or comprehension on the part of students. Only very small percentages of these items were at higher levels of the taxonomy. Sometimes, of course, this apparent imbalance makes sense. Certainly students must know and comprehend material before they can apply, analyze, synthesize, or evaluate it. But teachers, curriculum planners, and test developers need to remember the value of moving on from knowledge and comprehension to the higher levels of the taxonomy—the levels many teachers claim they really want to stress.

Widespread emphasis on lower-level objectives

Some researchers have raised questions about the taxonomy. Do the successive levels really form a hierarchy? If so, the highest level (evaluation) would require achievement of the next lowest (synthesis), which would require achievement of the next lowest (analysis), and so on down to the lowest level (knowledge). In fact, it has been demonstrated that the sequence is not rigid, that the taxonomy is not perfect in this sense. Nevertheless, many writers (for example, De Landsheere, 1977) have found the cognitive taxonomy satisfactory. Many users find it helpful because it organizes how we think about objectives. The practical gains seem to outweigh the imperfections.

Creating Cognitive Objectives

Behavioral objectives guide teachers and students through the curriculum. They help teachers decide what to teach, and they help students focus on what to learn. But they offer no information about how to teach because they say nothing about *how* learning might take place. To think about this issue, we need to create cognitive objectives.

The first step in developing cognitive objectives is thinking about the ways of behaving and thinking students must master to achieve stated objectives (Greeno, 1976). By carefully analyzing a learning task to specify the cognitive skills or mental operations necessary to perform it successfully, teachers can direct instruction to the areas that give students the most trouble. For example, suppose our objective is that students should be able to apply basic addition and subtraction facts when given word problems. Researchers who have analyzed this kind of task tell us that three basic kinds of problems are implied (see Riley, Greeno, & Heller, 1983):

1. *Change* problems (John had 10 marbles. He gave some to Mary. Now he has 5. How many marbles did he give to Mary?)
2. *Combine* problems (John and Mary have 10 marbles together. Three belong to John. How many marbles belong to Mary?)
3. *Compare* problems (John has 10 marbles; Mary has 4 marbles. How many more marbles does John have than Mary?)

Prototypic mental representations

Solving these different kinds of word problems requires certain kinds of language skills and mastery of basic counting facts in addition and subtraction. It also requires knowledge of how to separate a subset from a set of objects, how to match a set of objects with a subset of a different set of objects, and how to both identify and count a remainder. Students also need a *prototype,* a mental representation, of change, combine, and compare problems. Prototypes provide the fundamental understanding of the problem. They are built up only through extensive experience in solving problems of a similar kind. Gagné (1985) noted that students also need some additional cognitive processes in order to be successful learners. They need "plans" for taking action; that is, they need problem-solving strategies, not just knowledge of addition and subtraction facts. And he claimed that students need checking strategies so that when they arrive at an answer they can check that it "works," that it fits the available information.

Analyzing the learning task

The first step, then, in creating cognitive objectives is analyzing the learning task, deciding which prerequisite skills and which mental operations learners need to accomplish the task. From this analysis, teachers create cognitive objectives to guide their own instruction.

In our example, the cognitive objectives would include things like

- checking that the students have basic mathematics facts down pat, before moving to word problems.
- teaching the differences among change, combine, and compare problems.
- talking about mental representations of problems—helping students picture in their heads what is going on.
- if students give a wrong answer, probing to see whether they know how to check an answer.

Analysis is a difficult and creative task. But done well, it should affect students' thinking (an unobservable event) and help them perform in the way set forth in the behavioral objective (an observable event). Instruction guided by cognitive objectives—objectives that center on the skills and mental operations students need to learn the things we think they should learn—is likely to be better than instruction that ignores these factors.

SUMMARY

Before we begin to teach, we have to have some idea of what we want to teach. Objectives help us define the instructional program. Objectives of high quality have three characteristics: They describe the end product of instruction—what we want students to know or be able to do at the end of the unit or course; they define the conditions of performance; and they set forth acceptable levels of performance.

Objectives refer both to behaviors and subject matter (content). A behavior-content matrix is a table that shows what you want students to be able to do in each content area. It is a tool that functions in two ways: guiding your behavior and that of your students, and helping you construct tests that measure what has actually been taught.

Some writers have argued that objectives take too much time to develop and that they restrict learning. And certainly these problems may arise if we spell out too many objectives, too precisely. But a reasonable number of clearly stated objectives is a valuable guide for instruction.

The three domains of objectives—cognitive, affective, and psychomotor—reflect the three kinds of behaviors teachers may want to influence in their students. Taxonomies have been developed for each domain. The taxonomy of educational objectives in the cognitive domain helps us aim above the level of memorization, to see more clearly how information is processed through comprehension, application, analysis, synthesis, and evaluation. To form cognitive objectives, we have to analyze the content we are teaching, to determine the skills and mental operations students need to learn the material.

We are now at the end of Part I, which provides background on educational psychology. We have presented a view of educational psychology as a foundation discipline that helps to accomplish the tasks of teaching. We have discussed the content and the methods that educational psychology uses to help in gaining reliable information about educational problems. Finally, we have presented ideas about instructional objectives so that we can know how to think about the goals of education and teaching. Now we turn to the heart of the field of educational psychology—research on student characteristics, learning, motivation, teaching, and assessment.

Student Characteristics

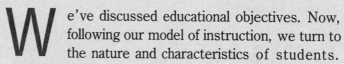

We've discussed educational objectives. Now, following our model of instruction, we turn to the nature and characteristics of students. We concentrate here on just a few of the educationally most significant characteristics, although there are literally thousands of characteristics that could concern us.

In Chapter 3 we deal with intelligence—one of the most thoroughly researched, educationally significant, and controversial traits studied in educational psychology. We introduce the determinants of individual and group differences in intelligence, as a basis for understanding the important controversies that surround them. We discuss here as well the many efforts to increase measured intelligence and achievement, especially in certain social groups.

In Chapter 4 we talk about cognitive development and how language, a critical part of that development, evolves. We discuss also how personality develops. The developmental changes in cognition, language, and personality that occur due to experience and maturation have fascinated parents, novelists, and psychologists alike. These changes have implications for teaching as well.

In Chapter 5 we look at individual differences due to culture, gender, and exceptionality. We discuss here how teachers should think and act given the cultural differences that characterize present-day students. We examine gender-related differences in abilities and traits and how sex roles develop. We consider too the school's role in gender stereotyping and some ways to teach without stereotypes. We discuss here as well how teachers should think and act about cultural differences.

We also look in this chapter at individual differences—the mental, physical, and emotional differences among students that create a need for special education.

3 ≡ Intelligence

OVERVIEW

It became possible during the twentieth century to measure individual differences in intelligence. Millions of intelligence tests are given each year. Yet controversy rages around whether these tests do more good than harm. In fact some major cities have banned the use of certain kinds of intelligence tests in the schools.

Intelligence is a serious matter, one that teachers need to be informed about. You may not need to know the intelligence-test scores of your students, but you do need to know about the concept of intelligence. This knowledge can help you understand what has long been seen as one of the major determinants of success in school and in life after school. In this chapter, we go into the definition, measurement, and organization of intelligence. We then discuss what is still, after a century of research and debate, a controversial issue: the role of heredity in intelligence. We deal briefly with current practice and the doubts that have been raised about that practice. We look at two contemporary theories of intelligence whose roots differ from those that gave rise to traditional IQ tests.

Then we continue our look at what determines intelligence: Evidence indicates that, *within* a group that shares a similar environment, *individual* differences are in good measure genetically determined. But what determines *group* differences in intelligence and scholastic achievement? That there are differences *among* racial, cultural, and social groups is well established. Why the groups differ has been the subject of debate for centuries.

So we examine the evidence and the causes of group differences in intelligence. Both evidence and causes are interpreted differently by people with different social and political ideologies. We believe that the degree to which the group differences are hereditary cannot be determined by any known methods, and that the critical question here is whether low group averages in intelligence and achievement—whatever the reasons for them—can be improved. We know that average height, a highly hereditary group characteristic, has been altered through improved diet and other treatments. It seems reasonable, then, that we can increase intelligence and achievement once we understand intellectual growth as well as we understand nutrition. We look first at the variables in the home environment that seem to make a difference in the intellectual achievement of children. Then we go on to the ways in which schooling, especially at the earliest levels, can help. We review the arguments for early intervention and the role of language in intervention programs. Finally, we look at how direct academic instruction in preschool and early grades affects the achievement of children from low-income homes.

The Definition of Intelligence

Everyone knows what intelligence is. It is brightness, "sharpness," the ability to understand things, solve problems and figure things out quickly, the capacity to learn from experience, and much more. Intelligence "explains" part of why some students seem to learn readily, while others in the same class, with the same books and teachers, have great difficulty.

We talk first about the definition and measurement aspects of intelligence; in fact the two aspects go hand in hand. Our traditional definition of intelligence evolved through the development of ways to measure intelligence.

Historical Background

Modern conceptions of intelligence and its measurement emerged early in the twentieth century. In the 1890s the French psychologist Alfred Binet took on the job of helping the schools of Paris identify students who needed special classes. Intelligence testing was not new. But tests that measured how quickly your hand can move 50 centimeters, or required you to estimate the difference in hand-held weights, or assessed your speed in reacting to sounds and in naming colors—not surprisingly—did not differentiate well in the intellectual domain. That is, children judged by their teachers to be dull did not perform less well on these kinds of tests than those judged to be bright. So Binet developed new tests, including some that dealt with higher mental processes—memory, imagination, attention, comprehension. At this point Binet and his colleagues tapped into what we now think of as intelligence.

Binet's job

The history of their efforts shows that they started with no clear definition of intelligence from which effective tests could be derived. Instead they worked in an almost trial-and-error way, gradually incorporating higher mental processes and using the test's differentiating power as their guide. To a large extent *intelligence* was defined as "what the intelligence tests test" (Boring, 1923, p. 35).

Intelligence = what test measures

Contaminated judgments by teachers

Notice the purpose of Binet's test development: to differentiate between dull and normal children as judged by teachers. Why was a test needed if teachers' judgments were going to be used as the *criterion* (basis or means) for judging the validity of the test? The answer gives us additional insight into the nature of intelligence. Teachers' judgments of the children's dullness or brightness were indeed determined largely by the children's intelligence—but not largely enough. Social skills, appearance, sprightliness, docility, and other factors not related to intelligence were suspected of spuriously raising teachers' judgments. Children who were quiet, creative, independent, or aggressive or who had defects in language, vision, or hearing had been labeled dull. A "good" test would help people identify children who had inappropriately been labeled "retarded" because their teachers could not cope with their behavior.

Present-Day Conceptions

Three aspects of intelligence

The hit-or-miss approach to the definition and measurement of intelligence has been improved on, although no scientific consensus about the nature of intelligence in Western culture has been reached (Sternberg & Detterman, 1986). But we do find agreement on certain elements. Snyderman and Rothman (1987) asked a group of experts in psychology and education to rank important aspects of intelligence (Table 3.1). The group agreed overwhelmingly on three abilities:

- The *ability to deal with abstractions* (ideas, symbols, relationships, concepts, principles) more than with concrete things (mechanical tools, sensory activities).
- The *ability to solve problems*—to deal with new situations, not simply to make well-practiced responses to familiar situations.
- The *ability to learn,* especially to learn and use abstractions of the kind involving words and other symbols.

Intelligence is behavior

These ideas are brought together in a brief definition by Estes (1982): Intelligence is "adaptive behavior of the individual, usually characterized by some element of problem solving and directed by cognitive processes and operations" (p. 171). Anastasi (1986) pointed out that definitions like this one remind us that intelligence "is not an entity within the organism, but a quality of behavior" (p. 19).

Nonintellectual Components of Intelligence

Intelligence is more than the ability to reason, to solve problems, and to learn. It also involves what appear to be many nonintellectual qualities—emotional, social, and sensory abilities and skills. For example, some definitions of intelligence include the ability to withstand stress and distraction, which in turn demands emotional stability and self-confidence. Other definitions include social

Descriptor	Percent Rating as Important
Abstract thinking or reasoning	99.3
Problem-solving ability	97.7
Capacity to acquire knowledge	96.0
Memory	80.5
Adaptation to one's environment	77.2
Mental speed	71.7
Linguistic competence	71.0
Mathematical competence	67.9
General knowledge	62.4
Creativity	59.6

TABLE 3.1

Expert Opinions About Important Elements of Intelligence

Source: Adapted from M. Snyderman and S. Rothman, "Survey of Expert Opinion on Intelligence and Aptitude Testing," *American Psychologist, 42,* 137–144. Copyright 1987 by American Psychological Association.

competence, character, interest in learning, achievement motivation, and visual acuity. There is less consensus about the nature of these characteristics than there is about the intellectual components of intelligence, but most scholars believe it takes more than just brain power to be intelligent (Snyderman & Rothman, 1987; Sternberg, Conway, Ketron, & Bernstein, 1981).

Intelligence more than brain power

It is traditional to distinguish intelligence, or general mental ability, from other abilities and skills. Therefore, many abilities—artistic, commercial, athletic, musical, mechanical—have been placed partly outside the boundaries of what we ordinarily define as intelligence. On the other hand, some argue (as we will discuss later) that a definition of intelligence that leaves out athletic ability or musical ability, for example, is too narrow (H. Gardner, 1983). For the present we use the traditional definition of intelligence. But remember that this definition is not all-inclusive; it omits many important kinds of abilities, capacities, skills, and capabilities.

Culture and Intelligence

The definition of intelligence used in this text stems from the intellectual tradition of the developed nations. That tradition represents only one approach to human learning and instruction—namely, that appropriate to a middle-class segment of an industrial society in which learning takes place in a certain kind of classroom in an institution called school. If our society were different or if education were to take a different form, we probably would have to redefine intelligence, making it more relevant to that society and that form of education.

Consider, for example, the American Indian cultures. Some of these cultures place high value on the skills required in weaving: Some of them depend on spearfishing for much of their food. If industrial society valued these skills in the

• Some definitions of intelligence include social competence and social skills. (© Jean-Claude Lejeune)

Culture defines intelligence

same way, our educational system would focus on them, and our definition of intelligence would give them greater importance.

Some researchers studying the sorting behavior of Kpele tribespeople in Africa saw firsthand the effect of culture on a society's definition of intelligence (Cole, Gay, Glick, & Sharp, 1971). Educated North Americans generally sort along taxonomic lines, categorizing a set of objects or pictures as animate objects or machines or musical instruments. Less educated individuals and youngsters ordinarily sort by function—grouping together pictures of a dog and a bone because dogs chew bones, or grouping together pictures of a man and a hammer because men build houses. The Kpele sorted primarily by function. But when the researchers asked them to sort in the way unintelligent people would, they easily began to sort taxonomically! The moral of this story is clear: Intelligence is culturally specific, not universal. To determine the intelligence of any individual, we must first understand how that individual's culture defines intelligence.

Human behavior is culture bound

No intelligence test is, and none may ever be, culture free. Human behavior is culture bound. This boundedness may not create a problem as long as we remember that the appropriateness of any test for any individual depends on that individual's access to the culture that developed the test. A society will always have a problem testing the intelligence of minority-group members because, by definition, they do not belong in important ways to the majority culture that usually develops the tests.

The Measurement of Intelligence

We measure intelligence with tests. The tests use questions or exercises that call on the individual to make a response. The questions are arranged in groups that increase in difficulty. At the 6-year level of the Stanford-Binet there are several items like these:

- "A table is made of wood; a window of _____ ."
- "A bird flies; a fish _____ ."
- "The point of a cane is blunt; the point of a knife is _____ ."
- "An inch is short; a mile is _____ ."

On another subtest of intelligence, designed for an older group, subjects are asked to repeat backward a series of digits that increases in difficulty. The person being tested may start with 1, 3, 7 and try to advance to 1, 5, 4, 2, 8, 6, 3. Or a vocabulary subtest may require a definition for a word like *pen* at the beginning and a definition for a word like *alienation* at the end. Most intelligence tests combine different ways to measure intelligence and are made up of a number of subtests.

The responses in these tests are usually scored right or wrong and are given a certain number of points. All the points earned are added, and the total is the individual's *raw score*. Usually the raw score is then converted into a more meaningful standardized score and interpreted in light of the test's norms. The

Raw scores

• The individual testing of intelligence—a scene repeated many thousands of times each year. (© Mimi Forsyth/Monkmeyer Press Photo Service)

Norms

norms show the frequency with which various scores have been obtained by the members of some norm group, say, "a representative sample of five-year-olds in the United States" or "adult males" or "high school seniors taking the Scholastic Aptitude Test."

Intelligence Tests and the Normal Distribution

During the first half of the twentieth century, thousands of IQ tests were given to large representative samples of children and adults. Partly because of the way the tests were made, and partly because of the way human intelligence functions, the resulting IQ scores, or their equivalent standard scores, fell into a *normal distribution,* which has the bell shape shown in Figure 3.1. The bell-shaped curve has been found to describe the frequency distribution of many human characteristics. Mathematically a normal distribution occurs whenever the magnitude of a variable is determined by many independent factors of roughly equal importance.

The normal or bell-shaped curve

Developing a normal distribution

Why do IQ scores tend to be normally distributed? Is it simply because the test is rigged? Not entirely. Remember that the test consists of many items, each designed to differentiate among individuals. That is, the items are written so that on some items only about half of a given age group responds correctly, while on other items a higher or lower percentage of that age group responds correctly. Also, the goal of test developers is to have each item measure an ability that is only moderately correlated with the abilities measured in any other

FIGURE 3.1

Normal Curve with Corresponding Standard Scores

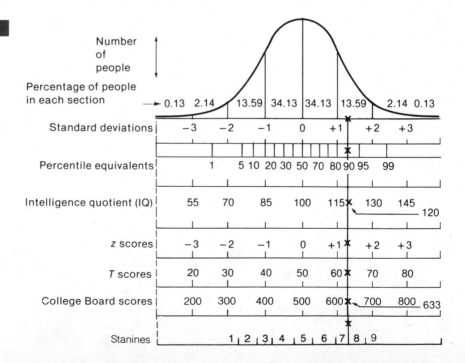

item. The magnitude of the score is determined by responses to many items. The correctness of each response is relatively independent of that of the other responses. In this kind of situation, a normal curve results. Height is also determined by many relatively independent anatomical factors. Both measured intelligence and height are normally distributed within any specific age, ethnic, and gender group, such as twelve-year-old Japanese boys.

Using age-group norms, the test authors prepare one or more tables for converting raw scores into percentile ranks or one of the various kinds of standardized scores (z scores, T scores, stanines). Figure 3.1 shows the percentile ranks associated with various IQ scores that have a mean (average) of 100 and a standard deviation (a measure of variability) of about 15. (Standard deviation is discussed in the Appendix, pages A1–A2.) Percentile rank—a widely used score because it is easy to understand—tells what percentage of the norm group is excelled by a person with that rank. The other types of scores, which we discuss later, have specified means and standard deviations.

Percentile ranks and standardized scores

College Board examination raw scores are converted to scores with a mean of 500 and a standard deviation of 100. The score of 500 represents the average of all high school seniors taking the test. Scores of 600 and 400 are 1 standard deviation above and below the mean, respectively. If the scores fall into the kind of distribution shown in Figure 3.1, it is easy to interpret standard scores in terms of percentile ranks. The figure shows several percentile ranks and their equivalents in various standard score systems. The Xs indicate where a person with an IQ score of 120 or a College Board score of 633 would fall on the various distributions. This person would be at about the 90th percentile rank. Roughly, this means that a 120 on an IQ test or a 633 on a College Board examination exceeds 90 percent of the scores of those in the norm group used as a reference; only about 10 percent of the norm group does better on either test. Most standardized IQ and achievement tests are reported in some form of standard score. These are all relatively easy to interpret with the information in Figure 3.1.

The Stability and Reliability of Intelligence Test Scores

Is intelligence stable? Or does it change from day to day, season to season, year to year? B. S. Bloom (1964) reviewed the evidence from several longitudinal studies of *individual* intelligence tests—that is, studies in which the intelligence of the same people was measured at intervals over a considerable period of time. These studies showed how the correlation between intelligence at a given age and intelligence at maturity (ages 16 to 18) increases as age increases. "Nearly 50 years of research shows that prediction coefficients from infant behavior to later IQ are sufficiently low to be conceptually uninteresting and clinically useless" (McCall, 1981, p. 141). Before age 7, the correlations are below .70 (see also Hopkins & Bracht, 1975; Petty & Field, 1980). This means that for most

Longitudinal studies

Stability of IQ

people intelligence begins to be stable by age 7. By age 12, intelligence is very stable. The rank order of individuals in intelligence at age 12 is much the same as their rank order at any subsequent age.

Reliability

This degree of stability also means that intelligence tests are highly reliable. *Reliability* is a technical concept that refers to the degree of consistency, dependability, or stability in a test's results. The correlation between scores on two or more testings tells us about the reliability of a test. If the correlations are high, the rank orders of individuals on the two testings tend to be highly similar. That is, a person who scores high on one administration of the test will score high on another administration of the test. The fact that we find reasonably high stability when we measure intelligence at, say, age 10 and again at age 18 means that at least equal stability will be found over shorter intervals—say, a month or a day. We can depend on the fact that for almost any test-retest interval, the results of the tests yield about the same rank order.

Shift in IQ scores

Most standardized tests of general intelligence, scholastic aptitude, mental ability, and the like are highly reliable. That is, few individual scores shift dramatically from one testing situation to another. But some do. A 20-point shift in IQ score from one testing session to another for a *particular* individual is not unheard of. Especially for younger children, the reliability of the tests is not as high as it is for older children. Petty and Field (1980) found that as many as 50 percent of their sample of 235 Australian children in grades 3 through 6 changed as much as 16 points in IQ scores in consecutive years, and 69 percent changed that much between any two years in those grades; 14 percent changed as much as 32 IQ points. At higher age levels, the amount of fluctuation decreases. For 10 percent of the children, the changes from grades 3 to 6 were steadily upward; for another 10 percent, steadily downward. For the majority of people IQ scores are highly stable, but for particular individuals IQ scores may vary considerably from one testing to another.

The Organization of Intelligence

Is there only one kind of intelligence? What about the people who are good at handling words but not mathematics? What about those who can see complex spatial relationships readily but not complex verbal ones?

Is intelligence *general* mental ability? Do we tend to show the same relative level of ability in dealing with verbal, mathematical, and spatial problems? Or is ability in one area relatively independent of ability in the others?

General mental ability (g)

Most psychologists believe that there is a general mental ability (*g*) simply because *all tests of cognitive ability tend to correlate positively with one another.* This finding holds for all tests of cognitive abilities whether they differ in content (verbal, mathematical, spatial) or reasoning process (deductive, inductive, analogies, memory, discrimination). At the same time researchers have discovered that tests of mental abilities can be grouped in clusters that are highly inter-correlated. These clusters of related tests are called *group factors*. For example,

Group factors

tests of analogies, comprehension, vocabulary, and dozens of other tests that rely on language are highly intercorrelated—they cluster together and form for us the *verbal factor* in intelligence. Researchers have consistently identified verbal, *mathematical,* and *spatial* group factors. We certainly can think of each group factor as a specific ability—a distinct aspect of intelligence. But we must remember that the scores a student gets in each area are usually correlated positively, although not at high levels, with scores in other areas. This means that all scores probably have in common g, the general mental ability factor, as well.

Distinctive aspects of intelligence? Yes and No

"Well," you might say, "so what?" Does it really matter how we think of intelligence? Why do we need to know about the organization of mental abilities? Understanding how intelligence is organized is important to teachers because of the implications for educational practice. If a single general ability accounts for most of the differences we see among students, we would quickly identify our bright and dull students and expect that the rank ordering of students in any one task would be similar to their rank ordering on any other task. Some have more ability, some less. On the other hand, if group factors are at work, we probably would look for, and fully expect to find, unique talents and abilities in each individual, somewhat independently of that person's rank in mathematics or verbal skills.

Some combination of the general mental ability conception and the group factor conception may be what you need to keep in mind as you think about educational alternatives for your students. Don't disregard the general intelligence so necessary for abstract reasoning. At the same time, don't neglect the more specific (or group-factor) abilities and potential of each student in some area, whatever his or her ability in other areas. We shall discuss different conceptions, or types, of intelligence further in a subsequent section of this chapter.

Intelligence and School Success

From the historical sketch we've given, you might guess that intelligence correlates with school success, and you would be right. If school success is measured in terms of grades or marks or grade-point average, we always find a positive correlation between scores on a general intelligence test and such school-success measures. Thousands of such correlations have been computed throughout the twentieth century, and we know of none that has been negative. Depending on how varied the students are in terms of their intelligence (here often called scholastic aptitude), the correlations range from about .2 to about .6 with an average value of about .4. Within the same class, course, or curriculum, students with higher scholastic aptitude tend to get higher grades. If scholastic success is measured not with grades but with achievement tests, the correlations tend to be somewhat higher, partly because both variables entail skill with paper-and-pencil tasks and partly because test scores are less affected by nonintellectual factors (such as participation and conduct in class) than grades are.

The correlations are not so high, however, as to rule out the possibility that students with high scholastic aptitude can get low grades (perhaps for lack of motivation) and others with low aptitude can get high grades (because of strong motivation, good study habits, and the like). The correlations are low enough to leave a lot of room for exceptions to the general trend.

Remember, here especially, that correlation does not mean causation. The correlations between IQ and school achievement do not necessarily mean that the IQ level tends to determine or influence the achievement level. It may well be that both variables are determined by a third variable such as home environment. Homes and parents that provide intellectual stimulation and motivation tend to bring about both higher IQs and higher achievement. Or it may be that the higher school achievement, resulting from better teaching and curricula, tends to raise IQs. Keep these ideas in mind as you read this chapter.

Intelligence and Job Success

Do more intelligent people do better in the real world of jobs, that is, in performance on the job, making a living, producing goods and services? The way to find out is (a) to give a group of workers in the same job an intelligence test so as to obtain a measure of each worker's intelligence, (b) to obtain a measure of how well each worker is doing the job, and (c) to obtain a coefficient of correlation between the intelligence measure and the job performance measure.

More than a thousand studies of this kind have been reported, and Hunter (1986) has summarized their methods and results, using meta-analysis (see Chapter 1). *He adjusted the obtained correlations so as to obtain estimates of the correlation that would be obtained if the tests and performance measures were perfectly reliable (see Chapter 12). These adjustments made the correlations higher than those usually reported.* He concluded that general cognitive ability predicts supervisor ratings and training success and that it also predicts work performance with even higher validity. Going further, he generalized that "general cognitive ability predicts job knowledge ($r = .80$ for civilian jobs) and job knowledge predicts performance ($r = .75$) verifying job analyses showing that most major cognitive skills are used in everyday work" (p. 340).

The kinds of jobs for which these generalizations hold are highly varied. They are both complex and simple jobs. They hold for mechanical, electronic, skilled services, and clerical jobs. And the correlations are not merely greater than zero; they are fairly high and have considerable practical significance.

Thus the evidence is strong that what is measured by intelligence tests (or cognitive ability tests) relates not only to academic success but also to job success. More intelligent workers tend to learn more about their jobs (have greater job knowledge). Those with greater job knowledge tend to do better work. And those with higher general cognitive ability tend to do better work. Thus we can say that the following picture holds:

Job success and IQ

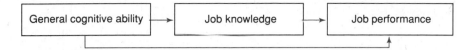

In short, the importance attached to tested intelligence by parents, teachers, and people in general is well justified. We are dealing in this chapter with a human characteristic that makes a big difference in how well people get along in school and on the job.

None of this rules out the importance of other kinds of intelligence, such as those described by H. Gardner (1983) and discussed later. General intelligence or cognitive ability tells an important story but not the whole story.

So far we have talked only about intelligence-success relationships *within* the same job. What about intelligence differences *between* jobs? Here, data from a variety of sources show clearly that certain levels of intelligence are typically found in some occupations and not in others. Writers, accountants, engineers, and teachers typically average over 120 in standardized tests of intelligence; teamsters, lumberjacks, and cobblers often average under 90 (N. Stewart, 1947). Occupation-based differences in average intelligence of adults or their children have been found in England, Hawaii, Soviet Russia, and the Netherlands, as well as in the United States, and for both African-Americans and whites.

Occupation and intelligence

Certain occupations seem to require or attract people at certain levels of measured intelligence, or academic aptitude. If environmental factors keep certain groups from achieving at higher levels, these groups are likely to remain in lower parts of the occupational structure (Herrnstein, 1971). What is operating here is something called the *poverty circle:* Parents low in scholastic ability and consequently in educational level create an environment in their homes and neighborhoods that produces children who are also low in scholastic ability and academic attainment. These children grow up and become parents, repeating the cycle. Like them, their children are likely to have only occupations at lower levels of pay, prestige, and intellectual demand.

The poverty circle

Recent research has shown, however, that intelligence, or general cognitive ability, is less important than "domain-specific knowledge" in correlating with memory, performance, and comprehension in a specific domain of subject matter (e.g., Schneider, Körkel, & Weinert, 1989). German elementary school boys and girls were asked to read a detailed narrative about a soccer game and its young hero's physical and psychological condition after the game. It turned out that their previous knowledge about soccer was much more highly correlated with their memory for and comprehension of the narrative than was their score on a German cognitive ability test. So "rich domain-specific knowledge can compensate for low overall aptitude on domain-related cognitive tasks" (Schneider et al., 1989, p. 311). Other studies have yielded similar results. These studies suggest that low-aptitude learners can do excellent work in domains in which they know a lot. Instruction should be aimed at getting learners to use in other domains the same capabilities that they use in the domains (soccer, baseball, or whatever) in which they have much knowledge.

Domain-specific knowledge

Heredity and Environment in Intelligence

Heredity and environment both important

Two factors determine any human characteristic: heredity (nature) and environment (nurture). Both are indispensable to human development. The question of which factor is more important is as meaningless as asking whether the length or width of a rectangle contributes more to its area. Without hereditary factors, no food, air, education, or other environmental factors would produce growth. And without the proper environment, hereditary factors would be impotent.

So the sensible question is, what is the relative weight of *variation* in each factor (heredity or environment) in producing *variation* in a given characteristic? For variation in eye or skin color, variation in heredity predominates; for variation in language spoken, variation in environment is the sole factor.

When there are no variations in hereditary factors—as is the case with identical twins—all variation in intelligence results from variation in environmental factors. Similarly if there were no differences in environmental factors—a condition that does not exist even for identical twins brought up in the same family—all variation in intelligence would result from hereditary factors. One problem in getting clear answers here is that heredity and environment usually vary together, making it difficult to separate their effects. Thus people who are relatives (parents and their children, siblings, twins) tend to have the same environment. So it becomes hard to tell whether their similarity (in IQ) results from their similarity in genes or their similarity in environment.

Social policy

The degree to which variation in heredity and variation in environment determine variation in human characteristics has major implications for social policy. If we believe that variations in intelligence are determined by variations in heredity, it *may* be futile to attempt to increase intelligence by improving the environment. And it becomes correspondingly futile to try to improve chances for the good life in modern society, insofar as those chances depend on intelligence. The "disadvantaged" tend to have lower intelligence-test scores. If these scores are determined by hereditary factors, the problems of the disadvantaged in gaining equal education, jobs, income, social status, and self- esteem *may* not be solved by improving the environment (schooling, housing, welfare, family life). Only insofar as lower intelligence is caused by inferior environment can environmental factors be changed to improve intelligence and the corresponding ability to gain the good things, material and cultural, that society offers. At least this is the reasoning of certain writers (see, for example, Eysenck, 1979).

The Nature-Nurture Issue and Ideology

Reasoning of this kind accounts for the passion that the issue of heredity versus environment arouses. Before we get too far into our discussion, however, you should know that there are questions about scientific objectivity in this area. Pastore (1949) looked at the positions of twenty-four American and British scientists on the nature-nurture issue and compared those positions to the scientists' political conservatism or liberalism. Of the twelve liberals,

● *When raised together, identical twins have nearly identical IQs; when raised apart, they show the effects of different environments. (© Shirley Zeiberg/ Taurus Photos)*

eleven were environmentalists, and of the twelve conservatives, eleven were hereditarians.

Pastore's findings suggested a link between views on the nature-nurture issue and on basic social and political issues. Related findings were reported by Sherwood and Nataupsky (1968). They surveyed eighty-three American researchers who had studied race differences in intelligence. Some had made hereditarian interpretations of the differences; others interpreted their findings along environmentalist lines. When the two groups were compared, it turned out that the hereditarians more often were firstborn, had grandparents born in the United States, had parents with higher educational levels, had higher grades in college, and had grown up in rural homogeneous communities. In some ways the hereditarians were themselves more advantaged. Perhaps for this reason they tended to believe that intelligence is innately determined; their own good fortune thus seemed to be a natural right rather than the result of good environment to which others might have equal rights.

IQ Differences as a Function of Genetic and Environmental Differences

When nature manipulates the genetic and environmental similarity between two people, we can examine the relative effects of heredity and environment on their similarity in measured intelligence. First we list pairs of people in order from least different (most similar) to most different (least similar) in heredity and environment. Then we look at the differences in their IQ scores as measured by the correlations between the pairs.

Levels of Genetic and Environmental Similarity.

There are nine levels, ranging from least different to most different:

1. *Identical twins reared together.* Identical twins are two people born of the same ovum fertilized by the same sperm. Their genetic similarity is complete; they have the same genes and, if raised in the same family, highly similar environments.
2. *Identical twins reared apart.* These twins are separated in early childhood and raised in different homes.
3. *Fraternal twins of the same gender raised together.* Fraternal twins are born at the same time of different fertilized ova. Their genetic similarity is no greater than that of ordinary siblings of the same gender, but the environments of fraternal twins are probably more similar than those of ordinary brothers or sisters.
4. *Fraternal twins of different gender raised together.* Here the environments may be more different than when the twins are of the same gender.
5. *Ordinary siblings raised together.* For siblings, the environment differs in various ways, depending on the difference in their ages, their parents' attitudes toward them, their family's socioeconomic condition at various times, and so on. Genetically the similarity between two siblings is about the same as that between a parent and his or her child. So it is also of interest to determine the degree to which *parents and children* resemble one another in IQ scores.
6. *Ordinary siblings reared apart.*
7. *Foster parents and foster children.* In this case children are reared by adults who are not their biological parents but who are furnishing the home environment. Any similarity in IQ scores between foster parents and foster children reflects the similarity in environment, except insofar as *selective placement*—the process of placing children with foster parents whose cultural and educational level resembles that of the biological parents—occurs.
8. *Unrelated persons of approximately the same age, reared together in the same foster home or institution.* Here genetic similarity is simply a matter of chance, except for the operation of selective placement. But some environmental similarity presumably does exist.
9. *Unrelated persons reared apart.* The researcher matches these pairs by chance. We would not expect to find more than a chance—that is, zero—correlation between their IQ scores.

Selective placement

IQ Score Correlations.

Correlations between IQ scores tend to follow genetic and environmental similarity. The evidence was first assembled by

Erlenmeyer-Kimling and Jarvik (1963) and has been supplemented with data reported since then.

Figure 3.2 shows the eighty-eight correlation coefficients obtained in these studies for each kind of genetic and environmental similarity. It is clear that the correlations tend to decrease as genetic and environmental similarities decrease. At the highest level of genetic-environmental similarity, that of identical twins reared together, the median of fourteen correlation coefficients is .87, almost as high as the coefficient we would expect to get when we correlate the IQ scores of the same persons a few days apart.

For identical twins reared apart, the environments differ enough to lower the median correlation to .71. But this median correlation based on four studies is so high that many psychologists have considered it to be strong evidence of the importance of genetic variations (or lack of them in the case of identical twins) in determining IQ variations. Here, apparently, the environments of the twins differ, but the IQ correlations (similarities) remain quite high. The only explanation, many psychologists conclude, is that the genetic similarity (or identity) produces the IQ similarity and thus hereditary factors are highly influential in determining IQ. But this conclusion has been challenged. In particular, the

Heredity is greater than environmental influence on individual differences in IQ

FIGURE 3.2 *Correlation Between IQ Scores and Different Levels of Similarity in Heredity and Environment*

Category of Relationship	No. of Studies
1. Identical twins reared together	14
2. Identical twins reared apart*	4
3. Fraternal twins of same gender	11
4. Fraternal twins of different gender	9
5. Ordinary siblings reared together	36
6. Ordinary siblings reared apart	3
7. Foster parents and foster children	3
8. Unrelated children reared together	5
9. Unrelated children reared apart (0 correlation)	4

Notes: N and median r for category 6 are given as corrected by Kamin (1975. p. 141).

*Median for category 2 corrected by eliminating $r = .77$ (Burt, 1966) as suspect and retaining only rs from Shields (1962: $r = .75$); Newman, Freeman, and Holzinger (1937: $r = .71$); and Juel-Nielsen (1965; $r = .69$); and adding Bouchard, Lykken, McGue, Segal, and Tellegen (1990; $r = .72$).

assumption that the environments of the identical twins reared apart were indeed different has been questioned.

How Different Are the Environments?   The strength of the argument based on the IQ correlations of identical twins reared apart depends on the assumption that the twins' environments had only chance similarities between them. If a pair of identical twins was raised in similar environments, we cannot justifiably attribute the similarity of their IQs solely to their identical genetic make-up. Some writers (e.g., Lewontin, Rose, and Kamin, 1984, pp. 108–109) have seen serious weaknesses in the studies of identical twins because in some instances the evidence for uncorrelated environments seemed extremely questionable.

The issue can be seen in the most recent study (Bouchard, Lykken, McGue, Segal, & Tellegen, 1990). This study reported correlations for identical twins reared apart on a host of variables, ranging from physical measures (height, weight) through the physiological (blood pressure, heart rate) to the psychological (speed of response, IQ, personality) and the social (religious attitudes, social attitudes, traditionalism). It seems implausible that these social variables are genetically determined. Similarity between identical twins reared apart on such

Similarity in twins' environments

variables must surely be due to similarities in their environments (e.g., the attitudes of parents, foster parents, teachers, communities). The correlation between the identical twins reared apart on religiosity was .49, on nonreligious social attitudes was .34, and on traditionalism was .53. So the "apartness" of the rearing of these pairs of twins seems suspect. So we are justified perhaps in asking whether the correlations averaging about .72 for IQ variables were inflated by similarities in the intellectual environments experienced by each pair of twins.

Studies that deal with children raised from infancy by adoptive (or foster parents) also tell us a lot about the relative influence of heredity and environment. Whose intellectual status does that of these children resemble—their adoptive parents' or their biological parents'? If environment makes the greater

Adoptive and biological parents

difference, the correlation between the children's and the adoptive parents' IQ scores will be higher. If heredity makes the greater difference, the correlation between the children's and the biological parents' IQ scores will be higher. Skodak and Skeels (1949) reported the pertinent correlations (see Table 3.2). The correlation of the child's IQ score with the adoptive parents' education is close to or at zero. But the correlations with the biological parents' IQ scores or education range from .32 to .44. On the other hand, an earlier study of 312 adopted children yielded a correlation of only .13 between the IQ scores of adopted children and their biological mothers (Snygg, 1938). So the picture is far from neat.

By statistical methods that we cannot go into here, correlation coefficients for identical twins can be used to obtain *estimates* of the amount of influence attributable to environmental differences. Many researchers have concluded that it is about 25 percent. This means that 75 percent of the influence on IQ score differences comes from genetic differences. *The influence attributable to environmental differences would have been greater if the environments of the*

	Number of Cases	Coefficient of Correlation
Adoptive parents, with whom child has lived at least 10 years		
Mother's education and child's IQ score	100	.02
Father's education and child's IQ score	100	.00
Biological parents, with whom child has not lived*		
Mother's IQ score and child's IQ score	63	.44
Mother's education and child's IQ score	92	.32
Father's education and child's IQ score[†]	60	.40
Mother's IQ score and child's IQ score[‡]	312	.13

TABLE 3.2

Resemblances in Intelligence of Adopted Children to Their Adoptive and Biological Parents

Source: Adapted from D. Snygg, "The Relationship Between the Intelligence of Mothers and Their Children Living in Foster Homes," *Journal of Genetic Psychology, 52:*401–406. Copyright 1938. Adapted from E. R. Hilgard et al., *Introduction to Psychology,* 5th edition, Harcourt Brace Jovanovich, Inc. Copyright 1971.

*All children were placed for adoption before the age of 6 months. Children's IQ scores used in correlations were obtained at ages 10 to 18 (mean age = 13).

[†]Not given in the report, but computed from the data given there. The biological father's education was unkown for the other 40 cases in the sample of 100.

[‡]From Snygg.

identical twins reared apart had differed more. It would have been less if the separate homes in which the twins were raised had turned out to have more similar effects on IQ scores.

The same kind of statistical reasoning can be applied to the coefficients of correlation for the other categories of relationship listed in Figure 3.2. The estimates of *relative* influence have been made by various statistical methods applied to various sets of data. It seems clear that, within the limits of environmental variation that have occurred in various studies of kinship correlations in Northern Europe and the United States, genetic differences may determine up to 75 percent and environmental differences at least 25 percent of the variation between *individuals* (not groups) in measured intelligence.

But in a recent survey, about six hundred of a thousand experts would not even attempt to estimate these percentages (Snyderman & Rothman, 1987). Of those who were willing to do so, heredity was seen by the average respondent as accounting for 60 percent of the variation in IQ scores within the Western white population. The evidence simply does not support either pure hereditarianism or pure environmentalism. But it runs clearly against the notion that, under present-day conditions, all *individual* differences in intelligence are due entirely to environmental factors. In short, the evidence indicates that variations in hereditary factors are somewhat more powerful than are those in environmental factors in producing *individual* differences in intelligence *within the single racial and cultural group studied,* namely, whites in Northern

Heredity more powerful than environment in producing individual differences

Europe and the United States. As we see below, the determinants of *group* differences in IQ scores cannot be at all clearly allocated to hereditary and environmental factors. Thus there is no clear evidence that differences in average IQ between racial groups, for example, are genetically determined to any degree.

The Strange Case of Sir Cyril Burt

One of the most interesting sidelights on the nature-nurture debate is the story of Sir Cyril Burt. The first British psychologist to be knighted, Burt was a major figure in education and psychology—in part because his findings on the high correlation (.77) between IQs of identical twins reared apart constituted powerful evidence for the hereditarian view. But his data were sketchily reported: "[The] treatments seem brief, almost grudging, in view of the admitted importance of the data and the pages devoted . . . to other matters" (Gage, 1972, p. 309). Then Leon Kamin in a 1972 letter to Arthur E. Jensen (Joynson, 1989, p. 326) revealed that Burt's correlations remained exactly the same despite increases over the years in the numbers of pairs of identical twins reared apart. Jensen (1974) then examined all of Burt's kinship correlations and found many additional errors. Hearnshaw (1979) concluded in his biography of Burt that the evidence strongly suggested that Burt had concocted many of his data and had invented (nonexistent) collaborators of whom no trace could be found and who could thus not be asked to corroborate either Burt's data or their suspect character.

Fraudulent data?

Thus, for a decade, Burt's reputation as a scientific investigator of IQ heritability was seriously damaged. Then books by Joynson (1989) and Fletcher (1991) appeared, reappraising Burt's data as messily reported but not necessarily dishonest. The latest installment consists of various reviews of Joynson's book. Two of these reviews consider Joynson's defense unsuccessful (Audley & Rawles, 1990; Clarke & Clarke, 1990). A third review (Ward, 1990) considers the case against Burt unproven.

Despite these ups and downs, the ironic fact remains that Burt's correlations, whether valid or fraudulent, do not differ substantially from those obtained in the four other studies of the IQs of identical twins reared apart.

High Heritability Does Not Mean Unchangeability

For educators, the question is whether intelligence, or, also important, achievement in school and job, can be improved. What many people erroneously assume is that the more heritable a trait or characteristic is, the less it can be changed or improved. Some traits, like eye color or hair color, are determined by genetic makeup almost entirely and are also unchangeable (ruling out colored contact lenses, hair dyes, and aging). Thus the high heritability of height shows up in the correlation of .86 between the heights of 56 pairs of identical twins reared apart (Bouchard et al., 1990, p. 226). But even such a highly heritable trait as height has changed remarkably; Angoff (1988) cited a Japanese study that showed an increase of $3^{1}/_{3}$ inches in the average height of young adult males in Japan between 1946 and 1982.

Similarly, Flynn (1987) found "massive IQ gains in 14 nations" from one generation to the next. The strongest evidence appeared in the Netherlands, which tests almost all 18-year-old men for military screening. Taking the same test (a form of the Ravens Progressive Matrices Test, which requires matching diagrams and patterns of increasing difficulty and uses no words or mathematics), the large populations showed an increase from 1952 to 1982 of about 20 IQ points. Because the samples were comprehensive, because the tests remained unaltered during this period, because the test was considered relatively free from cultural and educational influences, and because the men tested were relatively mature and so had reached their highest test performance, Flynn considered the evidence of a "massive IQ gain" from one generation to the next to be verified "beyond a reasonable doubt." Similarly strong evidence was available from Belgium, France, Norway, New Zealand, and Canada. The evidence went in the same direction, but was not as strong, in the United States, East Germany, Great Britain, Australia, Japan, West Germany, Switzerland, and Austria.

Flynn concluded from his careful analyses that "The Ravens . . .does not measure intelligence but rather a correlate with a weak causal link to intelligence; the same may apply to all IQ tests" (1987, p. 187). His reasoning was that, if the IQ gains reflected intelligence gains, the countries showing the gains should also have shown great improvements in the occurrence of outstanding real-life performances. Thus, "a generation with a massive IQ gain should radically outperform its predecessors" (p. 187). The percentage of men in the Netherlands showing IQs of 130 and above increased from about 2 percent in 1952 to about 25 percent in 1982. "The result should be a cultural renaissance too great to be overlooked" (p. 187) if the IQ gains reflect genuine intelligence gains. Yet no such "renaissance" occurred. Newspapers in these countries referred to no dramatic increases in genius, in mathematical or scientific discovery, in the number of superior schoolchildren, or in the number of patents granted. Hence, the test can rank people within 1952 and within 1982, but the "causal link [to intelligence] is too weak to rank generations over time" (p. 187). If the IQ tests do not measure intelligence, Flynn says, they should be regarded as measuring "abstract problem-solving ability." The problems solved in taking an IQ test are very different from the real-world problems that require genuine intelligence.

As for the causes of the IQ gains, Flynn can refer merely to "unidentified environmental variables" (p. 188). In the Netherlands, the data ruled out increased educational level and socioeconomic status (father's occupation and educational level) as the causes of any major part of the gain. Similarly, Flynn saw increased test sophistication as not the major cause. "At present, the Dutch data leave unknown the environmental factors responsible for about 15 points of a 20-point gain" (p. 189). Perhaps future research will show that television and other sources of increased information and intellectual stimulation have produced the gains. Whatever the causes, the average measures of this largely heritable characteristic are seen as changeable from one generation to the next.

The Distinction Between Intelligence and Achievement

Connotations of "intelligence" and "achievement"

Flynn's data suggest that intelligence test scores are weak correlates of what we really mean by intelligence. Perhaps the tests we use are more like achievement tests, and therefore scores are more modifiable. In fact, *intelligence* has long tended to suggest something determined by innate factors, while *achievement* suggests something acquired or learned. Intelligence appears to develop along a predetermined pattern, and not much can be done to improve it, at least according to some interpretations of past research. Achievement, on the other hand, is a product of instruction and educational activity. Test content and test results help us clarify the difference between the two concepts.

Test Content

Content similarities

First, some of the content of some intelligence tests resembles that of achievement tests. In a sense, intelligence tests *are* achievement tests—but of a special kind. Intelligence tests measure achievement of cognitive abilities "taught" by the total environment—the family, the home, the mass media, the neighborhood, the museum, the church—in family conversations, in books and newspapers, on television, *and in school.*

Items in intelligence tests vary as to how much they call forth the kinds of achievement aimed at in schools. Some types of items closely resemble some types of abilities and skills taught at various grade levels. For example, the ability to read and comprehend a paragraph of complex verbal material, as measured in some intelligence tests, looks much like an objective of reading instruction in the schools. Arithmetic-reasoning items also have much in common with what is taught in schools. But some intelligence-test items depart radically from school content. Unscrambling sentences, pointing out what doesn't belong in a picture, solving number-series problems, identifying analogies, and applying the principle involved in the relationship between two words or geometrical figures—these abilities are not taught directly in schools, although they obviously have been learned.

Intelligence tests and achievement tests similar

Intelligence tests differ from achievement tests only in the *degree* to which they measure what is taught in school. It is not an all-or-nothing distinction. The two types of tests do not differ qualitatively, one measuring some mysterious, biologically inherited, intrinsic essence, while the other measures acquired skills. Intelligence tests, then, *are* achievement tests in a way—tests of the achievement of knowledge, skills, and abilities that results from the informal interaction of individuals with the culture in which they live.

Cattell (1963) emphasized this difference when he distinguished between crystallized and fluid intelligence. *Crystallized* intelligence results from the application of general mental ability to subject matter fields such as verbal and numerical studies, geography, and history. *Fluid* general ability "shows more in tests requiring adaptation to new situations, where crystallized skills are of no advantage" (p. 3). Crystallized intelligence is measured by tests of reading, vocabulary, and arithmetical reasoning. Fluid intelligence is measured by tests that are relatively unaffected by education, tests that involve solving verbal analogies or mazes, predicting the next item in a series, or matching complex block designs, for example. Actual tests of scholastic ability, or aptitude, fall at various points along this spectrum.

Crystallized and fluid intelligence

Intelligence tests that require a good deal of academic knowledge are useful for predicting scholastic success. Tests that require little academic knowledge are probably more useful for detecting undeveloped talent on which special training could capitalize. These tests could reveal promise that has gone unrealized for lack of cultural advantage and educational opportunity. But when this kind of test yields a low score, it can lead to unjustified fatalism about the individual's future.

Uncovering talent

Test Results

The second question about the distinction between intelligence and achievement arises from the high correlation between group intelligence tests (the kind that can be given to more than one person at a time) and general achievement tests. Kelley (1927) estimated that, with age held constant, the overlap in results between two intelligence tests is about 95 percent; between intelligence tests and achievement test batteries, about 90 percent; between intelligence tests and reading tests, about 92 percent; between intelligence tests and arithmetic tests, about 88 percent. Later estimates have been equally high. William Coleman and E. E. Cureton (1954) noted that, despite Kelley's findings, "many psychologists as well as school people go on interpreting intelligence-test scores as measures of native capacity primarily, and achievement-test scores as measures of native capacity plus school motivation and effectiveness of instruction." They found a 95 percent overlap between a well-known intelligence test (the Otis Quick-Scoring Test of Mental Ability, Beta) and a well-known achievement test (three subtests of the Stanford Achievement Tests). For the most part, then, intelligence tests and general achievement tests usually lead to the same judgment about probable success.

Intelligence and general achievement tests highly correlated

But what if there is reason to suspect that a child has suffered an educational disadvantage? Or suppose the child has a language handicap, or comes from a different culture? Here an intelligence test whose content requires little educational experience may yield results appreciably different from, and more valid (i.e., relevant to intelligence) than, those of a general achievement test battery

When intelligence tests are more useful

because educational experience is more important for obtaining a high score on the achievement test battery.

For most students, intelligence tests have the slight advantage of taking less time. But achievement tests have the advantage of being less likely to lead to hereditarian, fatalistic, nothing-can-be-done interpretations. Low achievement test scores seem to call for remedial action. Low intelligence test scores seem to bring forth an attitude of resignation.

Remedy vs. resignation

Parents in low-income areas, whose children often tend to do poorly on intelligence tests, may believe that teachers and school systems hold hereditarian views. And they believe these views lead educators to stop trying to help their children. Actually most parents and teachers probably do not hold any purely hereditarian position about mental ability. One survey of parent and teacher opinion on the degree to which intelligence tests measure something innate or learned found that only 6 percent of American adults and only 1 to 2 percent of students and teachers believed that intelligence tests measure only inborn intelligence (Goslin, 1967). A large majority of American adults (78 percent) believed that the tests measure something both innate and learned, with greater emphasis on learning.

The Challenge to Intelligence Testing in Schools

The usefulness of group-administered intelligence tests in the schools has been severely challenged in recent decades. For example, the state of California has stopped using them. Individual intelligence tests for students who need special attention are still being used. But in 1979, in *Larry P.* v. *Riles,* Judge Robert Peckham ruled that even individual IQ tests should not be used as a basis for classifying children as educable mentally retarded (EMR) because the tests had resulted in the overrepresentation of minority-group children (African-Americans and Mexican-Americans) in EMR classes and had *not* been used together with evidence from developmental histories, adaptive behavior, and medical histories. Although the tests were written so as to eliminate gender differences in average IQ scores, the same effort was not made to eliminate racial and social-class differences (U.S. District Court, Opinion No. C-71-2270 RFP).

Overrepresentation of minorities

Self-Fulfilling Prophecies

The policy of using IQ testing has been criticized largely on the basis of the "self-fulfilling prophecy effect" of the IQ measure. (A self-fulfilling prophecy is one that tends to make itself come true.) As one teacher said, "Once you know the child's IQ score, you tend to see him through it, and you adjust your teaching to his ability or level of intelligence—as revealed by the test." In this way, IQ scores become the basis of a self-fulfilling prophecy for children as well as teachers.

Is the self-fulfilling prophecy powerful enough to influence students' IQ scores? Rosenthal and Jacobson (1968), in a widely publicized book, said yes, but their evidence for effects on IQ scores has been severely criticized (for example, by Elashoff & Snow, 1971).

Nonetheless, teachers' expectations on the basis of IQ scores have been found to have a somewhat consistent effect *not on IQ* but on teachers' behavior, students' behavior in class, and students' achievement (H. M. Cooper & Good, 1983). One estimate by Good (1987) is that a third of the teachers observed in a series of studies showed exaggerated responses to students whom they believed to be low achievers. Their responses to these children included the following:

- Waiting less time for them to answer questions.
- Giving them answers more frequently or calling on someone else when they were having difficulty. These students were not given additional clues or chances to respond as was often true when a student for whom a teacher held high expectations had difficulty in answering a question.
- Rewarding their incorrect answers or inappropriate behavior more often.
- Criticizing them for failure more often.
- Praising them less frequently for success.
- Failing to give them feedback after they had made a public response.
- Calling on them less often.
- Interacting with them less, and appearing less friendly in those interactions that did take place.
- Smiling at them less often.
- Seating them farther away from the teacher's desk.
- Demanding less work from them.
- Not giving them the benefit of the doubt when answers on a test were borderline.

These responses sustained, and at times even caused a drop in, the already low performance of these students.

Sustaining expectancy

The self-fulfilling prophecy is often a powerful shaper of behavior. Sometimes it is subtle; sometimes it is not. In one classroom, a teacher was overheard saying, "Hurry up, Robyn. Even *you* can get this right"; and another was heard to say, "Michelle, you're slow as it is. You haven't got time to look around the classroom" (Alloway, 1984).

When students are grouped (say for reading instruction) on the basis of IQ scores or achievement, teachers almost always treat the groups or tracks differently. Students thought to be less able often have less variety, less thought-provoking work, slower-paced instruction, less choice about what to study, and more drill and practice. And in their groups or tracks we see more

Low group gets different teaching

management problems and fewer opportunities to move up. This last is a particular problem. Once a child has been categorized, it may be very hard for the student to move out of that category. Assignment to a slow group early on can be like a life sentence with no likelihood of parole.

Given these findings about the ways some teachers respond to information about children's performance and test scores, it is no wonder that some parents are arguing against the use of intelligence tests. Because minority-group and poor children less often do well on these tests, their parents have a right to worry about how the information from these tests is used.

Getting Along Without Intelligence Tests

IQ tests and other information

Instructions to teachers usually caution against relying solely on group intelligence tests with children who are handicapped verbally, culturally, physically, socially, or emotionally. In 1982 a committee of the National Research Council judged standardized ability tests to be valid—useful in predicting an individual's school and job success and in doing so just as well for minority-group members as for whites. Rather than abandon the tests, we think they should be combined with other information that should be given at least equal weight in making decisions about people. In schools, widespread IQ testing is unnecessary; the tests are now used primarily for judging whether students need special education. These decisions should be reviewed periodically. In high schools, IQ tests should go hand in hand with opportunities for the additional or improved instruction they indicate is necessary. In colleges that do not practice selective admission, the tests are probably not needed.

Two Contemporary Theories of Intelligence

Debate continues about the importance in education of *g*, general mental ability. And debate continues as well about whether two or three or five major group or specific factors constitute intelligence. There is not necessarily a wrong or right here. The arguments simply focus on different aspects of the complex characteristic we call intelligence.

Recently two theories of intelligence have emerged that differ substantially from the various conceptions of intelligence held by psychometricians—the measurement specialists who design the kinds of intelligence tests we have been describing. One of these theories emphasizes the trainability of intelligent behavior; the other makes a case for multiple intelligences.

Intelligence and Information Processing

Components of information-processing conception

In a series of studies, Robert Sternberg (1982, 1985; Wagner & Sternberg, 1984) has pointed out that intelligent behavior of any kind can be broken down into a set of mental information-processing activities or components. He described three broad components of the overall process:

Meta components.   These are higher-order control processes that regulate all that we do, mentally and physically, to solve a problem or complete a task. Among the meta components of thinking are the overall strategies for attacking a task and for interpreting feedback while working at a task.

Performance components.   These are the mental processes we use in executing a task. These might include encoding the task, inferring relationships, and comparing possible solution strategies.

Knowledge acquisition components.   These are the mental processes for learning new things. They include such things as distinguishing relevant from irrelevant information and relating new information to old information.

We can see how this componential theory works by applying it to a common type of task, analogical reasoning. Imagine a test item: "Doctor is to patient as lawyer is to (a) judge, (b) client, (c) customer, (d) jury." What do you do to answer this question? You begin by bringing into play almost simultaneously certain meta components and performance components in order to solve the problem.

The *meta components* here might include *deciding* what kind of problem it is (fill-in or multiple choice), requiring a convergent (conventional) or a divergent (creative) response, having one right answer or several right answers; *choosing* an order of events (comparing before jumping to a conclusion); *monitoring* whether a solution seems possible and whether progress is being made; *keeping time* (if you can't come up with an answer quickly, you must decide whether to retrace your steps or to go on to another task); and *revising plans.* Meta components are all processes that help us think about our own thinking. Those who are able to monitor their thinking and activities are likely to appear to others to be acting more intelligently.

Monitoring thinking → better thinking

On the *performance component* side you must *encode* all the elements of the problem—a task not everyone is equally proficient at. But intelligent solutions clearly depend on getting all the important aspects of the problem represented in one's mind. The next performance component is inference. You must *infer* the relationship given in the first part of the analogy or you won't be able to complete the second part of the analogy correctly. You must "see" the relationship as that of provider to receiver of services—a relationship like banker to lender, or salesperson to customer. Then you must *apply* (or map) the inferred relationship about elements in the first half of the analogy onto the second half of the analogy (doctor-patient/provider-receiver/lawyer-_____). Then you search the four choices and *compare* each possible answer with the relationship. In this case, you'd quickly reject two choices—judge and jury are both irrelevant. Two choices seem to fit (client and customer), but only one—client—matches the ideal answer. You accept it and *respond.* To solve the analogy problem, then, you must at a minimum *encode, infer, map, compare,* and *respond.* Each of these component processes can be done well or poorly, and so each influences the making of choices from which we judge people as more or less intellectually able.

Knowledge acquisition components might be called for if a fifth choice in this problem was (e) maxlibs. To determine whether "maxlibs" is the right choice, you first have to define it. To do that requires knowledge you do not have. You might first try to break the word down. (Does *max* mean "maximum"? Does *libs* mean "libation" or "liberty"?) Or you may need to set up a routine to get to a dictionary or take some other action to acquire information about the word *maxlibs* (which is in fact a nonsense word).

Demystifying intelligence

The information-processing theory of intelligence has two important implications for education. One, it demystifies the mental processes that intelligent people use. Instead of being dumbfounded when students can or cannot solve a complex mental problem, we start to think: What mental processes lead to an acceptable solution to problems like this? What processes allow students to estimate answers when they are doing mathematics problems? What processes allow them to estimate the distance between Cairo, Egypt, and Cairo, Illinois, and actually be close? What gives them the ability to classify flora and fauna? How do students learn to check the accuracy of a news story?

Training intelligence

Having learned to think of intelligence as a series of distinct mental processes, we gain our second benefit. That is, we can think of training intelligence. We can think about how to debug problem-solving programs that do not work for students, concentrating on the components of the program that might produce intelligent behavior. We can work on meta components—how students monitor time, their strategy, or their sequencing—if we think that's where the difficulty lies. We can work on encoding skills or comparison skills, if that's where we think the difficulty lies. Armed with contemporary information-processing conceptions of intelligence, we can see that low general mental ability may not be a permanent condition but may be a behavioral pattern that can be remedied. Once we diagnose the problem accurately, we can prescribe ways in which students can learn to act more intelligently with items of a certain class or in a particular kind of context. This same approach to intelligence can of course be applied to teaching. What meta components are used in successful small-group discussions? What performance and knowledge acquisition components are needed to take part in classroom recitation (question-and-answer routines)?

Multiple Intelligences

Howard Gardner (1983) supplemented the psychometric tradition, which was based on the study of correlations between tests of various kinds. He asked how intelligence might be organized if we concentrated on

- literary accounts of intelligence;
- neurological evidence from studies of brain-injured people;
- descriptions of genius and deficiency as in prodigies, autistic people, idiots savants, and learning disabled children;
- anthropological reports of diverse peoples and practices in different cultures, species, and millennia.

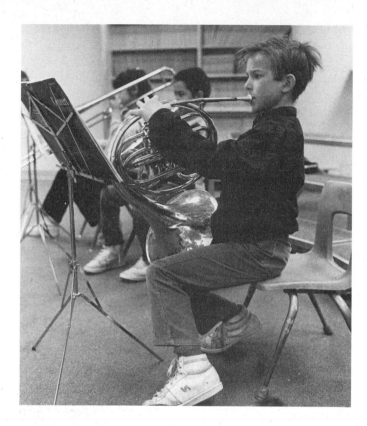

• *Should musical intelligence be any less of an educational concern than linguistic or logical-mathematical intelligence? (© Mimi Forsyth/ Monkmeyer Press Photo Service)*

Gardner sifted all these kinds of evidence. When a certain ability showed up in several of these kinds of literature, he accepted it into his categories of intelligence. His scholarship led him to theorize that there are at least seven distinct kinds of intelligence and that these are only slightly correlated, or interdependent:

Linguistic intelligence.   This kind of intelligence is seen in its extreme forms in the nuance of the poet or the writer, or in the inability of an aphasic to use language. It is what we commonly refer to as *verbal intelligence.* It includes the abilities to use vocabulary, do verbal analysis, comprehend complex verbal material, and understand metaphors.

Musical intelligence.   This shows up in the genius of a Mozart or a Lennon, or in the ordinary development of musical talent in ordinary young children following the Suzuki method. To develop musical talent in three-year-olds, as the Suzuki method does, argues well for the idea of a musical system being "wired in," waiting for the environment to influence it.

Logical-mathematical intelligence.   This appears in its extremes in mathematical genius, and in the long chains of reasoning seen in theorizing in high-energy physics or molecular biology. Arithmetic, algebra, and symbolic logic all demand this form of intelligence.

Spatial intelligence.   This is seen clearly in the work of architects and engineers, who demonstrate unique spatial ability. And it is deduced from the biographies of Rodin and other sculptors or Picasso and other artists. It is measured in tests where subjects look for hidden figures in diagrams, or mentally rotate objects in space and describe the changes they undergo in roll, pitch, and yaw.

Bodily kinesthetic intelligence.   This kind of intelligence is shown by athletes, dancers, and jugglers. It is an almost perfect awareness of and control of their bodies.

Intrapersonal intelligence.   This is the form of self-knowledge often seen in religious people, or in people with special knowledge of their feelings and control of their bodily functions (such as Indian fakirs). We have no tests of this ability.

Interpersonal intelligence.   This form of intelligence, often called *social intelligence,* has to do with the ability to make use of subtle cues in our complex social environments—our families, friendships, schools, clubs, and neighborhoods.

Different symbol systems

A modular theory of intelligence

Gardner believes that each kind of intelligence uses its own system of symbols as a fundamental unit for the processing of information. Musical intelligence, for example, is built up out of encoded rhythmic information; spatial intelligence uses a visual symbol system. For Gardner, each type of intelligence is self-contained but connected to other systems. Gardner also thinks of them as modular, like the systems that make up a car. The ignition system is related to, but clearly separable from, the propulsion system, the exhaust system, and the brake system.

We have good reasons for accepting Gardner's modular ideas. First, there is the evidence around us: the people who lose their speech but not their musical talent; the people who can correctly multiply seven digits by seven digits in seconds but are institutionalized for retardation; the people who can draw beautifully but can barely do anything else. These cases argue for separate musical, mathematical, and artistic processing systems in the brain. In the autobiographies of great musicians, artists, and writers we find descriptions in their earliest memories of a special sensitivity to rhythm and melody, to color and form, or to words and language. It may even be that there are specialized areas in the brain for the different systems.

This is only a brief account of Gardner's conceptions of the seven forms of intelligence. His conception means that a single measure of intelligence, such as the IQ, is grossly inadequate for describing people's capabilities. Even two scores, such as the Scholastic Aptitude Test's Verbal and Mathematics scores, are insufficient. Gardner and his co-workers have been developing ways of assessing all seven of his intelligences. They are using not only paper-and-pencil approaches but also performances with machines (taking apart a meat grinder), social tasks (telling a story), drawing a picture, dancing.

What is important for you to remember, however, is that the theory has implications for what a full school program might be if we tried to develop the talent of our youth (H. Gardner & Hatch, 1989). Right now our schools are designed primarily to support linguistic and logical-mathematical intelligences. We do not develop as well the musical and spatial forms of intelligence. We treat as extracurricular the development of bodily kinesthetic intelligence. And we generally ignore in formal schooling the two forms of personal intelligence—intrapersonal and interpersonal.

Schools nurture well only two intelligences

Some educators would say the schools should care as much for the other forms of intelligence as the linguistic and logical-mathematical forms. By nurturing many different kinds of intelligence we would allow many more students to succeed in learning. And that success would be a powerful motivator. Other educators say the school's main responsibility is to cultivate the intellectual outcomes and that other institutions (families, religious organizations, mass media, interactions with peers in the neighborhood and playground) can (and should be relied upon to) cultivate the other kinds of intelligence. They would also say that the different intelligences have different importances for society; thus, although music is a source of great beauty and satisfaction, it is less important than reading, writing, and mathematics for the economic, and hence overall, well-being of a modern industrial society. Also, the supply of and demand for the different kinds of intelligence are varied; our society may need scientists more than athletes. This debate about values and curriculum can now be more enlightened in view of the theory of multiple intelligences.

Ethnic Differences in Intelligence

Because "race" typically should refer solely to such psychologically unimportant characteristics as skin color, eye shape, and facial configuration, the term "ethnicity" has come into use. "Ethnicity" refers to the psychological and social differences between human groups—differences that are caused by and, in turn, influence the cultural forces operating in human societies.

We consider now a question of the most profound social importance: Are there ethnic differences in intelligence? Using *educability* as a synonym for *intelligence* reveals the seriousness of this question. The answer helps determine educational policies that shape the destinies of nations and their children.

Certain facts are clear. In the United States, African-Americans consistently score substantially lower on the average than do whites on intelligence tests. Shuey (1966) reviewed approximately 380 studies that dealt with all age levels, in all regions, using many different tests. In the vast majority of the comparisons, the mean IQ score of the African-Americans was 10 to 20 points lower than that of the whites. Shuey drew the hereditarian conclusion that these results "inevitably point to the presence of native differences between Negroes and whites as determined by intelligence tests" (p. 521).

Difference in average test scores between whites and African-Americans was not disputed by another major researcher, Klineberg (1963), who interpreted the results as environmentally determined: "As far as mental tests are concerned, the issue is not one of whether *on the average* Negro children obtain lower test scores than whites. Of that there can be no doubt" (p. 198). It is the cause of these differences that is in doubt.

Attempts to Control Environmental Differences

Differences in test scores signify hereditary differences only insofar as environmental differences are absent. Here is where much of the controversy arises. In most studies no attempt to control or adjust for environmental differences has been made. And even when attempts have been made to match the groups on measures of socioeconomic status and political and social advantage, a question remains. Environmentalists claim that the conditions under which African-Americans have been forced to live in American society make it impossible to equate environmental factors.

In an extensive review, Dreger and Miller (1968) tried to compare the intelligence of African-American and white children matched on economic status and going to integrated schools. They commented that

Caste factors in society

> "integrated" does not mean what it seems to mean. In any community of 50,000, North, East, or West, Negroes do not on the whole live where whites live because they are deliberately excluded from doing so; and other subtle, often major, discriminations exist. In other words, caste factors are still operating. . . . Even in school it would take more than the testimony of teachers or casual observation to demonstrate that the Negro children were "well accepted by the white children." (Dreger & Miller, 1968, p. 15)

It seems unlikely that any important comparison can be made against which a valid objection—that African-Americans suffer environmental disadvantages in the United States—cannot be raised. Are the environmental differences between African-Americans and whites in the United States large enough to produce average differences in IQ scores of about 15 points?

> Although we lack the data necessary for environmental comparisons of this kind, we can offer some reasonable conjectures based on the history of the two races, especially the blacks, in the United States. American history since 1700 has designed and executed a massive experiment in which radical manipulations of the environment constituted the experimental treatment. One substantial fraction of the population was enslaved, literally, not figuratively. Then, after being freed, it was subjected to an elaborate, pervasive, systematic, and rigorously enforced set of social, political, economic, and educational discriminations. The treatment operated so as to impair the fabric of that fraction's familial and educational life. The experimental group was deprived of books and access to opportunities to hear standard English. Its workers were kept so physically tired by hard labor

that they seldom could find energy for self-educative activities demanding intellectual effort. The experimental fraction was insulted, impoverished, made fearful, and instilled with self-hatred. In short, it would be difficult for psychologists, using what research has yielded concerning factors affecting cognitive functioning and development, to plan an environment better designed to harm the average intelligence of an experimental group consisting of about a 10 percent sample of the nation's population.

Unfortunately for the validity of the experiment, its design had a basic flaw: The subjects were not randomly assigned to the alternative treatments. Instead, the experimental treatment was confounded with the variable of race. All members of the experimental group were Negroes. Hence it has been impossible to determine, at least on the basis of the logic of experimental design, whether the resulting differences in the numerous dependent variables, including IQ, should be attributed to the treatment or to the race of the subjects.

A flawed experiment

Inasmuch as the experiment was flawed, it would seem to be bad research work to compound that error with another. If we cannot be sure that the educational and economic inequalities of Negroes result from the grievous experimental treatment to which they have been subjected, should we leap to the conclusion that it was their genetic makeup? For it should be recalled that all of the research on identical twins reared apart, and almost all of that on the other relationship and rearing combinations, has been done with white subjects only. Hence that research has dealt with only the environmental variances to which whites are subjected. We have no way of being sure that those environmental variances have been large enough to embrace, at the low end of the scale, the environments to which Negroes have been subjected. It thus becomes dubious in the extreme to conclude that Negroes cannot be helped, through better education, to achieve educational and economic equality. (Gage, 1972, pp. 311–312)

Attempts to Study Effects of Environmental Differences

Another approach to the problem of ethnic differences in measured intelligence is to allow environmental factors to vary widely, then see whether corresponding changes occur in IQ scores.

African-Americans in the northern United States have often been found to be higher in mean achievement and intelligence than those in Southern states (e.g., J. S. Coleman et al., 1966). The same is true for metropolitan as against nonmetropolitan African-Americans. The differences are the same for white students. Northeasterners score higher than Southerners, and urban students score higher than rural students.

Hereditarians would attribute these findings to *selective migration*. They would argue that the more able African-Americans migrated from the South to the North, that the migrating African-Americans were more able *before* they

Selective migration

moved to the North. But environmentalists would attribute the difference to educational opportunity. By this interpretation, the migrating African-Americans did not become more able until *after* they had moved to the North.

To test these competing explanations, Klineberg (1935) began work that culminated in a convincing study by Lee (1951). This was a longitudinal study, in which the same people—children in the Philadelphia schools—were tested in successive years. The IQ scores for children born in Philadelphia and for those born in the South who entered the Philadelphia schools in different grades were compared. The IQ scores of Southern-born African-American children improved regularly from the year in which they first entered the Philadelphia schools. With minor exceptions, the longer African-American students attended the Philadelphia schools, the higher their mean IQ score. This finding strengthened the environmentalists' argument. It is also strengthened by the facts about the IQ scores and scholastic achievement of Asian-Americans. Many of these people were at the bottom of the social system in their native countries. They came to the United States and found work as laborers. Yet once barriers to schooling were removed and these immigrants had acquired proficiency in the English language, their average IQ score moved beyond that of the white population by as much as 10 points (Ogbu & Matute-Bianchi, 1986).

All in all, the conclusion of most scholars is that it is impossible to tell whether hereditary or environmental differences are more influential as causes of the *group* differences between the average IQs of African-Americans and white Americans. The impossibility results from the confounding—the mixing together—of the two types of influence. The most thorough and thoughtful review of the issue (Loehlin, Lindzey, & Spuhler, 1975) reached the following conclusions:

1. Observed average differences in the scores of members of different U.S. racial-ethnic groups on intellectual-ability tests probably reflect in part inadequacies and biases in the tests themselves, in part differences in environmental conditions among the groups, and in part genetic differences among the groups. It should be emphasized that these three factors are not necessarily independent, and may interact.

2. A rather wide range of positions concerning the relative weight to be given these three factors can reasonably be taken on the basis of current evidence, and a sensible person's position might well differ for different abilities, for different groups, and for different tests.

3. Regardless of the position taken on the relative importance of these three factors, it seems clear that the differences among individuals *within* racial-ethnic (and socioeconomic) groups greatly exceed in magnitude the average differences between such groups.

Let us emphasize that these conclusions are based on the conditions that have existed in the United States in the recent past. None of them precludes the possibility that changes in these conditions could alter these relationships for future populations. It should also be noted that the probable existence of relevant environmental differences, genetic differences, and psychometric biases does not imply that they must always be in the same direction as the observed between-group differences.

On the whole, these are rather limited conclusions. It does not appear to us, however, that the state of the scientific evidence at the present time justifies stronger ones. (pp. 238–239)

Even with the usual difference in mean IQ scores between African-Americans, Hispanic-Americans, Asian-Americans, and Euro-Americans, we would find a large overlap in distribution. Suppose we have a difference of 10 points in mean IQ scores between two groups. As Figure 3.3 shows, many scores in the lower-mean (A) distribution fall above the higher mean; and many scores in the higher-mean (B) distribution fall below the lower mean. Although African-American children's mean score may be lower than that of white children, many African-American children exceed the mean for white children, and many white children exceed the mean for Asian children. Looking at it the other way, we see that many Asians score below the average of white children, and many white children score below the average of African-American children.

Overlapping distributions

FIGURE 3.3 *Distributions of Scores from Two Samples with an IQ Difference of 10 Points*

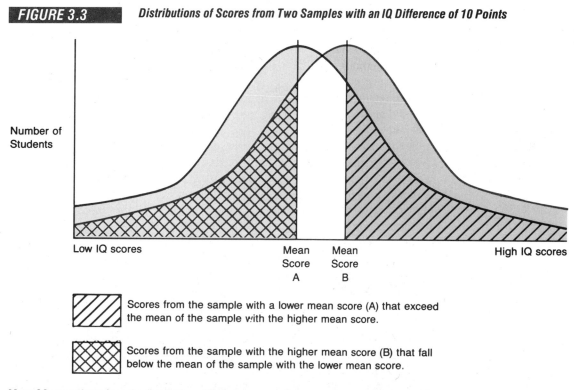

Number of Students

Low IQ scores

Mean Score A

Mean Score B

High IQ scores

Scores from the sample with a lower mean score (A) that exceed the mean of the sample with the higher mean score.

Scores from the sample with the higher mean score (B) that fall below the mean of the sample with the lower mean score.

Note: Many students from the distribution with the lower overall mean score exceed the mean of the students in the distribution with the higher mean score (and vice versa). Also, the number of students in the tail (at the extreme) differs substantially. The students from the lower distribution are less often among the highest scorers (and vice versa).

In dealing with any large representative group of children—Hispanic, African-American, Asian, or white—you cannot assume that a child from one ethnic racial group has lower or higher measured intelligence than does a child from another ethnic group. In different communities, with ethnic group members from different social classes, the mean differences between, say, Asians and African-Americans, may be of little use in predicting a particular child's ability. It is dangerous to generalize from ethnic *groups* to *individuals* within those groups. You have to look at individual students, not rely on inferences from skin color.

Group data vs. individual data

But we cannot discount the consequences of even a small difference between two distributions of IQ scores. A downward shift of 10 points, from the overall mean IQ score of 100, drastically changes the proportions found at the high and low ends of the intelligence dimension (Jensen, 1969). Fewer African-Americans, perhaps only 9 percent instead of 25 percent, have IQ scores above 110. More, perhaps 50 percent instead of 25 percent, have IQ scores below 90. And in the ranges above 115, where we usually find only about 15 percent of the general population, we find considerably more Asians than we do whites or African-Americans. The meaning of these figures in terms of job opportunities is considerable—a matter we discuss in more detail in the next section.

Social-Class Differences

Most comparisons show that middle-class children have higher average IQ scores than lower-class children, and that urban children tend to score higher than rural children.

Social class is measured by one or more of the following kinds of indexes: parents' occupation, family income, place of residence, and parents' educational level. For example, Waller (1971) compared the IQ scores of fathers and their grown-up sons—scores based on tests taken in high school. Figure 3.4 shows the mean scores of the generations categorized by the father's social class. For the fathers and sons alike, mean IQ score goes down regularly as the father's social class goes down. The differences are substantial—from means of 115 to 81 for the fathers and from 110 to 92 for the sons. Results of this kind have been obtained in many other studies (see Anastasi, 1958; L. E. Tyler, 1965).

Questioning the social importance of measured intelligence

Many educators believe that schools in general, and teachers in particular, have a responsibility to break the poverty circle, to eliminate or at least reduce the differences in educational achievement between lower-class and middle-class students. But how? The traditional view has been that special educational treatments—enriched curricula, new teaching methods, and the like—should be given students from low-income homes. These treatments should improve the students' scholastic aptitude and reduce and eventually eliminate their disadvantages, reflected in lower average IQ scores. This approach has taken the form of Project Head Start and Project Follow Through on a national scale and many similar programs in various cities and states.

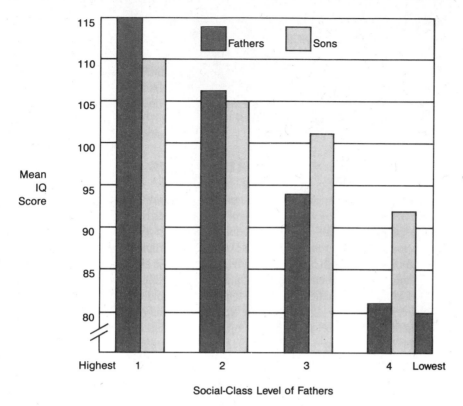

FIGURE 3.4

Mean IQ Scores in Different Social-Class Levels in Two Generations

Source: Adapted from Waller (1971).

Urban-Rural Differences

It is typical to find urban-rural differences in intelligence and achievement. In general, students in metropolitan areas show higher achievement than do those outside metropolitan areas. In the still-relevant 1966 study by J. S. Coleman and associates these differences were found at *all* the different grade levels studied (grades 1, 3, 6, 9, and 12) and on *all* the measures used in the study (verbal ability; nonverbal ability; reading comprehension; mathematics achievement; and general information in practical arts, natural sciences, social studies, and humanities).

That rural environments can be improved, with corresponding effects on IQ scores, was forcefully shown by Wheeler (1942). He reported the results of a wide-scale testing of East Tennessee mountain children in 1930 and again, "on children in the same areas and largely from the same families," in 1940. In the intervening years, the area was vastly improved, economically, socially, and culturally. Transportation, school enrollment, school size and equipment, teachers' educational level—all showed gains, largely as a result of increased industrialization. In 1930 the median IQ score of the 946 children in grades 1

Improved environment causes improved IQ scores

● *They come from every race and social class; of both genders; of all abilities; and every size, shape, and hue. The job is the same. Start where they are and teach them what they need. (© 1987 Susan Lapides)*

through 8 was 82.4. In 1940, for 3,252 children, it was 92.2. The gains were much the same at all age and grade levels. Improvements in the environment of the rural area affected IQ scores an average of 1 point a year.

The Causes of Group Differences

We have looked briefly at differences in intelligence scores between races, social classes, occupational groups, and urban and rural communities. What causes these differences? Three explanations have been proposed: selective migration, environmental influence, and test bias.

Selective Migration

The explanation based on selective migration says that more able people move into the more advantaged social classes, occupations, and communities. Their superior intellectual ability makes them better at competing for social advantage. Their higher intelligence makes them more able and interested in the kinds of activities and situations found in these more favorably placed parts of society. According to this explanation, the differences in intelligence exist *before* a group or individual moves into the more advantaged social category or location. Evidence in favor of this explanation would show that initially more intelligent persons migrate from lower-class to middle-class life situations, from the South to the non-South, from rural to urban communities.

Anastasi (1958), after summarizing the evidence, concluded that "in general, studies on adults do show a tendency for migrants from rural to urban areas to constitute a superior sampling of the rural population" (p. 530). But these results do not necessarily support hereditary explanations because the initially superior groups may have had an *environmental* advantage in their original rural setting. Also, in some situations, selective migration might operate so that those who migrate are less able. For example, in the Great Depression it was the hillbillies and sharecroppers who headed toward the cities, not the landed or higher-income classes. Those who are more able have achieved an advantageous position in their communities so that, when there is a famine or a depression, they have less incentive to migrate.

Environmental Influence

According to the environmental-influence explanation, white, non-Southern, urban or suburban, middle-class communities and families provide better environments for developing the abilities measured by intelligence tests. These environments expose children more often to the sights and sounds, words and ideas, problems and solutions that nourish the skills and knowledge measured by intelligence tests. The exact nature of this stimulation is still not known in any detail. No research has yet pinpointed the specific experiences that give city children an advantage in intelligence over farm children. But the suspicion has long persisted that hereditary factors alone cannot explain the differences.

Jensen (1969), despite his preference for hereditarian explanations of IQ score differences, has provided a striking example of how environmental influences can operate in the testing situation:

> When I worked in a psychological clinic, I had to give individual intelligence tests to a variety of children, a good many of whom came from an impoverished background. Usually I felt these children were really brighter than their IQ would indicate. They often appeared inhibited in their responsiveness in the testing situation on their first visit to my office, and when this was the case I usually had them come in on two to four different days for half-hour sessions with me in a "play therapy" room, in which we did nothing more than get acquainted by playing ball, using finger paints, drawing on the blackboard, making things out of clay, and so forth. As soon as the child seemed to be completely at home in this setting, I would retest him on a parallel form of the Stanford-Binet. A boost in IQ of 8 to 10 points or

Familiarity with testing setting

● *Rural and urban environments teach different things. But the urban environment teaches things that provide an advantage on tests. (Right: © Everett Johnson/Southern Light. Facing page: © 1985 Rick Friedman/ The Picture Cube)*

so was the rule; it rarely failed, but neither was the gain very often much above this. (p. 100)

Thus a substantial amount of the usual difference found between white and African-American, middle-class and lower-class, and urban and rural students can be eliminated by simply improving the test-taking environment. It is little wonder that environmentalists believe the "race" difference is environmentally induced. They argue that the home and community environments, combined with the testing conditions and the test-content bias (which we talk about next) are enough to explain the various group differences in IQ scores without invoking genetic factors at all.

Test Bias

Tested intelligence vs. practical intelligence

Think about the traditional task on an IQ test. It has been formulated by other people, is of little or no intrinsic interest, includes all the information necessary to solve it, is removed from the real world, is well defined (as opposed to being "fuzzy"), has one correct answer, and usually has one correct strategy that leads to that answer (Neisser, 1976; Wagner & Sternberg, 1986). Now think about intelligent performance as it takes place in the real world. Getting cars started and keeping them running with limited equipment, tools, and money is one test of intellect. Practical intelligence is at work in handicapping horses at racetracks

or navigating the open ocean in a small boat without instruments or finding the fastest route to the airport at rush hour. Intelligence comes in many forms, and tested intelligence in schools may not be the most appropriate measure of the intellectual functioning of people who are not participating in schooling to the same extent as those in the majority culture (see Chapter 5). Thus the tests themselves may give a distorted or limited picture of cognitive ability for rural, lower-class, or certain ethnic or racial groups.

The test-bias explanation, then, rests on a belief that intelligence tests involve content and processes that are more accessible to children in advantaged groups. The words, ideas, and problems used in these tests are drawn from situations of the kind more likely to be met by children in middle-class families, in urban environments, or in the non-South. Andersen (1970) noted that the Stanford-Binet Intelligence Scale (one of the most prestigious IQ tests) contains test items that refer to toys, clothing, household goods, cars, trees, trains, and houses—all things with which white middle-class children have more contact. In one study of nursery schools, a nursery with mostly white children had many playthings similar to the toys, dolls, and blocks used in the Stanford-Binet; a nursery with mostly nonwhite children had only one of these creative playthings (Andersen, 1970). The same kind of bias appears in the vocabulary items used at the higher age levels of the Stanford-Binet.

Much of the more blatant form of test bias can be avoided. Many test items intended to call for abstract thinking require knowledge that lower-class children

Middle-class test content

Avoiding more blatant bias

do not typically have. We do not have to test with an item like "Symphony is to composer as painting is to (*artist*)" when we could use "Corn is to farmer as cake is to (*baker*)." If we want to measure reasoning ability rather than knowledge, we have to free tests of their most obvious middle-class, white, urban and suburban, Northern bias. And in fact tests have been getting better in this sense.

Various group differences in intelligence might disappear, or at least become much smaller, if bias in test content was removed. But here we run into a problem. Intelligence tests are intended to measure what is important to success in twentieth-century American society. That society is itself oriented toward middle-class urban concerns. Removing this "bias" from the tests would make them less relevant to their purpose, a point that was emphasized in *Equality of Educational Opportunity:*

> The facts of life in modern society are that the intellectual skills, which involve reading, writing, calculation, analysis of information, are becoming basic requirements for independence, for productive work, for political participation, for wise consumption. . . . Such tests are not in any sense "culturally fair"; in fact, their very design is to determine the degree to which a child has assimilated a culture appropriate to modern life in the United States. (J. S. Coleman et al., 1966, p. 218)

Culturally fair tests

During the 1950s a careful effort was made to develop "culture-fair" intelligence tests, free of middle-class bias. Davis and Eells (1953) constructed and standardized a test intended to eliminate much of the disadvantage to lower-class urban children that previous tests seemed to improve. The test required reasoning about everyday events rather than abstractions; its language was nonacademic and nonbookish; it looked like a comic strip and was administered like a game. Unfortunately the test did not achieve its purposes (Charters, 1963). Middle-class children still did better on it, and the test did not correlate as highly with school achievement as did more conventional tests.

Bias or relevance?

Middle-class bias has proved much more difficult to eliminate than was anticipated. For tests of the intellectual abilities useful in modern American society, a "middle-class" and "urban" orientation may constitute not bias but relevance. An emphasis on verbal facility and the ability to solve abstract problems, like that found in intelligence tests, may be just what industrialized, technical, mercantile urban societies require. So we may not want to change the tests so much as we might want to change the environments that promote low test performance.

Improving Intelligence: The Home Environment

Can intelligence be improved by changing the environment? This is the major question in today's studies of intelligence. We do not yet have methods for increasing intelligence substantially and dependably. As yet no one has developed successful, clearly defined methods that can be repeated by other researchers with the same results.

This can also be said, but to a much lesser degree, about achievement in school. The same ethnic, social-class, rural-urban, and regional differences are found for achievement as are found for intelligence. The problem, then, is one of reducing or eliminating group differences in school achievement as well as in intelligence. The problem has been explored, progress has been made, and additional work may be expected in the years ahead. The social and educational problems at stake are so important that educators and psychologists should understand what is being done.

Differences of from 8 to 20 points separate the mean IQ scores of African-American and white children, of lower-class and middle-class children, of rural and urban children, and of Northern and Southern children. Similar differences are found in what is even more important—their achievement in school. Suppose we grant that genetic factors will always make for substantial individual *within-group* variability in IQ scores—that is, variability that occurs *even when the group (ethnic, social class, urban-rural, or regional) is held constant.* The question remains: Are there ways to manipulate environmental variables to reduce or eliminate major *between-group* differences that put a given segment of society at an intellectual disadvantage? The social concern with group inequalities in intelligence and achievement arises from our ideals of social justice. When whole groups—African-American, Chicano, rural, Southern, or lower-class children—are found to be handicapped by lower average intelligence and achievement, it is plausible to expect that broad social forces are at work. For African-Americans, these social forces include tragic parts of American history—slavery, residential and educational segregation, and job discrimination. As these injustices are eliminated, African-American disadvantages in average intelligence and achievement should be lessened. For educators, the task becomes one of improving education to make up for centuries of deprivation and neglect.

Reducing group differences

Much evidence indicates that home environment can affect IQ scores. "Whereas compensatory educational programs involve the child for a few hours per day . . . adoption alters the entire social ecology of the child. Parents, siblings, home, peers, school, neighborhood, and community—the child's rearing environment—are transformed by adoption" (Scarr & Weinberg, 1976, p. 736). Good adoptive homes and adoptive parents can turn out children whose IQ scores are substantially higher than we would predict from the biological parents' IQ scores.

Scarr and Weinberg (1976) studied 130 African-American or interracial children who had been adopted by advantaged white families. The adoptees scored on the average 106 in IQ and at the 55th percentile in achievement— above the mean IQ score and mean school achievement of African-American children reared in their own homes and of the white population. Early-adopted children did even better. "This mean represents an increase of 1 standard deviation above the average IQ of 90 usually achieved by black children

Interracial adoption

• *What happens to youngsters at home with their families correlates with IQ and achievement test scores. (Right: © 1979 Joel Gordon. Facing page: © Jean Claude Lejeune)*

reared in their own homes in the North Central region" (Scarr & Weinberg, 1976, p. 736).

Adoption across social classes

In a study in France of children of thirty-two "working-class" mothers—children abandoned, then adopted before 6 months of age into upper-middle-class families—it was found that the rate of school failures (repetition of grades or placement in a class with a simplified curriculum) was only 13 percent, much lower than that of a group of thirty-nine children of the same mothers who had not been abandoned, namely, 56 percent. Only 17 percent of the adopted children had IQ scores below 95, while 49 percent of the children who had not been abandoned had IQ scores below 95 (Schiff, Duymé, Dumaret, Stewart, Tomkiewicz, & Feingold, 1978). The estimated increase in IQ score for the adopted children was 14 points (Schiff, Duymé, Dumaret, & Tomkiewicz, 1982).

The evidence tells us that home environment affects intelligence, but it tells us relatively little about the processes involved. Just what variables in the home make the difference? If we knew, we could try to help other parents use them and try to incorporate them into our classrooms.

Measuring home environment

Sophisticated attempts have been made to analyze the home environment variables that affect cognitive development. R. M. Wolf (1964) tried to measure variables that *directly* influence specific characteristics. He measured what parents *do* in interacting with children rather than what parents *are* in terms of status and the like. He sampled a number of what he felt were influential

processes rather than a single feature of the environment. His procedure resembled that of test builders who use several items to measure a given ability or trait. He then determined whether his measures of the environment correlated with the specific characteristic of the individual.

For the characteristic of general intelligence, Wolf identified several potentially important environmental areas (B. S. Bloom, 1964, p. 78), among them:

- *Parents' pressure for achievement motivation* in the form of their intellectual expectations of their child, their aspirations for the child, the amount of information they have about the child's intellectual development, and the kinds of rewards they give for intellectual development.

Parental pressure for achievement

Parental pressure for language

- *Parents' pressure for language development,* which included their emphasizing the use of language in a variety of situations, providing opportunities for enlarging the child's vocabulary, emphasizing correctness of usage, and the quality of the language models the parents make available to the child.

General learning opportunities

- *Parents' provision for general learning opportunities in the home* and outside the home (excluding school) through making available learning supplies, books (including reference works), periodicals, and library facilities, and otherwise facilitating learning in a variety of situations.

Wolf checked these areas of the home environment through a ninety-minute, sixty-three-question interview with the mothers (or sometimes with both parents) of sixty representative fifth-grade students from several social-class levels in a medium-sized Midwestern community. The measures, when added together with the proper weightings, correlated .76 with the students' IQ scores. This high correlation, however, may not reflect cause-and-effect connections. It may have stemmed from both the genetic effect of parents' intelligence and the environmental effect of the parents' values and behaviors. Still the correlation between parent IQ score and child IQ score is usually only about .50. So Wolf may have revealed some of the environmental processes through which parental intelligence can operate.

In recent years the home life of Asian-American students has been analyzed because of the generally high IQ scores and school achievement of these students. The *New York Times* (Why Asian Students Excel, 1986) reports that more than 20 percent of the freshmen at the Massachusetts Institute of Technology and more than 25 percent of the freshmen at the University of California at Berkeley, both highly selective schools, are Asian-Americans, who constitute only about 2 percent of the American population. The source of Asian-American achievement apparently is related partly to family factors. Asian-American mothers, for example, stress hard work and the economic benefits of school success, hold high expectations for performance, and are regularly dissatisfied with their children's level of performance. They expect children to get and do homework, they limit television viewing, and they delay dating.

Cultural differences in home life

A simple set of comparisons makes clear the differences in home life in different cultural settings. Stevenson, Lee, and Stigler (1986) compared mathematics achievement in Chinese children in China, Japanese children in Japan, and American children in the United States. Sixty-three percent of fifth-grade American (Anglo) children had a desk at home, but 95 percent of the Chinese students and 98 percent of the Japanese students had desks at home to work at. Twenty-eight percent of the American children had mathematics workbooks, purchased by their parents to help extend the children's knowledge. In both China and Japan that percentage was doubled—around 57 percent. In science, only about 1 percent of American parents purchased, on their own, workbooks for their fifth-graders; 51 percent of the Chinese parents and 29 percent of the Japanese parents bought and expected their children to use workbooks. Though modified in the American setting, these are often the cultural ways of Asian-Americans, and Asian-American performance reflects this heritage.

RECAP

The parental behaviors associated with student intellectual achievement can serve as guides to teachers. Whether these behaviors are causally related to the child's intellectual development remains to be seen. Certainly some home advantages result form the parents' own intelligence, which influences both their style of life and their child's inherited intelligence. But some of the variation in children's IQ scores results solely from variables in the environment. The experimental search for reliable cause-and-effect relationships will greatly occupy teachers and educational psychologists in the years ahead.

Can Schooling Improve Intelligence?

So far we have considered only the effects of the home environment—either an adoptive home or the natural home—on children's IQ scores and achievement. This research is important to educators because it tells us that these things we call IQ and achievement can be changed, at least to some extent. Of course we cannot intervene directly in the homes of our students, except through programs of parent education and involvement. But we can accomplish a great deal by what we do at school.

The Argument for Early Intervention

It has long seemed reasonable that attempts to improve intelligence are more effective at earlier ages. It is for this reason that many programs focus on nursery school children.

Using the nursery school

Economic deprivation means inadequate opportunity to have the rich and varied experiences that promote the ability to learn. Crowded homes may provide these kinds of experiences during the first year of life, but they can suppress intellectual growth in subsequent years. During the third year, the child in a very low-income family has adult models who are more likely to provide only limited and nonstandard linguistic patterns, to answer the child's questions inadequately, and to inhibit the child's curiosity. So the child may begin a long slide into academic inferiority during early childhood. The clear implication is that preventive measures should be taken during these early years.

Economics and opportunity to learn

This kind of reasoning and evidence led to the proposition that early schooling can prevent the slum child's entering the first grade with a handicap that prevents adequate achievement in that grade and all subsequent grades. In early schooling, the preschool child should learn to handle language, evaluate information, use probable cues as well as completely certain ones, and otherwise grasp general principles and methods of dealing with the environment.

• *Nursery school experience prepares a child for elementary school. It has enduring effects, especially for low-income children. (© Carol Palmer)*

Exposure to a rich environment and taking part in the trial-and-error process should further such learning.

Attempts to Raise Intelligence

How have educators tried in recent years to improve intelligence? They have worked at both the early education and adolescent levels.

Early Education Programs

Educators have for many years advocated early education as a way of reducing the handicaps of children from low-income families—handicaps that show up in the first grade and become more severe with each additional year. In the 1960s many programs to remedy this problem were put into effect. They were based on the best ideas then available—a variety of theoretical models, curricula, and delivery systems.

The results of a follow-up study of children who had participated in eleven of these programs are available (Lazar & Darlington, 1982). Some of the programs were "center based," located in nursery schools; others were "home based," directed toward the parent, usually the mother; still others combined both approaches. Most of the children were African-American and poor; the sexes were about equally represented. The study tried to assess the long-term effects of the programs on a variety of possible outcomes: the children's intelligence, achievement, school success, goals and aspirations, and feelings about themselves and the school environment. It also assessed their parents' goals and aspirations for their children.

We give here a summary of what was a complex technical task, the "bottom line" of a series of tables, which themselves summarized much information. Table 3.3 shows the name of each outcome measure and the values of the measures for "program" and "control" children across the studies. The results indicate that the program children did better than the control children in the following ways:

- Staying out of special education classes
- Avoiding being retained in grade
- Avoiding either being retained in grade or special education classes or both
- Stating achievement-related reasons for being proud of themselves

TABLE 3.3

Lasting Effects of Early Education: Summary of Comparisons of Program and Control Children

Outcome Measure	Median of All Projects	
	Program	Control
Percent of students placed in special education classes	13.8	28.6
Percent of students retained in grade	25.4	30.5
Percent of students who failed to meet school requirements (placed in special education or retained in grade)	25.4	44.1
Percent stating achievement-related reasons for being proud of themselves	78.4	66.0
Mean of students' self-evaluations of their school performance relative to peers (1 = much better; 5 = much worse)	2.69	2.74

Source: I. Lazar and R. Darlington, "Lasting Effects of Early Education: A Report from the Consortium for Longitudinal Studies," *Monographs of the Society for Research in Child Development, 17* (2–3), Series No. 195. Copyright 1982 by The Society for Research in Child Development. Used by permission.

But they did not evaluate themselves more favorably than the control children in relation to their peers in school performance. (There the result could easily have been due to chance.)

Table 3.4 shows the results of comparisons of program and control children on a series of achievement and ability tests given in grades 3 through 6. These comparisons were adjusted statistically for variations, within each of the different studies, in the students' pretest scores, mother's education, number of siblings at entry into the research project, and father's presence. Here we give the outcome in our own terms: "Yes" (the programs overall did have a desirable effect as compared with the control group) or "No" (they did not). We use "?" if we cannot make a decision. With only two exceptions, it is clear that the program students did better on math, reading, and IQ tests and that the programs resulted in greater maternal satisfaction with the child's school performance.

The authors of this massive follow-up study concluded that "When evaluated over a period of years, early education had significant effects in the four outcome areas studied: school competence, developed abilities, children's attitudes and values, and selected family outcomes" (Lazar & Darlington, 1982, p. 55).

The results of a longitudinal study of extremely poor minority-group children in the Perry Preschool project in Ypsilanti, Michigan, were also impressive (Berrueta-Clement, Schweinhart, Barnett, Epstein, & Weikart, 1984). Three- and four-year-olds were followed through to age 19. Approximately two-thirds of these students finished high school, compared to 50 percent of a control group. About twice as many of the preschool group, as compared to the control group, started postsecondary education. The preschool group showed 20 percent fewer arrests, 20 percent fewer on welfare, and about 20 percent greater employment than did the control group.

Lasting effects of early education

The results are even more impressive when we analyze the economic benefits to society (Barnett, 1985). One year of the preschool, with about a 5 to 1 student-teacher ratio, cost almost $5,000 a child (in 1982 dollars). The return to society, by age 19, exceeded that amount. That is, reduced remedial programming, reduced crime, increased earnings, and the like, resulted in a small net gain for society. Moreover, if we accept some reasonable estimates that include lifetime reduced welfare, increased payments of taxes, and the like, we see a return to society of many tens of thousands of dollars. Looked at this way, society's return is probably at least $5 for every $1 put into good preschool programs for low-income children.

Concerns About Effectiveness

Transfer from developers to users of programs

One issue with all the claims for the effectiveness of schooling with low-income students is, Can a program that seems to work be transferred successfully from the developers to other users? We have not had great success in doing so.

Another issue is one of which Hebbeler (1985) reminded us (while reporting on a study done in a regular school district that showed positive long-term

TABLE 3.4
Lasting Effects of Early Education

Outcome Measure	Was Program Outcome Superior to Control After Adjusting for Other Variables?
Math achievement tests	
Grade 3	Yes
Grade 4	Yes
Grade 5	Yes
Grade 6	?
Reading achievement tests	
Grade 3	Yes
Grade 4	Yes
Grade 5	Yes
Grade 6	?
Stanford-Binet IQ	
Posttest	Yes
1 year after	Yes
2 years after	Yes
3 or 4 years after	Yes
Maternal satisfaction with child's school performance	Yes

Source: I. Lazar and R. Darlington, "Lasting Effects of Early Education: A Report from the Consortium for Longitudinal Studies," *Monographs of the Society for Research in Child Development, 17* (2–3), Series No. 195. Copyright 1982 by The Society for Research in Child Development. Used by permission.

Long-term effects of programs

effects for preschool and low-income children): There are two kinds of effects to consider. One is the comparison with a control group. The other is the comparison with national norms. When the experimental group does better than the control group, we should rejoice—education makes a difference! But it is also important to compare results with national norms for achievement, welfare, income, pregnancy, and crime. If the experimental group is not performing well in terms of national norms, we need to continue to be concerned about what education and other institutions in society can do.

Still we need not withhold the verdict on whether we can systematically increase intellectual ability and achievement. Some programs of early childhood education, particularly those with a direct instructional emphasis, are clearly superior to others in increasing intellectual achievement and in paying back society for the investment it makes in these programs.

We disagree with Jensen's premature conclusion that "compensatory education has been tried and it apparently has failed" (Jensen, 1969, p. 2). In 1969 research-based early education programs had rarely been adequately tried. Since then, more adequate trials have yielded impressive results. Much more effort should be put into these programs. The improvement of the achievement of children from low-income families is now within our reach.

Adolescent Education: Feuerstein's Programs for Improving Learning Potential

The work of an Israeli psychologist, Reuven Feuerstein (1980; Feuerstein, Jensen, Hoffman, & Rand, 1985), has yielded promising results for the improvement of intelligence. Feuerstein's approach to the measurement of intelligence is dynamic rather than passive. The measurer tests, then trains the person being tested, then tests again. Rather than allowing an incorrect response to persist, the measurer takes the role of teacher and uses a variety of strategies to build the understanding and self-criticism that lead to a correct response. In Feuerstein's view, cognitive growth results both from incidental learning in interaction with the environment and from *mediated learning*—learning assisted by an adult who focuses, sharpens, elaborates, emphasizes, provides cues, and corrects as he or she tries to get the learner to understand and solve a problem. Suppose one father says to his child, "Go to the store and get two loaves of bread," and another says, "Go to the store and get two loaves of bread so we'll have enough on Monday when the stores are closed for the holiday." The child learns a good deal more from the second adult than the first. This father has mediated the learning event in ways that, if done regularly, can make a big difference in the child's intellectual functioning. The child deprived of mediational conditions, over time, shows cognitive rigidity, inflexibility, a lack of openness to new situations. The good news, however, is that deficiencies caused by too little mediated learning experience are often remediable.

Mediated learning

Feuerstein's program, designed for ten- to eighteen-year-olds, is made up of abstract problem-solving materials totaling about five hundred pages and taking two to three years to complete if done two or three times a week. His materials, especially designed for culturally deprived adolescents, take the form of exercises in perceptual and cognitive skills. Believing that many adolescents score low on intelligence tests because their parents—through neglect, ignorance, or indifference—have deprived them of consistent mediated learning, he has developed an instrumental enrichment (IE) program. The materials resemble some of the problems used in traditional intelligence tests—analogies, embedded-figures, number series, and the like. The training procedures emphasize self-control and self-regulation; the teacher tries to make the learner aware of what the learning activities mean and of the student's need to carry out his or her own cognitive monitoring and regulation. The student is kept aware of what is to be learned, focused on, perfected, and applied to new problems (transferred). Like Sternberg's information-processing theory of intelligence, which we sketched above, Feuerstein's analysis yields the subskills needed to solve complex classification problems, transitivity problems (inferring whether two relationships, such as $X > Y$ and $Y > Z$, imply a third, $X > Z$), and spatial-relations problems. Then he teaches the students to think in ways that solve such problems.

Feuerstein's approach, developed and widely applied in Israel, has been imported into other countries. Evidence on its effectiveness is promising but not definitive (see Bransford, Arbitman-Smith, Stein, & Vye, 1985; Campione,

Brown, & Ferrara, 1982; Snow & Yalow, 1982). Still the work appears to be so valuable that Venezuela's government—combining into one national program the ideas of Sternberg, H. Gardner, Feuerstein, and others—created a ministry of human intelligence. Venezuela's program assumed that we now know enough to raise intelligence among schoolchildren. As the first minister said:

> In the same way that investments of resources and political strategy are
> planned, so should the different nations, by means of a common effort,
> plan the attainment of a higher degree of intelligence in the least time pos-
> sible and by all mankind. . . . And those political leaders who do not real-
> ize the magnitude of this possibility, would be unable to avoid having their
> countries, no matter how important now, be inevitably left behind. . . .
> When the necessary means are organized to systematically improve the in-
> telligence of all people, mankind will have taken the most important step to-
> ward progress. Then, the greatest revolution in history will be achieved.
> (Machado, 1981, pp. 3–4)

Unfortunately, for political and economic reasons, the program was discontinued in the late 1980s.

SUMMARY

Intelligence is one of the most important determinants of educational achieve-ment. We define it here as the ability to solve problems involving abstractions and symbols, especially verbal ones. Because our definition focuses on general mental ability, it is important to remember that it leaves out many other abilities and skills. Also this definition is culture bound.

We measure intelligence with tests. Students' answers are scored. The scores are then converted into some kind of standardized score and interpreted in terms of the tests' norms. Intelligence measured in this way is stable; by the age of 12, there is usually little change in one's rank from one test to another.

How is intelligence organized? Is it just a general mental ability? Or is it a set of fairly distinct dimensions, of group factors? Current research seems to point toward mental ability that is both general and more specific.

The debate over the number and kinds of human intelligence is second in interest only to the debate over the role of differences in heredity and environ-ment in determining differences in intelligence. Although there is no question that both factors influence intelligence, there is a large question about their relative influence. Research is clear that under certain conditions, genetic differ-ences account for as much as 75 percent of individuals' variation in intelligence. But the research is equally clear that these findings apply only to individuals *within* culturally homogeneous groups, not to differences *between* groups.

Current practice is to use intelligence tests to select, place, and counsel students because the tests predict success in educational programs. Here, intelligence tests differ from achievement tests, which measure actual performance in school subjects. The content of intelligence tests is usually not taught explicitly; the content of achievement tests is, or certainly should be, taught in school. Intelligence tests measure more fluid ability; achievement tests, crystallized knowledge. Yet we find a high correlation between the results of the two kinds of tests.

Many people argue that intelligence tests create a self-fulfilling prophecy—that children who receive low IQ scores are taught in ways that prolong poor achievement. Where low scores on achievement tests are interpreted to show a need for improved teaching and more effort in learning, low scores on intelligence tests are often interpreted fatalistically, as if nothing can be done to help the child with a low IQ score. It is probably a good idea, then, to get along without intelligence tests except *as part of* a diagnostic process, to identify the need for special education, in combination with other kinds of information.

Our definition of intelligence is based in large part on what intelligence tests measure. Two new conceptions of intelligence go beyond the tests. One evolved its definition from the components of information processing. The other has used a wide range of sources to identify seven relatively autonomous intelligences. Both of these ways of thinking emphasize teachability: Intelligent behavior can be taught; it is not fixed. And the multiple-intelligences theory has a second implication as well—that our schools should broaden their definition of intelligence, to tap the potential in as many students as possible.

Turning now to group differences, we find that there are ethnic and social differences in measured intelligence. The average IQ score is lower for African-Americans than for whites, for students from lower-income homes than for those from middle-class homes, and for those from rural areas than for those from metropolitan areas. Why? We know that individual differences *within* groups are in good part a function of heredity. But how can heredity explain differences *between* groups whose environments also differ greatly. Whatever the heritability of measured intelligence *within* a social group whose members share the same culture and history, the relative importance of heredity and environment to differences *between* groups is not determinable because the two kinds of factors cannot be separated.

Hereditarians believe that group differences in intelligence are largely genetically determined, and they use the concept of selective migration to explain why some social advantages are related to measured intelligence. Environmentalists argue that environmental deprivation and test bias are responsible for the lower IQ scores of certain ethnic, social, and geographic groups. There is evidence that the home environment can affect both measured intelligence and academic achievement. The difficulty here is determining which variables are at work. Using correlations with IQ scores, researchers have identified several factors that seem to relate positively with measured intelligence: parental pressure for achievement and for language development, and the provision of general learning opportunities outside school. Studies of Asian-American homes and comparison of Asian and American cultures show the importance of the home environment in fostering intellectual achievement.

The effect of the home environment on intelligence and achievement is important because it tells us that change here is possible and gives us clues to the kinds of changes we must make in schools. To overcome the economic deprivation of children from poor homes, intervention must be early.

Evidence over many years indicates that nursery school programs do improve both intelligence and achievement. Moreover, these programs have been found to be effective in cost-benefit terms. Programs aimed at improving the measured intelligence of culturally deprived adolescents are also being developed, implemented, and evaluated. And the results here too are promising.

One country (Venezuela) is on record as saying that *we do know how to improve intelligence!* It is time for American educators to examine this evidence and see if they reach the same conclusion. If so, pressure must be brought on government to enhance the services for low-income students. Improving these students' intellectual functioning may well be an economic and political necessity for the United States.

The Development of Cognition, Language, and Personality

OVERVIEW

Intelligence tests were originally developed to resolve a practical problem, and they served that purpose fairly well. Their developers noted, as did everyone else, that people seem to become intellectually more capable—more capable of seeing the way the world really works—as they get older. But the developers of intelligence tests did not describe coherently the ways in which mental functioning at one age differs from that at another. Instead their tests simply identified relatively miscellaneous sets of intellectual tasks that people at various ages could perform.

A coherent description of the changes that take place in intellectual functioning as children develop was in large part the contribution of Swiss psychologist Jean Piaget. Beginning in the 1920s, he observed and interviewed children, presented them with intellectual tasks, and recorded their answers. He reported his sensitive insights, unique data-gathering procedures, and wide range of interests in many volumes, among them *The Language and Thought of the Child* (1926), *Judgment and Reasoning in the Child* (1928), *The Child's Conception of Physical Causality* (1930/1951a), and *The Moral Judgment of the Child* (1932). His later work is closely aligned with that of his colleague, Barbel Inhelder (for example, Inhelder & Piaget, 1958, 1964). Piaget's work was relatively unknown to American psychologists until the 1950s. After his ideas were summarized in English by Flavell (1963), they received much more attention (for example, Bybee & Sund, 1982; Elkind, 1976; Furth, 1981; Furth & Wachs, 1982; Ginsburg & Opper, 1988). A comprehensive collection of original source documents is provided in *The Essential Piaget*, edited by Gruber and Vonèche (1977).

Piaget's theories have helped us understand how one behavior must develop in order that another can follow; how children incorporate experience into their own very personal conceptions of the world; how children's moral values develop sequentially; how imagination is formed and how it changes; how logical thought (such as scientific thought) develops; how the ability to categorize, generalize, and discriminate grows with children's experience; and how children learn symbol systems.

Cognitive development has also been described by Bruner (1966) and Vygotsky (1978), and we talk about their work too in this chapter. Then we examine the recent work on the development of language. As Piaget, Bruner, and Vygotsky would agree, when language is learned, cognitive development is changed. The development of this sophisticated symbol system makes possible the complex reasoning that is characteristic of humans, and that is so important to the learning process.

But cognition is only one part of personality, which is the integration of all our traits, abilities, and motives as well as our temperament, attitudes, opinions, beliefs, emotional responses, cognitive styles, character, and morals. In fact, the concept of personality encompasses all aspects of human behavior, and so we also need to understand how aspects of personality other than cognition develop.

We begin by examining Erik Erikson's theory of how personality is formed, a general theory that describes personality development from birth to old age. Erikson believed that personality develops through a series of crises. He focused on adolescent crises, showing how youngsters develop trust, autonomy, initiative, and identity. He also explored how, in the wrong circumstances, mistrust, shame, guilt, a sense of inferiority, and confused identity can be the outcomes of the early years and adolescence.

Next we talk about a more specific theory of personality. It focuses on one aspect of personality development—the growth of moral reasoning.

Finally we look at the aspects of personality called traits, which for most people are the names used to communicate our descriptions of one another. We examine the traits of honesty, creativity, self-concept, and anxiety. And we emphasize both the variability and the modifiability of personality traits as we encounter them in the classroom.

In this discussion of personality, then, we move from the general to the specific. We go from an all-encompassing theory, to a theory concerned with the development of a single aspect of personality, to individual personality traits and their variability and changeability.

Piaget's Stages

In general, Piaget saw intellectual development as having four main stages: sensorimotor, preoperational (which he subdivided into preoperational and intuitive), concrete operational, and formal operational (Figure 4.1). The age designations for each stage are approximate, not hard and fast. Moreover, a stage

FIGURE 4.1

Piaget's Concept of Stages of Cognitive Development at Various Chronological Age Ranges

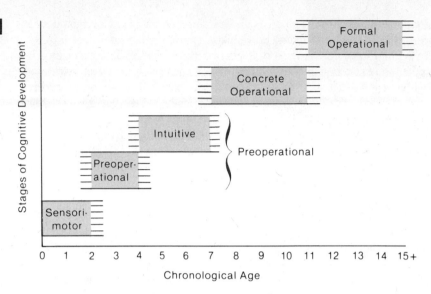

FIGURE 4.1

Piaget's Concept of Stages of Cognitive Development at Various Chronological Age Ranges

does not end suddenly. Rather it trails off. A child may still think preoperationally in some areas while performing more logically in others.

First Stage: Sensorimotor

Covering roughly the ages from birth to 2 years, the *sensorimotor stage* is characterized by the child's growth in ability in simple perceptual and motor activities. This stage covers the period during which children move from a newborn's reflexive activity to a more highly organized kind of activity. In this stage children learn to

- see themselves as different from the objects around them.
- seek stimulation in the light and sound around them.
- try to prolong interesting experiences.
- define things by manipulating them.
- regard an object as constant despite changes in its location or in their own point of view.

One example of changing behavior in the sensorimotor stage is that of an infant who tries to suck from the bottom of his bottle when it is given to him upside down. Perhaps just a month or two later the baby learns to turn the bottle right side up because he sees the bottle as the same object, regardless of the way in which it is given to him. Similarly a baby at the age of 5 months stops looking for a ball when it rolls under a blanket. But at 8 months she continues to look for it, having learned that objects do not cease to exist when they suddenly go out of her direct observational field. This important feat is called the development of *object permanence*. When you think about it, some remarkable achieve-

Object permanence

ments take place in the sensorimotor stage. Children from birth to about 2 years of age change enormously through maturation and learning.

One reason Piaget's work was unique is that he observed more carefully than his predecessors the remarkable cognitive changes that take place in children. An instance of the discriminative learning that goes on in the sensorimotor stage is found in Piaget's notes on his own child, Laurent, when he was between 3 1/2 and 4 months old.

> When, after being dressed as usual just before the meal, he is put in my arms in position for nursing, he looks at me and then searches all around, looks at me again, etc.—but he does not attempt to nurse. When I place him in his mother's arms without his touching the breast, he looks at her and immediately opens his mouth wide, cries, moves about, in short reacts in a completely significant way. It is therefore sight and no longer only the position which henceforth is the signal. (1952, p. 60)

You were probably wondering why we sit back and watch children change? Does it really matter that a baby changes a bottle around? That a child continues to look for an object after the object is out of sight? Or that an infant sucks under one set of circumstances and not another? Knowledge for children under 2 years **Knowledge is action** of age consists of their repertoire of actions on objects in the environment. What children do, from the simplest graspings through the most complex examinations of things, is designed to give them mastery over the world. In part they acquire this mastery by building internal (mental) representations, *schemata*, for **Schemata** the objects and events that they experience in the external world. Examining minute changes in behavior gives us clues to what children are learning and how that learning fits within the still more complex learning that follows.

Piaget was trained as a biologist, a fact that explains his way of looking for how one behavior fits within another, evolving in ways to help the organism adapt to its environment. If young children engage in some activity, that activity must serve a function. By carefully watching children we may learn how they come to see themselves as different from their environment and why that differentiation is important for the later development of their image of self. We may learn how and why children seek stimulation. We may learn the ways in which the manipulation of objects—the sheer joy children take in repetitive activities—helps the development of skilled motor performance and, later, symbolic thinking. We may learn that without babbling, children would never learn to speak. Piaget was searching for patterns in behavior, for the ways in which even the simplest behavior of an organism is organized and adaptive.

Second Stage: Preoperational

In the *preoperational phase* of the second stage, which covers the ages from 2 to **Preoperational phase** 4, children are busy using language to help themselves develop concepts. Their concepts are very private and often unrealistic. Experience is crucial for learning linguistic forms. You may say to a child, "Too much water. You'll spill it!" and the

Using language to develop concepts

child promptly spills it. Is the child testing your patience? Or is the child incapable of understanding a complex relational term like *too much* until a later stage, after much experience with the environment? Piaget insists that children need extensive experience to understand complex relational terms. Because our own thought patterns are relatively sophisticated, we overestimate the depth of understanding of young children.

In the preoperational phase of development, children

- are markedly self-centered and often incapable of putting themselves in another person's shoes, that is, taking another person's point of view in perceiving the physical world.
- can classify objects on the basis of a single conspicuous feature (redness, all metal objects).
- are unable to see that objects alike in one respect may differ in others (green squares and green triangles are grouped together).
- are able to collect things according to a criterion, including a shifting criterion.
- can arrange things in a series, but cannot draw inferences about things that are not adjacent to each other in the series. They cannot usually infer from the facts that if John is taller than Joe and Joe is taller than Jim, then John is taller than Jim.

Multiple classifications

The inability of a child in this phase to handle multiple classifications is seen in the nursery school child who meets his teacher in the supermarket and either fails to recognize her or is shocked to discover that she also eats! Piaget reported a similar observation made on his daughter, Jacqueline (J.), at age 2 years, 7 months, and 12 days:

Seeing L. in a new bathing suit, with a cap, J. asked: *"What's the baby's name?"* Her mother explained that it was a bathing costume, but J. pointed to L. herself and said: *"But what's the name of that?"* (indicating L.'s face) and repeated the question several times. But as soon as L. had her dress on again, J. exclaimed very seriously: *"It's Lucienne again,"* as if her sister had changed her identity in changing her clothes. (1951b, p. 224)

Intuitive phase

In the *intuitive phase* of the preoperational stage, which covers the ages from 4 to 7, children reach conclusions based on vague impressions and perceptual judgments that are not put into words. These give ground, but only slowly, to more logical, rational understanding. Perception without words—that is, without symbolic mediation—often leads children to misunderstand events in the world around them. As language becomes more and more important, more mediation can take place.

A good example of the way children's abilities change in the period of preoperational thought was given by G. A. Miller (1962), reporting Russian investigations. Suppose you give children two pictures to look at, one with a bright red circle on a pale yellow background and the other with a bright green circle on a gray background. Now ask the children to raise their right hands when the picture with the pale yellow background is shown and their left hands when the picture with the gray background is shown.

With these instructions, you've focused the children's attention on the least salient characteristics of the pictures. After practicing a while, test the children to see whether they are reacting to the background, or to the bright circles. The test is easy: Simply switch the circles. When you show the picture with the green circle (now on the pale yellow background), will the children raise their right or left hands?

Children who are 3 years old pay attention to the bright colors, ignoring the verbal instructions. They raise their left hands. They are dominated by the perceptual field (what they see), not the verbal system (what they are told). Four-year-old children appear to be confused, first doing one thing, then the other.

> Not until the child is five will a verbal command produce a stable reorganization of his perceptual field.
>
> Experiments of this sort illustrate the fact that long after a child has mastered the basic skills needed for social communication there are still important changes going on in the way these linguistic skills modify and control other aspects of his cognitive life. (G. A. Miller, 1962, p. 305)

Slowly, perhaps by age 7, children learn to react to symbol systems in a reliable way and to override their intuitive perceptual impressions. More important, by age 7 children can use symbol systems to transform the contents of their minds. But this can happen only if they have had extensive experience with the world at large. **Symbol system overrides perception**

In the intuitive phase of development, then, children

- become able to form classes or categories of objects, but are not necessarily aware of them.
- become able to understand logical relationships of increasing complexity.
- become able to work with the idea of number.
- start acquiring the principle of *conservation,* that is, the idea that **Conservation** the amount of something stays the same regardless of changes in its shape or the number of pieces into which it is divided. Children begin to acquire the conservation of mass at about age 5, weight at about age 6, and volume at about age 7. They may not completely master these concepts, however, for a year or two.

The mental processes required to recognize that the amount of liquid stays the same regardless of the shape of the beaker it is in, or that changes in the shape of a clay ball do not affect its weight, are relatively sophisticated. It is the acquisition of these concepts that tells us that the child is leaving the preoperational stage of thought and entering the operational stage. By introducing **Leaving preoperational thought**

• Sets in mathematics are a problem of classification—so easy for adults, so difficult for children. (© Susan Lapides 1987)

these kinds of tasks into the study of development, Piaget gained understanding of the growth of logical, abstract, and scientific thought processes. His goal was to probe fundamental aspects of thinking—the basic processes of mental life, not so much their products. Piaget's approach went considerably beyond a concern with the mere rightness or wrongness of answers to test questions, a concern that had dominated American psychology.

Mass

To study the conservation of mass (see Figure 4.2a), Piaget gave a child some clay to roll into a ball the same size as another clay ball. Then he rolled one of the balls into a long cylindrical shape. At the age of about 4, the child believes that the longer of the two objects contains more clay. But at the age of about 5, roughly half of the children recognize that the amount of clay is the same. In studying the conservation of weight (see Figure 4.2b), an understanding acquired at about the age of 6, Piaget first asked a child to balance two balls of clay on a scale. After changing the shape of one of the balls, Piaget noted whether the child realized that the ball whose shape had been changed would still balance the round ball. In studying the conservation of volume (see Figure 4.2c), Piaget first showed a child that balls of equal size make the water level in a cylinder go up by the same amount. Then he asked the child whether a clay ball whose shape had been changed, perhaps elongated, would cause the water to rise the same distance. Typically about half of the children give the right answer, a conserving answer, at about the age of 7.

Weight

Volume

Mass-weight-volume

The sequence in which these kinds of conservation are learned (first mass, then weight, and finally volume) seems to remain the same in many studies and in different cultures. It is possible, with a lot of work, to train children to understand conservation at earlier ages than they would normally do so. But

FIGURE 4.2   *Examples of Conservation Tasks*

	Suppose you start with this:		Then you change the situation to this:		The question you would ask a child is:
(a) Conservation of Mass	A ● ● B	Roll out clay ball B	A ● 〰 B		Which is bigger, A or B?
(b) Conservation of Weight	A ● — ● B	Roll out clay ball B	● A 〰 B		Which will weigh more, A or B?
(c) Conservation of Volume	A B	Take clay ball B out of water and roll out clay ball B	A B		When I put the clay back into the water beakers, in which beaker will the water be higher?
(d) Conservation of Continuous Quantity	A B C	Pour liquid from beaker A into beaker C	A B C		Which beaker has more liquid, B or C?
(e) Conservation of Number	A B	Break candy bar B into pieces	A B		Which is more candy, A or B?

Smedslund (1961) believed that earlier induced understanding is fragile. For example, a group of children were trained to respond correctly to problems involving the conservation of weight. Then Smedslund, without letting his action be seen, removed a very small quantity of the clay. Now the two pieces of clay were no longer balanced on the scale. Children who understood the conservation of weight as a result of their normal development resisted the experience, accusing the experimenter of trickery, searching the area for missing clay, challenging the accuracy of the scales. They kept on looking for an explanation longer and more persistently than did children who had received their understanding through experimental training. That is, children who had acquired the concept of conservation through training, not through natural experience, began acting as they had in pretraining sessions, unable to demonstrate the concept of conservation of weight. There is considerable controversy about whether you can really speed up the learning of certain kinds of concepts. Piagetians, as a rule, believe that the process is difficult and the results suspect.

Fragility of trained conservation

In the intuitive phase, the child becomes able to form classes or categories of objects, see relationships, and work with the idea of number. Children are not usually conscious, however, of the categories they are using, which is why we describe their thought processes as intuitive.

Third Stage: Concrete Operational

Operational thought

In the *concrete operational stage,* which covers roughly the ages from 7 to 11, children become capable of various logical operations but only with concrete things. An *operation* is a type of action—a manipulation of objects or their internal representations. It calls for transforming information so that it can be used more selectively. Operations make trial and error unnecessary because the child can think through certain actions and the results of those actions. Operational thought replaces the impressionistic leaps from data to conclusions with a series of small-scale reversible steps, each of which can be judged as reasonable or unreasonable. If information is concrete, comparisons can be made accurately. Thus children are not taken in by changed beaker shapes as liquid is poured back and forth. They can imagine operations and anticipate results. For example, until this stage is reached, a child cannot tell you with any conviction what the other side of the moon is like. But in the stage of concrete operations a child can "manipulate" the moon, turning it around in her mind, and will tell you that it probably looks just like this side of the moon.

During this stage children become able to handle classification systems like the one shown in Figure 4.3. This means that children become able to handle complex logical ideas:

Composition

Composition.   The idea that whenever two elements of a system are combined (for example, gasoline engine cars, *A,* and other cars, *A'*), we obtain another element of the system (that is, cars, *B*). Or if we combine cars *(B)* and other means of transportation *(B')*, we obtain means of transportation *(C).*

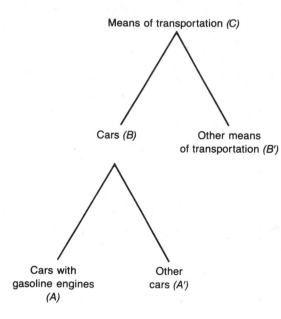

Means of transportation *(C)*

Cars *(B)*   Other means
of transportation *(B')*

Cars with
gasoline engines
(A)   Other
cars *(A')*

FIGURE 4.3

Classification Scheme Showing Kinds of Operations That a Child Can Handle in the Concrete Operational Stage

Associativity.   The idea that the sum is independent of the order in which things are added. In the example above, $A + A' = B$, and $A' + A = B$.   **Associativity**

Reversibility.   The idea that not only can we add noncars *(B')* to cars *(B)* to obtain means of transportation *(C)*, but also we can subtract noncars *(B')* from means of transportation *(C)*, to get cars *(B)*.   **Reversibility**

Although children in the concrete operational stage can handle classification, grouping, and ordering problems they are not fully aware of the principles involved. Still their thinking is at a very high level. They are not centered on salient perceptual characteristics; they can think through a number of problems independent of their perceptual dimensions. Their limitation in this stage is the need for concrete representations to tie their thinking to. The 7- to 11-year-old child, however, still has problems with highly abstract thought.

Fourth Stage: Formal Operational

In the *formal operational stage,* which covers the ages from about 11 to 14, children become capable of logical thinking with abstractions—that is, with the "possible" as well as the "here and now." They can think scientifically: draw conclusions, offer interpretations, and develop hypotheses. Their thought has become flexible and powerful. Youngsters in the formal operational stage can   **Scientific thinking**

- work out all logical possibilities without having to determine which ones actually occur in the real world. This capability is more than simple imagination; it is the systematic exposition of logical alternatives.

Combinational analysis

- conduct a combinational analysis of possibilities. Given two possible causes, C_1 and C_2, and a result, r, students can formulate the possibilities that

  either C_1 or C_2 causes r,
  both C_1 and C_2 cause r,
  neither C_1 nor C_2 causes r,
  C_1 could cause r, but C_2 could not,
  C_2 could cause r, but C_1 could not,
  C_1 and C_2 could cause r, but neither one alone could,
  C_1 could cause r, but only if C_2 is absent,
  and so on.

Propositional thinking

- do propositional thinking. Adolescents can take propositions like the ones about C_1, C_2, and r and combine them into new, higher-order propositions ("either p_1 or p_2 can be true, but not both").
- generalize from propositions based on one kind of content, say, clay or beads, to many other kinds of content, say, water, wood pieces, checkers, physical objects in general, all liquids, and all numerically denotable quantities.

Adolescents who are capable of formal operational thought can organize information in markedly different ways than were possible when concrete operational thought was being used. For example, in one experiment Inhelder and Piaget (1958) gave children four flasks that were perceptually similar, containing odorless, colorless liquids. The flasks contained (1) diluted sulfuric acid, (2) water, (3) oxygenated water, and (4) thiosulfate. A bottle, with a dropper, containing potassium iodide (g) was added. Oxygenated water (3) oxidizes potassium iodide (g) in an acid medium (1). That is, $1 + 3 + g$ yields a yellow color. The water (2) is neutral; it does not change the color when it is added to a mixture. The thiosulfate (4) bleaches out the yellow mixture of $1 + 3 + g$.

An experimenter gave the subject two glasses. In one glass was the mixture $1 + 3$; in the other glass was 2. The subject was not aware of which combinations were in each glass. While the subject watched, the experimenter put several drops of g in each glass and noted the different reactions. The subject was asked to reproduce the same yellow effect using flasks 1, 2, 3, 4, and g in any way he or she wanted. The records of two subjects in this experiment are given below.* The first describes a seven-year-old.

Subject: (Tries $1 + g$, then $2 + g$, and then $3 + g$.) I think I did everything. I tried them all.
Experimenter: What else could you have done?
Subject: I don't know.
Experimenter: (Gives the glasses to the subject again.)
Subject: (Repeats $1 + g$, $2 + g$, and so on.)

*Adapted from *The Growth of Logical Thinking*, by Barbel Inhelder and Jean Piaget, pp. 111, 117. © 1958 by Basic Books, Inc., Publishers. Reprinted by permission of the publisher.

Experimenter: You took each bottle separately. What else could you have done?

Subject: Take two bottles at the same time. (Subject then tries $1 + 4 + g$, then $2 + 3 + g$, failing to cross over between the two sets of bottles: $1 + 2$, $1 + 3$, $2 + 4$, and $3 + 4$.)

Experimenter: (Suggests that subject add other bottles.)

Subject: (Puts $1 + g$ in the glass already containing $2 + 3$, which results in the appearance of the color.)

Experimenter: Try to make the color again.

Subject: Do I put in 2 or 3? (Subject tries with $2 + 4 + g$, then adds 3, then tries it with $1 + 4 + 2 + g$.) I don't remember any more.

The seven-year-old's behavior was not random. It showed elements of systematic thought and organized planning that are considerably above the preoperational level of behavior. Still this child's attempts were inadequate. He could deal with only a few of the possible combinations at once. Environmental supports—the experimenter's hints and motivating statements—were needed to keep the subject searching for a solution. In contrast, here is the record of a fourteen-year-old facing the same problem:

Subject: You have to try it with all the bottles. I'll begin with the one at the end. (Subject goes from 1 to 4 with g.) It doesn't work anymore. Maybe I have to mix them. (Subject tries $1 + 2 + g$, then $1 + 3 + g$.) It turned yellow.

Experimenter: Are there other solutions?

Subject: I'll try. (Subject tries all six combinations of flasks, taking two at a time.) It doesn't work. It only works with $1 + 3 + g$.

Experimenter: Yes, and what about 2 and 4?

Subject: Two and 4 don't make any color together. They are negative. Perhaps I could add 4 in $1 + 3 + g$ to see if it would cancel out the color. (The subject pours 4 into the yellow mixture.) Liquid 4 cancels it all. I'll have to see if 2 has the same influence. (He pours 2 into a mixture of $1 + 3 + g$.) No, it doesn't, so 2 and 4 are not alike because 4 acts on $1 + 3$ and 2 doesn't.

Experimenter: What is there in 2 and 4?

Subject: In 4 certainly water. No, the opposite, in 2 certainly water since it didn't act on the liquids. That makes things clearer.

Experimenter: And if I were to tell you that 4 is water?

Subject: If the liquid 4 is water, when you put it into $1 + 3$ it wouldn't completely prevent the yellow from forming. It isn't water. It's something harmful.

The adolescent's ability to use formal operational thought led him right at the start to cross each element with all of the others. He used a method for determining causal relationships. Both his thinking and his language were scientific, mental and verbal "if . . . , then . . ." statements. In Piaget's theory, this kind of scientific thinking cannot be done by very young children. Only through experience and maturation does this kind of reasoning develop. Teachers should keep this developmental fact in mind: The kind of adult logic that teachers have may be beyond the capabilities of young children. In fact Peel (1976) has evidence of continued change in the complexity of adolescent thinking through age 17, and there is little doubt that some kinds of cognitive functioning change even later than that. All this means that sometimes we should be careful about the level of maturity we expect from our students in logic and scientific thinking.

The Developmental Process

Equilibrium

Children develop progressively more complex intellectual capabilities through the process of seeking an equilibrium between what they presently perceive, know, and understand on the one hand, and what they see in any new phenomenon, experience, or problem on the other. If their present condition can handle the new situation, their equilibrium is not disturbed. If it cannot, then some intellectual work is necessary to restore the equilibrium. That is, the organism must adapt in some way to the new environment.

Adaptation

Assimilation

Accommodation

Adaptation takes two forms—assimilation and accommodation—that occur simultaneously. *Assimilation* is the process of changing what is perceived so that it fits present cognitive structures (the representation, in cognition, of a concept, say, man or car or food); *accommodation* is the process of changing the cognitive structures so that they fit what is perceived. Suppose you've never seen a bat, and one flies by you for the first time. If you had to tell a friend what you saw, you'd probably describe something like a bird. You would change your perception to fit an existing cognitive structure. This is the process of assimilation. Suppose your friend, after hearing your description, tells you about bats. Now you would have to change your cognitive structure of the concept "mammal" to include a new characteristic—flight. A flying mammal requires accommodation—changing cognitive structures to fit what was perceived.

Assimilation is like chewing and digesting food in order to transform it into something the body can use. Assimilation transforms new ideas into something that fits into already-existing cognitive structures. Accommodation is like the adjustments the body makes in eating and using food: opening the mouth; contracting the muscles of the throat, esophagus, and stomach; and secreting digestive juices. In the same way, an existing cognitive structure must be modified, extended, or refined to come to grips with a new or unusual idea.

Assimilation and accommodation can be hard to tell apart. They go on simultaneously. And in the processing of ideas, they are two sides of the same coin—the process of maintaining equilibrium between people and their environment. When we interpret, construe, and structure, we are changing the nature of reality to make it fit into our own cognitive structure. This is assimilation. When we adjust our own ideas, calling up a memory, a similarity, or an analogy in order to make sense of reality, we are accommodating.

The processes of assimilation and accommodation have somewhat lasting effects on cognitive structures. As ways by which an organism adapts to its cognitive environment, they are comparable to the biological processes of adaptation that affect the structure and functions of an organism's body. So children's schemata, that is, their cognitive organizations and structures, gradually change as a function of experience, as they go through the four stages of cognitive development.

Disequilibrium and Piagetian Theory

Disequilibrium occurs, said Piaget, when we are confronted by new events that do not fit neatly with what we already know. In recent years, researchers have created disequilibrium for those who adhere closely to Piagetian theory.

For example, Brainard (1978a, 1978b) claimed that the stage theory is just descriptive, that it does not explain anything. He noted that multiplication ability always follows the development of the ability to add, but no one presumes that this sequence has any biological origins. The biological implications of Piaget's stage theory, then, may be superfluous.

Many researchers have pointed out that Piaget often underestimated the complexity of children's cognitive achievements at a particular age (Boden, 1980; Carey, 1985; Gelman, 1985). Dozens of studies show, for example, that newborns can display more complex behavior than Piaget (or the rest of us) believed possible. "Not only do children understand more than previously thought, they also can learn more" (Siegler, 1991, p. 53). Piaget also made much of children's egocentric speech and perception. But many researchers have now demonstrated that children can be very social in speech at very young ages and, when given appropriate instructions, are able to take different perspectives in perception. These are characteristics that Piaget believed to come much later in development.

Another issue being reexamined is the role of motor experience in cognitive growth. To Piaget, early motor activities are the basis for cognitive growth. Yet multiply handicapped children who have little motor experience in infancy show normal cognitive development.

And another issue has to do with Piaget's definition of formal operations. Only a small percentage of the general population appears to have formal operational abilities as Piaget defined them. The fault here seems to lie in Piaget's use of abstract tasks in investigating formal operational thought. For example, in two tasks requiring exactly the same logical processes, one presented abstractly and one presented with concrete referents, the percentage of people showing formal operational thought changed from 19 to 98 (Boden, 1980). This kind of study reveals the crucial role of context in people's judgments. Different tasks, instructions, social settings, and the like, influence greatly whether we find different kinds of thought processes when we study children's thinking (Gelman, 1985; Nagy & Griffiths, 1982). In fact, it may only be children's lack of knowledge in particular domains that leads us to believe that

Abstract vs. concrete referents

they think differently than adults. Carey (1985) believed this to be the case, and concluded that young children and sophisticated adults really think alike—one just knows a lot more than the other, and this difference in knowledge confuses the issue. Where children take on complex knowledge, as did a 4 ½-year-old who was fascinated by and became an expert on dinosaurs, we see evidence of developmentally advanced complex scientific thought, *in that domain* (Chi, 1985). The implication here, for teaching, is clear. Our students (and we, their teachers) may act like sophisticated thinkers in one area of the curriculum and be much less developed in the cognitive processes we use in another area of the curriculum. Development is a spotty phenomenon. Cognitive processes in various areas of the curriculum do not change at the same rate.

Domain-specific abilities

Cognitive change uneven

Finally, we have a conflict with Piaget's training studies, once thought to demonstrate that children could not really be taught certain kinds of things before they reached certain ages. This age requirement appears not to be true. Carefully designed training programs show that concrete or formal operational thought can occur much earlier than Piaget thought possible (Brainard, 1978a; Case, 1978; Scandura & Scandura, 1980; Siegler, 1991).

The problems with Piagetian theory have led to alternative theories about the development of children's thought (Siegel & Brainard, 1978). Cognitive psychology, which we talk about in Chapter 7, uses information-processing theory as an alternative to Piaget's thinking (see Case, 1978, 1985; Klahr, 1980; Pascual-Leone, 1980). This view considers the information-processing demands of the task (such as the number of bits of information that must be carried along to solve a problem, the number of transformations of data necessary, the number and complexity of the rules to be learned, the number of items that must be in working memory simultaneously, and so on). These demands are thought to be more important in the production of logical thought than are the mental structures that the child has built up through experience. Piagetian theory emphasizes the nature of the child's internal mental structures more than the demands of the task. Thus information-processing theory and Piagetian theory differ most in their relative emphasis on the roots of problems in the development of logical thought: The information-processing theorist more often emphasizes the nature of the tasks to be mastered; the Piagetian tends to stress the structure of the individual's thought process. The most recent theorizing of the neo-Piagetians (e.g., Case & Griffin, 1990; Case, 1991) has merged these emphases. Central ideas, or conceptual structures—in mathematics, social relations, physics, geography, time, and so forth—are found to change with age and experience. These central conceptual structures are mental entities consisting of meanings, representations, concepts, and their relationships to each other. Rather like the notion of schema, discussed again in Chapter 7, but neither biological nor logical as in Piaget's system, these central conceptual structures are semantic in nature. They are built out of experience in a particular domain *and* the state of the information-processing system at a particular stage of development. Thus, 4-, 6-, 8-, and 10-year-olds display different abilities in different areas depending on their experience and their central conceptual

Central conceptual structures

structures. The structures develop in an ordered way but are acquired through socially mediated processes (see the discussion of Vygotsky later in this chapter) and are potentially teachable.

Here is where Case diverges in an important way from Piaget. The broad central conceptual structures underlying the ability to solve problems in mathematics or physics and to understand the concepts of time or of geographical perspective are *teachable*. Although constrained by the information-processing system at certain stages (e.g., available memory), there is no need in Case's theory to believe that advanced levels of thinking (what Piaget called formal operational thought) are unlikely to occur if instruction is appropriate. While Piagetian theorizing allowed for underestimation of ability, or promoted the idea that teachers must wait for certain developmental characteristics to emerge, Case returns responsibility to parents, teachers, and schools. And that, we believe, is appropriate.

Children can be taught complex ideas

Is Piagetian theory, after all this criticism and reevaluation, still valid? Yes. Piaget's ideas are being refined and clarified, but because they form a remarkably adaptive theory, they are still robust after sixty years of development (Beilin, 1980).

Bruner's Theory of Cognitive Growth

Jerome Bruner (1966) has also examined the development of cognitive functions. His theory is concerned with the way children come to represent cognitively the world into which they are born. He believes that any theory of developmental processes must take into account the following points:

- Intellectual growth is characterized by increasing independence of responses from stimuli. Children are at first under rigid stimulus control: They respond in set ways to various stimuli. Over time they become increasingly independent of stimuli in the responses they make and the form those responses take. As they acquire a language system, they learn to mediate the relationship of stimulus and response. With mediation, they learn to defer gratification, modify their responses, or keep their responses invariant in changing stimulus situations.

Independence of response from stimulus

- Growth depends on the development of an internal information-processing and storage system that can describe reality. Unless children learn a symbol system, such as language, with which to represent the world, they can never predict, extrapolate, or hypothesize novel outcomes. To go beyond immediate sensory data and experiences requires mental—verbal, visual, mathematical, or musical—representations of the world.

Mental representations

- Intellectual development involves an increasing capacity to say to ourselves and others, in words or with symbols, what we have done and what we will do. This point really deals with

Self-consciousness

self-consciousness. Without the development of abilities to describe past and future actions, we cannot direct analytic behavior toward ourselves or toward the environment.

Tutor-learner interactions

- Systematic interactions between a tutor and a learner are necessary for cognitive development. Bruner's point is that father, mother, teacher, or some other member of society must teach a child. Simply being born into a culture is not enough for full intellectual development. A designated teacher must interpret and share the culture with the child. This point is an important element in Vygotsky's theory, which we discuss next.

Language as key

- Language is the key to cognitive development. It is through language that others communicate with us, teaching us their conceptions of the world. It is also through language that we communicate our conceptions of the world to others and question the way the world functions. Most important is the fact that as we grow older we learn to use language to mediate events in our world. This ability to provide linguistic mediation ties one event to another in a causal way, links the new to the familiar, and allows us to code events so that we can deal with these internal representations. (We talk about language development in more detail later in this chapter.)

Simultaneity in cognition

- Cognitive growth is marked by the increasing ability to deal with several alternatives simultaneously, to perform concurrent activities, and to pay attention sequentially to various situations.

Bruner noted these characteristics of cognitive growth as he worked with children in a manner similar to Piaget's. Both were concerned with the ways information about the world is coded, manipulated, stored, and ordered. From his observations Bruner identified three stages of growth in the ways that children come to represent in their minds the world around them. The first is the *enactive* stage, in which the child understands the environment through action.

Enactive stage

For example, there is no imagery and there are no words that can help you teach a child to ride a bicycle. It is psychomotor knowledge alone that gives the child mastery of a bicycle. At this stage, Piaget and Bruner have said, objects are what the child does with them. The enactive stage is where holding, moving, biting, rubbing, and touching provide needed experience with the objects of the world. It is this form of representation of knowledge that is at the root of Gardner's bodily kinesthetic intelligence (Chapter 3).

Iconic stage

The next cognitive level—the *iconic* stage—is a great advancement. It is the level at which information is carried by imagery. Visual memory is developed, but the child still makes decisions based on sensory impressions, not language. (Piaget's descriptions of preoperational thought overlap with Bruner's iconic stage.) The child is a prisoner of his or her perceptual world, swayed by brightness, vividness, noise, and movement. It is this form of representation of knowledge that Gardner calls spatial intelligence.

● *Looking, hearing, touching, feeling, chewing, squeezing, smelling—the ways in which children in the sensorimotor (and enactive) stage gain their knowledge. (© Gloria Karlson)*

Symbolic stage

Finally the child reaches the *symbolic* stage, where understanding through action and perception give way to understanding of the world by means of symbol systems. Language, logic, and mathematics come into play here. The symbolic stage allows us to translate experiences into formulas [$F = MA$, $E = MC^2$, $B = F(P \times E)$] and into semantically rich statements ("A stitch in time saves nine," "Too many cooks spoil the broth"). These formulas and sayings, communicated by symbol systems, allow us to condense ideas and thus store vast amounts of information that can be retrieved easily and that can represent the world accurately.

Bruner believes that children move from enactive to iconic to symbolic stages of representation. This statement does not mean that adults no longer code their experiences by enactive or iconic systems. It means that, with age and experience, the symbolic system usually becomes dominant. However, it is possible that great surgeons, athletes, and violinists have highly developed enactive coding systems, and that great artists are still dominated by their iconic processes.

Vygotsky's View of Cognitive Development

Russian psychologist Lev Vygotsky (1978) attributed a special role in cognitive development to the social environment of the child. He noted that children begin learning from the people around them, their social world, which is the source of all their concepts, ideas, facts, skills, and attitudes. That social world, one's culture, determines which stimuli occur and are attended to. Each culture selects differently. From the unique social-cultural patterning of events, children come to internalize selected aspects of the world. Cognitive development, then, has its origins in interaction among people in a culture before the psychological process—representing those ideas, events, attitudes, and strategies—becomes possible within children. All personal psychological processes begin as social processes, shared among people, often among adults and children. Language, of course, is the clearest example of this series of events. Social interactions determine what we find funny and sad. They determine what we are anxious about. They determine whether we hold cognitive categories (tall, brave, wealthy, and so on) that are very wide or very narrow. That is, our personal psychological processes begin as social processes, patterned by our culture.

Psychological processes start as social processes

Vygotsky's emphasis on the role of adults in influencing the cognitive development of children is the origin of Feuerstein's ideas about mediated learning (see Chapter 3). In this view cognitive development should be enhanced when children work cooperatively or collaboratively with adults and other children. And such enhancement does appear to be the case. Cognitive development proceeds from other-regulated behavior to self-regulated behavior.

From other-regulated to self-regulated behavior

> Teachers, tutors, and master craftsmen in traditional apprenticeship situations all ideally function as promoters of self-regulation by nurturing the emergence of self-control, as they gradually cede external control. In short, in a variety of learning situations, experts model many forms of control over their thinking and problem-solving activities, the controls that others must internalize if they are to become successful, independent thinkers and problem solvers. (Campione & Armbruster, 1985, p. 339)

To help a child or novice go from a social to a personal psychological form of knowledge requires, in Vygotsky's view, that the adult determine two things: first, the child's actual developmental level, by learning about the child's problem-solving capability as he or she works without any adult help; and, second, what the child can do with adult guidance. When a child is working independently, we see the actual developmental level of the child. When a child is working with an adult, we see the potential development of the child under optimum circumstances—learning with a competent, nurturing mediator. The difference between these two levels of functioning is called the *zone of proximal development*.

Zone of proximal development

● *All our personal psychological processes begin as social processes.* (© Elizabeth Crews)

Instruction is good, Vygotsky said, only when it proceeds ahead of development. Instruction must awaken and bring to life those functions that are in the process of maturing, that is, those functions in the zone of proximal development. It is in this way that direct tutelage and other forms of instruction play an important role in the cognitive development of the child (Moll, 1990; Vygotsky, 1986).

Instruction should precede development

The key to advancing the cognitive development of the child, then, is to find out the dimensions of the zone within which a teacher should work. Schools, noted Vygotsky, leave too much for the child to do independently, and this tendency slows the child's cognitive development. To develop fully, a child must be led systematically into more complex areas. The mastery of more complex levels of functioning can proceed with the help of an adult or anyone else who has expertise in the area. It is the more knowledgeable person who provides the intellectual scaffolding for the child to climb. In the zone of proximal development social knowledge—knowledge acquired through social interaction—becomes individual knowledge, and individual knowledge grows and becomes more complex. Ultimately development leads to a successfully functioning adult *in a particular community*.

Independent schoolwork can slow development

Intellectual scaffolding

Implications of Piaget's, Bruner's, and Vygotsky's Ideas for Teaching

What does all of Piaget's, Bruner's, and Vygotsky's work imply for teaching and teachers? Their findings have a bearing on what teachers ought to do. How children think and how their thinking changes as they get older should affect how children are taught. Here are some of the implications for teaching that derive from the study of cognitive development.

Understanding How Children Think

Intellectual empathy

Children do not think like young adults; they think in ways that adults can no longer remember. They make mistakes that most adults have difficulty predicting. Accordingly educators need to make a special effort to understand the child's mental operations, to see phenomena and problems in the way the child sees them. This kind of intellectual empathy is not easy, but it can be achieved through interviews, observation, and questionnaires. An understanding of children's cognitive processes is helpful in teaching the children.

Using Concrete Materials

Children, particularly in the preschool and early elementary school years, learn especially well from working with concrete objects, materials, and phenomena. Words and other kinds of symbols are less effective than things in promoting understanding at these ages. Giving children a chance to manipulate, act, touch, see, and feel things helps them acquire an understanding of concepts and relationships more effectively than the more abstract forms of learning that work well in later childhood and adolescence.

Discovery learning

In some ways the subsequent kinds of understanding based on words and symbols require the earlier kinds of understanding based on both direct and internal manipulation of objects. Children who have not acquired a "feel" for the laws of the lever by playing on seesaws may have difficulty understanding those laws in their high school physics class. Children who have not played with beads, rods, and lumps of clay may have difficulty understanding addition, subtraction, multiplication, and division. For example, to teach the concept of number, we must begin by classifying objects on the basis of color, size, form, weight, or coarseness. Without practice in seriation ("this stick before that stick"), it is hard to understand that 5 comes before 6 (Elkind, 1976). Indeed the effect of Piaget's and Bruner's ideas is to encourage "discovery" and other inductive approaches to teaching and learning. In these approaches children acquire an understanding of concepts and principles through personal discovery. Whatever the limitations of these methods at later stages of cognitive development, they have special value at preschool and early elementary levels.

• Exploration of the environment ("messing around") is necessary for cognitive growth. (© Elizabeth Crews)

Vygotsky probably would not argue this point with Piaget or Bruner. He would, however, stress the unique role of adults and older children in learning. He might stress the important role of direct tutoring. Thus a teacher must think of balancing the two kinds of educational experience—discovery learning and direct instruction. Overwhelming predominance of either is probably a mistake.

Sequencing Instruction

The idea that cognitive processes develop has implications for sequencing instruction across semesters or even for sequencing instruction within a small unit in your classroom. Instruction of children should begin with a "messing around" stage, a hands-on stage that builds enactive representations. You could do this with visits to rivers or valleys in geography, car parts in an auto

"Messing around" stage

Developing perceptual clarity

mechanics class, block letters in kindergarten, counting stadium seats in early arithmetic, and surveying a field in plane geometry.

The second part of the sequence should focus on developing perceptual clarity. You should point out salient features of objects or events, use audiovisuals extensively, and provide concrete, pictorial, and diagrammatic rather than abstract referents for things. This part of instruction is concerned with building iconic representations but in a social environment, with knowledgeable adults. Using time-lapse photographs to show a flower growing, pointing out the parts of an airplane, and color coding a molecule of salt to show both of its elements are all ways to strengthen iconic representations.

Concrete and iconic referents may be needed to help learners work with more abstract information, which they must do in the next stage of this instructional sequence, the verbal stage. Verbal discussions provide symbolic experiences for students.

Proximal experience before distal experience

A sequence of instruction that moves from hands-on experience with objects, to attention to their perceptual characteristics, and finally to verbal discussion of events seems to make sense. A teacher working with a student who is having difficulties learning some subject matter might try to use a sequence of instruction like this. Unless the appropriate kinds of preliminary experiences have taken place, it sometimes is hard for a student to understand abstract verbal discussions. Elkind (1976) wrote that "proximal experience must precede distal experience." For children to understand the map of the United States, they must first understand the map of their own city, town, or neighborhood. They can learn more in some important ways from observing live guinea pigs than they can from studying about dinosaurs. Children need to learn the near at hand before they venture out to learn things further from their own experience. Sometimes a teacher who is having difficulty explaining something should think about backing up to enactive and iconic levels of experience. This backing up can help students handle the more abstract verbal items with which they are having difficulty. Vygotsky would state it differently, but with similar implications—you must know your students' zone of proximal development and not exceed it.

In the symbolic stage, as in Piaget's formal operational stage, language becomes the instrument of thinking, taking precedence over enactive and iconic representations of knowledge. Sophisticated linguistic systems allow propositional thinking, if-then formulations, and deductive scientific thought. Once symbol usage is developed in students, and formal operations are the means by which the world is ordered and represented, teachers can discuss abstract knowledge with their students. Until children are able to process the curriculum at this symbolic level, a good deal of what goes on in schools must confuse them.

Introducing New Experiences

Fitting new experience to old

New experience, whether social or individual, interacts with cognitive structures to arouse interest and develop understanding. A new experience must fit to some extent with what children already know. But it should not fit so thoroughly that it prevents disequilibrium. Moderate novelty helps, zero novelty bores, and radical novelty bewilders.

Setting the Pace of Learning

Children ought to be allowed to proceed through the sequence of development at pretty much their own pace. They should have some chance to regulate their own learning rather than have it forced. This points toward individualized instruction rather than methods that carry a whole group of students along at the same rate. Some children need more help, different kinds of help, and more time to work alone on their own projects. They must be allowed the time they need to construct their own knowledge. The implication here is that children need "occasions for learning" more than they need formal teaching. Providing these occasions, or settings, and materials gives the teacher plenty to do in helping the child acquire understanding (Forman & Kuschner, 1977).

Student self-regulation

The Social Side of Learning

The teacher must also see to it that the Vygotskian view of cognitive development is represented by ensuring that the social side of learning is not neglected. Interaction with others—with teachers and other students—has both cognitive and affective consequences. Young children are very self-centered. This self-centeredness gives way as children are forced, through social interaction, to confront other people's points of view. Children receive information about how other people see things. They have to express themselves clearly, to defend their own views against questions, arguments, and opinions. Children's inconsistencies are seen less tolerantly by others than by themselves. Because social interaction goes on primarily by means of words, it adds a verbal level to children's understanding—thus going beyond the motoric, or manipulative, and intuitive levels.

Value of social interaction

Analyzing Errors

Piagetian tasks, like those shown in Figure 4.2, can reveal something about the cognitive strategies of children as they acquire concepts such as cause and effect, conservation, and number. For teachers with the time and the curiosity, guides to charting intellectual growth by means of Piagetian tasks have been developed (for example, Formanek & Gurian, 1976). Whether you use natural or contrived situations to probe a student's reasoning ability, Piaget made it clear, there is more information for the tester when the child makes an error then when the child is correct. Piaget worked for a while (in the school used by Binet, the developer of the intelligence test) trying to standardize a British intelligence test on Parisian children. He became fascinated with the children's errors, particularly the reasoning behind them, and never got around to finishing his standardization task. It was these errors that more than anything stimulated Jean Piaget's interest in the development of logical processes. If you take the

Information in errors

time to analyze and interpret the errors of your students, rather than simply informing students that they are wrong, you can learn a great deal.

The Development of Language

At around age 2, the sensorimotor, enactive, and iconic stages of development begin to be overwhelmed by the symbolic—the beginnings of language. This symbol system tends to replace the preverbal ways of knowing. The impact is swift, so that by 4 or 6 years of age the primary medium of human thinking, learning, and communicating is language. It is this extraordinary tool that makes human experience so different from that of other animals.

Language acquisition device

Rationalist view

There is some evidence that the ability to acquire language is innate (for example, Chomsky, 1957, 1968). A language acquisition device present in all of us and activated by exposure to spoken language has been suggested (McNeil, 1970). This rationalist (innate or nativistic) view holds that our minds contain a system of common preconceptions or ideas about the formal nature of language through which the informal linguistic data of our speech community are filtered. As they develop, children in possession of this kind of mechanism can implicitly determine what rules are operating in their language community. The rationalist view is supported by the relationship between language development and physical and motor development (Lenneberg, 1967), cross-cultural analyses of language that point to the universality of certain linguistic features and events (Slobin, 1970), and observation of the orderly acquisition of grammatical structures and use of syntactic rules by children (R. Brown, 1973).

Whether nativistic explanations are required to account for the spectacular and universal growth in the linguistic competence of children is, in part, irrelevant to our purposes. All linguists agree that it is experience with language that elicits and modifies language behavior. Variations in environment, particularly variations in the interactions between the primary care-giver and the infant, influence language and thought (Anastasiow, Hanes, & Hanes, 1982). As a listener and speaker interacting with mature language users, the child quickly learns an enormously complex set of rules and an even more complex set of exceptions to rules.

The One-Word Stage

Language in the form of single-word utterances typically starts after the first year of life, give or take a few months. By about 15 months a fifty-word vocabulary is evident. Most of this early vocabulary consists of referents *(shoe, milk, cookies, dog, car)* and action verbs *(go, push, blow)*. These are the things and events in the environment that the child acts on or that move and demand the child's attention (P. S. Dale, 1976). Children's early speech is also characterized by emotion. A child may say "cookie" loudly, meaning "I want something to eat," or "cookie" softly, meaning "I am content." The child at this stage is busy labeling things that have been enactively known and emotionally felt. Many of the action verbs are used as imperatives. The child says "push," meaning "push my swing some more." Or the child says "go," meaning "I want to go now." Sometimes the imperatives are self-directed. As the child moves from one room of the house to another, he might say "go," using the word to define the event because action alone is no longer definable without language.

First words are often overgeneralized because meaning is so difficult for a young child to determine. So *ball* is used to label all round objects, and *dog* describes a horse, a cow, and a rabbit. This period of overgeneralization ends when the child is a little older and deduces something of great importance—that everything has a name. Parents are familiar with the "What's that?" question, repeated over and over, all day long, as the child learns to name her world and build vocabulary.

Overgeneralization

No one believes that children have the detailed and differentiated ideas of adults. But the single-word utterances of a child are thought to be *holophrastic*, that is, one-word expressions of complex ideas, equivalent to the full sentences of adults. Even the first use of referents, action verbs, and imperatives seems to imply a rudimentary knowledge of grammar.

Holophrastic speech

Differences in the kind of words we first learn appear to be related to our linguistic community. In a study of the initial fifty-word vocabularies of children, K. Nelson (1973) found that the firstborn of highly educated parents use more words referring to things; later-borns of less educated parents use more words referring to self and people. The linguistic community we grow up in affects *what* we learn, and this fact has implications for education. But the rationalist view would point out that *how* learning takes place does not depend on characteristics of the linguistic community. Thus cognitive development and linguistic competence should not be affected by differences in those characteristics. In this view the linguistic competence of all speakers is equal; it is performance that differs from speaker to speaker. Cazden (1966) defined *competence* as "the speaker-learner's knowledge of his language—the finite system of rules which enable him to comprehend and produce an infinite number of novel sentences" and *performance* as "the expression or realization of competence in behavior" (p. 136). Performance is affected by our linguistic community, setting, topic, attention, memory, anxieties, and many other factors. But competence for development of a completely utilitarian language system is not in question, except for those who are brain-damaged or retarded.

Linguistic competence and linguistic performance

The Two-Word Stage

One-word utterances give the child a sense of the power, social significance, and functional importance of language. Eventually of course, and usually between 18 and 24 months of age, words get combined. The child begins to speak the way adults write telegrams. Instead of saying, "The car broke down," the child simply says, "Car broke." When Kathy wants to claim possession, she says, "Kathy sock" not "This is my sock." The child also learns to use *pivot words* (*more, allgone*), which are easily combined with other words. "More juice," "more ball," and "more giggle" communicate well, even though by means of

Telegraphic speech

TABLE 4.1			
Examples of the Semantic Relations That Can Be Expressed by Two-Word Utterances			
Semantic Relations	**Examples**	**Semantic Relations**	**Examples**
Identification	See doggie	Agent-action	Mama walk
Location	Book there	Action-object	Hit you
Repetition	More milk	Agent-object	Mama book
Nonexistence	Allgone thing	Action-location	Sit chair
Negation	Not wolf	Action-recipient	Give papa
Possession	My candy	Action-instrument	Cut knife
Attribution	Big car	Question	Where ball?

Source: Adapted from D. I. Slobin, "Seven Questions About Language Development," from P. C. Dodwell (Ed.), *New Horizons in Psychology,* No. 2. Copyright © P. C. Dodwell and contributors, 1972. Reprinted by permission of Penguin Books Ltd.

Pivot words

telegraphic sentences. The common pivot word *allgone*—"allgone sticky" or "allgone milk" (meaning "I have cleaned my hands of the sticky stuff" or "I have finished my milk")—is a way of expressing nonexistence. Even with beginning utterances, then, a sophisticated concept like the null (nonexistent) set can be communicated. This reflects remarkable growth, cognitively and linguistically, for a 2- to 2 1/2-year-old-child. The range of semantic relations displayed by a typical child in this stage is shown in Table 4.1. This is also the time when adjective use develops (Cruttenden, 1979). Children's first adjectives are often related to size ("little boy"), color ("red dog"), and affect ("pretty baby").

More-Than-Two-Word Stage

The child progresses, but quite unevenly, from the simple "go," to "go car," to the more sophisticated "go car house," which conveys both complex syntax and semantic knowledge. When more-than-two-word chains are formed, a new stage of linguistic development begins, marked by the introduction of inflection.

Inflection

In English an *inflection* is an ending of a word stem that expresses grammatical relationships. The plural *-s* and the past tense *-ed* are inflections. As children learn the rules of inflection, in order of their syntactic and semantic complexity,

Overregularization

they *overregularize* their language. For example, when the child uses *-ed* to express the past tense of *break (breaked), come (comed),* or *go (goed),* we see evidence of overregularization. Of course this is also evidence of the child's growing cognitive ability, because the child is applying rules to unfamiliar words and expressions. It may take the child a number of years to use the rules of inflection correctly.

Between approximately 2 and 5 years of age, children often display a highly creative use of language. The Russian writer Chukovsky (1968) wrote that beginning at age 2, every child becomes, for at least a short time, a linguistic genius. During this stage a child might say, "I'm barefoot all over!" or "I'll get up so early it will still be late." Children at this stage love nonsense verse. Chukovsky studied children's love of "topsy-turvies," a special form of nonsense, illustrated by "The rooster goes meow" or "The cow jumped over the moon." These are sources of hilarity to children. And they are ways to play with the cognitive representation of the world and the linguistic system that describes that world. As Piaget noted, this kind of play is really the "work" of children because it provides the experience they need for further development.

Topsy-turvies

By age 5 or 6, children typically lose some of this linguistic creativity. But children have mastered most of the adult syntactic relations by this age, although other aspects of language development continue for many more years.

The Adult and Language Development

It is interesting to watch how adults communicate with young children. First, adult speech is relevant to the here and now. Middle-class adult Americans usually comment on what children do ("That's right, eat your potatoes"), what exists ("That's a dog"), properties of things ("The puppy is furry"), and location relationships ("Baby is *in* the playpen"). When talking to children, they speak slowly, use short sentences, and frequently repeat words and sentences. They usually select words that they believe are useful, less difficult to understand, and easy to pronounce (H. H. Clark & E. V. Clark, 1977). Adults take turns with children, providing a model for social discourse. They check the truthfulness of children's statements much more often then they correct grammatical errors. They are likely to respond to "Doggie eat" by saying, "No, that's a horse," simply not commenting on the fact that the plural verb is wrong. This factor was studied in the acquisition of speech by three children:

> In general, the parents fitted propositions to the child's utterances . . . and then approved or not, according to the correspondence between proposition and reality. . . . It seems, then, to be truth value rather than syntactic well-formedness that chiefly governs explicit verbal reinforcement by parents, which renders mildly paradoxical the fact that the usual product of such a training schedule is an adult whose speech is highly grammatical but not notably truthful. (R. Brown, Cazden, & Bellugi, 1969, pp. 70–71)

The data are sketchy but consistent in indicating that parents' training procedures (modeling, reinforcement, punishment) have little or no effect on children's grammatical knowledge. It is probable that children's grammatical knowledge builds as their cognitive and intellectual abilities grow. When they are cognitively able, children can learn and generalize complex rules. As with the acquisition of conservation, directed training before certain ages is not as powerful as widespread experience.

Parental training in grammar not effective

Language Development and the Schools

Preschool and elementary school teachers would, at first glance, have the most concern with language development. But because bilingual, special, and minority-group education programs exist at all levels of schooling, all teachers need to have some awareness of what the study of language implies for education (Bierly, 1978).

Nonstandard English

There is continuing public controversy about whether nonstandard English is inferior to standard English. For most linguists, however, the issue is closed: There has yet to be found a dialect or language that is associated with some cognitive deficiency. There is no dialect or language that is more accurate, logical, or capable of expressing thought and feeling than any other language or dialect (Edwards, 1979). The rationalist position emphasizes that the surface structure or phonological sound of the language used by any speaker of nonstandard English is different *but not deficient*. The question is really whether the surface differences in the structural system of the language of nonstandard English speakers have educational and economic implications. This is a social issue, *not* a cognitive one.

Different language ≠ deficient language

Bilingualism

The debate on how to teach non-English-speaking students is also a social issue, not a cognitive one. As a teacher you will almost surely come across students whose primary language is not English. The number of non-English-speaking school-age children is surprisingly high. Although most of us are familiar with the large American Indian, Chinese, and Spanish-speaking communities of the United States, we tend to forget the Russian-speaking settlements of Brooklyn, New York; the Portuguese enclaves in Massachusetts; the Korean speakers of Los Angeles; the Samoans and the Southeast Asian immigrants of the San Francisco Bay area. By the time the children of these linguistic communities come to school, they have mastered most of the complexities of their native language. Now the challenge begins: How can the schools help these children master English and other school subjects so that they have a chance to achieve in the economic sphere *without destroying their native language competence, their self-image, or their cultural identity?*

Bilingualism superior to monolingualism

Educational research has unequivocally shown that the belief that bilingualism results in lower competence in both languages is false. Bilingual children of Montreal, of the same socioeconomic standing as a comparison group of monolingual children, were far superior in measured intelligence, with higher levels of school achievement, and had more positive attitudes toward members of the culture whose language they had mastered (Perl & Lambert, 1962). Other data consistently support the positive effects of early, balanced, bilingual education

● Bilingualism—full competence in two languages—enhances cognitive development. It is valuable for everyone not just for those lucky enough to learn their heritage language at home. (© Paul Conklin)

on students' cognitive abilities and attitudes (T. Anderson & Boyer, 1970; Lambert & Tucker, 1972; U.S. General Accounting Office, 1987). Bilingualism, then, is not necessary just for minority-group students. It is a better way of educating majority-culture students as well. This research background and the desire of many cultural groups to maintain their language community and cultural heritage have been part of the force for building bilingual education programs. But the primary factors in the growth of bilingual education are (a) the intense cultural shock experienced by non-English-speaking youngsters on entering school; and (b) the academic retardation that takes place because class time is used to teach English, while the child's regularly used, already-mastered language is ignored as a medium for teaching reading, social studies, science, and other subjects.

Cultural shock

The cultural shock of the non-English-speaking student was vividly described by L. M. Salisbury of Alaska:

By the time the native child reaches the age of seven, his cultural and language patterns have been set, and his parents are required by law to send him to school. Until this time he is likely to speak only his own local dialect of Indian, Aleut, or Eskimo or, if his parents have had some formal school-ing, he may speak a kind of halting English.

He now enters a completely foreign setting—a Western classroom. His teacher is likely to be a Caucasian who knows little or nothing about his cul-tural background. He is taught to read the Dick and Jane series. Many things confuse him: Dick and Jane are two gussuk [the Eskimo term for "white person"] children who play together. Yet, he knows that boys and girls do not play together and do not share toys. They have a dog named Spot who comes indoors and does not work. They have a father who leaves for some mysterious place called "office" each day and never brings any food home with him. He drives a machine called an automobile on a hard-covered road called a street which has a policeman on each corner. These policemen always smile, wear funny clothing, and spend their time helping children to cross the street. Why do these children need this help? Dick and Jane's mother spends a lot of time in the kitchen cooking a strange food called "cookies" on a stove which has no flame in it, but the most bewildering part is yet to come. One day they drive out to the coun-try, which is a place where Dick and Jane's grandparents are kept. They do not live with the family, and they are so glad to see Dick and Jane that one is certain that they have been ostracized from the rest of the family for some terrible reason. The old people live on something called a "farm" which is a place where many strange animals are kept: a peculiar beast called a "cow," some odd-looking birds called "chickens," and a "horse" which looks like a deformed moose. (Quoted in T. Anderson & Boyer, 1970, pp. 79–80)

It is not surprising that a large percentage of the native youngsters never reach the eighth grade.

Programs for the linguistically and culturally different vary from community to community. A program usually starts in the child's native language, eventually shifting to English. Whenever possible, education is provided initially by bilingual native-language speakers until, after a few grades, more instruction in English can take place. Then special education programs to maintain students' native language and to teach them more about their own cultures should be instituted, but usually are not. In an analysis of existing research, bilingual education showed positive effects on tests of reading, language skills, mathematics, and other curriculum areas when the tests are in English. But the programs also produced higher achievement in mathematics, writing, social studies, listening comprehension, and attitudes toward school when tests were in the student's native language (Willig, 1985). The data suggested that the average student in a bilingual program scores higher than 74 percent of the students who speak a foreign language but are placed in an all-English immersion program.

The teacher's role in bilingual education is typically defined by a committee in charge of the bilingual program. Educational psychology gives us some in-sights into teaching of this kind:

- Linguistic competence and intellectual competence are not the same. English-language tests of intelligence may seriously underestimate the intelligence of bilingual students. Students with language problems in English may have no difficulties expressing themselves in their native languages. They are also likely to withdraw from discussion and other classroom activities if teachers or other students treat them as though linguistic and cultural differences are synonymous with inferiority.

  Linguistic competence ≠ intellectual competence

- Bilingual students are also bicultural students. Particular attention should be paid to matching curriculum materials and methods of instruction to bilingual students. For example, it makes no sense to teach spelling by means of spelling bees and contests to students who belong to certain American Indian tribes that look down on individuals who achieve at the expense of others.

  Bilingual also means bicultural

- Bilingualism—the development of full competence in two languages—in no way hampers cognitive development. On the contrary it appears to enhance this development. Thus bilingual education is also recommended for native English-speakers.

- Bilingualism enhances economic opportunity. Corporations are multinational and need native speakers of other languages. The tourist industry also requires multilingual personnel.

- After their transition to English, students need opportunities to express themselves in school in their native language to help maintain their native linguistic competence and cultural identity. Only a short time ago teachers in the Southwest would send home Chicano children who "dared" speak Spanish in school. Instead the schools must see to it that facility in students' native language also grows by providing, for example, time for academic discussions in the native language.

  Maintaining native language skills

Metalinguistic Awareness

Metalinguistic awareness is the ability to think at a conscious level and talk about the sounds in words, the ordering of words in spoken or written sentences, and the selection of the linguistic form most suitable for conveying a given meaning. Metalinguistic awareness emerges in most children by about age 6. Cazden (1972) suggested that differences among children in metalinguistic awareness probably account for more of the differences among them in performance on school tasks than can be accounted for by differences in their language usage.

Children may implicitly know pluralization and some other rules, and their comprehension and production of spoken utterances may be correct. But school tasks may also require explicit awareness of rules. For example, a child may need to know consciously that the plural of most nouns ending in *y* is formed by replacing the *y* with *ies*. To succeed academically, children must make explicit their implicit knowledge of language. To participate in certain kinds of social

Explicit awareness of language rules

encounters also requires metalinguistic skills. For example, to laugh at a pun or a knock-knock joke requires the ability to be playful with sounds or word meanings—a metalinguistic skill (Anastasiow, Hanes, & Haynes, 1982). Metalinguistic awareness is necessary, too, to develop certain creative and scientific responses. Metaphors and subtle distinctions in language usage, so necessary for creative and scientific work, are best understood when metalinguistic awareness has been developed. And that awareness allows students to act on possible rather than actual information. Without some sophisticated metalinguistic awareness, then, children cannot function at the formal operational level.

A growing body of evidence suggests that bilingual education develops metalinguistic awareness, ability in concept formation, and divergent thinking (Diaz, 1983; Hakuta, 1986). In fact, the evidence for sophisticated cognition among balanced bilingual students is overwhelming (Kessler & Quinn, 1987). And in addition to these cognitive advantages, bilingual speakers also have economic advantages.

Why, then, are we not fostering bilingualism in our schools for both majority Anglo monolingual speakers of English and for minority speakers of another language? One reason is that Americans attach social status to their own and other languages. We seem to believe the rest of the world should speak English. Thus we stifle the heritage language of some children and foster monolingualism despite its recognized disadvantages. By doing so we fail to make use of one of the most obvious and effective ways to develop metalinguistic awareness in our children.

Individual Differences

The rationalist position expects individual differences in linguistic comprehension and performance. It does not attribute these differences to competence; instead it attributes these differences to personal characteristics (memory, anxiety) or to environmental differences (setting, social status). By assuming that individual differences in children's linguistic functioning can be changed, that they are not the result of innate differences in competence, a teacher is better able to adjust programs to shape students' linguistic performance.

You can accommodate students' individual differences in several ways:

- Remove sources of anxiety about communicating.
- State and adhere to explicit rules about language use. (For example, don't act when a student says, "I want that"; act only when she says, "I want the blue book.")
- Engage in more dialogue and less lecture.
- Reward reflective speech, not impulsive speech ("Let's try it because . . ." versus "Go for it!").
- Teach and use mnemonic devices to help students remember (see Chapter 7).

Sociolinguistic Competence and Schooling

It is now evident that the language development of many children outside of school may not prepare them for school. This is so because schools have a culture of their own, with special rules for communication. Children who have not mastered the etiquette of language called for in school are not able to understand and participate fully in their own education (Schultz, Florio, & Erickson, 1982). It's like visiting a foreign country—they can probably get by, but they blunder often and miss a lot!

The effects of the home-school gap have received a lot of attention (see Guthrie & Hall, 1983; Philips, 1983). We now understand that a problem exists, for example, if a student has not learned the structure of classroom lessons—a structure that often calls for a teacher initiation act (I), a student reply (R), and a teacher evaluation (E) (Mehan, 1979; 1982). (Such IRE units resemble the structuring-soliciting-responding-reacting units to be discussed in Chapter 11 when we consider classroom teaching.) A child may deviate from what is *expected* when this repetitive recitation pattern is used—responding to a teacher's question with a question, giving too lengthy an answer, or challenging the teacher's evaluative comment. These responses, although perfectly appropriate at home, are not appropriate in the classroom. Students may have to learn a new set of social rules for using language in school.

Structure of classroom lessons

Sociolinguists see the classroom linguistic environment as rule governed. Rules tell us how to speak, to whom, when, and for what purpose. But like other aspects of the process of learning language, rules are not posted on bulletin boards—children must infer them from what goes on in the classroom. Not every child does this well. Also classrooms differ in their rule structures. Some teachers ask "pseudoquestions," in which they have a right answer in mind; others ask "real" questions designed to be truly informative (Morine-Dershimer & Tenenberg, 1981). Students need to learn which kind of question is being asked. The rules also vary according to what teachers think about their students' ability. Low-ability students are not expected in reading lessons to spend much time on content or meaning; they are expected to spend their time on decoding and pronunciation problems (see J. L. Green, 1983). Rules differ, also, for different activities within classes. That is, the rules governing participation in the lesson, and the definition of appropriate content for discussion, differ markedly for large-group instruction in mathematics and small-group instruction in reading.

Classroom language is rule governed

Many different social rules for discourse in classrooms must be learned by schoolchildren. Being academically talented is not enough. Students need to present information in an appropriate form at the appropriate time (J. L. Green, 1983). "Competent membership in the classroom community, then, involves weaving academic knowledge and interactional skills together like strands of a rope, providing factually correct academic content in the interactionally appropriate form" (Mehan, 1979, p. 170). Teachers can help in the development of sociolinguistic competence by making explicit the rules for talking out, taking turns, participating in recitations, displaying factual knowledge, responding to comments by others, and so forth (see Morine-Dershimer, 1987). To expect every child to come to school with this knowledge, or to pick it up quickly once in school, is not realistic.

The Development of Personality

Schools have responsibility for developing more than cognition—they necessarily are concerned with the "whole child." Cognition and the tool it uses, language, are parts of personality, and the other parts also develop with age. We start looking at this broad area by examining one general theory dealing with development throughout the life span.

Erikson's Theory of Personality Development

Crisis in development

How do I acquire a sense of what I know to be the "real me"? Erikson (1968) believed that personal identity grows out of certain crises in psychosocial development. These crises lead to personality growth or regression. They influence whether our personality becomes more or less integrated. Erikson's underlying assumption is that as we grow we are forced to become aware of and interact with a widening social community. In the course of these interactions, first as children and later as adults, we have a chance to develop a "healthy" personality—one characterized by mastery of the environment, unity of functioning, and the ability to perceive the world and ourselves accurately. These are the qualities of the self-actualized individual described by humanistic psychologists Carl Rogers and Abraham Maslow (see Chapters 8 and 10).

For Erikson, self-actualization takes place only after the acceptable resolution of certain crises, or basic psychosocial problems (Table 4.2). A *crisis* is a time of increased vulnerability to a particular psychosocial challenge. Each crisis is related to the others. Each exists in some form before the decisive moment for its resolution arrives. And each, as it is positively resolved, contributes to the ultimate strength and vigor of the growing personality (Erikson, 1963).

Trust vs. mistrust

The *trust versus mistrust* crisis occurs in *infancy*. The quality of life during infancy—including love, attention, touch, and feeding relationships—influences the child's fundamental feelings of trust or mistrust of the environment. These feelings pervade all of later life. A favorable ratio of trust to mistrust is a form of psychosocial strength, the foundation of traits like optimism and hope.

Autonomy vs. shame and doubt

The crisis of *autonomy versus shame and doubt* occurs during *early childhood*. The child tests his parents and his environment, learning what he can control and what he cannot. Developing a sense of self-control without loss of self-esteem is necessary to his feelings of free will. Overcontrol by parents gives

TABLE 4.2
*Erikson's
Developmental
Sequence of Crises*

Age of Occurrence	Crisis to Be Resolved
Infancy	Trust vs. mistrust
Early childhood	Autonomy vs. shame and doubt
Middle childhood	Initiative vs. guilt
Elementary school age	Accomplishment vs. inferiority
Adolescence	Identity vs. role confusion
Young adulthood	Intimacy vs. isolation
Adulthood	Generativity vs. stagnation
Old age	Integrity vs. despair

Source: Extracted from *Identity, Youth and Crisis* by Erik H. Erikson, by permission of W. W. Norton & Company, Inc., and Faber & Faber, Limited. Copyright © 1968 by W. W. Norton & Company, Inc.

the child lasting feelings of doubt about his capabilities and shame about his needs or body. A child's feeling of autonomy grows out of the initial emancipation from his mother. It depends on the earlier development of trust rather than mistrust.

The crisis of *initiative versus guilt* occurs in *middle childhood*. With a sense of trust and a feeling of autonomy, the child can develop a sense of initiative. She can go on her own into strange places and let curiosity run its course. A realistic sense of purpose emerges along with rudimentary forms of ambition. A healthy resolution of the challenges at this age leads to a sense of responsibility. It is at this time that the development of initiative and the consequent experience of guilt begin to form the conscience. The parents deny the child permission to do certain things as part of their response to her unbridled curiosity. Thus the child learns the meaning of "No!" As she transgresses these prohibitions, in reality or fantasy, she feels guilt. The parent or teacher who blocks initiative too often may raise a guilty, constricted child. The parent or teacher who rebukes too rarely may raise a child without a fully developed conscience. A balanced resolution of the initiative-versus-guilt crisis frees

Initiative vs. guilt

> the child's initiative and sense of purpose for adult tasks which promise (but cannot guarantee) a fulfillment of one's range of capacities. This is prepared in the firmly established, steadily growing conviction, undaunted by guilt, that "I am what I can imagine I will be." (Erikson, 1968, p. 122)

The crisis of *accomplishment versus inferiority* occurs during the years *between kindergarten and puberty*. The child must become able to do and make some things well or even perfectly. Being denied feelings of accomplishment leads to the development of feelings of inferiority and inadequacy. Teachers in these years have the responsibility of creating successful experiences for each child, of keeping feelings of ineptness from forming. This requires knowing each student's capabilities and controlling the student's working environment. One

Accomplishment vs. inferiority

particular danger, noted by Erikson, is that doing the work becomes an end in itself, stifling the child's further growth. Feelings of worth based *only* on work—which can lead to the "rat race" in which so many business and professional workers find themselves—must be avoided. Healthy resolution of the crisis at this stage leads to a sense of competence.

Identity vs. confusion

The crisis of *identity versus confusion* occurs in *adolescence,* that period of "storm and stress." At this stage, some delay in the integration of personality elements must take place. Boys and girls are becoming men and women and cannot help but feel estranged and unattached. Their bodies and hormones change so that sexual forces often overwhelm other concerns, capture the imagination, and arouse forbidden desires. A new intimacy with the opposite sex approaches or is sometimes forced on the inexperienced young person, adding to the confusion.

The central problem of this period is establishing a sense of identity. For adolescents this means a series of questions to clarify who they are and what their role in society should be. Am I a child or an adult? Do I have what it takes to someday be a husband and father? A wife and mother? What work will I do? How am I going to earn a living? Do I matter, even though some people look down on me because of my race or religion or national background? Will I be a success or a failure? Adolescents are sometimes morbidly preoccupied with how they appear in the eyes of others as compared with their own conceptions of themselves, and with how they can make the roles and skills they have learned earlier match those that are currently in style (Office of the President, 1951).

The inability to come to an understanding of self—a lack of identity—leads to confusion. Failure to resolve this crisis prolongs adolescence and limits the ways in which people function in adult roles. These individuals do not cope effectively with later crises in the life cycle. On the other hand, a healthy resolution of this crisis leads to confidence in oneself and a sense of security that the future is going to be good.

Sometimes adolescence looks like a period of fun. One psychologist, rejecting the current view that adolescence is a time of great stress, wrote that "adolescents, as a whole, are not in turmoil, not deeply disturbed, not at the mercy of their impulses, not resistant to parental values, not politically active or rebellious" (Adelson, 1979). We tend to agree more with a psychiatrist who responded:

> To know that a teenager is doing well behaviorally in academic, athletic and social activities, as viewed from the outside, does not correlate . . . with knowledge about the mental and emotional experiences of that same young woman and man. The moods, fantasies, dreams, secret fears and wishes, that is, the painful conflicts of normative adolescence, are detectable in psychoanalytic treatment, even when they are not observable in research efforts based on one or two clinical interviews, group observations or questionnaire data. (Solnit, 1979)

• *Adolescence, a joyful and painful period in the search for identity. (© James L. Shaffer/Lightwave)*

Intimacy vs. isolation

The crisis of *intimacy versus isolation* arises in *young adulthood* after identity is functionally established, if not fixed. Can the young adult share by giving some piece of his own identity over to another, so that "we" supplants "I" in thinking about the present and future? The inability to develop intimate relationships leads to psychological isolation, which is less desirable, perhaps less healthy, for the individual. A healthy resolution of this crisis results in the person's ability to confidently give and receive love.

Generativity vs. stagnation

The crisis of *generativity versus stagnation* is the crisis of *adulthood*. *Generativity* refers to creativity, productivity, and an interest in guiding the development of the next generation. Maturity requires a dependent, one for whom you are mature. It also requires caring for and nurturing what is in your environment—ideas, things, and people. Without a certain amount of generative responses, the adult suffers boredom, apathy, pseudointimacy, an impoverishment in interpersonal relationships, and a pervading sense of stagnation. A healthy resolution of this crisis results in a *caring,* socially involved person.

Integrity vs. despair

The crisis of *integrity versus despair* occurs in *old age*. The personality is fully integrated when one develops a sense of acceptance of this one and only chance at life on earth and of the important people in it. People and events must be taken at face value. One's children, spouse, parents, and job are what they are. And most important, in recognizing this, one can say, "I am what I am!" Responsibility for what you are is your own. At this stage you can come to have dignity. On the other hand, the development of despair, of unhappiness with yourself and with what you have accomplished, can lead to a troubled, self-contemptuous, desperate end to the life cycle.

As C. S. Hall and G. S. Lindzey (1978) note, few theories of personality are supported by a firm body of quantitative and experimental data. Erikson's theory is no exception. Still it does have a ring of truth. Embedded in this general theory of development are all the possibilities of personality formation that we see in the people around us. Characteristics like trust, stinginess, creativity, altruism, complacency, and wiliness, assertiveness, precociousness, sensuality, and desperation appear to have roots in the various crises and resolutions Erikson described (P. H. Miller, 1989).

Teachers must be aware of the changes going on within their students, particularly at the stage of the adolescent identity crisis. Sometimes the newspapers report a series of teenage suicides. Family, friends, and teachers did not realize the terrible stress some of these youngsters were feeling. It reminds us again of how difficult adolescence can be in American society. A teacher's guidance, friendship, and caring can help students through this stressful period. We are in classrooms to do more than teach fractions or the causes of World War I. We are there to foster the social development of our students, to help them develop healthy and integrated personalities.

The Development of Moral Reasoning

Erikson's description of how personality develops was based on his clinical experience, his insight into the lives of Gandhi, Shakespeare, and other great people, and his psychoanalytic training. His theory rests on intuition, logic, rational analysis, and painstaking observation of his clients' reactions to society and its institutions.

Another way to study personality development focuses on the way in which some smaller part of the total personality changes over time. Because of its importance to educators, we have chosen to look at one of these approaches to the development of personality—the growth of moral thought.

How Morality Develops

How does morality develop? At what ages do we acquire ideas about right and wrong? Does our thinking about moral issues develop in stages, in a process like the one Piaget described? Kohlberg (1963, 1981) found three levels of moral thought, with two stages of development characteristic of each level (Table 4.3).

Levels of Moral Thought	Stages of Moral Development	
A. *Preconventional level.* The child responds to cultural labels of good and bad, but looks mainly at the physical effects of action (pleasure or pain) or at the physical power of the rule givers.	1. *The punishment-obedience orientation.* The individual tries to avoid punishment and defers to power in its own right.	2. *The instrumental-relativist orientation.* Right is what satisfies one's own needs, or sometimes others'. Human relations, as in the marketplace, are strictly a matter of reciprocity (You scratch my back and I'll scratch yours). This is a practical morality.
B. *Conventional level.* Meeting expectations of family, group, or nation is valuable, regardless of immediate consequences. Loyalty to and support of the social order are valued beyond mere conformity.	3. *The interpersonal-concordance orientation.* Good behavior is what pleases or helps others. Much conformity to stereotypes of "appropriate" behavior. Intentions are important. One earns approval by being "nice."	4. *Authority and social order–maintaining orientation.* Right behavior consists of doing one's duty, respecting authority, and maintaining the given social order for its own sake.
C. *Postconventional, autonomous, or principled level.* Effort is made to define moral principles that are valid apart from the authority of persons holding them or one's identification with these groups.	5. *The social-contract legalistic orientation.* Utility of laws and individual rights is critically examined. Societally accepted standards are important. Personal values are relative. Procedural rules for reaching consensus are emphasized. Hence laws may be changed democratically. Rational consideration of laws and rights can improve their usefulness.	6. *The universal-ethical principle orientation.* Right is defined by conscience, in accordance with self-chosen, logical, and comprehensive ethical principles. Right is abstract and ethical (e.g., the Golden Rule), not concrete and moral (e.g., the Ten Commandments). There is emphasis on reciprocity and equality of human rights. There is respect for the dignity of the individual.

TABLE 4.3
Kohlberg's Levels of Moral Development

Source: Adapted from E. Turiel, "Stage Transition in Moral Development," in R. M. W. Travers (Ed.), *Second Handbook of Research on Teaching* (Chicago: Rand McNally, 1973), pp. 733–734. Copyright 1973 American Educational Research Association. Also adapted from F. Oser, "Moral Education and Values Education: The Discourse Perspective," in M. C. Wittrock (Ed.), *Handbook of Research on Teaching* (3d ed.) (New York: Macmillan, 1986), pp. 923–924. Copyright 1986, American Educational Research Association.

Levels and stages of moral thinking

Kohlberg identified these levels and stages from the verbal responses of children and adults to hypothetical moral dilemmas. One of these dilemmas is: Should a civil defense worker leave his post to help his own family members, who may have been injured in a disaster, or should he stay where he is and help others? Responses to this kind of dilemma could be based on a number of beliefs:

Level A: Preconventional
Stage 1.   *The punishment-obedience orientation:* The worker should *stay,* or he'll be punished by the authorities.
Stage 2.   *The instrumental-relativist orientation:* He should *go* to his own family members because he'll worry himself to death if he doesn't find out what's happened to them.
Level B: Conventional
Stage 3.   *The interpersonal-concordance orientation:* He should *go* because good husbands and fathers care about their families.
Stage 4.   *Authority and social order–maintaining orientation:* He should *stay* because the rules say he should not leave his post.
Level C: Postconventional, autonomous, or principled
Stage 5.   *The social-contract legalistic orientation:* He probably should *stay* because he agreed to man his position in an emergency, but if some special circumstances come up, he might justify his leaving.
Stage 6.   *The universal-ethical-principle orientation:* He should *stay* because if he left he would be putting the safety of the few over that of the many, and that's not right. The people near him who are in trouble are someone's family also, and he is ethically bound to take care of them. If he doesn't, he will probably feel miserable the rest of his life.

The percentages of students of various ages who show these levels of moral thought are presented in Figure 4.4. Between ages 7 and 16, the percentages of level A go down, those of level B go up sharply, and those of level C go up moderately. Similar percentages have been found in places as different as a Malaysian aboriginal village, a Turkish city, a Turkish village, a Mexican city, and a Mayan village (Turiel, 1973). These ages for development of different kinds of moral reasoning parallel closely the preoperational, concrete operational, and formal operational levels of thought Piaget described. Kohlberg and Piaget hold similar views about the process of development, particularly the view that young children are virtually incapable of handling the abstractions of the higher stages, and that formal operational thinking is necessary to achieve level C—a level characterized by principled reasoning.

Formal operations and high levels of moral thought

Using a different way to assess moral development, the Defining Issues Test (DIT), researchers have done over five hundred studies of moral development (Rest et al., 1985). The DIT is an objective test that also assesses how the subject resolves moral dilemmas. In general, work with the test supports some of Kohlberg's assertions about development (older people score higher, show-

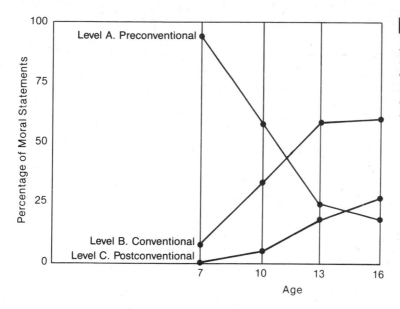

FIGURE 4.4

Age and Relative Percentage of Moral Judgments That Fall into One of Three Levels of Moral Development

Source: From *Introduction to Psychology,* 5th ed. by Ernest R. Hilgard, R. C. Atkinson, and R. L. Atkinson, copyright © 1971 by Harcourt Brace Jovanovich, Inc. Reproduced by permission of the publisher.

ing more principled reasoning), about education (better educated individuals show more principled reasoning), about family influence (child-rearing practices that are warmer, democratic, and highly verbal, and that model rational behavior and thought seem to produce children who show higher levels of moral reasoning), and about religion (no differences in moral reasoning are found among the major religious groups).

Kohlberg's dilemmas and the DIT define as "high" morality notions about abstract social justice. Some writers thought this was discriminatory against women. Gilligan (1982) made the point that women care more about social relationships and responsibility for care-giving than do men, who come to adopt a more abstract view of rights and obligations under law. Women *do* think differently about moral dilemmas, adopting a more personal view, more in tune with maintaining social relationships. Nevertheless, even with a test constructed with a decidedly male bias, when male-female comparisons are made so that educational levels are held constant, females actually score higher than males (Rest et al., 1985). Apparently women not only think differently about moral issues, they usually think at a slightly higher level if they have had the same educational opportunities as men.

Gender differences in moral concerns

Training in Moral Thinking

Can we use special school experiences to increase the rate of moral development? The answer at first appeared to be that training programs made little

Training-program effectiveness

long-term difference (Blatt, 1969; Turiel, 1966). But the more recent evidence is far more positive. For example, Schlaefli, Rest, and Thoma (1985) analyzed fifty-five studies that tried to stimulate the development of moral judgment. All of the studies used the DIT as the measure of change. (The DIT, unlike Kohlberg's stages, has a continuous scale. This allows us to detect small changes that might go unnoticed if we looked only for large changes from one stage to another.) They found that when students from junior high school age and up discussed the dilemmas over time—say, in a program lasting from eight to twelve weeks—a definite change in their moral reasoning occurred. The same effect has been found for programs designed to intensify self-reflection and personal psychological growth, particularly as it relates to how one interacts with others and society in general. Students in these kinds of programs show more principled reasoning. Average students in a control group would be expected to score at the 50th percentile rank on a test of moral-reasoning ability. These same students would be expected to score at about the 60th percentile rank after a training program.

Moral discourse

The components of a training program to increase the rate of moral development have been outlined by Oser (1986). He suggested moral discourse (discussions) between teacher and students as a means of raising the level of moral thinking. This discourse should be

- directed toward moral conflict and the stimulation of higher levels of moral thought.
- analytical about the student's own beliefs, reasoning, and theoretical positions.
- directed toward moral role-taking and moral empathy.
- directed toward an understanding of shared norms and the meaning of a moral community.
- directed toward moral choice and moral action.

No one is sure of the relationship between moral reasoning and moral behavior. Certainly, simply discussing moral issues does not lead everyone to act in moral ways. But moral discourse is a way to think critically about the important issues we face as individuals and as a society. To let education in this area happen by accident seems less sensible than to try programs that might move students more quickly to a postconventional level of moral thinking.

Morality vs. convention

One last thought. You must keep in mind your students' readiness for training in moral thinking. For example, you will want them to learn the distinction between morality and convention. *Morality* defines what is intrinsically just and fair because of its effect on the well-being of others; *convention* defines what is right or correct based on social consensus. Stealing is a moral issue; how we dress is an issue of convention. Children usually are not able to differentiate between these concepts before age 7 or 8 (Nucci, 1982). Although young students can profit from exposure to beliefs at one stage above their own, you might not want to go beyond that. Presenting moral beliefs at high levels of abstraction and complexity, which require relativistic thinking, probably is not effective with young children. Adolescents, on the other hand, are typically ready to explore moral questions because these kinds of questions occupy a good deal of their attention (J. J. Mitchell, 1975).

Personality and Traits

Personality is a concept derived from behavior. We see only behavior. But we create names for that behavior to talk about the different kinds of behaviors we notice. Our names for behavior—*honest, aggressive, hot-tempered, cheerful, serene, naive, creative*—are often the same words we use to describe personality. Psychologists have studied these descriptive words, called *trait names,* to understand the way personality is organized and maintained.

Trait names

A *trait* is an enduring aspect of a person's behavior, generally consistent across a wide variety of settings and situations. Allport and Odbert (1936) found 17,953 English-language adjectives that could be used to describe traits. Many tests are designed to measure traits. The Gordon Personal Inventory is aimed at "cautiousness," "original thinking," "personal relations," and "vigor"; the Edwards Personal Preference Inventory is aimed at some of our social needs, such as affiliation and achievement. The California Personality Inventory is intended to measure "sociability" and "tolerance," among other things. Almost all of these tests are designed to locate people on trait scales so that we can say that Suzi Johnson is very "sociable," Henry Washington is extremely "cautious," and Mary Lowenstein is neither high nor low in her "sense of personal worth."

Personality-trait measures

A profile of scores from a personality test that provides these kinds of descriptions might look like Figure 4.5. Ideally we would use these measurements to understand a student's personality, to help us diagnose and prescribe for that student. That is, trait scores should give us additional insights into a student's behavior.

Profile of scores

But this logical approach to traits and their measurement runs into problems. Unless we understand the environments we are dealing with very well, the consistency in behavior that we expect when we talk about traits may be largely illusory. The behavior of people with supposedly stable traits has not been studied nearly enough in *different* environments. Behavior is a function of *both* personality and environmental factors.

Consistency of traits illusory

Do people behave consistently? There is some evidence that they do not (see Mischel, 1973). Many correlations between individuals' scores on an objective test of personality given at two different times are relatively low. For the Rorschach Inkblot Test and other projective tests of personality, the reliability over time is even lower. This low consistency may result from characteristics of the test (say, the number and content of test items) or from genuine inconsistency over time in how people respond, even to identical items. Prediction from trait tests to behavioral situations is also often poor.

But we do find consistency in behavior when situations are similar. If students act up at one school dance, they are likely to act up at another. When situations differ, consistency may be low. Acting up at a dance does not neces-

FIGURE 4.5

*Sample Profiles of
Personality from a
Fictitious Personality
Test*

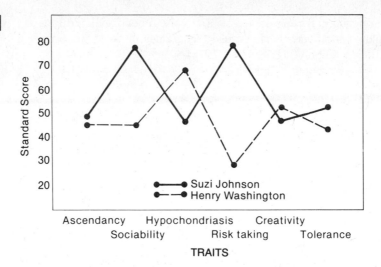

sarily mean that students will act up on the playground, on the job, or in family situations. We need to emphasize more that behavior is controlled, to a large degree, by the way rewards and punishments occur in the environment. As Mischel (1973) noted, if the rewards and punishments for behavior in different situations are largely uncorrelated, the behavior itself should not be stable from setting to setting—and indeed it is not in most empirical studies. We do not find high generality in behavior because the consequences for behavior vary so widely from one situation to another.

Let's look now at four of the hundreds of traits that are relevant to teaching—honesty, creativity, self-concept, and anxiety. We examine their consistency across settings as we describe them.

Honesty

Teachers value honest children—those who do not take money from a teacher's wallet, remove chalk, steal pencils, cheat on tests, or lie. The classic studies of honesty and deception in children were conducted by Hartshorne and May (1928). Among the tests they used were these four:

Copying.   For example, giving IQ tests to children, collecting the tests, secretly scoring and recording the answers, giving the tests back, and having the children score their own tests. The discrepancy between the experimenter's secret scoring and the child's self-scoring provided a measure of cheating.

Speed.   For example, giving two practice sessions in digit cancellation, then asking the child to take a third trial and report the number he or she did in a given period of time. Because this ability is rather stable, the increase in self-reported performance on the third trial over that measured on the second trial was used as a measure of the student's tendency to exaggerate his or her actual performance.

Peeking.   For example, asking a blindfolded child to pencil some dots within certain boundaries drawn on a piece of paper. Good performance in this task can almost always be attributed to peeking.

Stealing.   For example, giving students the opportunity to remove some coins from a box in the belief that only they can tell how many coins should be in the box.

The intercorrelations among these four kinds of tests are positive but low (Table 4.4). A student who cheats by changing an IQ score does not very often peek or steal. Yet these correlations do indicate some consistency; so a general factor called "honesty" probably does exist (Burton, 1963). The point is that consistency in the trait, from setting to setting, is *not* as great as everyday usage of the term *honesty* implies.

Low level of consistency

How widespread is this kind of cheating? In one of the peeking tests, 79 percent of the boys and 85 percent of the girls cheated. On another test, cheating was measured by the discrepancy between the experimenter's scores and the student's self-graded schoolwork. Of the boys, 30 percent cheated, as did 37 percent of the girls. In general, in elementary schools, girls had higher reputations for honesty but actually cheated more than boys. More recent studies (Bushway & Nash, 1977) suggest that high school boys are more likely to cheat than are girls.

Over the series of tests, the number of times some form of deception—cheating, peeking, stealing—took place is shown in Figure 4.6. Fewer than 8 percent of the students never cheated, and about 4 percent of the students cheated at every opportunity. For the remaining 88 percent of the students, honesty was not an all-or-nothing trait, consistent across all situations. Rather it was behavior that depended, in ways we do not understand, on the interaction between environmental circumstances, particularly the immediate demands of the task, and previously learned behavioral tendencies.

This emphasis on the dependence of behavior on both personality and environmental variables is important for teachers: Be careful about the labels you apply to students. Herman may cheat in your English class but not in science

Caution in labeling students

Area of Honesty	1	2	3	4
1. Copying (sum of 3 tests)		.45	.40	.14
2. Speed (sum of 6 tests)			.37	.17
3. Peeking (sum of 3 tests)				.20
4. Stealing (1 test)				

TABLE 4.4
Average Intercorrelations Between Tests in Four Areas of Honesty

Source: Adapted from H. Hartshorne and M. A. May, *Studies in the Nature of Character*, Vol. 1, Macmillan, 1928, as cited by R. V. Burton, "Generality of Honesty Reconsidered," *Psychological Review*, 1963, p. 484.

FIGURE 4.6

Percentage of Tests on Which Children Cheated

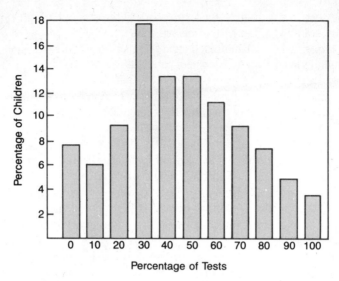

Source: Adapted from Hartshorne and May (1928), p. 386.

class. Luanne may steal some pennies from Ms. Murphy's class fund but would not peek in the blindfold task. Honesty, like many traits, may be fairly consistent over similar situations but more changeable in different situations.

You should use the same caution in dealing with all categories of behavior, or traits—outgoingness, emotional stability, dominance, conscientiousness, and the like. There is evidence that expert teachers understand this principle. In a comparison of expert teachers with novice teachers, the experts paid almost no attention to the notes left by a previous teacher about students they were planning to teach. Why? Apparently because they understood that each child may act differently in each class. Novice teachers tried to learn all they could about students before meeting them, apparently believing that a previous teacher's notes are valid and student behavior is consistent across settings (Carter, Sabers, Cushing, Pinnegar, & Berliner, 1987).

All of this does not mean that we have to give up the notion of consistency in human behavior. We still need to be able to predict behavior on the basis of past behavior. But you should not infer from limited observations of behavior in unique environments that your students have broad dispositions to act a certain way. You may not only be wrong, but, worse, you may communicate your beliefs through your behavior, creating a self-fulfilling prophecy. Your behavior can exert subtle pressure on students to act in accordance with your beliefs.

Creativity

Creativity is another trait name commonly used to describe behavior. We talk of the creative teacher and the creative child. We have tests of creativity and

• *Creative work in writing, architecture, mathematics, problem solving, or sculpting all share the same qualities— originality, suitability, validity, and somehow elegance, or being "just right." (© Elizabeth Crews)*

special programs in creative art, music, writing, and mathematics. The school, like society in general, values and feels it must nurture creativity.

Important elements in our definition of creativity include flexibility in thinking and fluency in the production of ideas. But central to the idea of creativity is originality. What we consider to be creative may vary greatly: a new way of solving a problem in logic; a new tool or chemical process; a musical composition; a work of poetry or fiction; a painting; a way of reasoning in law, philosophy, or religion; a new insight into a social problem; a way of diagnosing or curing a disease. Creative work is original, suitable, valid, and somehow elegant, or just right.

Originality

Suitability and elegance

Creativity and Intelligence. Is creativity the same as intelligence? Torrance (1967) concluded from a review of the literature that the best estimate of the correlation between creativity and intelligence was about .20 when verbal IQ measures are used and .06 when nonverbal intelligence measures are used. But this estimate may have been lowered by the homogeneity of the groups studied (Ripple & May, 1962). The prevailing view is that creativity is relatively independent of intelligence (for example, Getzels & Jackson, 1962; Hattie &

Creativity not correlated intelligence

Rogers, 1986). Clinical insight and testing suggest that the children in each of the four possible combinations of creativity and intelligence have certain related characteristics (Wallach & Kogan, 1965):

- Children with *high creativity* and *high intelligence* can vary how much control and freedom they allow themselves. They can exhibit both adult and childlike behavior.
- Children with *high creativity* and *low intelligence* are in angry conflict with their schools and often themselves. They feel inadequate and unworthy. Their best performances are given in stress-free environments.
- Children with *low creativity* and *high intelligence* are addicted to school performance. They must strive for traditional academic excellence, and they suffer greatly when they fail.
- Children with *low creativity* and *low intelligence* engage in various defensive activities as they try to adapt to a school environment that is basically bewildering.

Wallach and Kogan believe these two dimensions of personality, intelligence and creativity, are substantially different but pervasive sources of individual differences among children.

Training Creativity.   At one time researchers believed that creativity, like intelligence, was a relatively unmodifiable trait, highly consistent from one situation to the next. Yet environmental events can affect creative behavior. Maltzman (1960) examined the hypothesized thought processes that underlie performance on tests of originality. He designed a series of experiments in which students were trained in originality; then he measured the effects on **Unusual-uses test** originality of responses in an unusual-uses test. The training consisted of presenting a word to a respondent and asking for an association, then asking the respondent to provide four more associations with the word. This request for repeated responses produced more and more uncommon, that is, more and more original, responses. The trained students, compared with untrained controls, scored higher in originality on a new test. It appears then, that environments that elicit and reward original behavior can produce original behavior on tasks that are different from the ones on which a person trained.

Creative problem solving   Instructions to be creative also seem to affect creative problem solving. Maier (1933), using what he knew of creative problem solving, lectured 78 subjects on how to reason. His lecture made the following points:

1. Habitual ways of doing things do not solve difficult problems.
2. Problems would not be difficult if they could be solved through habitual ways of handling problems.
3. A person should not stay in a rut but should keep his or her mind open for new meanings.

4. The problem solver should try to locate a difficulty and overcome it.
5. If this fails, the problem solver should put the problem completely
   out of his or her mind and look for a new challenge.
6. Solutions to problems appear suddenly; they cannot be forced. The
   problem solver should just keep his or her mind open and not spend
   time following up unsuccessful leads.

Then he presented the tasks. A control group of 206 students who were not
given the lecture also tried the tasks. The difficult reasoning tasks required
ability to see common things in new ways and to do uncommon things with
simple objects. Clear differences emerged. And a replication of the study gave
similar results.

Maier's work in problem solving and other research indicates that students
can be made "more creative" in their solutions to problems, primarily by teaching them not to do things that inhibit creative solutions. You should be alert to
opportunities to provide an environment that elicits creative behavior from your
students. And when you find that behavior, be sure to reward it.

Despite their stated values, many schools seem to stifle creativity. In **Anticreative**
providing helpful hints to beginning teachers, one authoritative manual recom- **actions**
mended: "Be ready to use the first minute of class time. If you get Johnny busy
right away, he has no time to cook up interesting ideas that do not fit into the
class situation" (M. W. Hunt, 1969). This kind of "helpful hint" may make
classes more manageable, but many educators would see something perverse in
sacrificing Johnny's "interesting ideas" for the sake of discipline.

Teachers may do better in fostering creativity if they adopt the idea of
creativity as problem solving (see Torrance, 1962). Creativity here requires (1)
sensing gaps, or feeling that the elements in a situation do not fit together
correctly; (2) forming hypotheses about the solution of the problem; and (3)
testing each hypothesis and evaluating the results. Creativity becomes advanced problem solving of the type Maier was able to improve with instructions.
This notion of creativity agrees with the techniques of *How to Solve It,* a guide
to the solution of mathematical problems developed by the mathematician
Gyorgy Polya (1954). It also fits the analysis of problem solving by John Dewey
(1933) and other philosophers.

Instructional materials have been designed to teach creative problem solving
on the basis of these ideas. Perhaps the most widely studied is the Productive
Thinking Program—programmed instruction on how to recognize incongruity
and generate hypotheses (Covington, Crutchfield, Davies, & Olton, 1974).
Developed in the form of sixteen cartoon-text booklets, it is designed to teach
fifth- and sixth-graders to think like imaginative scholars, detectives, or scientists. The program did improve problem-solving skills applicable to a broad
range of tasks. Crutchfield's (1966) research with these materials led him to **A governing skill**
hypothesize a governing skill in problem solving—a skill that helps organize and **in problem solving**
manage the problem-solving activities necessary for productive or creative
solutions:

This governing skill has many aspects. It involves an understanding of the nature of different types of problems and of the appropriate skills required in their solution. It involves the grasp of general strategies of problem-attack, the use of a "planning method" for breaking the problem up into manageable sequential steps. It involves a highly developed sense of timing—an inseparable attribute of almost all skills—and an ability to assemble component skills in an optimal pattern. It involves an ability to be flexible and adaptive in the use of one's often competing skills—being able to be alternatively intuitive and analytical, engaged and disengaged, serious and playful, creative and critical, seeking for complexity and striving for simplicity. And above all, it involves an understanding of how to compensate for deficiencies in certain of one's skills and how to exploit one's special talents, not only in the choice of the mode of attack on a problem, but also in the very choice of problems to work on. (pp. 66–67)

Tested creativity vs. real-life creativity

This kind of skill is not often thought of as something that can be taught. But lacking evidence that this skill is entirely hereditary, teachers should assume that elements in the environment account for it. After reviewing the research, Mansfield, Busse, and Krepelka (1978) concluded that this kind of governing skill in problem solving can be taught. But they questioned whether the Productive Thinking Program and eight other programs improve "real-life" creativity:

This is a largely untested question. The implicit assumption of most training programs is that divergent thinking abilities are of central importance to real-life creativity. At least among adult professionals this does not appear to be the case. . . . [In general] the relationships have been too small to provide grounds for optimism that increases in divergent thinking ability alone will affect real-life creativity. (p. 532)

Classroom atmosphere for creativity

Creativity in the Classroom.   Although the relationship of creativity training to real-life creativity is debatable, such training seems worthwhile. Torrance (1962) offered suggestions about how to develop a classroom atmosphere in which creativity can flourish:

- First know what creative thought is. This means knowing definitions, examples, and tests of originality, fluency, flexibility, elaboration, divergent thought, and convergent thought.
- Using this knowledge, reward the expression of new ideas or creative acts. Encourage the manipulation of objects and ideas and the systematic testing of ideas.
- Do not try to force your own solutions on students. Instead provide a model of open-mindedness and tentativeness in appropriate areas. Show how curiosity and inquiry help solve problems by commenting on your thought processes as you solve a problem.

• *A common element in the careers of creative and talented people—heart surgeons, athletes, scientists, and artists—is a mentor. (© Carol Palmer)*

- Create situations where creativity can come forth, provoke students with incongruous ideas and seeming paradoxes, give open-ended assignments, and be controversial.
- Be sure that students do not hold creative artists, writers, inventors, and scientists in such great awe that their own creativity is paralyzed.
- Encourage children to keep track of their own ideas by using notebooks, idea cards, and the like.

Direct observation of master teachers of the gifted by Silverman (1980) indicated that these teachers provide *less* information to their students. They spend more time questioning their students instead of instructing them. They often refuse to answer students' questions, reflecting questions back to the students by asking, "What do you think?" Their questions are often divergent ("What would happen if . . . ?"). They often ask students, "What made you think that?" They have a habit of not giving judgmental feedback: They accept students' responses, showing interest, but manage at the same time to be nonjudgmental. The result, of course, is that students tend to evaluate themselves. These teachers genuinely enjoy their students. They spend time with them before and after class; they often make discoveries with them. They reveal a good deal of personal information about themselves while they observe and work with the gifted students. In short, they are not so much information-givers, trainers, and evaluators as they are mentors or counselors.

Nonjudgmental feedback

Using mentors

It appears that creativity is nurtured by using mentors in a systematic way. Torrance (1986), in a twenty-two-year longitudinal study of creative achievement, found that mentors make a big difference in the life of youngsters, particularly students from minority-group or low-income families. B. S. Bloom (1985), in looking at similarities in the upbringing of extremely successful swimmers, pianists, surgeons, mathematicians, and sculptors, noted the crucial role of teacher-mentors in the development of an individual's unique talent. Different kinds of mentors are needed at the beginning, middle, and later stages of the development of an Olympic swimmer or world-class mathematician. But in all cases the personal involvement of a caring, knowledgeable teacher—a mentor—makes a big difference. Finding appropriate mentors for gifted science, mathematics, art, and music students is not easy. Public schools alone usually cannot nurture the extremely talented student. The schools are too big, and teachers' time often too limited. But other community resources can be used: employed or retired scientists and engineers, college students with athletic or artistic talent. Science, art, and other special interest clubs, with small groups of highly motivated students and knowledgeable interested mentors, are also a source of fun and learning for both students and mentors. (See Chapter 6 on mentoring.)

Intolerance

Blocks to Creativity.   One block to creative problem solving is the intolerance of fellow students. We have to help these students develop tolerance for novel, unique, even bizarre ideas. More important, we have to get them to encourage the creative problem solvers among them to work out the implications of their ideas. Another major block to creativity is the way students think about themselves ("I'm not creative," "I never do anything out of the ordinary"). By getting students to stop making negative self-evaluations—by getting them to say to themselves, "I'm original," "I won't worry about what others think," or "I'll break out of the commonplace," we can increase their creativity (Meichenbaum, 1975). People can learn to teach themselves to act differently in certain situations. This fact has implications for developing creative thought, enhancing self-concept, and reducing anxiety in our students.

Teachers' bias

In short, remember that creative behavior and the environmental factors associated with that behavior can be changed. Be aware that you may hold slightly negative feelings about gifted and talented students. Cramond and Martin (1985), repeating a study first reported in the 1960s, found stability over twenty years in how athletic ability among students is admired and how intellectual ability is not. The attitudes of adolescents, preservice teachers, and experienced teachers were virtually identical and consistently negative about brilliant, studious nonathletes. Because of this bias, teachers have a special responsibility to understand themselves and what their creative students need in order to function well in school.

Self-Concept

When we say, "Brett doesn't think he can do well," or "Sarah won't even try it," or "Tippi can't stand herself," we are talking about characteristics often grouped together under the heading of self-concept. *Self-concept* is the totality of the perceptions that we have about ourselves—our attitude toward ourselves, the language we use to describe ourselves. For example, we can infer a part of self-concept in the area of mathematics ability from a student's response to this question:

"How do you rate yourself in mathematics ability, compared with others in your class?"

a. I am among the best.
b. I am above the average.
c. I am at the average.
d. I am below the average.
e. I am among the poorest.

If we change "mathematics ability" to "general academic ability," we could use the same item to measure a part of general academic self-concept.

We can think of self-concept as a hierarchy (Figure 4.7). At the top of this hierarchy, at level 1, is *general self-concept,* the set of beliefs we hold about ourselves, beliefs that are relatively difficult to modify. At the next level there are two major areas of self-concept for students: academic and nonacademic (social and physical). Finally we come to more specific areas of self-concept, related directly to a subject matter or a kind of activity. These specific self-concept areas are probably the most likely to change as a function of our everyday experiences. If students' performances in mathematics or dating or baseball improve, their attitudes toward themselves in these areas are also likely to improve.

Three levels of self-concept

Does a change in behavior lead to a change in attitude more readily than a change in attitude leads to a change in behavior? Evidence indicates yes. In changing self-concept, "the relative superiority of a behaviorally oriented approach stems from the fact that a basic change in behavior provides an objective and genuine basis by which one feels self-respect, self-confidence, and dignity" (Bandura, 1969, p. 91).

Changed behavior → changed self-concept

Short-term behavioral changes in ability do not always affect self-concept, however. In fact students who have acquired poor self-concepts in some areas seem to reject their own success at first. Presumably they do so because these experiences are not congruent with their self-concepts. But long-lasting behavioral changes in areas of concern do lead to changes in attitudes toward self.

Changes in verbal behavior about oneself can change self-concepts, as illustrated by the simple method Homme and Tosti (1971) reported. In this case the "behavior modifier" identified a child with good academic potential but poor academic self-concept. The teacher announced recess and let everyone go outside except this child. The child was told, "You cannot go outside and play until you say something good about your work in school today." If the child then said something like, "Today I really understood my English grammar lesson!" he was allowed to go out and play. Positive statements about self and reinforcement (reward) for making those statements resulted in a more positive

FIGURE 4.7   *Three Levels of Self-concept for Students*

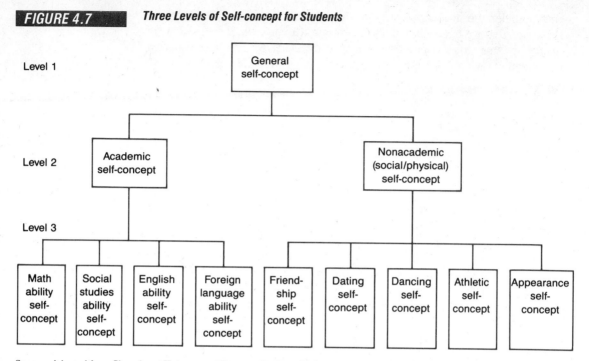

Source: Adapted from Shavelson, Hubner, and Stanton, *Review of Educational Research.* © 1976 American Educational Research Association. Used by permission.

self-concept. Helping students extinguish negative statements about themselves and replace those negative statements with positive statements can help to change their self-concepts. But we emphasize that changes in self-concept follow changes in verbal behavior only if the latter accord with reality. Procedures to induce change work best when a low self-concept is unrealistic. It is difficult, unwise, and perhaps unkind to try to develop a positive self-concept about physical attractiveness or agility when an individual is really homely or clumsy.

Reality and self-concept

Self-concept seems to grow out of interactions with significant people in our lives—usually parents, teachers, and peers. Evidence does exist that teachers can affect their students' self-concepts (Davidson & Lang, 1960; Staines, 1956). This is important to remember when working with minority-group students. African-American self-concept has undergone massive positive changes in recent years. Several surveys have found that African-American children show higher general levels of self-esteem than do white children (Christmas, 1973; Rosenberg & Simmons, 1973; St. John, 1975; Stephan & Rosenfield, 1979). But the problem of poor minority-group self-concepts in particular areas (for example, schooling and employment) still holds for many African-Americans and other minority-group members in American society. To be different—whether African-American, Native American, Chicano, Jewish, Italian, or Croatian—is likely to mean being "less than" the majority group. Consequently students who

Minority-group self-concept

belong to a minority group are especially likely to have negative self-concepts in at least some respects. Teachers must be aware of this problem and carefully monitor the school environment to guard against incidents that could harm self-concept.

Does self-concept affect educational outcomes? Or do educational outcomes affect self-concept? Correlational studies show substantial positive relationships between achievement and self-concept measures (Byrne, 1984). But these data cannot tell us which variable is causally affecting the other. The evidence is accumulating, however, to indicate that level of school success, particularly over many years, predicts level of regard for self and one's own ability (Bridgeman & Shipman, 1978; Kifer, 1975); whereas level of self-esteem does not predict level of school achievement. The implication is that teachers need to concentrate on the academic successes and failures of their students. It is the students' history of success and failure that gives them the information with which to assess themselves. This is consistent with Erikson's notion of the crisis of accomplishment versus inferiority, which takes place in the elementary school years. A sense of inadequacy and inferiority can arise if children do not receive recognition for their efforts (Hamachek, 1978). The recognition of accomplishment by parents and teachers often leads to positive self-concept.

> **Self-concept and achievement**

In projects aimed directly at improving self-concept, strong effects on achievement have seldom been obtained. Scheirer and Kraut (1979) reviewed twenty-six studies of this kind and concluded that the

> underlying theory is wrong. In all the theories reviewed here, self-concept is viewed as a variable necessarily intervening between various sources of self-concept formation and the student's performance on academic achievement measures. An alternative view is that . . . self-concept change is likely to be an outcome of increased achievement with accompanying social approval, rather than an intervening variable necessary for achievement to occur. (p. 144)

It should follow that teaching that improves achievement should also improve student self-concept. And in fact it does (Crawford et al., 1978). From students' self-appraisals it was learned that better teaching was positively associated with higher student self-esteem and attitude toward school, and a reduction of anxiety (Corno, Mitman, & Hedges, 1981).

Anxiety

Anxiety is both a trait (a relatively stable characteristic) and a state (a temporary characteristic) (Spielberger, 1966). As a trait, anxiety is a general disposition to feel threatened by a wide range of conditions. As a state, anxiety is related to particular situations. For example, a person may at a particular time be anxious about a job, a spouse, a child, or an examination. One's feelings of apprehension and tension are, to some extent, focused and localized.

> **Trait vs. state anxiety**

Sarason and his associates (Mandler & Sarason, 1952; Sarason, Lighthall, Davidson, Waite, & Ruebush, 1960) examined anxiety as a trait, asking these

FIGURE 4.8

Performance on Two Tasks of Children with High and Low General Anxiety

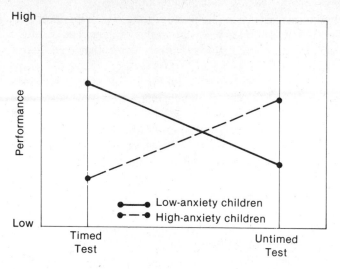

FIGURE 4.8

Performance on Two Tasks of Children with High and Low General Anxiety

Source: Adapted from Sarason, Lighthall, Davidson, Waite, and Ruebush (1960), p. 181. Reprinted by permission of the authors.

kinds of questions: Do you worry about accidents? Do you worry more than other children? They also examined anxiety as a state, particularly in relation to taking tests: Are you afraid of school tests? When taking a test, do you worry that you are doing poorly? The general (trait) anxiety and the test (state) anxiety scales correlated about .60. Thus the two kinds of anxiety have something in common, but they are also fairly distinct.

Anxiety and thinking under pressure

Evidence has accumulated that high-anxiety students do not perform as well at certain kinds of tasks as do low-anxiety students. These tasks are characterized by challenge, difficulty, evaluation of performance, and time pressure. Figure 4.8 shows the performance of high- and low-anxiety children on two tasks that required analytic thinking, one under pressured (timed) conditions, the other under unpressured (untimed) conditions. The high-anxiety children performed worse on the timed test; the low-anxiety children performed worse on the untimed test. This interaction clearly shows the disadvantage of the high-anxiety person in high-pressure situations. It also reveals the positive effect of anxiety, promoting strong motivation, in unpressured situations.

If general anxiety reflects a state of high motivation, we could predict that in a college environment, where course work is stressful, low-anxiety students should perform better than high-anxiety students. Figure 4.9 presents pertinent data collected by Spielberger (1966). The hypothesized difference occurs at all but the very lowest and very highest aptitude levels. At the levels where college work is most challenging to students—neither so difficult that it cannot be completed nor so easy that there is no challenge—low-anxiety students perform better in their course work than do high-anxiety students. These results are typical at all age levels. Thus Corno and her colleagues (1981)

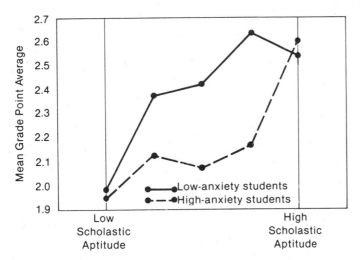

FIGURE 4.9

College Performance of High- and Low-Anxiety Students of Various Levels of Scholastic Aptitude

Source: Adapted from Spielberger (1966).

reported that anxiety correlated negatively with general mental ability ($r = -.26$), scholastic achievement ($r = -.25$), self-esteem ($r = -.38$), and favorability of attitude toward school ($r = -.15$) among the 634 third-graders studied in their experiment.

These findings mean that teachers need to examine the learning situation for high-anxiety learners. For example, the extent to which academic programs are structured in various classrooms and schools has been shown to interact with anxiety levels (Dowaliby & Schumer, 1973; Grimes & Allinsmith, 1961). Unstructured learning environments and teaching methods may create difficulties for children with high anxiety levels. Tobias (1979) suggested that anxiety can affect how well students (1) receive information, (2) process information, and (3) retrieve processed information. To help with problem 1, anxious students need to be able to go back over the input—to rewind a tape, reread a passage, or review notes. To alleviate problem 2, students need better-organized material of lower difficulty, requiring less reliance on long-term memory. To reduce problem 3, anxious students may be helped by take-home exams instead of in-class tests, or many short quizzes, which arouse less anxiety than a single final exam.

Anxiety and structure

Tryon (1980) reviewed attempts to treat test anxiety through systematic desensitization. This procedure entails getting physically relaxed, then thinking of anxiety-producing situations, beginning with the lowest one in the anxiety hierarchy and proceeding upward until, eventually, the highest one no longer produces anxiety. The results require us to make a distinction between emotionality and worry, two separate components of test anxiety (Schwarzer, 1982). In general, desensitization reduced the emotional (physiological, affective) aspect of anxiety but not its worry (cognitive) component. Treatment through cognitive procedures aimed at helping students focus on the task—say, by imagining reinforcement for doing so—was effective in reducing the worry

Systematic desensitization

Worry vs. emotionality

component. Improving study skills alone tends to be ineffective for the highly test-anxious student unless such effort is combined with desensitization or some other procedure.

Remember that memory aids, careful instructions, and practice sessions can help remove some of the pressure felt by high-anxiety students. Getting the students' private conversations with themselves under control is also important. What we say to ourselves in different situations ("I feel nervous" or "I can handle this") determines to some extent what we do. Remember too that the application of some stress raises motivation levels in low-anxiety students, thereby enhancing their performance. To reduce the state anxiety generated by tests, by certain subject matters (chemistry, mathematics), or by settings (the gymnasium, a science laboratory), desensitization procedures—a form of behavior modification—can be used by teachers and school psychologists.

The Teacher and Trait Theory

Overattribution of consistency

In a previous section of this chapter, we argued against the tendency to think of traits as relatively fixed dispositions to act consistently in certain ways. This tendency constitutes an overattribution of consistency to the behavior of others. As E. E. Jones and R. E. Nisbett (1971) pointed out, "actors [in the sense of persons behaving] tend to attribute the causes of their behavior to stimuli inherent in the situation while observers tend to attribute behavior to stable dispositions of the actor" (p. 8). So Jill says, "I tripped because it was dark," while her teacher may say, "Jill tripped because she is clumsy."

Labeling as false generalization

The distinction here is a crucial one. Labeling a student as honest, creative, self-confident, anxious, or anything else could amount to a false generalization, because these kinds of behaviors are often specific to a given situation. Moreover, labeling can operate as a self-fulfilling prophecy, exerting subtle pressure on students, literally forcing them to play out their attributed role as sneak, dummy, clown, or aggressor. Most traits can be changed, depending on environmental factors that call forth and reinforce the kinds of behaviors we identify with trait names. If we think a kind of behavior is bad because it interferes with a student's and others' achievement of educational objectives, we should try to modify the behavior before we label the student.

SUMMARY

The importance of Piaget to teachers arises from his analysis of thought processes in children and adolescents. He built a cohesive and persuasive theory that identifies four stages of intellectual development. Important behaviors that take place in the first stage, the sensorimotor stage, are the base from which more complex behaviors can emerge. In the preoperational stage children are conceptually confused. Although they talk and apparently reason, in fact they are not able to think operationally. That is, children before about age 7 cannot internally transform and manipulate the world; they do not have the symbolic representations with which to engage in abstract, logical, and scientific thinking. Some of this ability appears in the concrete operational stage. But it is rudimentary, and the experience gained is only a prelude to the development, from about age 11, of formal operational thought. The thought patterns of adolescents are very sophisticated compared with those of younger children.

Piaget's theory, although it has been attacked on several points, gives us some useful insight into intellectual development. The theory and data point out that development goes on through a process of constant adaptation to the environment. When a new phenomenon disturbs the equilibrium of their environment, children restore balance by assimilation (changing what is perceived to fit what they already know) and accommodation (changing cognitive structures to fit what is perceived).

The three stages of representation of information described by Bruner overlap considerably with Piaget's developmental stages. In the enactive stage, which is much like Piaget's sensorimotor stage, knowledge and action are synonymous. In the iconic stage, knowledge is coded by perceptual characteristics, much as it is in Piaget's preoperational stage. Finally, in the symbolic stage, understanding comes through symbol systems, especially language.

Vygotsky pointed out the importance of our social community in the development of cognition. The directed learning he advocated demands an understanding of what a child can do alone and what a child can do under the guidance of a knowledgeable tutor. The difference between these two levels of functioning is the zone of proximal development. And the key to enhancing the child's cognitive development is determining the dimensions of the zone in which to work.

The theories put forth by Piaget, Bruner, and Vygotsky have implications for how we teach. They tell us the importance of understanding how children think, of using concrete material in teaching young children, and of sequencing instruction. And they give us insight into the ways to introduce new material and set the pace of learning. They suggest a social element in learning, one that influences both cognitive and affective processes. Finally, the research methods of these scholars point to the importance of analyzing and interpreting students' errors.

The development of language is probably the most important factor in the development of cognitive abilities. Rationalists believe that we have an innate system that allows us to determine implicitly the rules operating in our language community. As we interact with others in that community—as we experience language—our language becomes more complex. Although development of competence in a language may be biologically based, language performance is affected by experience. Here, too, we see a progression from one-word holophrastic speech, to two-word telegraphic speech, to multiple-word inflected speech. This progression is reflected in the way adults speak to and with young children.

Despite lingering public debate, most linguists agree that no dialect or language is any more or less accurate, logical, or capable of expressing thought than another. For us, the question of nonstandard English centers on educational and economic implications, not cognitive ones. For bilingual students, the challenge is to help them master English and other subjects without destroying their cultural identity. Bilingual programs offer an effective means for developing metalinguistic awareness.

When you teach, you will see individual differences in the use of language. Remember that these differences do not mean a lack of ability; they rest on personal and environmental characteristics. Try to accommodate these differences. At the same time, you have to help students understand the special language requirements of the classroom.

Don't think of children as young adults. Their ways of thinking and their ability to communicate are very different at different ages. They need a wide variety of experiences, including interaction with others and a good deal of time in order to develop formal operational thought and a linguistic system for expressing that thought. Remember that thinking is a process that develops over time. Your methods and expectations must match the level of cognitive development of your students.

Simultaneous with the development of language and cognition is the ongoing process of personality development. Erikson believed that our psychosocial development is a response to crises we face at different stages in life. The way in which we resolve these crises affects our personality. That is, proper resolution allows us to develop a "healthy" personality. In infancy we learn trust rather than mistrust; in early childhood, autonomy rather than shame or doubt; in middle childhood, initiative rather than guilt; and in the elementary school years, accomplishment rather than inferiority. In adolescence we face a special crisis: the development of an identity. Who are we? What will become of us? These are the kinds of questions we ask and need to resolve, if only in a preliminary way, when we are in our teens. If you work with high school-age students, remember that they are going through a time of turmoil. Understanding their confusion is an important part of helping them learn. In young adulthood comes another crisis—the challenge of sharing our lives with someone else. To resolve this in times of changing roles and social values is a difficult problem. Many beginning teachers face this crisis at just the time they begin their careers, and it often is a source of great stress for them. In adulthood, we face the problem of generativity rather than stagnation; and in old age, integrity rather than despair. Although we can't prove them empirically, Erikson's insights appear to have validity as we look around and analyze the ways we and our families, friends, and students function.

Moral knowledge also grows as the child progresses through stages of development. Young children are governed by a primitive system of morality, their behavior motivated by avoiding punishment or getting something in return. The conventional level of morality is held by most people from about age 13. It is characterized by conformity and a sense of doing one's duty. As a result of experience and growing older, a small percentage of people develop a principled morality, governed by legal and ethical beliefs. Contrary to earlier work, it appears now that teachers can influence the moral development of their students, that they can foster higher levels of moral thinking.

A trait is a stable aspect of behavior that is generally consistent across a variety of settings. Notice the qualification in our definition. Traits are not as consistent as many people believe. Our honesty, creativity, self-concept, or anxiety at a particular time depends, in part, on the environment in which we are operating. Therefore, teachers can modify traits by changing factors in the environment. It also means that labeling a student could harm that student. A student may have been dishonest or felt inferior under certain circumstances. But by attributing general dishonesty or general low self-esteem to that student, we could be exerting pressure on the student to conform to our beliefs. It's fine to identify an unwanted behavior and try to modify it. It's wrong, however, to use that behavior as a basis for labeling our students.

5

Human Diversity and the Schools: Culture, Gender, and Exceptionality

OVERVIEW

Understanding diversity—particularly the variations among our students owing to culture, gender, and exceptionality—has become a major focus of social science and educational research. The research on cultural differences has been stimulated in part by the recognition that the typical urban school-child is not a white Anglo-Saxon Protestant. The United States has become increasingly a multicultural society. The research on gender differences has been stimulated in part by the feminists of recent years who have raised angry voices to communicate their dissatisfaction with the roles prescribed for women in American society. The research on exceptionality has been stimulated by parents of the handicapped and the gifted, as they push schools to provide special programs to meet the needs of their special children.

In this chapter we look at cultural differences—how culture affects intellectual functioning, communication, language use, and the development of talent, and how these elements relate to schooling. And we look at programs that respect cultural differences and how they seem to improve the social adjustment and academic performance of children from different cultures. We review the research on gender-related differences in intelligence and personality. We talk about the areas in which differences have been found and the significance of those differences. We explore the relationships between personality and intelligence. And we examine how home and school affect sex-role development and particularly how sex-role stereotyping in schools can be reduced.

Finally, we consider the nature of *exceptional students*. The information we present here can give you only a working familiarity with this complex varied group and with possible ways of meeting its educational needs, but it is information that you will be able to build on as you meet and begin to teach special students. We also introduce you to the topic of aptitude-treatment interactions—a way of thinking that requires teachers to consider differences among students and teaching methods in order to match individual students with instructional treatments that are most effective for them.

Cultural Differences

Intelligence, cognitive development, personality, and sex roles all contribute to the differences we find among students. Each of these factors is affected by the context in which children develop. That context is called *culture*. It is powerful. And it influences all of us, most often in ways we are unaware of. Making the influence of culture more visible is our goal in this section.

We've talked about some of the obvious ways in which culture acts on the individual in the home environment and in language. But culture is also at work in very subtle ways. Think for a minute about personal space, the physical space you need to feel comfortable when you are near another person. Most North Americans prefer to stand no closer than an arm's length from someone else when they are talking. In fact, "keeping someone at arm's length" is a common expression in the United States. Latin Americans, and many Mediterranean peoples, prefer to stand closer when they speak. What happens when a North American and Latin American are talking? One keeps pulling away and the other keeps moving closer. Communication is going on at two levels: verbal and nonverbal. Whatever the words are saying, the actions are communicating a message, a message that usually is not true. The North American may interpret the moving closer as disrespect or even as a sexual advance, and the Latin American is likely to interpret the pulling back as aloofness and unfriendliness (E. T. Hall, 1976).

Culture and personal space

Culture is an integral part of any person. Cultural differences therefore play a large role in determining individual differences. Culture announces our membership in particular groups, our values, and our biases. And most of this happens without our realizing it, because so much of our culturally conditioned behavior is unconscious. The way you greet someone, the way you use language, your opinions about what and when it is appropriate to eat, and many of your other personal preferences are all culturally conditioned. The influence of culture on thinking has led some scholars to argue that culture determines learning (Vygotsky, 1978) and shapes intelligence (H. Gardner, 1983).

Culture influences learning and intelligence

Changing and Enduring Effects of Culture

Culture and ethnicity are integral parts of all of us, not special characteristics of people who are different from us. In fact, 83 percent of all Americans in the 1980 Census reported identification with at least one ethnic group, and about 40

• *School is a cultural setting, with rituals and customs, with rules for speaking and taking turns. Some students come with knowledge of that culture, others struggle to learn its ways. (© David S. Strickler/The Picture Cube)*

percent of those identified with more than one ethnic group (Hernandez, 1989). Different ethnic groups provide their members with different cultures. Culture includes all the ways in which we think, feel, and act as we try to solve particular problems in a given environment. These things change; so our view of culture must change. We expect the food and dress of immigrants, for example, to change drastically across generations, and usually they do. But these kinds of behaviors are easy to change; others—because they are virtually unconscious—are much more difficult to change. Communication patterns, linguistic styles, rules of politeness, a preference for looking directly at or away from the person to whom one is speaking—these are ingrained behaviors that change only slowly. Remember that the effects of culture are often not obvious, that the child who loves hamburgers and wears sneakers also shows behavioral characteristics and modes of thinking that are representative of his or her cultural heritage.

Enduring effects of culture

A Word of Caution

Any discussion about cultural differences is dangerous because we are talking about group characteristics, and group characteristics can easily turn into stereotypes. It's important to remember four things:

Culture masks individual variation

- Differences between cultural groups tend to mask individual variations within each group.
- We still know little about the sources of most individual differences within groups and cannot always interpret them. For example, we

know that amid the most impoverished communities in the United States—communities ravaged by drugs, unemployment, family disintegration, and disease—emotionally well-balanced, academically and artistically gifted children arise. Simultaneously, in American communities that are highly advantaged we find that emotionally disturbed academic failures are produced with regularity.

- The value we attach to particular behaviors or characteristics is not inherent in those behaviors or characteristics but is ascribed to them by people in a particular social context. Suppose you ask two children a difficult question. One looks up, appearing to get inspiration from the heavens. The other stares down at the ground. Would you assume that the second child is working as hard at the question? Is he avoiding the task? Or is he, perhaps, shy or embarrassed? The expectation that people will look up when they are thinking hard about something is culturally conditioned. It may represent religious traditions that lead us to seek heavenly assistance. Some American Indian children believe that spirits live below the earth. They expect the source of wisdom to lie underground. For them looking down is the culturally appropriate response to a difficult question. The point is that we interpret behavior in light of our own cultural context. This is natural, but it does not make for effective teaching. It clouds our judgments of students' behavior and, more important, can act as a restraint on their creativity.

Culture determines appropriate behavior

- Often we think that because children live in the same city, wear the same clothes, listen to the same music, and speak the same language, they are alike. This just isn't so. Teachers tend to overestimate the power of the American melting pot and the supposed effects of television as a homogenizing influence. All of us are individuals, affected by different cultures, and how we learn is much influenced by those cultures.

Cultural homogeneity overestimated

Culture and Schooling

A basic understanding of how cultural differences influence school learning is a necessary component of teacher preparation in a country distinguished by its cultural diversity. Children are products of a home culture that has helped to shape them for at least five years. Their culture has prepared them to act, to speak, and to relate to others in specific ways. Actually all children encounter a different culture when they enter school: Schools are themselves cultural settings—places where certain behaviors are accepted and others are not, where rituals and customs determine appropriateness. Think about some of the common school behaviors of having children stand in line to go from one room to another, of having them raise their hands when they want to speak, of expecting them to go to the bathroom in groups at predetermined times. All of these are arbitrary customs and rituals that define the culture of the school. Children entering school must learn these customs and many others to navigate the

School as a different culture

The fit between home and school

school experience successfully (Tobin, Wu, & Davidson, 1989). Many scholars argue that the accommodation necessary for success in school is easier for children whose home environment is most like the school environment (Erickson & Mohatt, 1982; Philips, 1983). The difference between home and school environments is often cited as a major cause of low academic achievement and high dropout rates among ethnic minorities in the United States (Heath, 1986).

When children's home culture differs in significant ways from the school culture, miscommunication is likely to occur. In the classroom, miscommunication may play a decisive role in decisions teachers make about their students' competence and behavior. As a result of cultural discrepancies certain children may be labeled "slow learners," "learning disabled," or "behavior problems."

Expressed and hidden curricula

Some critics also argue that schools, in their expressed and "hidden" curricula, reflect almost exclusively the majority culture and values. It is easy to see oversights and discrepancies in the expressed curriculum. We might notice the exclusion of material on African-Americans from an American history textbook, for example. It is more difficult to attend to the implicit, but no less important, messages carried by the hidden curriculum. The teacher's large desk and its position at the front of the classroom silently underline the teacher's higher status in relation to the students. And when students see that the only minority-group members working in a school are a janitor or a cafeteria worker, they learn something about social class that is not being taught in social studies.

Historical Background

Ethnic diversity is not a new phenomenon in the United States. The country's founders recognized this diversity when they chose not to establish a national religion or language through the Constitution. In 1776 what is now the United States was a region composed of many nations: American Indian, British, French, Spanish, and Mexican. Hundreds of languages were spoken, and customs and religious expression differed widely. Things are not very different in America today. The social isolation of some ethnic and racial groups, as well as continuing immigration, means that cultural differences are still very much a part of American society.

Education for the culturally different

One reason we must deal with these issues is that educational opportunities for different cultural groups in the United States have not been equal. African-Americans, as we noted in Chapter 3, were either forbidden to participate in educational activities or restricted to separate and unequal schools. American Indians were removed from their tribal homes and sent to distant boarding schools, where their names were changed, their hair was cut, and the use of Indian languages was prohibited. The goal was to reduce their "Indianness" and force them into mainstream society (Foreman, 1972). Mexican-Americans in the Southwest also faced cultural rejection and limited opportunities in the schools, as did many European immigrants. The legacy of these policies remains with us today.

During World War II, African-Americans in the U.S. Navy served primarily as officers' stewards, and Japanese-Americans fought in a segregated battalion in Europe. In 1948, President Truman ordered an end to segregation in the United States armed forces. The post-World War II situation served as a catalyst for efforts to improve the educational opportunities of ethnically diverse students. A major milestone in these efforts was the dissolution of racially homogeneous school districts by the Supreme Court's decision in *Brown* v. *Topeka* in 1954. This decision paved the way for racial integration in the schools and increased public awareness of the extent of educational inequality in America. But change has come much more slowly than expected.

Recognition in the late 1950s and early 1960s of disproportionate academic failure among minority-group students, particularly among African-Americans, led to well-meaning but, in retrospect, patronizing efforts to provide compensatory education. As the name implies, *compensatory education* was an official response to compensate for the deficit of students. The assumption was that poor minority-group children arrived at school with an "educational disadvantage" that had to be compensated for through educational intervention. This disadvantage was thought to be due to environmental deficiencies that left the child "culturally disadvantaged" and speaking a nonstandard language (Baratz & Baratz, 1982). The assumption was that children must adapt to the school setting; the school did not have to adapt to the children.

A deficit model of education

Recent decades have seen a gradual change in the understanding of cultural differences and the role of the school in adapting to these differences. Findings from cross-cultural, classroom-based, and sociolinguistic research have made many scholars aware of the subtle and pervasive influence of culture on school performance. This research has also begun to sensitize educators to the unconscious biases that affect the supposedly objective assessment of qualities like "ability," "intelligence," "linguistic competence," and "learning disability."

Learning and Cognition in a Cross-Cultural Perspective

Many psychological researchers have ventured beyond familiar Western middle-class locations to study learning in widely different settings, both in different countries and in the United States. In doing so they have sometimes joined with anthropologists and linguists, integrating the methods of the other disciplines with their own. They have discovered some things that are both simple and profound: First, there is a danger in generalizing across cultural contexts. And second, understanding the context within which behavior occurs is of great importance in trying to interpret behavior.

A study of two neighboring communities by Heath (1983) gives us a good example. The people in one of these communities are African-American; members of the other community are white. Although these people live only a short distance apart and most work in the same textile mill, children in each of these

• *Students from all cultural backgrounds should be encouraged to develop knowledge in all areas of the curriculum. (© 1987 Jonathan A. Meyers)*

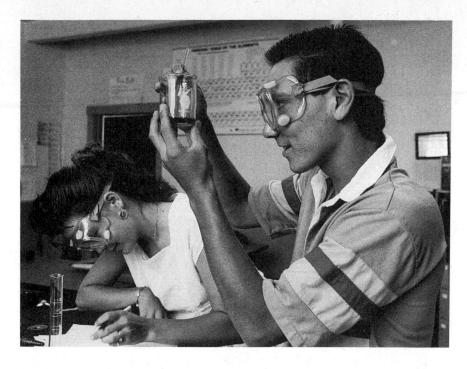

communities learn very different sets of rules as they learn to speak. The researcher asked residents in the two communities to explain how children learn to know and talk. In the African-American community of Trackton, Annie Mae explained that her children must learn on their own to a large extent, while Peggy, in the white community of Roadville asserted that it was up to her to give her children a good start by talking to them "all the time" and by buying them books and educational toys.

"Comin' up" and "bringin' up" children

In Trackton, Heath concludes, adults talk of children's "comin' up"; in Roadville, they speak of "bringin' up" their children. The two communities hold different concepts of childhood and development, and each provides roles for adults and children that fit their notions of who can and should teach children to listen, talk, read, and write. By the time they go to school, the children have learned their own community's ways of using language to get along and to attain their social goals (Heath, 1983).

The adult assumptions influence the language development of children in these communities. In Trackton, children have rich and varied experiences with language, but their perceptions of things and events are not guided by adults. They have to find their own patterns in the complex, multichannel stream of stimuli that surrounds them because time, space, and talk are not set aside especially for them. Parents in Roadville do set aside special time and space and talk for their children, but they focus the children's attention mostly on labels and descriptions. They give their children opportunities for extended narratives, creating new contexts, or manipulating elements of an event or item.

Trackton children come to school with experience in a world of discontinuities. Their ability to *contextualize*—to understand an item or an event in relation to the context in which it occurs—which has served them well in their community, is useless in the school, where correct responses require students to lift items and events out of their context, to *decontextualize*. Trackton children have a problem separating letters and their sounds from words, and words from sentences. And so they learn to read only slowly. Their ability to contextualize could help them in upper grades where relationships become important to understanding. But the initial difficulty they experience in school discourages them from further developing that ability.

When they first enter school, Roadville children experience success. Their home world and that of the school appear well matched. They have been accustomed to a structured linear world, where time is divided into blocks and there are limits on the use of space. They know about bedtime stories and coloring books. But theirs is a limited readiness that does not prepare them for higher-level academic tasks—tasks that demand an understanding of relationships, the ability to predict outcomes, and a synthesis of knowledge. They know less about how to contextualize.

The researcher found still other patterns of language use in a third community nearby. African-Americans and whites here look beyond the boundaries of their region for rules and guidance in fashion, entertainment, and decision making in their jobs. Children from these homes are taught relationships *and* labels. They are asked not only "what" but "why." These children are not exposed to a large quantity of language, but the *quality* of their language interactions is different. Their parents, successful students themselves, provide them with opportunities to practice the skills valued in the classroom, both initially and later on.

Culture and Communication

How we communicate is in good measure a function of culture. Even something as simple as asking and answering questions is culture bound. In most parts of the United States and in many European countries, we help students learn by asking them questions. This method would probably not be effective for the Athabaskan Indians of Alaska. Their *participant structures*—the rules that govern conversation in their community—are unlike those that guide most verbal interaction in the United States. Among the Athabaskans it is the subordinate person who is expected to ask questions and the superordinate who responds. The rhythm of Athabaskan conversations is also different. Athabaskans tend to make long pauses between statements (Scollon & Scollon, 1981).

These may seem to be minor differences. Yet, as the Scollons noted, they can impair communications. Think, for example, about the interaction of visiting federal officials and Athabaskan community leaders. The Athabaskans expect the visitors to answer, not to ask, questions. But the bureaucrats are there to get answers. The result: Communication is hampered. And what happens when

Contextualization

Limited readiness for higher-level tasks

Participant structures

Miscommunication

the visitors move quickly through conversation while the Athabaskans pause again and again. The visitors don't understand why the Athabaskans are silent, and the Athabaskans find the visitors rude. You can see how easy it is for typical American teachers to have problems if they ask lots of questions to keep the pace rapid, as in the standard recitation format or drill-and-practice exercise so common in our classrooms. Notice also that we may have miscommunication, even though everybody is speaking English. Scollon and Scollon (1981) argued that problems of miscommunication are often overlooked when participants speak the same language. We tend to assume that using the same grammar and vocabulary guarantees effective communication. In fact, it doesn't.

Native American rules for turn-taking

Work by Philips (1983) also shows how a common language does not guarantee effective communication. She found that conflicts in participant structures contributed to problems in the classroom. One set of these guides the taking of turns. In the Warm Springs Indian Reservation, children learn three rules of turn-taking: (1) speakers are more likely to address a group rather than a specific individual; (2) it is not always necessary to respond immediately to a speaker's statements; and (3) speakers control the ends of their own turns (no interruptions). Within this community, the organization of verbal interactions maximizes individuals' control over their own turns at talk. When these children enter school, they come up against different rules of turn-taking. Here the teacher, not the individual student, decides who should speak and when and for how long. The teacher also addresses students directly and directs individuals to respond on command. These children are faced with a wide discrepancy between their own expectations and the teacher's expectations. Although they speak English, their confusion about the rules operating in the classroom leads them to withdraw from participation (Philips, 1983).

It is interesting to note that Anglo students in the same classrooms have no problem with classroom interaction. Also the teachers' expectations, given traditional training, are not unreasonable. And the Warm Springs children are not consciously aware of the reason for their discomfort. In this situation, as in so many others that involve cross-cultural participation, everyone is acting in good faith and, simultaneously, misunderstanding one another.

Violation of linguistic rules

Obviously communication is more than speaking. It is all the ways in which conversation between individuals is structured, and these structures are part of our earliest socialization (Gumperz & Gumperz, 1981; Hymes, 1972). As we learn the language of our parents, we also learn the rules that guide conversation in our cultural context. These participant structures become so deeply embedded that we do not recognize them as rules, although we operate by them. We react when they are violated, but our reaction usually is not directed to the source of the problem, the sociolinguistic violation. Instead we react to the person who is breaking the rules or to the group or institution that person represents. In the case of schoolchildren, their reaction can take the form of silence, restlessness, or other behaviors we think of as inappropriate to the classroom. These behaviors are often symptoms of confusion, not of learning problems or lack of discipline.

Culture and Testing

One problem in cross-cultural studies has implications for teachers as well. The problem arose when researchers interpreted a lack of competence on specific tasks, particularly on testlike laboratory tasks, as an indication of cognitive deficiencies (Sigel, Anderson, & Shapiro, 1966). The groups being studied were African-Americans from lower socioeconomic backgrounds. Findings from the research appeared to indicate that these children, when compared to children from higher socioeconomic settings, used fewer descriptive and categorical groupings and relied more on relationship groupings when classifying pictures in a test of conceptual ability. For example, the children might classify two pictures, one of a woman and one of a girl, as mother and daughter instead of "woman" or "female." The researchers concluded that these differences reflected social-class differences in the ability to categorize—a cognitive ability—the result, they claimed, of fewer opportunities for "distancing" experiences in lower-class homes. Simmons (1979) challenged that conclusion. He constructed a similar test using more culturally relevant items and demonstrated that differences in performance in the earlier test were due to cultural not cognitive differences.

Cultural difference vs. cognitive deficit

Serpell (1979) designed a study in response to conclusions that African children lack certain general cognitive abilities. These conclusions had been drawn from studies that required the children to reproduce patterns while using paper and pencil or blocks. Serpell's study incorporated four perceptual tasks:

- *Mimicry,* which required the children to copy the position of the researcher's hands.
- *Drawing,* which required copying two-dimensional figures using pencil and paper.
- *Molding,* which required constructing copies of two-dimensional wire objects using strips of wire.
- *Modeling,* which required the children to use clay to copy three-dimensional objects.

Serpell chose these particular tasks because he knew that the two cultural groups he wanted to compare had had different opportunities for prior experience with each of them. He predicted that a group's prior experience would affect performance on each task.

Prior experience and performance on tests

The results of this study comparing English and Zambian children supported Serpell's hypothesis. The two groups of children performed similarly in those tasks in which they had comparable experience: mimicking hand positions and modeling with clay. English children had the advantage in the drawing task, which required the use of pencil and paper. Zambian children performed better in the wire-molding task, an activity that is common to them but not to English children.

Clearly the performance of a specific group on an experimental task cannot be taken as evidence that group members lack a specific ability or process (Cole & Means, 1981). We can only conclude that the group does not show that particular ability or process when performing that particular task under those specific conditions. This is an important piece of information for you to remember. Cole and Scribner (1974) have also asserted that it is safe to assume that no cultural group lacks any general cognitive abilities. Apparent lacks are due to differences in practical experience. Cognitive abilities are in part culturally determined and are intended to be useful within the system in which they are supposed to operate.

No deficient cultural groups

A study by Luria (1979) shows the way cognitive ability is intimately tied to culture. He presented members of rural Russian communities with the task of grouping a set of pictured articles by categories. One of the sets included pictures of a tree, an ax, a saw, and a boy. They could be grouped together along the organic-inorganic dimension: tree and boy, and ax and saw. Or they could be grouped by function: tree, ax, and saw—all for cutting wood—as one group, boy as another. These are common ways in which educated people categorize things. But Luria's unschooled subjects insisted that these items all belonged in one group. Luria could have concluded that these people lacked categorization skills. Instead he chose to find out more. He asked the respondents their reasons for grouping what seemed to be disparate items together. They explained that all the items in the group were needed to make a fire: The ax and the saw were needed to cut the tree, and the boy was needed to bring lunch to the workers in the forest. All were necessary to get firewood and survive the winter.

Functional cognitive ability

Our cognitive skills are not learned in a vacuum; we acquire them in the process of learning how to function in our culture. Thus the same general cognitive ability appears in different forms, or may be more or less developed, within different cultural groups. South Sea Islanders demonstrate what to us appear to be incredible feats of navigation. They cross the open ocean guided by their ability to notice minute changes in the sea, the wind, and the sky, without the help of mechanical instruments or charts. Yet, if they were tested for navigational skills by the U.S. Coast Guard, they would fail because they do not know how to make use of all the instruments and charts we find necessary for navigation. This does not mean that they lack the cognitive ability to understand maps any more than our inability to navigate without maps means we do not have the cognitive capacity to do so. Pulawat navigators of the Pacific have learned to use perceptual and memory skills within a system that rewards those skills (navigators have high status in their society). We have learned to use our cognitive perceptual skills within a system that rewards us for using written and graphic material, mathematical formulas, and mechanical devices. In each culture similar skills are used, but within different systems.

If you are working with students from a culture different from your own, remember to be careful not to assume a lack of ability in individuals whose performance fails to meet your expectations. What you are seeing may be the product of the system by which your students operate, not a deficiency in their cognitive capacity.

Culture, Expectations, and School Success

The expectations of teachers for their students can have powerful effects on student achievement (Good, 1987). These expectations are shaped in large part by cultural norms. If we have grown up believing that punctuality demonstrates interest and concern, we are offended when someone is late. In cultures where time is a resource to be conserved, punctuality is important. In cultures where time is just a convenient reference for organizing activities, punctuality is far less important and being late is not a sign of disrespect. We may think that children who consistently arrive at school late are unmotivated or uninterested. But we should ask whether time simply has a different meaning for them. Although lateness may be disruptive in school and we may want to correct the problem, we have to be careful about our attributions. Our response to the children should vary according to the causes to which we attribute their behavior.

By the year 2000, 5 billion of the 6 billion people on earth will be nonwhite (Hernandez, 1989). In the United States, minority-group populations are expected to increase at a much faster rate than the white majority population (Hodgkinson, 1981), and the school population will reflect these international and national trends. In fact, by the mid-1980s, twenty-two of the twenty-six largest school systems in the United States already had enrollments in which more than half of the students belonged to minority groups. At the same time, the percent of teachers that belong to minorities has been dropping. Thus many teachers will not be familiar with the particular cultural group they will be teaching. When we lack experience with groups different from our own, or with people who speak different languages or dialects, we tend to impose expectations based on our own cultural norms. We are very likely to judge their behavior on the basis of our expectations rather than their own standards. And this tendency can limit our effectiveness as teachers.

Minority enrollments growing

Expectations and Language

In Chapter 4 we talked about language. We said there that almost all linguists agree that no language or dialect is more effective than any other. The issue here is not whether black English or some other nonstandard English should be used in the schools; it is whether our judgments of students' competence are based on their use of language. We simply cannot assume that students who speak nonstandard English are less competent than their peers.

Unfortunately this assumption is often made during the assessment of academic needs in populations of students whose home language is not English. Apparently many teachers confuse the knowledge of English as a language with academic competence. This confusion is evident in the extreme overrepresenta-

Language ability and academic competence

**Nonstandard
English and
special education
placement**

tion of non-English-speaking students in special education categories. In the state of Texas, 300 percent more Hispanic students than would be expected, based on their numbers in the population, have been classified as learning disabled (Ortiz & Yates, 1983). And at the national level, among one hundred school districts that appeared to show discrimination in the placement of children who spoke languages other than English, sixteen had placed *all* of these students in special education classes, and more than forty had placed over 50 percent of these students in special education classes (Dew, 1984). We also find confusion between language and academic competence in the English reading instruction of many non-English-speaking students who are already literate in their native language. Instead of giving these students instruction at a level of comprehension comparable to the level achieved in their native language, teachers sometimes begin in English and with oversimplified texts of the type used to teach much younger children (Diaz, Moll, & Mehan, 1986). This practice seems to say to a student, although unintentionally, "You haven't learned anything worthwhile in your native language."

Expectations and the Development of Talent

Co-membership

We are usually unaware of our expectations, and so they are hard to control. They can influence our thinking and our behavior in invalid ways. Erickson (1975) found that school counselors, while consciously trying to be fair in their advice to students, were nonetheless affected by *co-membership,* that is, shared cultural norms and values. Students who demonstrated co-membership with a counselor—Italian background, for example—were able to get more useful information than those who did not. The counselors' expectation—that students who were not like them in some way were also not interested in everything the counselors could present—apparently influenced the counselors' behavior. Er-

Gatekeepers

ickson pointed out the importance of this influence to students outside the mainstream culture, who depend on the information these "gatekeepers" can provide in making career decisions.

Almost all educators function as gatekeepers. This means you must learn to recognize the influence of irrelevant student characteristics on your decisions about students. Sometimes these influences lead us to misjudge a student's competence. Other times they keep us from recognizing and nurturing a student's abilities.

An interesting example of a valued characteristic that has been neither recognized nor nurtured comes from a study that measured intelligence among Hopi Indians (L. Thompson, 1951). On the Grace Arthur Intelligence Test one group of Hopis achieved a mean IQ of 111; another group scored 115. On the Goodenough Intelligence Test, the same groups had average IQs of 117 and 111, respectively. All of these average scores exceed the average performance of white populations by a considerable amount. And the performance is all the more impressive when we consider the relative isolation of the Hopi tribes in the early 1950s.

What happened? These impressive scores went unnoticed. The Hopis have not achieved the level of academic and economic rewards we would expect for a population demonstrating such high levels of general intelligence. It seems that intelligence-test scores, usually a trusted predictor of academic success, were not given the same importance when manifested by a population that is not expected to demonstrate high levels of success in the general society.

We find another example of the failure to recognize and nurture some students' abilities in the work of scholars who have tried to understand how children become literate. They suggest that a child's potential for successful acquisition of literacy is closely related to the ability to see language as an object that can be manipulated: "a conscious awareness, on the part of the language user, of language as an object in itself. The person who is linguistically aware will recognize that language . . . is a manipulative system" (Olson, 1984, p. 160). The close fit between this definition and the language games played by urban African-Americans ("jivin'," "playing the dozens," "signifying") is striking. Researchers have pointed out the extensive metaphorical use of language by African-American children in games like these (Delain, Pearson, & Anderson, 1985; Taylor & Ortony, 1980). But educators for the most part have not made the connection between these linguistic skills and the metalinguistic skills said to be necessary for successful school performance. The creativity and imaginativeness of these street games is often considered no more than an intriguing nuisance to be controlled in the classroom.

Language as manipulable object

Children who have developed bilingual competence are also likely to display behavior that conforms to Olson's (1984) definition of a linguistically sophisticated person. These children learn to shift from one language to the other. They learn the relative usefulness of one or the other language in different settings. They also learn that some things can be said more effectively in one language than in the other. All these behaviors demonstrate metalinguistic skills, the ability to see language as an object that can be manipulated. But in the vast majority of schools, these children, like their African-American counterparts, are thought to be disadvantaged, and their linguistic skills become instead a "language problem" (Cummins, 1986).

What Schools and Teachers Can Do

The possibilities for miscommunication and misunderstanding we've been talking about may seem overwhelming. It may also seem impossible to overcome the unconscious cultural biases we've described. Fortunately many individuals, programs, and institutions have managed to minimize the problems inherent in cross-cultural situations. Here we look at some of the strategies that are working.

Cooperative learning is a method of getting students to work together in the classroom. It makes use of groups and teams to reduce competition. (We talk in detail about the method in Chapter 9.) Cooperative learning may be an important innovation in terms of education and culture for two reasons: First, it may be more compatible with the cultural norms and values of some ethnic groups. Second, it may contribute to better interethnic relationships in the classroom. Kagan (1986), for example, has argued that at least part of the reason why the

Cooperative learning

democratic goal of equal educational opportunity has not been realized in the United States is the competitive structure of most classrooms. He claims that a competitive environment biases educational outcomes against minority-group and low-income students.

The preference for a cooperative environment among minority populations may be related to their preference for different participation structures. Certainly this would seem to be the case with Athabaskan and Warm Springs Indian children. Kagan, Zahn, Widaman, Schwarzwald, and Tyrrell (1985) have argued that Mexican-American students also have a similar aversion to competition. For many minority-group students, a cooperative learning environment provides a more compatible social context.

Parental involvement

Understanding that, in many urban areas, low-income and minority-group parents have had limited schooling, some educators assume that these parents have no interest in school and are unable to help their children. These assumptions have been challenged. Recent research shows that these parents have high expectations for their children, that they value education, and that they communicate their values to their children. Also, when they receive clear explicit requests for assistance from schools, they respond effectively (R. Clark, 1982; Epstein, 1984; Goldenberg, n.d.). Moreover, the studies found that parents' efforts to help their children led to student achievement gains. In some cases, parental help appeared to determine whether a child succeeded in early literacy learning. Parental involvement programs take time and effort from teachers, who are already busy. But the benefits of such programs are clear.

Bilingual education

Bilingual education, discussed in Chapter 4, has also been found effective with language minorities. It makes sense to begin instruction by acknowledging what students already know—their culture and their language. Ignoring students' home language means discarding about five years of learning, probably the most significant learning in an individual's life. This is not a new insight. In the seventeenth century the great European educator Comenius (1596–1670) advocated the use of the native language in initial instruction. And bilingual education has one more advantage: It demonstrates respect for a student's language heritage and, by association, respect for the student's cultural heritage.

Heath (1983) and the teachers who participated in the study of language development in Trackton and Roadville attempted to use the knowledge they gained to improve the effectiveness of their instruction. Heath describes the work of Mrs. Gardner, who was assigned a class of nineteen African-American first-graders. All the students had been designated "potential failures" on the basis of reading readiness tests. Mrs. Gardner visited her students' communities before school started and made simple maps of the communities. She picked up old tires and, with the help of some parents, attached the tires to pieces of wood to make letters. The letters were then scattered about the yard outside the classroom. The children had many opportunities to pick up and play with these "toys" informally.

Mrs. Gardner used the knowledge gained from her visits to the students' communities and from the research to develop a program that built on her students' skills at noticing similarities between items and events. One example of her efforts to integrate the students' early learning with school activities was the way in which she introduced the letters of the alphabet. She did not limit herself to presenting the letters only as symbols on paper; these symbols appeared in structures all around the children: I's as telephones poles, L's as upside-down streetlights, and, of course, the toys in the schoolyard. The children were encouraged to search for the letters all around them and bring their findings to the classroom.

Instruction in that first-grade classroom was drastically changed by the teacher's knowledge of her students and her integration of their skills into the instructional effort. Her goal was academic excellence. She did not change her expectations; she only modified instructional practices. She met her students halfway.

Mrs. Gardner's efforts were amply rewarded. By the end of the first grade all but one of the potential failures was reading at grade level. (The one exception was a child diagnosed as having serious emotional problems.) Six of the nineteen were reading at second-grade level, and eight were reading at third-grade level.

These examples of what schools and teachers can do about cultural diversity have two characteristics in common. First, the strategy begins with the assumption that all children are capable of learning. Second, it is assumed that instruction must be adjusted to students. Too often we assume that lack of academic progress is the student's fault. So we try to remediate the student. Vygotsky (1978) had a better idea. He spoke of "re-mediating," of restructuring the instructional process to provide more effective mediation for the student. Remediation assumes that one strategy may succeed where others fail. This view of learning is particularly useful for teachers who work with children from different cultures. To succeed with these children, teachers need to learn how to withhold judgment, to observe, to modify, and to re-mediate. The reward here is twofold: an increase in student achievement and an increase in self-knowledge from examining our behavior in relation to that of people from a different culture.

Adjusting instruction to children

Gender Differences

We turn now to differences between males and females, especially the differences that affect education. Before we begin, it is important to remind ourselves of two well-established facts: First, individual differences *within* a group are almost always greater than differences *between* groups. For most gender differences in intellectual areas, as for most racial and ethnic differences, there is marked overlap of the distributions of the variable we are measuring, even though the means may differ. Second, in interpreting studies that compare the sexes, we seldom can separate genetic from environmental influences on behavior. This was true when we examined race differences; it is also true of gender differences.

Individual vs. group differences

Genetic and environmental contributions

Cultural conditioning starts early

We have to begin with the admission that we can never really know what the sexes would be like if there were no cultural conditioning, if we did not begin with pink and blue blankets in the nursery, dolls and trucks in the pre-school, ballet and basketball in the pre-teens, cheerleaders and football players in high school, and so on. Since children cannot survive outside of a cultural matrix, by the time we can examine them we have already begun to shape them. (Bernard, 1973, p. 7)

And one more thing. Studies that show sex differences on a particular variable get printed in journals and presented at meetings far more often than do studies that show no differences. Thus reviews of published literature tend to overestimate any gender-linked differences in intellectual functioning (Jacklin & Maccoby, 1972).

Gender Differences in Intellectual Functioning

What follows is a list of general and specific cognitive abilities and a short discussion of the gender-related differences we find in each. More complete reviews of the research we talk about here have been written (Hyde & Linn, 1986; Linn & Hyde, 1989; Maccoby & Jacklin, 1974; Sadker, Sadker, & Klein, 1991; Spence & Helmreich, 1978; and Wittig & Peterson, 1979).

General intelligence. Studies to determine whether or not males and females differ in general intelligence have not yielded consistent findings. Mean differences, when they occur, are small. In the preschool years girls score higher on intelligence tests; in the high school years boys score higher on these tests. The latter difference may be due to the higher dropout rate of low-ability boys in high school, leaving behind an unrepresentative group of relatively high-ability male students. Overall no dramatic differences between the sexes are noted when we measure general intelligence.

Verbal ability. Because girls learn to talk, to use sentences, and to use a greater variety of words a little earlier than boys, they were believed to perform better on measures of verbal fluency. Furthermore, it is generally agreed that they speak more clearly, read earlier, and do consistently better than boys on tests of spelling and grammar. A likely cause of all this is that they pay more attention to what is being taught. Later research, however, has questioned the early superiority of females in the verbal domain and argued that such superiority emerges only at about puberty and continues thereafter. But even these results are now no longer so clear. In tests of verbal reasoning, verbal comprehension, and vocabulary, the findings are not usually consistent. In her 1981 analysis Hyde estimated that only about 1 percent of the variation in verbal ability in the general population can be attributed to gender. But in more recent analyses (Hyde & Linn, 1986) it was concluded that later studies showed even smaller differences, and it is appropriate to conclude that there are no longer any gender differences in verbal ability worth discussing.

Mathematical ability. During the preschool years, no important gender-related differences in mathematical ability appear. At the end of elementary school, boys begin to excel in mathematical reasoning, and the difference becomes greater in high school, college, and adulthood (Fennema, 1987; Maccoby, 1966). This difference has led some (e.g., Benbow & Stanley, 1980) to suggest that there are genetic differences in the mathematical ability of males and females. But the evidence is weak. Recently far more studies have shown no male superiority in mathematics (Hyde, Fennema, & Lamon, 1990). Also, new studies show that any male superiority in mathematics may be related to the way mathematics is traditionally taught—as a competitive individual endeavor rather than a cooperative small-group learning activity. When basic mathematics is taught in cooperative small groups, girls do better than boys (Fennema & Peterson, 1987). Hyde (1981) estimated that if gender differences exist, these differences would account for only about 1 percent of the variation in quantitative ability that we see in our population.

The differences in mathematics achievement we see in our culture may be nothing more than the result of different role expectations. These expectations for men and women play a part in decisions to take mathematics and to achieve well in it (see Fennema, 1982; Fox, Tobin, & Brady, 1979). Evidence for this idea comes from two sources: First, in cross-national studies we find in Sweden, where sex-role differences are smaller, that the male-female differences in mathematics achievement also tend to be smaller (Svensson, 1971). And in all-female schools, where women do not as consistently experience the marked differences in role expectations held for males and females, women show higher performance in math and science than they do in coeducational schools (Finn, Dulberg, & Reis, 1979).

Role expectations and mathematics

These comments on mathematics ability and achievement can be extended to science ability and achievement. Since a good deal of science is related to mathematics, any changes in mathematics achievement will affect science achievement. M. C. Linn and J. S. Hyde (1989) note that gender differences in science achievement are decreasing.

Spatial ability. This is the ability to recognize a figure when it is rotated, detect a shape when it is hidden within some other figure, or

• *Limiting a person's choices about what to excel in, based on gender, simply wastes talent. (Right: © Jean-Claude Lejeune. Facing page: © Jean-Claude Lejeune)*

Spatial ability and genetics

effortlessly take a three-dimensional object and sketch it with accurate perspective. Here males have consistently done better than females. In fact, of all the gender-related differences in intellectual activity, the difference in spatial ability seemed to be the most consistent and thus, perhaps, the most likely to have a genetic origin. Still, although evidence for some kind of genetic sex linkage of this ability can be found (for example, Stafford, 1972; Vandenberg & Kuse, 1979), that evidence is hardly overwhelming (Fennema, 1981; Sherman, 1978). Moreover, and as usual, the magnitude of gender differences is small, accounting for no more than 5 percent of the variation in spatial ability that we see in the population before 1980 (Hyde, 1981). More recent analyses have shown (1) that gender differences in spatial ability are declining and (2) that the differences that exist can be removed through special training programs. These two factors make it unlikely that any genetic explanation for the differences can be defended.

Problem solving.   We find mixed results when we examine problem solving, creativity, analytical skill, and cognitive styles (such as field independence, described below), probably because these are complex concepts. What consistency there is points to greater ability in males (1) to break sets, that is, to try new approaches in problem solving, and also (2) to be generally more "field independent," that is, freer of the effects of the context in which a problem is placed. This latter characteristic means that males are less likely to be influenced by irrelevant cues in certain kinds of learning tasks. Males tend also to exhibit wider "category width" in concept-learning tasks; that is, they are likely to use broader conceptual categories, focusing more on common features and ignoring irrelevant features. Males also show more curiosity and markedly less conservatism than women in risk-taking situations (D. B. Lynn, 1972; Maccoby, 1966). These characteristics give males an edge in most problem-solving tests.

But when it comes to problem solving in the area of human relations, women's performance usually exceeds that of men (Garai & Scheinfeld, 1968; see also Gilligan, 1982). In fact, in studies of problem solving related to the school principalship in education,

Ability to break sets

Field independence

Solving problems in human relations

females consistently show superior performance, despite the fact that the principalship is still a male domain (Sadker, Sadker, & Klein, 1991).

School achievement.   Almost without exception the studies show that girls do better on the average than boys in school achievement (grades), particularly in the elementary grades—even in the mathematics and science areas. These differences narrow considerably in high school. But throughout the school years, the scholastic performance of girls seems more stable—that is, less fluctuating—than that of boys.

Differential treatment unwarranted

Our examination of gender-linked differences in important areas of cognitive functioning—general intelligence; verbal, number, and spatial ability; problem solving; and school achievement—*has uncovered no compelling evidence that indicates teachers should treat boys and girls differently. The overlap of the distributions for most cognitive variables is great,* even when nonchance (statistically significant) differences are found.

Gender Differences in Personality

We find gender-related differences on many personality variables. We can't examine all of these variables here, but we do talk about some characteristics of personality that are related to performance in school.

Males more aggressive

Aggression.   Of all the gender differences related to personality, those related to aggression are the most consistent. Males of all ages and in most cultures are generally more aggressive than females. Margaret Mead (1935), in her classic *Sex and Temperament,* described the wide variation in male and female roles in different cultures. Most of the variation in behavior seemed attributable to environmental influences. Later thinking—based on more extensive anthropological examination and studies of animals and human hormones—suggested that aggression is probably genetically sex-linked (see R. Brown, 1965). But the argument goes on, with Tieger (1980) attacking the position that there is a biological basis for differences in aggression. His review of aggression in young boys and girls revealed no association with either sex until about age 5. His findings pointed out that social learning (see Chapter 6), rather than biology, could result in the differences we see. What is clear is that male and female roles differ widely in most cultures, and that males usually are found to be more dominant, assertive, energetic, active, hostile, and destructive.

Conformity and dependence.   Females generally have been found to be more conforming and suggestible than males (H. M. Cooper, 1979; Eagly & Carli, 1981). But the biases in these studies make them suspect (Maccoby, 1966). For example, Eagly and Carli (1981) noted that male researchers find women more easily persuaded and more likely to conform; female researchers do not.

Emotional adjustment.   The emotional stability of the sexes is about the same in childhood, but we do see differences in how emotional problems are manifested (temper tantrums for boys, thumb sucking for girls). Personality inventories, however, indicate that adolescent and adult females have more neurotic symptoms than males. This difference may occur because our society defines mental health in ways that go along with male roles (Broverman, Broverman, Clarkson, Rosenkrantz, & Vogel, 1970), or because the tests have usually been designed by men.

Values and life goals.   It is no surprise to find data from the 1950s showing men with greater interest in scientific, sales, mathematical, mechanical, and physically active occupations and expressing stronger theoretical, economic, and political values. Nor is it a surprise to find women tending to choose literary, social service, and clerical occupations and expressing stronger aesthetic, social service, and religious values (Anastasi, 1958). These differences have probably been smaller since the 1950s as women have begun to think about themselves differently.

Changing values and goals

Achievement orientation.   Females do not react in the same way as males in conditions designed to bring out achievement motivation. Stein and Bailey (1973) concluded that females are more likely to express their achievement motivation, that is, their desire to succeed, in the areas that American society has traditionally designated as appropriate for women—in social skills and social relations. Sex-role expectations are strongly communicated at very early ages. Studies of children from grades 2 to 12 show that mechanical, spatial, and athletic skills are considered masculine, and that social, verbal, and artistic skills are considered feminine. So a young woman with high achievement motivation would be likely to express it in areas where she will receive the greatest rewards—social areas.

Sex-role expectations

This hypothesis—that different school subjects bring forth achievement striving for the two sexes—has been confirmed in several studies (Battle, 1965, 1966; Stein, 1971; Stein, Pohly, & Mueller, 1971). So what has sometimes been interpreted as a fear of success (Horner, 1969; Komarovsky, 1950) or a lack of achievement motivation in women may simply be a different choice about the areas in which to display success orientation (Spence & Helmreich, 1978). As Gilligan (1982) showed, success in relationships and in working cooperatively may simply be more important to more American females (as compared with males) than trying to succeed in intellectual or competitive activities. Different areas of their human experience elicit success strivings for the two sexes, as one would expect given the different biological and social roles of women and men. Schools should foster self-discovery or self-understanding, in terms of these values, as much in girls as in boys. Girls, as well as boys, should choose the fields in which they wish to succeed *after* they have acquired the relevant self-understanding.

In summary, for personality and affective behaviors, most of the observed differences between the genders are, if not completely determined by culture, at least in large part the result of the interaction of environment and heredity. And because culture changes, sometimes very quickly, those behaviors that reflect culture also can and do change.

The Relationship Between Personality and Intellectual Achievement

The "oversocializing" of girls—making them overobedient—by parents and teachers who display too much warmth and too much restrictiveness is common in many families and classrooms. The tendency to value obedience, conformity, and passivity in females restricts them from taking responsibility and leadership (see Bronfenbrenner, 1961). Yet it doesn't have to be this way.

Pressure and female achievement

> Some female children are trained to be achievement oriented, and the literature is remarkably clear in indicating what parental characteristics are involved. The pattern that fosters achievement striving for females is not entirely consistent with the stereotypical notions of the best child rearing for happy, mentally healthy children. It involves some pressures on the child, some withholding of nurturance, and some punitiveness, although none of these characteristics appear in extremes. Moderate levels of warmth, a fair amount of permissiveness, combined with high standards and reinforcement for achievement efforts are likely to facilitate achievement behavior in female children, whereas their opposites are likely to lead to conforming, dependent . . . patterns of behavior. (Stein & Bailey, 1973, p. 363)

Distribution of traits

Maccoby's (1966) hypothesis about the relationship of personality to intellectual performance for girls is presented schematically in Figure 5.1. The distribution of boldness, impulsivity, and aggressiveness differs in the two sexes. For girls, when these traits are at higher levels than usual, we see evidence of higher levels of performance in a wide variety of intellectual tasks. If this relationship were causal, "it would follow that for optimum intellectual performance, most girls need to become less passive and inhibited" (Maccoby, 1966, p. 47). The findings are not as clear for males, although the evidence points to a similar relationship.

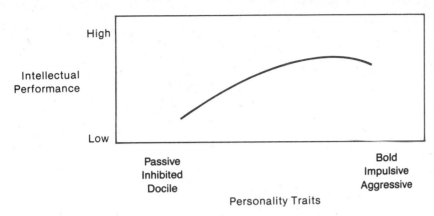

FIGURE 5.1

Hypothesized Relationship Between Personality Traits and Intellectual Performance for Girls

Source: Adapted from *The Development of Sex Difference,* edited by E. E. Maccoby. Used by permission of Stanford University Press.

Sex-Role Development at Home and School

The behavior of children is shaped by their gender, to some extent, right from birth. From the very first differentiation with pink or blue blankets, through different handling and expectancies, children come to acquire the sex-role behavior that society imposes.

Table 5.1 shows some of the dominant sex-role stereotypes in the United States. These stereotypes guide parent-child interactions at home, teacher-student interactions at school, and peer interactions in all settings. These stereotypes are commonly accepted; at least 75 percent of male and female respondents agreed that the description is masculine or feminine. Stereotypes can act as guidelines for behavior and also as norms against which we judge behavior. So these stereotypes, if applied blindly, can destroy both male and female potential. There is ample evidence that stereotypes like these are prevalent in the schools (National Education Association, 1980; Pottker & Fishel, 1977). For example, Kemer (1965) asked junior high school teachers to select adjectives that describe the "good" female and "good" male students. Table 5.2 lists their responses. As we might expect, teachers' values mirror the society in which they live.

Dominant sex-role stereotypes

Teacher's values mirror society's values

Parents start early to act in ways that foster a match between the commonly shared stereotypes and the behavior of their children. For example, Moss (1967) studied mothers' interactions at home with their 3-week-old infants. The study controlled for "irritability," because boys generally fuss more and girls sleep more. Mothers still gave significantly more attention to their little boys through holding, arousing them from sleep, attending to them, and standing them up. With their little girls, the mothers engaged more in cooing, talking, and making faces.

It seems the mothers systematically encouraged general activity in their little boys even though the boys were already more irritable, a behavior

TABLE 5.1

Sex-Role Stereotypes

Descriptions Related to Competence, Where the Masculine End of the Scale Is More Valued

Masculine	Feminine
Very aggressive	Not aggressive
Very independent	Not independent
Not emotional	Very emotional
Hides emotions	Does not hide emotions
Not easily influenced	Easily influenced
Very dominant	Very submissive
Likes math and science	Dislikes math and science
Not excitable in a crisis	Very excitable in a crisis
Very active	Very passive
Very competitive	Not competitive
Very logical	Very illogical
Very worldly	Home oriented
Very skilled in business	Not skilled in business
Very direct	Very sneaky
Knows the way of the world	Does not know the way of the world
Feelings not easily hurt	Feelings easily hurt
Very adventurous	Not adventurous
Makes decisions easily	Cannot make decisions
Never cries	Cries easily
Almost always acts as leader	Never acts as leader
Very self-confident	Not self-confident
Comfortable being aggressive	Uncomfortable being aggressive
Very ambitious	Not ambitious
Separates feelings from ideas	Cannot separate feelings from ideas
Not at all dependent	Very dependent
Not conceited about appearance	Very conceited about appearance
Thinks men are superior to women	Thinks women are superior to men
Talks freely with men about sex	Does not talk freely with men about sex

Descriptions Related to Warmth and Expressiveness, Where the Feminine End of the Scale Is More Valued

Masculine	Feminine
Uses harsh language	Does not use harsh language
Not talkative	Very talkative
Very blunt	Very tactful
Very rough	Very gentle
Not aware of feelings of others	Very aware of feelings of others
Not religious	Very religious
Not interested in own appearance	Very interested in own appearance
Very sloppy in habits	Very neat in habits
Very loud	Very quiet
Little need for security	Very strong need for security
Does not enjoy art and literature	Enjoys art and literature
Does not express tender feelings easily	Easily expresses tender feelings

Source: I. Broverman et al., "Sex-role Stereotypes and Clinical Judgement on Mental Health," *Journal of Consulting and Clinical Psychology* 34: 1–7. Copyright 1970 by the American Psychological Association. Adapted by permission.

"Good" Male Students	"Good" Female Students
Active	Appreciative
Adventurous	Calm
Aggressive	Conscientious
Assertive	Considerate
Curious	Cooperative
Energetic	Mannerly
Enterprising	Poised
Frank	Sensitive
Independent	Dependable
Inventive	Efficient
	Mature
	Obliging
	Thorough

TABLE 5.2

Descriptions of "Good" Male and "Good" Female Students

Source: Adapted from B. J. Kemer, "A Study of the Relationship Between the Sex of the Student and the Assignment of Marks by Secondary School Teachers," unpublished doctoral dissertation, Michigan State University, 1965.

which, if it persisted, would annoy a teacher. The mothers encouraged verbal behavior and social interaction in their little girls—both of these would give little girls a head start in nursery school and kindergarten. (M. P. Smith, 1972, p. 29)

In social learning situations in the schools, stereotypic sex-role behavior is learned early. In a study of nursery school play activities, boys were found to engage more in physical activity—block building, climbing, and tricycling; girls played more with paints, kitchen toys, dolls and doll houses, and modeling clay (Fagot & Patterson, 1969). Both boys and girls received reinforcement from their peers for playing with gender-appropriate materials. In fact 97 percent of the reinforcement received by 3-year-old girls from their teachers was for gender-appropriate, that is, feminine, play activity. From very early ages, girls are offered by their parents and teachers a highly consistent world that teaches stereotypical feminine role behaviors.

Stereotypic roles learned early

Interestingly, Fagot (1981) found that experienced male teachers are just as likely as experienced female teachers to reward feminine behaviors, regardless of a child's gender. One analysis showed that boys received most of their reinforcement (85 percent) for play rated as feminine. This finding supports Sexton's (1965) claim that schools try to "feminize" boys.

Boys and schools seem locked in a deadly and ancient conflict that may eventually inflict mortal wounds on both. In vastly disproportionate numbers, boys are the maladjusted, the inattentive, the rebellious . . . the problem is not just that teachers are too often women. It is that the school is too much a woman's world, governed by women's roles and standards. (p. 57)

School as a woman's world

• *Parents start early to act in ways that foster a match between stereotypes and their children's behavior. (© Michael Weisbrot)*

Despite this pressure in school, it appears that boys learn from other sources what role expectations to pay attention to. From their family, their peers, and the broader society comes reinforcement for masculine roles. The teacher becomes for boys, to a much greater degree than for girls, incidental. The school and home seem to restrict the total variance in role behavior for girls and to widen it for boys. One way in which the broader society communicates its expectations about sex-appropriate behavior is through textbooks and other instructional materials—films, workbooks, and the like. The common stereotypes for female and male behavior are communicated in hundreds of ways through these channels.

Stereotypes in Textbooks

When you were in elementary school, you probably used texts that had a decided bias. In the early 1970s, DeCrow (1972) analyzed the content of ten publishers' textbooks and found that the only women they portrayed outside the home were nurses and teachers, and these women were always "Miss." What these books were saying is that a woman's place is in the home, that women work only until they get a husband. In point of fact, however, about 50 percent of all American women work, usually outside their homes (Sadker & Sadker, 1982).

In the same textbooks, fathers drive cars, plan trips, and fumble doing the laundry. Mothers cook and tend babies, watch their husbands do things, and wait until their husbands come home to fix things. Men are doctors, women are nurses. Older children (boys) help younger children (girls). Boys show initiative, creativity, and the ability to make decisions. Girls are almost always fearful and dependent, watching others do things.

Another analysis of a sample of textbooks showed that for themes dealing with active mastery, where ingenuity, cleverness, industry, and bravery were called for, boys were the leading figures 1,004 times, girls 343 times (Women on Words and Images, 1972). When the themes dealt with passivity, dependence, incompetence, and humiliation, boys were the leading figures 182 times, girls 435 times. A more careful statistical analysis of grade-school readers was made by Jacklin and Maccoby (1972). Their content analysis revealed marked male domination in the stories. Males showed significantly higher frequencies of problem solving, physical effort, and appearances outdoors. Females were significantly more often directed in their activities by someone else, conforming, and shown working inside the home. The situation was the same in British texts and curriculum materials (Sutherland, 1981).

Male domination in readers' stories

Two additional interesting facts emerged from the Jacklin-Maccoby analysis. First, the content category called "expression of emotion" had to be dropped because it was used so infrequently. Boys and men were usually the central characters of the stories, and they were rarely allowed emotional expression. Psychotherapists and counselors often point out that the enforcement of this particular sex-role standard leads to more behavior difficulties in men than almost any other aspect of the socialization process. The constellation of factors that makes up the male sex role in school (and society) includes, besides hiding emotions, acting tough, earning a lot of money, getting the right job, competing intensely, and winning at almost any cost (Sadker & Sadker, 1982).

Boys and the expression of emotion

Jacklin and Maccoby also found that the stereotypic quality of the roles for males and females increased with the grade level of the textbooks. It was not just a peculiarity of the readers used in the early grades. Of ten problems on a page of a fifth-grade mathematics text, five dealt with girls cooking or sewing. In a set of problems dealing with club activities, boys built room dividers, girls made sandwiches. In twelve problems in a series, eleven had boys earning money, building things, and going different places, while one problem presented a girl buying ribbon to finish her sewing (Frazier & Sadker, 1973).

Sex-stereotyped texts, tests, and curricula are definitely changing. But the changes are slow, and problems still exist (e.g., see Powell, Garcia, & Denton, 1985; Sadker, Sadker, & Klein, 1991). Many textbooks and reading materials are less biased than they were. But middle-aged teachers were raised during an earlier time period and hold the values of their times. So when 254 elemen-

Curriculum material shape attitudes

tary school teachers were interviewed to find out their favorite books to read aloud in class, they naturally picked books that they had liked. Their top ten favorites included books with males as the main character 80 percent of the time. One book had a female main character, and one had both male and female main characters (N. Smith, Greenlaw, & Scott, 1987). Popular books from earlier times are in widespread use and are not as gender fair as contemporary books. However, there is no longer any doubt that gender, racial, and ethnic biases in curricular materials have an impact on student achievement and attitudes (Scott, 1980). So you need to be on guard about what materials you use in class.

At its roots American society may not have changed since the following editorial appeared in 1889 in the student newspaper of an agricultural college in Pennsylvania:

> A woman needs what will make her a queen of the household and of society, while man needs what will fit him for the harder, sterner duties of life, to which ladies should never be driven except in cases of exigency. She cannot afford to risk her health in acquiring a knowledge of the advanced sciences, mathematics, or philosophy for which she has no use. . . . Too many women have already made themselves permanent invalids by an overstrain of study at schools and colleges. (Cited in Frazier & Sadker, 1973, p. 146)

Nonstereotypical models

Members of the women's movement are quick to point out the damage this kind of stereotyping does to both girls and boys. Girls (and boys) much too seldom get to see or read about intelligent, powerful, creative, interesting, decisive, and charismatic women. And boys (and girls) much too seldom hear about admirable men who show strong aesthetic interests, sensitivity and kindness to others, and the ability and willingness to cry when hurt. The impact of these deprivations on the development of both sexes is hard to assess, but it is likely to be great. One effect is probably to restrict personal growth for those whose basic wants and interests do not conform to stereotypes.

Title IX

There is a legal issue here too. Title IX of the Education Amendments, federal laws passed in 1972, states that "no person in the United States shall, on the basis of sex, be excluded from participation in, be denied the benefits of, or be subjected to discrimination under any education program or activity receiving federal financial assistance." Title IX has had an impact. For example, women's participation in school sports rose 570 percent between 1970 and 1980 (Sadker & Sadker, 1982), probably as a direct result of this legislation.

Discrimination and economics

Restrictions on what students can participate in become particularly cruel when discrimination in school leads ultimately to economic discrimination. In most school districts, no one would any longer think of keeping African-Americans or Hispanics out of science courses because of a belief that they cannot do the work. Overt discrimination against these minority-group members has decreased as they made clear to the courts the discrimination they were experiencing. Yet even now, in some of the most racially integrated school systems,

● *Are all school activities, equipment, and facilities equally available to students of both sexes? (© Billy E. Barnes)*

young women are subtly counseled away from drafting and engineering courses. These vocational-technical courses hold the potential for greater lifetime economic return than do courses in cosmetology or clerical work. The subtlety of this kind of discrimination was indicated in a study where school counselors listened to audiotapes of high school girls talking about their career goals. Counselors of both sexes indicated that young women who had interests in "masculine" careers were in need of counseling but that young women who had interests in "feminine" careers were making appropriate choices (Bornstein, 1982). We are learning only slowly that discrimination because of race, sex, or nationality must be challenged. It robs society of human potential and the individual of economic independence and dignity.

Teaching Without Stereotypes

The universities, the educational profession, and social institutions reflect the customs and beliefs prevalent in their society. Teachers can change those beliefs by being acutely sensitive to their own classroom practices. Sadker and Sadker (1982) developed a series of exercises to help teachers toward this goal.

And teachers can think about their own attitudes and behaviors (Fillmer, 1974; see Frazier & Sadker, 1973).

- Do you usually ask boys to do the heavy work (carrying projectors, moving books), and girls to do the light work?
- Do you usually ask boys to lead groups and be executives, and girls to be secretaries in those groups?
- Do you use gender as a basis for splitting groups ("Boys line up to the right, girls line up to the left!")?
- Do you pit boys against girls (spelling contests where teams are male or female)?
- How often do you make remarks like "Boys shouldn't hit girls," "Ladies do not use such language," or "Big boys don't cry"?
- Do you intervene, or do you let children on the playground call one another "sissy" or "tomboy"?
- Do you worry more about career planning for boys than for girls?
- How often do you counsel girls to prepare for technical fields of employment?
- Does your school or district policy open courses to students regardless of their gender?
- Are all school activities, equipment, and facilities equally available to students of both sexes?

District office personnel and classroom teachers who serve on textbook adoption committees should ask other questions too. In these books are boys allowed to display emotion? Are girls rewarded for problem solving, decision making, and sound judgment rather than for beauty? Are derogatory remarks or pictures directed at females in general? Are mothers shown holding jobs outside the home? Are women shown working at jobs other than nursing, teaching, and secretarial work? Are one-parent families discussed? Are minority and ethnic groups treated nonstereotypically? Are women and minority-group members given places in history?

Sex discrimination, subtle sex bias, and unexamined but widely shared stereotypes about the sexes pervade American society and the educational system in that society from nursery school to graduate school.

Consequences of discrimination

The consequences for a boy who decides to be a kindergarten teacher or a girl who decides to be a physicist are severe. Even greater consequences are suffered by the boy who was never allowed to consider kindergarten teaching as a career, who had to hide poetry books in his locker, and who did not find out until he was forty that indoor cooking—or a conversation with a woman lawyer—could be fun; or by the girl who was told that it was OK for her to flunk algebra tests because girls were not expected to "do math," was ostracized by her friends because she excelled at baseball, and who was discouraged from entering graduate school because she was "too pretty"—and was left with two children to support when her husband was run over by a bulldozer. (S. B. Anderson, 1972, p. 104)

Educators should not base educational policies on gender differences because these differences are usually of no great educational consequence. Moreover, the practice is illegal. Instead, they should concentrate on eliminating stereotypes that restrict the variability and diversity that we prize in people. If teachers examine their attitudes toward their colleagues and students, they can eliminate the most unjust examples and consequences of sex-role stereotyping.

The Exceptional Student

Let us now consider one more kind of diversity among our students: exceptionality. And let us begin by asking: Who is the exceptional student? Although many definitions have been offered, it may be most useful to think of the exceptional student as one whose education must be specially designed to fit his or her particular

- mental characteristics.
- sensory abilities.
- neuromotor or physical characteristics.
- social behavior.
- communication abilities.
- multiple handicaps. (Kirk & Gallagher, 1986)

Some students require special attention because their unique blend of these characteristics has limited their ability to learn in traditional ways. One student may be learning disabled, which means you may have to collaborate with a specialist to develop and use specific activities to meet her needs. Another student may have a hearing impairment, which means you may have to arrange your classroom to heighten the effectiveness of his hearing aid. And another may be intellectually gifted, which means you may have to design special enrichment programs to challenge her learning.

Public Law 94–142

You may be wondering why you're expected to teach exceptional children in the regular classroom. In 1975, Congress passed Public Law 94–142, the Education for All Handicapped Children Act. Among other things, the act was designed to "assure that all handicapped children have available to them a free and appropriate public education." The law was a response to the concerns of parents of handicapped children about their unfair double burden. They were expected to bear the expense of educating their children in special schools and also pay taxes to finance public education. Also important here was the parents' belief that their

FIGURE 5.2   *The Purpose of Mainstreaming: Least Restrictive Environments*

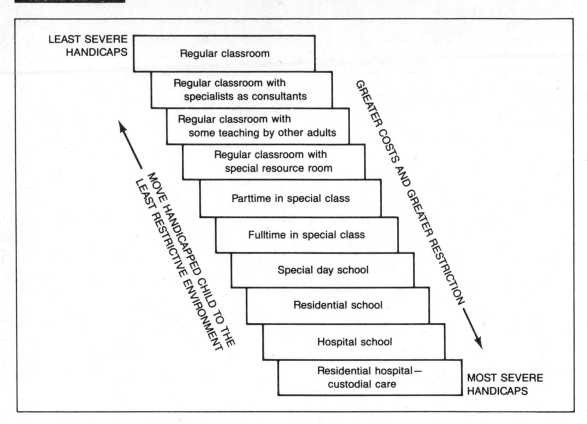

Source: Adapted from N. J. Long, W. E. Morse, and R. G. Newman, *Conflict in the Classroom.*
© 1980 Wadsworth Publishing.

Least restrictive environment

children would grow to their full potential only if they grew with other children. A key provision of the act thus mandates that exceptional children be placed in the "least restrictive environment" appropriate to their needs. This requirement means that exceptional children must be educated with their nonexceptional peers—to the maximum extent appropriate—in regular classrooms. (Although gifted students are not handicapped, we discuss them here because they are "exceptional" students who require special educational attention in classrooms.)

From PL 94–142 and amendments to it, educators have devised plans for *mainstreaming* exceptional children, for bringing them into the regular classroom. The plans call for a "continuum of services," as shown in Figure 5.2, for moving exceptional students from the most to the least restrictive environment. The idea is to meet students' special needs and to develop their abilities as fully as possible in the least restrictive environment. This approach means students cannot be moved to a special class if they can receive an appropriate education in a regular classroom, even though special services must be provided for them.

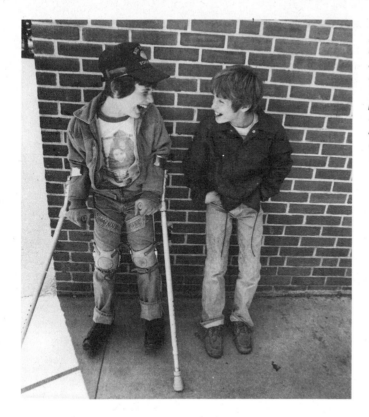

• Handicapped students are more like other "regular" students than they are different from them. They smile, laugh, pout, and respond like other students. And they can learn. (© David S. Strickler/ The Picture Cube)

The law requires that special services be integrated into a student's *individualized education program* (IEP). In addition to grouping students according to their abilities and needs—slow readers in the morning, faster readers in the afternoon, for example—teachers are expected to devise, in consultation with parents and special educators, an IEP for each exceptional student. That IEP will define the educational objectives for the student, outline the plans for reaching those objectives, and specify the criteria for measuring performance. The IEP builds on the student's present level of educational performance and helps the student achieve the agreed-on objectives. It sets forth and puts into effect educational and administrative services needed by the student.

IEP: individualized education program

The move to incorporate rather than exclude exceptional students has its base, of course, in American beliefs in equal opportunity and fair treatment for all citizens. But there were more specific problems and dissatisfactions that this legislation was meant to overcome. Many children, particularly those from low-income or bilingual homes, were mistakenly diagnosed as mentally retarded and placed in special education classes. The law states that evaluation of a student's performance must be based on several methods. Standardized test scores, for example, cannot alone determine placement. They must be used in combination with other criteria to diagnose needs, determine placement, and guide the planning of students' educational programs. The use of multiple

Multiple criteria for placement

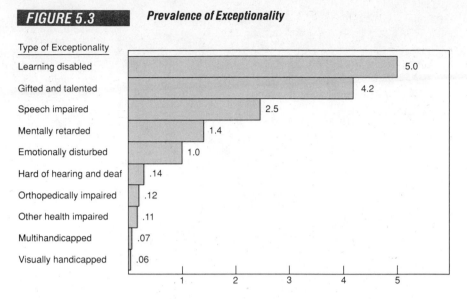

FIGURE 5.3   *Prevalence of Exceptionality*

Type of Exceptionality

Approximate Percent of School-Age Population

Sources: Haring and McCormick (1986), Kirk and Gallagher (1988), Ysseldyke and Algozzine (1990), U.S. Department of Education (1989).

criteria is especially important when evaluating students whose academic problems are caused by social, rather than emotional or physiological, factors. In the past, special education classes were the main method of educating exceptional students. They produced few beneficial results and often became dumping grounds instead of remedial centers for problem children (Kirk & Gallagher, 1986; Knoblock, 1982).

For these reasons and these purposes, you almost certainly will be teaching exceptional students in your regular classes. Figure 5.3 shows the estimated percentage of children in each broad category of exceptionality. It is not easy to get accurate estimates, so think of them only as a rough guide. Also, the number of school-age children varies from year to year. In the 1990s, that number is approximately 45 million. From the figure we see that the total percentage of those in need of special services is between 14 and 15 percent, or between 6 million and 7 million children. The odds, therefore, are that about 1 out of every 6 or 7 children in school has an exceptionality that requires special attention.

Research Results on Mainstreaming

Soon after the various federal laws promoting mainstreaming went into effect, studies pointing to problems began to appear. Linton and Juul (1980) found indications that, although social acceptance increased slightly for exceptional children in mainstreamed classes, the acceptance was less (or absent) for those with *severe* impairments. Although children with mild handicaps achieved as well in mainstreamed as in special classes, their chances of failure were greater in the competitive environment of regular classes. Normal children sometimes did less well in classes with exceptional students than normal children who did not have to share their teacher's attention with exceptional students. Exceptional children were usually not accepted socially by regular students because social acceptance depended in part on achievement, and exceptional students usually achieved less well than normal students. Regular teachers often had less favorable attitudes toward mainstreaming than did special education teachers because they felt that they were not trained to teach exceptional children, that the curriculum materials were inadequate, and that the children required amounts and kinds of attention that the teachers were unable to provide (Schmelkin, 1981).

Compliance with the law was far from complete because of lack of funds, facilities, and teacher training. Meade (1980) noted that "wrongly interpreting the Act as strictly a 'mainstreaming' law, many administrators are simply placing the retarded and learning disabled in regular classrooms and considering legal requirements met," even though an IEP had not been developed or put into effect for the students.

Much of the research on mainstreaming has had serious limitations. It lacked clarity about program specifics, took inadequate account of large variations in school contexts, lacked control groups, used inadequate definitions of the exceptional child, and used inappropriate tests. These limitations led Semmel, Gottlieb, and Robinson (1979) to conclude that there may be little evidence that mainstreaming practices improve the performance of exceptional children. But "until the context, nature of instruction, and other process variables can be identified, it appears useless to designate mainstreaming as a treatment variable in research studies" (p. 267).

Despite the best of intentions, in most cases mainstreaming does little to improve the achievement or the acceptance of children with cognitive and behavioral handicaps by their normal classmates (Macmillan, Keogh, & Jones, 1986). On the other hand, it appears that increasing the amount of interaction of physically and sensorily impaired children with normal children does improve their social acceptance. So mainstreaming seems to work with some kinds of handicapping conditions, but not with others. Special training for teachers and students, however, can turn the situation around. For example, Borg and Ascione (1982) trained teachers to use a classroom management program aimed at changing their use of specific practices in mainstreamed classes. From observations in the classroom, they found that the trained teachers used nine of the sixteen trained practices in better ways than did the untrained teachers and that the students of the trained teachers engaged more frequently in on-task behavior and less frequently in mildly or seriously deviant behavior. Also the exceptional students did not differ from the nonexceptional students on most comparisons of behavior. Training teachers to use peer tutoring (see Chapter 10) has also had some effects (e.g., Delguardi, Greenwood, Wharton, Carter,

Problems with mainstreaming

Cognitive handicaps and acceptance

Physical handicaps and acceptance

Need for teacher training

& Hall, 1986). And teaching teachers how to help mildly handicapped students acquire learning strategies (see Chapter 10) has also shown promise (e.g., Deshler & Schumaker, 1986; Palincsar, 1986).

In other studies, cooperative learning techniques (see Chapter 9) were taught to teachers and their students (Madden & Slavin, 1983). These techniques were used to replace the more common individualistic and competitive approaches to learning that are found in classrooms and that always place children with handicaps at an even greater disadvantage. In the cooperative environment, mainstreamed children showed more academic success and greater social acceptance. The overall conclusions about mainstreaming may be on the negative side—the program has not usually worked as well as was hoped for. But some environments that teachers can create do work; that is, cooperative environments yield more positive outcomes.

Cooperative learning and academic success

In addition to developing training for teachers, researchers have tried to develop social-skills training for children with handicaps. This kind of work, reviewed by Gresham (1981), "has the potential of facilitating mainstreaming efforts" in that "handicapped children are better accepted by their peers after social skills training" (p. 167).

Social-skills training

Mainstreaming requires going beyond simply putting exceptional children into regular classes. It calls for working actively to help these children take advantage of their opportunity to interact with other students and thus be better prepared to get along well in the world outside of school.

General Concerns of Teachers of Exceptional Students

As we discuss exceptional students, you should keep in mind several general concerns. These are normalization, attitudes, assessment, and instruction.

Normalization

Normalization.   Most exceptional students smile, laugh, pout, and respond like other students. They are like other students except for some particular area in which they require modification in the educational program.

It is important that you and your regular students learn to think of exceptional children as normal in those areas in which they are, in fact, like other students. A student who is visually impaired may have to read from special books with large letters, but this requirement need not exclude the child from show-and-tell sessions, the school play, or normal lunchroom activities. We must not think of exceptional children as special in all areas, when in fact their exceptionality is likely to require adjustments in only a few areas.

Attitudes

Attitudes.   Society—including administrators, teachers, and nonexceptional students—does not usually hold positive attitudes toward those with handicaps in general, or exceptional students in particular. All differences—even giftedness—seem to have some negative associations. Your task as a teacher is to help students value *all* people and to help dispel ignorance and prejudice about exceptionality.

Assessment.　　The education of special students requires careful attention to the students' strengths and weaknesses. You must know what to capitalize on and what to remedy by way of instruction. Usually the comprehensive assessment of students' abilities is the work of school psychologists, speech or language pathologists, resource teachers, and other specialists, and usually it will have been carried out before students enter your class. But you may be asked by specialists for periodic evaluations of particular skills.

Assessment

Instruction.　　Exceptional students may have problems in learning, but they *do* learn. Your job is to take children as they are and build on their strengths—to help them learn. A carefully constructed IEP, required for each exceptional student, provides guidelines for improving academic behavior and defines goals and checkpoints along the way.

Instruction

The good news about teaching exceptional children in the mainstream classroom is that the effective teaching practices we discuss in Chapter 11 improve the achievement of exceptional children also. Effective teaching practices—organization, management of time, maintenance of order, presentation of content, and so forth—combined with respect for the child and with some modifications to accommodate the child improve success. Successful teachers of mainstreamed students are almost always successful teachers of all their students (Larrivée, 1989).

Categories of Exceptional Students

In examining the major categories of exceptionality, you should be aware that many exceptional students do not fit neatly into them. Some students have more than one handicap—say, mental retardation and deafness. And not all students with the same exceptionality learn at the same rate—exceptional students vary in their abilities just as their nonexceptional peers do. You should also know that special educators disagree profoundly on the wisdom of labeling exceptional children "mentally retarded," "emotionally disturbed," "learning disabled," and so forth. Proponents of labeling (who have themselves become cautious in recommending labels) believe that labels help identify children with special needs and help in further diagnosis and treatment. They also believe that labels facilitate communication, legislation, and administration in serving exceptional students. Opponents of labeling argue that labels mislead—that they allow misdiagnosis and perpetuate stereotypes—instead of pointing the way to accurate assessment and treatment of the exceptional students' unique needs. We want to emphasize, then, that the categories described here are broad and

"Labeling" controversy

• A child can be exceptional in one area and a regular member of the classroom as well. (© Alan Carey/The Image Works)

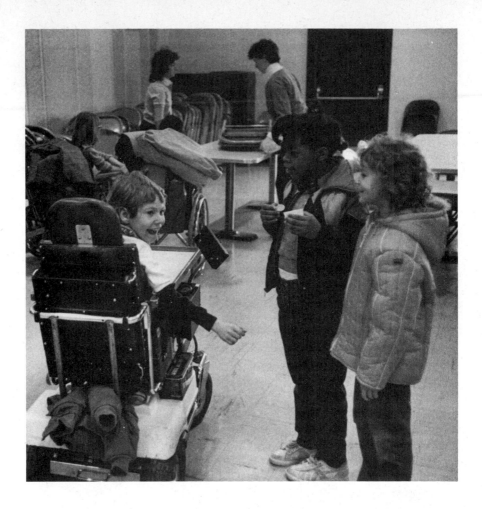

should not be allowed to conceal the range and complexity of the needs and abilities of exceptional students. What follows are the terms, and clusters of characteristics associated with those terms, in general use in schools today.

Specific Learning Disabilities

This relatively new category of exceptionality refers to students whose abilities are judged to be much higher than their actual performance. Their problem is a profound difficulty in acquiring and using abilities in listening, speaking, reading, writing, reasoning, or calculating. The problem is not due to economic or cultural differences, nor is it one of motivation (see Chapter 8). And the specific learning disability cannot be attributed to or explained by other handicapping conditions (mental retardation, visual or hearing impairments, emotional disturbance), although it may occur alongside these handicapping conditions. Usually, but not always, the difficulty goes hand in hand with significant discrepancies in a student's psychological or linguistic development. For example, a ten-year-old may not talk at all or may not talk like his classmates.

We should distinguish here between the *causes* of a disability and the *factors* that contribute to it. The causes are generally believed to be genetic disorders (DeFries & Decker, 1981), brain damage, environmental deprivation, and biochemical imbalance. Each has been shown to lead to a central nervous system dysfunction that underlies some learning disabilities.

Causes vs. contributing factors

It is important to understand the causes of a student's learning disability if medical treatment is necessary. But this information does not help you much in educating the student. As teachers, we are concerned with behavior, and so our focus here is on the *contributing factors*. We cannot change a child's genetic makeup or damaged brain, but we can change the behavior that interferes with learning. This behavior may originate in a physical factor (visual perception difficulties that limit reading achievement), in a psychological factor (inability to sustain attention), or in an environmental condition (faulty diet or home background) that has contributed to physical or psychological factors.

Focus on contributing factors

Specific learning disabilities have complex origins and manifestations. They are also widespread. Kirk and Gallagher (1988) estimate that 2 to 4 percent of the school-age population has severe learning disabilities, though many more children are classified as learning disabled. The number of students identified as learning disabled has gone up from about 120,000 in 1968 to 1.9 million today (Haynes & Jenkins, 1986; Ysseldyke and Algozzine, 1990). Our best hypothesis is that this dramatic increase is due to a misuse of the label! L. A. Shepard, M. L. Smith, and C. P. Vojir (1983) inform us that less than half of the large sample of students labeled "learning disabled" they studied actually fit the definition. Apparently, the pressure to do something with children who are not learning at the regular rate or in the regular way leads some teachers and administrators to grab hold of this medical-sounding term and use it as an excuse for a failure in instruction. One simulation study—a study that tried to copy or imitate teachers' decision making—showed that over 50 percent of normal children were evaluated as needing special education because of learning disabilities. These data and an intensive study of how we decide who is learning disabled led M. L. Smith (1982) to question whether the system of identifying and treating children who are learning disabled is in fact more harmful than helpful—a disturbing possibility.

Mislabeling

The best practical advice for dealing with the wide variety of problems labeled specific learning disabilities is to *describe, compare, evaluate and consult,* and *treat.*

Describe. It is all too easy and all too common to make clinical-sounding inferences about behavior. We say Johnny is *distractible* when all we observed is that Johnny paid attention to his workbook for only two out of fifteen minutes. Or we say that Heather has *perceptual problems* when a descriptive statement might report only that Heather reverses letters when she prints. To design effective educational programs, begin with careful observation and a clear, descriptive report of behavior. Many behavioral checklists have been published

Description vs. inference

for teachers' use. These lists allow you to check those items that describe a particular child. In the psychomotor area, for example, the items might be "has difficulty walking up stairs," "cannot skip," "has trouble with buttons and zippers," and "cannot control scissors properly." But accurate observation of a particular child, using notebook and pen, provides the same kind of information, maybe even better information because the descriptions deal with specific behaviors and provide the context of those behaviors. For example, you might record:

10/1 Reversed digits on his paper when copying math problems from the board.
10/3 Read "was" as "saw" during oral reading.
10/4 Drew a man with one arm during art period.

These descriptions of behaviors prepare you for consultation and for developing a prescription for treating the problem if necessary.

Determining typical behavior

Compare.   The reason for comparing the behavioral descriptions you have collected for a particular student with the behaviors of other students is that young students differ greatly from adults. What an adult thinks of as a problem may be normal for an age group. It is not the least bit unusual for children to confuse "was" and "saw." At certain ages youngsters understand only the literal meaning of the expression "Where there's smoke, there's fire." And younger students often fail to hear or follow a set of instructions. These kinds of behaviors become indicators of specific learning disabilities only when they are not part of the normal development of the individual or the age group. Many young students referred for treatment of specific learning disabilities are actually displaying typical behavior for their age. In one study of 284 second-graders, 184 were categorized by their teachers as "easily distractible," 157 were reported "repeating the same behavior over and over," and 96 were reported unable to sit still in class without shaking or swinging their legs or fidgeting (Meier, 1971). Distractibility, perseveration and repetition at tasks, and high levels of activity and fidgeting might be symptoms of learning disabilities or behavior problems. But they also might be descriptions of the behaviors of typical children trying to master school tasks whose relevance is hard for them to see. For this reason comparing a student's behavior with that of other students and with his or her own behavior in different tasks is necessary before deciding whether a student has a specific learning disability.

Evaluate and Consult.   After observing and comparing a particular student's behavior, you can judge the nature and severity of the difficulty and the possibilities for treating the problem. It is important to decide at this time whether you need outside consultation. Sometimes the student's problems require that a specialist—a school psychologist, a behavior modification practitioner, or other special education consultant—plan the treatment. The special education consultant may call for a complete testing program to evaluate the student's intellectual, perceptual, and psychomotor performance. Many specialized tests are available for use in identifying students' weaknesses and strengths, and in planning instruction. But as M. L. Smith (1982) reminded us, specialists make their living finding special cases to treat. Many perfectly normal students—shy, slow, excitable, a little odd—are diagnosed as special, giving clients to special educators, school psychologists, medical practitioners, and others who depend on referrals. *Beware of the danger of "overidentification."*

Overidentification

Treat.   At this stage of the process, federal law requires the development of an individualized education program for the systematic treatment of a student's disability. The IEP includes (1) a statement of the student's present educational performance, (2) a statement of the annual and short-term goals, including evaluative criteria, and (3) a statement of the educational and administrative services to be provided.

Usually it is more efficient to treat specific behaviors and not to try to change the underlying problems. So if a student regularly reverses words and letters when writing, it is usually better to treat that particular problem than to map out a whole curriculum to increase proficiency in perceptual-motor performance. To focus treatment on particular skills, pinpoint the areas of defective performance. This task calls for careful observation and description of behavior.

The treatment is then designed—a treatment that often relies in good part on the theory and practice of operant conditioning we describe in the next chapter. In operant conditioning, we use a system of reinforcement (and, perhaps, judicious punishment) to change behavior. Then we help students learn to generalize the changed behavior to similar but new situations. So teaching a child to pay more attention to details in people, in order to draw a human body that is neither distorted nor lacking parts, may also help that child learn to attend to other parts of the environment and draw other things with more accuracy (Stephens, 1977).

There are some general principles to keep in mind when teaching students with specific learning disabilities (Gearheart & Weishahn, 1980). First, there is no one right way to instruct a student with a specific learning disability. A student with unique behavior patterns may need to be taught by unique methods. You may have to experiment awhile before you find the right approach for a particular child. Even children with the same behavior pattern—say, the inability to repeat sentences—may need different treatment. Similar behavior problems sometimes have different neurological or psychological origins. Also the other skills and abilities of two students may differ. Thus a student with a high IQ score may profit from one treatment; a student with a low IQ score, from another.

No one right way to instruct

A second principle is that you be willing to use new methods of instruction. This does not mean that you should try the latest instructional fad. It means that you should discard the materials and approaches that have not worked in the past and try a set of materials or an approach that is new *for the student*. Specific learning disabilities pose unique problems that may respond only to particular teaching practices.

Try new methods

Restructure cognitive processes

Third, in using a new technique, approach, or set of materials, you should work on restructuring certain of the learners' cognitive processes. Students with learning disabilities usually are skeptical about instruction because of a history of failure in previous attempts to remedy their problems. When you are going to try a new method, tell students that earlier failures may have been due to the inappropriate matching of instruction to their individual style of learning. Because the new method has proved successful with other students, they should approach the learning task with positive expectations. Students need to be convinced that they are accepted, and that eventually the right techniques will be found to help them. Otherwise their negative expectations about themselves could become self-fulfilling and contribute to repeated failure to remedy the learning problem.

Use multiple senses

Finally, use as many senses as possible at the same time. Combining visual, auditory, body position, movement, and touch sensations when teaching some-times facilitates learning in ways that words alone cannot. This approach has a long history of success in special education, particularly with students of average or above-average mental ability who show specific learning disabilities in reading and mathematics (Gearheart & Weishahn, 1980).

Communication Disorders

The acquisition of speech and language is one of the most complex human functions. It is not surprising that one of the largest single categories of excep-tional students is that of speech and language impaired. About 3 percent of the school population is estimated to have speech disorders, though Kirk and Gallagher (1988) believe this figure underestimates by half those who at one time or another really need special attention.

Speech disorders

A *speech disorder* is speech that "deviates so far from the speech of other people that it calls attention to itself, interferes with communication, or causes the speaker or . . . listener to be distressed" (Van Riper, 1978, p. 43). The major speech disorders include problems in articulation (omissions, substitu-tions, distortions, additions of sounds), voice (pitch, loudness, quality), and

Language disorders

fluency (stuttering). *Language disorders* are those that arise in the basic under-standing of the symbols we use to convey ideas. These disorders include delayed language development and aphasia—difficulty in comprehending or for-mulating messages.

Children with communication disorders need special educational attention, ranging from a few exercises with the classroom teacher to extensive clinical treatment and even surgery. These children may have no difficulties in other areas, although communication problems often go hand in hand with cerebral palsy, hearing impairment, mental retardation, learning disabilities, and other conditions.

All of us teach speech and language and should be alert to children's difficul-ties. Some problems are due to central nervous system disorders; others are due to situational or environmental conditions. Notice the amount, rate, quality, clarity, and structure of each child's speech and language. If you find a problem, work with a speech or language specialist and the parents to develop an IEP. You may be able to help a student by rewarding appropriate communication, paying close attention to the student's efforts, providing activities that encourage communication, promoting classroom acceptance of different communication patterns, and encouraging the student to monitor his or her own communication skills. (See Wood, 1976, and Wiig, 1982, for more suggestions.)

You can help the consulting specialist most by accurately recording the conditions under which speech problems occur. These notes, with examples, help the clinician make a more accurate diagnosis.

Observe and record

> It is not enough to say the child lisps or stutters. Many other factors are important: the problem's consistency, the conditions of pressure or fatigue under which it occurs, whether it is noticed by other children, whether it is a true lisp or stutter. For each kind of speech problem, note specific points that will help . . . decide what to do next. (Gearheart & Weishahn, 1976)

Careful behavioral descriptions are the only basis for accurate diagnosis, which is in turn the only basis for intelligent prescriptions.

Mental Retardation

Many terms have been used to describe the child who is mentally retarded—*feebleminded, idiot, imbecile,* and *moron* among them. These terms, once believed to have a precise meaning, are no longer adequate or acceptable. More important, one crucial element in the current definition of mental retardation is the student's adaptive behavior in addition to his or her general intellectual functioning (Grossman, 1977). *Adaptive behavior* includes sensorimotor, communication, self-help, socialization, daily living, and vocational skills. A child must be well below average in *both* IQ score (below an IQ of, say, 70) and adaptive behavior to be considered mentally retarded.

Adaptive behavior

Although definitions vary by state, many federally funded programs are designed with three levels of mental retardation in mind. Students who are *severely and profoundly mentally retarded* need extensive training in self-care skills as well as some form of custodial supervision. They may display a variety of other difficulties stemming from cerebral palsy or physical disabilities. Despite these complications, which might tend to keep children who are severely retarded out of regular classrooms, the number of public school programs, specialists, and educational methods for these students has increased (Sailor & Guess, 1983; Snell, 1978; Sontag, 1977).

Severely and profoundly retarded

Children who are *trainable mentally retarded* (TMR) are usually identified at an early age. School programs for these youngsters should focus on developing skills in self-care, language usage, independent living, perceptual-motor abilities, and social interactions. Traditional academic subjects have limited value for these students (Berdine & Cegelka, 1980). The most important training is in

Trainable mentally retarded

vocational skills because these students often succeed in sheltered workshops and even in jobs in the community (Brickey, Browning, & Campbell, 1982; Wehman, 1981).

Educable mentally retarded

Those who are *educable mentally retarded* (EMR) are often identified first by a nursery school teacher or a teacher in a regular classroom. A key component in the definition of mental retardation is *inadequate adaptive behavior*. Intellectually subnormal students are "retarded" only while they are in school—only at school do they *behave* in nonadaptive ways. Be very careful in identifying these students. At present, African-Americans and other minority-group members are disproportionately often identified as EMR. Cultural differences and unwitting prejudice cloud many teachers' judgments of their students.

One characteristic of the EMR child is inability to profit from reading and math instruction on entering school. It may take three or more years for the child to catch on to the rudiments of these subjects. Moreover, the child's rate of progress, which reflects mental age not chronological age, may be only between 25 and 50 percent of the typical child's. The youngster's final level of achievement in academic areas ordinarily is only the sixth-grade level and may be only the second-grade level.

Some implications for teaching are immediately sensible. Instruction should be carefully sequenced, with lots of time for completion of the work and a very high success rate. Make the learning tasks uncomplicated and brief, with few new elements presented at once. Help retention by providing considerable overlearning (Sailor & Guess, 1983). These guidelines could apply to the teaching of all children, but are especially crucial for children who are educable mentally retarded.

Success of educable mentally retarded

In general these children can profit from remaining in the regular classroom. Numerous follow-up studies report the success of people who are mentally retarded in literally hundreds of occupations (Brickey et al., 1982). One long-term follow-up of children classified as educable mentally retarded showed that, during a period of high employment nationally, 83 percent were self-supporting, some even living in expensive homes; 80 percent were married; and their children were, as a group, progressing well in school and had a reported IQ range of 50 to 138, with a mean of 95 (Baller, Charles, & Miller, 1967). In short, sound diagnosis and prescription, following a carefully developed IEP, can help students who are mentally retarded gain enough academic and social skills to live useful lives.

Behavior Disorders

The United States government in Public Law 94–142 uses the phrase *seriously emotionally disturbed* to define the characteristics that we discuss here. We use *behavior disorders* so that we can keep our focus on what most concerns teachers—students' behavior. Behaviorally disordered students, according to the definition in PL 94–142, generally exhibit one or more of the following behaviors in a way that significantly affects educational performance over a long period of time:

- An inability to learn that cannot be explained by intellectual, sensory, or health factors
- An inability to build or maintain satisfactory relationships with peers and teachers
- Inappropriate types of behavior or feelings under normal circumstances
- A general pervasive mood of unhappiness or depression
- A tendency to develop physical symptoms or fears associated with personal or school problems

The causes of these behavioral problems are most often environmental—poverty, racial discrimination, lack of parental love, abuse, neglect, and a host of others. But physiological factors sometimes underlie the disorders, and drug abuse can be a causal factor as well. Although your primary concern as a teacher is students' behavior, not the causes of that behavior, you may be able to influence those causes (prevent a parent from further abusing a child, for example) by your careful description, comparison, and evaluation of the behavior. Many standardized checklists are available for recording student behavior. But again simple paper-and-pencil descriptions often provide the information a teacher needs to plan special instruction for individual children. These notes can be especially helpful in recognizing behavior that is situationally determined—that is, deviant behavior shown only in some situations, not others. One young student was found to be violent every Friday, the day her abusive father came home from weekly sales trips. Another student's severe withdrawal occurred in one class but not in another. This student came from a poor family, and a clique of wealthy students in that class intimidated her. Careful records of the behaviors and the context in which they occur may reveal patterns that help target treatments.

Situationally determined behavior disorders

Comparison is usually a necessary step in interpreting behavior. Unlike their age-mates, youngsters with behavioral disorders tend to exhibit behavior "in the wrong places, at the wrong time, in the presence of the wrong people, and to an inappropriate degree." These are children who are "too precise, too worried, too angry, too happy, too easily disappointed, and manipulate others too much" (Reinert, 1976).

Next you might evaluate your data and perhaps consult a specialist. Most school psychologists are trained not only to give tests. They can usually help treat a wide range of behavior problems. In developing an IEP you might consider the behavior modification procedures we talk about in Chapter 6. These procedures rely on positive reinforcement to increase wanted behaviors, and other techniques to eliminate unwanted behaviors. Some forms of contracting—setting forth objectives, evaluation criteria, and rewards—have been used successfully to improve the behavior of withdrawn, uncooperative, aggressive, overly controlled, phobic, and dependent students (Sulzer-Azaroff & Mayer, 1986). Reading about specialized techniques (Cullinan, Epstein, & Lloyd, 1982; Long, Morse, & Newman, 1980) and consulting with a specialist can help you learn effective methods for changing the ways students behave.

• *Technology is improving the instructional and vocational opportunities of the hearing impaired. (© Julie O'Neill)*

Hearing Impairment

Hearing impairment ranges from hard of hearing to deaf. Hard-of-hearing students, with some special care and amplification devices, can be taught through auditory channels. Deaf children must be instructed through other senses. Even mild auditory loss can result in speech and language problems that make teaching and learning more difficult. In fact the major problem for hard-of-hearing or deaf students is lack of proficiency in speech, language use, and reading. Because these learning tools are affected by hearing deficiencies, it is often assumed that the measured intelligence of deaf children is below normal. This assumption is not true. Rittenhouse (cited in Moores, 1982), for example, presented Piagetian conservation problems (see Chapter 4) to both hearing children and deaf children. The hearing group performed significantly better when standard procedures were used. But when the instructions were modified, the hearing and deaf groups performed equally well. Where deficits in general intellectual abilities are found among children who are hard of hearing or deaf, they are usually minor, or they exist in some areas of cognitive functioning but not in others (McConnell,

Language deficit ≠ intellectual deficiency

1973; Myklebust, 1960; Vernon, 1968). Nevertheless, the more profound and severe the hearing loss, and the earlier the age of its onset, the greater the deficiencies in reading skills and speech. Relative to their chronological age-mates and their measured mental ability, deaf children are ordinarily many grades behind in schoolwork in these areas.

Hearing (audiometry) tests are often given in school districts to help diag-nose hearing losses. But identifying children with mild hearing loss is difficult. Pay attention to complaints about earaches, discomfort, or noises; lack of attention; turning or cocking the head; poor articulation or omission of speech sounds; difficulty in following spoken directions; frequent requests to repeat spoken information; reluctance to participate in speaking activities; dependence on classmates for instruction; and better achievement and attention in small-group activities than in large-group activities, where hearing is more difficult.

The identification of hearing-impaired students is important because of the possibility of medical and surgical remedies. An alert teacher can help save a child from progressive impairment, difficulties in communication skills, and a loss of classroom learning. Hearing aids, speech (lip) reading, manual signing, auditory training, combined speech and manual communication (total communi-cation), speech therapy, and other approaches, if used early in a student's schooling can enrich the child's life.

Most school districts have specialists who can be consulted about students with hearing difficulties. Special programs, medical and educational, may be prescribed in addition to regular classroom instruction. In working with children who are hard of hearing, there are some easy-to-use devices available to teachers: repeating directions, placing assignments and directions on the chalk-board or writing them out on paper; using overhead projectors and transparen-cies and other visual aids; reducing general classroom noise (because hearing aids amplify all sound); seating students near the source of vocal instruction or group activities; avoiding visual distractions from or obstructions to speech reading; encouraging all classroom speakers to face the student as much as possible when speaking; and the student's learning how to make good use of new aids to hearing and communication. The continued refinement of personal com-puters with modems that send and receive messages over telephone lines, and captioned films and television, have increased instructional and vocational possi-bilities. As with all individual differences, we need special instruction that matches the unique characteristics of the learner and the task.

Identifying hearing loss

Accommodating the hearing impaired

Physical and Health Impairment

This diverse area of exceptionality—physical and health impairment—includes a wide variety of conditions. Some may be so mild that they need not concern the teacher. Or the conditions may require modifications in the physical environ-ment, additional means of communication, or aids to instruction and locomotion.

The guidelines established by PL 94–142 have divided this category of impairment into disorders of (1) the skeleton, joints, and muscles and (2) those health conditions that affect the student's educational performance. The first category includes amputations, cerebral palsy, muscular dystrophy, spinal cord injuries, spina bifida, and impairments caused by disease or burns. The second includes asthma, cystic fibrosis, diabetes, epilepsy, heart defects, hemophilia, lead poisoning, leukemia, nephritis, sickle cell anemia, rheumatic fever, and tuberculosis. We cannot attempt here to describe each of these conditions. But if you have a student with a physical or health impairment, you should review medical information in the student's record, general information about the condition, and specific teaching techniques described in specialized textbooks. Additional study by teachers is called for.

Many of these conditions can also cause secondary problems that affect learning. Students with cerebral palsy, for example, often have difficulty speaking. Try to encourage and understand the students' attempts.

In evaluating each student's needs, consider the student's

- ease of moving around within the classroom and the school.
- ability in and method of communicating with peers and teachers.
- ability to meet daily academic requirements.
- self-care skills within the classroom and the school.

Visual Impairment

A student who is visually impaired is able to read print; a blind student uses braille. Both are found more and more often in regular classrooms. For both, the principal concerns of the teacher are to help the student be oriented, move around, communicate, and get information.

Orientation and mobility

Helping the student know where things are and move around includes training the student's motor coordination, spatial orientation, and physical conditioning. And use of travel aids (a long cane, a guide dog, sighted guides) and sensor devices (sonic glasses, laser cane) also require training. Communication involves learning to read and type braille, if necessary, and to use a typewriter, telephone, and recording equipment. Access to information requires the use of all senses—including any remaining vision (Sykes, 1972). A child can be legally blind and still make certain visual discriminations. The way a child uses vision is more important than the child's measured visual ability.

Technological aids

The student's training in braille can often be supported by technological devices and optical instruments, which either magnify printed information or scan and translate it into other sensory channels. For example, the Visualtek enlarges the material for viewing on a television screen; the Kurzweil Reading Machine vocalizes printed matter; the Optacon converts letters of the alphabet into vibrations that pass across the fingertips; the talking calculator converts numbers and symbols into solutions; and talking books are available for all ages. The American Foundation for the Blind, the Library of Congress, and the American Printing House for the Blind provide recorded books and magazines and equipment on a free-loan basis. Children can be prepared to use these devices if they have had consistent emphasis on and training in listening skills.

TABLE 5.3
Common Indicators of Visual Disorders

Observable Signs	Visual Behavior
Red eyelids or reddened eyes	Rubs eyes excessively
Crust on lids or lashes	Shuts or covers one eye
Recurring sties or swelling	Is sensitive to light
Watery eyes or discharge	Squints, blinks, or frowns during reading
Crossed eyes	Holds reading material too close or too far when reading
Pupils of uneven size	
Drooping eyelids	Moves reading material close and far while reading
Eyes that move excessively	Complains of headaches, eye pain, dizziness, or nausea
	Has difficulty seeing distant objects
	Has tendency to lose place in sentence or page
	Has tendency to confuse letters, syllables, and words
	Uses poor spacing in writing and has difficulty "staying on the line"

Source: Adapted from B. R. Gearheart and M. W. Weishahn, *The Exceptional Student in the Regular Classroom*, 3rd edition, Charles E. Merrill Publishing Company, Columbus, Ohio. Copyright 1984 by Charles E. Merrill Publishing Company. Used by permission.

Numerous suggestions for regular classroom teachers are available in specialized texts. These also describe structured curricula designed to enhance the listening skills of students whose poor vision requires that they be read to.

Early identification of visual impairment is important. Look for symptoms and behaviors like those listed in Table 5.3. The regular classroom teacher is not required to teach orientation and mobility skills or the use of electronic aids. Specialists in the school system or other community agencies do those things. But the teacher can

Accommodating the visually impaired

- modify the classroom environment or structure to facilitate the student's use of aids.
- utilize special instructional materials, such as large-type texts, raised globes and maps, and audiotapes.
- encourage activities that improve fitness and experience with the physical environment.
- adjust the student's desk so that he or she receives enough light.
- describe class activities orally so that the student is able to follow the flow of events.
- encourage the student's use of any available visual ability.

- provide braille signs or large-print labels on important objects in the classroom.
- report to the student any self-stimulating movements like rocking or turning the head, to help reduce these unwanted behaviors.
- instruct other students on when and how it is appropriate to help the student who is visually impaired.
- address the student by name.

Teacher's role in attitude change

Students who are visually impaired have grown up to be accountants, carpenters, physical education teachers, lawyers, judges, entertainers, computer programmers, and homemakers. Technological improvements and special instructional techniques are available. But attitudes and reactions to these children must also improve. For example, teachers and students often raise their voices when talking to a blind student. This kind of reaction persists because of lack of familiarity with people who are blind. The regular classroom teacher plays a vital role in changing the attitudes of students toward those who are visually impaired.

Giftedness and Talent

Giftedness and talent are wanted forms of exceptionality. Definitions vary, but the category of gifted and talented students usually includes those demonstrating high performance in one or more of the following areas: general intellectual ability, specific academic aptitude, creative or productive thinking, leadership, or the visual and performing arts.

The first study of people reputed to be geniuses was published by Galton (1952) in 1869. Later interest in giftedness was strengthened by advances in the measurement of intelligence (see Chapter 3). A major milestone in the field was reached when Lewis M. Terman (1925), the Stanford psychologist who with Maud Merrill transformed the Binet-Simon instrument into the Stanford-Binet Intelligence Scale, initiated a longitudinal study of approximately fifteen hundred gifted students. His five volumes of research, published between 1925 and 1958, helped disprove many misconceptions about gifted people. As a group they are equal to or better than average in physical stature and health, popularity and social acceptance, emotional health and freedom from behavioral disorders. They also maintain or increase their intellectual ability and productivity as they grow older.

Classroom teachers have not done well at spotting gifted students. One study at the junior high level showed that about 30 percent of the students nominated by teachers failed to meet the criterion of giftedness used by the researchers; moreover over 50 percent of those identified as gifted by the researchers were not nominated by the teachers (Pegnato & Birch, 1959). Teachers often confuse conformity, including neatness and good behavior, with giftedness.

Conformity ≠ giftedness

To help you identify exceptional children, we offer the following signs of giftedness and talent:

- Demonstrated talent in performing or creating
- A wide variety of interests and information
- Ability to concentrate on a problem, task, or activity for long periods
- Ability to engage in abstract thinking and to construct relationships between problems and solutions
- Independent thinking characterized by creative ideas
- Extensive curiosity
- Early reading ability
- Use of a large vocabulary
- Rapid learning of basic skills

When appropriate, and in consultation with a specialist in testing, you could begin with standardized tests to measure intelligence, creativity, and achievement. But these tests are only one method or criterion of identification. You should be alert to observations of parents, other teachers, and peers; information from interest inventories; and especially those unique products that spring from the student's desire to investigate, build, or create. Gifted students are found in both sexes, in all ethnic and socioeconomic groups, and in handicapped populations.

The two basic approaches to helping gifted students in their areas of high ability are acceleration and enrichment. The nine-year-old graduating from high school is an example of extreme acceleration. Accelerated students receive learning experiences designed for older students. Some forms of acceleration include skipping grades, special schools, early admission to or concurrent enrollment in high school and college, and rapid advancement in specific subjects. The basic argument for acceleration is that it prevents boredom, enhances motivation, and allows the student to enter a chosen field at an earlier age, thereby gaining years of productivity (Pressey, 1963). A meta-analysis of twenty-six studies of acceleration found that bright accelerated students (1) made about one grade level in growth over and above the growth of their equally bright non-accelerated peers, (2) performed about the same as the bright older students in the classes in which they were placed, and (3) showed neither positive nor negative effects on attitude, adjustment, or other social-emotional measures (Kulik & Kulik, 1984). Acceleration is not used as often as it could be, despite its consistent record of positive results.

Acceleration

Enrichment provides experiences and training that enhance regular classroom instruction. This approach includes special interest clubs or organizations, resource rooms, honors seminars, independent study, field trips, mentor programs, and summer camps (see B. Clark, 1979; Gallagher, 1975; Maker, 1987; and Sato, 1982, for methods and materials).

Enrichment

Gifted and talented students contribute greatly to society and should be considered a precious human resource. Our investment in identifying and developing these students should at least rival—in interest, time, and money—the investment we make in gifted athletes. It is certainly a reflection of the values of American culture that we have many more scouts and coaches for gifted football players than for gifted artists or scientists.

Aptitude-Treatment Interaction

Adaptive instruction

The individual differences that we have been talking about are somewhat extreme and obviously demand unique instruction. But all students are special in their own way, and it is important for us to think about how we can adapt instruction to their individual differences. Special educators are in the forefront in making these kinds of adaptations. But all instructors should think about finding the best ways to teach different kinds of students. Genuinely individualized, adaptive instruction is an ideal rarely achieved in the everyday classroom. But it is still an ideal. We should learn not to think of teaching methods as fixed treatments to which students must adapt. Instead we should think about the many alternative methods of instruction and our students' unique characteristics, and try to match the two. We discussed this topic earlier in this chapter when we noted that schools should try to adapt to culturally different students, instead of expecting those students to adapt to schools. We discuss adaptive teaching again in Chapters 10 and 11.

One conceptual and empirical orientation toward this important educational ideal is called aptitude-treatment interaction, or ATI (Cronbach & Snow, 1977). An ATI occurs when students high in a characteristic (aptitude) learn better when taught by one method (treatment) while students low in that characteristic learn better when taught by another method. Information about a student's aptitudes (that is, any characteristic, such as gender, intelligence, or anxiety, that helps predict achievement of an educational objective) is used to choose the most effective teaching method for the student. The uses of aptitude information are based on findings that an aptitude-treatment interaction exists.

Some ATI Findings

Anxiety and student-centered vs. teacher-centered methods

Aptitude-treatment interactions do exist. We have learned that when two treatments (methods) are available—for example, a discussion (student-centered) method and a lecture (teacher-centered) method—different kinds of students succeed with each of them (Dowaliby & Schumer, 1973). Low-anxiety students did significantly better than high-anxiety students in student-centered discussion groups. And high-anxiety students did better than low-anxiety students in teacher-centered lecture classes. Similar but more complicated ATIs between level of anxiety and the degree to which learning environments are structured have been found (Peterson, 1976; Snow, 1977).

Another ATI was found by Stallings and Keepes (1970), who studied aptitude in the form of auditory ability, and achievement in the form of vocabulary knowledge. Two treatments—methods of teaching beginning reading—were compared: the phonics and the whole-word methods. These two methods have been the subject of much controversy. It turned out that different kinds of students did better in one kind of treatment than the other—neither treatment was better than the other for everyone. Similar conclusions emerged from an aptitude-treatment interaction study of foreign language instruction. Chastain

(1970) found that one method, the audiolingual method, worked better for students low in verbal ability, while a different, more "cognitive," method was superior for students with high verbal ability. And Janicki and Peterson (1981) showed that a small-group approach to instruction in mathematics worked better for students who had positive attitudes toward mathematics and who took responsibility for their own behavior. For other kinds of students the traditional form of direct instruction was superior, or either instructional method worked. In our discussions of gender and mathematics and of ethnicity and achievement, we noted how cooperative learning environments may favor the less aggressive and competitive students (females, American Indians, Chicanos), whereas traditional instruction may provide a better environment for the more competitive students (often Anglo males).

The implications for research here are significant. We no longer are looking for the "one best way" to teach. Instead ATI researchers are investigating many ways to teach, each of which may be "best" for particular types of learners.

There is no one best way to teach

What ATI Means for Teachers

For the teacher the idea of ATI serves as a reminder that different kinds of students learn better in different ways. If a particular method of instruction or curriculum fails with a student, perhaps another method or curriculum will succeed.

Time and again we hear teachers, parents, and administrators tell us that method A is better than method B. They should add "for some students." When people argue about which of two methods is "better," chances are that *both* methods are "better" for some students. No one method, no one text, no one curriculum, no one version of any teaching-learning activity is likely to be most effective with all students. The many variables on which children differ interact with the many different methods we might use to teach them. You should never lose sight of the need to monitor learning and then match treatments to students in some fashion that best fits each student. In this sense, every child needs special education.

Every child needs special education

SUMMARY

Culture affects our intelligence, cognitive development, and personality. It is a powerful and often invisible force. When children enter school, they bring with them the cultural heritage of their home. In school they find another culture to which they must adapt. Their success in school, at least initially, is a function of their adaptation to its culture. And that adaptation is a function of the similarity between the home and school environments.

Cross-cultural studies have pointed out the differences among cultures in the ways children are reared and taught to communicate, and in their life experience. More important, these studies show how these differences affect children's learning, verbal interactions, and test taking.

Teachers' expectations for their students affect their students' achievement. And these expectations also reflect culture. Teachers should separate their culturally based expectations from their judgments of how students use language and what students are capable of doing.

Although the job of working against custom is not an easy one, it can be done. Cooperative learning, parent involvement programs, and bilingual education programs are ways of accommodating cultural differences in the classroom. All of these strategies share two characteristics: They assume that all children are capable of learning, and they adapt instruction to children's needs. Teaching children from different cultures is a challenge. The rewards of meeting that challenge are great.

Our discussion of gender-related differences in intellectual functioning gave us little reason to believe such differences are important. The tendency for boys to be more aggressive than girls is the most consistent of the gender-linked differences in the personality domain. In other areas—emotional adjustment, values and life goals, and achievement motivation—the differences appear not so much in the level of the characteristic as in its expression. Most differences here are in large part, if not completely, determined by culture.

Culture defines our sex-role behaviors at home and in school. The problem is that the stereotypical sex roles in American society may not meet the wants and needs of the individual children. The teacher's responsibility to help children develop to their full potential, in the face of custom, is not easily met. But it is possible, by avoiding the use of stereotypes in the classroom and by monitoring instructional materials.

Exceptional students are those whose education must be designed to meet their special mental, physical, or emotional needs. The responsibility for teaching many of these children now lies with the regular classroom teacher. Mainstreaming is the end product of legislation that mandates instruction in the least restrictive environment. A critical component of mainstreaming is the individualized education program, a program that sets forth the educational objectives for each exceptional student, the plans for achieving those objectives, and the criteria for measuring achievement.

Does mainstreaming work? Although research shows that the interaction of children who have physical and sensory impairments with their normal peers does improve the social acceptance of these children, it does little to improve the acceptance or achievement of youngsters with cognitive and behavioral handicaps.

There are four primary concerns for teachers of students with special needs. The first is normalization, an awareness that a handicapping condition is only one aspect of an otherwise normal child. The second has to do with attitudes, with freeing yourself and your students from the ignorance and prejudice that usually surround exceptional students. The third is assessment, knowing students' strengths and weaknesses, so that you can build on or remedy them. And the fourth is instruction, taking the information you have about your exceptional students and using it to choose the right teaching methods for each of them. Teachers should not be the sole judges of a student's exceptionality, but their observations can help reveal giftedness, low intelligence, behavior problems, learning disabilities, and problems in speech, vision, and hearing. They should cast their observations in the form of clear behavioral descriptions, and these should be compared with the behavior of other students. Consultation with specialists may then be needed to develop an IEP (individualized education program).

Special education is a recognition of the right of all children to receive instruction appropriate to their unique characteristics. Aptitude-treatment interaction takes the notion of adapting instruction to individual differences out of the realm of special education and reminds all teachers to look for better ways to teach *each* student, not just exceptional students. There is simply no one best way to teach all students.

Learning and Motivation: Theories and Applications

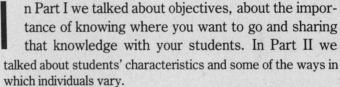

In Part I we talked about objectives, about the importance of knowing where you want to go and sharing that knowledge with your students. In Part II we talked about students' characteristics and some of the ways in which individuals vary.

Here in Part III we look at the ways students acquire the behavior, skills, and ideas we want to teach them. Chapter 6 begins with a discussion of operant conditioning. This theory gives us a methodology for modifying students' behavior. Although operant conditioning explains a wide variety of phenomena, it does not easily explain how we learn from watching others, how we learn to judge ourselves, how we learn from meaningful prose, or how we solve complex problems. So we also talk about a theory that combines ideas from operant conditioning and cognitive psychology—social learning theory.

In Chapter 7 we introduce ideas from cognitive psychology, examining how information is processed, remembered, and applied to the solution of a wide variety of problems. Here we explore the meaning of transfer—how things learned in one setting are used in another. Transfer is extremely important in education, because schooling is intended to help with life beyond school.

Finally we discuss motivation, without which learning rarely takes place. We look at internal motivators—such as the need for achievement—as well as external motivators—incentives and reinforcers. We go into procedures and programs for improving motivations and attributions, and conclude with a set of practical techniques. Together these three chapters should help you understand how learning takes place and how our teaching can be made compatible with the learning process.

6 ≡ Operant and Social Learning

OVERVIEW

Many different kinds of learning take place under many different conditions. It is no wonder, then, that many different theories of learning have been proposed. We start with three behavioral theories that help explain why we learn. The first is respondent conditioning. The second is contiguity learning. The third—and the most important and well-developed of the behavioral theories of learning—is operant conditioning. This theory informs us about practical things: how to create a learning environment that builds and maintains a student's correct responses, how and when to reward a student for appropriate behavior, and how to set up a learning contract. Punishment is another element in the process. Hardly a teacher lives who hasn't wished at one time or another to send a student away or put one in the stocks for all to scorn! But does punishment work? Should it be used? We end with a moral question: Although operant conditioning gives us the tools to modify our students' behavior, is it ethical to use those tools?

We are also concerned with social learning. Here we use both the external reinforcement and internal cognitive explanations of learning (discussed in Chapter 7) to account for how we learn from other people. Humans are social animals. Through observation of our social world, through cognitive interpretation of that world, and through reinforcement or punishment of our responses in that world, we learn enormous amounts of information and complex skills.

In the social learning view "people are neither driven by inner forces nor buffeted by environmental stimuli. Rather, psychological functioning is explained in terms of a continuous reciprocal interaction of personal and environmental determinants" (Bandura, 1977, pp. 11–12). Social learning theory emphasizes that the environments we are exposed to are not random; they often are chosen and changed by us through our own behavior. A social learning perspective helps analyze the continuous interplay among environmental variables, our personal characteristics, and our covert and overt behaviors. And this perspective gives us interpretations of how observational learning takes place and how we learn to regulate our own behavior—two processes that are important for teachers to think about.

Learning: A Definition

Before we discuss the different kinds of learning we need a definition of learning. *Learning* is the process whereby an organism changes its behavior as a result of experience. A simple definition, but deceptively so. Let's examine it.

The idea that learning is a *process* means that learning takes time. To measure learning, we compare the way in which the organism behaves at time 1 with the way it behaves at time 2 *under similar circumstances*. If the behavior under similar circumstances differs on the two occasions, we may infer that learning has taken place.

Further, it is a change in *behavior* that occurs in the process of learning. Changes in physical characteristics (height, weight) do not count as learning. Nor do changes in physical strength (lifting ability, endurance), which occur as a result of physiological change in the size of muscles or the efficiency of circulatory and respiratory systems.

Learning is what we infer has taken place when the behavior of animals, including humans, has changed. *Behavior* refers to some action, muscular or glandular, or combination of actions. One kind of behavior is verbal—our spoken and written actions. The changes from "dada" to "father," from an essay about "How I Feel Today" to one about "Transcendental Meditation," from writing "sorlool" to "school," allow us to infer that learning has taken place. The overt behaviors of talking, writing, moving, and the like allow us to study the cognitive behaviors that interest us—thinking, feeling, wanting, remembering, problem solving, creativity, and so on. The overt behaviors of the organism—pigeon or school-age child, dog or teacher—are always our starting point. Some psychologists focus exclusively on overt behaviors; they are often called *behaviorists*. Other psychologists use overt behaviors as a clue for inferring what goes on in a person's mind; they are called *cognitive psychologists*. But all psychologists need to observe overt behaviors in order to determine whether change has occurred.

Typically, in school learning, the change in behavior we are looking for is the ability to remember, understand, and apply various things and the tendency to have certain attitudes and values, of the kind set forth in our educational objectives. And we want these kinds of learning to be relatively permanent.

The final component of our definition of learning is *experience*—interchange with the environment whereby stimuli take on meaning and relationships are

Process means time

Behavior change

Behaviorists and cognitive psychologists

Learning and experience

established between stimuli and responses. We want to exclude behavior changes due primarily to other maturational processes, such as a baby's learning to stand and walk. We also want to exclude behavior changes that are due to alcohol or other drugs. And we want to exclude purely physiological changes, like the behavior changes we show when we are overtired.

Learning is the process whereby an organism changes its behavior as a result of experience. Not such a simple definition after all. But it is one we come back to again and again as we talk about learning theories and their applications.

Three Behavioral Psychologies

Three relatively distinct theories have been put forth by behavioral psychologists to describe how we learn. All three theories have applications to learning in schools.

Respondent Conditioning

Respondent (or classical) *conditioning* was one of the first of the modern behavioral learning theories. It focuses on the behavior of organisms, on changes in muscle or glandular responses. It has never accounted very well for cognitive kinds of learning. Some of the clearest examples of respondent conditioning are the classic studies by the famous Russian physiologist Ivan Pavlov. A review of the procedures he used in his historic studies can help clarify some terminology.

Unconditioned stimulus

Unconditioned response

A dog is given some meat and starts salivating as it eats. The meat is called an *unconditioned stimulus* (US), and the act of salivating is called an *unconditioned response* (UR). This particular stimulus elicits this particular response. The response to this stimulus is unlearned.

Now suppose we turn on a light in the presence of the dog. Turning on the light has a minimal effect on the dog's salivation. But what if we turn on the light and then quickly give the dog some meat (US)? If we repeated this action a number of times and then, on a particular trial, did not give the dog any meat, we would still notice the salivating response. The light, a to-be-conditioned stimulus, after several associations with the meat is capable of eliciting in the organism a response very similar to the one given when meat is presented. The light, a previously neutral stimulus, has become a *conditioned stimulus* (CS), and the response that it elicits is called a *conditioned response* (CR). Figure 6.1 shows the relationships among these terms.

Conditioned stimulus

Conditioned response

In the situation we've just described, behavior changed as a result of experience. Learning took place. Now let's move from dogs to people and use this model of learning in a more general form. The unconditioned stimulus-response linkage is operating whenever a stimulus (the US) elicits an instinctive or emotional reaction (the UR), such as fear, anger, vomiting, revulsion, or joy, pleasure, happiness, or ecstasy. Pairing the conditioned stimulus, a previously neutral stimulus, with the unconditioned stimulus leads to a conditioned response (such as fear or joy) to that conditioned stimulus.

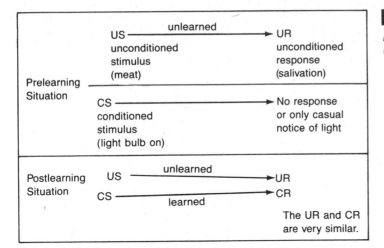

FIGURE 6.1
Model of Respondent Conditioning

For example, imagine a five-year-old girl going to school for the first time. She meets her teacher and receives a smile, a hug, and a compliment. In a few days, she begins leaving for school earlier than necessary and tells her mother that she wants to be a teacher when she grows up. In this case the teacher's smile, hug, and compliments can be interpreted as the unconditioned stimulus. They elicit in the child feelings of pleasure, which we can interpret as the unconditioned response. The previously neutral teacher and school, the conditioned stimulus, are associated with the unconditioned stimulus and soon come to elicit the same feelings of pleasure (now, a conditioned response).

Conditioning positive responses to school

But what if this child had come to school and found the teacher threatening, the routine rigid, or the remarks of other children hurtful? The respondent-conditioning model still helps explain what might happen. The school and all its components—teachers, books, students—might in time come to elicit feelings of fear or revulsion because they have been connected in time and space with the stimuli that induced these feelings. The negative feeling toward traditional schooling held by many students from ethnic and cultural minorities and from poor families may have its roots in their perceptions of teachers, schools, and other students as threatening. Teachers must be sensitive to the special needs of these students.

Conditioning negative responses to school

Some students experience nausea as a direct result of test anxiety. Early in their school careers these children learned the linkage between the test result and feelings of failure, real or imagined—the disappointment of teachers and parents, the ridicule from other children. The conditioned stimulus, either the announcement or the administration of a test, elicits the conditioned response—anxiety.

The "symbol shock" that many students experience when they first come across mathematical symbols like α, β, or $r = ax^2 + bx + c$ is probably based on the respondent conditioning of fear responses to mathematical problems. The sight of the unknown symbols, which previously had been paired with difficult

Symbol shock

● *Some children are anxious about school. A caring teacher can soon change that. (© David S. Strickler/The Picture Cube)*

subject matter, elicits negative emotions in the students and often blocks effective learning.

Henderson and Burke (1971) described a situation in which a number of students from poor homes regularly came to school with no breakfast:

> They come to school reluctantly—generally viewing it as a necessary evil. As the morning goes on each day, however, they experience increased discomfort, particularly during science class that just precedes the lunch hour. The students' hunger brings increased anxiety and tension that makes it difficult for them to concentrate and attend to their work. (p. 66)

Hunger in school   Here hunger is the unconditioned stimulus. The combination of discomfort, anxiety, and tension, with little concentration or attending, is the unconditioned response. The conditioned stimulus is the science class. Paired together are hunger and the science class. The conditioned response is the feeling of discomfort, anxiety, and tension that occurs as a response to the science class alone.

If we understand this phenomenon, we can use it as a basis for taking practical action. Knowing that the science class elicits the conditioned response means that changing science to another time will not necessarily change student behavior. The CS-CR link is well established, although in time it certainly could be extinguished. Providing food during science class, however, would break the relationship and establish positive emotional responses to science by association with relief from hunger.

Perhaps an even better strategy would be to establish a breakfast program. Reluctance to come to school, evidenced by tardiness, absence, derogatory comments, and vandalism, would be reduced by this kind of program. Here breakfast serves as the unconditioned stimulus. The pleasure that stems from the relief from hunger is the unconditioned response. The conditioned stimulus is coming to school. If we pair together receiving food and coming to school, in time we might elicit the conditioned response (pleasure) with the conditioned stimulus (coming to school). Although human behavior is often difficult to predict, and this simple model of learning has severe limitations when applied to human beings, we might very well see a decrease in the students' tardiness, absence, and vandalism and an increase in favorable statements about school. And the problem of the negative responses to science, resulting from the association of science with hunger, should disappear.

Virtually anything in the environment can be paired with a stimulus that elicits emotional responses. A teacher's kind or harsh words can elicit feelings of happiness or fear. Associated stimuli—say, mathematics, the gymnasium, the principal, or the school—eventually may elicit a response similar to the unconditioned response simply by closely preceding the unconditioned stimulus. And remember that conditioning often occurs without the student's awareness, making it very hard for the learner to understand how his or her responses were acquired. If you can examine the learning environment with the respondent-conditioning model in mind, you may be able to help your students understand their feelings and achieve certain outcomes more efficiently. You may also prevent them from learning unwanted responses.

Breakfast program

Awareness unnecessary

Contiguity Learning

The pairing of an unconditioned stimulus and a conditioned stimulus is part of the requirement for respondent conditioning. Some learning theorists point out that just the simple pairing of events, any events, can result in learning. It is not necessary that there be an unconditioned stimulus-response connection. Simple contiguous (close together in time or space) association of a stimulus and a response can lead to a change in behavior.

Pairing events

How does it work? Look at these incomplete statements:

- Don't make a mountain out of a _____.
- He's crazy as a _____.
- May the force be with _____.
- Nine times five is _____.

By filling in the words *molehill, loon, you,* and *forty-five,* we demonstrate that we learn things simply because events or stimuli occur close together in time.

Sometimes repetition is necessary, but sometimes such learning takes place in a single trial. Notice we have no need to assume unconditioned stimulus-response connections. We simply are stating that people change as a result of experiencing events that occur together.

Drill

In school situations we see contiguity learning used in drill. From repeated pairing, students learn that "2 + 2" on a flash card means "4" and that the written word *cat* is pronounced "cat." A good deal of foreign language vocabulary is learned this way. Instruction by means of drill, although often tedious, can be an efficient means of learning rote responses to simple questions. And we can make this kind of learning more efficient and less tedious by using contingent reinforcement (for example, giving gold stars, or points that can be used to get some prize, for correct responses) or by building more activity into the learning situation (using games and team competition for learning spelling or math facts).

Stereotypes learned from contiguity

Stereotypes—oversimplified rigid beliefs about groups of people—are often learned through the simple pairing of events. When movies regularly show a black woman as a maid, a bigot speaking with a Southern drawl, a banker as hardhearted, or an artist with a beard, they are setting conditions for the learning of stereotypes. Not all black women are maids, all bigots Southerners, all bankers hardhearted, or all artists bearded. But by experiencing the frequent pairing of these categories, people come to believe that they go together. Often the communications media, including textbooks, perpetuate stereotypes—both negative *and* positive. That is, paired words or events can also help people learn flattering stereotypes ("black is beautiful," "polite Japanese," "friendly Americans," "peace-loving Quakers").

In some degree, generalizations are valid and necessary for understanding people. Women do tend to be shorter, to be physically weaker, and to have higher-pitched voices than men. College students tend to wear jeans; bankers do not. But stereotypes are overgeneralizations, generalizations that have become too rigid and lacking in complexity. Be aware of how students learn by contiguity. Examine instructional materials and your own behavior to avoid teaching stereotypes to your students.

Operant Conditioning

Learning as a result of reinforcement, another basic type of learning, has been widely applied in what is called *behavior modification*. Learning of this kind is called *operant conditioning* because the behavior of interest appears spontaneously, without being elicited by any known stimuli, while the organism is "operating" on the environment. Unlike respondent conditioning, where behavior is elicited, in operant conditioning, behavior is *emitted* (spontaneous). And it is the *consequence* of that behavior that is the crucial variable in operant learning. Behavior that has as its consequence some reinforcer often is strengthened in frequency, magnitude, or probability of occurrence.

Emitted vs. elicited behavior

The consequence of behavior

Reinforcer

What is a reinforcer? A *reinforcer* is an event or stimulus that increases the strength of behavior. If you are feeling that our definition here is a circular one, you are right. But the fact remains that it is possible to change behavior by manipulating—giving or withholding—reinforcers.

The simplest example of operant conditioning is the rat in a so-called Skinner box (named after B. F. Skinner, the psychologist who developed operant conditioning theory most fully and used this kind of equipment to study it). The Skinner box is a small enclosure, empty except for a food tray and a lever. When a hungry rat is first placed in the box, it emits a wide variety of responses, or operants—getting up on its hind legs, sniffing around, and trying to climb the walls. Eventually, more or less by accident, it presses the lever. Later it presses it again. Then again. The frequency with which it presses the lever under these conditions, where nothing reinforcing happens as a result of the lever pressing, provides a baseline that we call the *operant level*—the frequency of this kind of behavior before conditioning.

Baseline, or operant level

Suppose the experimenter throws a switch that connects the lever to a food-releasing apparatus. Now as soon as the rat presses the lever, a pellet of food drops into the food tray. The rat, of course, will sniff the food and eat it. Sooner or later, the rat will press the lever again, and again food will drop into the tray. Each time it presses the lever, the rat gets another pellet of food. The reinforcement is *contingent* on pressing the lever. What has been found, almost without exception, is that the rate of the rat's lever-pressing response increases. The rat has been conditioned to press the lever by contingent reinforcement with food. In terms of our definition of learning, we see that a change in behavior, an increased rate of lever pressing, has taken place as a result of experience—the sight and taste of food.

Contingent reinforcement

Operant conditioning has been demonstrated in the behavior of many other animals—a pigeon pecking a key, a dog raising a paw, a horse nodding its head. In principle any operant behavior can be made more frequent by being reinforced soon after it occurs.

In human beings, the same model applies. All of the infinite variety of human behavior can be made more or less frequent or probable by the use or nonuse of reinforcement, contingent on some response. The response can be anything—an action, a statement, or even inaction. For example, the response may be volunteering to answer a teacher's question or the answer itself. Or the response may be a student's sitting quietly and apparently doing nothing.

If the response is volunteering to answer a question, one likely reinforcer of that response is being called on by the teacher. If the response is the actual answer to the question, the reinforcer is likely to be the teacher's saying "Right" or "Correct" or "That's good." If the response is sitting still and doing nothing, a reinforcer might be some kind of indication of the teacher's approval, either in words or by means of a smile or some other nonverbal behavior. Or it might be relief from the anxiety of being called on and possibly giving a wrong answer.

Because teachers, especially, find great practical value in operant conditioning, we give much more attention to this learning theory than to the other theories of learning put forth by behavioral psychologists.

Reinforcement in Operant Conditioning

Reinforcement is a key element in learning because behavior that is followed by reinforcement is strengthened. A reinforcer is any event that can be shown to strengthen a response. There are two major kinds of reinforcers: positive and negative.

Positive and Negative Reinforcers

Both positive and negative reinforcers can strengthen responses. Figure 6.2 shows a four-celled table, of which cells A and D interest us here. (We examine cells B and C later.) Providing something of positive value (a stimulus) following behavior (a response) is *positive reinforcement* (cell A). Giving food when a lever is pressed, saying "Good" after a student's response, giving candy for obeying rules, smiling after a joke, and looking attentive during someone's speech—all are ways of providing a positively valued stimulus. In turn, these kinds of positive reinforcement may cause an increase in lever pressing, student responding, obedience, joke telling, or speech giving.

Positive reinforcement

If you want to strengthen a particular behavior, you should define the behavior carefully and apply an appropriate reinforcer when that behavior occurs. Fortunately many children respond positively to a smile, a nod, an exclamation of "Good," "Great," or "Fine job." But for a particular child, a teacher's saying "Good" for obeying rules may not serve as a positive reinforcer. For that child, candy, permission to go to gym early, or being allowed to conduct a physics experiment may be the "right" reinforcer. We know with considerable certainty that if we can find the right reinforcer, we can strengthen behavior.

Appropriate reinforcers

In Figure 6.2, cell D is labeled "negative reinforcement." When something of negative value is removed or stopped after a response, the result is a strengthening of the response that preceded the removal. Because it strengthens behavior, the event that resulted in removal is a reinforcer; but because it is associated with something unpleasant, something of negative value, we call it a *negative reinforcer.* (Examples of things of negative value include an annoying noise, a harsh criticism, a boring assignment.) Reinforcement, whether positive or negative, always increases or strengthens behavior.

Negative reinforcers

Suppose that just as a test is about to begin, an anxious child gets sick. What happens? The child is sent to the nurse's office and does not have to take the test. The response of becoming sick has been followed by a negative reinforcer—removal of the test. We might expect "getting sick" behavior to increase in frequency in similar situations.

The test here is an aversive event. Other aversive events might be a parent's or a teacher's nagging a student to be neater, being made to attend a school dance, or being assigned to a low-achieving English class. Because students often try to escape from these negative events, negative reinforcement is also called *escape conditioning* (Sulzer-Azaroff & Mayer, 1977).

Escape conditioning

The Value of What Is Given or Taken Away

FIGURE 6.2

Types of Reinforcement

	Positively Valued	Negatively Valued
Something Given	Cell A Positive Reinforcement	Cell B
Something Taken Away	Cell C	Cell D Negative Reinforcement

What Happens After A Response Is Made

Responses associated with the removal of negative events—that is, responses that are negatively reinforced—are likely to be strengthened. For example, if a student was neater and the nagging stopped, the neatness response would be strengthened. The neatness behavior, because it would lead to the removal of the aversive stimulus (nagging), is likely to increase. Neatness becomes the way to obtain the reinforcement—less nagging. If a boy who has been forced to go to a school dance leaves the dance or associates only with other boys at the dance or asks a girl to dance and she accepts, he may no longer be frightened or embarrassed about school dances. Any of these responses could end an unpleasant situation. Through negative reinforcement, the response that ended the boy's fear or embarrassment is likely to be strengthened. Finally, if a student feels a low-level English class is aversive, the behaviors that could remove her from the class are likely to be strengthened. She may study hard to improve her writing or her ability to identify nouns, gerunds, and pluperfect subjunctive cases. And if studying gets her moved up to a higher-level class, then studying behavior may increase. It is the response that leads to the reward. Escape from the aversive event is contingent on the correct performance of certain tasks in the English class. When those tasks are performed correctly and the student is moved back to the regular class, she is negatively reinforced, and we can expect an increase in the behaviors that led to the change.

RECAP

"Events which are found to be reinforcing are of two sorts. Some reinforcements consist of *presenting* stimuli, of adding something—for example, food, water, or sexual contact—to a situation. These we call *positive* reinforcers. Others consist of *removing* something—for example, a loud noise, a very bright light, extreme cold or heat, or electric shock—from the situation. These we call *negative* reinforcers. In both cases the effect of reinforcement is the same—the probability of response is increased" (Skinner, 1953, p. 73).

Primary and Secondary Reinforcements

The distinction between primary and secondary reinforcement is useful. Positive primary reinforcers are stimuli such as food, water, sex, and other events that satisfy physiological needs. By satisfying physiological needs, we can strengthen behavior, particularly the behavior of lower organisms. Human beings, with their elaborate language system and highly developed intelligence, can be reinforced by positive secondary reinforcers like praise, money, gold stars, and movies. Secondary reinforcers may at one time have been linked in some way to the primary reinforcers. That is, money may be a reinforcer because it buys food or shelter. Gold stars may serve as reinforcers because they are linked to a person's basic need for security or safety. If you are earning gold stars, you are pleasing your teacher, thereby increasing your feelings of security and safety within the classroom environment.

"Look for the reinforcer"

Because money and other secondary reinforcers can become powerful reinforcers, the distinction between the two types of reinforcers is blurred when we set out to *use* reinforcement techniques. The operant conditioner's motto in practice should be "Look for the reinforcer"—find the event that is acting or can act as a reinforcer for a particular person. Whether it is primary or secondary, positive or negative, the appropriate reinforcer can be used by one person to change the behavior of another. If a teacher is the person responsible for student learning, and learning is defined as a change in behavior, then a primary function of a teacher is to change student behavior. Used correctly and for the right purposes, operant techniques can help us change the behavior of students in good ways.

Schedules of Reinforcement

Continuous vs. intermittent reinforcement

Ratio schedules

Interval schedules

Fixed vs. variable schedules

Reinforcement can be continuous or intermittent. With *continuous reinforcement* we reinforce every response of a given type; with *intermittent reinforcement* we reinforce only a fraction of these responses. This fraction of responses can be based on the number of responses made. Here we are using a *ratio schedule* of reinforcement, in which one of every N wanted responses is reinforced. We may reinforce every second response, every tenth response, or every hundredth response. Or we can use intermittent reinforcement by varying the time interval between reinforcements. Here we have an *interval schedule* of reinforcement. We might reinforce the first response made after an interval of ten seconds has elapsed since the preceding reinforcement. Or we might reinforce every sixty seconds, only once every five minutes, or once every hour, regardless of the number of responses made during that time.

Both ratio and interval schedules can be fixed (constant) or variable. So we can use fixed-ratio, variable-ratio, fixed-interval, or variable-interval schedules of reinforcement (see Figure 6.3). These and many other possibilities have been studied by Ferster and Skinner (1957). They found that the various schedules of reinforcement had different effects on rate of responding, number of responses

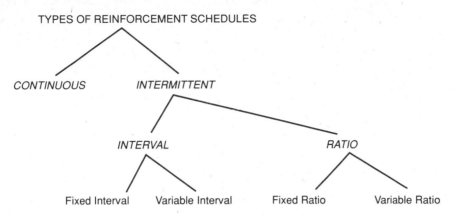

TYPES OF REINFORCEMENT SCHEDULES

CONTINUOUS   INTERMITTENT

INTERVAL   RATIO

Fixed Interval   Variable Interval   Fixed Ratio   Variable Ratio

FIGURE 6.3

Types of Reinforcement Schedules Possible in Operant Conditioning

per reinforcement, and the number of responses made after reinforcement was stopped. The Ferster-Skinner research was conducted with rats and pigeons. But it has been found that learning in school is affected in much the same way by the common schedules of reinforcement.

Fixed-Ratio Schedules

We might find a fixed-ratio schedule, in which a student is reinforced on, say, every fifth correct response, in programmed learning materials or in computer-assisted instruction. For example, every fifth correct answer might be met with a new unit or new page, or a statement like "You're doing fine." Fixed-ratio schedules can result in stable responding, particularly when the ratio of reinforcements is low, say, 1 in 100, 1 in 500, or even 1 in 1,000 (Ferster & Skinner, 1957). The lower the ratio, the more stable the responding because the individual is conditioned to make many responses in order to obtain reinforcement.

Stable responding

In some situations the goal of the instructor is to phase out the reinforcement. This method forces students to work on their own, or for reinforcers that they control, rather than for those from external sources. To practice this approach, you might start with continuous reinforcement for correct responses, then use a series of decreasing fixed-ratio schedules until reinforcement can be eliminated completely. This procedure was used in the case reported by Whitlock (1966). A normal six-year-old boy was not acquiring reading skills. The experimenter taught the child a token reinforcement system—a system in which objects (for example, poker chips, redeemable for candy, toys, or pleasant events) are used as reinforcers. When he made a correct response, the child received a plastic token. The tokens were put into jars holding thirty-six tokens each. When one jar of tokens was turned in to the experimenter, a storybook was read to the child. For three jars of tokens, the child could listen to records; for seven jars he could see a cartoon. At first the experimenter used continuous reinforcement. For each correct word identification from a flash card, the child received a plastic token (a ratio of 1:1). The student soon began to read in storybooks, with a fixed-ratio schedule of 1:2—that is, 1 token for every 2

Phasing out reinforcement

Token reinforcement system

words read correctly. That was changed to 1:4, then 1 per page (about 1:20), 1 per story (about 1:60), and eventually 1 per 4 stories (about 1:240). Behavior was effectively maintained as the experimenter stretched the ratio, eventually phasing out reinforcement altogether after the fifteenth hour of special treatment. In fact,

> in about four weeks a child's reading performance changed from "below normal" to a level which enabled him to be placed into the regular reading program of his class. After the twenty-third session, the study was terminated. Three months after completion of the study his teacher reported that the S [subject or student] read with ease and accuracy both alone and in a group and has been placed in the normal reading group within his class. The S's mother recounted a distinct change in his attitude toward reading and in his actual reading behavior since the beginning of the study. Prior to this study she characterized him as "having a fear of words; therefore being uninterested to the point of refusing to try to read." (Whitlock, 1966, p. 84)

Persistence and intermittent schedules

Obviously a switch from continuous to intermittent reinforcement is necessary in operant conditioning because it is nearly impossible outside the laboratory to reinforce every correct response. Moreover, the use of intermittent schedules in training results in behavior that persists longer without reinforcement than does training with continuous reinforcement. The ratio has an effect on the rate of response too. With a high fixed-ratio schedule, say 1:2 or 1:5, responding is fast, and further responding usually begins right after reinforcement is given. With a lower fixed-ratio schedule, say 1:30 or 1:100, there is a characteristic pause after a reinforcement, as if the pigeon or person were resting. It is as if the organism knows that it takes a certain large number of responses to earn reinforcement. Yet once the animal begins to respond, it is likely to do so at a high rate, so that the reinforcement can be obtained as quickly as possible. Factories use the fixed-ratio schedule in what they call piecework. Farmers often pay their workers so much per bushel of picked fruit. These fixed-ratio schedules require a certain fixed amount of work or picking before some amount of money is credited to the worker.

Variable-Ratio Schedules

In the variable-ratio schedule, responses are reinforced on a certain *average* ratio, but each individual reinforcement comes after a different number of correct responses. That is, if the individual ratios are 1:5, 1:10, 1:15, 1:13, and 1:7, the variable-ratio schedule averages 5:50, or 1:10. *A variable-ratio schedule induces the organism to make many more responses than a fixed-ratio schedule of about the same mean level.* Slot machine gamblers are a good example of the way we respond to variable-ratio schedules. Slot machines pay off on a variable-ratio schedule. This schedule keeps people pulling the slot machine handle hour after hour. It is well established that behavior that has been maintained by a variable-

•Hand-raising behavior is maintained on a variable-ratio schedule of reinforcement. (© Paul Conklin)

ratio schedule is the hardest to extinguish. That is, after variable-ratio reinforcement, many unreinforced trials may be necessary before a rat finally stops pressing a bar or a gambler finally stops putting coins into a slot machine.

In school we might find a variable-ratio schedule in the reinforcement of volunteering behavior. Some children always put up their hands to volunteer to answer a question or perform a task. Suppose 20 of 30 children in a class raise their hands whenever there is a chance for students to respond. One particular child, other things being equal, would be called on 1 time out of 20. Unless the teacher goes alphabetically or by rows, the probability of a child's being chosen is more variable, perhaps *averaging* 1:20, but sometimes 1:3, 1:30, 1:7, or 1:40. In other words, volunteering behavior is reinforced on a variable-ratio schedule. The persistence of hand raising among students may be due to this variable-ratio reinforcement schedule—a schedule that makes any behavior, including hand raising, hard to extinguish. Notice, however, that although it is hard to extinguish this kind of behavior, it is not impossible. By consistently ignoring the raised hands of some students, a teacher can eventually eliminate this behavior on the part of these students. When a behavior is not reinforced, it is likely not to be emitted.

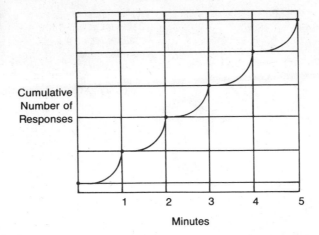

FIGURE 6.4

Characteristic Pattern of Responding Under a Fixed-Interval Schedule of Reinforcement

Fixed-Interval Schedules

When reinforcement is provided on a fixed-interval schedule, a period of decreased responding occurs after each reinforcement. So when a rat is reinforced for the first response made after one minute, the rat is likely to be inactive for perhaps fifty seconds, then respond until reinforced. After this reinforcement, the rat is again inactive for a period. Figure 6.4 shows the response curve under a fixed-interval schedule.

Cramming

We find this same effect in human behavior. Think about the way most students study for regularly scheduled tests. When a midterm and final examination are the only two tests scheduled, the responses required (studying) to get reinforcement (a good grade) increase in magnitude and frequency just before a test. We call it cramming. Immediately after a test, many students enter an inactive period, rarely studying. The major portion of study behavior occurs at fixed intervals, halfway through the course and again at the end of the course. If tests are given every Friday, it is common to find a cycle of rest (Monday through Wednesday), study (Thursday), and test (Friday). We could change the vertical axis of Figure 6.4 to read "Hours of study" and the horizontal axis to "Weeks" or "Fridays," and then use the same general curve of responding to describe the study behavior of students that we used to show the lever-pressing behavior of rats. Both curves would show the scalloping effect—relatively little responding for some time period, followed by a sharp rise in responding when it is nearly time for reinforcement to take place if a response is emitted, followed by another period of minimum responding.

Scalloping effect

Variable-Interval Schedules

The fourth reinforcement schedule is the variable-interval schedule. An interval of, say, five minutes might be the time span used as an average. Actually the interval during which no reinforcement is given for responding can vary greatly.

It may be thirty seconds or ten minutes. The major characteristic of behavior maintained by a variable-interval schedule is its regularity. Stable and uniform rates of responding occur in rats and pigeons on this kind of schedule. Moreover, the response is hard to extinguish; it lasts a considerable time after all reinforcement stops. **Regularity of responding**

A variable-interval schedule might be used in a language laboratory where students respond to audiotaped lessons. Suppose the instructor, by operating a master console, can listen in to students' pronunciation and tell them whether they are doing well or poorly. If the instructor randomly chooses which students to listen to, he or she is creating for a particular student a variable-interval schedule. The student has no way of knowing when reinforcement (being listened to) will take place. In what looks like an effort to ensure reinforcement, the student responds at uniform rates, with no scalloping effect—even when reinforcement does not occur for a considerable period of time. The student has no way of knowing whether the situation has changed or the reinforcement interval has become much longer. So behavior continues long after it stops being appropriate for obtaining reinforcement. We find the same situation in classes where surprise quizzes are given. To be sure that they are prepared, students must study regularly—a very different study pattern from the one we found in a fixed-interval schedule. If a teacher actually stopped giving surprise quizzes after students had taken some, the students would continue to study regularly for a long time. That is, the study behavior would be extinguished only slowly.

You are probably thinking that surprise quizzes are the way to go, and certainly you could use them to keep the study behavior of your students at a high level for extended periods. But there is a danger here of creating high anxiety levels in students. Therefore, you probably should not use surprise quizzes as a general strategy.

Contingency Management

Contingent Reinforcement

The term *contingent reinforcement* means that reinforcement depends on certain conditions. When we say, "You will earn one gold star *for every spelling paper that is at least 80 percent correct*" or "I'll allow you to play with the others *if and only if you finish your homework at home,*" we are making the reinforcement—the gold star or the play activity—contingent on a particular response—spelling correctly or finishing a homework assignment. Research has shown that the clarity of the contingency and the consistency with which it is applied have great effects on the process of changing behavior.

Contingent reinforcement is simply reinforcement that depends on the occurrence of a certain response. Contingency management is providing reinforcement under the proper circumstances and withholding reinforcement when those circumstances are not appropriate.

•*The Premack principle: Preferred activities, such as games, can be used as reinforcers for engaging in less preferred activities, such as spelling. (© Elizabeth Crews/The Image Works)*

The Premack Principle

What kinds of stimuli or events can be used as reinforcers? Long lists of them have been collected by Sulzer-Azaroff and Mayer (1977) and by R. V. Hall and M. C. Hall (1980a). The latter list contains dozens of verbal reinforcers (praise, encouragement), physical reinforcers (hugs, smiles), activity reinforcers (listening to records, playing), and token reinforcers (points, chips). Consumable reinforcers can also be used (cookies, candy). Just observing what children like gives us insight into what to use as a reinforcer.

Probability of a behavior's occurring

Premack (1965) offered the principle that an activity more preferred at time X can reinforce an activity less preferred at time X. That is, when people are free to choose their activities, a behavior with a higher probability of occurrence can be used as a reinforcer for a behavior with a lower probability of occurrence. Playing on a playground (high preference, or high probability) can be used as a reinforcer for spelling practice (low preference, or low probability). When a father says something like "Eat your spinach, and I'll read you a story," he invokes Premack's principle.

It is easy for teachers and parents to misunderstand the method, however. Homme and Tosti (1965) provide the illustration:

A child is seated at the dinner table. Dinner is served. The other members of the family are eating. The child, however, does not eat. She plays with her shoes. The usual way to solve this problem is obvious: "Stop playing with your shoes! Eat your dinner!"

"Playing with shoes" is a high-frequency behavior and eating is a low one. When the problem is viewed this way, the contingency manager says, "Eat one bite of potatoes, then play with your shoes some more." It may be startling to spectators, but the latter method worked. Instead of having an emotional scene, with both parent and child upset, the contingency manager has a child cooperating in a gamelike atmosphere. What stimulus set off the playing-with-shoes operant in the first place? It is impossible to say. But it does not matter. If this higher frequency operant follows a lower frequency one, the latter will get strengthened.

In the classroom the teacher who says, "Let's play outside now, so we'll be less restless for arithmetic" or "Stop playing around, and do your chemistry" has missed the point. We must use the more preferred activity to get students involved in the less preferred activity. The teacher should say, "Let's do a little math now, then we'll go outside and play" or "Let's do a little chemistry now, then everybody can play around." For one teacher we know, this technique succeeded in motivating a group of students from low-income families. The state curriculum required the students to read Dickens's *David Copperfield;* the students preferred to read comic books. The teacher, intuitively applying the Premack principle, said, "For five minutes of reading *David Copperfield,* you can read twenty-five minutes of comic books." Soon the contingency was changed to ten minutes of Dickens for twenty minutes of comic books. Eventually, fifteen minutes were given for each activity. As time passed, most of the students became so engrossed in *David Copperfield* that they finished it on their own during the reading period. The students who did not become absorbed in the book were kept at a 50 percent ratio of text reading to comic book reading. It is doubtful that any of these students would have read any of Dickens without the use of contingency management.

Homme (1966) first became aware of the power of the Premack principle while working with an out-of-control class and a distraught teacher. Children were running, screaming, pushing chairs noisily, and doing puzzles. The teacher's requests for order seemed to have no effect on the class. Faced with the problem, Homme took the approach of making the running and other disruptive behaviors contingent on doing only a small amount of whatever the teacher wanted the students to do. For example, the pupils were asked to sit quietly in chairs and look at the blackboard. Then, almost immediately, they were told, "Everybody, run and scream now." This kind of contingency management enabled the teacher to take control of the situation. Subsequently, Homme reports, the teacher was able to teach everything ordinarily taught in first grade in about one month.

Classroom management of contingencies

The Contingency Contract

Contingent reinforcement gives us a procedure to use to modify student behavior. The Premack principle gives us an effective guide for choosing the right reinforcer. We use both in creating contingency contracts—written or oral agreements with students and their parents that specify what responses must be made and what reinforcement will be earned.

Homme, Csanyi, Gonzales, and Rechs (1970) offer teachers and parents nine suggestions for making systematic contingency contracts with students:

1. The contract payoff (reward) should be immediate, particularly early in the learning situation.

Successive approximations

2. Initial contracts should call for and reward small and easy approximations of the wanted behavior. This is the idea of shaping behavior by successive approximations.

   For example, if you want a child to do cursive writing, you might begin by reinforcing any kind of pencil-and-paper contact. Next you reinforce rough approximations to the letters. Then you reinforce fairly accurate imitation of the letters. Finally you reinforce connected letters. In teaching children to talk, we first reinforce babbling, then approximations to words. Eventually, the magic day comes when a baby utters "mama" or "dada." Typically this accomplishment brings massive amounts of reinforcement—from parents and grandparents who convey to the child their conviction that he or she is a genius. The child's speech is shaped by reinforcing successive approximations to the wanted sound patterns. At first "gamps" may be reinforced, but in time reinforcement may be withheld until "grandpa" is said.

   Many teachers and parents set first tasks that are too difficult. The result is that no amount of reinforcement can induce a child to accomplish the task. Instead of asking students to do twenty mathematics problems, perhaps a teacher should assign just one or two at first. Instead of offering reinforcement to a child for cleaning an entire room, perhaps a parent should ask that socks be picked up off the floor. The idea is to find an appropriate starting point for shaping the terminal behavior, then, during later stages of training, to change the criterion for reinforcement so that the wanted behavior is approximated more and more closely.

3. In the beginning the teacher should give rewards frequently, though in small amounts. (Eventually the teacher may change to a less frequent schedule of reinforcement.)

Accomplishment, not obedience

4. The contingency contract should call for and reward accomplishment, not obedience. We do not want children to learn to do what we tell them to do in order to get a reward. What we really want to say to them, as clearly as possible, is that for their *accomplishment* of particular tasks they will be reinforced. The learning situation should be task oriented; it should not demand obedience to the contingency manager as a person.

"First work, then play"

5. The teacher should reward the wanted performance *after* it takes place. This "first work, then play" rule is often violated. When a study hall teacher says, "You can have free reading another five

minutes, but then you've got to do your homework," the free reading time (a reinforcing activity) does not occur after work on the homework. First work, then play, is a rule that, when systematically used, can help students achieve their goals.

6. The contract between teacher and students must be fair. The reinforcement should have a good relationship to the effort required to obtain it. Telling a student that if she passes French you will take her to the movies does not seem fair. The effort to achieve in French is much greater than the magnitude of the reinforcer.

Fairness

7. The terms of the contract must be clear. Students must always know how much or how well they should perform and what they can expect to receive in return. A good way to see to it that all parties to the contract (teachers, students, and parents) understand what is expected and what will occur is to write out the contract. Use simple language and brief statements. Written versions of contingency contracts often work better than oral versions (Kazdin, 1980).

Clarity

8. The contract must be honest. That is, the contract must be carried out immediately as specified.

Honesty

9. The contract should be positive. The shaping of behavior through positive reinforcement is the goal. Certainly contracts can be offered to children where the responses receive negative reinforcement. For example, you can say to a child, "If you do your homework, I'll stop nagging you." This kind of negative reinforcement can work. But it is better to make a contract that takes a positive form: "If you do your homework, I'll take you to the hockey game."

A positive contract

Kazdin (1980) described a contingency contract for a child named Andrew—a contract that resulted in a reduction of school fighting behavior from nine fights per week to none, over an eighteen-week period. The written contract specified what Andrew would do; what his teacher, Mrs. Harris, would do; and what Andrew's parents would do if Andrew could go through a school day without a fight. The behavior was clearly described, and the reinforcers were clearly specified. And the teacher, parents, and Andrew all signed the contract. The contract was never thought of as a legally binding document; it was a commitment of goodwill among parties who cared about one another. Seven months after the end of the contract, Andrew was still doing well. A sample contract is shown in Figure 6.5.

The Elimination of Responses

In this section, we talk about several ways to eliminate unwanted responses. Learning how *not* to behave can be just as important as learning how to behave.

FIGURE 6.5   *Sample Contract*

•>> OFFICIAL <<•
CONTRACT

This contract is between ___Van Thu Hue_____ (student)

and ___Ms. Lepeto_____ (teacher, ~~friend, other~~)

Date: from ___October 1, 1991_____ to ___November 15, 1991_____

       (this date)   (contract expiration)

Following are the terms of the contract:

___Van Thu Hue_____ (student) will _Not engage in any physical fighting on school grounds. All disputes will be verbal. Anger will be discussed with Ms. Lepeto._

___Ms. Lepeto_____ (teacher, ~~friend, other~~) will _provide to Van Thu Hue 4 movie tickets, the job of school messenger for 1 month, and a chance to work in the school shop during free time._

When this contract is completed, the contractee will be able to _control his temper with the other students, respond verbally instead of physically to other students' behavior, discuss freely the feelings of anger generated at school and alternatives to violence._

___Van Thu Hue_____
Contractee

___Ho Thu Hue, brother___
Witness

___Virginia Lepeto_____
Contractor

OFFICIAL SEAL

This contract may be terminated by agreement of parties signing this contract. New contract(s) may be negotiated by the same parties.

Source: Adapted from *Achieving Educational Excellence* by B. Sulzer-Azaroff and G. R. Mayer, copyright © 1986 by Holt, Rinehart and Winston, Inc., reprinted by permission of the publisher.

Extinction

Extinction is the process by which the rate of occurrence of a response decreases as a result of nonreinforcement. Being called on reinforces a student's volunteering to recite. The student has acquired the habit of frequent volunteering because, over time, she has been reinforced for this response. But what if she is no longer called on when she volunteers? Her volunteering behavior would be extinguished; that is, it would become less and less frequent, until the behavior returned to its prereinforcement frequency, or operant level.

Extinction is the opposite of response acquisition. It is the weakening of a response by nonreinforcement, just as acquisition is the strengthening of a response by reinforcement. Usually when nonreinforcement begins, there is a temporary increase in the rate and intensity of the response. But soon the rate begins to decline until, if the nonreinforcement continues, the rate of response becomes very low or even zero.

How quickly extinction occurs depends on whether the previous reinforcement has been continuous or intermittent. Again, extinction occurs more slowly after a history of intermittent reinforcement than it does after continuous reinforcement, other things being equal. Among the "other things" would be the amount of positive reinforcement given after each response and the total number of reinforcements received before the beginning of the extinction process.

Examples of acquisition and extinction can be found in many operant-conditioning studies. To show that an increase in the frequency of a behavior is causally related to the reinforcement procedures used, experimenters often include an extinction period in their research design. If during the extinction period the behavior decreases in frequency, then increases again during a period of reinforcement, we have convincing evidence that the behavior changes are causally related to changes in the reinforcement contingencies. Figure 6.6 is a graph of just such a situation recorded by Schmidt and Ulrich (1969). During the baseline period, the noise level of 29 fourth-grade students was measured. During phase 1, extra time in the gymnasium was given to the class for keeping the noise level below 42 decibels. No such positive reward was given if the 42-decibel level was exceeded in a ten-minute period. Obviously the procedure worked. The mean noise level of the class was considerably reduced during phase 1 of the study. To strengthen the evidence of the causal relationship between reinforcement and the change in classroom noise level, the researchers instituted an extinction period. During this period, called the *reversal period,* the newly acquired quiet behavior was not reinforced. The noise level increased. If being quiet had been ignored for a longer period, the noise level would probably have gone back to the baseline level. But the experimenters reinstated the positive reinforcement, ending the extinction period and reestablishing quieter classroom behavior during phase 2 of the study.

Notice that in this study a group contingency was used. The group, not an individual, was the subject of behavior modification. When group contingencies are used, group members often take on roles to see to it that the group succeeds. For example, members can be quite supportive, reinforcing and

Nonreinforcement

Extinction rate and reinforcement schedules

Reversal period

Group contingency

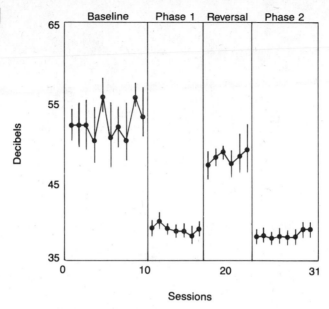

FIGURE 6.6

Effects of Sound-Control Procedures on Classroom Noise Levels

Source: G. W. Schmidt and R. E. Ulrich, *Journal of Applied Behavior Analysis*, 2, 1969, pp. 171–179. Used by permission.

Note: Each point represents the average sound-level reading for one session; vertical lines denote the mean deviation.

helping one another to achieve the reinforcement. Members can also exhibit threatening behavior toward those who endanger the group's chances at reinforcement (Sulzer-Azaroff & Mayer, 1977). The latter side effect does not happen often (Sulzer-Azaroff, 1981), but you should watch for it and eliminate it when you try to shape the behavior of groups.

Unintentional reinforcement by teacher attention

Another thing to watch for when you are trying to shape the behavior of an individual student or a group is unintentional reinforcement. Many disruptive classroom behaviors—students' getting out of their seats, talking out of turn, pencil tapping, making strange noises, crying, hitting, and a host of others—are unintentionally reinforced by the teacher's attention. Sending a student to the principal or yelling at him can have the same effect as praising him if the student is looking for your attention. This is why it seems to teachers that the more they reprimand a student for not raising her hand when she wants to talk, the more she seems to speak without permission. To extinguish a response, you often do better to ignore it. If attention is the positive reinforcer that maintains the behavior of speaking out of turn, ignoring the behavior will reduce its frequency.

Reinforcement of Other Behavior and Reinforcement of Low Response Rates

Although it may seem paradoxical, reinforcement can be used to reduce or eliminate behavior (Kazdin, 1980). The technique of differential reinforcement of other behavior (DRO) requires reinforcement of all other kinds of behavior

DRO

The Value of What Is Given or Taken Away

	Positively Valued	Negatively Valued
Something Given	Cell A Positive Reinforcement	Cell B Punishment 1
Something Taken Away	Cell C Punishment 2	Cell D Negative Reinforcement

What Happens After A Response Is Made

FIGURE 6.7

Types of Reinforcement and Punishment

except the one that you want to suppress or eliminate. If you want to eliminate a student's talking out of turn, you would reinforce every behavior you can that is incompatible with that behavior. You might reinforce the student when she is writing or staring into space or doodling or reading or doing workbook problems. Over time the unwanted behavior should be reduced or even eliminated.

The differential reinforcement of low rates of responding (DRL) also can reduce or eliminate unwanted behavior. Here we reinforce any reduction in unwanted behavior. So when a student who talks too much begins to talk less, we use DRL, reinforcing the reduction in talking. This is a bit like the process of shaping behavior through successive approximations, but, instead of trying to use reinforcement to increase a response, we use it to help decrease a response.

DRL

What is so appealing about DRO and DRL procedures is that they are positive ways of suppressing or eliminating unwanted behavior. Extinction, DRO, and DRL are preferable to punishment, the topic we examine next in our discussion of how to reduce or eliminate unwanted behavior in students.

Positive way to eliminate responses

Punishment

Another way to eliminate a response is to punish the student when the response occurs. Figure 6.7 shows the relationship of reinforcement and punishment to stimulus events and their value. Let's examine cells B and C.

Punishment 1.   Cell B is labeled "punishment 1." It is the giving of something of negative value after an unwanted response. Getting your wrist slapped for reaching across the table, being yelled at for going into the street, receiving an F on a composition, being suspended from school for fighting—all are punishments intended to decrease the frequency of a particular response.

Presenting negative stimuli

Does punishment work? Is it a good thing? Answers to these questions have varied in recent decades. Most recent research shows that, under appropriate conditions, particularly when intense punishment is presented, behavior can be permanently suppressed (Matson & DiLorenzo, 1984). Can punishment reduce behavior? "A definitely affirmative answer may be given" (Azrin & Holz, 1966,

p. 426). As Johnston (1972) summarized the evidence, other ways of reducing the frequency of behavior (for example, extinction, DRO, and DRL) are less immediate, enduring, and effective than punishment properly used.

In some research with human beings punishment has simply not been severe enough to reduce behavior. In other cases punishment has failed because it has satisfied needs for attention, paradoxically serving as a reinforcer. Teachers who pay attention to students only when they misbehave and then provide what they think is punishment may actually be reinforcing rather than punishing.

Punishment as paradoxical reinforcer

Although punishment can be effective, is it a good thing? The answer here depends on a variety of factors. If the behavior to be suppressed is sufficiently dangerous or undesirable, then punishment as a way of eliminating that behavior is a good thing. Parents and teachers would appear to be justified in punishing children who run into the street, who push nails into electrical outlets, who continuously violate the rules necessary for orderly classroom work, who misuse power tools in shop, who bully weaker students, who try dangerous activities in the gym, or who destroy school property.

Justifying punishment

A controversy has arisen among people concerned, as either parents or therapists, with autistic (unresponsive, nonspeaking, seemingly lost in thought) and retarded children. Some such children engage in head banging of a violent, constant, and self-injurious kind. Such children may hit themselves hundreds or thousands of times per day, injure their nerves and eyes, and suffer bruises, open wounds, and even detached retinas leading to blindness.

Research showed that 60 percent of such persons were significantly improved by means of various kinds of reinforcement, positive or negative. But what about the other 40 percent? Alternatives for them were (1) permit the self-injury to continue, (2) use heavy doses of tranquilizing drugs, (3) use physical restraints, hand and foot, all day, and (4) use unpleasant, but not painful or damaging, aversive procedures (Rimland, 1990).

One example of the fourth alternative is the Self-Injurious Behavior Inhibiting System (SIBIS). This device uses an electrical shock that is brief and uncomfortable (like a hard pinch), but mild and noninjurious. It works through a device attached to the head. In one study of five cases of head banging, SIBIS greatly helped four with only a few shocks totaling about 2–3 seconds; the fifth case required 3,000 stimulations before reducing head banging to near-zero levels (Linscheid, Iwata, Ricketts, Williams, & Griffin, 1990).

Is such use of punishment 1, in the form of SIBIS, justifiable? Some people say no; only positive or negative reinforcement or punishment 2 (see the next section) is justifiable. Others say that when nothing else has been found effective, SIBIS should be used, but only with the consent of the parents or guardians, and only when carefully monitored.

In any case, the example of SIBIS clarifies the issue of punishment. Many psychologists—including B. F. Skinner—who emphasize the desirability of positive approaches nonetheless accept the justifiability of punishment, or "aversive treatments," under such circumstances, namely, when they are "brief and harmless stimuli, made precisely contingent on self-destructive or other excessive behavior, [which] suppress the behavior and leave the children free to develop in other ways . . ." (Skinner, 1987). But in using punishment to suppress behaviors, the punisher (that is, the parent or teacher) can acquire negative stimulus properties. Children who claim to hate their parents and teachers are demonstrating a common response to negatively valued stimulus objects. Another problem here is *generalization,* whereby the same response is made to stimuli associated with the stimulus to which one was first conditioned. So a child may extend an intense dislike of the teacher to a particular subject matter or to school itself. Then too we have the problem of *avoidance*—the cheating, truancy, lying, sneaking, and hiding that students do to avoid the punishment that goes along with being wrong, failing, misbehaving, or getting caught. All in all, punishment is a weapon that can be as risky for the teacher as it is distasteful to the student.

How should we use punishment? Research indicates that punishment is most effective when

Punishing effectively

- it is presented immediately after a response.
- it cannot be escaped.
- it is as intense as necessary.
- an alternative and desirable response is available to the student.

If possible, instead of punishing, warn the student. But if a warning does not suppress the behavior and if nothing positive works, follow the behavior with a punishment. Repeated often enough, this procedure will make the warning effective, eliminating the need for continual punishment. Punishment 1 can be effective, but it must be used carefully to do more good than harm. And because students are so sensitive about it, you must be prepared to use punishment fairly. *All* students who deserve punishment must receive the same degree and type of punishment. Students are quick to spot favoritism and discrimination. Fairness is one of the characteristics of teachers that students prize most.

Punishing fairly

Punishment 2.   Another kind of punishment is generally more acceptable in school settings. As shown in Cell C in Figure 6.7, punishment 2 consists of taking away something of positive value. Here we discuss two kinds of punishment 2: time-out and response cost.

- *Time-out* is a procedure whereby we deprive students of the opportunity to obtain reinforcement if they misbehave (R. V. Hall & M. C. Hall, 1980b). We can deprive a student of an opportunity to see a movie, watch a television program, work on a project in shop, participate in games during gym period, or have some other kind of fun. This kind of punishment often seems more acceptable because it does not force us to impose negative stimuli or events— we simply remove the student from positive ones. Also physical punishment (punishment 1) violates present-day ideas about good teacher behavior and makes the teacher a model of aggressiveness.

Time-out

Response cost—removal of particular reinforcers

- *Response cost* is another way to use punishment 2. Response cost is the contingent removal of particular reinforcers. The 15-yard penalty in a football game for roughing the passer is an example of a response cost. It removes, for an inappropriate behavior, some of the reinforcement previously attained, and is unlike punishment 1, which presents an aversive event for an inappropriate behavior. If the penalty for jaywalking was being sent to jail, we'd have an example of punishment 1—the giving of something of negative value. But if the penalty for jaywalking was a $5 fine, we would have an example of response cost—the removal or withdrawal of something of value already earned, a case of punishment 2.

  In school, if we take away tokens or the free time a student has already earned when the student misbehaves, we are using response cost to control unwanted behavior. For example, Rappaport, Murphy, and Bailey (1982) studied two boys who were being given methylphenidate (Ritalin) to control their hyperactivity. The researchers obtained both increased attention and increased rates of completion of academic tasks by taking away free time from the boys when they did not do their academic work. This response-cost procedure was far more effective than the drug in controlling hyperactivity.

Reasoning as an Alternative to Punishment.

What about reasoning? Can't we reason with a student who is misbehaving? The answer is yes. Always try rational explanations for behavior. Sometimes they work. But some writers hold that an analysis of reasoning techniques in the suppression of behavior shows that

> children respond to reasoning either to reduce anxiety or to not be punished. [A teacher] . . . who relied solely on reasoning as a disciplinary technique would not be very successful in obtaining response suppression. Reasoning becomes effective only when it is supported by a history of punishment. (Walters & Grusec, 1977, p. 207)

Reasoning and punishment

What do you do if reasoning and a given punishment don't work? What do you do if a student continues to misbehave? First, you should review the way you are using punishment. Is it immediate, inescapable, and of the right intensity? And are alternative behaviors available to the student—ones that offer a chance for reinforcement? Next, think about unintentional reinforcement. Is the punishment unintentionally satisfying the student's need for attention? If so, perhaps you should be ignoring, not punishing, the unwanted behavior. Is positive reinforcement coming from another source—possibly the attention of other students—outweighing the effect of the punishment?

If you find you are using or want to use punishment a lot, you should examine the total teaching-learning situation. What is causing the unwanted behavior? Is the work too difficult, lasting too long? Is it boring or irrelevant to the student's interests and needs? Are you meeting the student's need for activity? The frequent use of punishment is a symptom of something wrong in your approaches and methods or in the total school situation. The challenge for you as an educator is to discover and correct the problem, to reduce the need for punishment.

Ethical Issues

We know that people learn through operant conditioning. But is the process ethical? Some charge that conditioning techniques are manipulative and controlling. Others insist that it is the teacher's function to arrange and manipulate the environment to bring about learning.

For many kinds of learning, objections to the use of conditioning methods seem unjustified. When a child is cured through conditioning procedures of bed-wetting, excessive withdrawal, fighting in nursery school, or stuttering, hardly anyone objects that the child's behavior has been manipulated. When conditioning techniques are used to reduce a child's hyperactivity so that he stays in his seat longer and learns more, almost everyone would agree that the techniques are justified means toward a proper end. But when the techniques are misused—say, to reduce the normal activity levels of children because they make the teacher "nervous"—there is valid reason for complaint.

Justified uses of conditioning

The greatest objection to conditioning techniques comes when they are used to change attitudes, values, beliefs, and knowledge that should be based on rational, intellectual processes. The process by which a person becomes either liberal or conservative should stem from logic applied to correct information, not operant conditioning. We shudder at the thought of a person's political views being "shaped" by conditioning processes that the individual is not aware of and cannot control. Such processes smack of brainwashing. Unwanted behavior should not be taught by any method, conditioning or others. And even certain wanted behaviors should not be fostered through conditioning processes. Why? What criteria do we use to make decisions here?

One criterion is that whenever a behavior or attitude can in principle be learned through rational processes, these processes should be used. Certainly we can condition children to say "One of the angles in a right triangle equals ninety degrees" or "Democracy is the best system of government." But instead we should present information and instruction that leads children to understand the defining characteristics of right triangles and what democracy means. These teaching and learning processes, sometimes called *reflective thinking*, are based on the assumptions that human beings are rational and that it is immoral to treat them irrationally. The teacher must, if moral, engage a student's reason. A simple change in behavior is not enough for the teacher. The change must be brought about intentionally on the part of both teacher and student, and it must be based on rational processes. By this model, "the teacher's prime task is to ensure that when a change occurs in the beliefs or behavior of the students, it occurs for reasons which the student himself accepts" (Nuthall & Snook, 1973, p. 66). Teaching, then, is different from training and conditioning, which focus

Rational processes and operant conditioning

on performance, not belief and rational action. We do not want students to be patriotic, altruistic, and democratic because they've been conditioned to be so. We want them to arrive at these objectives by considering the issues and reflecting on their meaning.

Awareness and cooperation in conditioning

A second criterion for determining when the ends do not justify conditioning procedures is the degree to which students are aware of the procedures. To be ethical, conditioning must have student cooperation in and awareness of its use to change behavior. (In many instances, effective conditioning actually requires students' willing cooperation.) Of course we assume here that students are capable of understanding conditioning procedures. For young children or those who are mentally retarded, others must decide on the ethics of using conditioning methods.

Behavioral humanism

Behavioral and humanistic concerns can be merged (Thoresen, 1972). Operant techniques are being used to develop self-regulatory mechanisms in people whose freedom of choice has been limited by self-impairing behavior. Bad "habits" are being eliminated through conditioning procedures. Not only are individuals fully aware of these procedures, they are applying the procedures to themselves. For example, there are programs to develop self-assertiveness that use conditioning methods to help those who cannot change their behavior by purely rational processes or by the exercise of willpower.

A third criterion for some is that conditioning methods should rely on intrinsic rewards and incentives. Rewards are *intrinsic* when they arise in a way that is naturally a part of the learning activity itself. If a student gets the right answer to an arithmetic problem, the intrinsic reward is a feeling of satisfaction at having applied the principles of arithmetic correctly. Many educators argue that intrinsic rewards are better than extrinsic rewards (praise, gold stars, money, high grades) and that extrinsic rewards debase learning. But most proponents of conditioning believe that intrinsic rewards are often inaccessible to students in the early stages of the learning process. Intrinsic rewards do not occur simply because, in many situations, learners cannot make the appropriate response. Should these students go unreinforced? Or should we give them an extrinsic reinforcer that will induce them to continue responding, thereby changing their responses in the wanted ways? The answer here depends on what works. Certainly we should not insist on intrinsic reinforcement to the point where students experience prolonged frustration and failure. If intrinsic reinforcers work, fine. If not, use extrinsic rewards.

Reinforcement ≠ bribery

Some educators charge that the use of positive extrinsic reinforcers is a form of bribery. But bribery means using rewards to get a person to do something dishonest or unfair. When positive extrinsic reinforcement is used to promote honest and wanted behavior, with the student's awareness and cooperation, it cannot be considered bribery. We also think that most teachers probably would not teach if they were not paid. Should we expect higher levels of behavior from students?

Reinforcement and independence

Another objection to operant conditioning is that it makes students dependent on others and thus subverts their independence. But students can learn to

● *Rewards are intrinsic when they arise in a way that is naturally a part of the learning activity itself. (© Jean-Claude Lejeune)*

reinforce themselves, to become independent of an external agent. Also they can be weaned away from dependence on reinforcers of any given kind (for example, approval by the teacher) by having reinforcers of some kind (approval by their peers) substituted. Finally, students can learn to respond on a very low ratio of reinforcers to responses.

In short, although the issues are complex and not all educators and psychologists agree, we believe that conditioning procedures can be used ethically in educational settings. These procedures offer teachers effective and humane methods for changing student behavior in desirable ways.

Limits of the Theory. The operant conditioning model of learning focuses on how the environment affects emitted behavior. It is concerned with increasing, eliminating, shaping, and improving behavior. It assumes that no learning takes place without reinforcement or punishment.

But can that be true? Don't people learn how to act in a restaurant, airport, hockey game, or wedding without first emitting behavior and then getting reinforced or punished? Didn't you learn to drive a car by watching other people more than by having your behavior "shaped"? How do operant conditioning theorists explain such facts? They try, but we think their explanations are inadequate.

Another theory has been put forth to account for observational learning and other aspects of learning in social settings. Much of what we master comes to us through interacting with other people, whom we simply observe. So we need to think more about how that kind of learning takes place and what it means for education. We turn to those matters now.

Observational Learning

It would be sad if we could not learn from observing others in our social world. We would spend much more time and make many more mistakes in our attempts to acquire the knowledge, skills, and attitudes of our culture. But fortunately we learn approximately correct responses from our friends, parents, and teachers by observing both their behavior and the consequences of their behavior.

When you received your first baseball bat, you probably held it by the correct end, stood in a reasonably correct way, and swung the way baseball players do. When you first learned to drive a car, most likely you knew where and how to sit and, by observing your instructor, what you had to do to start the car and drive. If you ever go to a formal dinner, replete with extra spoons, forks, and glasses, you will probably wait until some brave or knowledgeable person begins to eat and use that person's behavior to guide your own. These are examples of how we depend on observational learning. *Behavior models*—baseball players, drivers, people with social graces—guide our behavior. And because our observations change our behavior, we learn through them.

Behavior models

In a single study, Bandura (1969) illustrated the impact of and conditions for observational learning. He assigned nursery school children to one of five treatments. In treatment 1, children watched a human adult model who physically and verbally attacked a life-size inflated soft plastic doll. In treatment 2, children saw a film of the same event. In treatment 3, they saw a cartoon character carrying out the same aggressive actions. The children in treatment 4—the control group—had none of these experiences. Those in treatment 5 saw a human model of subdued temperament, one who was inhibited and nonaggressive. After exposure to the treatment, each child was placed in a situation similar to the one in which the model performed. Observers watched through one-way windows and for a short period of time counted each child's aggressive verbal and physical acts. Figure 6.8 shows the mean number of aggressive responses exhibited by the children in the various treatments. All groups that saw an aggressive model made more aggressive responses than did the control group. The group that saw the inhibited, nonaggressive model made fewer aggressive responses than did the control group. Clearly, watching the model affected behavior.

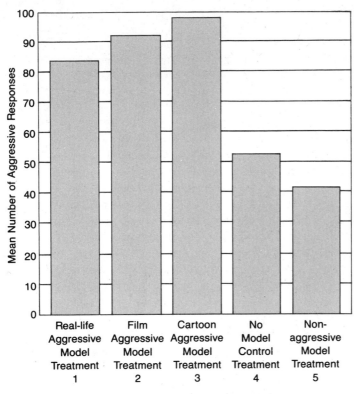

Source: A. Bandura, "The Role of Imitation in Personality Development," reprinted by permission from *Journal of Nursery Education*, vol. 18, no. 3 (April 1963): pp. 207–215. Copyright © 1963, National Association for the Education of Young Children, 1834 Connecticut Ave., N. W., Washington, D.C. 20009.

We know that exposure to a model can affect a person's behavior in at least three ways: (1) learning new behavior, (2) facilitating already learned behavior, and (3) inhibiting or disinhibiting already learned behavior.

1. An observer can learn new behavior from a model. In the Bandura study, the children often said things like "Pow" or "Sock 'em," repeating verbatim the aggressive model's unusual language.

   Models teach new behavior

2. A model can also facilitate the learner's response repertoire. When the model's behavior resembles behavior the learner has previously mastered, the model's performance may simply elicit a previously learned response. For example, the aggressive responses of the control group (treatment 4), when confronted with a large, air-filled, plastic doll that seems to beg to be pushed and pounded, appear, as shown in Figure 6.8, to be well established and of high frequency. The higher frequency of aggressive responses

   Models facilitate behavior

by children in treatments 1, 2, and 3 shows that a model, in addition to teaching new behaviors, can elicit behavior that the learners already have but would not demonstrate or perform as frequently.

Models inhibit and disinhibit behavior

3. Exposure to a model can inhibit or disinhibit an observer's responses. To *inhibit* is to restrain a response or make it less frequent; to *disinhibit* is to free from restraint and thus allow a response to occur. A comparison of the treatment 5 group with the control group in Figure 6.8 shows that models can inhibit responses. The mean number of aggressive responses of the children in treatment 5 is below the mean of the control group, which is our estimate of the baseline or operant level of aggressive responding in this environment. So observing an inhibited model can inhibit responses that the observer is known to possess. In treatments 1, 2, and 3, children watched aggressive behavior that had no unpleasant consequence. The increased frequency of aggressive responses demonstrated by these children (in comparison to the control group) was due, at least in part, to *disinhibition*. Here the absence of any constraints apparently removed inhibitions. Well-established aggressive behaviors are partially held in check by the many constraints imposed by the environment. A particularly forceful constraint on aggressive behavior is the consequence of that behavior when parents or teachers are present. Usually parents and teachers act to extinguish this kind of behavior. When these constraints are absent, as appeared to be the case in the situation where the model was not punished for his activities, the inhibitions against aggressive behavior are removed. Inhibitory and disinhibitory effects are most pronounced when an observer sees the consequences of a model's actions. The model's punishment or reinforcement for the behavior greatly affects the observer's own activities.

Consequences of model's behavior

No-trial learning

One interesting aspect of observational learning is that it is no-trial learning. A response does not have to be made by the learner as is necessary in respondent and operant forms of learning. The most likely mechanism by which people acquire behavior through observation is the immediate association of the model's behavior with a cognitive event, say, a sensory event (a visual coding of model, doll, and hitting behavior, for example), or with a symbolic response (a verbal coding of the propositions "doll = hitting behavior = okay to do"). The observer records and stores the sensory event or symbolic response at the time of the model's performance. These sensory events or responses serve as cues for later performance, when the learner is called on to make an overt response.

Sensory and symbolic cognitions

Vicarious reward or punishment

Reward or punishment of behavior can be vicarious (by mentally substituting oneself for another), by watching the consequences of the model's performance, or the result of the observer's own actions. In either case, reward and punish-

● *Models can teach new behavior, facilitate behavior that is already learned, and inhibit or disinhibit behavior. (© 1983 Peter Menzel)*

ment markedly affect the *performance* of behavior; they do not seem to affect the *acquisition* of behavior. Complex behavior repertoires can be acquired by simply observing another person. The learner need only pay attention to the model's activities—and the model must be credible—but beyond these variables, no others need to be offered to account for observational learning.

Studies of observational learning demonstrate that people often learn to do what they see others doing. So we must deal with social situations when we try to understand observational learning. Moreover, this kind of learning is powerful. So we need to provide children with models of wanted behavior and to reduce their exposure to models of unwanted behavior. One source of the latter appears to be television. Students in recent years have been exposed to many more aggressive and violent models than they were a few decades ago. We look at how this exposure is affecting students' behavior later in this chapter. Now, however, let us see how observational learning in social situations goes on.

Performance vs. acquisition of behavior

A Social Learning Analysis of Observational Learning

How is observational learning—this basic and pervasive form of learning—viewed from a social learning perspective? The theory states that there are four phases of learning from models: an attentional phase, a retention phase, a reproduction phase, and a motivational phase (Figure 6.9).

Attentional Phase

Teachers = high-status models

Without attention, there can be no learning. Obviously, then, attention is a necessary condition of observational learning in social settings. Research shows that we pay attention to models with high status, high competence, and expertise—attributes that teachers are often thought to have (thank goodness!). Consequently, students are likely to pay attention when a teacher solves a two-column addition problem, decodes a word phonetically, demonstrates a field hockey pass, lists the steps required to identify a wildflower, or dissects a frog. A good deal of what students learn in school they learn by watching their teachers.

Incentives for attending

Students' own characteristics—their dependency needs, their self-esteem, and their perceptions of their own competence—determine to some extent the likelihood of their paying attention to a model. But often overriding the model's attributes and the students' characteristics as determiners of attending are the incentives for attending (Bandura, 1969). Teachers control rewards and punishments for attending or nonattending. When a teacher says, "This will be on the test," and proceeds to demonstrate how to convert Fahrenheit to Celsius and vice versa, the teacher is manipulating the incentives for attention. By making the incentives obvious, we can override other factors that might lessen attending.

Distinctive cues

Repetition

Finally, the distinctiveness, rate, and complexity of the stimuli to be attended to affect whether or not attentiveness can be maintained. Teachers who have their students' attention can make the imitation easier by seeing to it that the important cues in the learning situation are clear. (For example, "Now notice how I am changing the sign, and taking the numerator and denominator of this fraction and reversing them.") The models' identification of important aspects of the instructional situation can greatly facilitate imitative learning. So can repetition. This kind of facilitation is especially important when working with very young children or with retarded or learning disabled students, who have a limited capacity for attention.

Retention Phase

Contiguity

Observational learning takes place by contiguity. The two contiguous events that are necessary are attention to the model's performance and the representation of that performance in the learner's memory. Verbal or visual mnemonics

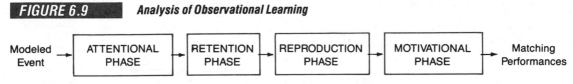

FIGURE 6.9   *Analysis of Observational Learning*

Source: Adapted from Albert Bandura, *Social Learning Theory*. © 1977. Used by permission of
Prentice-Hall, Inc., Englewood Cliffs, New Jersey.

(memory aids) and schemata (the mental structures that allow people to learn)
for dismantling an engine in automobile shop, for doing long division, or for giving
an oral report must be developed by the observer at the same time that the
observer watches how a model takes apart an engine, divides polynomials, or
gives a classroom talk. These mnemonics and schemata are recalled at a later
time, when newly learned behavior is enacted.

    We retain material to be learned better when we rehearse it overtly ("All **Rehearsal**
together now, the four phases of observational learning are _____,
_____, _____, and _____"). But rehearsal need not
always be overt. For example, student teachers preparing their first lesson or
lesson segment often use covert rehearsal to practice what they've learned
through observation.

Reproduction Phase

In this phase of learning from models, the verbal or visual codes in memory guide
the actual performance of the newly acquired behavior. It has been found that
observational learning is most accurate when overt enactment follows mental **Overt enactment**
rehearsal. We can see the advantage of enacting a newly learned behavior in a
study with Papago Indian children (Swanson & Henderson, 1977). The Papago
typically ask few questions in their interactions with Anglos. Their culturally
preferred way to obtain information and acquire skill is through observation and
imitation, not direct questioning. Papago children, then, suffer a handicap in
school, where their Anglo peers do use questions to get information.

    Preschool Papago children were pretested on their question-asking ability.
They were shown pictures and requested to ask as many questions about the
scene as they could. The children were then assigned to one of three experimental conditions. One group was exposed only to television models. In one of
many sequences viewed, a Papago woman and puppets depicting Papago children named Laura and Norbert were shown asking questions and being praised
for doing so. A series of similar tapes were administered twice.

    Children in a second group also saw the series of tapes. But instead of a
second viewing, they were given practice in and praise for asking questions. The
third group was the control group. These children saw television tapes that had
nothing to do with asking questions.

    The results (see Table 6.1) showed that on the pretest all three groups were
about equal, scoring quite low in question-asking behavior. At posttest, and on

TABLE 6.1

Effects of Modeling and Modeling with Practice on the Acquisition of Questioning Behavior

Treatment Group	Pretest Mean	Posttest Mean	Retention Test Mean
Model and practice	1.76	82.70	93.70
Model only	3.13	29.73	19.40
Control	2.00	2.00	2.50

Source: Adapted from R. A. Swanson and R. W. Henderson, "Effects of Televised Modeling and Active Participation on Rule-Governed Question Production Among Native American Preschool Children," *Contemporary Educational Psychology*, 2:345–352. Copyright 1977. Used by permission.

a delayed retention test given about two weeks later, differences among the groups were obvious. The data from the model-only group, in comparison to the control group, show how observing models can lead to the acquisition of new behavior. That effect, however, was markedly heightened when enactment and feedback were also part of the learning program. The posttest and delayed retention test scores of the children who learned question asking through modeling and practice are clearly superior. A reproduction phase is necessary.

Similarly, a study by Schunk (1981), in which long division was taught to children who had difficulties in learning mathematics, illustrates this point. Modeling was used during instruction and again during the reproduction phase if students made any errors. Compared with a group that had no exposure to models during instruction, the students who learned from models showed greatly improved achievement. They also showed increased persistence and self-confidence when tackling long-division problems.

Corrective feedback

Note here the importance of corrective feedback for shaping wanted behavior. Operant conditioning is greatly concerned with reinforcement and punishment, whose powerful effects on behavior we have already described. But many of the statements made by teachers to students about their classroom performance seem to be neither reinforcing nor punishing—just informative. Knowledge of results, simple feedback, has a strong effect on subsequent behavior. Letting learners know quickly about their inappropriate responses—before they develop bad habits—is sound instructional practice. This kind of corrective feedback is not punishment. It is crucial in the development of skilled performance. When we tell students to hold their pencils tighter when they write, to remember to count the number of lines in their sonnets, or to spring higher off the board when they dive, we are giving them information that helps them learn the skills they must master.

Motivational Phase

The Distinction Between Performance and Learning.   Behavior acquired by observing others is enacted if it is reinforcing to do so. If it is punishing to perform the behavior, it will not usually be forthcoming. In this sense social

• *Overt enactment—matching the model—is most important when body-position cues must be learned.* (© Paul Conklin)

learning theory and operant conditioning are alike. Both recognize how reinforcement and punishment can shape and maintain behavior. But in observational learning, reinforcement and punishment are seen as affecting the learner's *motivation* to perform; they do not account for *learning* itself. Moreover, the social learning view recognizes the importance of covert cognitive activity, not just overt behavior. So the social learning theorist believes that vicarious reinforcement and punishment—observing the consequences of the behavior of others—can also shape and maintain behavior. When an older sibling is praised for receiving a good report card or sent away from the dinner table for using a vulgar word, youngsters are often affected as much as if they were the one being reinforced or punished.

Bandura's experiments showed that learning can occur without any overt responding by the learner. Observing and coding behavior in memory are sufficient to ensure its being learned. The learner's overt performance of what has been learned may occur only when the appropriate environment is encountered by the learner. In social learning theory, the positive or negative consequences of behavior, then, are *motivators* of performance. They are *not* determiners of learning, as was claimed by the adherents of operant conditioning theory.

Reinforcement and punishment as motivators

Learning without overt responses

One other pair of factors enters into the motivation to perform activities learned from models. That pair consists of self-reinforcement and self-punishment. As we behave, we judge ourselves. In this way we come to regulate our own behavior—something we talk more about later in this chapter.

A Note on Television Viewing.   Intuitive understanding of the distinction between performance and learning, and the effects of vicarious reinforcement and punishment, has led many parents and teachers to worry about violence on television and in the movies. Concern about violence began in the earliest days of television. But, as a government report concluded:

> The violence on television that began in the 1950s has continued. There have been a few changes and fluctuations, but, in general, television, despite the concerns of Congressmen and citizens' groups, remains a violent form of entertainment. (*Television and Behavior,* 1982, p. 37)

Estimates indicate that violence occurs in Saturday morning cartoons about *twenty to thirty-five times an hour* (National Coalition on Television Violence, 1981).

Violent models

Children learn by observing, and if violent models are shown receiving no punishment or receiving some form of reinforcement for their behavior, some children may learn dangerous things. These socially undesirable behaviors could be enacted in the future. A case in point is the highly acclaimed movie *The Deerhunter,* which has played in theaters and on television. A scene in the movie shows a character playing Russian roulette. There is confirmed evidence that at least twenty-two people who saw the movie shot themselves while "playing" Russian roulette (National Coalition on Television Violence, 1981). Although the interpretation of the data continues to be argued, the relationship revealed is clear: The evidence accumulated in the 1970s seems overwhelming that viewing televised violence and committing aggressive acts are positively correlated in children (*Television and Behavior,* 1982). To explain this clear positive correlation, researchers have suggested, among other processes, observational learning. The social learning perspective makes it sensible to keep children away from certain films or television programs and to insist that film and television producers end their stories with the villain paying for the crime. Keep in mind that from kindergarten through the twelfth grade, the typical student will spend

Twelve thousand TV hours

about twelve thousand hours in front of a television set. The medium is "teaching," and the viewer is "learning."

A Note on Cognition

Social learning is affected by the learner's conceptions of the learning event. Learners need sensible reasons to build clear conceptions about what they are doing and why. Modeling is not effective if the observer's beliefs, attitudes, sense of efficacy, and sense of purpose are not congruent with the learning task. In both operant conditioning and social learning theory, the mechanisms by which we learn are not beyond cognitive control. We exert personal control through reflective self-consciousness. Change in behavior of any lasting kind always means a change in cognition has taken place. Students think about what they do and what we want them to do, and those thoughts affect what the students do. The idea that the processes of operant conditioning and social learning are mechanical is erroneous. Thoughts are always influencing actions, and actions are always influencing thoughts (Bandura, 1986a; 1986b).

Change in behavior = change in cognition

The Teacher and Modeling

A primary definition of *teaching* is "to show." So we should think about how to show, demonstrate, or model so that we optimize conditions for our students' learning. We often worry more about what we teach than how we teach. But by using information about observational learning, you can do a better job of teaching skills. In a study in which social learning theory was used to teach teachers how to teach (Zimmerman & Kleefeld, 1977), the researchers studied ways of teaching young children to order objects from longest to shortest. One group of teachers read about the instructional task, examined the materials to be used for instruction, and saw a sample of the test items to be used to evaluate how well the children had learned. A second group received the same background information as the first plus simple instructions on how to model when teaching: See that the child is attending; describe each action as you do it; teach memory aids to help learners code activity (for example, "See if they go down like stairs"); use the same procedure each time you order a scrambled array of objects; have the child judge his or her performance; and so on.

Learning how to model

The children were divided into three groups. Group 1 was taught individually by the first group of teachers and group 2 by the second group of teachers. The third group of children, not taught at all, served as the control group. All children were pretested and posttested on two types of items: judgment items (Is this group of objects in order from longest to shortest?) and ordering items (Can you put these objects in order from the longest to the shortest?). The results showed clearly that teachers who do not know much about how we learn from models do not produce much learning in the children they teach. The students of the untrained teachers showed less learning in judgment items and only slightly better learning in ordering items than did the children who received no instruction at all. The teachers trained in modeling, however, had a great effect on student learning on both judgment and ordering items.

From teachers' helping other students, classmates can learn attitudes toward those students. Indeed, the teacher's help can make classmates think less of the students being helped. This effect of the teacher's helping showed up in an experiment by Graham and Barker (1990). They showed videotapes of two boys working on math problems: One boy was helped by his teacher or classmates; the other was not. The viewers subsequently rated the helped boy as lower in ability than the nonhelped boy. The teacher's help may thus tell classmates that the helped pupil is low in ability. Similarly, when a child fails on a task, sympathy can tell the child that the teacher regards the child as having low ability, whereas anger can indicate that the child should try harder.

The same kinds of learning from observation can take place when pupils observe how their fellow pupils behave toward pupils. In the kind of cooperative learning we discuss in Chapter 9, pupils help one another. And being helped makes pupils be perceived by other pupils and by themselves as having lower ability. These "side effects" of well-intentioned behaviors of the teacher or classmates—praise, minimal criticism, helping, and sympathizing—are effects that teachers should be aware of.

Self-Regulation of Behavior

Self-chastisement and self-reinforcement

Some of the things we do in life are not very important to us. So they don't usually lead to much self-reinforcement or self-punishment. But if the things we do really matter to us, we tend to engage in some kind of self-appraisal. For example, if we are diet conscious or concerned about the food we eat, we might evaluate our activities and chastise ourselves for going to a fast-food outlet. This self-punishment or self-reinforcement, like direct or vicariously experienced punishment and reinforcement, affects our performance. By means of our cognitive activity and the management of our own environment, we can motivate ourselves through self-generated reward and punishment. In this way we can regulate our own behavior.

The Processes in Self-Regulation

Three processes in self-regulation

Bandura (1978) provided a simplified conception of the process of self-regulation. This conception sets up three covert processes in learning to regulate our own behavior. These processes can be thought of as a subset of the motivational phase of observational learning shown in Figure 6.9. First, we observe our own performance. We examine our behavior in terms of its quantity, quality, originality, rate, and so on. Second, we judge our performance. We evaluate how well we did against our personal standards. Third, we determine the consequences for ourselves. On the basis of our judgments of our own behavior, we might generate self-satisfaction (personal pride) or self-dissatisfaction (self-criticism).

Record keeping

Observing One's Own Performance.   If a teacher wants to regulate the amount of lecturing he does, if a student wants to regulate the amount of time she spends off-task, or if your Aunt Mary wants to regulate how many pieces of candy she eats each day, the first step is observing the responses of interest. We make this observation by timing or counting the responses. Good record keeping, using graphs or schedules, is necessary to monitor our behavior (or to teach others to monitor their behavior). Many studies have shown that just knowing about our own behavior can result in behavioral change (R. D. Nelson, 1977; M. S. Rosenbaum & Drabman, 1979). In one experiment with eighth-graders, the study behavior of one student and the disruptive behavior of another were modified by having them monitor their own behavior (Broden, Hall, & Mitts, 1971). Similarly, the novelists Trollope, Hemingway, and Irving

Wallace each reported using daily logs when they were writing, in order to monitor the number of words or pages they produced each day (Wallace & Pear, 1977). Such self-observation leads to self-evaluation and self-determined reinforcement: The students did increase study behavior and decrease disruptive behavior as a result of their record keeping, and the novelists finished their novels more or less on schedule.

Judging Performance.

Where do we get the standards against which we judge our performance? Sometimes they appear to be self-generated, as when a painter, writer, or teacher works over and over to get a painting, chapter, or lesson right. But social learning theory points out that many of the standards we have for performance are learned, like so much else, from models in our social world. For example, how long we may be willing to work on tasks that are hard to solve is influenced by models, as shown by Zimmerman and Ringle (1981). Children in their study watched models who tried to solve a problem and failed. The models, however, showed either high or low persistence at the problem and talked aloud, making either highly optimistic or highly pessimistic comments about their problem-solving behavior. The lowest levels of persistence were found in students exposed to models who themselves showed low persistence and who were pessimistic about their chances for success.

> **Self-generated standards**
>
> **Standards learned from models**

A note of caution is in order here. High personal standards are a good thing, but standards that are too high are harmful. "Austere systems of self-reinforcement (usually owing to unrealistically high standards) may be causally linked to depression, feelings of despair, aimlessness, self-injury, or suicide" (Karoly, 1977). People who aspire too high and constantly disparage their own accomplishments live in a state of anxiety and depression. We have all come across students who have received a 99 on a test and were crushed that they didn't get 100. These students need as much help in setting realistic performance standards as do students who are happy with a barely passing grade.

> **Unrealistically high standards**

Determining Consequences for Ourselves

People who reward their own behavior achieve significantly higher levels of performance than those who perform the same activities under instruction but receive no reinforcement, are rewarded noncontingently, or monitor their own behavior and set goals for themselves but do not reward their attainments (Bandura, 1978, p. 351).

People who punish themselves, particularly for behavior that they do not want to engage in (stuttering, obsessive thoughts) or for behavior that will be punished by others (cheating, stealing), can also modify their behavior. You can reward or punish yourself cognitively, consciously saying, "I really aced that exam" or "I sure acted stupidly." And you can reward or punish yourself by arranging your own environment—going to a movie after you study hard or skipping a meal after you cheat on a diet. One well-known writer described his self-reinforcement system like this: "I pour a drink of scotch every morning,

> **Self-reinforcement and self-punishment**

put it on the table in front of me, and drink it only after 10 handwritten pages are finished." The classroom version of this technique would be to give students access to reinforcers (free time, candy, games, comics) when they are satisfied that they have met some behavioral goal. Self-reinforcement turns out to be one of the most powerful agents in learning self-control (S. G. O'Leary & Dubey, 1979).

The Teacher and Self-Regulation

Using self-regulation in teaching

Not all programs for teaching self-regulation show effects, and not all programs that do work show that change is maintained over time and in different environments. But the work is promising. We saw the process in action recently, when we visited a teacher who was having difficulty working with a student he disliked. First we asked the teacher to monitor the frequency and types of contact he had with the child. Then we asked him to evaluate the data he had collected. After acknowledging that he was avoiding the child, interacting with him only when he was fighting or talking or otherwise misbehaving, the teacher agreed to try to catch the student doing something right. He began to reinforce the child for cooperating, for doing assignments in his workbook, and for not talking. And the teacher patted himself on the back whenever he did this. He had lunch with the student one day, and reinforced himself for spending time with the student. The student's behavior changed somewhat for the better. The teacher's attitude and behavior also changed. The teacher no longer harassed the student. He also found that he didn't dislike the student as much. In a short time the teacher had regulated his own behavior and had begun to treat the student more fairly.

Guidelines for teaching self-regulation

The following guidelines emerge for teaching students self-regulation:

1. Be sure students are monitoring themselves *accurately*. At first have them compare their records with your own or those of an outside observer.
2. Establish contingencies for behavior changes.
3. Eventually transfer control of the contingencies to the students.
4. When self-determined contingencies begin to operate, teach students some verbal instructions and praise statements to use in guiding their behavior.
5. When students are controlling their own behavior, withdraw extrinsic contingencies (see Rosenbaum & Drabman, 1979).

Mentoring

Most of our examples of social learning thus far have involved relatively brief observations of others, such as the teacher and classmates, and of oneself. What about learning from many such observations of another person, continuing over a period of months or years? Social learning in such situations may constitute learning from a mentor—a wise and trusted senior person. Student teaching experiences in teacher education programs serve as learning experiences featuring a mentor-protégé relationship. Many writers have urged that beginning teachers be paired with experienced teachers who will serve as mentors. Mentoring can take place in any field—baseball rookies with veterans, graduate students with professors, budding actors with stars, or in general, mentors and protégés.

Not every superior-subordinate relationship is a mentoring one. First, in mentoring, the relationship is two-way, in that the mentor as well as the protégé benefits from it. Second, mentoring goes on in relation to some kind of work, that is, in a work environment. Third, mentoring promotes advancement in the mentor as well as the protégé. Not just skills but ways of perceiving, thinking, feeling, and acting are changed in both. The mentor sees her ideas of what is important become adopted by the protégé, and the protégé inevitably modifies those ideas in a way from which the mentor also benefits. Finally, a mentoring relationship goes through stages. It has a beginning, in which the two persons are getting acquainted, feeling each other out, making silent judgments about the promise of the relationship. In its middle stage, the relationship is in full swing, with the protégé learning from the behavior, suggestions, and evaluations of the mentor—repeatedly going through the sequence of four steps in observation learning that we have described—while the mentor is benefiting from seeing how her behavior is imitated, her suggestions prove fruitful, and her evaluations are validated. Finally, the mentoring relationship declines and ends, as the protégé breaks away from the mentor, strikes out on her own, becomes a mature professional, and perhaps begins to serve as a mentor for a next-generation protégé.

Stages of mentoring

Mentoring at the highest level of scientific achievement—that of Nobel Prize winners—can be seen in descriptions of the many instances in which both the mentor and his protégé have won this honor. Zuckerman (1977) in her *Scientific Elite* described many mentor-protégé (or master-apprentice) pairs. "More than half (forty-eight) of the ninety-two laureates who did their prize-winning research in the United States by 1972 had worked either as students, postdoctorates, or junior collaborators under older Nobel laureates" (p. 100). Fifteen of these forty-eight had had two or more laureates as mentors. And ten Nobel mentors had produced thirty laureates. Clearly it helps to have a Nobel mentor, and Nobel mentors clearly produce more than their share of Nobel protégés.

This Nobel "inbreeding" results from the two-way mentoring process. The mentors seek out and select extremely promising protégés, and the protégés seek out and apprentice themselves to extremely productive, stimulating, demanding, rigorous, and exciting mentors. In at least one case, a protégé moved away from an already-Nobel possible mentor and into the fold of a more exciting mentor (who won a Nobel *after* his protégé had been so honored). Unlike biological heredity, as Zuckerman pointed out (p. 104), mentoring heredity allows "children" to choose their "parents," and part of the success of the "children" results from their wisdom in choosing their "parents."

"Children" choose their "parents"

The Nobel inbreeding might have resulted from political forces, as when Nobel laureates nominate their own students for the prize. But Zuckerman shows that such factors played only a minor role, if any. Sixty-nine percent of the Nobel apprentices had mentors who won the prize only after the master-apprentice relationship had ended. Both sides of the relationship know what is important, where to find it, and how to nourish it. The Nobel-winning protégés were not mere passive recipients of good fortune; they were "tuned in" to promising lines of work and they actually sought out mentors who could help them in these lines.

At less exalted levels of mentoring, the same processes operate. Once the mentor-protégé pair have come together, they engage in the social-learning-from-observation processes we have already described. It is not the substantive knowledge that is so important in what is learned. Rather it is "a method of work that really got things done," "a style of qualitatively distinctive thought," "a wider orientation that included standards of work and modes of thought" (pp. 122, 123). In a word, the protégé in mentoring acquires "socialization": norms, standards, values, and attitudes, as well as the knowledge, skills, and behavior appropriate to a given role, whether it is that of student, adolescent, plumber, mother, teacher, mechanic, ballet dancer, or scientist.

Socialization

How do the mentors foster such learning? (1) By their own example of how good work is done, that is, by providing a model of what is desirable; (2) by expecting such work from the protégé; and (3) by evaluating the work of others according to their (the mentors') standards. Zuckerman quotes a physicist talking about his teacher: "You tried to live up to him. It was wonderful to watch him at work. Sometimes I eventually did things the way he did" (p. 125).

When coaching the girls' basketball team, giving students extra help in mathematics during lunch period, or helping children prepare for a school play, you enter into personal relationships with students, and you inevitably take on a mentoring role. Your students learn from your habits of mind, your ways of solving problems, your standards of performance. You will enjoy being a mentor, but you need to be aware of what you are doing as mentor and let your students influence you as well. Both mentoring and teaching are enhanced when influence goes both ways.

Two-way influence

SUMMARY

There are three behavioral theories of learning. Each of these theories applies to some learning tasks but not to others. With *respondent conditioning,* a neutral stimulus is paired with an unconditioned stimulus and in time can elicit the unconditioned response. *Contiguity learning,* the kind of learning that goes on with drill instruction, rests on the simple pairing of events. The broadest theory to come out of the branch of psychology called behaviorism is *operant conditioning*—learning as a result of reinforcement. Here behavior is initially spontaneous. But with reinforcement we can strengthen and shape (modify) that behavior.

There are two major kinds of reinforcement. If we give something of positive value (success, praise, a good grade) after a response (behavior) is made, we are using positive reinforcement. If we take away something of negative value (failure, nagging, a threatening situation), we are using negative reinforcement.

Choosing a reinforcer is one critical part of the process. Another is choosing a schedule of reinforcement; the schedule affects both the rate of responding and the strength of the response after reinforcement ends.

In contingency management, reinforcement is made to depend on a certain response. If that response takes place, we given reinforcement; if it does not, we withhold reinforcement. Premack's suggestion that behaviors with higher probabilities of occurrence can be used to reinforce behaviors with lower probabilities of occurrence, coupled with the concept of contingency management, can guide us in making contingency contracts with students.

We also need to do something about unwanted responses, such as student misbehavior. Extinction is the process of weakening a response by non-reinforcement. The speed with which we can extinguish a response depends in good measure on whether reinforcement has been continuous or intermittent. It is much more difficult to extinguish a response that has been only intermittently reinforced than one that has been continuously reinforced.

There are several other ways to eliminate an unwanted behavior: reinforce other behaviors that are incompatible with the unwanted behavior; reinforce reductions in frequency of the unwanted behavior; or use punishment. Punishment 1 is giving something of negative value (a critical comment, a bad grade) after the response is made. To be most effective, this kind of punishment must come immediately after the response, must be inescapable, must be as intense as necessary, and must be used only when an alternative response is available to the student. Punishment 2, generally more acceptable in schools, takes away something of positive value (free time, tokens) after the response is made. Using punishment requires a special vigilance on the part of the teacher. It's very important that we do not satisfy a student's need for attention when we punish, a kind of unintentional reinforcement of the unwanted behavior. And the overuse of punishment is a symptom that something is wrong with the educational environment.

Turning now to social learning, we emphasize that we learn much by watching those around us. Behavior models help us learn new behaviors, and they can facilitate, inhibit, and disinhibit behaviors we have already learned.

Social learning theory identifies four phases of observational learning: attention, retention, reproduction, and motivation. Attention is a necessary condition of observational learning. In the retention phase, students use verbal or visual codes to help them remember what they have learned through observation. Rehearsal—both overt and covert—also helps here.

In the reproduction phase, verbal and visual codes guide the performance of the newly learned behavior. This phase is especially important where body-position cues are needed to master behavior. It also allows the teacher/model to identify and correct problems. Corrective feedback has a strong impact on performance, particularly early in the reproduction phase.

Students may pay attention to a modeled behavior, try to remember it, even practice it, and still not perform it. The motivation phase focuses on the reinforcement that encourages students to enact a behavior, and on the punishment that discourages them from performing. Effective here are actual and vicarious reinforcement and punishment, and self-regulation. Notice that social learning theory distinguishes between learning and performance.

Our cognitive responses to our own behavior allow us to regulate that behavior. By observing, we collect data about our responses. With our personal standards, often learned through observation, we judge our behavior. And by rewarding or punishing ourselves, we can effectively control our behavior. We need not be controlled by environmental forces or inner urges. Instead we can learn to become self-directed social beings. Helping our students learn the self-regulation process is a critical part of teaching.

Mentoring is a two-way relationship between an experienced model of excellent performance and a relative newcomer to the field of practice—a relationship in which much social learning takes place. During the course of the mentor-protégé relationship, socialization into the perceptions, beliefs, values, and actions of the profession, or other kind of work, results.

Memory, Cognitive Processing, and the Transfer of Learning

OVERVIEW

In this chapter we examine a particular kind of learning, cognitive learning, especially from meaningful verbal or mathematical material. Operant conditioning is concerned with overt behavior; it is not useful when we try to understand how we manipulate verbal material cognitively. Social learning theory, although it clearly is concerned with cognitive processes, does not focus on how we learn, use, and remember the verbal and mathematical symbol systems we depend on for communication. Because teachers spend so much of their time with facts, concepts, principles, and cognitive skills that are important in our culture, they should understand the ways in which meaningful information is learned and processed.

Research on cognitive learning typically has not been aimed at explaining all learning through a single integrated theory. Instead it has focused on describing and understanding the cognitive processes of learners primarily as they engage in meaningful verbal learning. To study *cognition* we need to study attention, memory, rehearsal, forgetting, retrieval, and a host of other mental processes. We are concerned with how attention and memory work because we want what we teach to be attended to and remembered. In this chapter we ask many questions. Are stimuli that elicit emotions or provoke mental imagery remembered better than other kinds of stimuli? Does anything ever get lost from memory once it is stored there? Are there ways to improve memory? What about the order of the material we present—does the way we arrange material affect retention? As cognitive psychologists learn more and more about the way the mind works, we can often learn better ways to teach. Our instruction becomes compatible with the ways in which knowledge is organized and processed.

Regardless of whether we use operant conditioning, social learning theory, or cognitive and information-processing approaches in our teaching, we share a single goal: to have our students show evidence of learning in new situations— those not quite the same as the situation in which they originally learned. That is, we want our students to transfer learning. If what is learned in school is not generalizable to situations outside of school, of what value is it? Thus transfer must be a central concern of teachers.

The Information-Processing Approach

A model of memory

Between a stimulus and a response, there are elaborate mental processes. We use the information-processing model of memory, shown in Figure 7.1, to help us think about how we think, how we process information cognitively. That model differentiates between the external world and internal cognitive events (the area inside the broken line).

Information processing often begins with the stimulus—with input from the external environment—for example, light, heat, pressure, or sound. In order for the stimulus to work its way through the information-processing system, it must first elicit an orienting response (OR), a response that focuses our attention on the stimulus. This begins the internal mental process.

Brief sensory storage

The stimulus or information from the environment is stored briefly—maybe for less than half a second—in our short-term sensory storage (STSS). The capacity of the STSS system is probably unlimited, and it may include a separate "store" for each sense. Our attention determines what happens next. This is a particularly important point in the process because what we currently are processing in our working memory is a chief factor in determining the stimuli we attend to. If we do not pay attention to the new information coming in, it's forgotten; if we do pay attention to it, it moves from STSS to the short-term memory (STM) and working memory (WM) storage systems. Short-term memory is conscious memory—all that we are aware of at one time. The capacity of this store is limited to about seven chunks of information. The information here is not in the raw sensory form in which it exists in the STSS. And it can be bumped out by new information, that is, forgotten. Working memory is very much like short-term memory; in fact, it may be just a part of STM. If we think of short-term memory as conscious memory, working memory is like a scratch pad we use to do mental arithmetic or to make a list of persons we want to invite to a party. Information in STM or WM, if rehearsed or encoded, remains the focus of attention or is passed along to long-term memory (LTM). The capacity of long-term memory, like that of STSS, is probably unlimited. The information stored in long-term memory is almost never forgotten, although we may be unable to retrieve it because of a failure in the way we search for it. Any response we might make—say, answering the question "What caused the

FIGURE 7.1   *An Information-Processing Model of Memory*

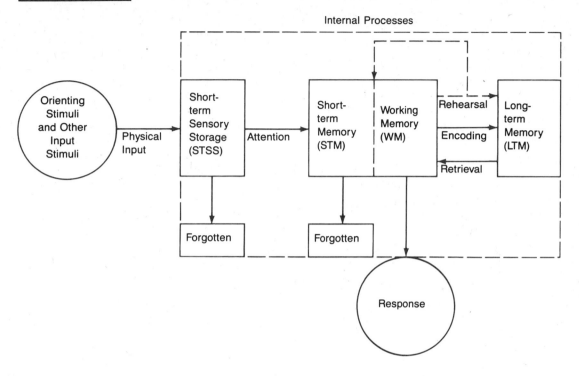

eclipse?"—stems from working memory, either directly or through retrieval from long-term memory. Let's now look more closely at elements of this model.

Orienting Stimuli and Responses

Of the stimuli in the environment, some succeed in eliciting an orienting response; others do not. An orienting response arouses our interest, makes us curious, makes us want to know more about the stimulus. It is made to changes in stimuli or to their unique characteristics. Perhaps the simplest way to take possession of students' thoughts—to gain their attention—is to use a command. *Commands* are verbal statements that have a highly probable consequence associated with them (Skinner, 1957). When a person yells, "STOP!" people usually stop what they are doing and check around them for further commands or more information. A teacher has available a set of commands that can arouse. The teacher can say, "Now listen closely" or "This is really important" or "Pay attention to this!" or "Look at that!" These are commands with a highly probable consequence on the part of students—attention to what is happening.

    Variation in the stimulus offered to students also can gain attention. When teachers (like actors) vary their volume, pitch, or rate of speech, they are

Commands

Variation in stimulus

varying the stimulus in ways likely to arouse the orienting response. When teachers write on the board in

different colors

or places

words in

unusual

patterns

Emotional stimuli

they are more likely to elicit attention; that is, more of the information they want to be attended to ends up in working memory. *Emotional stimuli* also can capture attention. For example, words like "blood" or "gold" or our own name are likely to elicit an orienting response. Vivid similes and metaphors have the same attention-grabbing properties. Who would not attend further after hearing, "My love is like a red, red rose" or "He was known in the field as Doctor Death."

Other attention-arousing stimuli depend for their effect on *novelty* (the teacher sits down on the floor, instead of at the desk); *surprise* (the teacher solves a mathematics problem in an unusual way); *complexity* (the teacher follows a series of two-digit addition problems with one containing five-digit numbers); *ambiguity* (the teacher provides students with a map that has no cities indicated and asks where cities are likely to develop); or *incongruity* (the teacher discusses a mammal that lays eggs, that is, a platypus). Thoughtfulness about the ways to control your students' attention will pay off in getting what you want into their information-processing system. Teachers and parents are quite right when they say to their children, "Pay attention or you won't learn anything!"

But teachers should use these attention-getting stimuli sparingly. All the forms of eliciting attention share a common problem: Once students get used to them, they are no longer effective. Don't cry "Wolf!" too often. Remember that novelty overused becomes commonplace. Students can become accustomed to changing voice levels. They can lose their emotional responses to words like *murder* and *ice cream* when they hear or read them often. Use techniques to elicit orienting responses only to attract attention to important information or events.

Novelty can be overused

Short-Term Memory and Forgetting

We now move a little further along the path shown in Figure 7.1. We assume that something in the physical world entered short-term sensory storage and was attended to. When we pay attention to a stimulus, the information represented by that stimulus goes into short-term memory or working memory. This is where we store information that needs to be available for just a few seconds. For example, when you look up a telephone number that you are not going to need

• *A teacher or a student can say, "Now listen closely" or "This is really important"— commands with a highly probable consequence. (© 1986 Susan Lapides)*

again, it is stored in STM or WM and forgotten a few minutes or even seconds after you dial.

The speed with which we forget material in STM or WM was illustrated in an experiment by L. R. Peterson (1966). The data are shown in Figure 7.2. Subjects in this experiment learned meaningless trigrams (sets of three letters), such as *XJR* and *YGM*. When asked to recite the list of trigrams immediately, most subjects could recall about 88 percent of them. When rehearsal was prevented (by asking subjects to count numbers immediately after the list was presented), only about 62 percent of the trigram list was retained at the end of 3 seconds. When rehearsal was prevented for 6 seconds, another group could recall only 41 percent of the trigrams. When rehearsal was prevented for 18 seconds, the rate of retention of another group was reduced to 15 percent. Unless certain things happen to the information held in STM or WM, that information is quickly forgotten.

Of course it's not surprising that subjects in Peterson's study forgot nonsensical trigrams. What is interesting is that we all tend to forget familiar things as well, things we've come across thousands of times. Nickerson and Adams

Forgetting is rapid in STM

FIGURE 7.2

**Amount Retained
After Various
Intervals Between
Learning and Recall
of Lists of Nonsense
Trigrams**

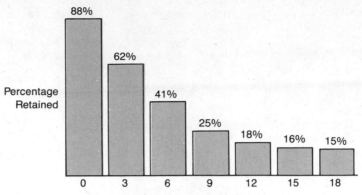

Source: Adapted from L. R. Peterson and M. J. Peterson (1959).

(1979) asked subjects to do the following: "In the circles below draw a penny."
Try it before you go on.

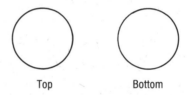

The researchers scored eight characteristics of a penny: on the top is the head,
"In God We Trust," "Liberty," and the date; on the bottom is the building,
"United States of America," "E Pluribus Unum," and "One Cent." If you are like
most of the subjects in the study, you did not score very high. This is an example
of what happens when we do not encode or rehearse stimuli in STM or WM—no
matter how often we come across them, we forget them!

**Forgetting serves
a purpose**

Forgetting serves a good purpose. Without forgetting, our minds would
become hopelessly cluttered. We would not want to keep in memory all the
information we receive each day. To survive, people need to forget most of what
they initially process. For teachers, this useful forgetting creates a challenge: If
we feel the information we teach is worthy of retention, we must combat the
natural forgetting process.

**Decay of memory
trace**

Sometimes we are unable to retrieve information from long-term memory.
That inability may result from new information interfering with attempts to recall
old information. Or we may have trouble remembering because there was a
quick decay of the physical memory trace in STM. In either case, a lack of
retention is functional, natural, and universal. As a teacher, you should know
that your students are going to forget most of the specific facts you teach them.
This is the reality of the situation. Guilford (1952) used a graph like that
presented in Figure 7.3 to show the retention over time for various kinds of
material. For nonsense material, the ability to recall words declines very fast,

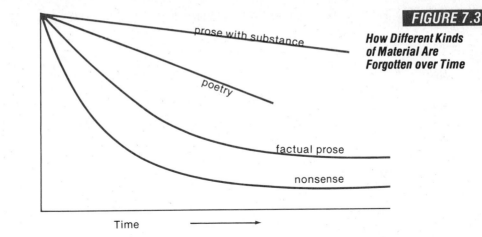

FIGURE 7.3

How Different Kinds of Material Are Forgotten over Time

Source: Adapted from Guilford (1952, p. 408).

often within minutes. "Well," you may be saying, "we don't teach nonsense words in school." But you should realize that words like *algorithm, mores, evolution, radium, quadratic,* and *sonnet,* on first encounter, are nonsense words for many students. And, as the figure shows, we find a considerable drop in retention even when the material is factual prose or poetry.

R. W. Tyler (1934) measured various kinds of knowledge and skill of college students before, immediately after, and one year after a course in zoology. Figure 7.4 shows some of his data. A test that measured the correct naming of parts of animals showed an increase during the course, from 22 percent correct to 62 percent correct. But 77 percent of that gain was lost one year after the final examination, as the score dropped back to 31 percent correct. Of the gain in the ability to identify technical terms, 26 percent was lost (mean scores on the test dropped from 83 percent to 66 percent over the twelve months). But the students' ability to apply principles or interpret new experiments showed no loss or even a gain. A principle of teaching can be seen in these results: Factual and isolated bits of information are forgotten much more easily than are principles and meaningful (interconnected) kinds of information.

For single lectures, in contrast to a whole course, the loss in retention over a week's interval is also remarkable. The kind of retention you can expect for facts presented in a lecture takes the form shown in Table 7.1. Obviously a lot of information is lost quickly!

You should know one other factor about the loss of retention over time. The drop-off probably differs for students of varying ability. Bright students retain more than average-ability students, and average-ability students retain more than low-ability students (Royer, Hambleton, & Cadorette, 1978). This difference appears even if bright and less bright students are brought to the same initial level of learning.

But even though forgetting is natural and functional, there are ways to combat losses in attention. We talk of them in the next section of this chapter.

FIGURE 7.4   *Forgetting of Different Types of Material and Skills Learned in a Zoology Course*

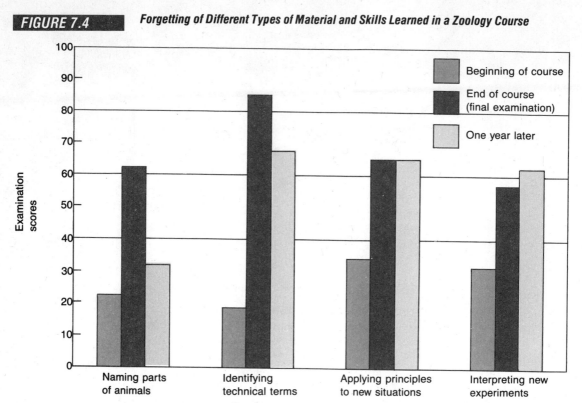

Source: Adapted from R. W. Tyler (1934).

Long-Term Memory

To get material from short-term memory and working memory to long-term memory need not be a big problem. It is necessary only to enhance the material in some way or see that it is held as the focus of attention for a period of time.

Retrieval   Retrieving information from long-term memory is another matter. Let's assume that almost any verbal, visual, or auditory information of real or potential significance can get into long-term storage. Let's also assume that the information in the long-term store is permanently recorded. Our problem resembles that of the chief librarian of the Library of Congress. Many documents of many kinds are coming in with great frequency. Storage facilities in the library are virtually unlimited since the advent of microfilm and similar systems. When someone requests a particular book, the main problem for the librarian is not one of storage but of retrieval. A smoothly functioning card catalog for locating items is what is needed most.

Long-term memory: unlimited and permanent   We can think of long-term memory in the same way. Research has shown us that LTM is virtually unlimited in storage capacity and that we do not often forget information once it is there. So storage is not the problem. The problem

	Presentation of Lecture Material			
	First 25 minutes	Next 15 minutes	Final 15 minutes	Total 55 minutes
Immediate recall	44%	25%	48%	41%
Recall after one week	14%	17%	20%	17%

TABLE 7.1
Immediate and Delayed Recall of Lecture Material

Source: Adapted from J. McLeish, *The Lecture Method*, p. 10. Cambridge Institute of Education. Copyright 1968. Used by permission.

is one of retrieval, locating the information in LTM and bringing it up as the focus of attention in STM or WM.

Information Storage in Memory

How does the brain store information? In pictorial form? In verbal form? In both? In neither? Dual-code theorists believe that all information is tied to sensory input: that things we see are stored in pictorial form, and that things we hear or read are stored in verbal form (Paivio, 1971; 1978). This theory has a common-sense ring to it. But before we close the issue, we should describe a study by Bower, Karlin, and Dueck (1975). They asked their subjects to remember pictures like those shown in Figure 7.5. The subjects in one group used their own pictorial representations, or verbal representations, or both to store and retrieve the pictures. They generally were able to reconstruct from memory about 50 percent of the pictorial stimuli that they were shown. The subjects in a second group were told that picture A was a midget playing a trombone in a phone booth, and that picture B was an early bird that had tried to catch a very large worm. These subjects were able to reconstruct about 70 percent of the pictorial stimuli correctly.

Dual-code theory

How do we explain this increase in retention? It seems that information is stored in visual form or verbal form or both, and that it also is stored by its meaning. Regardless of whether the stimulus is visual or verbal, its meaning to the person determines how it is to be stored, retrieved, and used.

Storage can be verbal, visual, or by meaning

 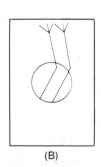

(A)   (B)

FIGURE 7.5
Two Pictorial Stimuli Used by Bower, Karlin, and Dueck (1975)

Declarative knowledge

Episodic memory

Another useful distinction in thinking about what is stored, is that between declarative knowledge and procedural knowledge (Squire, 1987; J. R. Anderson, 1985). *Declarative knowledge* and information is about factual things. It may be thought of as composed of two types—episodic and semantic. *Episodic memory* refers to the personal, dated, autobiographical memories that we all have stored. Events such as our first kiss, the time we were stopped by the police, and a vacation in Mexico are the kind of personal factual episodes to which we refer. A particular episode marked by place or time is the kind of memory we denote by the term "episodic" memory. Our students remember spelling bees, field trips to the woods, sporting achievements and failures, the time the principal called them in, and so forth. When a child reports on his field trip (sometimes with endless description of extraneous material), we have evidence of how vivid and filled with visual and verbal information such memories can be.

Semantic memory

Semantic memory is about concepts, principles, and characteristics of objects, all without personal involvement. The characteristics of mammals, the color of a nectarine, the relation between pressure and flow are all bits of semantic memory—the kind of memory schools especially reward.

Procedural knowledge

In contrast to declarative knowledge—either the episodic or the semantic forms of information—is *procedural knowledge*. Memories for procedures include starting your car, multiplying fractions, preparing a meal, and finding the meaning of a word in the dictionary. These are the almost automatic procedures that we use to go about our business every day. Declarative knowledge is knowledge that something is the case. It is what we believe to be factual. Procedural knowledge is knowledge about how to perform some activity, either physical or cognitive (make a decision, solve a problem). The two forms of knowledge are related, not separate. One should know how to compute simple interest or write a report (procedural knowledge) but could not do either without a good deal of semantic, factual information (the kind we call declarative knowledge). Different neural structures may be involved in the storage of declarative and procedural memory (Squire, 1987). A student's failure to perform well, therefore, may be due to inadequate information in the declarative or the procedural memory storage system, and teachers will need to find out which is the case.

Meaningfulness

Meaningfulness is one of the most overused words in education. To say that teachers must promote meaningful learning suggests that they go out of their way to teach meaningless material. And of course this assumption isn't so. But teachers often forget to take into account the differences between what they find meaningful and what their students find meaningful. Remember, much of what we teach is new information. In and of itself, it may have no meaning for our students. To make unfamiliar material meaningful for our students, we must provide them with *associations*.

The greater the number of associations, the more meaningful the information. One type of association is familiarity. For example, suppose we were to test individuals on the truth or falsity of syllogisms. We would find one error rate for "All bogs are sketen; no sketen are lechts; therefore no bogs are lechts." We would find another error rate for "All dogs are canines; no canines are men; therefore no dogs are men." The first error rate would be higher. Although these two syllogisms do not differ in level of difficulty as judged by formal logic, they do differ greatly in the familiarity of their terms.

Number of associations

Familiarity

A teacher's concern for meaningfulness, associations, and familiarity helps learners find meaning in information so that, if needed, it can be retrieved. *The richer the network of associations, the quicker the learning and the more efficient the retrieval.* In the paragraphs that follow, we talk about ways in which teachers can help students form associations to make information meaningful for them.

Mediators.   One way to add meaning to apparently meaningless material is *mediation,* the process of creating meaningful links between unrelated items or ideas. Suppose a student is trying to learn a list of paired words, say *comb-cup, foot-chair,* and *hammer-clock.* Here the first word is a stimulus for the learner to give the second word as a response. This kind of learning (called *paired-associate learning*) can be difficult for children who are retarded or disadvantaged. But this task is not difficult for normal middle-class children (Jensen, 1967). Middle-class children have learned to provide themselves with mediators (connectors). They think to themselves, "The comb is in the cup," "Her foot is on the chair," or "The hammer hits the clock." Evidently the middle-class culture teaches children, formally or informally, to supply mediators and provide more associations for remembering the information that is present in the world around us. When retarded and disadvantaged children learned a mediational strategy, their performance in paired-associate learning tasks became about as good as that of normal middle-class children.

Paired-associate learning

Teachers can help students by demonstrating mediational behavior, that is, by providing specific examples of the technique. When teaching that Israel is a diamond-cutting center in international trade, the paired associates are "Israel–diamond cutting." To help students connect the two, we might say that Israel receives diamonds to be cut; that diamonds are shipped to Israel and cut there; that uncut diamonds enter Israel, and cut diamonds leave; or that Israeli diamond cutters are among the most talented in the world. In every case we are providing mediators linking Israel and diamond cutting. This should help students code, store, and retrieve the information. These techniques are obviously valuable in learning codes, foreign language vocabularies, and similar collections of more or less arbitrarily paired associates.

Almost any paired stimulus-response learning event is more easily remembered when mediators are used (see Russell & Storms, 1955; Underwood & Schulz, 1960). When studying for your next examination, try them. You will probably find that mediational processes—giving yourself some verbal connectors or links for memorizing or taking certain actions—are helpful in learning and retention.

Advance Organizers.

A technique proposed by Ausubel (1968, 1978) for helping students learn and retrieve information also arises from the concepts of meaningfulness and familiarity. The instructor provides students with an *advance organizer*—a brief introduction about the way in which information that is going to be presented is structured. The advance organizer is like a set of general concepts that helps students organize the more specific material that follows. It assumes that if we give students an abstract, hierarchically structured preview of what we are going to teach, one that is compatible with their memory storage system, we can make the material easier to learn and retrieve.

Mental scaffolding

The advance organizer for particular material may be a brief written or oral presentation, far more general than the material itself. It should act as a kind of mental scaffolding, identifying concepts to which new information is related. Empirical evidence suggests that a teacher who begins an instructional session with an advance organizer can make new material more familiar and meaningful and, therefore, easier to retrieve (Luiten, Ames, & Ackerman, 1980). (We return to advance organizers in Chapter 9.)

Hierarchical Structure.

Gagné (1985) has talked about hierarchical structure as a way of developing instructional materials. *Hierarchical structure* is a sequence that orders material from simple learning events (specific ideas and concepts) to complex ones (abstract concepts and principles). Research on the effectiveness of sequencing is encouraging. Both Ausubel and Gagné assume that general principles encompass specific ideas, and both use this assumption to make information more meaningful and familiar. But Ausubel's advance organizer works from the top down: By identifying the most general and abstract principles, an advance organizer helps students give more meaning to the specific concepts and facts that make up the new material to be learned. Gagné's theory about the importance of specifying how information is hierarchically organized is compatible with Ausubel's thinking, but it is more of a bottom-up theory. It creates meaning and familiarity in sequential steps, requiring that students master a lower-order concept before moving on to a higher-order one. In teaching that "intermittent reinforcement strengthens resistance to extinction," Gagné would concentrate on teaching the component concepts: distinguishing between the terms *continuous* and *intermittent*, identifying instances of positive and negative reinforcement, and teaching the differences in the ways response strength is measured (magnitude, frequency, and probability of response). Using Ausubel's advance organizer, we could begin with a presentation of the goals of behavior modification, the need to be assured that responses once learned are not extinguished easily, and note some hypotheses about the effects of reinforcement when people are trained under continuous versus intermittent reinforcement. Both researchers recognize the importance and effect on retention of familiarity, meaningfulness, and order in instruction.

Bottom-up and top-down organization

Organization.   The effectiveness of advance organizers and hierarchical structure may be due to their emphasis on "organization" (see Mandler, 1969). As Bower (1970b) pointed out, the factor of organization is extremely important in aiding retrieval from memory. In one study, Bower, Clark, Winzenz, and Lesgold (1969) worked with hierarchical knowledge and the ability of certain general concepts to encompass more specific ones. The task for the learner was to remember certain lists of words. For example, suppose you were asked to memorize a list like this:

platinum	silver	gold
aluminum	copper	lead
bronze	steel	brass
sapphire	emerald	ruby
limestone	granite	slate

Now look at Figure 7.6. The researchers have taken the same list and, using the hierarchical form, have organized it from general to specific. In an experiment in which they presented subjects with four separate lists of twenty-eight words—all random or all organized—the results were striking, and supported the theories of Ausubel and Gagné. Figure 7.7 presents the data for subjects in the two treatments. These data come from four learning trials, each of which exposed subjects to the four lists for approximately a minute per list.

> [In Trials 1 and 2] it is obvious that subjects having the organized presentation are recalling about three times as many words as are subjects in the random condition. By Trial 3 all subjects in the organized condition were recalling all 112 words, whereas recall by subjects in the random condition by Trial 4 had not yet reached the Trial-1 score of the organized subjects. (Bower, 1970b, p. 39)

The data have clear implications for curriculum development or for any teaching activity in which knowledge is to be communicated to and retained by

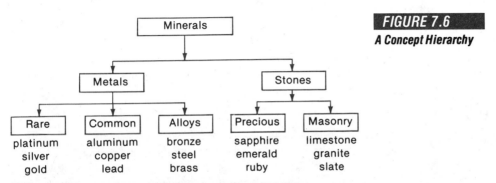

FIGURE 7.6

A Concept Hierarchy

Source: Adapted from Bower, Clark, Winzenz, and Lesgold (1969).

FIGURE 7.7

Effects on Memory of Learning Lists of Words in Random or Organized Form

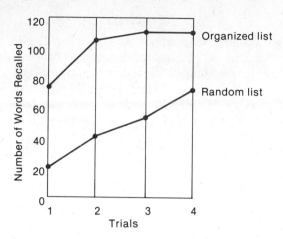

Source: Adapted from Bower, Clark, Winzenz, and Lesgold (1969).

Organization aids retention

the learner. Simply put, organization aids retention. Making use of the relationship between concepts of wide generality and less general concepts substantially improves learning.

A special case of organization has been studied in many real-world classroom situations, sometimes demonstrating remarkable effects. This is the case of *semantic maps*—organized visual and verbal maps of the declarative and procedural knowledge to be remembered (Lambiotte, Dansereau, Cross, & Reynolds, 1989). Figure 7.8 presents two examples of semantic maps. Maps like these have been used to increase reading comprehension and to improve both learning from lectures and writing. They have been generated by teachers or students, used before or after instruction, generated by groups and individuals. Teachers claim they have found such maps helpful in organizing their own presentations, allowing them also to spot difficulties in instruction, and useful also for designing tests. The best ways to develop and use maps are not yet known. You will have to experiment. But in some studies they seem to aid in encoding information by adding a visual representation to the verbal knowledge that is to be learned. In some studies they seem to aid in retrieval, increasing the cues available to the person trying to remember. And in some studies, they aid in comprehension, helping students see what is important and the relations between different areas of knowledge. The use of semantic maps to organize knowledge particularly helps students with low prior knowledge in an area, those with low general ability, and those with problems in reading comprehension.

Semantic maps

Abstract knowledge structures: schemata

Schemata.   *Schemata* (singular: *schema*) have been proposed as a way of understanding how the mind organizes information. They are abstract structures that represent the knowledge stored in memory (Rumelhart & Ortony, 1977). For some psychologists, they are the building blocks of cognition. They are the existing mental structures that allow us to learn new information and that guide us through the day, providing us with the theories and behavioral scripts

FIGURE 7.8   *Two Semantic Maps: Graphic Organizations of Knowledge*

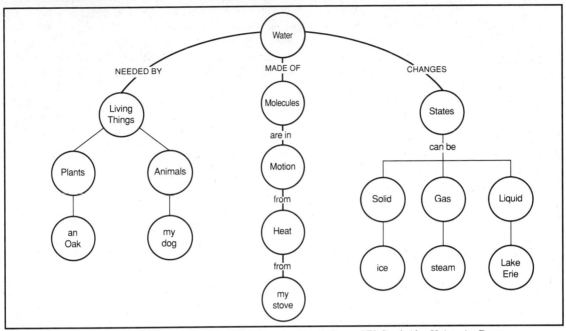

Source: Adapted from Novak, J.D. & Gowain, D.B. (1984) *Learning How to Learn*. NY: Cambridge University Press

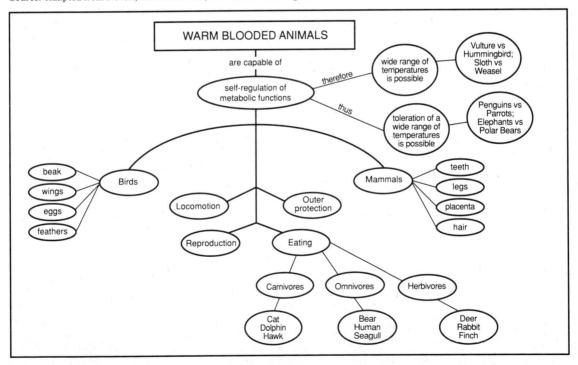

Source: Adapted from "Multirelational Semantic Mapping" by J. G. Lambiotte, G. K. Dansereau, D. R. Cross, and S. R. Reynolds, *Educational Psychology Review*, 1989, pp. 331–368. Used by permission of Plenum Publishing Corporation.

we need to interpret our world (Rumelhart, 1980; H. Gardner, 1985). We have schemata for eating in restaurants, attending hockey games, and visiting our grandmothers. The knowledge associated with each of these activities is our schema for the activity. That knowledge also connects with other schemata. It is the intersection of schemata that defines our world. A schema for student, for example, would intersect with schemata for schooling, reading, and teaching. It would consist of the information, in an abstract form, on the customary associations we have with the word *student*. A schema differs from a concept: A concept provides a formal definition; a schema underlies the concept. Our concept of student is a definition of the attributes of students and nonstudents; our schema for student is our more general knowledge associated with the word *student*. The schema contains slots or placeholders into which we fit our experience. For example, we might expect the occupations of an eighteen-year-old and an eighty-year-old to be "student" and "retired," respectively. Our schemata, the knowledge structures we have about students and retired persons, contain slots for age, which is customarily associated with these occupational titles. Yet neither the concept of student nor the concept of retired person requires age as a defining characteristic. There are some retired eighteen-year-olds and many eighty-year-old students. Our schemata, which we bring to our experience, determine how we interpret that experience.

Schemata more general than concepts

In fact, some theorists believe that the schemata we bring to an instructional situation are as important as the actual oral or written message that makes up instruction:

> A general implication for education is that the schemata a person already possesses are a principal determiner of what will be learned from a text. Imagine a section from a geography text about an unfamiliar nation. An adult would bring to bear an elaborate nation schema, which would point to subschemata representing generic knowledge about political systems, economics, geography, and climate. Each subschema would have its own infrastructure and interconnect with other subschemata at various points. . . . The young reader, on the other hand, may not possess a nation schema adequate to assimilate the text. In the worst case, the material will be gibberish. . . . More likely, the young reader will have partly formed schemata that will allow him or her to make sense of the passage but will not permit the construction of mental representatives of great depth or breadth. (R. C. Anderson, Spiro, & M. C. Anderson, 1978)

Meaningfulness = engagement of appropriate schemata

What this comment implies is that meaningfulness depends on engaging appropriate schemata. If a relevant schema does not exist, then a teacher needs to provide a context or schema for what is to be learned. In this way the new material can be assimilated into existing knowledge structures and "cross-listed" with other schemata. Unless the teacher provides these contexts, the students will provide their own, which may be inappropriate.

An example of the power of schemata to influence what is learned comes from an experiment by R. C. Anderson, Reynolds, Schallert, and Goetz (1977). Suppose, like their subjects, you read the following story:

Rocky slowly got up from the mat, planning his escape. He hesitated a moment and thought. Things were not going well. What bothered him most was being held, especially since the charge against him had been weak. He considered his present situation. The lock that held him was strong, but he thought he could break it. He knew, however, that his timing would have to be perfect. Rocky was aware that it was because of his early roughness that he had been penalized so severely—much too severely from his point of view. The situation was becoming frustrating; the pressure had been grinding on him for too long. He was being ridden unmercifully. Rocky was getting angry now. He felt he was ready to make his move. He knew that his success or failure would depend on what he did in the next few seconds. (p. 372)

Is this a story about a prison break, yes or no? Suppose we had multiple-choice items to test your recall of this story and one item asked: Was Rocky punished for aggressiveness by (a) being imprisoned or (b) losing points to his opponent? If you think this story is about a prison break, you would choose *a.* If you were a physical education major, however, as half the subjects in this study were, you might choose *b,* interpreting the entire story as concerned with a wrestling match. Sixty-four percent of the physical education majors made this choice. Reread the story from that perspective. Only 28 percent of the subjects who were music majors interpreted the story theme as a wrestling match. The point of this and similar experiments (for example, R. C. Anderson & Pichert, 1978; Bransford & Johnson, 1972) is to demonstrate how the schemata one brings to a learning experience influence what is learned and what is retrieved.

Providing schemata or helping learners bring their own appropriate schemata to an instructional situation is an important way in which teachers can ensure meaningful learning. One way to provide schemata is to use similes ("Electric current is like flowing water," "Long-term memory is like a giant card catalog"), which allow us to incorporate new information into an already existing schema with only some minor modifications (Ortony, 1975). As a teacher, whatever you can do to tap into the already existing knowledge structures that the learner brings to the instructional situation can help you make the material more meaningful for the learner.

Using similes in teaching

Generative Model of Learning.
Many of the ideas we've just talked about fit into what Wittrock (1989) calls the *generative model of learning*—whereby cognitive learning is seen as taking place when learners actively construct or *generate* meaning for themselves out of what is presented to them. Wittrock refined his ideas after discovering that the insertion of one familiar word into each sentence of a reading text that was in common use in schools increased story comprehension an amazing 50 percent and retention an amazing 100

Learners generate meaning

percent (Marks, Doctorow, & Wittrock, 1974). For example, suppose a story reads: "Nimuk wanted to be a shaman. He wanted to talk with the deities." This could easily be changed: "Nimuk wanted to be a religious leader. He wanted to talk with the gods." When you ask, "What did Nimuk want to be?" or "Who did Nimuk want to talk with?" you get very different answers from youngsters who read the first version and those who read the second version. The familiar words make things more meaningful for students by enabling them to relate new material to their own personal schemata. This technique helps learners generate their own meaning, almost always increasing learning. But it is the *active* generation by students themselves that provides the largest gains. In a study with junior high school students, students generating summaries, constructing topic sentences, or relating what they read to their own experience increased their performance on comprehension and retention tests by about 25 percent— sometimes even by more than 100 percent! These effects were replicated in other grades, with other samples, including those containing low-ability students. In virtually every case, when students are required to make meaning—to generate paragraph headings, summaries, interpretations, and images and to relate what is read or heard or experienced to one's own preexisting knowledge—comprehension is significantly increased.

Relate new learning to pre-existing knowledge

How do we help learners generate meaningful ties between what is to be learned and their own memory storage system? We can remember to use vivid mental imagery; cue learners about organization; provide advance organizers; teach students about mediators; have students write out their own one-sentence summaries of paragraphs; use analogies, similes, and metaphors during lectures; and induce appropriate schemata. These kinds of activities clearly increase reading comprehension (Linden & Wittrock, 1981) and probably can increase learning from field trips, movies, television, and other sources. In the generative model "instruction involves stimulating the learner's information-processing strategies . . . and stores of relevant specific memories in relation to the information to be learned" (Wittrock, 1978, p. 26). The trick to being an effective instructor, suggests Wittrock, is to identify those students who do not naturally know how to generate relationships between what is to be learned and their own knowledge and experience. If we can teach them how to create these associations, we can do much to improve classroom learning. But whenever possible, we should remember to let the learner do the work. We could draw a graph, or they could. We can make a table, or they could. We could write out questions, or they could. We can summarize, or they could. The more we involve them in making meaning, the more they are likely to learn. It is they who should draw inferences, paraphrase difficult ideas or passages, draw pictures of the situation, come in with classroom demonstrations, solve practical problems. The generative model reminds us that learning is not like digestion—just put stuff in, and the system takes over. Learning requires an active neural process, one that bestows meaning and significance on that which is attended to, or it will not get to long-term storage and will not be retrieved from long-term storage. This view of learning—also called a constructionist view—stands in marked contrast to the notion that learning is, somehow, "passive," a view that was

Make students make the meaning

A constructionist view of learning

characteristic of educational psychology and curriculum developers for the last few decades (P. L. Peterson, Clark, & Dickson, 1990).

RECAP

The development of an efficient retrieval system is the crux of remembering. Hardly anything is forgotten, but things sometimes cannot be retrieved. How can you help your students with the development of a retrieval system? You can relate what is new and unfamiliar to what is well learned and familiar. Examine what you teach, and if you have new words, phrases, ideas, and concepts, tie them to things your students already understand. Help students mediate things. When you teach, say, the procedures for the impeachment of a president, put events in sequence: "First the House, then the Senate" or "The recommendation goes from the representatives to the senators." Build a visual structure:

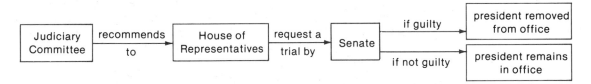

Try to organize phenomena in ways that will help your students learn and retain material more easily. And keep in mind the generative model of learning as you try to engage or provide schemata in which to embed what is to be learned. You need to teach in ways that are compatible with helping students construct their own knowledge, for ultimately it is constructed by them, not handed over to them.

Active Learning

We can state as a principle of instruction that active learning is more likely to result in longer and greater retention than is passive learning. The activity may provide more associations with which material to be retained can be coded, perhaps simply by focusing attention on the material to be learned. All of the studies reported in this section are concerned with active techniques to improve at least that aspect of learning that can be measured by recall.

Active learning promotes retention

Recitation.   A classic study of recitation and its effects on learning was reported by Gates (1917). Subjects learned a list of nonsense syllables or short biographies. Various amounts of the material to be learned were recited out loud. In this way auditory stimuli and the psychomotor responses involved in speech were associated with the symbolic verbal material, increasing the ways the material could be coded. Recall was measured immediately and four hours after instruction. Using either the percentage of nonsense material remembered or the percentage of information learned in biographies as a measure of achieve-

● *Active learning and heightened imagery result in better learning. (© Andrew Brilliant)*

ment, Gates examined the effects of recitation during learning. His findings were unambiguous: The more recitation during learning, the higher the test scores, both immediately and after four hours.

Seibert (1932) demonstrated the beneficial effect of recitation in learning foreign vocabulary, and Forlano (1936) did the same for learning arithmetic and spelling. Even though Berelson and Steiner (1964) believed the effect is diminished for highly meaningful material, it is clear that recitation helps learning. Perhaps it focuses the learner's attention; perhaps it forces some kind of review by the learner; perhaps it increases the codability of the material by adding an auditory and a physical dimension to the learning task. Whatever the reason, the addition of recitation to a learning task that usually is done silently increases the amount learned and makes retrieval more efficient.

Recitation helps learning

Physical Activity. In their interesting study of the value of physical activity in teaching, Kunihira and Asher (1965) assumed that language is initially learned by associating a set of activities with a set of commands. The initial association probably occurs when someone says, "Stand up," and someone else then stands up. Eventually, through exposure to models and the cues they respond to, children learn the same stimulus-response connections. These stimulus and response connections are learned long before the children need talk for themselves. As many parents know, children can respond to a complex command like "Get your red socks" long before they can talk.

• *Drawing objects, which involves motor activity and pictorial representation, is a way to enhance learning. (© James Carroll)*

Kunihira used simple stimulus-response connections to teach a second language. While sitting down, he would say, *"Tate,"* and then stand up. Acting as a model, he would then say the Japanese word *aruke,* and walk forward. Eventually when he said, *"Tate,"* the students stood up, and when he said, *"Aruke,"* the students walked forward. After twenty minutes of intensive exercises of this type, the students had no difficulty in responding to the command *"Isu kara tate, kokuban no anata no namae o kese"* ("Stand up and erase your name from the blackboard"). None of the students had had any previous experience with Japanese. The data on amount of material learned, speed of learning, and long-term retention of the vocabulary—all learned without speaking or written instruction—were impressive.

The psychological reasons for the effect may be related to the enhanced associations that occur. A more efficient coding scheme may be developed because a relatively meaningless term like *tate* has been given both a meaningful association ("stand up") and a physical referent (the psychomotor experiences associated with getting up). There is now a growing body of research indicating that almost any form of motor enactment during learning improves performances on subsequent tests. Getting students up and about, moving and gesturing, may make an environment far more conducive to learning than keeping students at their desks, passively responding (R. L. Cohen, 1989).

Enactment during learning is helpful

We should mention here a person on whom Luria (1968), the distinguished Soviet psychologist to whom we return later, reported—a man who never forgot

Synesthesia

anything. He seemed to have a memory system that depended on extreme *synesthesia,* a condition in which stimuli of one sensory system produce images in another sensory mode. This kind of person "hears in color" or sees numbers arranged geometrically—skills that can result in perfect codability and retrieval from memory.

Combining sensory responses

Perhaps teachers should learn to foster the combining of physical, auditory, gustatory, and visual responses to stimuli whenever they can be brought together in a particular learning task. Kunihira's effectiveness may have resulted from this combining. Or the physical activity may simply have kept his subjects awake. Whatever the reason, we know that physical activity can help in mastering a second language and other verbal material.

Overlearning.   There have probably been times in your life when you've been asked to continue to study material that you thought you had mastered. Perhaps you even chose to do so rather than risk forgetting something important. For example, maybe you repeated an important phone number a few times after you had successfully remembered it. The process of continuing to study material after it has been mastered is called *overlearning.* Overlearning works (Krueger, 1929). And the more time one spends overlearning, the more likely one is to score well on some test, either immediately or sometime after one has studied. But repetition does not simply result in *more* learning or simple rote learning; it can result in *different kinds* of learning. As they repeat learning trials with unfamiliar, technically complex material, learners appear to focus better on the main ideas in the material. The repetitions help them reorganize and transform the ideas and make them more meaningful. In a study by Mayer (1983), measures of verbatim learning actually *decreased* over repetitions. But measures of problem-solving skills and the ability to apply what was learned increased over learning trials. Repetition and overlearning, then, are likely to have benefits beyond that of helping students just to learn more or to learn simple things by rote. Repetition and overlearning may be necessary for real understanding of technically complex material and for learning how to solve problems with that understanding. Expert problem solvers—radiologists, physicists, or chess players—all have acquired extensive knowledge in the domain in which they are expert. Thus teachers need not apologize for trying to have students master large bodies of information in, say, chemistry or geography. Problem solving in a domain is, without question, knowledge based. Our problem is to teach in ways that make the knowledge accessible (Prawat, 1989).

Overlearning and recall

Mnemonic Devices.   Techniques to help us remember are called *mnemonic* devices. Careful observation of teachers in classrooms reveals that they provide very little instruction in how to memorize (Moely et al., 1986). Not every child stumbles onto and develops mnemonic strategies for learning. So teachers should provide more direct instruction in these skills. Efficient routinized memory strategies help the student to learn the basic knowledge in a curriculum area and free the student to concentrate on more complex behaviors. Here we look

TABLE 7.2

Nonsense Syllables Memorized by S

(1)	ma	va	na	sa	na	va
(2)	na	sa	na	ma	va	
(3)	sa	na	ma	va	na	
(4)	va	sa	na	va	na	ma
(5)	na	va	na	va	sa	ma
(6)	na	ma	sa	ma	va	na
(7)	sa	ma	sa	va	na	
(8)	na	sa	ma	va	ma	na

Source: Reprinted by permission of the publisher. From *The Mind of a Mnemonist: A Little Book About a Vast Memory* by A. R. Luria, New York: Basic Books. © 1968 by Michael Cole.

at three mnemonic devices: imagery, the method of loci, and the keyword method.

Imagery. A case studied by Luria (1968) shows what imagery was like for S, a man who never forgot anything, who possessed a so-called photographic memory. One of S's most remarkable feats of memory was to reproduce a list of closely related nonsense syllables, some of which are shown in Table 7.2. Not only was S able to reproduce this list perfectly after a short study period, but four years later he recalled it with equal precision. After eight more years S was asked, without warning, to recall the list, and once again he gave a faultless recital. In his record of how he recalled lines 3 and 4 of the list, we find the ability to generate pictorial representations clearly present. This was his imagery for line 3 (sa na ma va na):

Pictorial representations

> This is where Slizkaya Street begins. Near the gates to the tower there's a sleigh (SANA) (Russian: *sani,* "sleigh") in which my landlady (Mava) is sitting. She's holding a long white slab with the letters *na* (Russian: *na,* "on") written on it. (Luria, 1968, p. 54)

And this was the imagery associated with line 4 (va sa na va na ma):

> Aha! Here on the corner of Kolkhoznaya Square and Sretenka is the department store where the watchman turns out to be my friend, the pale milkmaid Vasilisa (VASA). She's gesturing with her left hand to indicate that the store is closed . . . (the Yiddish *nava*), a gesture that's intended for . . . the wet nurse NAMA, who has turned up there wanting to go to the store. (Luria, 1968, p. 55)

S was an oddity. His coding of his environment was so complete that he was unable to forget any aspect of it. The mechanism underlying S's ability was synesthesia. He had no demarcation between vision, hearing, touch, taste, or smell. Images in any form were coded in several ways. Lines and blurs and splashes of color occurred from sounds and colors in S's environment; figures danced in his mind from numerical stimuli; tastes were associated with letters; and so on.

Multiple coding

I recognize a word not only by the images it evokes but by a whole complex of feelings that image arouses. It's hard to express . . . it's not a matter of vision or hearing but some over-all sense I get. Usually I experience a word's taste and weight, and I don't have to make an effort to remember it—the word seems to recall itself. But it's difficult to describe. What I sense is something oily slipping through my hand . . . or I'm aware of a slight tickling in my left hand caused by a mass of tiny, lightweight points. When that happens I simply remember, without having to make the attempt. . . .

Even numbers remind me of images. Take the number 1. This is a proud, well-built man; 2 is a high-spirited woman; 3 is a gloomy person (why, I don't know); 6 a man with a swollen foot; 7 a man with a mustache; 8 a very stout woman—a sack within a sack. As for the number 87, what I see is a fat woman and a man twirling his mustache. (Luria, 1968, pp. 28, 31)

S was speaking literally when he turned to another famous Russian psychologist, Lev Vygotsky, and said, "What a crumbly yellow voice you have!"

Left hemisphere: verbal; right hemisphere: nonverbal imagery

Evidence suggests that functions relating to verbal and visual coding abilities are separated in the two hemispheres of the brain. Speech is organized chiefly in the left hemisphere; nonverbal imagery, in the right hemisphere. As we noted earlier, at least two systems for representing information in the brain may be operating. People may use both an imagery store and a verbal store for encoding input. The imagery system works better in processing concrete and spatial information (the story of Paul Bunyan, geometry); the verbal system works better in processing abstract and sequential information (a definition of morality, a computer program in BASIC). The two systems are richly interconnected. When we can attach verbal material to pictorial images and pictorial images to verbal labels, we can usually retrieve information better (Bower, 1970a), as with semantic maps.

Because most school learning is verbal, students should learn how to associate imagery with verbal material. In part this may be good advice because the storage capacity for pictorial information appears to exceed the very large storage capacity for verbal material (see R. N. Shepard, 1967).

Concrete words = high codability

Using concrete (nonabstract) words helps provide imagery. Paivio (1969) hypothesized that concrete terms like *zebra* and *house* produce both perceptual and verbal codes, while abstract terms like *justice* and *freedom* produce only verbal codes. Thus concrete terms are as a rule easier to learn. This was found to be the case by R. C. Anderson (1974), who saw clear educational implications: Whenever you can, be as concrete as possible and use concrete words that have image-evoking powers.

Age and imagery

Can imagery techniques be taught to help children learn more efficiently? Rohwer (1972), after several unsuccessful attempts at training young children in imagery, concluded that children must be of a certain age before they can learn the strategy. J. R. Levin (1976) found that below the age of 7 or so, instructions to use imagery are not generally helpful. Above this age, particularly with adults,

Rattey's ice cream		Narragansett Park Race Track
Major's barber shop		→
Fire station		To Boston
Home		Fish and chips
Bumpy's house		The monastery
The market		El. Gas Co. ballpark
The druggist		Dentist
←		The bully's house
To New York		
South Woodlawn Elementary School		Piano lessons
Book store	Haunted house	Bicycle shop

FIGURE 7.9

A Sentimental Map of West Avenue, Pawtucket, Rhode Island

Source: From Herbert F. Crovitz, *Galton's Walk*, p. 43. Copyright 1970 by Herbert F. Crovitz. Used by permission of HarperCollins Publishers.

these instructions usually have a pronounced positive effect. However, even with young children, if you can get them to draw objects, providing them with both motor involvement and pictorial representations, as well as verbal coding, you should be able to facilitate learning (Varley, Levin, Severson, & Wolff, 1974).

The method of loci. A trick of the ancient orators, the method of loci relies on imagery. It can increase recall from two to seven times over customary ways of memorization. To use the method, first imagine and learn, in order, the location of objects or places, creating a set of "memory snapshots." Figure 7.9 is an example. It shows a sentimental map of one person's childhood home and the surrounding area. This person could use the map to apply the method of loci. You can also use the train stops on the subway, a path through the woods that you know well, or the different rooms in a house—virtually any familiar ordering of things with high imagery value.

Memory snapshots

Now place the things you want to remember in these loci. You could place the tragedies by Shakespeare; the fifteen stanzas of a poem; the twenty-one significant events in a reign, war, or congressional session; or the nations that are permanent members of the United Nations Security Council. Distribute the images and the verbal labels of the new material at the imaginary locations in memory. Once you've memorized the loci—a task requiring a good deal of time and effort—it is relatively easy to "walk" down the street or through the woods, and "pick up" the information you want to remember.

J. Ross and K. A. Lawrence (1968) had students study many lists of nouns, each forty items long, using as loci forty familiar places on their college campus.

The forty nouns were studied once, each for thirteen seconds. Immediate recall averaged thirty out of forty nouns correct, in serial order. The next day, delayed recall scores averaged thirty-four out of forty items correct.

> In comparison to the scores usually observed in rote learning experiments, such recall performances are quite exceptional, if not staggering. Such demonstrations of the effectiveness of the procedure are important in indicating the magnitude of the mnemonic effect. (Bower, 1970a, p. 500)

The keyword method. J. R. Levin (1981; Pressley, Levin, & Delaney, 1982) and his associates have developed the keyword concept at great length. Suppose you had to learn a foreign word, say, *carta,* Spanish for "(postal) letter." With this method you are taught to find an English keyword that comes to mind when you hear *carta.* Suppose you pick *cart.* You learn to visualize "cart" and put a letter into it. Then when someone says *carta,* you see

and can easily respond "letter." When students are learning vocabulary in their own language, the procedure works, as well. For example, Pressley, Levin, and McDaniel (1987) pointed out that the two key stages of the keyword method are an "acoustic-link" stage and an "imagery-link" stage. Thus, if a fifth grader were trying to learn the word *persuade,* she might acoustically pull out "purse" from "persuade," and then use as the imagery link a woman being persuaded by a salesperson to buy a purse. The next time the word *persuade* is encountered, the term *purse* comes to mind, the visual image follows, and the meaning is recalled. Mnemonics in general and the keyword mnemonic in particular have been helpful for poor learners, the mildly retarded, and learning disabled students, who usually do not have effective learning and memory strategies of their own (Mastropieri & Scruggs, 1989).

Acoustic links and imagery links

In dozens of studies Levin and his colleagues have shown how the keyword method can improve the learning of foreign language vocabulary, English vocabulary, the presidents of the United States, the fifty states and their capitals, and so on. J. R. Levin (1981) and Bellezza (1981) have similar comments to make about mnemonics in education: They (1) are consistently effective, (2) show large effects, (3) are usable in many different curriculum areas, and (4) take little time to teach.

Concern with mnemonic devices, particularly with the role of imagery in memory, has had a long history. But scientific study of this psychological phenomenon has until recently been neglected. Nevertheless it now appears that forgetting can be fought by using a coding system that, through extensive use of imagery, systematic ordering of loci, and keyword methods, makes possible vastly improved information retrieval. Of particular interest is the demonstration that simple rote learning of elements is not all that is greatly facilitated by mnemonics. M. E. Levin and J. R. Levin (1990) have evidence that mnemonic instruction can improve students' problem solving in tasks where creative integration of information is required. This conclusion holds for both analytical thinking tasks (e.g., figuring out analogies) and formal reasoning tasks (e.g., predicting results). Efficient memory strategies seem to facilitate students' performance in a number of higher-order thinking and transfer tasks, where success depends on remembering factual knowledge relevant to the task. And higher-order thinking and problem solving almost always require access to such basic factual knowledge.

Mnemonics and creative problem-solving

Teachers can use these mnemonic techniques in their own learning and can teach these devices to their students. In fact, you have probably used memory aids in many subject matter areas. Remember the "famous Indian tribe" that got you through trigonometry? The SOHCAHTOA tribe (Sine = Opposite/Hypotenuse; Cosine = Adjacent/Hypotenuse; Tangent = Opposite/Adjacent). And most astronomers when first learning the order of the planets from the sun would have been greatly helped to know that "Men Very Easily Make Jugs Serve Useful Nocturnal Purposes" (Mercury, Venus, Earth, Mars, Jupiter, Saturn, Uranus, Neptune, Pluto). We even have a couple for teachers-to-be. Remember HI and UMF—Heighten Imagery and Use Mnemonics Frequently.

Insights of Cognitive Psychology

If a child does not add quickly, you might think about giving him more addition problems to solve, in the hope that with more practice, his speed will improve. If a child is not reading well, you might break up reading tasks into smaller units, so that the subskills that make up reading can be learned in isolation and combined later. If a student appears time and time again to be unable to profit much from instruction, you might be justified in concluding that he just isn't very smart. If a second-year college physics student gets a simple problem in Newtonian physics wrong, you might conclude that he has a terrible memory or never was taught that aspect of physics, and so you might choose to reteach it.

Cognitive psychologists have a very different view of these problems in learning from that of the behaviorists or general educational psychologists of just a few year ago (Gardner, 1985). Before prescribing more problems, breaking up reading tasks, concluding that a child is not smart, or reteaching the principles of physics, cognitive scientists would try to understand the kinds of thinking associated with the particular content to be learned. They would ask what is

Understanding how students think

● *What the text presents is important, but perhaps more important is what the reader brings to a learning situation. (© Mimi Forsyth/Monkmeyer Press Photo Service)*

going on in the heads of these students to help us understand how they learn to add, read, understand instruction, or do physics.

Mental Models of Addition

Learning to add, for example, can be done a number of ways. Suppose you try to add 2 and 6. You can start by setting a place in your mind at zero, go up 2 units, then go up 6 more, and mentally see what you get. Or you can start with the 2, as given, go up 6 units, and see what you get. Or you can start with the larger number, the 6, and go up 2 units, and see what you get. All three methods give you the correct answer. But a student who learns to add using the first is going to work slowly because that model of arithmetic, although correct, is inefficient. On the other hand, the student who learns the last of these models works quickly because it is the simplest way to reach the solution. In this case, having a child do more problems would probably not be as effective as finding ways to understand the cognitive strategies used by the student in solving addition problems, then helping the student make those strategies more efficient.

The point hammered home again and again by cognitive psychologists is that practice and reinforcement may not be as likely to increase a student's mathematics skills as is modifying the cognitive strategies the student uses to perform those skills.

Other cognitive studies of mathematics learning by youngsters find that some kinds of problems that look similar are in reality very different types of problems for young students. For example:

Modifying cognitive strategies

A. Joe has 3 marbles. Tom gives him 5 more marbles. How many marbles does Joe have now?

B. Joe has 3 marbles. Tom has 5 more than Joe. How many marbles does Tom have?

Both of these problems can be solved with the equation $3 + 5 = 8$. But kindergarten and first-grade children who get problem A correct cannot always get problem B right. Type-A problems are of a class called "causing a change" problems; type-B problems are called "comparison" problems. Different kinds of thought patterns are needed to solve the two types of problems.

Cognitive scientists are working to identify the kinds of problems that require different kinds of student cognitions (see Mayer, 1986; Nesher, 1986; Riley, Greeno, & Heller, 1983). If we can understand how successful and unsuccessful learners think about different kinds of problems, we can do more than model, reinforce, and provide practice for our students. We can teach them to think in better ways, and we can learn to instruct in better ways. For example, suppose a group of teachers learned how to think about students' thinking in mathematics and to understand the different kinds of difficulties that are encountered when mathematics problems are taught? Suppose they learned about memory problems of young children, as the following dialogue illustrates (adapted from Romberg & Collis, 1987).

Teacher: What number equals $2 + 4 + 3$?
Student (7 years old): $2 + 4 = 6$. What was the other number?
Teacher: I said, What number equals $2 + 4 + 3$?
Student: Now, 2 plus . . . uh . . . say the number again, please.

Is this a defect in mathematical understanding or a limitation in the memory span of young children? Probably the latter. Let's assume our teachers learn also about how children stop thinking about problems as "real" and adopt strategies to solve problems that are used in school. For example:

"Real" vs. "in-school" problems

It takes Bill 12 hours to cut a lawn. Bob can cut the same lawn in 8 hours. How long will it take them to cut the lawn if they work together and each has his own mower?

Students often answer 10 hours. They look for some key operations to perform, like "get simple average," and do so, because that often works (Shoenfeld, 1985). They rarely seem to check the logic of the answer, apparently finding nothing wrong with concluding that 10 hours of work is needed by two people to cut the lawn, although one of them can do it himself in 8 hours! Learning in school is seen by students as remarkably different from learning and problem solving in the real world (Reed, 1989; Saye, 1988).

Problems in mathematics instruction, like these, were actually taught to teachers. Those teachers began to understand mathematics as students in school might learn mathematics, and it affected their teaching. The result was that significant gains in mathematics learning were achieved by the students of teachers who took a short course in how students think mathematically (Carpenter, Fennema, Peterson, Chiang, and Loef, 1989). More practice wasn't what their students needed to learn better. Greater understanding of how they learned was the key to improvement.

Schemata and Reading Achievement

You are now probably thinking that our sensible-sounding prescription for the child having trouble learning to read should be modified. What the text presents is important, but perhaps more important is what the reader brings to a learning situation. Without rich schemata for incorporating the text, not much will be learned. We find from cognitive studies, for example, that students who do not have a schema for a story often cannot remember stories well. Some children enter school with sophisticated ideas about the nature of stories. They know, for example, that stories have beginnings and ends, are usually presented in chronological order, have a hero or heroine, put an obstacle in his or her way, and **Story schemata** arrive at a solution to a problem. A child without a story schema is at a disadvantage. Even if this child could decode every word as well as someone who has a well-developed story schema, he or she would probably be found to comprehend less when tested.

Reading, then, is more than decoding. There is no doubt that teaching decoding and word recognition skills—a practice prevalent in schools—is helpful in making reading more automatic. But reading is now seen also as a sense-making process, with meaningfulness at its core. Strategies for remedial reading, based strictly on having children read bits and pieces of words or do worksheets often devoid of meaning, are probably emphasizing the wrong thing. Yet such strategies are commonly used in instructing low-achieving or low-income children. It seems that those children with the most problems in learning in schools are assigned materials and activities that are *harder* to learn from. They get the most rote, decontextualized materials to learn from—materials most devoid of everyday meaning. From the perspective of cognitive psychology, where there is an emphasis on how we make meaning, such learning activities are not seen as very sensible.

Meaning-based instruction The same perspective has implications for teaching vocabulary or spelling, which are often taught in rote ways. Since meaning-based instruction is our goal, we should probably emphasize the teaching of vocabulary and spelling words that children encounter and use in their reading, writing, and speaking. It is words in meaningful contexts, not isolated words, that are learned best (Duin & Graves, 1987).

Cognitive psychologists tell us now that the meaning of text is really in the minds of the readers. Because readers construct the text for themselves, teachers must also be concerned about a child's knowledge base for interpreting stories and often must provide more practice in reading meaningful material. Thus students often need more comprehension training than reading-skills training, at least after they have some initial skills (see R. C. Anderson & Pearson, 1985; Beck & Carpenter, 1986; A. L. Brown & Campione, 1986; Paris, Wixson, & Palincsar, 1986; Perfetti & Curtis, 1986).

Meaning is in the mind of the reader

Student Misperceptions

And what of our physicist? Suppose we ask him to imagine a coin being flipped and to freeze the motion about halfway up to the highest level the coin will reach. Now we ask what forces are acting on the coin at that moment. A large percentage of second-year physics students would assert that two forces are operating on the coin—a force from the flip, sending it up, and a gravitational force, which acts to bring it down (Clement, 1982). In reality, once set in motion, there is no force acting on the coin other than gravity. Cognitive scientists tell us that misperceptions of this kind are widespread. Many children believe that sugar ceases to exist when it is dissolved in water, that styrofoam has no weight, and that shadows are made of "stuff." There are even sophisticated adults who believe that electric current is used up in a light bulb, that a light from a candle goes farther at night, or that heavier objects fall faster than light objects.

These intuitively satisfying concepts, wrong though they may be, are held through all kinds of ordinary instruction. Students easily pass through university courses, many with A's, still believing that the world operates as they intuit, not as it really does (Carey, 1986; Linn, 1986). If we do not interview, question, and probe our students to confront their naive theories and misconceptions directly, those wrongheaded ideas may last despite our best efforts at instruction. Roth and Anderson (1990) have evidence that after six to eight weeks of instruction on photosynthesis with fifth-graders only 7 percent of them were able to explain that plants make their own food. It sometimes seems as if you have to hit them over the head to get them to give up their beliefs that water or soil or fertilizer, or all of these, are what plants use as food. We need to develop teaching strategies that (1) reveal the student's misperceptions, (2) create conceptual conflict, and (3) encourage accommodation to new information.

Intuitively satisfying but erroneous concepts

Strategy Use

Sometimes, despite our best efforts at instruction, students do not learn. The fault may lie with the students' motivation or intellect, but it could also lie with their failure to use a learning strategy while instruction is occurring. Before we decide that students do not have the interest or intellectual ability to learn something, we need to be sure that students know how to learn what it is we are trying to teach them. We all know that the world is filled with people who are smart outside of school but who never learn how to do well in school subjects.

One way to achieve well in school subjects is to use learning strategies. A learning strategy is "composed of cognitive operations over and above the processes directly entailed in carrying out a task" (Pressley, Woloshyn, Lysynchuck, Martin, Wood, & Willoughby, 1990). If you are attending to this sentence, turning the pages of this book, and "absorbing" what you can, you are reading. No strategy use is apparent. On the other hand, if you underline, use highlighter, stop and ask yourself what the authors mean, try to relate the notion of learning strategy to your own meaning of "having a strategy," and so forth, you are using learning strategies. You are more active cognitively than if you were merely reading what is before you. More effective learners—readers, writers, mathematicians—are strategy-using learners. Less effective learners have been found to use learning strategies less. What is important to remember is that some students have hardly any such strategies to rely on when trying to master a school subject.

Effective learners = strategy-using learners

In learning from reading, a cognitive strategy can take the form of creating first-letter mnemonics to remember something (Roy G. Biv = red, orange, yellow, etc.—the colors of the rainbow) or using imagery and the other generative techniques that we noted previously. A cognitive strategy can also include learning to summarize, which is a simple yet marvelously helpful strategy for learning from prose. Many effective school learners have mastered the four major rules of *summarization:* (1) Identify the main information; (2) delete trivial information; (3) delete redundant information; and (4) relate main and supporting information. When students who did not know how to do such summarization were trained in this learning strategy, they learned more from a text than students who did not use such strategies (Pressley, Burkell, Cariglia-Bull, Lysynchuck, Martin, Wood, & Willoughby, 1990). It may be hard for you—the readers of this text—to believe that some people do not know how to do such simple summarization. But there are! You are, but virtue of getting this far in your academic career, a sophisticated learner. You probably possess an extensive repertoire of cognitive learning strategies. But many of your students will not have acquired such strategies. If students do not learn these strategies, they will struggle needlessly.

Summarization as a strategy

Students could also learn another simple strategy, namely, to ask questions (see Davey & McBride, 1986; Raphael & Wonnacott, 1985). Students who ask good questions of text often find similar questions on their tests. And then they are ready for them. Also, students who do poorly on comprehension questions can be taught to "look back." Students between 9 and 13 years of age were taught by Garner and her colleagues a simple *look-back strategy* (Garner, Hare, Alexander, Haynes, & Winograd, 1984; Garner, Macready, & Wagoner, 1984). They taught students why they should look back, reminding them that they cannot remember everything. They taught the students to look back when the questions were factual, when they were about what the author said. And they also taught them not to look back when the questions were about students' thoughts. In addition, the students were taught to skim the text to find the part that might have the information needed. Students trained in lookbacks did so more often than untrained students, and they scored higher on a posttest. For some students, what might have appeared to be a deficit in motivation or intellect was simply a deficit in strategy: the lookback.

Questioning as a strategy

The look-back strategy

Deficits in motivation or in strategies

Still another learning strategy is based on the realization that some students have not acquired the understanding of a *story grammar*. Stories have main characters that do and feel things in time and space, and the stories start and end in particular ways. So if you teach students to keep track of five questions (Who is the main character? When and where did the story take place? What did the main character do? How did that character feel? How did it all end?), they might be able to keep the main points of the story straight. And the story might be more memorable for them, as well. In fact, that is exactly what happens. If some students are somehow unaware that stories are organized in certain recurring ways, they are bound to have difficulty answering comprehension questions. The questions about textual material that are asked on tests usually are created by someone who assumes that "everyone" knows how stories are organized. For students who do not know the concept of the story grammar, training in identifying the story grammar helps them do better on tests (Short & Ryan, 1984). The story grammar can also be mapped. Idol (1987) demonstrated positive effects among students who learned the strategy of mapping a story, as shown in Figure 7.10.

Story grammars

Story maps

There are also strategies in learning to write. One of them can be summed up as T-P-W: Think (who is my audience, what do I want to say); Plan (use a TREE to plan: T = note Topic sentence, note Reasons for writing, Examine your reasons, and note Ending); Write, and rewrite, and rewrite again. Many students have no idea of how to take the perspective of a reader, nor do they understand that writing is a process usually requiring much revision. But such strategic writing skills are teachable (see Fitzgerald & Markham, 1987).

Think-plan-write (T-P-W)

Strategies for doing mathematics also exist, perhaps the simplest being estimation of an answer, as a way of checking whether you are in the right "ball park." (The answer to 161.4 – 19.175 has to be around 160 – 20, or around 140; 96 divided by 18 is like 100 divided by 20, so the answer must be around 5.)

Estimation as a strategy

In all school subject areas there are cognitive strategies to enhance learning. But in 10,000 minutes of observation in elementary reading, social studies, and science classes (Durkin, 1979), in 13,000 minutes of observation of high school writing instruction (Applebee, 1981), and in 9,000 minutes spent observing general elementary instruction (Moely et al., 1986), *virtually no evidence of strategy teaching was found!* Teachers in the past simply have not made explicit the strategies that exist, and it is time to change that situation. But Pressley, Burkell, and associates (1990) have warned us that strategies are sometimes difficult to teach. Some students find them hard to remember, or extra work, or leading to just a little gain for a lot of time expended. Of interest also is that students who have had successful experiences in using learning strategies are remarkably inconsistent in their use of them afterward (Tobias, 1989). Also, many students have developed their own successful strategies. They already know how to learn effectively in school, and trying to teach them new or more efficient strategies may interfere with their methods for learning.

No evidence of strategy teaching

Nevertheless, we should remember that for some students strategies make schoolwork that was difficult much easier to learn. And, for some learning-

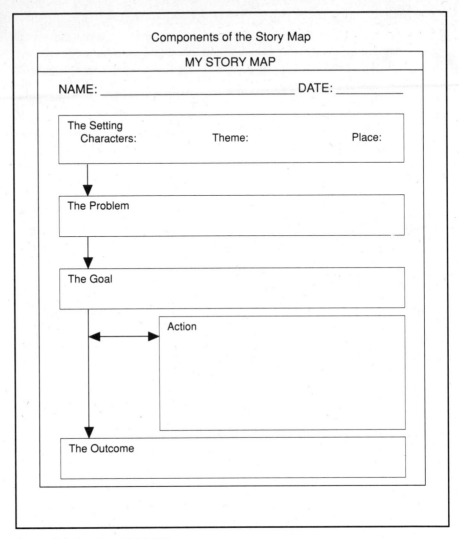

Source: Reprinted from Idol (1987).

disabled students, mastery of learning strategies can yield substantial gains in achievement. Strategy learning programs with special education students have been successfully field-tested by Deshler and his colleagues (e.g., Deshler & Schumaker, 1988).

Problem Solving

Recent years have seen much research on how people learn to solve problems. These studies have led to a wave of programs for teaching problem solving, thinking, and reasoning—what are often called the higher mental processes (Segal, Chipman, & Glaser, 1985; Chipman, Segal, & Glaser, 1985).

One simple model of problem solving identifies five critical cognitive processes: Identification, Definition, Exploration, Action, and Looking and learning—an IDEAL approach to problem solving (Bransford, Sherwood, Vye, & Rieser, 1986; Bransford & Stein, 1984).

First, to solve a problem, one must recognize that a problem exists. Readers who read a nonsensical passage but miss seeing that it is nonsense, writers who write an incomprehensible sentence but don't notice it, distance runners who change stride but are unaware that they are running a bit differently, babysitters in a cluttered environment who see no dangers for toddlers—all are failing to *identify* problems. Less mature and less able learners often simply fail to see that a problem exists. Thus they do not feel the need to change their behavior. If we can't sense a problem, obviously we can't solve it.

Identifying a problem

Once a problem is identified, it must be *defined*. Expert problem solvers in physics or mathematics may take much time to define problems. They try to classify problem types. (Is it a Newton's third-law problem? Is it an inclined plane problem? Could the problem be addressed by solving for two unknowns?) And they try to build representations—in their minds or on paper—of the problem. This kind of representation is crucial in successful problem solving (Larkin, 1985; Siegler, 1985). Inadequate representation can mean the retrieval of the wrong knowledge from long-term memory. It makes a big difference in how we solve a problem if we code it as one kind or another. Suppose a babysitter is having a problem with a toddler's exploration of the house. The representation of the problem in the mind of the babysitter might be that the child is curious, or it could be that the child is defying adult rules. The representation determines what knowledge will be brought up from long-term memory to address the problem. If the sitter believes the problem is one of curiosity, he can simply rearrange the environment, keeping the child occupied with toys and play. If he believes the problem is one of defiance, he has to begin working on a program of behavior modification. Different mental representations of a problem lead to different attempts at solutions.

Defining a problem

Mental representation

Different representations → different solution strategies

Next comes some kind of *exploration* of strategies for solution. Of the many different strategies for solving problems, one may be more appropriate for a mathematics word problem (for example, break the problem into parts); one may be more appropriate for physics (start at the goal you want and work backward); and one may be more appropriate for English literature (list all possible motives for a character's action).

Explore solution strategies

After exploring the possible strategies, we begin to try to solve the problem. That is, we *act,* then *look* at the effects of our actions. More successful problem solvers revise or abandon faulty strategies. They apparently monitor what they are doing while they are doing it. Less successful problem solvers keep on working with inadequate strategies. They may act, but they do not look and learn from their actions. Lochhead (1985) stated that "students' stubborn adherence to ineffectual . . . strategies may be the single most important deterrent to effective education" (p. 109).

Action

Looking and learning

These general problem-solving techniques are derived from hundreds of studies of how experts, students, artists, and practitioners process information

• The new version of formal discipline: Will this activity develop reasoning ability? Improve observational skills? Enhance the powers of communication? Strengthen the scientific intellect? (© 1984 Jerry Howard/Positive Images)

for solving problems. The good news is that teachers who spend time learning some of the techniques of problem solving can also learn how to model and reinforce problem solving in their students. Because the goal of teaching general approaches to problem solving is to have the students transfer what they learn to new situations, we turn now to the topic of transfer.

Transfer of Learning

The process that enables us to make previously learned responses in new situations is called *transfer*. Transfer often, but not always, allows us to perform sensibly and adequately in a new task. Learning about pulleys in physics should help a student lift a car engine onto a chassis. Learning how to make a shirt on a sewing machine in home economics should help a student sew a pair of pants at home. Learning English grammar should help a student write correct English. If not, why is this material in the school curriculum? The things learned in schools are intended to prepare students for life outside the schools. That is, education should foster transfer.

To understand transfer we must understand how learning to perform one task gives us the ability to perform another. This problem was addressed early in the twentieth century by several eminent American educational psychologists, among them E. L. Thorndike and Charles Judd. Their views of transfer have stood up reasonably well over the decades.

Traditional Views of Transfer

Thorndike and Woodworth (1901) reasoned, quite sensibly, that if the stimuli in two situations are similar and the same responses are called for, transfer should take place. The more the elements of one situation are identical with those of another, the greater the transfer. This theory of *identical elements* as the basis for transfer stemmed from a series of experiments Thorndike performed to see whether practice in one test, say, crossing out all the *E*'s on a page, would influence performance on another test, say, crossing out the *S*'s on the next page. The studies revealed that except for shared perceptual abilities or motor behaviors, or whatever was common to the two tests, no general transfer was present. Positive transfer, such as transfer from playing a piano to typing, takes place only insofar as eye-hand coordination skills are present in both tasks. Thorndike stated his findings clearly: "A change in one function alters another only insofar as the two functions have as factors identical elements" (1913, p. 358).

Identical elements

Thorndike's thinking was very different from the doctrine of *formal discipline,* which upheld the value of studying certain subjects because they train the mind. For example, one book of those times stated that

Formal discipline

> the value of the study of German lies in the scientific study of the language itself, in the consequent training of the reason, of the powers of observation, comparison and synthesis; in short, in the upbuilding and strengthening of the scientific intellect. (cited by Thorndike, 1913)

In the 1920s, Thorndike set out to disprove the doctrine of formal discipline. In a series of studies at the high school level he found no evidence that Latin was superior to French, or that geometry was superior to bookkeeping, or that any one course of study was superior, in terms of transfer, to any other. He concluded that those who have the most intellectual ability to begin with gain the most during the year. Whatever studies they take always seem to produce large gains in intellect:

> The chief reason why good thinkers seem superficially to have been made such by having taken certain school studies, is that good thinkers have taken such studies, becoming better by the inherent tendency of the good to gain more than the poor from any study. When the good thinkers studied Greek and Latin, these studies seemed to make good thinking. Now that the good thinkers study Physics and Trigonometry, these seem to make good thinkers. If the abler pupils should all study Physical Education and Dramatic Art, these subjects would seem to make good thinkers. These were, indeed, a large fraction of the program of studies for the best

thinkers the world has produced, the Athenian Greeks. (Brolyer, Thorndike, & Woodyard, 1927)

The theory of formal discipline almost disappeared after these studies were presented. It still keeps popping up, however, usually in different forms in different decades. To hear the advocates of computers talk, learning to program can improve students' performance in dozens of areas. This expectation is based on the old formal discipline doctrine, with the learning of programming substituted for the learning of Greek and Latin. Thorndike would have taken a dim view of these claims.

Identity of substance

Thorndike's theory that identical elements account for the phenomenon of transfer was widely advocated, but mainly in its narrowest form—*identity of substance*—one-to-one correspondence between the elements of what was studied and what was to be done in real life. Thus analysts of curriculum believed that learning addition helps in learning multiplication only because part of multiplication requires the ability to do addition.

Identity of procedure

But Thorndike had also pointed out that there could be *identity of procedure,* whereby the general habits, attitudes, principles, patterns, and procedures we have learned can facilitate performance in a wide variety of situations. Some educators believe Thorndike's identity-of-procedures form is the more prevalent way in which transfer takes place. These educators argue that principles and generalizations are the key elements in the transfer of what is learned in one situation to performance in another situation. For example, a child learns that breaking words into syllables can help in the phonic analysis of words. To the word *ossify,* the child learns to say ŏs ʃ-fī'; to the word *terminal,* the child says tûr'mə-nəl. The stimuli and responses are different in the two situations. No one would claim that there are identical elements in the two tasks. Yet the child's learning of the *principle* of syllabication in one task probably facilitates the learning of the other task.

Transfer value of principles

The transfer value of principles was first upheld by Judd (1908), then by others (for example, Hendrickson & Schroeder, 1941). These researchers did not analyze stimulus-response relationships, but they experimented with the teaching of principles of such generality that they facilitated solving many problems and learning many things that seemed very different. If children learn by rote that the number after 4 is 5, then are asked what is the number after 4,723, they may be completely stumped. But suppose the teaching they have received has concentrated on principles. Suppose the children have learned that the next number, whatever it is, is always 1 more than the last number, whatever that was. Then they may deduce that the proper response is 4,724. Knowledge of principles, compared to factual knowledge, holds up well. Principles have "staying power."

Principles, although usually helpful in providing positive transfer, can also result in negative transfer. That is, a principle that is helpful for one set of problems can mislead you when you try to solve a new problem. Luchins (1942) presented subjects with a set of problems of the following type: Given a 3-quart jar, a 21-quart jar, and a 127-quart jar, how would you measure out 100 quarts? One solution to the problem is to fill the 127-quart jar and, from that jar, fill the 21-quart jar and then the 3-quart jar twice. Or $X = C - B - 2A$, where C equals the third jar, B equals the second jar, and A equals the first jar. Now suppose the problem reads: Given a 6-quart jar, a 9-quart jar, and a 42-quart jar, how would you obtain 21 quarts? Again the problem is solved with the formula $X = C - B - 2A$, or $21 = 42 - 9 - 2(6)$. But what if in a later problem in the series you are asked to measure 20 quarts of water with a 3-quart jar, a 23-quart jar, and a 49-quart jar. Try the problem before you read on.

If you solved this problem by using the same formula, you have demonstrated *negative transfer*. The principle you learned in previous tasks has influenced you to solve the problem inefficiently. It really is simpler to fill the 23-quart jar and remove 3 quarts. In other words, the formula $C - B - 2A$ was misapplied because under these conditions the formula $B - A$ would suffice. When previous learning hinders new learning or problem solving, or leads us to respond incorrectly, we have negative transfer. Breaking a *response set*—a tendency to respond in the same way despite new conditions—is hard to do. But unless you make a conscious effort to build into students' lessons some experiences to get them to think more flexibly, they may not do so. When teaching students about the characteristics of fish, for example, you should also introduce students to whales and dolphins, to teach the principle that not everything that swims in the sea is a fish. When teaching about birds, you should discuss the kiwi, a flightless bird, and the bat, a flying mammal. If the point of a lesson is to teach the concept that most things contract when cold, fill a glass container with water and freeze it. Negative transfer can be avoided only by conscious attempts to teach flexibility in applying principles.

To this point we have talked about how principles are involved in positive or negative transfer. Principles can also take the form of *rules*. Children can be taught rules that prevent them from learning new responses (e.g., "Always color in the lines"), or they can be taught rules that facilitate new responses (e.g., "Say the first thing that comes into your mind").

Clearly the principles you teach and the rules you set will affect the future learning and problem solving of your students. Therefore you must give considerable thought to the transfer value of the principles and rules with which you work. And you should point out the transfer value to students; indicate where there are similarities between new tasks and old ones. Never take it for granted that they can apply what they learn to new situations. Help your students see those applications.

We can conclude from the older studies of transfer that positive transfer takes place when the elements of two tasks are similar. These similarities can occur in simple eye-hand coordination acts or in complex mathematical skills. When two tasks have identities of substance or identities of procedure, there will be positive transfer between them *if* the learner recognizes the similarities. An important principle of teaching is "Point out the similarities in different tasks so that transfer can take place."

Negative transfer

Response set

Flexibility

Transfer of rules

Make transfer explicit

Contemporary Views of Transfer

The traditional view is that transfer occurs when elements in a new task resemble elements in the original learning task or when principles learned in one task can be used in another task. Current research accepts these findings but seems to blur the distinction. Cognitive psychologists, in studying the thought processes of people who demonstrate an ability to transfer learning, ask two major questions:

1. What is it that people who show transfer do that helps them bridge the gap between the original learning and the new situation?
2. If we find out what these people do, can we teach it in such a way that we can help those who do not spontaneously show evidence of transfer?

The research on metacognition, use of models, and expert-novice differences in problem solving tells us that the cognitive skills of people who show transfer are indeed different from those of people who do not show transfer, and that some of the positive-transfer skills can be taught.

Metacognition.   Knowledge about one's own cognitive system is called *metacognition*. Metacognition during learning and transfer is of two kinds: thoughts about what we know and thoughts about regulating how we go about learning (A. L. Brown, 1978; Chipman, Segal, & Glaser, 1985; Flavell, 1976).

Metacognitive knowledge includes the ability to ask ourselves these kinds of questions:

- What do I know about this subject (a self-administered achievement test)?
- How much time will I need to learn this?
- What is a good plan of attack to solve this?
- How can I predict or estimate the outcome of this task?
- How should I revise my procedures?
- How can I spot an error if I make one?
- Did I understand what I have just read?

Monitoring skills   Metacognitive skills are monitoring skills that are activated during learning and instruction. If we did not know how to check our answers, allocate enough time to study, or check to see if we have relevant knowledge already stored, we would have to face each learning task as if it were our first. Learning would always be very difficult. Metacognitive skills make learning easier.

Although metacognitive skills usually develop slowly as we get older, the process is not simply part of the natural developmental process. Experience and explicit instruction seem to play a much more important role in the development of these crucial cognitive skills than does maturity alone. As a consequence,

• *From extensive experience, expert chess players learn tens of thousands of game types. (© 1987 Ulrike Welsch)*

teachers have a responsibility to help students develop their metacognitive skills.

When compared with average students, children who are mildly retarded and learning disabled sometimes show metacognitive deficits (A. L. Brown & Palincsar, 1982). Suppose you accept the hypothesis that students with learning disabilities have different and deficient monitoring processes for learning. You might try to handle the problem by simply instructing these students to think in the ways that others think when they engage in metacognition. By doing just that, Palincsar and Brown (1981) illustrated the importance of metacognition to learning and transfer. These researchers identified some junior high school students with IQ scores of about 90. The students could decode prose when they read but had comprehension scores at about the 7th percentile rank on national norms. They lacked a skill most of us take for granted: using the reading of the words to understand and learn from the text. These students read words but seemed unaware of what and how to learn from the words they read. To make up for what seemed to be a lack of metacognitive skills, Palincsar and Brown first gave the students intensive corrective feedback when they tried to answer comprehension questions. They praised the students for correct responding and taught them how to change their responses when they were wrong. Then the students learned study strategies: how to paraphrase main ideas, how to classify information, how to predict the questions that might be asked about certain segments of the prose material, how to clarify what confused them, and how they might solve their own problems. That is, they learned metacognitive skills to use when learning.

As shown in Figure 7.11, the percentage of correct responses to comprehension questions for one student was about 15 percent before the special instruction. After corrective feedback, the percentage went up to about 50 percent. And after metacognitive strategies for learning were taught, the student was generally able to answer about 80 percent of the comprehension questions correctly.

In addition, the metacognitive strategies learned by these students transferred to their work in the regular classroom. The students showed improvements ranging from 20 to 46 percent in classroom performance. After a brief reinstatement of training sometime later, evidence for sustained improvement in learning and transfer was found months later.

Every teacher's goal is to have comprehension skills transfer this way, but not every student shows the ability. How did these researchers do it? They assumed, as you can, that many learning and transfer problems are due to deficits in metacognitive skills. Many students need training in self-regulation (see Chapter 6), self-monitoring, self-checking, problem identification, and the like. They can learn to learn only when they have mastered generalized cognitive strategies. Otherwise, each new learning task is nearly insurmountable in its complexity. Learning to comprehend and transfer what is learned from text material is how much school learning takes place. For this kind of learning students need metacognitive skills to

Learning to learn

- make and refine predictions about what they are reading.
- maintain focus during instruction and problem solving.
- know how to vary their focus and break set when they are doing something wrong.
- relate ideas to existing knowledge structures.
- ask questions of themselves.
- pick out and attend to the important information or characteristics of the text or task.
- dismiss irrelevant information or characteristics of the text or task.
- recognize when a relationship occurs or is implied.
- use visualization when reading and problem solving.
- consider the worth of ideas.
- know when to ask for help. (See Tierney, 1985, for additional skills; see also A. L. Brown, Armbruster, & Baker, 1985; A. L. Brown, Bransford, Ferrara, & Campione, 1983.)

The point of all this is that we do certain things when we teach novices to play chess or poker; to ride a horse, a bike, or a skateboard; or to drive a car. We

Record of the Percentage of Comprehension Questions Answered Correctly by a Student Before, During, and After Metacognitive Training

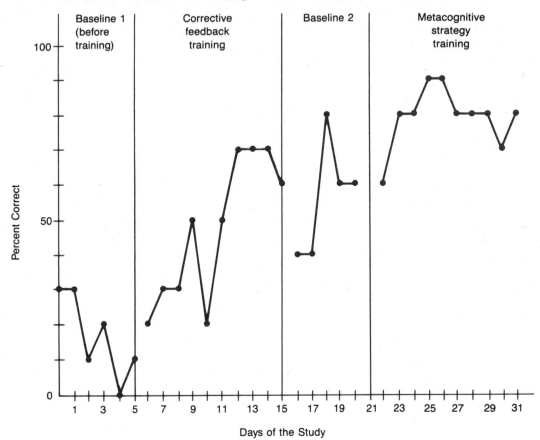

Source: Adapted from Palincsar and Brown (1981).

usually model for them; we teach them strategies for learning in that area; we give them a vocabulary to use in describing their performance; and we teach them how to regulate and monitor their own performance. Along with teaching them a strategy for doing something—say, asking questions while reading text—we teach them strategies for monitoring what they do. The monitoring part of instruction is what we mean by metacognition. Too often in schools we provide direct instruction only in areas where behavior is easily observed; we spend much less of our time on instruction in metacognitive skills. As A. L. Brown noted, "Metacognitive deficiencies are the problem of the novice, regardless of age. Ignorance is not necessarily age related; rather it is more a function of inexperience in a new (and difficult) problem situation" (1980, p. 475). Experts in areas such as chess, automobile driving, poker, horseback riding, or teaching may be experts because of their metacognitive skills. Those

Novices have metacognitive deficiencies

skills allow them to apply what they know to problem areas, to transfer their knowledge. Perhaps the greatest benefit of mentoring relationships is that they enable novices to learn how their mentor thinks about problems. It is the mentor's habits of mind as much as his factual knowledge that novices need to master.

Conceptual Models for Understanding and Transfer.   A *conceptual model* consists of the words or diagrams used in instruction to help learners build mental models of what they are studying. For example, not all information about, say, how radar works or how brakes work in an automobile is worth remembering. Ideas are not all created equal, though novices do not seem to know this fact and cannot always distinguish the important ideas from the unimportant ones. What conceptual models do well is to highlight the main ideas or objects or actions in a system. They are accurate and useful representations of knowledge that is needed when solving problems in some particular domain. Figure 7.12 shows three conceptual models used by Mayer (1989) in an informative series of studies. One model is for understanding how radar works, one for understanding how brakes work, and one for understanding the nitrogen cycle. As part of instruction, conceptual models like these were taught to some students, while other students, those in control groups, received instruction without having conceptual models presented and discussed.

In the study that focused on the learning of radar, for example, both groups heard a lecture. But one group of students had one minute to study the conceptual model that was developed, a model that featured the main steps and processes in the conversion of time to distance. The model attempted also to make the major elements in the system more concrete: the radar pulse, the remote object to be sensed, the transmitter, the receiver, the clock, and the converter. What did a minute's worth of studying the model yield? Compared to the control group, the students who studied the model before the lecture recalled 57 percent more conceptual information, scored 14 percent lower in verbatim information, and scored 85 percent higher on problem-solving transfer tasks (e.g., answering questions like, How can you increase the area under radar surveillance?).

When the topic taught was how automobile brakes work, the models were included within the instructional passages that were read by students. The control group of students had no such diagrams accompanying the text they studied. Compared to control students, and averaging over two separate studies, the model-reading students scored about 35 percent higher on conceptual information, about 7 percent lower on verbatim retention tests, and about 63 percent higher on a test of creative solutions to transfer problems (e.g., What could be done to improve the reliability of brakes?).

In another study a conceptual model of the nitrogen cycle was included as a supplement to a passage from a high school biology text, which, like many science texts, was densely packed with information. With such texts, students have a hard time deciding what is and what is not important. The model detailed the five steps in the cycle: *fixation*, whereby bacteria take and convert atmo-

Representations of knowledge

Verbatim scores down; transfer scores up

FIGURE 7.12   *Three Conceptual Models for Promoting Transfer*

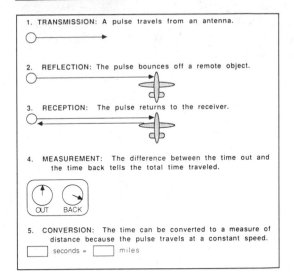

1. TRANSMISSION: A pulse travels from an antenna.

2. REFLECTION: The pulse bounces off a remote object.

3. RECEPTION: The pulse returns to the receiver.

4. MEASUREMENT: The difference between the time out and the time back tells the total time traveled.

        OUT   BACK

5. CONVERSION: The time can be converted to a measure of distance because the pulse travels at a constant speed.

        seconds =   miles

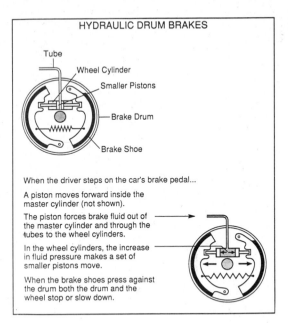

HYDRAULIC DRUM BRAKES

Tube
Wheel Cylinder
Smaller Pistons
Brake Drum
Brake Shoe

When the driver steps on the car's brake pedal...

A piston moves forward inside the master cylinder (not shown).

The piston forces brake fluid out of the master cylinder and through the tubes to the wheel cylinders.

In the wheel cylinders, the increase in fluid pressure makes a set of smaller pistons move.

When the brake shoes press against the drum both the drum and the wheel stop or slow down.

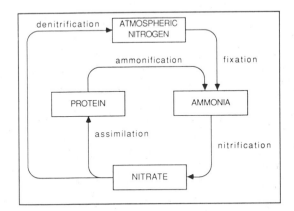

Source: From Mayer (1989).

spheric nitrogen (N_2) into ammonia (NH_3); *nitrification,* whereby bacteria in the soil convert the ammonia (NH_3) into nitrate (NO_3); *assimilation,* whereby plant cells take in the nitrates (NO_3) and convert them into protein (NH_2); *ammonification,* whereby bacteria in the soil convert the protein (NH_2) from decaying plants and wastes into ammonia (NH_3); and *denitrification,* whereby the bacteria in the soil convert nitrates (NO_3) in the soil back into atmospheric nitrogen (N_2). Compared with students in the control group, students who had the conceptual model to use as they read the passages on the nitrogen cycle from the textbook scored 73 percent higher on conceptual information, 14 percent lower on verbatim retention, and 42 percent higher on transfer problems (e.g., If you used only natural means, how could you make the soil richer in nitrogen for use by plants?).

These studies are intriguing. They show, of course, that verbatim information scores may go down when conceptual models are used. Apparently, when the information is reorganized into a conceptual model for the students to remember, some of the factual information is lost. But that may not be much of a loss. The studies show also how the models helped students retain the major conceptual information in the area they were studying. Apparently the models direct attention to the key objects, locations, and events. That is probably more important than having attention drawn to all of the declarative knowledge in that domain. Most important of all is that the studies reveal that problem-solving tasks requiring transfer are performed remarkably better by students who have been exposed to conceptual models. These students probably used those models to build mental representations of great parsimony and power in the domain studied. Students who build a personal mental representation based upon the conceptual model presented to them, and who learn to manipulate those models cognitively, appear to be far better able to solve transfer tasks.

Mental representations of parsimony and power

For students who already have a lot of information about some area, or for students who have a good deal of intellectual ability, we would expect the models to be less effective. Such students may have developed their own effective strategies for connecting and remembering information that is important to them. And the data confirm this expectation. Using conceptual models primarily affects the performance of those with little knowledge in the area, or those of lower ability. Furthermore, the models work best when used before a lesson (like a visual advance organizer) or during the lesson (like an illustration that presents the important elements, processes, or events to be learned). The models do not work well when presented after instruction occurs.

The Seven C's

Mayer suggested that teachers build models using the Seven C's as a guide (notice the mnemonic aid). Such models should be

- Complete, having all the important information within them;
- Concise and not contain an overwhelming amount of information;
- Coherent, holding together in a rather transparent way, with the logic of the model apparent to students who do not know a lot about the area they are studying;
- Concrete, rather than abstract;
- Conceptual, that is, explaining something, not just listing things;
- Correct, that is, really correspond to the processes or relationships under study, not like some useful but incorrect models (e.g.,

explaining that electricity is like water flowing) that, under certain circumstances, can be misleading;

- Considerate, using a learner's vocabulary and an organization appropriate to the learner's ability and age.

In sum, conceptual models of the type described by Mayer could enhance transfer of school knowledge for many students. Yet in thousands of hours of classroom observation, investigators have seen little use of such models.

Expert-Novice Differences in Problem Solving.   What makes an expert an expert? One answer is that experts have an uncanny ability to solve unique problems. That is, they can organize their previously acquired knowledge in such a way that they can apply it to seemingly new situations and resolve them. This application to the new is, of course, what we mean by transfer. So if we study how experts and novices differ in problem-solving processes, we may learn something about how transfer takes place.

For example, how do expert chess players differ from novice chess players? The research suggests that one of the ways in which they differ is that experts, over the years they have played, have stored in long-term memory as many as 50,000 familiar patterns. These 50,000 perceptually distinct and familiar configurations of the chess board are the expert's "vocabulary" for playing chess. It is like having a vocabulary of 50,000 nouns and verbs for describing your environment. Each of the 50,000 patterns has associated with it certain moves. The expert knows that for a certain kind of game, certain subroutines must be used to win. The expert, when playing ten chess games simultaneously, is in fact playing ten distinct patterns. The expert seems to know that on board 1 is game type 6,974 and that it can be won by concentrating on how the bishop moves; or that on board 2 is game type 12,074, which calls for queen and rook attacks if the opponent moves the queen's knight. Each game is classified as a game type. The new, first-time-ever-seen configuration of the board in a game of chess is translated by the expert into a recognizable "old friend"—a pattern that is known (see de Groot, 1965).

Classifying problem types

How do expert physicists differ from novices? One difference is that experts take more time than novices in studying a problem. But once they start to work, they solve problems faster than novices do. The experts also seem more often than novices to construct an abstract representation of the problem in their minds. That is, in their working memory they hold mental representations of the blocks, pulleys, inclined planes, levers, or whatever they need to solve a problem. Expert physicists also tend to classify new problems more frequently. They may decide a problem is a type-X problem, to be solved by using the laws of inclined planes. Or they may see the problem as belonging to the type that deals with forces, pulleys, and blocks, which are always solvable by using some version of Newton's second law, $F = MA$ (force = mass × acceleration) (Chi, Glaser, & Rees, 1982).

Problem representation

After extensive experience in their areas of interest, experts in chess and experts in physics seem to show positive transfer—the use of old information in

Use of routines

a new context to solve problems—by very similar mechanisms! Experts in both fields attempt (1) to classify a problem as a particular type, (2) to represent the problem visually in their minds, and then (3) to use well-known routines to solve the problems.

Classification is very important here. Once we know what kind of problem we're dealing with, the solution seems to follow easily. Research on college students solving algebra word problems and physicians solving medical problems, as well as the work on chess and physics experts, shows that experienced problem solvers work with a "problem" schema. Once they find the schema—the abstract representation of the phenomenon—in long-term memory, it directs the solution. Novices do not appear to have developed elaborate schemata. So each problem they face is truly new and therefore extremely difficult. Experts, on the other hand, have stored in memory many problem schemata and the associated moves that generally produce a solution. They've acquired these schemata as a result of extensive experience with the phenomena on which they are expert. Expert teachers, auto mechanics, chefs, and tailors—no less than chess masters and theoretical physicists—seem to show transfer in the same way.

All experts alike

For teachers there are two important implications here:

Lengthy experience is necessary for expertise

- Students must have lots of experience with a domain of knowledge in order to learn the skills needed for transfer. The "smorgasbord" and "surface" education we sometimes give our students (one unit of this, one unit of that; one hour of this topic, thirty minutes of that topic) will not be enough to produce expertise. This kind of education develops students who are *familiar* with a vast array of events and domains of knowledge, but who are experts in none of them.

Modeling of problem solving

- Teachers can help students solve problems by purposefully modeling the problem-solving strategy needed. The teacher might say, "Look everyone! When a block of mass M1 is put on top of a block of mass M2, a horizontal force F1 must be applied. Picture it in your mind! When we face problems of mass and force, we should decide whether the laws of force or energy take precedence. If energy, then . . ."

Evidence is mounting that problem-solving and transfer abilities can be markedly improved by teaching students self-monitoring, self-regulating, and self-management skills for supervising their own learning and their application of learning to new situations (Belmont, Butterfield, & Ferretti, 1982). We have always hoped students would *learn* to think, to solve novel problems, and to show transfer. But we have not really known how to *teach* these skills. Today the cognitive sciences are giving us information that points to how such thinking skills can be developed.

Teaching for Transfer

We have two basic ways of teaching for transfer. We can concentrate on substantive transfer, using the theory of identical elements to guide our teaching. Or we can concentrate on procedural transfer, using our knowledge about how principles and rules can apply across a wide variety of situations. These two approaches are not mutually exclusive; both are important in teaching for transfer.

Teaching for Substantive Transfer

When we concentrate on substantive transfer, we might argue that we try to teach directly whatever it is we want the person to learn. If you need computer programming in your job, you should study programming during training, preferably the same type of programming you are going to need on the job. (How much knowledge about the history of computers is necessary for a programmer to be efficient is a highly complex question.) If you want to study Plato in the original, learn Greek. But don't expect that experience to help you in learning German. To learn German, you would do better to study German directly. Training in statistics might help you solve research problems because statistics is a tool for solving such problems, but it certainly will not help you by sharpening your general reasoning power.

These statements agree with that part of the theory of identical elements that is concerned with identity of substance. Be careful, then, that curriculum intended to improve the students' readiness for learning a particular skill or subject can be defended as having positive transfer for that skill or subject. Often we do better to teach children exactly what we want them to know. You might find that the time spent in readiness training is better used for direct training in the curriculum area you want your students to master. As Hudgins (1977) noted, in the upper elementary grades sentence diagramming has been defended because it "prepares" students for and improves their mastery of sentence structure. Yet the empirical research reveals that "pupils can be taught diagramming rather efficiently, but there is very little benefit in terms of sentence mastery. In fact, in one of the studies . . . the control children actually improved a bit more in sentence mastery than the children who had been taught diagramming" (p. 153). But the myths about transfer linger on, despite empirical evidence that disproves them.

On the other hand, a complex activity such as reading can be broken into subtasks that can be learned more easily because they have been made simpler, and these simpler tasks can then be combined intact into greater and more complex activities. In this situation, the idea of readiness training makes better sense.

Readiness

**Teach exactly
what's needed**

• *Library skills—a highly transferable tool. (© Mimi Forsyth/Monkmeyer Press Photo Services)*

Teaching for Procedural Transfer

When we concentrate on procedural transfer, we often are concerned with the way we teach broadly applicable concepts, principles, and procedures. Learning the meaning of words like *untie* and *unfair* is perfectly appropriate, but notice how much more useful it is to learn that the prefix *un* means "not" or "contrary to." With this knowledge, students can try to find meaning in many more words: *unaffected, unaccompanied, unarmed,* and so on. You should make it a point to

Transferable tools   teach such highly transferable tools as library skills, the Venn diagrams and truth tables used in logic, and algorithms. All these have wide utility if, and perhaps only if, they are taught in such a way that students can recognize new situations to which these skills are applicable. Our abstract knowledge structures, our schemata, should be built to accommodate the widest range of examples and applications. That is, you should always try to present a wide array of examples in which the student can see how new principles and techniques can be used. Many of those examples should be placed in real-world settings. Ultimately much of what is learned in school must meet some criterion of usefulness or value in the nonschool world.

We have emphasized the transfer value of general skills and techniques. But we also must note that attitudes toward self and toward areas of learning are among the most transferable phenomena. If children think of themselves as competent and of an area of learning as "knowable," we can expect them to attack problems vigorously rather than to exhibit withdrawn, noncreative approaches to new situations. For this reason, we pay much attention in Chapter 8 to the students' attitudes toward achievement in general and to the kind of explanations (attributions) they make for their own success and failure.

Attitudes are transferable

Mindfulness and Transfer

Substantive transfer happens because social situations or physical environments are similar, or because the skills needed in two settings are alike. This kind of transfer is almost mindless. It's what allows you to rent a Toyota and drive off without difficulty even though you usually drive a Buick. Procedural transfer, however, often calls for effort, for *mindfulness*. We usually have to take principles and concepts deliberately from one area of knowledge and apply them to another (Salomon & Perkins, 1989). Suppose you've learned in educational psychology the importance of "controlling reinforcement contingencies." You can apply this strategy to running a newspaper as its editor, or to selling a consumer product line as a sales executive. This is procedural transfer. But it demands conscious effort. You have to *decontextualize,* or separate the idea from its original associations, so that you know and understand its essential elements and can apply them to a new context. For example, you probably learned the concept of rhythm from banging a spoon on a plate, or in a music class very early on. And it was probably not long before you were using the concept to discuss dance, poetry, plays, the graphic arts, the shape of a seashell, and a method of contraception. To apply the concept of rhythm correctly across contexts, you had to decontextualize it, separating it from its original context.

Mindfulness = effort

Decontextualization

Because transfer across dissimilar contexts requires so much effort, so much mindfulness, it is often avoided. Students who have strategies to help them learn effectively in school do not always use them at home. Students who can compute the area of a rectangle in math class cannot figure out at home how much carpeting is needed for a room. And students who cook meals for five siblings and parents at home cannot measure at school. Their knowledge is inert, unusable outside of the context in which it was learned (J. S. Brown, Collins, & Duguid, 1989; Cognition and Technology Group at Vanderbilt, 1990). It is now clear that the usual case is that knowledge in one context is not freed: It is bound to a single situation and does not easily transfer for use in dissimilar contexts. One reason for this lack is that we don't make the effort—we are not usually mindful (Salomon & Globerson, 1987; Salomon & Perkins, 1989).

Our job as teachers is to encourage students to work at generalizing and applying what they know, to be active transferrers. If we are not ourselves more deliberate, more mindful, in our attempts to foster transfer, we can expect only a limited amount of substantive transfer to take place and even less procedural transfer.

General Guidelines for Transfer

How do we help our students become active transferrers? Here are some general guidelines:

Real-world similarity

1. *Make the training situation as similar to the real-world situation as possible.* At the beginning you may teach in a simplified situation. But you are not finished with your teaching job. If typists usually type in noisy typing pools, don't train them only in a quiet room. You'll end up with a problem of transfer. Don't teach children how to build a sundial only in the classroom out of store-bought materials. Take them to a field, where they'd use a sundial, and let them build it out of the sticks and stones they find there. Don't ask your journalism majors only to write a story in twenty days if in the real world they would have only twenty minutes. If you cannot simulate real-world conditions, at least describe them, so that students are not confused when they come up against the real-world situation. One factor that prevents novices from solving problems as well as experts is that novices have only encountered textbook problems, not "real" problems. Textbook problems are neat and clean; problems in the real world are often messy and complex. Let your students know what to expect out there.

Practice opportunities

2. *Provide lots of practice on the original task before you ask students to transfer their learning.* This guideline is adhered to strictly in flight training. Landings, simulated and real, are practiced over and over on the training field before a student pilot is allowed to try to land at another field. Experts get to be experts only after much experience!

Practice on related tasks

3. *Provide lots of practice on related problems.* If you're teaching about contracts, give your students many examples of many different kinds of contracts with different wording to make them aware that even in the midst of changing conditions, there are some constants: the contractor, the contractee, the terms, the price, and so on. Try to teach students how to break apart—to decontextualize—an idea, to separate its abstract qualities from the immediate situation so that the idea can be applied in more than one situation.

4. *Watch for negative transfer when stimuli are similar but the responses required are different.* For example, to the novice learner 3 + 2 and 3 − 2 may appear to be similar, even though the responses called for are different. *Rome* and *Romania* are easy to confuse; so are the words *ethnography, ethnology,* and *ethology.* If you recognize the

potential for confusion, you can spot areas where students may have difficulty. When stimuli are similar, spend some time differentiating among them—a process called *stimulus predifferentiation* when it is done early in a sequence of learning. Remember that if students can't differentiate the similarities and differences among stimuli, they can't determine what kind of response to make.

Stimulus predifferentiation

5. *Emphasize the early learning of prerequisite skills or knowledge.* If you are teaching students to identify igneous, metamorphic, and sedimentary rocks, teach the identifications early in the learning unit. Once students master initial required tasks, they can better transfer their knowledge to related tasks. For example, if you teach students how to solve a problem like $8\overline{)56}$, that knowledge can help them solve $83274\overline{)93254031.2}$. Learning what happened to the Soviet Union during World War II gives students a basis for understanding Soviet policy during the cold war. And learning the movements necessary to turn on skis when on a slight grade is immensely useful—that is, these skills do transfer—when students have to turn on a steep and icy ski run.

Teach prerequisites early

6. *Give your students conceptual models.* As noted earlier, either you or they can construct a model that captures the essence of what it is that needs to be learned. The models help students in problem solving and transfer tasks.

Conceptual models

7. *Whenever you state a principle or generalization, give students a wide variety of examples.* If you are teaching the concept of community, you can talk about ants, bees, and Eskimos, as well as the country club, small town, tenants' association, neighborhood association, and Alcoholics Anonymous. When you say that geometry and trigonometry are useful, show students how they can use these subjects to measure distances between places in town, estimate the height of buildings, determine the number of tiles needed to cover the floor of a room, or navigate a boat across a lake.

Examples

8. *Ask students to make some applications themselves.* Have them determine how learning to measure the speed of sound can be used. Ask them whether a new writer resembles anyone else they know, or whether the new novel's plot refers to events with which they are familiar. Try to get young students to think of the kinds of measuring they do in their homes and to think of how often they need to measure. In short, help your students link what they learn in the classroom to the world outside of school. Get them to act mindfully. Have them act in a generative manner.

Applications

9. Get students to think aloud when they are trying to solve problems. Use what they say as a basis for learning about their metacognitive strategies. What skills do they appear to have? What skills do they lack? If a student has not learned some important self-governing, self-monitoring, and self-checking skills, learning and transfer will be hampered. You can help teach these skills by explicitly

Thinking aloud

modeling how you go about solving problems and getting students to imitate you.

SUMMARY

The information-processing model explains how information from our external environment enters memory. The process begins with a stimulus that elicits an orienting response—a response that makes us want to know more about the stimulus. Attention is critical here and often is the response to the psychophysical, emotional, discrepant, or commanding properties of the stimulus.

Once we respond to a stimulus, the stimulus (the information from the environment) briefly enters our short-term sensory storage system. Again attention is important. If we don't attend to the information, we forget it. If we do, it moves into short-term memory or working memory. Short-term memory is conscious memory, a store that's limited to about seven bits of information at a time. Working memory, which may be a part of short-term memory, is a sort of mental scratch pad. The information held in short-term memory and working memory must be encoded or rehearsed to move on to long-term memory. If it isn't, it's forgotten. The challenge for teachers is to trigger the encoding and rehearsal processes, to get what they want students to learn into long-term memory, then to help them retrieve it.

The first part of this challenge is relatively easy. To get material from short-term or working memory into long-term memory we just have to see to it that the student focuses attention on material for a period of time. Much more difficult is retrieval. The first step in the retrieval process is making the information meaningful. We do this by making associations—by tying something that is to be learned to something the students already know. How? Analyze the material for associations that could help students learn more efficiently. Use mediators to create meaningful links between unrelated ideas. Advance organizers and hierarchical structure help to organize material in ways that are compatible with how memory works. Schemata—abstract structures that represent the knowledge stored in memory—are also important here. Where a relevant schema does not exist, you must provide it for the material you are teaching. Most of these ideas fit into the generative model of learning. When we can relate new material to what students already know, they can generate their own meaning for the new material, and learn and retrieve it more easily.

Active learning—recitation and physical activity—also makes retrieval easier, perhaps because it adds another basis for coding new material. The overlearning helps students to understand complex material, not just to remember simple facts. Mnemonic devices—imagery, the method of loci, and keywords—are strategies that improve retrieval and free students to concentrate on complex material. Don't forget to HI and UMF!

The insights of cognitive psychology also inform us that learning is a process of making meaning. The ways students think about problems, the schemata they invoke, and the naive misperceptions they hold must be understood if one is to teach effectively. Furthermore, the strategies students use or don't use in learning need to be assessed. If missing or inappropriate, those strategies need to be taught. Not everyone is likely to be a great problem solver. But methods for solving problems better do exist and are worthy of being taught. In sum, studying our students' thinking is as worthwhile as studying their behavior. Teachers don't have the luxury of being either a behaviorist or a cognitivist. They are inevitably *both*.

Transfer enables us to use previously learned knowledge and skills in new situations. The greater the number of identical elements, both in substance and in procedure, the greater the transfer. Principles and rules usually transfer well, but when misapplied, they can cause negative transfer, hindering new learning.

Metacognition helps in transfer. Metacognitive skills are the monitoring processes we use when we learn. They develop through experience and explicit instruction. They are necessary for classifying problems, representing problems visually in our minds, and retrieving from memory the solutions to problems. Conceptual models also help in fostering transfer.

Teachers have two general responsibilities: to teach material thoroughly and to model problem-solving behavior. Meeting these responsibilities is in part determined by the type of transfer for which you are teaching. To teach for substantive transfer, it may be best to teach exactly what you want students to know. For procedural transfer, you should usually emphasize broad concepts and highly transferable skills. Unlike substantive transfer, which is almost unconscious, procedural transfer demands mindfulness—an effort to decontextualize ideas.

There are several guidelines you can use: Make the training situation as much like the real-world situation as possible; give students lots of practice on the original task and on related tasks; guard against negative transfer; emphasize prerequisites of what you want students to learn; teach students conceptual models; give students a wide variety of examples; ask students to make some applications themselves; and get students to think aloud when they are working, so that you can "view" their metacognitive processes.

8 ☰ Motivation and Learning

OVERVIEW

Everyone knows what motivation is, how it makes a difference between resentful boredom at one extreme and ravenous interest at the other. Shakespeare wrote of "the whining schoolboy, with his satchel and shining morning face, creeping like snail unwillingly to school." And most of us have known a time of ardent learning, when we could not get quickly enough to the truth of a matter about which we were deeply concerned, when we were altogether entranced. *Motivation* is what moves us from boredom to interest. It is what energizes us and directs our activity. Motivation is sometimes likened to the engine and steering wheel of an automobile. Energy and direction are at the center of the concept of motivation.

Motivation is a broad concept. It embraces several other terms that describe influences on the energy and direction of our behavior: *needs, interests, values, attitudes, aspirations,* and *incentives.* Our needs and the urge to satisfy them are a primary source of motivation. But we follow as well the paths picked for us by our interests, our values, and our attitudes toward activities or events. Our aspirations, and the incentives we are interested in, influence our behavior as well.

In this chapter we first examine both internal and external influences on motivation. Then we discuss how motivation affects behavior and learning in our students and our schools. We explore one of the most important of the internal variables, achievement motivation—the need to succeed, to be good at something. Without a personal need to achieve, economies would not function, scholarship would be reduced to pedestrian levels, and scientific and artistic projects would stop. We also discuss attributions, how teachers and students assign responsibility for their successes and failures at the tasks they try. We then briefly discuss the needs for affiliation (friendships, social contacts), power, and approval, and how these needs affect learning in our classrooms.

Then we look at variables that are mostly external to the person, though the distinction between personal and environmental variables is easily blurred because a personal variable can also be shaped and maintained by our environment. In particular we explore the operant-conditioning approach to the understanding and improvement of motivation. This approach concentrates on the environment—particularly the reinforcement contingencies in the environment. We also present some ideas about the motivating effects of frustration. Like the rest of us, students are energized and directed by frustration, but often that leads toward aggressive behavior.

Toward the end of this chapter we focus on how to change motive patterns by changing either the attributions persons make or the environmental contingencies that shape their behavior. We also examine two behavior-modification approaches—token economies and contracts. Both have been highly effective in improving the performance of unmotivated students. Finally we present fifteen ideas about how to control certain classroom variables to increase student motivation.

Personal (Internal) and Environmental (External) Influences on Motivation

Behavior depends on properties of the person and the environment in interaction with one another and in interaction with one's thinking and judgments about one's own behavior. This view of behavior, called *reciprocal determinism* (Bandura, 1978), is often shown as follows:

Reciprocal determinism

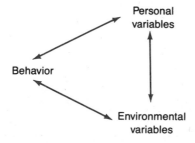

Personal variables include both *traits,* which are stable long-lasting dispositions, and *states,* which are temporary short cycles of arousal. Some personal variables are learned; some are unlearned. Table 8.1 lists several personal variables of each type.

Trait and state variables

Environmental variables include school grades and other incentives, frustrating situations, richness of environment, and dissonant situations. All of these

Motive Pattern	Usually Learned	Usually Unlearned
Traits (usually stable)	Need to achieve Need for power Need for affiliation	Exploratory drive Fear of loss of support Attraction to opposite sex
States (usually temporary)	Test anxiety Curiosity Stage fright	Hunger Thirst Need for tobacco

**Personal vs.
environmental
variables**

are external to the person but influence the energy or direction of behavior, or both.

Personal variables can lead to purposeful activity. For example, when you're hungry, you look for food; when you want to achieve, you study hard. Environmental variables can also arouse purposeful activity. A steak brings people to the table, or a chance for a high grade makes a student work harder. When personal and environmental variables are at work together fostering behavior leading to the same goals, the kind of purposeful activity engaged in is clear. Under these conditions we can say that a person is highly motivated.

We are not likely to get students to work constantly at the highest peak of motivation. But we do want students to be interested and to think of their schoolwork as somehow "relevant." And we want to avoid the negative extreme, where students become so frustrated and dissatisfied that they drop out of school.

The Role of Motivation in Behavior and Learning

The concept of motivation helps us understand and explain certain intriguing facts about behavior and learning. We need the concept of motivation to account for what makes a reinforcer, the goal orientation of behavior, and the amount of time spent on different tasks. Motivation is also causally related to achievement, acting both as a means to educational achievement and as an end (objective) of the educational process.

Motivation Determines What Makes a Reinforcer

Suppose the school newspaper reports that Bart King, the new center on the basketball team, has received a multivolume set of the *Story of Civilization* from grateful fans for his performance in the first game of the season. And suppose another story tells us that Helen Lee, head of the science club, has been awarded a year's membership at a health club by the alumni boosters for her entry in the state science fair. Sound odd? Yes, because we know that motives determine what makes a reinforcer. If we want behavior to increase in frequency, duration, or magnitude, we need to reinforce the behavior, and to do

● *Motivation energizes and directs behavior. It sustains our attention and maintains our effort in the activities in which we engage.* (© *Jean-Claude Lejeune*)

that, we need to choose as reinforcers those things that individuals value positively. It is likely, though not certain, that the athlete would prefer the membership in the health club and the scientist the books. Their motives (needs, values, incentives, aspirations, attitudes, interests) determine what is and what is not a reinforcer for them. Remember this idea when you are trying to find reinforcers for a particular student. A pat on the head may work as a reinforcer for a child who has a high need for approval; it may have no effect on the child with a high need for autonomy; and it may have a negative effect on a child with a high need for peer approval.

Fitting reinforcers to students

Motivation Accounts for Goal Orientation

Apart from its value in determining what operates as a reinforcer, the concept of motivation is required by the fact that behavior is *goal oriented.* We behave as if we were "going somewhere." We sit down at a desk, pick up a pen and a piece of paper, write for a period of time, then put the paper in an envelope, which we stamp and address. Later we drop the envelope into a mailbox. All these separate acts are organized into a larger unit that has an evident purpose. In fact many philosophers point out that one of the distinguishing characteristics of human behavior is that it is purposeful, that is, goal directed. This is why human behavior can be sustained over much longer periods of time than animal behavior.

Motivation Determines the Time Spent in Different Activities

Atkinson (1980) noted that one of the most important conclusions drawn from motivation research is that the relationship of time spent in particular tasks and motivation for those tasks is almost linear, as Figure 8.1 shows.

This linear relationship allows us to estimate the amount of time students will commit to learning a particular task from what we know about their motives. And one estimate of the strength of their motivation is the amount of time learners are able and willing to spend on a learning task (Carroll, 1965). The amount of time a student spends in academic pursuits has been found to be one of the better predictors of student achievement (Berliner, 1990). In studying this issue we find that perseverance or time commitments to academic pursuits can be **Perseverance** reduced by lowering the value of completing the learning task, by impairing the self-esteem of the student, and by making the learning task unpleasant. Perseverance can be increased by increasing the expectation of reward and the bad consequences of failure. Perseverance in learning is not always of positive value. To a clinical psychologist, it can be a sign of a problem. Because of neurotic needs to achieve or because of a kind of learned helplessness, a child may spend inordinate amounts of time on an insoluble problem. Here perseverance is a hindrance, not an aid, to learning.

Motivation and Achievement

The concept of motivation helps us account for differences in school achievement beyond those that result from differences in intelligence or scholastic aptitude. The correlation between intelligence and school grades—typically about .45—is low enough that we can find many students of low ability with relatively high achievement and vice versa.

Overachievement and underachievement

These exceptions to the generally positive correlation between intelligence and school achievement have given rise to the concepts of *overachievement* and *underachievement*—achievement that is greater or less than that predicted on the basis of an individual's intelligence or scholastic aptitude. The concepts of overachievement and underachievement get involved with sticky methodological problems (see R. L. Thorndike, 1963), but they are useful in describing motivation to succeed academically. They help us explain why students with the same level of intelligence have different levels of school achievement. The

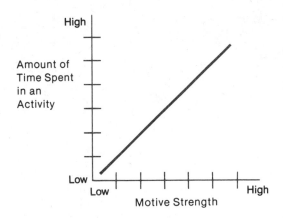

FIGURE 8.1

The Relationship of Time Spent in an Activity to Motive Strength

overachiever may try harder and the underachiever less hard than do students whose achievement agrees closely with what is predicted from their scholastic aptitude. Ringness (1965) looked at motivational differences in students of the same IQ level. He identified a group of normal achievers—thirty ninth-grade boys with IQ scores of 120 or above and grade point averages of 3.0 or above. He also found thirty underachievers matched in IQ scores, sex, age, school, and academic load; their grades averaged 2.0 or lower. He measured the motivation of the two groups using various tests and an interview. It turned out that the higher-achieving boys had higher motivation to achieve and lower motivation to affiliate. The underachieving boys did not accept school and parental standards of achievement as well but valued popularity with their peers to a greater degree. Their motive to affiliate was higher than their motive to achieve. In addition, when compared with overachievers, underachievers have poorer study habits and study skills, apply themselves to academic matters less diligently, and set lower vocational and academic goals for themselves (R. R. Mitchell & Piathowska, 1974).

Achievement vs. affiliation

Motivation as Means and as Ends

For a teacher, student motivation is important because motivation can serve as both an objective in itself and a means for furthering achievement of educational objectives. As an objective, motivation becomes one of the purposes of teaching. We want our students to become interested in certain intellectual and aesthetic activities and to retain that interest after formal teaching has ended. We want adult citizens to be interested in art and music, science, and public affairs. Certain kinds of motivation are among the goals for which schools strive. Interests and values of various kinds are outcomes of schooling that we try to foster.

Motivation as an outcome

As a means, motivation becomes one of the factors—like intelligence or previous learning—that determine achievement. In one review, the many correlations between measures of motivation and achievement averaged about

• Experiences outside the regular classroom can be enriching and motivating for students of all ages. (© Beringer/Dratch, The Image Works)

High motivation →
high achievement

+ .34, indicating that high levels of achievement and high levels of motivation tend to go hand-in-hand (Walberg, 1986).

Types of Motivation

Single-motive conceptions

How many different kinds of motives are there? How are they related to one another? Some theorize that there is a single, pervasive kind of motivation. Freud's notion of the libido—a basic kind of sexual energy underlying all human striving—is one example. He believed the libido influences both conscious and unconscious processes in an irrational and instinctual way. Both scholars and writers (see Hermann Hesse's *Demian,* for example) have used the concept of

Dual-motive conceptions

duality in motivation. They believe that the interplay of two opposing forces— maleness and femaleness, good and evil, yin and yang—give us our energy and direction. Others claim that there are many different types of motives and offer

Multimotive conceptions

long lists of them. Murray and associates (1938) offered one of the best known lists, which included many social needs, among them the need for power, the need to play, the need to affiliate, and the need to achieve—a motive of particular importance to teachers and society.

Maslow's hierarchy

Still another way to think of motives is to group them, as Maslow (1954) did, into a hierarchy (see Figure 8.2). Maslow's hierarchy includes five basic levels of needs: At the bottom, needing satisfaction first, are physical needs—needs for food and safety. Once these needs are satisfied, social needs come into play.

FIGURE 8.2   *A Hierarchy of Needs*

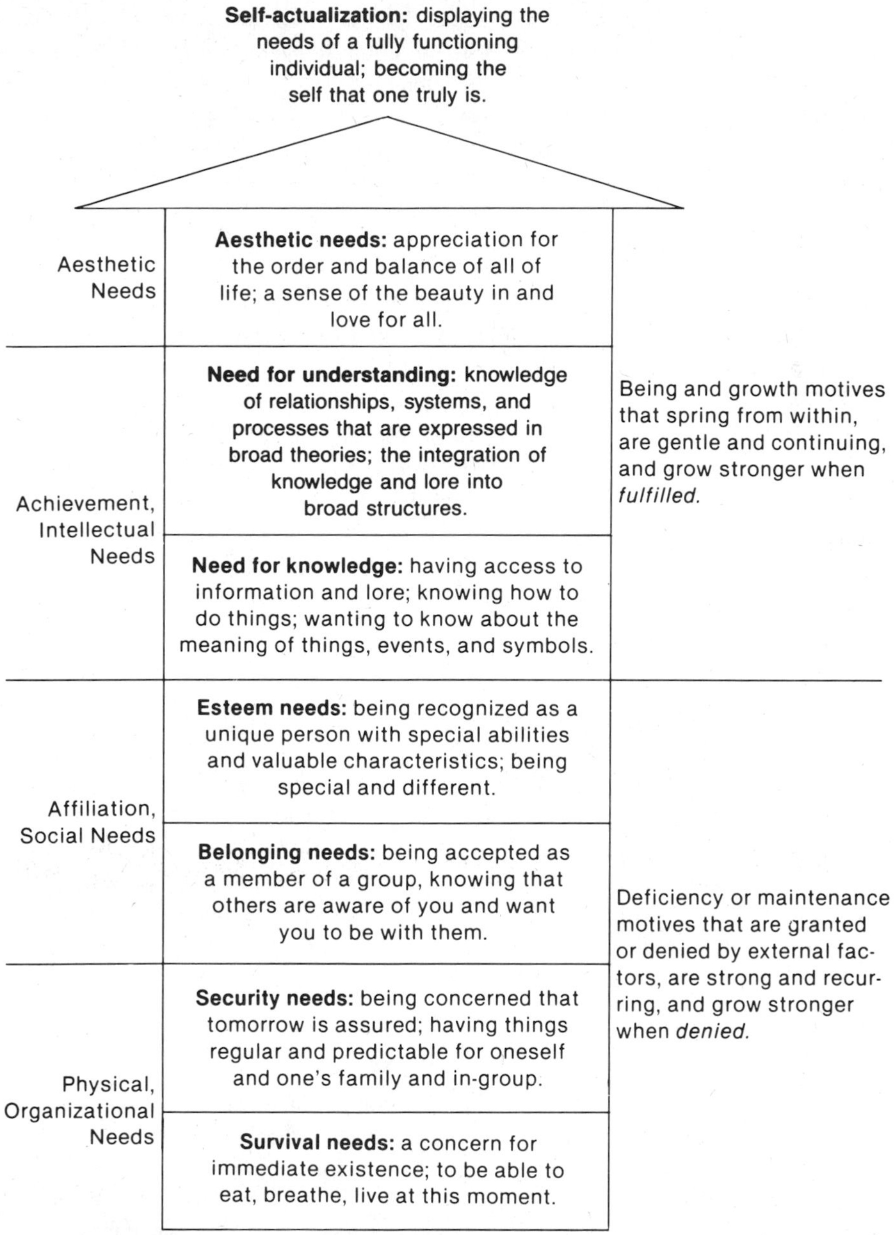

Self-actualization: displaying the
needs of a fully functioning
individual; becoming the
self that one truly is.

Aesthetic Needs	**Aesthetic needs:** appreciation for the order and balance of all of life; a sense of the beauty in and love for all.	
Achievement, Intellectual Needs	**Need for understanding:** knowledge of relationships, systems, and processes that are expressed in broad theories; the integration of knowledge and lore into broad structures.	Being and growth motives that spring from within, are gentle and continuing, and grow stronger when *fulfilled.*
	Need for knowledge: having access to information and lore; knowing how to do things; wanting to know about the meaning of things, events, and symbols.	
Affiliation, Social Needs	**Esteem needs:** being recognized as a unique person with special abilities and valuable characteristics; being special and different.	
	Belonging needs: being accepted as a member of a group, knowing that others are aware of you and want you to be with them.	Deficiency or maintenance motives that are granted or denied by external factors, are strong and recurring, and grow stronger when *denied.*
Physical, Organizational Needs	**Security needs:** being concerned that tomorrow is assured; having things regular and predictable for oneself and one's family and in-group.	
	Survival needs: a concern for immediate existence; to be able to eat, breathe, live at this moment.	

Source: Adapted from a formulation by Maslow (1954) as modified by Root (1970).

Self-actualization

Once these are reasonably satisfied, intellectual needs will develop, followed by aesthetic needs. The highest level is *self-actualization,* where the need to be everything you want to be is evident in your behavior. The self-actualized person is motivated by needs to be open, not defensive; to love others and self without yielding to aggression or manipulation; to act in ways that are ethically and morally good for society; to express autonomy and creativity; to be curious and spontaneous in interacting with the environment (Maslow, 1971). (In Chapter 10, which deals with humanistic approaches to teaching, we discuss the classroom environment that is intended to develop self-actualized adults.)

The theory of motivation we adopt can have an impact on what and how we teach. If, for example, we accept Maslow's hierarchy, we must address its implications as well. We cannot expect to meet students' intellectual needs (or develop their aesthetic ones) until their physical and social needs have been met. When a child comes to school hungry, ill, abused, or feeling uncared for, it is difficult if not impossible to motivate that child to achieve academically. Schools may have to become more oriented to childrens' social welfare than they are now. Until they address the hunger and the medical and social problems of children, schools cannot hope to educate children very well. And worse, the highest levels of human potential are not achieved—a personal and societal loss that should concern all educators and political leaders.

Schools and social problems

Achievement Motivation: A Personal Variable

Personal variables are the factors "inside" students that affect their motivation. Among these variables is one of considerable importance to teachers and society—achievement motivation—the motivation to succeed, to be good at something. This kind of motivation can be as important to hairdressers and Navajo sheepherders as it is to artists and scientists. The ways we choose to do well—to achieve—are influenced by our culture and work. But the motive to achieve can be present in anyone, in any cultural or occupational group. We discuss here how the achievement motive is measured, how it relates to other motives, and what it means for education.

Measuring the Motive to Achieve

Motives in fantasies

Suppose you believe, as Freud did, that you can glimpse what people want—their motivational patterns—in their fantasies. You might want to construct a standardized situation for bringing out and examining people's fantasies. A test was designed to do just that. It involves a series of ambiguous pictures and a set of questions about each picture that guides the subject in creating a fantasy. For example, one picture shows a boy at a table looking up from a book. The tester would ask several questions:

1. What's happening? Who is the boy?
2. What's happened in the past? What led up to this situation?

● *Students with high achievement motivation choose work-oriented partners.*
(© 1987 Joel Gordon)

3. What is the boy thinking? What does he want? Do others want things from him?

4. What's going to happen? What is the boy going to do?

Through these questions, the subject creates a story—a fantasy—that can be analyzed and scored (McClelland & Atkinson, 1948; McClelland, Atkinson, Clark, & Lowell, 1953). The scores are indicators of a person's basic need to achieve.

Relation Between Need for Achievement and Performance

Estimates of students' need for achievement should be reflected in some other measure of their performance. Otherwise the scores are worthless. As it turns out, the strength of the motive to achieve is correlated with a number of interesting performance measures.

Suppose a student high in achievement motivation is given a choice of work partners. One of them is friendly; the other is good at the task. The achieve-

Choice of work partners

Task persistence

ment-motivated student tends to choose the person who is good at the task. Students high in affiliative needs but low in achievement needs tend to make the opposite choice (French, 1956). In a different study, French and Thomas (1958) gave subjects complex problems to solve. Their data clearly indicate that people with higher achievement needs have greater task persistence and are more likely to reach a solution to a problem.

Rate of performance

Wendt's (1955) study is typical of these investigations. It yielded data from a small sample of high school students (see Figure 8.3). The level of achievement motivation was related to quantity (number of tasks attempted) and quality (percentage of tasks completed correctly) in performance on arithmetic tasks. Subjects high in need for achievement performed well even during an unscheduled period when students could determine their own rate of performance. Their achievement orientation led subjects to maintain high levels of performance without external monitoring. The positive relation between need for achievement and task persistence (number of tasks attempted) emerged clearly. Other studies (Weiner & Kukla, 1970) have shown that individuals high in achievement motivation also persist longer than those low in achievement motivation even when they are failing at a task. Those high in achievement motivation often see failure as a result of their own lack of effort, rather than some external force. So they reason that, by increasing personal effort, they can perform most tasks.

Personal effort

Completion of interrupted tasks

High achievement motivation has also been clearly linked to a tendency to complete interrupted tasks. Seeking to resume the main thread of activities is characteristic of students with high achievement motivation. These students create a complex, long-lasting mental structure made up of main activities, side activities, and subactivities. This structure guides them through an orderly series of steps to some goal, even when the process must be sustained over long periods and thus may be interrupted often (Heckhausen, 1967).

Risk taking

And high achievement motivation has been linked with risk taking. Those motivated to succeed more often seek tasks of intermediate difficulty. Apparently their purpose is to get the maximum realistic estimate of their own ability. With this knowledge they can set goals and plan routes to success more accurately. Those without a strong achievement motive more often choose tasks of low or high risk, avoiding the realistic self-appraisals necessary for sensible goal setting and planning (Heckhausen, Schmalt, & Schneider, 1985).

Sex differences in achievement-motivation correlations

Not every study of achievement motivation gives us evidence of a positive relation with student performance in terms of choosing partners who can get the job done, task persistence, rate of performance, task completion, the ability to keep up orderly progress toward distant goals, or risk taking. Particularly hard to find are studies that show similar relationships for the two sexes. Most of what we have been discussing applies to males, not females. But the social roles for females have changed quite a bit since the first wave of studies in achievement motivation was completed. Today the data from females may be more similar to those for males. To complicate matters of interpretation even more, achievement motivation may be of two types: *autonomous,* in which we compare

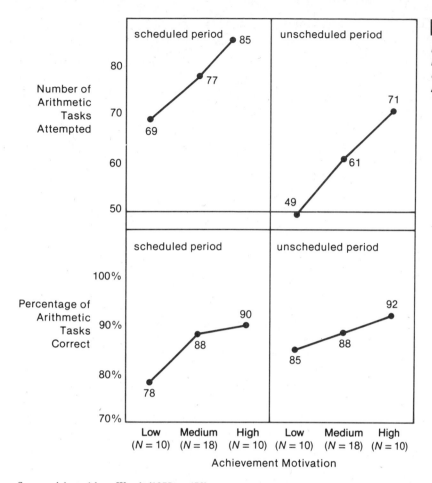

FIGURE 8.3

Relation Between Need for Achievement and Performance on Arithmetic Tasks

Source: Adapted from Wendt (1955, p. 452).

our performance against our previous performance, using our own "inner" standards for comparison; and *social,* in which we compare our performance against that of others. Autonomous achievement motivation develops early and is prevalent until a child enters school. Then, as you might predict from our competitive scholastic system, achievement motivation that is influenced by social comparison develops, becoming more prevalent around second grade (see Feld, Ruhland, & Gold, 1979; Ruble, 1980).

Autonomous vs. social achievement motivation

In any case, available studies show the value of thinking about the achievement motivation of students. In fact some intriguing evidence suggests a relationship between the level of achievement motivation and the productivity of a society. This evidence hints that achievement motivation can foster economic and technological progress (DeCharms & Moeller, 1962). Thus society depends on the schools not just for the teaching of subject matter but for instilling in students the need to succeed.

Achievement motivation and a society's productivity

Achievement Attributions and Affect

Attributions about responsibility

Performance is only the visible indicator of achievement motivation; it is supported by a complex system of thoughts and feelings. When we succeed or fail at a task, we naturally think about who or what was behind our success or failure. We look to assign responsibility, to understand the causes of our performance. That is, we make *attributions* about who or what was responsible for how we performed. These attributions are systematically related to different kinds of subsequent behavior. Attributions are also the source of our feeling good, bad, or indifferent after we succeed or fail. That is, attributions have affective (emotional) consequences. Because our attributions influence both our subsequent behavior and our feelings, we need to study them more closely.

Locus of control

We can classify attributions along three dimensions: the source of control, stability, and controllability (Weiner, 1986). The *locus* (source) *of control* can be internal or external. If you say you did well on a test because you're "good in math," you are attributing your success to an internal characteristic—your ability. If you believe you did well because the teacher was lenient, you are attributing your success to an external factor—the teacher.

Stability of factors

Stability or the lack of it is another characteristic of attributions. That is, some attributions refer to a temporary factor, relating only to a specific task; others refer to more lasting factors, relating to a series of tasks. Suppose you fail an exam. An unstable attribution might refer to your effort ("I didn't study as much as I should have"); a stable attribution might refer to perceived discrimination on the part of the teacher ("This teacher is always tough on girls").

Controllability of factors

Attributions also vary along a dimension called *controllability*. If you feel, for example, that the difficulty of the task was responsible for your failure ("I didn't do well because the questions were too hard"), you're describing a cause that is beyond your control. If you failed the test because you lost your notes and couldn't study, you're attributing your failure to a factor that you can control.

From the three dimensions—source of control, stability, and controllability—we can create eight different categories of attribution. Table 8.2 lists these categories. In using the table, assume that both teacher and student are assigning responsibility to explain the student's poor performance on a test.

Attributions affect performance

How we classify attributions can affect our performance on future tasks. If you believe a failure is controllable—say, the result of low effort—you may be spurred on by that failure to do better next time. If you believe, however, that you cannot control who or what caused the failure, you may not even try to improve your performance. Failure itself, then, is not harmful; it's attributing failure to causes over which you have no control that does the damage.

Students' Causal Attributions

The research on student attributions reveals that only a small number of categories—effort, ability, mood, task difficulty, and luck being among the most prevalent—are regularly used by students to account for their success or failure

TABLE 8.2	Attributions That Might Be Made by Teacher and Student After Student's Low Performance on a Classroom Test	

Characteristic of the Attribution			Teacher's Attributions	Student's Attributions
INTERNAL	STABLE	Uncontrollable	"I'm simply not an effective teacher." (ability)	"I just have no head for numbers." (ability)
		Controllable	"I never prepare well enough to teach this unit." (effort)	"I'm too lazy to study much." (effort)
	UNSTABLE	Uncontrollable	"I was too sick that week to teach it right."	"When I have to work late, I'm sometimes shot the next morning."
		Controllable	"I was too tired from partying that week to teach it well."	"I was too tired from partying the night before to do well."
EXTERNAL	STABLE	Uncontrollable	"This school's standards for passing a test are too high." (difficult task)	"This teacher hardly passes anyone—she's too tough in grading." (difficult task)
		Controllable	"These kids don't like me."	"This teacher doesn't respect any of us."
	UNSTABLE	Uncontrollable	"I must have been unlucky in my choice of questions." (luck)	"Sometimes you hit it right, when you study, sometimes you don't." (luck)
		Controllable	"My aides didn't show up this week to help prepare the students."	"Too many people were visiting the family this week."

(Bar-Tal & Darom, 1979; Frieze & Snyder, 1980). And we know from an analysis of dozens of studies by Whitley and Frieze (1985) that children (as well as adults) usually hold to an egotistic attribution system. That is, they ordinarily attribute success to internal factors (effort, ability) and failure to external factors (task difficulty, luck). But some students do not always use this ego-maintaining strategy. And many students who perceive a lack of ability as the cause of their failure come to expect failure regularly. They come to believe they do not have the ability to succeed, and so they often avoid achievement-oriented activities or fail to work hard in achievement-oriented tasks. One study analyzed the attribution patterns of 743 subjects from fifth to twelfth grade (Fyans & Maehr, 1980). It found that students' attribution patterns were good predictors of whether students would choose tasks calling for skill, for effort, or for luck.

Attributions and achievement motivation

Besides attributing failure to an internal characteristic—say, a lack of ability—some students simultaneously attribute their success to an external characteristic—say, the ease of a test or good luck. With this kind of attribution for success, these students cannot find any sensible reasons to make a great effort to succeed in school tasks. Bar-Tal (1979) noted that attribution patterns that assign responsibility for failure to a stable internal cause, such as ability, and for success to an unstable external cause, such as luck, are maladaptive.

Maladaptive attribution patterns

• *Trying to teach children that their failure has more to do with effort than ability isn't easy—but every teacher must try! (© Elizabeth Crews)*

We find maladaptive attribution patterns to be most prevalent among people for whom some members of society hold negative stereotypes: members of some minority groups, students from low-income families, students who are handicapped, and women, for example. Some researchers argue that more members of these groups reject effort as a causal factor in success or failure. If less powerful members of society feel that their effort is useless, that it cannot give them a chance to succeed, the schools (and all of society) have a problem. In such circumstances we can expect maladaptive achievement-oriented behavior to be perpetuated in many areas of the school curriculum (Frieze, 1980). Because attribution patterns are fairly stable over time and situations, training programs are necessary to break self-defeating attribution patterns in schoolchildren (Bar-Tal, Raviv, & Bar-Tal, 1982).

Teachers' Causal Attributions

Of course teachers also succeed and fail at what they do in schools. To what do they attribute their success and failure? Commenting on students' test performance, teachers often attribute student success to the students' home conditions, effort, and interest, and—as you might expect—their own excellent teaching skill. But when students fail, teachers blame the students' preparation, ability, poor home conditions, and the difficulty of the test (Bar-Tal, 1979). In other words, teachers tend to share credit with students for success on a test but to blame failure on external (nonteacher) causes. This tendency is understandable—it is the ego-maintaining mechanism in all of us—but it is probably not appropriate professional behavior.

R. Ames (1982) noted, however, that teachers can range from low to high in their commitment to excellence in teaching. Teachers who value teaching highly take personal responsibility for student failures. Teachers who have less commitment to excellence in teaching attribute student failure more often to student characteristics. Teachers in the former group increase their effort to help students succeed; those in the latter group do not.

Teacher's commitment and attribution

Internal and External Attributions

Those who generally attribute their success or failure to their own behavior (personal effort or ability) are said to have an *internal* locus of control. Those who generally attribute their success or failure to luck or task difficulty are said to have an *external* locus of control. These relatively stable patterns of behavior are associated with many other personal characteristics.

Internal locus of control

External locus of control

> Causal attributions in part determine the affective consequences of success and failure. Pride and shame . . . are absolutely maximized when achievement outcomes are ascribed internally and are minimized when success and failure are attributed to external causes. Thus, success attributed to high ability or hard work produces more pride and external praise than success that is perceived as due to the ease of the task or good luck. In a similar manner, failure perceived as caused by low ability or a lack of effort results in greater shame and external punishment than failure attributed to the excessive difficulty of the task or bad luck. In sum, locus of causality influences the affective or emotional consequences of achievement outcomes. (Weiner, 1977, p. 183)

Pride and shame

Besides having emotional consequences, the degree of internality-externality, like achievement motivation, has been associated with speed of performance, choice of tasks, and persistence on tasks (Bar-Tal, 1978; Weiner, 1974; Weiner & Sierad, 1975). Self-concept as a learner also appears to be related to a student's attribution pattern. The student with an internal locus of control for success ("I succeed because I have ability or put in the proper amount of effort") and an external locus of control for failure ("I messed up because my luck was bad") enters learning tasks with a positive self-concept (D. Johnson, 1981). Learned helplessness, the extreme negative self-concept as a learner, is also related to attribution patterns. Students with learned helplessness do not believe effort is related to achievement. They think that nothing they do will lead to success. Typically these students believe in an internal locus of control for failure ("I am dumb!"), which induces intense feelings of shame and self-doubt,

Locus of control and self-concept

Learned helplessness

particularly in the face of cumulative failure (Covington & Omelich, 1981). Their belief that they don't have the ability to succeed often means they don't even try. There is method here. By not attempting school tasks, their poor performance can be attributed to low effort, which is less shameful in American society than is low ability (Covington & Omelich, 1979). Teachers need to be on the lookout for children with learned helplessness. Attribution patterns can be changed to give those who avoid school and those who fail at it new ways of coping with the educational system.

Perhaps the best known example of the importance of internality or externality as a personal characteristic was the finding of J. S. Coleman and his colleagues (1966) that black children, more often than white children, believe that success is caused by luck (an external factor) rather than by effort (an internal factor). This attribution pattern—an external locus of control—appears to affect academic performance. The black students who believed that success

Hard work vs. luck

was due to hard work had higher reading scores than did students who believed in luck. The mean verbal achievement of believers in the importance of hard work was higher than the mean of *all* children who believed in luck as the cause of success, whatever their race or geographic origin.

Teachers should be concerned about students who are high and consistent in "externality." Such students seem to lack the beliefs that make them take responsibility for their academic achievement. As a result, their level of motivation to achieve in academic tasks may seem low. But, again, students' attribution patterns, and their achievement motivation, can be modified.

Attributions and Emotion

We know a teacher who gets angry every time a student fails a test. How would you explain the teacher's behavior? We know another teacher who usually is sympathetic to students who fail. How would you explain her behavior? Take a minute and think about these questions.

From studies by Graham (e.g., 1986, 1988) we learn that a teacher who expresses anger at a student who has failed a test probably acts that way because he or she believes that the student made too little effort to achieve.

Lack of student effort and teacher anger

That is, when a teacher attributes poor performance to a characteristic that is under the student's control, as student effort is, the emotion of anger is linked with the attribution. Children learn very quickly in school that there are differences between the concepts of ability and effort (Blumenfeld, Pintrich, & Hamilton, 1986). In Graham's study, even five-year-olds recognized the appropriateness of the link between an attribution of lack of effort and the emotion of anger. They also recognized that when a teacher expresses sympathy for poor

Lack of student ability and teacher sympathy

performance, the attribution behind the emotion is probably linked to a belief that the student lacks ability.

Accepting the attributions of others

What happens to children who are the target of a teacher's anger or sympathy? They often accept the attribution they think is behind the anger or sympathy (Graham, Doubleday, & Guarino, 1984): They come to believe that they have made too little effort or have too little ability to succeed. And they expect to perform accordingly. By attributing a student's failure to lack of effort and expressing anger, a teacher can make the student feel guilty (Weiner, 1986). That guilt—the feeling that he or she has let self or teacher down—is usually a positive motivating force when the student next attempts a task. But by attributing failure to low ability and expressing sympathy, a teacher ordinarily makes a student feel shame. And shame is not a positive motivating force. Instead it can lead a student to withdraw, to feel inferior and helpless. The point of all this is that sympathy can backfire. It may be a genuine emotion. It may express sincere caring about the schoolwork of low-achieving students. But it can work great mischief when students think that behind the sympathy is a teacher's belief that they don't have the ability to succeed.

Guilt vs. shame

Sympathy can backfire

Sympathy is not the only emotion that can backfire. So can (1) praise for a student's success and lack of criticism for a student's failure when a task is very easy and (2) providing excessive help, particularly when it is not sought (Weiner, Graham, Taylor, & Meyer, 1983). The moral here is not to prevent justifiable anger or to stop praising your students' performance when that is appropriate. It is to remind you that our self-esteem and self-confidence as learners are built out of the way others treat us. All teachers make attributions about their students' behavior. More important, all students make attributions about their teachers' behavior! When you criticize, sympathize with, praise, or offer to help your students, you must be sensitive to how they might perceive your actions.

Self-esteem derived from others

Classroom Structure and Attributions

Can classroom structure affect students' sense of self-worth and competence? Earlier, we talked about the autonomous versus the social need to achieve. There is a parallel in attribution patterns, and it too is linked with age and school. When children are very young, learning on their own, they usually think about their performance without thinking about how anyone else is doing. They often seem pleased with their own learning. They show what some call "intrinsic" or "autonomous" motivation to learn. Later, once they enter school, they begin to compare their own performance with that of others to determine how well they are doing. The typical child, then, goes from an individual approach to judging learning to some kind of social-reference approach for judging learning. The social-reference approach can and often does lead to competition in the classroom, to "winning" and "losing." In classes with a competitive structure, a student's ability takes on special status. High-ability students will feel pride. But what about low-ability students? They will feel shame, especially when they fail after making a strong effort. This kind of failure is humiliating because it "proves" they don't have ability. If you try hard and still fail to achieve a goal, it seems that the only reason for that failure is low ability (Covington, 1984). As C. Ames and R. Ames (1984) noted:

Competitive structures

> Failing in a competitive setting elicits strong negative affect that is directed at oneself, and because competition necessarily involves a situation of many losers and few winners, most children undoubtably experience

• *The differences in competitive and cooperative classrooms are sometimes obvious. (Right: © Dennis Mansell. Facing page: © Dennis Mansell)*

threats to self-esteem. We cannot help but speculate that declines in children's self-perceptions of their ability over the elementary school years may, in part, be a consequence of the competitive nature of many classrooms and the increased emphasis placed on social comparison as children progress through school. (p. 45)

Noncompetitive structures

But some classroom structures are not based on competition or on a single notion of ability. These different kinds of structures increase the number of winners in the class and allow more students to feel competent. The effects of failure, even after high effort, are not as devastating. For example, there are classroom structures that emphasize individual learning, where individual learning contracts or mastery approaches (see Chapter 10) teach students that self-improvement comes from self-effort. Here students assess their performance using personal guidelines, not someone else's performance. Figure 8.4 shows how the motive to achieve is fostered in classrooms that stress individual learning and is stifled in classrooms where social reference groups are used to judge performance. There were thirteen teachers in each of the two groups in the study. Researchers measured the achievement motive of 311 students in the twenty-six classes. The data show clearly that over four years the teachers who used a social-reference norm for judging performance had students with significantly lower achievement motivation than did teachers who had created ways for children to judge themselves. And, as we noted earlier in this chapter,

Negative effects of social referencing

high achievement motivation is associated with many desirable school-related behaviors.

Cooperative learning

Still another kind of classroom structure that affects motivation is cooperative learning (see Chapter 9). In a cooperative-learning structure students usually work in small groups for group rewards. The high-ability members and the low-ability members of the group must work together to achieve a reward. The structure encourages and enables higher-ability students to help lower-ability students. At the same time, it removes negative consequences for the higher-ability students: They can do their best; they do not have to hide their talent, as happens in some schools. A key factor in the success of cooperative classroom structures seems to be that genuine cooperation is the only way to get rewards (Slavin, 1984). The effects of failure are moderated and can be externalized a bit ("We *all* messed up!"), and low-ability students can be part of a successful cooperative group ("We did it!"). In fact, in this kind of structure, students may learn that it feels just as good to contribute to the well-being of others as it does to triumph over them (Covington, 1984).

Unidimensional classrooms

We should note one other kind of classroom structure—the multidimensional class. Rosenholtz and Simpson (1984) have observed that most classrooms are *unidimensional*—all students work on similar academic tasks most of the time. In this structure social comparisons are common, and the meaning of the term *ability* is narrow but widely shared. In elementary classes of this kind, reading ability is often equated with intelligence. Students here do not believe that art

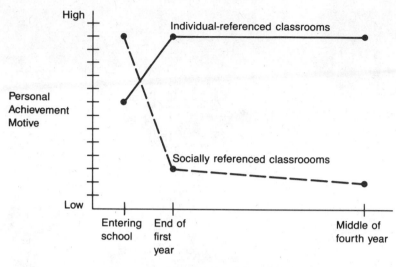

Source: Adapted from Heckhausen, Schmalt, and Schneider (1985) from data in Trudewind and Kohne (1982).

FIGURE 8.4

Effects of Two Types of Classroom Structures on the Motive to Achieve

Multidimensional classrooms

ability, athletic ability, or interest in science is equivalent to "being intelligent" or "being a good student." But in *multidimensional classrooms* this view seems to change. Here, students often work at different tasks. While some students are reading, some are doing science projects, and some are painting. Because there are many different academic and social tasks in which a student can achieve, the multidimensional class structure allows more different kinds of ability to be recognized, and more students end up feeling they are competent.

Affiliation, Power, and Approval Motives

We have concentrated on one motive, achievement, because of its central importance to success in schools and other areas of society. But dozens of other motives are also important. We discuss here only three of them—the need for affiliation, the need for power, and the need for approval.

The Need for Affiliation

The affiliation motive represents the degree to which students want and need friendly relationships with other people. McKeachie (1961) has shown how this motive can affect academic achievement. He reasoned that the academic achievement of students with a strong affiliation motive would be higher in classes high in affiliative cues than in classes with weak affiliative cues, and that the achievement of students with a weak affiliation motive would be relatively

● *Schools satisfy affiliation needs, but sometimes those needs compete with the academic curriculum. (© 1987 Ulrike Welsch)*

lower in classes high in affiliative cues than in classes with few affiliative cues. *Affiliative cues* consist of opportunities to call out, to take part in discussions and small-group work, to be called on to answer questions posed by other students, and to receive displays of personal interest.

Affiliative cues

McKeachie assumed that affiliation cues will occur more frequently with teachers who are warm, friendly, and personally interested in students than with those who are subject-matter oriented or self-oriented. He measured the strength of students' affiliation motive with a projective test of motive strength like the one described earlier. He measured the teacher's warmth by means of observers' records and students' responses to a questionnaire about the characteristics of the classroom. The sample consisted of thirty-one college classes in general psychology and other subjects.

As Figure 8.5 shows, those psychology students who had high affiliative motivation received higher grades in classes with warmer instructors, while students low in affiliative motivation achieved better in classes with less warm

FIGURE 8.5

*Interaction of
Teacher's Warmth
and Students' Need
for Affiliation in
Determining
Achievement*

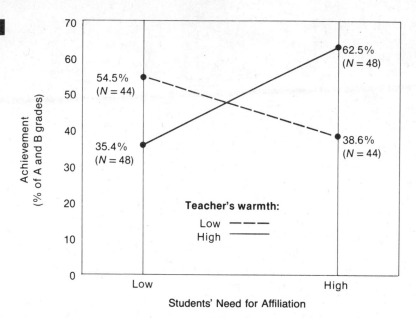

FIGURE 8.5

Interaction of Teacher's Warmth and Students' Need for Affiliation in Determining Achievement

Source: Adapted from McKeachie (1961).

instructors. A partial confirmation of this finding was reported by McKeachie, Lin, Milholland, and Isaacson (1966).

The Need for Power

Student volunteering

To examine the need for power—the need to influence other people—McKeachie looked at teachers who encouraged students to volunteer their ideas freely. (Volunteering, it was hypothesized, gives students an outlet for their need to influence others.) As Figure 8.6 shows, male students high in the power motive did achieve higher grades in classes in which student volunteering was prevalent. Males low in need for power received more A's and B's in courses where volunteering was not encouraged. These differences did not appear for female students, perhaps because their need structures differ from those of the males, a point made persuasively by Gilligan (1982) and discussed in Chapter 5.

Interaction of teacher's behavior with students' motives

Once again we note the importance of the teacher's understanding students' motives. A teacher's characteristic behaviors appear to interact with students' motivation systems. The environment the teacher creates can help some students and hinder others. Matching the teaching environment to students' motive patterns in order to maximize their achievement was implied by the concept of aptitude-treatment interaction we talked about in Chapter 5. At this point, however, we must rely on our intuition in deciding how to make the right match. Someday, we hope, more objective methods for making these kinds of decisions will be available.

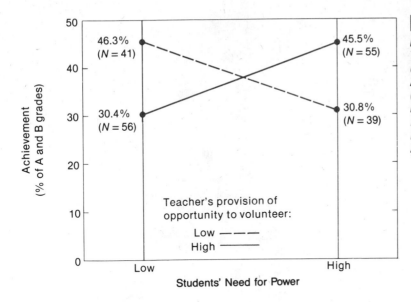

FIGURE 8.6

FIGURE 8.6

Interaction of Teacher's Provision of Opportunity for Assertion (Volunteering) and Male Students' Need for Power in Determining Achievement

Source: Adapted from McKeachie (1961).

The Need for Approval and Other Personal Motive Patterns

One motive that every teacher recognizes in students, especially when it is at a high level, is the need for approval or recognition. Although all of us need approval, most of us are not overdependent on it. Approval-dependent students, as described by Crowne and Marlowe (1964), are highly conformist and submissive to authority. They take the fewest possible risks of social rejection or threats to their self-esteem. Research with students high in the need for approval indicates that they give more word associations that are like those of other students, rather than unconventional associations; that they are conditioned more easily; that they are more easily persuaded; that they set more cautious goals in risk-taking situations; and they express more positive attitudes toward dull and boring tasks. Approval-dependent students characterize themselves in very desirable terms, make less accurate self-assessments, and protect their self-esteem from potentially hostile evaluations. Although individuals with high approval needs are affiliation oriented, they are often disliked by others. The child who tries to be the teacher's pet may have these tendencies.

Conformity and submissiveness

Teacher's pet

Indeed many other motives, among them conformity, dependency, ingratiation, and aggression, create problems for the teacher when they become too strong. Overconformity, overdependence, preoccupation with ingratiating oneself with others, and verbal or physical aggression toward oneself or others—all require the teacher's understanding. The origins of these motives and the training that can reduce their intensity are not as well known as those for

● *Intrinsic motivation to learn is wonderful to behold. But its roots often lie in extrinsic reinforcement, received when the activity was first started. (Right: © Paul Conklin/ Monkmeyer Press Photo Service. Facing page: © Paul Conklin)*

achievement motivation. But we know that factors in the immediate environment can influence motivational levels and subsequent behaviors.

So let us now switch our focus away from internal and personal variables in order to examine environmental and external factors that energize and direct our behavior. As you might expect, operant conditioning, with its focus on environmental contingencies, has much to contribute in this area. To discuss the operant conditioning approach, we must first discuss the concepts of intrinsic and extrinsic motivation. The kinds of contingent rewards and punishments that we discussed in Chapter 6 can affect these kinds of motive patterns.

Intrinsic and Extrinsic Motivation

At times behavior appears to be unaffected by environmental variables. A person seems to maintain energy and direction simply as a result of some unknown drive, without apparent reinforcement from outside. Motivation without apparent reward is sometimes called *intrinsic*. (This is different from another meaning of *intrinsic*, which refers to rewards inherent in the activity itself.) Some claim that intrinsically motivated behavior is better than extrinsically motivated behavior, which depends on observable rewards. These critics of operant methods say things like "Rewarding children spoils them; it makes them work only for rewards," "The kind of children we *really* want do not need rewards," "Paying children to read or play the piano destroys their chance to develop their own love of reading or piano playing," "Reinforcement is bribery!"

We believe that people are motivated in large part by the reinforcing consequences of their own or an observed model's past behavior. Often reinforcement is obvious, but even when it is not, it is there. No one reads or plays the piano without reinforcement. A reader or pianist who appears to be motivated from

Apparently unrewarded behavior

Self-reinforcement

within actually has developed self-reinforcement processes derived, most likely, from earlier external reinforcement. Initially, the reading or piano playing may have been fostered by the social approval of parents or teachers—a hug for reading the words *cat* and *hat*, applause from a small but important audience when the first song was played. From these external rewards, the reader or piano player generated self-reinforcement. Eventually the fascinating facts about Hemingway's life or the pleasure of playing the piano so as to produce beautiful music replace the hug and the applause.

Motivation—intrinsic or extrinsic—affects both our self-perception and our attribution pattern. If we see ourselves as the cause of our own behavior—that is, if we believe we are "origins," in control of our own behavior—then we believe we are intrinsically motivated. When we believe our behavior is determined by external forces, that we are "pawns," we think of ourselves as extrinsically motivated (Calder & Straw, 1975).

Extrinsic rewards may undermine intrinsic motivation

Our perceptions of our motivation for a particular behavior are important because they affect behavior in interesting ways. In one series of studies (Lepper, Greene, & Nisbett, 1973; Lepper & Greene, 1975), the researchers measured children's initial interest in an activity. The children were then allowed to continue that activity. The children in one group were told they were going to be rewarded for their efforts. Other groups of children either got no reward or were rewarded unexpectedly. The group that was expecting a reward showed a relative drop in performance. It was as if the youngsters' intrinsic motivation was somehow undermined by the reward. Their attributions may have changed from thinking of themselves as origins to thinking of themselves as pawns.

> To the extent, for example, that many of the activities we ask children to attempt in school may be of some initial interest to at least some of the children, the effect of presenting these activities in the context of a system of extrinsic incentives . . . may be to undermine that intrinsic interest in those activities. Unwittingly, these studies suggest, we may often turn activities of initial interest into drudgery which children engage in only when external pressures are present to force or lure them to do so. (Lepper & Greene, 1975, pp. 484–485)

It is important to remember that some students in some situations actually show decreases in performance because of extrinsic rewards. This decrease is most likely to happen when initial interest is stimulated by the complexity or novelty of a task (Lepper & Greene, 1978).

Verbal vs. tangible rewards

Informative vs. controlling verbal rewards

The effectiveness of rewards is also related to the form of the reward. Pittman, Boggiano, and Ruble (1982) point out that verbal rewards (praise) appear to undermine interest less than do tangible rewards (grades, candy). But we should note some distinctions here. Verbal rewards that attempt to control behavior are not effective; those that provide information about performance are (Weiner, 1990). That is, we may be undermining a student's interest if we say, "Thanks, that's the way I like the job done," and we may be fostering that interest when we say, "Thanks, you're doing a fine job. You are neat and fast." Control statements lead to an external orientation and lower motivation; informational statements lead to an internal orientation and enhanced feelings of competence (Deci, 1975; Deci & Ryan, 1985). If this principle were to hold in schools, a teacher's task-related comments about students' performance (informational statements) would enhance the intrinsic motivation of students more than would grades (which imply external control). This is exactly what happened when Butler and Nisan (1986) studied intrinsic motivation (desire to keep working, interest in a task) after grades and informational feedback were given to sixth-graders.

Task-related comments vs. grades

Our point is not that rewards are bad. For the most part, when used and monitored carefully, they are usually effective. But students who are already intrinsically motivated will not become more motivated through the use of extrinsic rewards. Furthermore, if extrinsic rewards are used with tasks students would have done anyway, they are likely to undermine motivation. Extrinsic rewards may be beneficial only to those whose level of motivation is initially quite low (Lepper & Hodell, 1989; Stipek, 1988). We simply must keep in mind that we cannot always assume that grades, praise, money, or any potential reinforcer will act as they are supposed to—increasing performance (Morgan, 1984). Under some conditions the motivation to perform a task actually decreases following reinforcement. The message here is that things don't always work as they should or the way we expect they will! Just as sympathy and help can backfire (as we noted above), so can reinforcement. Teaching often calls for subtlety and understanding that are far from obvious.

Effects of reinforcers unpredictable

Operant Conditioning and Motivation

Strictly speaking, for psychologists who adhere closely to operant-conditioning concepts, the term *motivation* is superfluous. Motivation shows up as a response, and, like any other response, it is learned and strengthened through reinforcement.

So, if we wish to inquire which students become truly motivated, the operant conditioning theorist would have us rephrase the question to read, Which students exhibit the behavior they have learned long after their schooling is over? These people are of interest because they have learned to get along for long periods without much apparent reinforcement. They persist at tasks although the ratio of reinforcers to responses has grown smaller and smaller over a long period of time. Scientists and artists may spend years working on projects with no success or acclaim. Through the accidents of their experience, they have learned to continue working despite greatly stretched out reinforcement schedules. Educators who want to produce this kind of dedication in students somehow must arrange for a high ratio of reinforcers to responses in the early stages of learning, then a gradual thinning out, or lowering, of the reinforcement ratio as the students mature.

Stretched-out reinforcement schedules

Stimulus Control

Chances are, if you are teaching arithmetic and make the sum of the homework grades equal 50 percent of the final grade, your students will do their problems (that is, make the desired responses) regularly. By simply bringing the learners' behavior under the control of a reinforcing stimulus you can regulate their production of arithmetic. Manipulating stimuli in the environment is enough to change behavior. These stimuli in the environment are "motivators." And when we respond to them in particular ways, we are under stimulus control.

Incentives

Stimulus control can be exerted by reinforcing stimuli or incentives. An incentive is not the same as a reinforcer. An *incentive* is the promise or expectation of reinforcement. The expectation of praise is the incentive; the praise itself is the reinforcer. Expectations of receiving grades, money, or social approval are powerful incentives. Those under the stimulus control of one of these incentives show increases in energy expended and changes in the direction of their behavior.

What makes something an incentive is a previous history of association with reinforcement. Food can be an incentive because people have a consistent history of associating food with the satisfaction of hunger drives. Incentives in classrooms include all the events that promise reinforcement. An approving glance as the teacher passes by could be a contingent reinforcer for some activity the student is engaged in. Or it could serve as an incentive—a cue that the student is liked and can expect to receive attention and friendship from the teacher. If the student is under stimulus control, the expectation of reinforcement, provided by the approving glance or its equivalent, is a motivator.

Reinforcers and Stimulus Control

How do we find out which reinforcers and incentives will motivate particular students? How do we determine whether some stimuli are already exerting control? Knowing students' preferences for reinforcers means knowing the environmental stimuli and incentives for which the students will work.

Preferences for reinforcers

One method of determining the appropriate reinforcers for children is to observe the children. The Premack principle we talked about in Chapter 6 is useful here. The principle implies that what children do on their own initiative can be used as a reinforcer for activities they do not engage in spontaneously. Another way to determine the appropriate reinforcers for students is simply to ask them—in an informal discussion. Still another way to determine reinforcers is to develop a reinforcement menu, listing lots of activities, tangible items, and consumable items that a teacher can provide. The students, like patrons at a restaurant, consult the menu and choose a reinforcer before they take part in productive activities.

Reinforcement menu

Reinforcers must theoretically be determined for each individual child. But in practice children may be very similar in what will reinforce their behavior. Gender, ethnicity, social class, and age do not necessarily lead to differences in preferred reinforcers. Although there is a widespread belief that different kinds of reinforcers work with children of different social classes, this appears not to be true (Schultz & Sherman, 1976).

A few cautions: The procedures for determining reinforcers are far from infallible. Students are not always able or willing to talk about what is reinforcing for them. Also motivational systems change over time. And it is important that the reinforcers be in line with your own values. Do you really want to reinforce a young student with an A or candy? You may choose to play down adult approval or consumable rewards, substituting free time for reading or some other reinforcer more compatible with your values. The idea is to find a simple way to uncover the preferences of individual students, then tailor incentives so that the students will be motivated.

Tailor incentives

Frustration and Motivation

Incentives provide control because the expectation of reinforcement is usually followed with actual reinforcement. What happens when expected reinforcement does not come or reinforcers cannot be obtained? The student is frustrated. This frustration motivates students' behavior, but not in good ways. (If nonreinforcement continues, the behavior is eventually extinguished, a process we described in Chapter 6.)

Frustration can stem from many sources. One common source is the assignment of material that is too difficult for students to complete. Large numbers of students experience failure because homework is too difficult to do independently, classroom questions are too hard to answer during recitation, or worksheets are too complicated to finish quickly and accurately. These students aren't allowed to succeed, and success is important here. High success rates in the classroom are a positive predictor of student achievement (Marliave & Filby, 1985; Rosenshine & Stevens, 1986). Low success rates—in homework or classroom discussions or seatwork—are a predictor of lower achievement and a likely source of frustration for students as well.

Overly difficult material

Success rate and achievement

Frustration can also stem from the teacher's failure to provide reinforcement. If you don't take the time to go over students' papers, they cannot receive the expected reinforcement—a grade they were expecting or the praise they were hoping for.

Withholding reinforcement

Another source of frustration is the teacher's preventing completion of responses that lead to reinforcement. If you move a student from a group in which she is doing well to one in which she does less well, you are keeping her from receiving reinforcement. If you don't allow a student to finish a task he is engrossed in because time has run out, you are frustrating him. In both these examples, the students find it more difficult to obtain reinforcement than they had expected.

Preventing completion of responses

And frustration can be the unintended by-product of preventing the initiation of a response that would lead to reinforcement. For example, if you excuse a student from a spelling contest because he is a good speller, you are preventing him from making responses that will obtain reinforcement.

Preventing initiation of responses

• *Reinforcement—a powerful motivator.* (© Carol Palmer)

Frustration leads to regression and aggression

How does frustration, from whatever source, show up in students' behavior? In a classic study by Barker, Dembo, and Lewin (1943), thirty children (two to five years old) were allowed to play with desirable toys. After a period of time the children were frustrated by being moved into another area with a wire-net partition that blocked them from (but let them see) the toys. The researchers recorded, among other things, the constructiveness of the children's play. Following frustration, the children regressed; that is, they showed behavior patterns characteristic of a younger age level. The regression averaged 17.3 months in mental age. That is, their play after frustration was, on average, like that of children about 1.5 years younger. They showed less free expression, less friendly conversation, and fewer signs of happiness. There was more restlessness, loud singing and talking, stuttering, thumb sucking, hitting, and the like.

Frustration happens when expected reinforcement does not take place—when material is too difficult for students to complete successfully, when a teacher fails to provide reinforcement, or when a teacher prevents the comple-

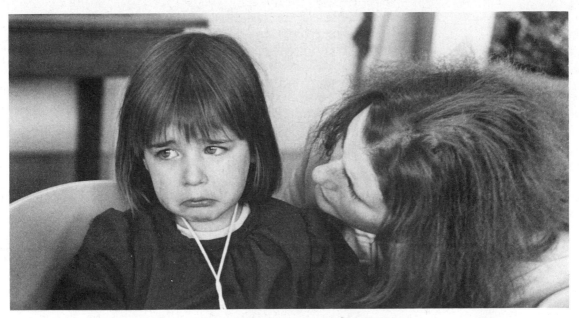

• *Frustration can lead to aggression. But gentle probing may reveal the problem that is preventing goal attainment. (© David S. Strickler/Monkmeyer Press Photo Service)*

tion or initiation of responses that would be reinforced. Frustration does motivate: It does change students' energy level and direction. But it usually motivates unwanted behavior. It has proved to be a source of emotionality, withdrawal, regression, hyperactivity, and particularly aggression in rats, primates, and humans (Lawson, 1965). When we see these behaviors in our students, we have to recognize them as symptoms of frustration, caused, perhaps, by some problem in the reinforcement system. If we can identify the source of frustration, we can work to rectify it.

**Frustration →
unwanted
behavior**

Changing Motivational Patterns: Cognitive Approaches

The findings and concepts derived from discussions of motivation, both personal and environmental, have influenced some researchers to try to change motive patterns. Obviously, if we can increase achievement motivation or change self-defeating attributions into ego-enhancing attributions, we have a chance to change achievement-oriented behavior. Similarly, if we improve the contingencies in a clever way, we should be able to affect behavior in ways we desire.

 Training programs for fostering achievement-oriented behavior have been developed. One kind of program, based on the achievement-motivation approach, emphasizes changes in cognition and behavior and rewards these changes. Another kind of program, based on the attribution approach, is highly cognitive in its orientation. It strives to change the ways in which people think about their behavior. Both programs show some evidence of success.

Achievement-Motivation Training Programs

One such program was developed by Aronoff, Raymond, and Warmoth (1965) for lower-class youngsters. They developed special case studies to be read and discussed and achievement-oriented games and exercises to try out new ways of thinking and behaving, and they modeled the behaviors and expectations needed to achieve well. They ran the achievement-motivation course for twenty-one high school juniors chosen from fifty-six potential dropouts. A year later, only one of the twenty-one students had dropped out of school, while eight of the thirty-six untrained students used as a control group had dropped out (Alschuler, 1967). The average grades of the trained students went up about half a letter grade, despite their taking more difficult courses than the untrained students. Furthermore, members of the trained group reported more new interests and activities, reflecting a greater feeling of control over their own lives, than did those in the control group. Alschuler (1973) has described many other successful studies of achievement training with adolescents.

Origins and pawns

DeCharms (1976) concentrated on changing motivation in children from low-income black families. His program emphasized becoming an "origin," not a "pawn." *Origins* feel that they themselves are in control of their fate, that they originate their own behavior patterns; *pawns* feel that they are pushed around by others, that their fate is in the hands of others. The program focused on aspects of personality similar to the internal-external locus of control variable. The students were helped to learn their own strengths and weaknesses, choose goals realistically, determine concrete actions that they could carry out immediately to achieve their goals, and determine whether their goals were being met. Personal responsibility was stressed. From the first year's training, the children improved in achievement motivation, realistic goal setting, and freedom from feelings of helplessness. They also showed less absenteeism and tardiness. Data on vocabulary, reading, language, and arithmetic achievement for students with two years in the training program (see Figure 8.7) show that the training was effective in important ways. Follow-up of these students found that the training had significantly increased the probability that these low-income children would graduate from high school (DeCharms, 1980).

Summarizing about twenty years of these kinds of motivation-change studies, Heckhausen and his colleagues (1985) point out that they often result in more realistic goal setting, less fear of failing, increased hope for success, higher opinions of one's own competence, and less general anxiety and dislike of school. The point is that the motive to achieve is not fixed. It can be changed, perhaps not easily, or in everyone, but under the proper conditions many who are not now motivated to achieve can be transformed.

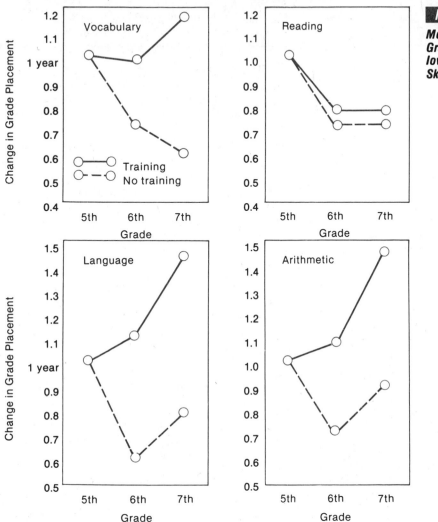

FIGURE 8.7

Mean Change in Grade Placement on Iowa Test of Basic Skills

All subjects began at an equal point in fifth grade. Deviations above and below that point indicate an increase of more or less than one full year in one-year elapsed time. Thus in vocabulary, the trained group has gained 2.2 years by grade 7 (1.0 in grade 6 and 1.2 in grade 7), while the untrained group had gained only 1.3 years by grade 7. (.7 in grade 6 and 6 in grade 7).

Source: Adapted from DeCharms (1970).

Attribution Training Programs

As we have noted, people tend to see the causes of their success and failure in systematic ways. The goal of attribution training programs is to change those ways if those interpretations are leading to counterproductive emotions and

TABLE 8.3			Wanted and Unwanted Feelings and Behaviors Following Success and Failure		

	Event	→	Attribution	→	Emotion/Expectation	→	Behavior
UNWANTED PATTERN	Success	→	Luck	→	Indifference/minimally increased expectation of success	→	Lack of willingness to engage in achievement tasks
	Failure	→	Lack of ability	→	Shame, incompetence, depression/decreased expectation of success	→	Avoidance or lack of persistence at achievement tasks
WANTED PATTERN	Success	→	High ability	→	Pride, self-esteem/increased expectation of success	→	Willingness to engage in achievement tasks
	Failure	→	Lack of effort	→	Guilt/relatively high expectation of success	→	Persistence and willingness to engage in achievement tasks

Source: Adapted from F. Fosterling, "Attributional Retraining: A Review," *Psychological Bulletin,* 48:495–512. Copyright 1985 by the American Psychological Association. Adapted by permission.,

behavior (see Fosterling, 1985; Weiner, 1982, 1986). Table 8.3 shows the wanted and unwanted attribution patterns we are concerned about.

These kinds of changes are probably what made Dweck's (1975) attribution training program successful. Dweck tried to change the attribution tendencies of children manifesting learned helplessness, or resignation to failure. After daily exercises over a period of twenty-five days, Dweck's subjects took more responsibility for their failures in mathematics problem solving, having learned to attribute their failure to insufficient effort. G. R. Andrews and R. L. Debus (1978) extended and verified Dweck's work. It now appears that some aspects of internality can be learned from teachers who systematically reinforce and model internal attributions. Andrews and Debus found that training effects endure and that these attributional strategies are generalizable to a wide range of school activities.

Learning internality

What does this mean for teachers? When a child seems resigned to failure and appears to lack a sense of personal responsibility, you should set up a program of systematic reinforcement for that child. The idea is to get children to attribute their problems to their own lack of effort and to reinforce that insight. Diener and Dweck (1978) also have pointed out how the kind of self-monitoring, self-instruction, and self-reinforcement strategies we talked about in Chapter 6 can be used to teach children with faulty attribution patterns to "talk to themselves" in ways that might be more appropriate. Fowler and Peterson (1981) showed that this approach can increase persistence at reading tasks. The verbal behaviors of the children change, and eventually so does their actual performance. They appear to be more achievement oriented. Rohrkemper (1986) described how students talk to themselves while solving mathematics

Teachers should model internality

problems. The messages they send themselves as they work ("Try harder" or "Try a new strategy" versus "I give up" or "I'll never solve this") are crucial factors in their motivational systems. We as teachers need to know about these thoughts and feelings and the attribution patterns they reflect and try to change those that are maladaptive.

Retarded children's attributions

Nowhere is the need to change unwanted personal attribution patterns clearer than in studies of mentally retarded children. Many of these youngsters have learned to be helpless, given the expectations held for them by others and their own difficulties in achieving because of real deficits in ability. Yet changing their attribution patterns can result in surprising increases in performance (Gold & Ryan, 1979). Effort, not just ability, can accomplish a lot! All the members of groups that must fight stereotypes of low ability—African-Americans, women, the learning disabled, and others—can profit from attribution improvement.

Changing attribution patterns

From his review of fifteen studies, Fosterling (1985) concluded that attribution training programs work. There is an important lesson to be derived from the projects he reviewed: Regular classroom teachers, given just a little training or opportunity for study on their own, can probably improve the attribution patterns and achievement motivation of their students. What teachers say and do influences the attribution patterns their students develop (Bar-Tal, 1982).

Changing Motivational Patterns: Environmental Approaches

Imagine you have been given responsibility for teaching thirty-six teenage boys, most of whom—about 85 percent—are school dropouts. All have been found guilty of crimes from stealing cars to rape and murder. Their achievement in five curricular areas—reading, English, science, mathematics, and social studies—at the beginning of your program is shown in the "before" columns of Table 8.4. What would you do if you had between three and eighteen months to work with these boys? Would you expect the improvements shown in the "after" columns?

Token Economies

The impressive data on achievement gains for institutionalized boys shown in Table 8.4 were reported by H. L. Cohen (1973). His program consisted of a learning environment in which academic achievement, as measured by regular tests, bought points that could be exchanged for goods, services, and special privileges. The students had to pay "fees" to get into a course. That is, the students used points advanced to them in order to gain admittance to a course in which they could earn additional points by performing well. The boys could use the earned additional points to purchase recreational time in a lounge, books, magazines, extra clothing, mail-order supplies, a private shower, a private room for sleeping and entertaining, and restaurant-style meals. They could even purchase time out of the institution to shop, go sight-seeing, or visit their

| TABLE 8.4 | Percentage of Delinquent Boys Achieving at Particular Grade Levels in Five Curriculum Areas Before and After Training |

Achievement (Grade Level)	Reading		English		Science		Mathematics		Social Studies	
	Before	After	Before	After	Before	After	Before	After	Before	After
1–4	22	3	97	8	22	14	72	14	33	6
5–7	36	28	3	33	78	28	28	8	67	36
8–10.5	39	39	0	25	0	44	0	53	0	19
10.6–12	3	30	0	33	0	14	0	25	0	39

Source: Adapted from H. L. Cohen, "Behavior Modification and Socially Deviant Youth," from C. E. Thoresen (Ed.), *Behavior Modification in Education: Seventy-Second Yearbook of the National Society for the Study of Education,* 72 (Part I). Copyright 1973. Used by permission.

Note: $N = 36$

families. This economic system, which provided reinforcement contingent on academic achievement, motivated the students to achieve at a level unprecedented for alienated and delinquent youth.

Characteristics of token economies

This economic system, called a *token economy,* has often been found to be effective in improving the academic and social behavior of students of many kinds (O'Leary & Drabman, 1971). The dramatic results in an institution for delinquent boys have their counterparts in regular school settings. Typically a school-based token economy includes (1) a set of behaviors that earn tokens, (2) a set of rules for students by which they exchange their tokens for wanted reinforcers, (3) a set of rules for awarding the tokens for appropriate behavior, and sometimes (4) a set of rules for taking back tokens for inappropriate behavior. McLaughlin (1975) has found that the systems in use have proved to be generally effective in public schools, easier than teachers think to implement and manage, relatively inexpensive, compatible with most school and community attitudes, and liked by the learners. But these programs have not often been used. Perhaps you will find a time and place to try out such a program.

Contingency managment techniques

Cohen, who first worked with institutionalized delinquents, extended his work to regular school environments using a model called Programming Interpersonal Curricula for Adolescents (PICA). Contingency-management techniques are the heart of the program, which reinforces appropriate academic and social behavior. The program also contains short courses on how to cope with schools, authority figures, parents, drugs, and sex. Although intended for adolescent students considered delinquent or about to be expelled from school, PICA was designed for use by regular classroom teachers. A preliminary effort with "problem" students yielded impressive results. As shown in Figure 8.8, one year of the program brought about remarkable changes in students' verbal and mathematical achievement. The students also became less disruptive, attended school more, and improved in a wide range of other social behaviors. Cohen's work gives us an answer to the question of whether there is some way to motivate disaffected youth. These young people initially were not controlled by stimuli that the teacher could identify or use. The program created a system

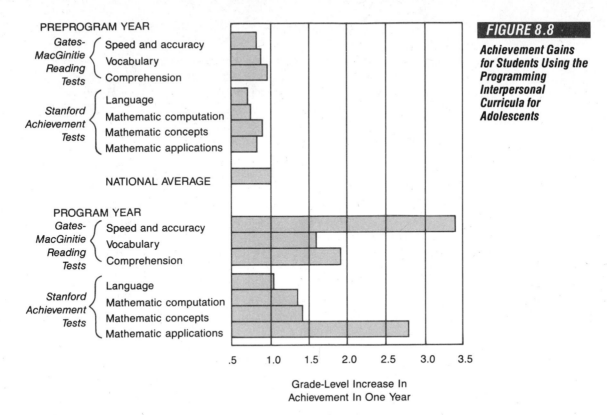

FIGURE 8.8

Achievement Gains for Students Using the Programming Interpersonal Curricula for Adolescents

Source: Adapted from H. L. Cohen, "Behavior Modification and Socially Deviant Youth," from C. E. Thoresen (Ed.), *Behavior Modification in Education: Seventy-Second Yearbook of the National Society for the Study of Education,* 72 (Part I). Copyright 1973. Used by permission.

of incentives and rewards that satisfied the students, teacher, parents, and general community.

Working with adolescents can be difficult because so many of the important reinforcers for high-school-age students (cars, money, dates) are outside the teacher's control. Even praise and attention from adults, so useful with younger students, can acquire negative value for motivating high school students. Peer approval takes on unusual significance during adolescence. But parents do control some important reinforcers, and they can be enlisted by the teacher to help motivate high school students. Home-based reinforcers include money, use of the family car, signing work and driving permits, and granting permission to work part-time or take a day off from school. Tokens of some sort (stars, check marks, points) can be used to obtain these reinforcers. Notes or telephone calls from the teacher can keep the parents up-to-date so that reinforcement is contingent on appropriate school behavior. None of this concern with "extrinsic" reinforcement means less concern with making schoolwork more interesting and important to students in its own right. The token economy is merely a powerful supplementary approach to be used if it is needed, if more traditional approaches don't suffice.

Parental control of reinforcers

Motivational Contracts

The kind of systematic approach developed by Cohen often involves formal or informal contracts between teachers and students. The pay for fulfillment of the contract takes the form of points or tokens, consumables, or simply praise—a very powerful reinforcer and incentive some of the time. Contracting of various types, for different ends, and with students of all age levels, seems to be an unusually promising educational invention.

Motivating games

Contracting for Mathematics in the Elementary Grades.   A motivational contracting system in the form of a game was developed by Alschuler (1968) as part of a method for improving achievement motivation. Each child in the class was advanced $2,000 in play money. Children could "get rich" or "go broke" by playing the game. Table 8.5 shows the schedule of payments. The greater the risk—say, trying to get 100 percent of the problems attempted correct—the greater the payoff. Students lost "money" for incorrect answers, for revising their contracts, and for late work, which incurred the severest penalty. The contracts were drawn up in a form like the one shown in Figure 8.9 with the teacher the government contract officer.

Children kept their own achievement charts, and the teacher never saw them. End-of-year prizes (gerbils, slot cars, and the like) chosen by the class were given to the six highest money winners. All students who finished the text received an award. Children were encouraged to take moderate risks, revise their plans on the basis of feedback, and make their own decisions about assignments, pacing, and the need for help from friends and teachers. The teacher's job was to coach—not to give information—to provide the social approval necessary for building and maintaining achievement behaviors. The teacher was to be warm, friendly, and encouraging, and to concentrate on helping children "win" at the game.

Did the game work? During the previous year, in the fourth grade, 17 percent of the students achieved gains on a standardized mathematics test equal

TABLE 8.5

Schedule of Payments for Mathematics Game

Percentage of Problems Done Correctly	Cost to Try Problem Set	Return to Investor for Success	Rate of Return
100	$500	$2,000	4:1
90	$450	$1,350	3:1
80	$350	$700	2:1
70	$250	$400	8:5
60	$150	$250	5:3
50	$100	$150	3:2

Source: Adapted from A. S. Alschuler, "How to Increase Motivation Through Climate and Structure." Cambridge, Massachusetts: Achievement Motivation Development Project. Graduate School of Education, Harvard University. Working Paper No. 8, 1968.

FIGURE 8.9

Math Contract

The undersigned will attempt to do correctly _____ percent of the problems in Chapter _____.

The sum of $_____ has been deposited with the government of the class for materials and franchise.

I understand that 10% of the gross return will be deducted from my payment for each day the contract goes unfulfilled after _____.

I also understand that the contract may be revised at any time prior to one week before due date for a fee of $10.00. One percent of the gross return will be deducted for each wrong answer below the number intended.

Date: _____.

_____

Contractor

_____

Govt. Contract Officer

FIGURE 8.9

Math Contract

Source: Alschuler (1968).

to or greater than that expected (that is, 1.0 year of grade-equivalent growth). During the fifth grade, when the contracting game was instituted, 100 percent of the students exceeded the national norm for expected gain. Indeed an average gain of three years' growth for one year's work was noted. Because only a few students from one class were involved, and an appropriate control group was not used, the results need further support. But these data are impressive and in line with what has been obtained by others.

Did the children become grasping and overcompetitive because they were working for material rewards?

Children who did nothing in mathematics in fourth grade, except under duress, suddenly began taking their books home on weekends. Very few deadlines were missed. Many students began assessing themselves more optimistically, yet realistically, and they performed up to those standards. One boy fidgeted through the entire year in mathematics in fourth grade. Threats and stern words could not focus his attention, nor could they keep him in his seat. His total output reflected a small percentage of his ability. Within the new structure, however, he chose his first goal of 70 percent with two weeks to finish the contract. Within three days he revised his goal upward to 100 percent, paid the extra fee, and did all the problems with only 11 errors out of almost 400 problems. A student was considered by the teacher to be mathematically slow in the fourth grade. She was consistently at the bottom of the class and seldom handed in assignments at all. Her 100 percent contract for the first chapter was the first completed and with only six errors. Her error total was the lowest in the class. Four other girls in grade four found math an excellent time to do other things, such as writing notes to one another and surreptitiously playing with clay. In grade five they still clustered around each other, but when asked to be quiet, it was generally for disagreeing too loudly over mathematics problems (e.g., the exact way to program a function machine). All were punctual and accurate. . . . It was the teacher's impression that in the first half of fifth grade, enthusiasm was generated more by the game than by intrinsic interest in mathematics. However, in the second half of the year, buoyed by new found competence, the game, prizes and play money became more or less irrelevant while the pace of work continued. Mathematics itself had become more interesting. (Alschuler, 1968, pp. 57–58)

We do not know whether these students will become cutthroat entrepreneurs. But we do know they have become better mathematicians. And we can see how intrinsic motivation develops out of systematic application of contingent reinforcers, an extrinsic motivation system. Our guess is that motivating games of this kind are not harmful and can be altogether beneficial.

Contracting and Individually Guided Motivation. Another approach to bringing about behavior change through contracting is called Individually Guided Motivation (Klausmeier, Sorenson, & Ghatala, 1971). It makes much use of conferences between the teacher (or teacher's aide) and the student. In the conferences, the teacher and student arrange contracts, and the student is reinforced for completed work, receives feedback, and sets new goals. The program is aimed at developing academic self-direction among students. Students would work with the teacher or aide to set realistic goals, to learn why it is important to do work outside of school, and to express that learning in words. And students would receive positive reinforcement for reaching their goals.

Teacher-student conferences

The procedure depends heavily on a one-to-one relationship. In one study of reading, materials and books for various reading levels were made available in the school library and classroom. Rewards (crayons, pencils, erasers) were given first for reading two books, then for reading five books. Individual conferences were conducted by adult volunteer aides who visited the classroom once a week. Individual aides worked five to fifteen minutes with each child, listening to the student read, receiving a synopsis of the books read, and finally setting, with the student, some goals for the following week.

The results of this program were promising. Over the nine months of the school year, seventy-two third-grade inner-city students had read an average (median) of twenty-one books each. These children had been doing almost no independent reading before the program began. Despite the success of such programs, we rarely see them used in schools.

Contracting systems, used with clearly stated objectives and incorporating personal contact between adult and child, have been shown to improve motivation. Reinforcement may be given freely for task-oriented behavior and goal attainment. Achievement, even with students whose predicted performance is low, seems to be affected favorably.

The two contracting systems we've been discussing were undertaken with young students. But the token economy for adolescents devised by Cohen also used a contracting system. Some version of contracting has a place at all levels of schooling. We talk again about this kind of individualized instruction in Chapter 10.

Nonetheless, token economies and contracting systems can be misused. If rewards become excessive, they can destroy intrinsic motivation. If we want children to enjoy reading for itself, apart from the teacher's approval or school grades that might reward it, we must withdraw extrinsic rewards gradually as the child begins to learn about the fun of reading for its own sake. Earlier we described research that shows intrinsic motivation toward an activity may be reduced by rewards that are artificially attached to it. But even Lepper, Greene, and Nisbett (1973) noted that such effects will not always "or even usually, result in a decrement in intrinsic interest in the activity" (p. 136).

Misuses of token economies and contracting

Moreover the effects of token economies appear to be long-lasting if attention is given to making the programs more generalizable (Wildman & Wildman, 1975). In one study, where fifth- and sixth-grade students had participated in a token economy, their eighth-grade junior high school achievement was evaluated. They had not been in a token economy for two years. Still, because of naturally occurring reinforcers in their environment (parent and teacher praise, special privileges for academic performance, and the like), the students maintained their high achievement. In comparison with control students, those who had had a reinforcement program two years earlier showed significantly greater growth in reading achievement, were more often on the honor roll with a B or better average, and had fewer referrals to deans or principals for behavior problems (Dickinson, 1974).

Stability of token economy effects

Token economies and contracting systems have their place in initiating learning activity that might not occur otherwise and in building competence to a point where students begin to reinforce themselves. In this way students sometimes learn to enjoy the activity and engage in it for its own sake.

Fifteen Motivational Techniques in Classroom Teaching

There are a number of environmental factors that classroom teachers can use to increase student motivation. Many of them do not require the classroom reorganization demanded by token economies or individual guidance systems. We offer here some guidelines and the reasons why they are effective.

1. Begin the Lesson by Giving Students a Reason to Be Motivated

When Brophy, Rohrkemper, Rashad, and Goldberger (1983) looked at six upper-elementary classrooms eight to fifteen times each, they never once heard a teacher say a student might receive some personal satisfaction from a task. Only about a third of the comments teachers made to introduce new tasks were motivating ("I think you'll like this—and it will come in handy at home as well!"). Most new tasks were introduced neutrally or even negatively ("I know you won't like this, but . . ."). Brophy (1987) noted that, in general, even teachers who are usually effective do not do and say the things that could motivate their students to learn academic content. Students really do deserve a reason to be motivated. We owe it to them. Try to tell them what the tasks they are doing are good for, how the tasks prepare them to do other things, and why they are important and interesting.

2. Tell Students Exactly What You Want Accomplished

Energizing and directing student behavior calls for a clear statement to students of what you want accomplished. In many classes teachers do not give clear directions about what must be done (Berliner, 1982). They plunge into a task without telling students what the goal of the task is and what students need to do to complete the task successfully. The students of teachers who do not provide this kind of information perform less well than do those of teachers who do provide this kind of information. No matter how well motivated students are, if they do not know what is expected of them, they start slowly, feel uneasy, may feel anxious, and may do the wrong tasks.

Guidelines 1 and 2 together mean you should start out, as often as you can, with clear statements of your expectations for students and some reason about why they should want to meet those expectations.

3. Have Students Set Short-Term Goals

Bandura and Schunk (1981) studied forty elementary-age students with substantial deficits in and an intense dislike of mathematics. Some learned to set short-term goals for learning; some set long-term goals; some had no goal-setting practice. At the end of seven learning sessions, the students who set short-term goals found they actually liked the activities they once thought were so dreadful. They were dramatically higher in measured intrinsic interest and substantially higher in feelings of self-efficacy and mathematical skill (Zimmerman, 1989). Morgan (1984) also obtained this result with college-age students. Once again attainment of short-term goals seemed to enhance both learning and motivation. The sense of mastery, of meeting goals successfully, seems to make tasks that once were seen as drudgery much more interesting.

4. Use Spoken and Written Praise

In many cases tangible reinforcement is not as important as a teacher's spoken praise. Saying "Good," "Great," "Wonderful," or "Fine work," contingent on appropriate performance or approximations to appropriate performance, can be a powerful motivating device.

Crandall (1963) described how the environmental variable of social approval can increase achievement motivation. Reimanis (1968) verified Crandall's ideas with kindergarten children, and Stein (1969) verified them with fourth-graders. It seems clear that social approval can strongly influence the achievement of schoolchildren.

Social approval

Praise is the easiest to use and most natural of the motivational devices available to a teacher. Most important, praise contingent on a certain behavior increases the frequency of that behavior. That is, social approval in its many forms is a relatively consistent reinforcer or incentive. You should remember, however, that too much praise is counterproductive. Praise can be so much a part of communication in some classes that it loses its utility as a motivating force. And there is "good" praise and "bad" praise (something we talk about again in Chapter 11). Brophy's (1981) study of how praise is used in classrooms yielded guidelines for the effective and ineffective use of praise. These guidelines are listed in Table 8.6. Study them carefully.

Effective vs. ineffective praise

One set of studies showed that teachers' written academic comments have a small but positive effect on subsequent test performance (Page, 1958; L. G. Stewart & White, 1976; Elawar & Corno, 1985). Although the effort required is substantial and the effects small, we agree with Page that "when the average . . . teacher takes the time and trouble to write comments (believed to be 'encouraging') on student papers, these apparently have a measurable . . . effect upon student effort, or attention, or attitude, or whatever it is which causes learning to improve, and this effect does not appear dependent upon . . . student ability" (p. 181).

Comments on homework and tests

The kind of social approval, social reinforcement, praise, and encouragement that Page studied showed that students can be motivated by these practices. Sometimes teachers forget how important their comments are to students. We have seen teachers who indiscriminately praise all sorts of student behavior, and other teachers who never seem to say a good word to students. Both extremes are inappropriate.

Remember, too, that some students are less responsive to praise than others. For example, extroverts (persons interested in things outside themselves and in social life) may be motivated more by blame than by praise; for introverts (persons interested in their own feelings and thoughts), praise may be more effective (see Kennedy & Willcutt, 1964). Also some praise-givers are more effective in motivating students than other praise-givers (see Lipe & Jung, 1971). They may have more status, appear more genuine, or offer praise less often so when they do praise a student it seems to carry more weight. But despite these restrictions, social approval contingent on wanted behavior can serve well when academic achievement or academic behavior needs to be improved.

Introverts and praise

TABLE 8.6
Guidelines for Effective Praise

Effective Praise	Ineffective Praise
1. is delivered contingently.	1. is delivered randomly.
2. specifies the particulars of the accomplishment.	2. is a general positive reaction.
3. shows spontaneity, variety, and other signs of credibility; suggests clear attention to the student's accomplishment.	3. shows a bland uniformity that suggests a conditioned response.
4. rewards attainment of specified performance criteria (which can include effort criteria).	4. rewards mere participation, without consideration of performance processes or outcomes.
5. provides information to students about their competence or the value of their accomplishments.	5. provides no information at all or gives students information about their status.
6. orients students toward better appreciation of their own task-related behavior and thinking about problem solving.	6. encourages social-reference comparisons.
7. uses student's own prior accomplishments as the context for describing present accomplishments.	7. uses the accomplishments of peers as the context for describing students' present accomplishments.
8. recognizes noteworthy effort or success at tasks that are difficult (for *this* student).	8. is given without regard to the effort expended or the meaning of the accomplishment.
9. attributes success to effort and ability, implying that similar successes can be expected in the future.	9. attributes success to ability alone or to external factors (luck, the ease of the task).
10. leads students to believe that they expend effort on the task because they enjoy the task and/or want to develop task-relevant skills.	10. leads students to believe that they expend effort on the task for external reasons (to please the teacher or win a competition or reward).
11. focuses students' attention on their own task-relevant behavior.	11. focuses students' attention on the teacher as an external authority figure who is manipulating them.
12. fosters appreciation of, and wanted attributions about, task-relevant behavior after the process is completed.	12. intrudes into the ongoing process, distracting attention from task-relevant behavior.

Source: Adapted from J. E. Brophy, "Teacher Praise: A Functional Analysis," *Review of Educational Research*, 1981, Vol. 51:5–32. Copyright 1981 American Educational Research Association, Washington, D.C. Used by permission.

5. *Use Tests and Grades Judiciously*

In Chapter 14 on the assessment of students, we discuss some arguments for and against the use of tests and grades. Despite the many strong criticisms of tests and grades, we believe they should be used. The fact that tests and grades are bases for various kinds of social rewards—approval, promotion, graduation, certification, admission to colleges and professional schools, better jobs, higher

Social rewards

prestige, more money, more interesting work, greater responsibility—gives tests and grades motivational power. Grades become incentives and reinforcers. Students learn that there are benefits associated with getting high grades. So the giving of tests and the assigning of grades come to have the effect of motivating students to learn.

But the criticisms of tests and grades are not without merit. The most important to us is that evaluation of student efforts has a potentially harmful effect on *continuing* motivation—the tendency to return to and continue working on tasks away from the instructional context in which they were initially confronted (Maehr, 1976). Here again we face a problem of balance. Using tests and grades probably motivates many students to study—those who value the grades—and thus is likely to improve learning. But for some students, externally imposed grades are likely to result in a decrease in their desire to work on tasks outside of school. Although "external evaluation by the teacher emerges as a potentially dangerous tool" (Salili, Maehr, Sorensen, & Fyans, 1976, p. 99), it is useful when judiciously used. A teacher who explains to students what tests are for, how they are constructed, and how to interpret them; who uses tests and grades to provide students with *information,* not to punish them; who sees tests and grades as evidence of mastery and growth, not as evidence of how one student compares with other students; and who sees tests and grades as indicators of effort, not unchangeable evidence of mental ability, has available a motivational device of considerable power.

Continuing motivation

6. Capitalize on the Arousal Value of Suspense, Discovery, Curiosity, Exploration, Control, and Fantasy

We talked about the arousal value of novel stimuli when we discussed cognitive learning in Chapter 7. Stimuli that are novel, surprising, complex, incongruous, or ambiguous give rise to a kind of cognitive arousal that Berlyne (1965) called *epistemic curiosity.* This is behavior aimed at acquiring knowledge, the means to master and understand the environment. When our epistemic curiosity is aroused, we are motivated to find ways to understand a novel stimulus.

Epistemic curiosity

Berlyne categorized some of the ways in which epistemic curiosity can be aroused:

Surprise.   Slip a brass ball through a metal ring. Heat the ball and try again. It won't fit. (Heat expands the ball.)

Doubt, or conflict between belief and disbelief.   Asking students whether the interior angles of triangles always total 180 degrees.

Perplexity, or uncertainty.   The condition that arises when a number of possible solutions are available but none seems absolutely right. Have students try to predict where crime will be most prevalent in a city, given only various sociological and economic facts about its different neighborhoods.

Bafflement, or facing conflicting demands.   Duncker (1945) described
a classic problem: treating a patient's tumor with radiation strong
enough to kill the tumor but not so strong as to harm adjacent tissues. (The solution: Focus weak X rays from different directions
onto the tumor so that the amount of radiation where the rays intersect is high, while that on intervening tissues is much lower.)

Contradiction.   Here we are talking about a finding that seems to fly in
the face of a general principle or common sense. One example is the
notion that resistance to extinction is greater after partial reinforcement than after continuous reinforcement (see Chapter 6).

**Conceptual
conflict**

When we use surprise, doubt, perplexity, bafflement, or contradiction, we
are arousing a kind of conceptual conflict. The motivation lasts until the conflict
is resolved or until students give up. Remember, if students cannot resolve the
conflict, they will become bored or frustrated, and these methods will eventually
fail to arouse any positive responses in them.

Lepper and Hodell (1989) have discussed how school tasks, such as learning
geometry, can be embellished to increase intrinsic motivation. They have noted
how Berlyne's ideas, plus two others, can produce increases in motivation and
achievement. One of these ideas is about *control*. Students who feel they can

**Giving students
control**

control the situation for learning (where, when, how) and the outcomes of
learning (seeking the level they want to achieve), are more intrinsically motivated. In addition, when learning tasks involve *fantasy,* intrinsic motivation is

Using fantasy

often aroused. Thus trying to determine how the "space invaders" can find
the distance from their spaceship to the tower of knowledge is more interesting
to most students than doing a workbook page with geometry problems devoid of
meaning.

7. Occasionally Do the Unexpected

Here also you can take advantage of epistemic curiosity. Use whatever has
become ordinary and usual as a cue for what you can do that is extraordinary and
unusual. If students have been talking about their own learning problems,
suddenly talk about your own. If the discussion has been at an extremely
"applied" level in a class in science, give it a theoretical turn. If you usually
prepare test questions, ask the students to prepare them. If you usually test
your students, have them give you a test. An occasional departure from what
students have come to expect has the effect of attracting their attention and
getting them involved.

8. Whet the Appetite

Give students a small sample of the reward before they make an effort to learn
(Marx, 1960). Show students what social approval is so that they know what
they are working for. Read to them so that they know the enjoyment of reading.
Use a reinforcer early in the learning sequence in the same way that you plan to

use it later in the sequence. This procedure gives the reinforcer incentive value that can influence performance.

One implication of this idea is that you should make the early stages of learning a task easy. Design a sequence of instruction so that students have some initial success—an important motivator. And be sure that all students get an opportunity to receive a "taste" of reinforcement. Brophy and Evertson (1976), for example, found that third-graders learned more when teachers called their names first, then asked questions, instead of waiting for volunteers. By calling names first, the teachers were able to control participation (and hence reinforcement). The brighter and more eager pupils did not get a disproportionate share of opportunities to respond and be reinforced.

Beware of contests, "bees," and games that require some students to "lose" unless you can predict that the same students will not always be the losers. This theme has applications in the design of curriculum and the assignment of grades. The curriculum should make room for a variety of talents and skills. The grading system should avoid distribution curves that allow only a fixed number of students to pass or earn an A.

Make early stages easy

Distribute reinforcers

Competition narrows spread of reinforcers

9. Use Familiar Material for Examples

When you give examples, use things that are familiar. If you're making up a set of arithmetic problems, use the name of a teacher or student, not the hackneyed John Jones or Mary Smith. In teaching students how library catalogs are alphabetized, use titles from books the students have read or list biographies of their heroes in sports or movies (Speeth & Margulies, 1969). Remember that familiarity, meaningfulness, and associations can improve learning and retention (see Chapter 7).

10. Use Unique and Unexpected Contexts When Applying Concepts and Principles

Apply the law of supply and demand to the price of tickets at rock concerts. Apply the inverse-square law to the number of decibels of sound at various distances from the stage of a rock group. Notice the difference between this point and guideline 9. When you want to build interest, use familiar things to motivate the students. For applications, after learning has taken place, use the unique and unexpected to keep students' interest high and to help them transfer what they've learned.

11. Make Students Use What They Have Previously Learned

By forcing students to use what they have learned before, you reinforce previous learning, strengthen previously acquired responses. You also build an expectation that what is currently being learned will have some subsequent use.

•*Simulations and games motivate students. They can instruct if they sustain attention and require information to be processed at more than a surface level. (© 1981 Susan Lapides)*

Never limit instruction to new learning. Whenever possible, call for previously acquired facts, concepts, and principles.

12. Use Simulations and Games

In the past two decades, teachers have increased their use of games and simulations. As microcomputer use increases, opportunities for instructional gaming also increase. Games and simulations motivate students, promote interaction, present relevant aspects of real-life situations, and make possible direct involvement in the learning process. We can only marvel at the intensity with which students play Nintendo or Space Invaders. This kind of intensity is what the designers of learning games and simulations are looking for.

There are two good questions you should ask to help you decide whether a learning game is effective—that is, whether it improves learning:

1. Does the game increase and sustain attention?
2. Is the student keenly involved in the game, processing information and making responses where more than just a surface kind of commitment is called for?

If attention is high and processing deep, chances are the game will enhance learning (Lepper & Chabay, 1985).

Learning requires attention and deep processing

Many games that do not require computers are available. *Disunion* is a three-week game that simulates the constitutional crises in the United States between 1776 and 1789. Research activities and role-playing help students learn parliamentary procedures, speech making, the problems of the thirteen states, and early political philosophies. The game seems to involve students in a way that traditional history courses do not. *Drug Attack* is a three-class-period game that teaches about the roles of pushers, addicts, the mayor, police, and citizens. *Ghetto* takes four hours to play and helps students learn about the emotional, physical, social, and economic forces that affect poor people as they try to improve their lives. *Roaring Camp* takes twenty minutes a day, continues as long as the teacher finds it useful, and develops an understanding of the gold rushes of the Old West and the life and times of the miners. Students, given a grubstake, file claims and strike gold or go broke. *Queries 'n' Theories,* playable at various levels of complexity, improves skills in scientific theorizing and experimental design as students learn to ask the right kinds of questions and also acquire an understanding of Noam Chomsky's theory of linguistic structure.

This brief sample suggests the variety of games already available to educators. And the list is growing. Most of these games are fun, provide important learning experiences, keep students highly involved, and involve the teacher in the learning experience in new and enjoyable ways. Using and even developing interactive games almost surely increases the classroom motivation of students *and* teachers. One reminder, however, is in order. Any game or activity can be played too long at a time or used too often. Watch out that enthusiasm doesn't turn to boredom.

13. Minimize the Attractiveness of Competing Motivational Systems

Sometimes a student, in order to gain acceptance by other students, may feel pressure to put down the teacher, do poor schoolwork, cut classes, smoke, or otherwise defy authority. What can you do to make these behaviors less desirable from the student's point of view? Getting student leaders involved in student activities (for example, administering tests or representing the school at a science fair) can help. Concentrating on keeping the most prestigious and popular leaders of a clique from smoking and using drugs is likely to be more effective than trying to convince an ordinary member of a clique not to conform to the group.

Get student leaders involved

To minimize the attractiveness of competing motivational systems, you might have to use punishment for inappropriate behavior along with reinforcement for appropriate behavior. The important task here is to identify and analyze competing motivational systems. Then use that information to strengthen positive motivation or to reduce the influence of those systems. For a particular student, the need for acceptance by fellow students may be competing with the need for approval by teachers and other adults. Or the need for achievement in athletics or hobbies may compete with schoolwork. Or the need for money can cause a student to take a job when there is homework to be done. By analyzing these competing systems you may be able to devise ways of reducing their anti-educational effects.

14. Minimize Any Unpleasant Consequences of Student Involvement

Aversive effects

Positively reinforce students' involvement with the subject matter. And minimize the factors or events that have aversive—that is, disliked—effects on their involvement. What are some aversive effects? Once pointed out, they are obvious:

- Loss of self-esteem (from failing to understand an idea or solve a problem correctly).
- Physical discomfort (sitting too long, straining to hear in a room with poor acoustics, peering at a blackboard or a screen that is too far away for the size of what is being shown).
- Frustration from not being able to obtain reinforcement.
- Being told that one is unlikely to understand something.
- Having to stop work in the middle of an interesting activity.
- Taking tests on material and ideas that have not been taught.
- Trying to learn material that is too difficult for one's present level of ability or understanding.
- Having a request for help go unmet by the teacher.
- Having to take a test made up of trivial or incomprehensible questions.
- Not being told by the teacher how well one is doing except at the end of a course, when it is too late to remedy problems.
- Having to go too fast to keep up with students better than oneself at what is being learned.
- Having to compete in a situation where only some of the students can succeed (for example, get an A or B), no matter how well one learns or achieves the objectives of a course; in short, being graded on a curve.
- Being grouped in a section of inferior students.
- Having to sit through a dull presentation—one that is repetitive, boring, or unchallenging. (A teacher's reading aloud from a textbook or manuscript is likely, in most instances, to be aversive.)

- Being exposed to a teacher who seems personally uninterested in the subject matter.
- Having to behave in a way other than the way a prestigious model (the teacher or a student leader) behaves.

15. Understand the Social Climate of the School

The school is a small society. It creates a social climate that has motivational effects. Teachers should understand this climate because it influences motivation within their classrooms.

J. S. Coleman (1960) studied the status systems of high schools to examine their effects on individual students. Some of his findings are dated—but one is still relevant. Students in his survey were asked how important grades were to social status. That is, could you be a popular cheerleader or athletic star and not do well in school? Or do you have to do well in school to also be a member of a "star" crowd? This is one way of measuring the climate of the school for academic achievement. The higher the percentage of students agreeing that good grades are necessary, the more the climate fosters academic achievement. The relation between (a) the IQ scores of the students receiving A's in a school and (b) the percentage of students in that school who said good grades were an important criterion for being in the leading group is given in schematic form in Figure 8.10.

The figure clearly shows that in schools where academic achievement is valued by students (where good grades are a sign of status), the students who go after and receive A's as grades tend to have higher IQ scores than do other

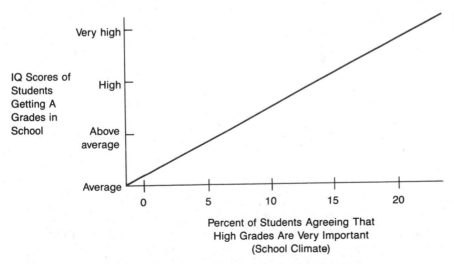

FIGURE 8.10

Relation Between School Climate and IQ Scores of Highest Performing Students

Source: Adapted from J. S. Coleman. Copyright 1960, *American Journal of Sociology* 65, pp. 337–347.

students in the same school. But where academic achievement is not highly valued, less able students receive the best grades. It seems that here the more able students are motivated to seek peer reinforcement through some other means than school performance.

Adolescent subcultures

The implications for American society as a whole are clear. Because high schools allow the adolescent subcultures to divert energies into athletics, social activities, and the like, they recruit into adult intellectual activities people with a rather mediocre level of ability. In fact, the high school seems to do more than allow these subcultures to discourage academic achievement; it aids them in doing so. . . . These results are particularly intriguing, for they suggest ways in which rather straightforward social theory could be used in organizing the activities of high schools in such a way that their adolescent subcultures would encourage, rather than discourage, the channeling of energies into directions of learning. One might speculate on the possible effects of city-wide or state-wide "scholastic fairs" composed of academic games and tournaments between schools and school exhibits to be judged. It could be that the mere institution of such games would, just as do the state basketball tournaments in the midwestern United States, have a profound effect upon the educational climate in the participating schools. (J. S. Coleman, 1960, pp. 344, 347)

Scholastic fairs

Coleman's words were prophetic. Today we find many more "mental olympics," "problem-solving tournaments," and other forms of academic competition than we did when Coleman was writing. And we find an increased awareness that high school athletes must do well in school subjects to compete. "No pass, no play" is now a part of many school policies. This shift is a big help to teachers. It is hard to teach Chaucer, trigonometry, genetics, or earth science to students whose popularity is based only on dating, grooming, athletics, clothing, cars, and the like. Just a few extra percentage points of students who value academics—as well as sports and the social aspects of school—change the climate of a school. That change fosters achievement among all students, but especially the achievement of the brightest.

Academic climate

There is evidence that the motivational patterns of many students can be changed if social approval depends on academic achievement. For example, a study of secondary schools serving low-income students in London, England, (Rutter, Maughan, Mortimore, & Ouston, 1979) found positive effects when an academic climate was created. Delinquency rates were lower, and attendance and academic performance rates were higher when the schools held high expectations for students' academic success and held the students personally responsible for their own behavior. In addition, these schools created a safe, orderly, and academically focused environment for the students to work in. Teachers were serious about teaching and expected students to be serious about learning. The effects of this climate were not limited to academic achievement. The students' pride and their responsibility to the school community also increased (Purkey & Smith, 1983).

The United States is concerned about the high dropout rate from its high schools. So it is important to note that researchers now have strong beliefs about how that situation can be improved. Finn (1989) pointed out that a "participation-identification" model of schooling explains well the dropout problem. Children who do not *participate* a lot in school activities do not *identify* with the school. If they do not feel close to their school, then school norms cannot influence, or exert pressure on, the behavior of such students, and they leave when they can (Nisan, 1990). Delinquency sometimes occurs as well. Both dropping out and delinquency are similar responses to conditions of alienation, nonparticipation, and nonidentification with the school. Finding ways to get students to feel close, or bonded, to schools so that the school can motivate their academic behavior is a big part of our challenge as educators. Development of extracurricular activities, student success in mastery-oriented rather than norm-oriented classes, and involvement in school decision-making, particularly in developing the school's disciplinary system, are all likely to lead to increased bonding. The development of "academic olympics" to recognize achievement and artistic accomplishments among the most talented may be precisely the kind of program most likely to increase dropouts among those who find no way to participate in and identify with the work of the school. So we must find ways for *every* student to be successful and involved in school. To maximize participation and identification means that rewards cannot go only to the brightest.

Participation and identification

Bonding to the schools

SUMMARY

Motivation is what energizes us and directs our behavior. It is what we use to explain how a student performs the same task in different ways, under different conditions, and how a group of students with the same learning history and aptitude perform the same task differently. Freud believed that a single motive—the libido—influences all human behavior. Others claim that two opposing forces motivate our behavior. Still others list many different motives. Maslow's hierarchy groups many different motives in five levels of needs, from basic physical needs to self-actualization. He claimed—and teachers of low-income and troubled students corroborate—that until students' lower-level needs are met, we cannot hope to be effective in helping them acquire knowledge, understanding, or appreciation of the world around them.

The measurement of the motive to achieve in the classroom is difficult. Teachers must usually estimate the needs of students by careful observation coupled with intuition and common sense. Why bother? Because we know that high achievement motivation goes hand in hand with important academic behaviors.

A primary influence on students' achievement is their attribution pattern—how they attribute responsibility for their successes and failures. Students who attribute their successes to internal factors (effort, ability) and their failures to external factors (task difficulty, luck) are using an ego-maintaining system. They believe they can control performance. Students who attribute their successes to external factors and their failures to internal factors often believe they don't have the ability to succeed. The result is they come to expect failure and often won't even try to succeed.

Another element that comes into play here is how the teacher attributes students' successes and failures. If you respond to a failure with anger, you are communicating to students that they can do better—that it is their effort, not their ability, that led them to fail. But when you express sympathy, you run the risk of making students feel that they cannot do better. What's important here is what the students believe your anger or sympathy means.

Classroom structure also affects students' self-concept. A competitive structure, although reinforcing for the few who are "winners," can be a source of humiliation for the many "losers." Individual learning, cooperative learning, and multidimensional classrooms reduce competition, and in the process promote self-esteem in students. Through the structures they use and the behaviors they exhibit, teachers also play an important role in helping students meet their needs for affiliation, power, and approval. What is important here is matching the teaching environment to the students' motive patterns. For one student you might increase social reinforcement; for another, you might require group work; for still another, you might talk about tendencies toward overdependence.

There is a distinction between intrinsic and extrinsic motivation. What appears to be intrinsic motivation, in the sense of not depending on external rewards, probably has its roots in extrinsic reinforcement systems. Over time, external reinforcement gives way to self-reinforcement. Both intrinsic and extrinsic motivation affect our self-perception. When we believe we are intrinsically motivated, extrinsic rewards can have a negative effect on performance.

Within the operant-conditioning framework, where extrinsic reinforcement systems are used, the key element is to bring learners under some sort of stimulus control. Incentives, for example, are controlling stimuli because students work to attain the reinforcer implied by the incentive. Learning about a student's preferences—sleeping late, building models, reading auto magazines, eating chocolate, collecting fashion books or baseball cards—can help you design a motivational program tailored for any student.

Frustration is a motivator, but generally toward negative behaviors. Aggression, regression, emotionality, withdrawal, and hyperactivity are all symptoms of frustration. When you find them, you should examine the environment you have created. Perhaps the material is too difficult; perhaps you are preventing students from finishing or even starting reinforcing activities. Once you find the source, you can attempt to remedy the problem.

Motives can be systematically changed. For example, the motive to succeed can be trained. Students can learn to want to do better at certain tasks. By helping students learn their own strengths and weaknesses, choose realistic goals, plan to reach those goals, and evaluate their work, you can help them take control of their behavior. Feeling in control is an important part of the motivation to achieve. You can also help students change their attribution patterns by teaching them and modeling self-monitoring, self-instruction, and self-reinforcement strategies.

One way to built a motivational system with incentives and reinforcers is to set up a token economy. Another is to create a contracting system for groups of students or individual students. Results from these kinds of programs indicate that they can be enormously effective when used properly. These programs imply using extrinsic rewards, but only to induce students to take part in a learning activity that they would otherwise avoid. As soon as intrinsic rewards, those inherent in the activity itself, begin to appear, you should withdraw the extrinsic rewards so that students will learn to enjoy the activity, as much as possible, for its own sake.

Many motivational techniques can be used in the classroom. Keep in mind the importance of giving students a reason to be motivated as well as telling students what is expected of them. Try to have students set short-term goals. Remember that there are ineffective as well as effective ways to use praise to influence learning and students' attitudes toward learning and toward themselves. Tests and grades can motivate most students, but for some students they probably have harmful effects to which you should try to be alert.

Try to capitalize on surprise—it's nice to throw students off a little by being innovative now and then. Give students a taste of reinforcement. Make the early stages of learning easy, and see to it that all students have an opportunity to be reinforced. Help ensure transfer as well as motivation by adding unique examples for applying concepts and principles, after you have used familiar examples to teach the concepts or principles. Encourage students to use what they have already learned as they learn new things. Try to incorporate games into your curriculum. Get your students to invent some if none exist.

Identify and work with competing motivational systems to strengthen motivation to achieve academically. Avoid a long list of aversive events, from physical discomfort to a loss of self-esteem. We don't want to punish students for their learning; we want to reinforce them. Finally, be sensitive to the social climate of your school and how it affects students' values.

You must be alert to what's going on in your classroom and how you feel when you teach a given topic in a certain way. Make your teaching experience cumulative. Don't be afraid to experiment, but be sure to learn from the experience. Keep records. If something works, use it again; if it doesn't motivate your students, drop it. Teaching is a process that demands constant and careful revision.

IV Teaching Methods and Practices

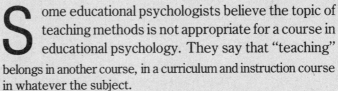

Some educational psychologists believe the topic of teaching methods is not appropriate for a course in educational psychology. They say that "teaching" belongs in another course, in a curriculum and instruction course in whatever the subject.

We disagree. First, research on teaching has increasingly occupied educational psychologists in recent decades. They have applied special ways of thinking and investigating to the phenomena of teaching. The result is a body of knowledge that has been well received and widely applied but typically is not used in curriculum and instruction courses. Second, and consequently, educational psychologists' treatment of teaching is much more research oriented than that of curriculum and subject-matter specialists. These specialists rely more on practical wisdom, philosophy, tradition, and untested common sense than on carefully conducted research. Third, educational psychologists point to what is generalizable across subject matters as well as to what is specific to teaching a certain subject matter and grade level. Fourth, educational psychologists, in referring to research, tend to describe teaching behaviors and practices in more specific, less ambiguous terms. Unless curriculum specialists are also researchers, they are not likely to be as specific. So we have chosen to include this section comprising three chapters on teaching methods and their relationship to learning.

What is a teaching method? It is a recurrent pattern of teacher behavior, applicable to various subject matters, characteristic of more than one teacher, and relevant to learning (Gage, 1969). The term *pattern* refers to a set of behaviors that occur simultaneously or in a unified sequence. *Recurrent* means that the pattern is repeated over intervals measured in minutes or weeks. *Applicable to various subject matters* means that a teaching method is more than a behavior that is useful in teaching only, say, the addition of fractions or the nature of a chemical bond. This kind of specific behavior is a *teaching technique*. We are interested here in methods, not techniques—in behaviors that cut across all or many subject matters. And these behaviors must be usable by more than one teacher; they cannot depend on the talents or traits of a single individual.

Lots of people use the term *teaching method* to describe curricular materials of some kind—say, the Initial Teaching Alphabet, the color phonics system, or chronological and topical approaches to teaching music appreciation. We shall not consider teaching methods in this sense.

We call the components of teaching methods—the specific things that teachers do that make up a teaching method—*teaching practices*. So the teaching method called "lecturing" consists of teaching practices like providing structure, clarifying content, explaining, and summarizing.

Not all teaching methods are equally appropriate for helping all students meet all instructional objectives. This general principle is often overlooked when students and teachers talk about teaching methods. What method of teaching is best? This question really has no answer unless we specify the characteristics of the students (age, intelligence, motivation, previous learning and achievement) and the objectives of the teaching. Some methods yield better results for students with certain characteristics; others produce better achievement in students with different characteristics. Individual instruction works best for some objectives, discussion for other objectives, classroom teaching for other objectives, and lecture for still other objectives. Adding to the problem is that, within any given method, there are scores of different practices that can be applied—even when the content of the material we are teaching is held roughly constant.

In this section we cannot give you a list of methods and practices and tell you that these always work and those never do. But we can give you some general guidelines to make your decision making easier. We begin in Chapter 9 with an examination of lecturing, explaining, and small-group teaching methods. In Chapter 10, we look at methods for teaching the individual and open and humanistic education, which is more a value system than a method of teaching. Finally, Chapter 11 discusses classroom teaching. Here we describe research-based suggestions for making both the preactive (planning) and interactive (contact) phases of classroom instruction more effective.

9 ≡ Lecturing, Explaining, and Small-Group Methods

OVERVIEW

A great deal of teaching still takes the form of a solo performance. There you are, all alone, lecturing, explaining, pointing out relationships, giving examples, correcting errors for one student or several hundred, for a minute or an hour. How do you go about establishing rapport with your students? Can you motivate them? Can you get them to pay attention to what you are saying? Can you organize your thoughts coherently? Can you put them into understandable terms?

In this chapter, we talk about these problems and many others and discuss ways to resolve them. We examine both lectures (the relatively long, uninterrupted talks frequently used by college or university instructors) and explanations (the shorter talks, lasting anywhere from a few seconds to several minutes, frequently used in elementary and secondary school classrooms). We deal in turn with objections to the lecture method and the reasons it has managed to survive despite them, with the preparation process, and with the various parts of the lecture (introduction, body, and conclusion). And we insert a word of caution. The lecture can be a valuable instructional tool, but it must be the right tool for the material, the educational circumstances, and, most of all, the individual teacher.

For teaching small groups (from two to twenty or so students), both the discussion method and cooperative learning are often used. We begin by looking at the educational objectives of discussion-group teaching—critical thinking, democratic skills, and other complex cognitive abilities—and the conditions under which this versatile method works best. Next we look at the process of teaching a discussion group:

what to do before, during, and after a meeting. And we consider the intellectual, social, and emotional pitfalls of the discussion method. Finally we turn to another form of small-group teaching, cooperative learning, and describe several techniques and their effectiveness.

The Lecture Method: Is It Effective?

Why Has Lecturing Lasted?

Samuel Johnson, the great English author, was quoted by his biographer as saying,

Antilecture arguments

> Lectures were once useful; but now when all can read, and books are so numerous, lectures are unnecessary. If your attention fails, and you miss a part of a lecture, it is lost; you cannot go back as you do upon a book. (Boswell, 1795/1953)

The point has often been made over the centuries (McLeish, 1976). What Johnson surmised has been confirmed time and again by research. After reviewing 208 studies made between 1890 and 1980, Welwert (1984) concluded that visual presentation is more effective than auditory presentation in improving retention and comprehension of hard or medium-hard text, especially for students over age 13, whose reading ability has developed fully.

Lectures have been called an anachronism. They've been criticized for fostering a passive role for students in the learning process. In any given year, it's not unusual to read a student's editorial that talks about "our absurd lecture system," or a news item that reports that "twenty-five medical students say their lectures are dull and a waste of time" or an article that laments that "only a very small number of students ever spoke or raised questions." Students regularly argue that lectures are boring, poorly organized, irrelevant or redundant. And they insist that lectures limit their involvement and fail to take account of individual differences among the students. But are these valid criticisms of the method? Isn't it the fault of the lecturer, not the lecture, if material is boring, poorly organized, or irrelevant? And aren't reception and listening important ways of learning? The failure to accommodate individual differences is indeed a flaw of the method, but it is a flaw in many other teaching methods too. We don't dismiss them out of hand; we try to adapt them.

The point about passivity is arguable. The process of following a lecture can be anything but passive. Just because the students are silent and almost motionless does not mean they are inactive. They may be working hard to follow the argument, comprehend its logic, judge its validity, evaluate the facts and evidence, separate the essential from the less important, and in other ways run alongside the lecture. Indeed, if one learns anything from a lecture, one has not been passive.

•The lecturer can give a framework, overview, and criticism unlike that found in any printed material. (© 1983 Walter S. Silver)

Although criticism has been loud and hard, there are those who defend lecturing, who find it valuable for surveying a whole field of knowledge through the medium of a living personality, and for arousing active interest that leads students to understanding. Lecturers can repeat material in different words, something books rarely do. They can introduce something from this morning's paper if need be, something that is a year away from publication in a textbook. Lecturers can compensate for the overabundance of books in some fields and the lack of books in others. They can give students a framework, an overview, a critique unlike anything in any available printed material. They can bring to their material their own aesthetic pleasure and enthusiasm to a far greater degree than can the printed page.

Prolecture arguments

The lecture method gives some teachers and students a kind of reinforcement that is not available in other educational procedures. A professor of art wrote:

The lecturer's reinforcement

I enjoy the lecture method. It is the most dramatic way of presenting to the largest number of students a critical distillation of ideas and information on a subject in the shortest possible time. The bigger the class the better I perform intellectually. How else in teaching can you share with so many a lifetime of looking at and loving art? You stand on a stage in front of a screen on which the whole history of art is projected. You can be an explorer of African art, an interpreter of Greek sculptures, a spokesman for cathedral builders, an advocate of Leonardo, a political theorist for palace architects, an analyst of Picasso and philosopher of Sung painting. No other subject is as visually exciting in the classroom, and this is what keeps me turned on lecture after lecture, year after year. With that supporting cast and if he knew his lines, who wouldn't want to perform in front of a large audience? (Elsen, 1969, p. 21)

Students' reinforcers

How are students reinforced? By the lecturer's warmth, humor, drama, intensity, logic, enthusiasm, and attention—to say nothing of the knowledge and comprehension they acquire. And there is the sense of security that comes from doing the right thing at the right time (being at a lecture), paying attention, perhaps taking notes, and responding with interest or boredom, in the same way that most of the other students are responding at that moment. We often measure the effectiveness of teaching methods by how much students learn in the form of knowledge. But the lecture situation may also provide social reinforcement, aesthetic pleasure, and emotional reassurance—a kind of coping with the essential loneliness of the human condition.

Cheapness and adaptability

Whatever its faults, whatever its benefits, the lecture method has probably persisted because it makes administrative sense. First, the method is cheap: It allows a single teacher to instruct a very large number of students. Second, the method is flexible: It can be adapted on short notice to a particular audience, subject matter, time, and set of equipment. It can also be adapted to a teacher's schedule to a degree that printed and programmed teaching materials cannot. Teachers cannot always plan to have materials run off. Sometimes an all-too-human inefficiency stops us from putting on paper and getting printed exactly the selection of ideas we want to present. No teaching method this adaptable will disappear in favor of methods that require more rigorous planning and that can be used only with a certain audience, subject matter, time allotment, or equipment (projectors, books, record players, computers).

Empirical Evidence

Whatever its advantages, the lecture method would probably not be used at all if experience and research had indicated that it was completely ineffective. But this evidence has not been forthcoming, despite scores of experiments.

Lectures Versus Other Teaching Methods.   In numerous experiments, students taught by the lecture method have been compared, on the basis of their achievement on final examinations, with students taught by other methods, especially the discussion method. The overall verdict is that lecturing is just about as effective as the other methods. Dubin and Taveggia (1968) reviewed the data (not just the conclusions) of nearly a hundred studies performed over a forty-year period. They tallied the results of eighty-eight independent comparisons of scores on final examinations of students taught by the lecture and discussion methods, as reported in thirty-six experimental studies. Of these, 51 percent favored the lecture method; 49 percent favored the discussion method.

Lecture vs. discussion methods

The differences between average final examination scores were so close to zero that they could be attributed to chance.

McKeachie and Kulik (1975) tried a different approach in examining these studies. They compared the lecture and discussion methods on three different types of criteria—a factual examination, a measure of retention and higher-level thinking, and measures of attitudes and motivation. As shown in Table 9.1, in twenty-one comparisons on a factual examination, the lecture method was superior in twelve, about equal to the discussion method in four, and inferior to the discussion method in five. In all seven comparisons on retention and higher-level thinking, the discussion method was superior. In nine comparisons on wanted attitudes and motivation, the discussion method was superior in seven.

Most of these studies run into a methodological problem that should be noted. Students who know they are going to take a final examination compensate for the inadequacies of the methods by which they are taught, whether lecture or discussion methods, reducing differences in the effects of the teaching methods on student achievement. McLeish called this the *equalization effect:* "Irrespective of differences due to the teaching methods used, the work which students do for themselves in preparation for an examination will tend to bring their scores close to equality" (1976, p. 271).

Equalization effect

Lectures and Thought Processes.   Teaching methods are often compared on their end product—the change in student knowledge, understanding, or attitude that follows a period of teaching. But they can also be compared on students' thought processes while the teaching is in progress. This criterion has the advantage of being less contaminated by other influences, such as the textbook or discussions with other students or teachers outside of class. B. S. Bloom (1953) studied these thought processes by the method of "stimulated recall." He played back a tape recording of an entire class period within twenty-four hours after the class. He stopped the tape at critical points and asked the students to remember what they were thinking at that point of the lecture or

Method of stimulated recall

	Criteria		
	Factual Examination	Retention and Higher-Level Thinking	Attitudes and Motivation
Lecture method superior	12	0	1
Lecture and discussion methods about equal	4	0	1
Discussion method superior	5	7	7

TABLE 9.1

Comparison of Lecture and Discussion Methods on Three Criteria

Source: Adapted from W. J. McKeachie and J. A. Kulik, "Effective College Teaching," *Review of Research in Education,* 1975, Vol. 3:165–209. Copyright 1975 American Educational Research Association, Washington, D. C. Used by permission.

discussion. During lectures, 31 percent of the students' thoughts were irrele-vant to the subject; during discussion, the comparable percentage was 14 percent. Other studies show that the relevance of student thought is substan-tially correlated with student achievement from lectures (Siegel, Siegel, Capretta, Jones, & Berkowitz, 1963). The implication is that lecturers should make an effort to keep their students' attention on the subject matter. Lecturers should realize they are competing with the students' tendency to think about irrelevant matters.

Proper Uses of Lecturing

When lectures are suitable

What does research tell us about when to use the lecture method? Many writers (Bligh, 1972; McKeachie, 1967; McLeish, 1976; Verner & Dickinson, 1967) have concluded from their reviews of studies that the lecture method is *suitable* when

- the basic purpose is to disseminate information.
- the material is not available elsewhere.
- the material must be organized and presented in a particular way for a specific group.
- it is necessary to arouse interest in the subject.
- students need to remember the material for only a short time.
- it is necessary to provide an introduction to an area or directions for a learning task that is going to be taught through some other teaching method.

When lectures are inappropriate

These authors believe that lecturing is *inappropriate* when

- objectives other than acquisition of information are sought.
- long-term retention is necessary.
- the material is complex, detailed, or abstract.
- learner participation is essential to achievement of objectives.
- higher-level cognitive objectives (analysis, synthesis, evaluation) are the purpose of instruction.

The often-maligned lecture method is probably here to stay. In choosing to use it or not to use it, it is important to evaluate criteria like those we have described here and earlier. It is equally important to separate faults of the lecturer from faults of the method. We turn now to ways in which lecturers can improve presentations.

Preparing a Lecture

How long you intend to lecture determines how or whether you should prepare. For a longer, formal lecture, you must prepare thoroughly. For a shorter, less formal explanation, you cannot prepare at all or must prepare in a different way.

Explanations are often spontaneous, unplanned. We talk about explanations and "preparing" for them later in this chapter. Here we concentrate on the formal lecture.

For the longer lecture, you should think about four factors; your knowledge of the subject, your comfort with the lecture method, the time available for preparation, and the use of media.

- Do you know your subject well enough? It seems obvious that the lecturer should have content knowledge—teachers must know their subject. But what does it mean to know the subject "well enough"? Knowledge at the low end can mean that you have read the textbook one step ahead of your students. Then you are limited in what you can offer. You will be shaky on other ways to present the material, on fresh examples and applications, on flexible ways of explaining the ideas, on metaphors and other rhetorical devices that may light up the content for your students. You will be weak on what Shulman (1987) called *pedagogical content knowledge*, that is, knowledge of *how to teach* the content knowledge you possess.

  At the high end, you have a lot of pedagogical content knowledge and can "move around" in the subject matter comfortably and flexibly. You will possess familiarity with alternative conceptions of the field. Thus you will know metaphors for elucidating the Bill of

Content knowledge

Pedagogical content knowledge

Rights, analogies for clarifying the Pythagorean theorem, convincing examples of inherited and acquired characteristics, mnemonics for remembering the sonnet's rhyming scheme, and wholly different conceptions of your subject—such as whether, in teaching computer programming, you should focus on "documentation and format" or on general concepts applicable to many settings (Baxter, 1987). Research on pedagogical content knowledge is still in its early stages. But enough has been done to indicate that this form of content knowledge can make a big difference in how well teaching is done. As your teaching experience increases, you should try to accumulate such knowledge so that your second effort will benefit from your first, and so on.

Speech fright

Systematic desensitization

- Are you comfortable lecturing? Many people are frightened at the idea of public speaking of any kind. And fright reduces the teacher's ability to communicate (Clevenger, 1955; Ellis & Jones, 1974). Speech fright can be overcome (Fremouw & Harmatz, 1975). Systematic desensitization is one effective technique. The subjects learn to relax. After they are able to relax on cue, a graded series of anxiety-producing events is presented for them to react to—from thinking about giving a lecture to actually standing in front of a large group and delivering a lecture. Each anxiety-producing situation in the hierarchy is considered neutralized when the subjects can stay relaxed in the imagined situation. Systematic desensitization works because relaxation and anxiety are incompatible. It can enable speakers to face an audience without fear.

- Is there time to prepare? Organizing a good lecture takes time for collecting information, determining emphases, organizing the sequence of ideas, and creating incisive and fresh examples. Teaching methods other than lecturing require a more general, less specific kind of preparation, namely, acquiring a broad knowledge and background in the whole curriculum area. Such general preparation allows explanations and examples to come readily to the teacher's mind in a spontaneous, seemingly unplanned and unprepared, way. The lecture, however, should be planned better.

Audiovisual media

- Will you use media? Are film, television, slides, or tape recordings available to help you teach? Many teaching aids exist, and it is usually worth the effort to examine catalogs of films and tapes to see whether appropriate material can be had. Preview any material and evaluate its relevance and cost. Prepare transparencies for an overhead projector.

Low-Inference Variables

In giving suggestions on lecturing, as well as other teaching methods, we try to focus on *low-inference variables* rather than *high-inference variables*. These terms refer to the amount of inference, interpretation, or extrapolation from

• *A variety of media that can aid and enhance teaching is available.*
(© Elizabeth Crews)

cues that a perceiver or practitioner must make to judge or act on the variable (Gage & Cronbach, 1955; Heyns & Lippitt, 1954). Teacher warmth, clarity, or enthusiasm, for example, would be high-inference variables because a judge of the teacher would need to infer a lot in going from cues (what the teacher does or says) to a judgment about these variables. And a teacher would not know exactly what to do or say if she wants to act in such a way as to be warm, clear, or enthusiastic. It is easy to tell an observer to judge these dimensions of teaching, but one judge may infer very differently from another on the basis of the available cues that reflect these dimensions. It is easy to tell a teacher to be warm, clear, and enthusiastic, but such high-inference advice is not very helpful.

So, in this section on teaching methods and practices, we try to talk in low-inference terms. When we talk about "clarity," for example, we try to boil clarity down to the kinds of things teachers can do or say in order to be clear.

The risk in talking in low-inference terms is that we may lose the "essence" of the high-inference variable. We may miss the complexities, subtleties, and nuances that clarity comprises. But we think the risk is worthwhile, as against the opposite risk of talking in high-flown, resounding, but not very helpful abstractions.

The Introduction to the Lecture

Every lecture has an introduction, body, and conclusion. The introduction serves several functions: motivating students, providing motivational cues, exposing essential content, and helping students to organize content. Although the techniques we talk about here are used primarily in the introduction to a lecture, they can also be put to work at any point at which a new topic is introduced.

Motivating Students Through Their Interests

Relevance to students' goals

Lectures should be *relevant* to students' goals—whether these goals are good grades, the solution to an intellectual problem, success in a career, satisfaction of curiosity, the ability to help other people, or a chance to earn more money. Lectures that are relevant to the students' motives become motivating in themselves.

Suppose your students are interested in good grades. If at the outset you tell them they will be tested on lecture material, you're motivating them to learn.

To make a lecture relevant, teachers must first determine what students find interesting. This isn't an easy job. Students can have very different interests depending on

- their age, sex, socioeconomic status, level of ability, previous educational experiences and success, ethnicity, nationality, religion, and so on.
- the times in which they live.
- changes in their circumstances and conditions of living.
- events in the world of art, politics, science, and technology.
- their stage of development (for example, adolescents may be more interested in the opposite sex than their careers; college students may be more concerned with their future occupation).

These kinds of factors have to be taken into account whatever the subject of the lecture—*Hamlet,* isotopes, marginal utility, or lepidoptera. As we noted in Chapter 8, your choice of words, examples, analogies, and supporting evidence should be drawn from fields that touch students' interests.

Providing Motivational Cues

Telling students that examination questions will be asked on specific topics, that certain ideas are important, that some ideas or techniques are difficult—all provide cues that motivate learning.

Telling students material is difficult

Hovland, Lumsdaine, and Sheffield (1949) showed that warning students that they will be tested on the content of a film or filmstrip tends to make the students learn more. Allison and Ash (1951) found that learning can be improved by telling students that the material in a film is both important and difficult. It is probably better to tell students, in lectures and other teaching situations, that a topic or problem is difficult but understandable than to say it is easy. Think about it. If students do manage to understand the topic or solve the problem, their self-reinforcement is greater; and if they fail, their loss of self-esteem is less. But if students succeed with what they have been told is an easy topic or problem, their self-reinforcement is less; and if they fail, their loss of self-esteem is greater. The attributions students make—attributing success to their own ability, not to the easiness of the task, and attributing failure to the difficulty of the task, not to their own lack of ability—can improve their subsequent effort. **Fostering the right attributions**

Creating a "feeling of disequilibrium, e.g., by suggesting that the topic is novel . . . or challenging them with one or more provocative questions" (Gregory, 1975, p. 59) can also motivate students. For example, you might begin a lecture on lecturing by saying that it is both the most criticized and the most widely used teaching method in colleges, then ask "Why?"

Exposing Essential Content

In a paragraph, it's a topic sentence; in a lecture it's an announcement of the topic:

- "Our subject today is the bimetallic standard."
- "This lesson is about the various kinds of money used during the history of our country."
- "In this lesson you will see that circumstances have forced our country to use many different kinds of money."

You can summarize the main points (two to four, at least) of the lesson or define terms related to the lesson topic.

A statement of objectives—"At the end of this lesson you should be able to describe five causes, besides slavery, of the Civil War"—is also part of exposing essential content.

Several studies found correlations of .50, .39, and .26 between student ratings of the "clarity of aims" for a lesson and a measure of student achievement (Belgard, Rosenshine, & Gage, 1971; Fortune, Gage, & Shutes, 1966). The studies used a rating instrument on which a high rating in "clarity of aims" meant that teachers have made explicit the objectives of the lesson they were teaching. **Clarity of aims**

Helping Students Organize Content

Advance Organizers.   Telling students in advance about the way in which a lecture is organized is likely to improve their comprehension and ability to recall and apply what they hear. Ausubel (1968) used the term *advance organizers* to describe this kind of preliminary material (see Chapter 7). Luiten, Ames, and Ackerson (1980), in a meta-analysis of the results of 135 studies, concluded that the "average advance organizer study shows a small, but facilitative effect on learning and retention" (p. 217). This average effect appeared in all grade levels, subject areas, and presentation modes (written or oral).

Ausubel (1978) has suggested that most people who have tried to use advance organizers don't understand them. They can be *rules of organization* that underlie a body of apparently unorganized ideas. For example, we can tell students that most psychological research reports are organized according to **Rules of organization**

Higher-level propositions

purpose, method, results, interpretations, and conclusions. Or they can take the form of *higher-level propositions*. For example, we can tell students that the depressions of 1919–1920 and the 1930s can be understood as instances of the general phenomena of primary and secondary postwar depressions. Or that Churchill's wartime role is understandable as charismatic leadership. Or that rocket power fits under Newton's third law of motion: For every action, there is an equal and opposite reaction.

The rules or propositions should help students learn by giving them, or helping them remember, concepts on which to hang or anchor new knowledge. These concepts help students classify, store, and retrieve the information they are learning.

Advance organizers can make material that seems to lack any clear meaning or organization more meaningful and more readily remembered.

Ideational scaffolding

With advance organizers, we do not give students a set of facts, then let them develop generalizations by inductive reasoning—the discovery method. We give them concepts by which to learn facts. But so long as we do not give students conclusions, advance organizers can still be used in discovery learning to help them form the concepts and categories needed to interpret discoveries. Providing "ideational scaffolding" for fitting experience into a preexisting structure is the purpose of advance organizers. They do not have to interfere with discovery processes.

Pretesting

Prompting Awareness of Relevant Knowledge or Experience.   Asking questions—informally or in a short written pretest—is another way to help students organize material, to make them aware of what they already know that can help them with new learning, and what is important (Hartley & Davies, 1976). Students' answers also give teachers an idea of the students' level of knowledge, as well as a basis for modifying instruction.

Prior knowledge

Ausubel (1968) claimed that the most important factor influencing learning is what the learners already know, and that teachers must determine that knowledge and teach their students accordingly. Similarly, Gagné (1970) argued that the major factor in learning is the prior learning of "prerequisite capabilities" (p. 470). Schemata—the ways in which knowledge is stored in memory—are also relevant here (see Chapter 7). Coding of the information to be learned appears to be more effective when appropriate schemata are deliberately brought to mind as learning begins. So, from a number of points of view, you are reminded to bring forth your students' related knowledge and experience before you begin your lecture.

The Body of the Lecture

From the introduction, the teacher moves to the body of the lecture—to covering content, creating order, clarifying both organization and content, and maintaining students' attention.

• *Not all lecturing and explaining takes place in the classroom before large groups of students. (© Michael Carpenter)*

Covering Content

It's obvious: Lectures should cover what we want students to learn. Many experiments have manipulated the degree to which teachers cover the material—that is, provide content relevant to a test. These experiments have found that students regularly do better on tests when content has been covered better. Content usually has "a large impact on achievement" (Abrami, Leventhal, & Perry, 1982, p. 454).

The same phenomenon was found in a twelve-nation study of achievement in mathematics (Husén, 1967). Questions rated by teachers and students as higher in terms of the students' opportunity to learn what the questions covered were indeed answered correctly more often by the students.

Opportunity to learn

In short, lecturers should provide the content (facts, concepts, principles) that they want students to learn, especially if the lecture is the students' only source of this content. This variable, sometimes called *time on target,* is always an important factor in learning.

Time on target

Creating Order

Almost everyone would agree that a lecture should be well organized. All of us have heard well-organized lectures—those whose structure made good sense, held together in a logical way, and seemed to be going somewhere. We have also

Does organization improve comprehension?

heard lectures that were hard to follow because the lecturer jumped around from one idea to another. Buxton (1956) put it this way: "The goal of lecturing is, after all, communication, and it is likely to be more effective if there is an evident order or sequence" (p. 148). Skinner (1968) stated that "material which is well organized is also, of course, easier to learn" (p. 107).

But Nisbet (1967) disagreed:

> I think irresistibly of three or four great teachers of this century I have been privileged to know: Gilbert Lewis in chemistry, Edward Tolman in psychology, Carl Sauer in geography, A. L. Kroeber in anthropology. Not one of them would have passed muster on clear organization of subject matter. Seminal minds are almost never very clear in their organization of subject matter. How could they be and at the same time leave generations of students . . . with the feeling that in knowledge as in a woman's beauty there is something wonderful and beckoning that eludes precise classification? (p. 31)

Of course, in the case of great scholars, students are willing to compensate mightily for shortcomings. John Dewey

> sat at his desk, fumbling with a few crumpled yellow sheets and looking abstractedly out of the window. . . . He hardly seemed aware of the presence of a class. He took little pains to underline a phrase, or emphasize a point, or so at first it seemed to me, to make any. . . . He seemed to be saying whatever came into his head next. . . . The end of the hour finally came and he simply stopped; it seemed to me that he might have stopped anywhere. But I soon found that it was my mind that had wandered, not John Dewey's. I began very soon to do what I had seldom done in college courses—to take notes. It was then a remarkable discovery to make . . . to find that what had seemed so casual, so rambling, so unexciting, was of an extraordinary coherence, texture, and brilliance. (Edman, 1938, pp. 138–143)

Most of us are not great geniuses, however. And we would do better making the organization of our lectures as clear as possible.

E. Thompson (1960) manipulated organization by taking a well-organized speech (version 1) and "randomly rearranging the order of sentences within each main point" (version 2). He then made the organization even worse by "randomly rearranging the order of sentences within the introduction, body, and conclusion of the speech" (version 3). Finally, he added transitions—simple statements describing the points to be covered—after the introduction and before and after the development of each point in the original, well-organized speech (version 4). (The organizational value of transitional statements that highlight and emphasize the structure of a message had been found by Thistlethwaite, deHaan, and Kamenetzky, 1955, to improve comprehension.)

After listening to the speech, Thompson's subjects, college students in a beginning speech course, were given a comprehension test. The average scores were ranked according to the amount of structure and transition in the speeches. That is, structure helped, and so did transitional statements. Also the students recognized and disliked the lack of structure in versions 2 and 3. (We talk about the important role of organization in fostering memory in Chapter 7.)

Structure and transitional statements

Organizational, or Outlining, Forms

Teachers can organize the body of a lecture, and thus its outline, in many different ways. Goyer (1966), in developing a test of ability to organize ideas, described some of them:

- Component (part-whole) relationships
- Sequential relationships
- Relevance relationships
- Transitional (connective) relationships

To these four, we've added comparisons, combinational devices, and explanations.

Component (Part-Whole) Relationships.   With component relationships the lecturer shows how a large idea is made up of several smaller ones. Once students understand this relationship, it is easier for them to understand the larger idea and to remember the smaller ones related to it. For example, if you were lecturing about fishing, a favorite hobby of yours, you might talk about why you like to fish, the equipment needed for fishing, and the best fishing spots. Under the heading "Why I like to fish," you might include the facts that fishing is an outdoor sport and that it is relaxing. Under "Equipment needed," you might discuss the casting rod for bait casting, the cane pole for still fishing, and the fly rod for fly fishing. And under "Best fishing spots," you might point to Smith's pond for panfish and Blue Lake for bass. Figure 9.1 shows how these topics and subtopics could be arranged. Notice the sub-subtopics under the fly-rod sub-topic.

Bligh (1972) calls this kind of organization a *classification hierarchy*. It groups together various items (facts, concepts, principles) under a common unifying heading. The grouping reduces the number of separate items, making comprehension easier. If the number of items under a single heading becomes too large—say more than about seven—it's a good idea to create new clusters if logic allows.

Classification hierarchy

In using component organization, be sure to let students know when you are moving to a new major heading. You can begin by announcing all of the major headings and saying that you are now going to deal with the first of them. When you've finished with the first heading, give the students a *signal of transition,* an indication that you are going to talk about the next heading now. Say something like, "We are through with that topic; now let's turn to the second major theme (topic, heading, purpose, problem)." Within each major heading,

Signal of transition

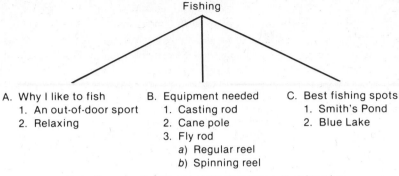

FIGURE 9.1

A Component Organization for a Lecture on Fishing

you may want to list each of the subheadings, to keep the students continuously informed of the level at which you are speaking.

Sequential Relationships.   Sequential relationships have some sort of order—chronological, cause and effect, building to a climax, or "con-pro"—as their basis. Once this basis is understood, the sequence is easier to remember. For example, you might say:

> In considering a problem for informal group discussion, we should proceed through the following steps in the logical order indicated. First, we should examine the facts out of which the problem arises. Second, we should state and define the problem. Third, we should consider the criteria to be used in evaluating solutions. Fourth, we should examine and appraise solutions. And fifth, we should consider the steps to be taken in carrying out the adopted solution. (See Figure 9.2.)

Problem-centered lecture

You begin with a set of facts that creates a question or problem. You then present information about and arguments for each of several possible solutions. Finally you adopt a solution and talk about its implementation. These kinds of problem-centered lectures can be highly motivating. And you can heighten interest through rhetorical questions, skillfully timed introductions of new pieces of evidence, and careful explanations of the way in which a hypothesized solution follows from evidence.

The con-pro sequence

A suspense-building sequence is con-pro: First, lay out all the arguments against your own position, as strongly as possible, perhaps with quotations from your opponents. Your students will be wondering how you will answer these arguments. Then, in the second part of the lecture, you present your evidence (logic and data) against your opponents' position and in favor of your own positions. Finally you sum up by indicating, as evenhandedly as possible, what remains to be done to buttress either your position or that of your opponents. Gage (1991) used this con-pro sequence in a lecture on the obviousness of social and educational research results.

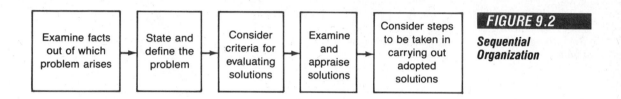

FIGURE 9.2

Sequential Organization

Relevance Relationships. Relevance relationships have a central unifying idea and a criterion that determines whether or not other ideas should be included as part of an argument. You begin by identifying the criterion. Then you show how its application results in including some ideas and excluding others. For example, suppose you were trying to convince an audience that American farmers should have price supports. Your most relevant argument—your central idea—is that stable farm prices influence the stability of our whole economy. It is relevant, then, that farmers are large-scale purchasers of the goods of others, that they provide food for all of us, and that they have as much right to economic aid as anyone. It is irrelevant that agriculture is a scientific and mechanical industry that requires expensive machinery, technical knowledge, and hard work.

Central unifying idea

Transitional (Connective) Relationships. Transitional relationships can be shown by using relational words and phrases that define the structure of your organization and make your students fully aware of it. By repeating certain phrases, you are teaching your students about the component parts of a series. You should also use a phrase of some sort to indicate that a summary is coming. For example:

Relational words or phrases

> Teaching can be analyzed in many different ways for different purposes. *It can be analyzed according* to the components of the learning process that it influences, when it is being related to the learning process. *It can be analyzed according to* the time sequence of the logical steps involved, when one is planning a teacher education program. *It can be analyzed according to* grade level or subject matter, when one is planning to speak to teachers of different grade levels or subject matters. *To repeat,* teaching can be analyzed in different ways for different purposes.

Here the repeated phrase "It can be analyzed according to" shows the parallelism of the series of ideas. The phrase "To repeat" signals the summary.

Comparisons. Comparing two or more things requires that you make explicit the bases of the comparison. That is, comparisons require bases, or dimensions, on which the comparisons are made. Your organization then takes the form of listing or defining basis 1, illustrating it, then indicating whether the things being compared are similar or different on basis 1. Then you list or define basis 2, and repeat the process. You continue this way until you've dealt with

The bases of comparison

FIGURE 9.3

Organization of a Comparison

Basis of Comparison	Thing A on Each Basis	Thing B on Each Basis	Conclusion as to Similarity or Difference
1	_____	_____	_____
2	_____	_____	_____
3	_____	_____	_____
4	_____	_____	_____

Overall conclusions as to similarity or difference
between Things A and B: [   ]

each of the bases for comparison. Figure 9.3 shows how to organize a comparison this way.

For example, suppose you are comparing tutoring (thing A) with film presentation (thing B) for teaching some concept. You might note that on the basis of encoding media they are dissimilar: The first is highly verbal; the second, highly visual. On a second dimension, whether they are transient events or persistent (like a text or photograph), you would note that they are alike: Both are transient events. You'd continue the process until you've examined all the bases for comparing thing A (tutoring) and thing B (film presentation). Then, you'd rate their overall similarity or difference. Your rating can be made using phrases such as "quite similar" or "highly similar."

Combinatorial Devices.   Whenever two or more distinctions can be applied to the same subject matter, they can be combined. When the combination is made, new insights into the structure and organization of the subject matter may emerge. This procedure can be seen in 2×2, or $N_1 \times N_2$ tables, like those shown in Figure 9.4. Here the two sets of distinctions are combined to yield $N_1 \times N_2$ categories; your lecture would deal with each of the categories in turn. You would tell the students each of the main distinctions and each of the combinations to which they lead.

$N_1 \times N_2$ **tables**

When you are considering each of a number of things (facts, concepts, principles) in relation to each of the other things in a set, networks of the kinds shown in Figure 9.5 may also be useful. These devices help speakers organize the material they want to cover. They also provide visual images and mnemonic systems that help students retain learning.

Networks

Explanations

These are usually shorter than lectures and have a narrower purpose: to clarify, to define, to account for, to reveal the cause of some single concept, event, or instance. Explanations can stand by themselves or be part of a lecture.

	Men	Women
Married		
Single		

An Organization for Describing Sex Roles

FIGURE 9.4

*Combinatorial
Organizations*

	Types of Team Sports	
	Noninteractive	Interactive
Contact	wrestling	football
Noncontact	gymnastics	volleyball

An Organization for Describing Team Sports

How do we know an explanation is a good one? One criterion is that students have a feeling of understanding. A second is that they can do something—apply a definition, use a concept, follow a set of directions, or solve a problem.

A good explanation

Explaining Behavior in Teaching Reading.   The explaining behavior of more and less effective teachers of reading has been studied by Duffy, Roehler, Meloth, and Vavrus (1986). They found that teachers' explanations are *physical,* through models and posters, or *verbal,* typically oral rather than in writing. Explanatory talk may be close to the heart of what we mean by *teaching.* It was this kind of talk by elementary school teachers of low-achievement reading groups that Duffy, Roehler, and their co-workers examined. The more effective teachers at each grade level (second, third, and fifth) were those whose student achievement and student awareness (measured by interviews) were higher. Their explanations were found through careful analysis to be

Physical and verbal explanations

- more responsive.
- more adequate for developing awareness of content.
- more complete in providing specific kinds of information.
- better in giving students devices to help them learn.

Being responsive means attending to students' needs for information useful in building or modifying schemata (see Chapter 7). This information tells the student about the academic task ("What are possessives?" "What are question marks?"), about the correctness of their answers ("That is a good clue"), and about how to refine understandings ("What do I do first? Look for clues?"). You can see responsive information-giving at work in this exchange between a fifth-grade teacher (T) and students (S):

Responsiveness

FIGURE 9.5

*Organizational
Networks*

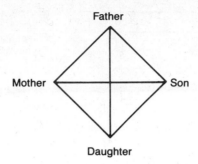

Relationships Within a Family

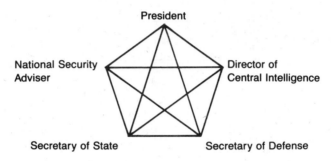

Relationships of the Executive Branch
in the Foreign Policy Establishment

Dialog Illustrating Responsiveness of an Explanation	*Aspect of Responsiveness Being Illustrated*
T: What we're going to talk about today is the punctuation that tells us when someone is speaking. How do we know, when we are reading, that someone is speaking?	Tells students about the academic task.
S: When it has . . . um . . . two parentheses around them.	
T: All right. (Teacher draws a set of quotation marks on the chalkboard.) These are called . . . does anybody know what these are called?	Tells students about the academic task.
S: Commas.	
T: Not commas. Not when they're up in the air like that.	Tells students about the correctness of their answers.

S: Brackets.

T: Not brackets. These are brack-   Tells students how to refine under-
 ets. (Teacher draws a pair of   standings.
 brackets on the chalkboard.)

S: Parentheses.

T: Not parentheses. These are up in   Tells students about correctness of
 the air above the words.   their answers.
 (Teacher points to the words
 within the quotation marks.)

S: Oooh, oooh, oooh. Quotation
 marks.

T: Perfect. These are quotation   Tells students about correctness of
 marks. And quotation marks,   their answers and how to refine
 when you run across them in a   their understandings.
 story, tell you that someone is
 speaking directly. (Duffy et al.,
 1986, p. 203)

Less effective teachers were not as responsive to students' misunderstandings and did not clarify those misunderstandings with new information.

Developing awareness refers to going beyond the students' finishing a task or answering questions correctly to reminding students of the usefulness and importance of what had been learned. For example, a teacher might say, "Now when you read, you can know when someone is talking. And, when you write, you should use quotation marks to show that someone is talking." Such awareness has metacognitive values (see Chapter 7). The more effective teachers wanted students to know when and how to use and interpret what was being taught. They made these goals explicit and provided reminders, reviews, and summaries.

Providing appropriate information means giving information that has declarative, conditional, or procedural value. *Declarative* information deals with the nature, characteristics, and structure of a task. The teacher could say, "Let's try to find quotation marks in our reading assignment for today to see whether you can recognize them."

Declarative, conditional, and procedural information

Conditional information provides awareness of when and why a given device is used to get at the meaning of what is being read, as in an explanation of indirect quotation: "You don't use quotation marks when what someone says is preceded by the word *that.* So if I wrote *John said that it is raining,* I wouldn't put quotation marks around *it is raining.*"

Procedural information tells students how to apply a device or strategy correctly. "Be sure to put the quotation marks above the line and not on the line you are writing." These three kinds of information, closely interrelated, help students understand the explanations involved in teaching reading.

Precise and explicit information

The information should be *precise* and *explicit,* not approximate and indirect. The more effective teachers, teaching how to use context to figure out the meaning of new words, for example, would follow a series of steps: (1) looking for clues in previous or subsequent sentences, (2) putting clues together with what students already know, and (3) going back and checking whether the meaning guessed at makes sense.

Conceptual accuracy

Similarly, the information should be *conceptually accurate.* Less effective teachers might describe the wanted outcome as "using context" or "memorizing a set of steps." But the more effective teachers correctly describe the objective as skill in using a thinking process for figuring out unknown words—a process to be used flexibly and adaptively.

Providing assistance to help students understand their objectives also was done more often by teachers who were more effective. These teachers presented information gradually and sequentially, and by giving students "hooks" for restructuring explanations along wanted lines. Help was abundant at first, diminishing as students acquired understanding. The teachers also showed their own reasoning in solving the kinds of problems the students were learning to solve, making the processes "visible" to the students.

Duffy and his colleagues (1986) focused on teaching reading to low-achieving elementary school students. But their findings probably apply more generally to the teaching of other subjects to other kinds of students at other grade levels.

Minilectures and microlectures

"Explaining" here refers to the brief statements—"minilectures" and "microlectures"—that teachers make as they work toward getting students to understand, not just to remember, the ideas they need in any discipline or subject matter. In this sense explaining takes place not only in lectures to large groups, but also in classroom teaching, discourse, recitations, and discussions of the kinds we talk about in later chapters.

A Model for Organizing Explanations.   It helps to have a model to follow in organizing your explanation. One common model attempts to show how the relationship between two or more concepts, variables, or events is an instance of a more general relationship or principle.

Instance of a general principle

Suppose you want to explain why it is colder in winter than in summer or why the time in San Francisco is different from that in London. You'd begin with a series of steps:

Step 1.   Be sure you understand the question that a student has asked or that you have raised in your lecture. What is the student's concern? What are you hoping to teach?

Step 2.   Identify the "things" (elements, variables, concepts, events) in the relationship that need to be explained.

Step 3.   Identify the relationship between the things identified in step 2.

Step 4.   Show how the relationship identified in step 3 is an instance of a more general relationship or principle.

Thyne (1963) offered an example of explaining that fits into this model (see Figure 9.6). What is important for teachers is that this kind of four-step strategy for explaining can be learned. Miltz (1971) taught the techniques to thirty teacher trainees. Table 9.2 summarizes judges' ratings of explanations given by the trainees before and after training. The explanations were rated in random order by ten judges who were "blind," that is, not told which explanations were made before training and which explanations were made after training. The ratings were used to assess whether or not there was a pretest-to-posttest change in the quality of the explanations. The training resulted in explanations rated significantly higher in organization, clarity, and overall quality. Doubtless, some good explainers are born. The rest of us can learn to be better explainers by following this four-step model.

FIGURE 9.6   *A Model for Organizing Explanations: How It Works*

Thyne's Example

One stormy winter evening my neighbour was puzzled by a strange low humming sound which seemed to come out of the walls of his house. After much searching he traced it to a draught-excluder on his front door—a device consisting of a wooden strip to which was attached a long rubber tube. . . . My neighbour understands the eerie noise, not just because he now perceives that it comes from the draught-excluder—for that in itself could be puzzling—but because he knows that an air current across the end of a pipe produces this sort of sound. . . . When my noise-haunted neighbour understands, it is not just because he appreciates that air is blowing across this particular tube and making this particular sound. If that were all he knew, he would, of course, know where the noise was coming from, but he would scarcely be said to have "understood" it. If that were all he knew, he might as well have discovered that the noise was coming from a piece of cheese in his pantry, for the one thing would make no more sense than the other. He understands the noise only in so far as he knows that an air current passing over the end of any pipe produces some sort of musical note, and he *sees this particular thing as an instance of that general principle.* (Thyne, 1963, pp. 127–129)

Our Use of the Model

Step 1. Be sure you understand the question being asked. *Why is the low humming sound coming out of the walls of the house?*

Step 2. Identify the elements, variables, concepts, or events in the relationship that need to be explained. *(a) The low humming sound, (b) coming out of, (c) the walls of the house, (d) draught-excluder on the front door, (e) wooden strip, (f) rubber tube.*

Step 3. Identify the relationship between the elements identified in step 2. *Air (draught) blowing across the end of the rubber tube causes the eerie sound.*

Step 4. Show how the relationship identified in step 3 is an instance of a more general relationship or principle. *The general principle is that an air current passing over the end of any pipe produces some sort of musical note.*

TABLE 9.2

**Mean Ratings by
Judges of
Explanations Given
by Teacher Trainees**

	Pretest*	Posttest*
Organization	2.92	3.62
Clarity	2.79	3.59
Overall quality	2.84	3.68

Source: Adapted from R. J. Miltz, "Development and Evaluation of a Manual for Improving Teachers' Explanations." Unpublished doctoral dissertation, Stanford University, 1971. Used with permission.

*In these ratings, 5 = excellent, 4 = good, 3 = average, 2 = poor, and 1 = very poor.

Clarifying the Organization

It is not enough for a lecture to be well organized. The organization must be made clear to students. There are several devices—explicitness, the rule-example-rule technique, explaining links, verbal markers of importance, and structural support—that do just that.

Explicitness.   Giving children instructions that were more explicit and detailed yielded better performance of tasks by eight-year-olds (Van der Will, 1976). Even when shorter instructions were presented more slowly, to take as much time as the more explicit instructions, the latter yielded more correct performances. It is more effective to say

> Pick up your blue pen. First draw a big blue circle and then draw a little blue circle next to it.

than to say,

> In blue, after you have drawn a big circle, draw a little one by it. (Van der Will, 1976, p. 195)

The Rule-Example-Rule Technique.   Explanations of highly effective lecturers contained many more instances of the rule-example-rule sequence than did those of less effective lecturers (Rosenshine, 1971a). For example, in explaining aspects of Turkish foreign policy, a highly effective teacher might say,

> Although it is an Islamic nation, Turkey wants to increase peaceful and friendly relations with the European Economic Community. How? By increasing trade, exchanging ideas, and arranging personal contacts with people in the other nations of Europe. The country's leaders believe that better relations must be established between the nations of the European Community and those in the Muslim world.

Here, the first and last sentences are rules. The material in the middle provides examples.

Explaining Links.   Good explanations also make use of explaining links (Rosenshine, 1971a). These are prepositions and conjunctions that indicate the causes, means, consequences, or purposes of an event or idea. Examples are *because, with (by means of), in order to, if . . . then, therefore, consequently,* and certain usages of *by* and *through*. Explaining links tie phrases together either within or between sentences so that one part of the sentence elaborates and expands on another part. The following five sentences contain essentially the same content, but only the last three make use of explaining links (in italics):

- The Chinese dominate Bangkok's economy, and they are a threat.
- The Chinese dominate Bangkok's economy, but they are a threat.
- The Chinese dominate Bangkok's economy, *therefore,* they are a threat.
- The Chinese are a threat *because* they dominate Bangkok's economy.
- *By* dominating Bangkok's economy, the Chinese are a threat.

Explaining links are important *because* (an explaining link!) they serve to tell us that a relationship is being presented.

Verbal Markers of Importance.   Verbal markers of importance cue students to material that is especially important (Petrie, 1963; Pinney, 1969). The cues act like "commanding stimuli" (see Chapter 7), letting learners know to pay close attention. Examples are "Now note this . . ."; "It is especially important to realize that . . ."; "It will help you a great deal to understand this if you remember that . . ."; "Now let me turn to what is perhaps the most important point of all, namely, that . . . ."

Pinney (1969) analyzed transcripts of the lessons of thirty-two inexperienced teachers, each of whom presented a forty-minute lesson to a different class of about twenty-five students assembled solely for the research. He found that the frequency of verbal markers of importance was consistently greater for those teachers who elicited higher student achievement. Petrie (1963) noted six other studies that indicate that this kind of emphasis, along with repetition, increases the comprehension of an oral message. The findings hold even though audiences dislike repetition. Maddox and Hoole (1975) demonstrated not only the value of markers of importance but also the value of nonverbal cues—say, the lecturer's walking away from the lectern for a moment or writing on the blackboard—for note taking.

Structural Support.   Whatever organizational scheme you're using, you generally should make it explicit at the outset. Providing this kind of insight is not necessarily incompatible with maintaining some suspense. You can still add details that are vivid, apt, and engaging.

If visual aids (charts, handouts, chalkboards, overhead projectors) are available, you can reveal your organization one step at a time, writing or projecting each heading and subheading as you come to it. An experiment yielded clear

Causes, means, consequences, and purposes

Commanding stimuli

Value of giving the structure progressively

evidence of the value of giving students the structure of a lecture, the transition between lesson segments, progressively, as the lecture unfolds (Cheong, 1972). This approach is probably more effective than explaining the underlying structure entirely at the beginning or end of the lecture.

Clarifying the Content

Almost everyone would agree that lectures should be clear. But how do we go about making them clear? How do we go about converting abstract advice into concrete behaviors? From their work, researchers have developed two suggestions: give examples and avoid vague language.

Giving Examples.   In one experiment, Evans and Guyman (1978) rewrote and redelivered a lecture to an equivalent set of students with "two examples to illustrate each major concept" (p. 5). They did not change the sequencing; they just added the examples. The students learned more and rated the revised lecture (with examples) more favorably.

Ambiguity → lower achievement

Avoiding Vagueness Terms.   *Vagueness terms* leave listeners with a feeling that the speaker is unsure of the subject. Words like *almost, generally,* and *many* are imprecise, indefinite, ambiguous. Several studies have shown that greater ambiguity, measured by the frequency of vagueness terms, is associated with lower student achievement on tests measuring understanding of what a teacher has presented. For example, L. R. Smith and M. L. Cotten (1980) tape-recorded four short mathematics lessons. One pair of lessons contained no vagueness terms; the other pair, 120 of them. This is what a no-vagueness paragraph looked like:

> The first theorem involves two chords intersecting at one point in a circle. Look at figure 1. AB intersects CD at point E. The length of line segment AE is 4 units. The length of line segment EB is 3 units. The length of line segment ED is 6 units. The length of line segment EC is 2 units. Notice that 4 × 3 = 2 × 6. (Smith & Cotten, 1980, p. 672)

The same content in its high-vagueness version went like this:

> The first theorem *sort of* involves a *couple* chords intersecting at one point in a circle. *I guess* we *probably* should look at figure 1. AB intersects CD at point E, *you see.* Look at figure 2. The length of line segment AE is 4 units. The length of line segment EB is 3 units. The length of line segment ED is 6 units, *as you see.* The length of line segment EC, *you know,* is 2 units. You *might* notice that 4 × 3 = 2 × 6. (p. 672)

The vagueness terms used in the experiment by Smith and Cotten (1980) include the following categories and words:

Ambiguous designations: conditions, somehow, somewhere, thing
Approximations: about, a little, just about, somewhat, sort of
"Bluffing" and recoveries: actually, and so forth, and so on, anyway,
       as you know, in a nutshell, in essence, in fact, in other words, of
       course, or whatever, to make a long story short, you know, you see
Error admissions: excuse me, I'm sorry, I guess
Indeterminate quantification: a bunch, a couple, a few, some, various
Multiplicities: kind(s) of, type(s) of
Possibilities: chances are, could be, may, maybe, might, perhaps,
       seems
Probabilities: generally, in general, often, ordinarily, probably, usually

The students took a twenty-item test after hearing a high-vagueness or
no-vagueness lesson. Each lesson was accompanied by projected figures showing the geometric content being taught. The students who received a high-
vagueness lesson had much lower average scores on the test than did those
who received a low-vagueness lesson. Furthermore, the students who heard
a low-vagueness lesson evaluated the teacher and his presentation more
favorably.

This experiment and additional studies stemming from the original work on
vagueness by Hiller (1968) have shown convincingly that vagueness hurts
student achievement and attitude. Teachers not only should know the subject
but also should avoid words and phrases that give an impression of vagueness.

Using Rhetorical Devices

Lecturing, like writing, can benefit from the same rhetorical devices that writers
on composition have described over many centuries. *Rhetoric* in this sense is not
empty or overblown language but rather the study of the elements used in
composition or lecturing—elements of the kind we have been describing. A
rhetorical device is any arrangement of ideas that makes an argument (a lecture)
more persuasive. Such devices were taught in ancient Greece and Rome
(Broudy, 1963, pp. 7–10) and are still part of what is taught in composition
courses. You are familiar with some of these devices: simile, metaphor, alle-
gory. Others may be less familiar:

Hyperbole.   An exaggeration or extravagant statement. (This book
       weighs a ton. This third-grader was a giant in his ingenuity.)
Irony.   A statement of the opposite of what you mean. (I just yearn to
       hear a lecture full of verbal mazes—half-sentences that lead me into
       a jungle. I was, of course, fascinated by the emptiness of his words.)
Metonymy.   Using an associated idea to stand for the idea it's associ-
       ated with. (He abandoned the laboratory [science], and took up the
       pen [writing]. She doffed the apron [homemaking] in favor of picking
       up the briefcase [an executive career].)

Synechdoche.   Substituting the part for the whole, or the whole for the part. (The school had a total of 1200 heads [students]. Pretty soon, the law [a policeman] appeared on the scene.)

Climax.   A series of words, phrases, or clauses in order of increasing importance or intensity. (She was a woman of beauty, dedication, productivity, rigor, and to cap it all, integrity. A lecture ought not merely to fill an hour; it should be interesting, capture attention, enlighten, and, if it is really exceptional, inspire.)

These rhetorical devices, among many others, should suggest ways in which you can enliven your lectures. They suggest that your language need not always be literal, plain, unadorned, prosaic, matter-of-fact. These devices can give your lecture flavoring, zest, and gusto. Just as with food, the nutritive value need not be sacrificed when you increase palatability. But, of course, like seasoning, these devices can be overused. A little may be better than a lot. And, as in cooking, planning helps produce a tasty dish.

Maintaining Attention

The best organizational structure is a waste if you can't maintain the attention of your audience. You will no doubt find your own favorite techniques. We mention some here.

Varying the Stimuli.   Always speaking in the same tone of voice, never moving or gesturing, using monotonous grammatical structure, an overly predictable pattern of speech, and lots of clichés—all these are good ways to lose an audience's attention. Variety has motivational effects. Rosenshine (1971a) found that a lecturer's changes in the form of movement and gesturing correlate positively with student achievement. Whatever the lecturer can change fairly often, without making the change so extreme that it distracts students from the subject of the lecture, probably helps students to pay attention. Video cameras are easily come by. Have yourself videotaped and critically analyze your lecturing.

Remember, of course, that stimulus variation can be overdone. Wyckoff (1973) found that stimulus variation had a curvilinear relationship with student achievement. Apparently at the highest levels of stimulus change—teacher mobility, gesturing, and pausing—achievement was lower. Furthermore, the relationship between stimulus change and achievement was negative for elementary school teachers, even though it was positive for secondary school teachers: "Stimulus variation apparently distracted the younger students" (p. 89).

Changing Communication Channels.   One form of stimulus variation is the use of slides, graphs, pictures, chalkboards, overhead projectors, and other visual media. By switching the channel of communication from oral to visual, even momentarily, you cause changes in the response patterns and attention

Auditory vs. visual information

mechanisms of students. Adults seem to prefer visual information, a preference that appeared in learning a concept-discrimination task (Lordahl, 1961). And there is evidence that as children grow older, they pay relatively more attention to visual information in films and less attention to auditory information (Stevenson & Siegel, 1969). But on achievement outcomes, and preferences, there is no clear evidence that the addition of visual information to written or oral presentations has an effect (see reviews by Allen, 1960; Carroll, 1971; Twyford, 1969).

May (1965a, 1965b) described several ways in which graphics can be used within lectures and explanations. The evidence suggests that the simpler the graph, figure, or table, the better. As a general rule, if you use visual aids, they should convey information quickly and simply, in summary form (see Wainer, in press). The diagram or chart that is simple and clearly labeled, and that has little accompanying text, can improve learning from oral instruction.

Use simple graphics

Remember, however, that even most adults cannot read graphs quickly or effectively. So graphs are almost sure to confuse young students. Students' intelligence and educational levels must be fairly high for them to profit from graphic enhancement of prose material (see P. R. Wendt & Butts, 1962). Still, the stimulus changes that result from using visual aids as well as their ability to communicate information efficiently make them worthwhile additions to the lecture.

Introducing Physical Activity.   The case for physically active learning applies especially to lecturing. Every one of us has nodded off at one time or another during a lecture, even when we were moderately interested in the topic and the lecturer was fairly dynamic. It is almost impossible to pay continuous attention to content in a lengthy lecture. Remember the success of active responding in Gates's (1917) study and the success of Kunihira and Asher's (1965) technique of using physical activity in language learning (both described in Chapter 7). Teachers can make their teaching more effective by giving learners the opportunity to make physical responses. Letting students in the middle of a lecture take a short break between a movie and a lecture, verbalize responses, call out names, repeat phrases—all are ways to improve learning. Allen (1957) reviewed twenty-six studies that examined student participation during learning from films. Of these, eleven were nonconclusive, two favored no participation, and thirteen favored participation of one sort or another.

Stretching, breaks, verbalization

Using Humor.   Should lectures be livened with humor? J. P. Powell and L. W. Andresen (1985) reviewed a large literature on the claims and the research evidence. Some of the claims refer to the value of humor in promoting comprehension and retention, creating good classroom atmosphere, holding students' attention, and enhancing students' and teachers' lives. But humor can also have a dark side: hostility and bigotry. This kind of humor—directed toward females in mathematics, or African-Americans in dance, or Jews in business courses—is not only in poor taste; it may be illegal if it can be construed as harassment.

Humor has a dark side

•*Students'
evaluations of their
teachers are
correlated with their
teachers' humor.*
(© Elizabeth Crews)

Students' evaluations of their teachers correlate with teachers' humor. In one study, recordings of class presentations in seventy separate courses were analyzed to determine the amounts and kinds of intentional humor: jokes, riddles, puns, funny stories, and humorous comments. The overall amount of humor correlated .31 with ratings of teachers' effectiveness by the individual students who had made the recordings without knowing the purpose of the study or the humor-analysis results. Strangely, this positive correlation appeared only for the forty-nine male teachers ($r = .38$), not for the twenty-one female teachers ($r = -.01$) (Bryant, Comisky, Crane, & Zillman, 1980). These correlations may mean simply that more effective male teachers use more humor, not that humor causes higher ratings of effectiveness.

But in an experiment, Kaplan and Pascoe (1977) did find a causal relationship between humor and student retention. They improved on earlier studies by experimenting with lectures whose humor was concept related or concept unrelated. Two groups that received these two kinds of humor were compared with a control group that received no humor. Six weeks later, the students in the concept-related group remembered more of the material than did those in the other groups.

Concept-related humor

Overall, in about two dozen studies reviewed by Powell and Andresen (1985), the effects of humor on recall, comprehension, and retention were inconsistent. Sometimes humor helped; sometimes it did not. But the results for attitudes and atmosphere were fairly consistently positive: Attention and interest were improved by humor. Also it seems plausible that by reducing anxiety, humor can improve students' creativity. Of course too much humor can boomerang, lowering the teacher's credibility and status.

Positive attitudes and atmosphere

Can teachers learn to use humor? Yes. Help can be found in collections of humor—both general and subject-specific (physics: Anonymous, 1968; science in general: Asimov, 1971, and Weber, 1982; chemistry: Read, 1947) and in anecdotes in the biographies of well-known individuals in the arts and sciences.

Showing Enthusiasm.   Lecturers have long been urged to "communicate enthusiasm for the subject of the lecture" (J. W. Brown & Thornton, 1963). Unlike many other kinds of advice for lecturers, this one has been validated correlationally and experimentally. Rosenshine (1971b) reviewed five correlational studies in which ratings of enthusiasm were related to measures of student achievement. The significant correlations ranged from .37 to .56.

Correlational and causal validation

The characteristics of the enthusiastic lecturer include gesturing, varied intonation, maintaining frequent eye contact, moving back and forth across the "stage," and using humor and lively examples. But enthusiasm in a broader sense may simply mean communicating feeling and conviction. Even the lecturer who is serious, who simply reads notes, is enthusiastic if he or she communicates a deep sense of the importance and fascination of the subject.

The correlational studies reviewed by Rosenshine deal with "natural" enthusiasm—the kind people show as part of their personal style. But can we generate enthusiasm where it is lacking? Larkins, McKinney, Oldham-Buss, and Gilmore (1985), in a review of several experiments, found that teachers can learn, if not enthusiasm itself, enthusiasm-showing behaviors. Trained groups of teachers showed these behaviors to a greater degree than did untrained teachers. The students of the trained teachers also rated their instructors and instruction more favorably. But these students did not necessarily learn more— that is, get higher scores on achievement tests. The advantage of teacher enthusiasm, then, lies more in attitude than in intellectual achievement. This is still an important advantage, of course.

Enthusiasm-showing behaviors

Some evidence suggests that enthusiasm can have negative effects in the earlier grades. In an experiment with fourth-graders, McKinney et al. (1983) found that achievement was unaffected and that classroom discipline was lowered by high enthusiasm.

> In the words of one of the teachers, children in the high-enthusiasm treatment were "climbing the walls." Furthermore, many students in the low-enthusiasm groups exhibited boredom. . . . Elementary students appear to behave more appropriately when the teacher conveys a medium level of enthusiasm. (McKinney et al., 1983, p. 252)

Asking Questions.   The idea of a lecturer's asking questions seems at first glance to be a contradiction in terms: We do not usually think of lecturers asking

Possible functions of questions

questions and students answering. But in fact students are responding—usually covertly, but sometimes overtly. The lecturer must try to keep the response level high because it promotes attention and learning.

Questions inserted into an ongoing lecture or explanation can serve a number of interesting functions (Berliner, 1968):

Emphasis.   Questions can serve to emphasize points in the instructional material that deserve special attention.

Practice.   Responding to questions allows students to practice recently acquired knowledge.

Self-awareness.   Questions can help students become aware that they do not really understand something. If questions are followed by information about the correct response, they should have direct instructional effects, increasing motivation to learn from subsequent sections of the lecture.

Attention.   Questions that require students to respond may heighten their attention during a lecture.

Diversion.   Questions are a form of stimulus variation, like a coffee break at work. A diversion also reduces the rate of new input, allowing more time for processing.

Review.   Questions can force students to review what they've been learning, to mentally "scan" all of the material the lecturer has presented to the point at which a question is asked.

Berliner (1968) compared the effects of asking questions in lectures with those of instructing students to take notes or just to pay attention. The students were given a short-answer recall test immediately after a forty-five-minute videotaped lecture on Chinese history, and again one week later. As shown in Table 9.3, the group that was asked questions and made responses during the lecture performed better on the tests than did the groups that took notes or just paid attention.

Student Self-Questioning.   Students can also be trained to ask themselves questions—a metacognitive strategy—while listening to lectures. Such questions can take general forms, such as "What is the main idea of . . . ? How does . . . relate to . . . ? What conclusions can I draw about . . . ?" (King, 1991). When college students in a remedial reading and study skills course were given training in such self-questioning, they did better on achievement tests than students who merely engaged in untrained note taking and note reviewing. The self-questioning students actually did less well on an immediate posttest than students trained in another metacognitive strategy, summarizing, but they did better than the summarizers on a delayed posttest given a week later. Teaching students both strategies should improve learning from lectures even more.

Metacognition during lecture

Promoting Intimacy.   Helping students get to know one another is likely to promote attention to the lecture. But this kind of intimacy can be hard to develop in a lecture class. Not surprisingly it is much easier to promote intimacy

Student Activity During Lecture	Test Given Immediately After Lecture	Test Given One Week After Lecture
Answers question every 2½ minutes	23.11 (N = 47)	19.98 (N = 42)
Takes notes	18.29 (N = 34)	18.14 (N = 28)
Pays attention	13.87 (N = 38)	13.96 (N = 27)

TABLE 9.3

Mean Scores of Students on Immediate and Delayed Tests of Learning

Source: Adapted from D. C. Berliner, "The Effects of Test-Like Events and Note-Taking on Learning from Lecture Instruction." Unpublished doctoral dissertation, Stanford University, 1968. Used with permission.

among students in classes where the teacher encourages discussion among students, and where the teacher is easy to talk with (Meredith, 1985). Here again, research points to the advantages of "informal lecturing," or lecturing combined with class discussion.

Note Taking.   Many lecturers seem to prefer that students take notes, perhaps because it is reinforcing for them to know that students are in some way valuing what they say. But the empirical evidence does not always support the value of note taking during lectures (see Hartley & Davies, 1977). Of thirty-four experiments, the results of sixteen were not statistically significant. But in correlational studies, where note taking has been measured as it takes place naturally (rather than being manipulated, as it is in experiments), the "results—reported over a period of fifty years—have been remarkably consistent, and they show that taking notes leads to enhanced performance in subsequent tests" (Hartley & Davies, 1977, p. 4). The issues concerning the effectiveness of note taking seem to revolve around *what* notes are taken and whether note taking helps in *encoding* (during the lecture) or in *remembering* (reading the notes before a test).

Encoding vs. remembering

The evidence suggests that some students take notes related to achievement test questions, and some do not. Obviously, those students who can pick out what is most important in a lecture will do better on subsequent achievement tests. So, if a teacher gave students cues about what was important, students should obtain higher achievement test scores.

Moore (1968) experimented with giving students such cues. A green card meant "take notes"; a red card meant "don't take notes." Compared with a control group, the cued students did better on an achievement test and evaluated the six-week course and the instructor more favorably.

The evidence also suggests that note taking during the lecture has only a small effect on comprehension. It is not much of an aid to encoding. Note taking's positive effect lies in its helping students remember the content of the lecture, through their studying the notes before an examination. Thus a teacher's notes

Cuing what is important

Furnishing outlines and notes

shared with students, or the notes of an official note taker, or even borrowed notes are all likely to improve achievement if the notes are studied before an examination. Actually taking notes during the lecture is not the important factor. Attending the lecture and studying a good set of notes before an examination enhance learning from lectures. Accordingly, more lecturers should themselves furnish their students with outlines and notes.

Using Handouts.   Outlines that show the organization of a lecture and other handouts can improve student achievement (Hartley, 1976). Handouts are more efficient, in the sense of improving achievement without requiring additional note taking, when they are filled with illustrative detail. A *spaced* handout—bare-bones outline that omitted any detail—stimulated more note taking but did not improve achievement over that of students given a detailed handout. *Incomplete* handouts, which omitted twenty key words or phrases (the omission was indicated by a line), produced better achievement than either a complete hand-out or no handout at all. The generative element in learning (see Chapter 7) would seem to explain this finding.

Generative learning

The Conclusion of the Lecture

You've finished the body of the lecture. Now what? How do you tie it all together? How do you finish up?

Functions of the Conclusion

From his analyses of videotape recordings of what some first-time teachers actually did, Shutes (1969) identified a number of functions that conclusions serve:

Social amenities

- They offer an opportunity to interact with students at a social level, something that has been shown to be related to better learning. ("It's been a pleasure to teach the class. I wish you all good luck.")

Questioning students

- They give us one more chance to see whether students understand the material, by asking them to recall specific ideas or give examples, definitions, or applications. ("I've talked about several learning theories. Can anyone describe them for me?")

Answering students' questions

- They allow us to clear up any misunderstandings by answering students' questions. ("No, individual and individualized instruction are not the same thing because . . .")

Reviewing or postorganizing

- They can act as a kind of "postorganizer," letting students know what they should have learned and identifying key points in the lesson. ("And you should now understand the various parts of a lecture and the functions each of those parts—introduction, body, and conclusion—serves.")

Should summaries come at the end of a lecture or at the beginning? At the beginning they help prepare students; at the end they act as a review. A summary differs from an advance organizer not only in position but also in *not* being more abstract, general, and inclusive than the lecture or learning material. Although results are conflicting and often based on printed rather than oral deliveries, they tend to favor summaries at the end. When students were given a 1,000-word article to read, they did better on tests of factual knowledge when the summary came at the end than when it came at the beginning or was omitted altogether. The results held for both men and women, and for both facts contained only in the article and facts contained in the summary as well as the article (Hartley, Goldie, & Steen, 1979).

Interlecture Structuring

The end of one lecture should tie the material to the preceding one and hint at the nature of the next. Lectures should form a chain, and the connections between links in that chain should be clear. It's the lecturer's job, then, to describe interlecture structure as well as intralecture structure. For example:

> As you will recall, this lecture is the fifth in a section of this course that deals with ecology. Last time, I dealt with the concept of an ecological niche, which led up to what I have discussed today. Next time, I shall go into the ways in which human beings have affected these niches. Those ways were implied by the conclusions I reached today on the fragility of the niche for most organisms.

This kind of interlecture structuring can give students a sense of direction that helps them tie the whole series of lectures together into a coherent whole.

A coherent whole

In this section we have talked about the teaching method that is most maligned and yet, at least at the college level, most used. Obviously we believe lecturing is a valuable method, or we would not have spent the time here on it. But despite our positive feelings about the method, we know it has drawbacks.

First, the lecture method is easily misused. It can be used too often, at too great a length, and too much to the exclusion of other methods better suited to certain kinds of objectives. It can encourage passivity and dependence on the part of students. It can become a vehicle for displaying the teacher's hobbies and pet interests rather than for fostering the achievement that students want and need. In heterogeneous classes, lectures can be aimed at too narrow a range of students, missing those who lack prerequisite knowledge or who already know the material.

Choose the best method for the objectives

Finally, the lecture method is not for every teacher. It depends on qualities of personality—voice, style, manner, pace, fluency, ease, and orderliness—that simply cannot be provided in the right mixtures by everyone. Not every role is

Lecturing not for every teacher

suitable for every actor; and not every teaching method matches the strengths and weaknesses of every teacher. A teacher whose personality is not suited for lecturing should choose another method—perhaps discussion or tutoring or small-group instruction or any of the many forms we describe in the next two chapters.

Objectives of Discussion-Group Teaching

Criticism of lecturing led educators to think about the possibilities and advantages of small-group teaching. Here was a method that brought students together face to face. Here one student could talk to another, who could then respond. Other students could also enter into the discussion. The teacher usually hovered over the whole complex interaction, acting as chairperson, guide, initiator, summarizer, and referee.

As might be expected, students sometimes reject discussion-group teaching just as they reject lecturing. The rejector may say, "I didn't pay all this money (give all this time) to listen to students who are just as ignorant as I am." Or, "I'd rather hear a poor lecture by an expert (a great woman, a renowned scholar, a professional teacher of the subject) than a lively discussion by my fellow novices."

Thinking critically

We believe that small-group teaching is useful in fostering the ability to think critically. It forces students to learn to support their opinions with reasoning based on facts, definitions, concepts, and principles. Another prime objective of small-group teaching is to foster students' participation in discussions. In an undemocratic committee, classroom, school, or nation, the ability to reason together is not essential. But in a democratic setting, skill in the free and rational examination of ideas is important. Working together in groups demands skills that must be learned, and small-group teaching seems especially suited for this learning. Our ability to listen to others, to evaluate their arguments, to formulate our own views in the give-and-take, to resist the influence on our reasoning of personal likes and dislikes and of pressure to conform, to focus on the problem at hand despite emotional arguments—these skills are all learned in discussion.

Democratic skills

Complex cognitive objectives

McKeachie and Kulik (1975) found that comparisons with the lecture method on measures of retention, higher-level thinking, attitudes, and motivation tended to favor the discussion method (see p. 389). Because discussion allows students more activity and feedback, it ought to be and actually is, according to McKeachie and Kulik, more effective than lectures in promoting an understanding of concepts and the development of problem-solving skills. But information is transmitted more slowly in discussion classes than in lecture classes. So the lecture ought to be and is more effective in promoting knowledge of information.

•*Small-group teaching is useful in fostering critical thinking. (© Paul Conklin/Monkmeyer Press Photo Service)*

Arranging Discussion in Large Classes

Although we associate discussions with small groups, such teaching can also be arranged in large classes (from 20+ students to hundreds) by breaking the class into small groups of 5 ± 2 students (Bergquist & Phillips, 1989). Such resulting small groups may be called "buzz groups," "panel discussions," "symposiums," "debating teams," "role-playing teams," or "circles (of discussants) within circles (of audience members)." Whatever the arrangement, it results in a group small enough to allow everyone to talk. What the smaller groups do often consists of formulating questions or topics, answers or solutions, analyses or syntheses, and prepared or spontaneous points of view. These small-group products can then be shared with the whole reassembled class either on paper or orally. Sometimes the small group is asked to select a spokesperson who will present its ideas to the whole class.

In short, large classes need not preclude small-group teaching methods. The objectives of such teaching can be achieved in large part in these whole-class-breaking ways. But the teacher cannot usually observe and participate in all of the many resulting small groups. So there are still advantages in having a single small class of about 10–20 students.

High-Consensus Versus Low-Consensus Fields

Any analysis of the value of discussion-group teaching should take into account the degree of consensus in the subject being taught. Some subjects are highly agreed upon—their major concepts, principles, and methods so well established

High-consensus fields

that no competent person can raise serious doubts about them. At the introductory level in mathematics, the natural sciences, and engineering, just about everyone agrees on what is important, on how the fields are organized, and on basic concepts and principles.

Low-consensus fields

In other areas there is not at present, and in principle may never be, a high degree of consensus. In the social sciences and humanities—in psychology, sociology, anthropology, history, economics, political science, literature, music, and art—we do not agree nearly so much about what is important, good, true, or beautiful. There are schools of thought here, controversy even at the introductory level about how these fields should be organized. What one teacher teaches in an introductory course in a low-consensus field may not even resemble what another teaches. The terms "hard science" and "soft science" capture some of this distinction between the natural and the social sciences.

Objectives and consensus

The objectives of teaching also differ in high-consensus and low-consensus fields. In high-consensus fields one major objective is to convey knowledge of a well-established body of facts, concepts, principles, and skills. In low-consensus fields the students also need knowledge, but not to the same degree. One expert's knowledge may be irrelevant, unacceptable, or less significant to another expert. Here students may need a broad sense of the nature of the field. They need to be able to find their way around in it. They need to understand the controversies. They need to be able to develop and defend reasonable positions of their own.

Discussion: a necessity in low-consensus fields

It follows, then, that one-way communication from books and lectures may serve better in high-consensus fields. But in low-consensus fields, discussion is more suitable. Only discussion can give students the kind of practice they need in formulating a position, examining different points of view, and marshaling facts from their reading and experience to defend a point of view. We are not saying that only lectures should be used in high-consensus fields or that only discussions should be used in low-consensus fields. By all means, use different methods; build variety into your instructional program. But remember what we've talked about here when you're creating a balance of methods.

Controversiality and Attitudes

Public decisions

Discussion-group teaching may also be better suited than the lecture method for changing students' attitudes and behavior. Discussions are public. Participants who make a decision, who take a stand, are committing themselves publicly to a course of action. This kind of commitment is missing in the lecture form, no matter how forceful the speaker. Research on this question has not yielded consistent conclusions, but the trend of the evidence makes the general proposition plausible. Lewin's (1947) classic experiment compared the effectiveness of the lecture method with a discussion approach (which included public commitment) in getting housewives to use unusual cuts of meat in their family meals. A follow-up showed that the percentage of housewives who actually used the new cuts after participating in the discussion and making a public commitment was

Discussion vs. lecture for changing behavior

much greater than the percentage of those who had simply heard a forceful, persuasive lecture. Similarly,

> group discussion has been successful in causing mothers to give their children orange juice and codliver oil, workers to increase their rate of productivity, students to volunteer for experiments, juvenile delinquents to improve their behavior patterns, and parents to change their expressed attitudes toward mental retardation. (Gall & Gall, 1976, pp. 201–202; references in original)

And discussion has been found to promote positive attitudes toward Native Americans among fifth-graders, greater change in attitudes toward ecological concepts among sixth-graders, and greater expressed tolerance for racial groups (Gall & Gall, 1976).

The Teacher's Personality

The success of discussion-group teaching also depends on the teacher's personality and temperament. Some teachers are better suited than others for this kind of teaching. The teacher's ability to tolerate a low degree of structure and organization can be important. If you are uncomfortable when discussion is not always organized, logical, and relevant, chances are the method is not a good one for you.

Tolerance of low structure

The discussion-group teacher needs "intellectual agility"—the ability to follow the twists and turns of a discussion without losing track of the argument or losing patience with its complexity. The teacher must be able to help students pull scattered points together and bring them to bear on the problem at hand.

Intellectual agility

The teacher also must be willing to relinquish some authority over what goes on in the classroom. During a lecture, the teacher has complete control over the ideas under consideration. In a discussion, every participant has some power to take off in a new direction. The teacher must share the authority to decide what is relevant and where the argument should go. And not all teachers are comfortable with the idea of sharing authority.

Relinquishing authority

Problem Solving

Discussion obviously involves solving problems that students have identified and chosen. This kind of teaching is tied in with the *discovery method,* which requires students to find their own concepts, principles, and solutions, not to adopt them from a teacher or textbook. The discovery method can be used by individuals or groups. An advantage claimed for the method is its effectiveness in helping students to apply what they have learned to the acquisition of new comprehension or a new skill. The same advantage seems to apply to the discussion method.

Discovery method

Problem solving can occur when students explore a topic's emotional significance for themselves. In an American history course, for example, the group

Affective outcomes

might talk about the Civil War and the controversy over slavery, and the treatment of African-Americans since the Civil War. Black and white students alike need discussion to explore these highly charged issues. Affective outcomes are influenced by this kind of discussion, and intellectual understanding is improved as the complexities of the topics emerge. A few studies have indicated that "students trained in discussion skills can use the discussion process more effectively as a learning and problem-solving tool than untrained students" (Gall & Gall, 1976, p. 208; references cited in original).

Speaking Ability

Finally, the discussion method can foster the ability to speak well. It gives students an opportunity to practice expressing themselves clearly, with good pronunciation and sentence structure, grammatically, and interestingly. Students who only read, listen, write, and recite get too little practice in self-initiated speaking.

Extemporaneous speaking

Speaking is at least as important in modern society as writing, and *extemporaneous speaking* is most important. Students need the ability to speak their minds thoughtfully and clearly "on the run," in the give-and-take of group discussion. This objective differs from the ability to participate in discussions themselves. The latter is more of a social and emotional objective. Speaking ability calls on cognitive and psychomotor skills—the ability to speak clearly, audibly, correctly, concisely, and logically, in a way appropriate to the occasion and topic. Group discussion gives students a chance to try out rhetorical flourishes and forcefulness, and, in observing the ways others speak, to become more sensitive to ways to improve their own speaking.

Before You Meet the Discussion Group

Before you meet with students for a discussion, you need to do some of the same kind of planning that's needed for any other kind of teaching. But that planning takes special forms here.

Setting Objectives: Choosing a Topic

Objectives as topics

To your students, your objectives may seem to consist merely of the topics you choose. Topics can take all of the infinite forms of human concerns. But topics for discussion have a number of dimensions that make them different.

Noncontroversial Topics.   First, topics differ in controversiality. On some topics all informed people agree. Here the teacher's function may be to have the students arrive at the same position held by informed persons. You might say that if acquiring knowledge and understanding is the objective, the discussion method is not the best way to teach. (Remember, lectures are more effective for this kind of learning.) But something can be gained from having students arrive at the uncontested correct position by themselves, through discussion. A discussion is a forum in which students can practice expressing themselves clearly and accurately, hearing the variety of forms that expressions of the same idea can take, and criticizing and evaluating successive approximations to an adequate statement.

Suppose your sixth-grade class is discussing the value of longitude and latitude—pretty much a noncontroversial topic. The first stab may be "They're straight lines on the earth's surface that divide the surface into small sections, by which different things like lakes or cities can be located." In the discussion that follows, students might in turn point out that the lines are not straight, that the sections can vary greatly in size, and that any given combination of a longitude and latitude defines a point, not an area or section. As these ideas come out, they are accumulated and arranged by the class into a coherent and correct treatment of the topic. Eventually the social context in which all science is embedded may be brought up. For example, what problems did nations face before they agreed on a standardized longitude and latitude system? Why was Greenwich, England, chosen as the origin point for longitude? You could find this same kind of questioning and evaluation in a discussion of the meaning of atomic number or the form of the sonnet or any number of noncontroversial topics.

Controversial Topics.   The discussion method is especially appropriate for topics in which there is no single true or correct position, in the sense of being accepted by all competent judges. The value of discussing controversial topics is not to establish the truth. Presumably if the truth about major problems could be achieved through discussion, it would have been arrived at long ago and the topics would no longer be controversial. The values of these discussions lie in (1) their motivational effect, (2) the need they create to withstand the pressure of another person's logic and information, and (3) the resultant process of sharpening students' understanding of their own logic, information, and position.

Motivational effect.   This takes the form of the *epistemic curiosity* we discussed in Chapter 8 (Berlyne, 1965; D. W. Johnson & R. T. Johnson, 1979). The conflict between ideas forces us to find new information, to reorganize our thinking, and to resolve the conflict.

Need to withstand another's logic and information.   This takes the form of seeking greater understanding of another person's perspective. Kurdek "found that good cognitive perspective-taking skill was related to quarreling and arguing with peers in students in grades one through four" (cited in Johnson & Johnson, 1979, p. 54).

Sharpening the understanding of one's own logic, information, and position.   This results from interaction with others. When children who understand the principles of conservation (discussed in Chapter 4) are paired with children who do not, and the pair are given conservation problems to solve, conservers usually prevail, not because of general social dominance but because of the "greater certainty and

Practice in expressing oneself, in hearing varied expressions of ideas, and in evaluating successive approximations

Motivational effect

Withstanding arguments

Sharpening understanding

superior logic of the conservers" (Johnson & Johnson, 1979, p. 55). The nonconservers learn from their controversy with the conservers. Similar results have been found in experiments with controversy-arousing discussions of moral dilemmas. "Taken together, the . . . studies do provide evidence that controversies among students can promote transitions to higher stages of cognitive and moral reasoning" (Johnson & Johnson, 1979, p. 55; Oser, 1986).

Staying away from controversial topics

Unfortunately teachers often stay away from controversial topics. What happens if teachers censor topics, if they refuse to deal with sex, politics, drugs, and schooling? Students get less useful practice in clarifying values, weighing evidence, hypothesizing, and relating facts when discussion centers on trivial issues. Yes, democratic ends may be served by hearing opinions about whether earnings from a car wash by a ninth-grade class should be used for a Christmas party. But this issue probably does not generate as much passion as would a discussion on abortion, grading, gender roles, teaching fifth-graders about safe sexual practices (as was advocated in 1987 by the Surgeon General of the United States), or African-American separatism—topics that have seldom been discussed in our schools.

Establishing Common Ground

After you've set the topic for discussion, you need to give your students and yourself some *common ground* from which to work on that topic. The common ground usually takes the form of a reading assignment, but it can be anything that provides information, perspective, or understanding on the topic—films, television programs, or a field trip to a museum, a farm, or a laboratory.

Focus on specific topic

You should also help students focus on the specific material you'll be discussing. For example, if the common ground (the reading assignment) is *Hamlet,* you'd tell the class that discussion is going to center on, say, Ophelia's sanity or Hamlet's conflicting loyalties to his father and to his mother. If you're using the film *Birth of a Nation* in a U.S. history class, you might suggest that students pay close attention to how blacks were perceived by the dominant population in the United States during the first quarter of the twentieth century. Or if you're taking a mathematics class to a museum to see an exhibit of marbles falling through a grid to form a normal distribution, you might ask students to focus on the choice of explanatory theorems.

Another approach to getting a common ground was described by Wilson (1980). First he described his previous methods: (1) Asking a student to write a paper on a set topic; this led to dialogues between the student and the teacher only. (2) Setting up a debate, with the students choosing sides, a chairperson, and a summarizer; this led too often to artificial controversies or overly subtle ones. (3) Getting all students to read something different but related to different aspects of a topic; here again the discussion too often became a series of teacher-student dialogues instead of a group discussion.

Finally, Wilson hit upon the idea of telling the students, at the end of the previous seminar, about the literature: key names and the schools of thought to which they belong. The students choose any of this literature and read it. At the beginning of the seminar, each of the students describes what he or she has read, his or her opinions of it, and whether he or she would recommend it to other students. Then,

> We create a pattern. . . . The topic for the session is placed at the centre, and then I will say something like, "So what are some of the things that we need to look at today?"—and the ideas will start to emerge. As they emerge I may say something like, "Is that a separate item, or does it belong with this idea we've already got?"—and so the main headings are identified, and subheadings placed with them.
>
> When we are running out of suggestions I will then usually ask a student to draw lines enclosing points that could be dealt with together. Often the other students will suggest how to do this. Then we can easily place these chunks in order ready for the discussion. (Wilson, 1980, p. 83)

Choosing a Physical Setting

The physical arrangement of the participants in a discussion affects how the group functions. Sommer (1967) compared a seminar, or circular, seating pattern with a lecture pattern, where the instructor faces students sitting in rows. In both settings, students who directly faced the teacher participated more than did students on the sides. In the lecture setting, students in the front and middle of the classroom participated more than did those in the back or on the sides. The variable that seems most important here is eye contact. Direct visual contact between members of a group, whatever the seating pattern, increases communication. And seating position in relation to the teacher affects eye contact (Caproni, Levine, O'Neal, McDonald, & Garwood, 1977).

Eye contact

Takanishi-Knowles (1973) studied twenty-four third- and fourth-grade classes. She found that when teachers organized their students into small groups, the students spent more time on task than when teachers had the students working in a large group. But how the groups are arranged also affects time on task. In a first-grade class, table-seating with pupils facing one another across the table resulted in less time on task than did a row arrangement with children sitting on the same side of the table, facing in the same direction (S. Axelrod, Hall, & Tooms, 1979). Similarly, in a seventh-grade class, the facing-one-another table arrangement led to consistently higher rates of *call-out*—"any audible verbal sound made by a student without the teacher's permission" (p. 33).

Work on task increases in small groups

At higher grade levels, however, or in teaching with the discussion method, being on task *requires* free communication with other students and calling out (that is, speaking without the teacher's permission). Here, then, eye contact between students is a good thing. At this point the differences between tradi-

FIGURE 9.7   *Three Seating Arrangements*

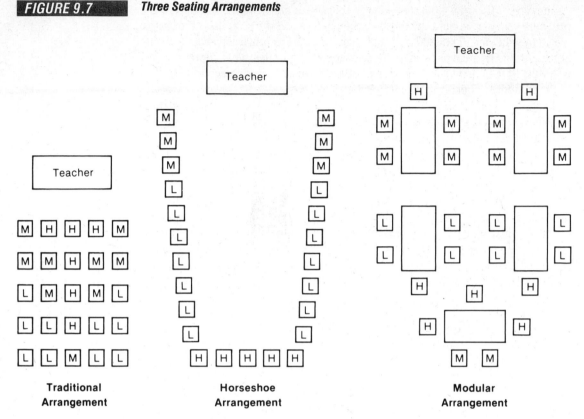

H = High Interaction Seat, M = Moderate Interaction Seat, L = Low Interaction Seat
Source: McCroskey and McVetta, 1980.

tional (straight row), horseshoe, and modular seating arrangements (see Figure 9.7) take on different meanings. For disseminating information and independent study, the traditional arrangement seems best; for discussion, the horseshoe arrangement seems to be more effective; for small-group work organized to carry out a particular task, the modular arrangement seems to work best (Hurt, Scott, & McCroskey, 1978).

Student preferences depend on type of course and communication apprehension

Students' preferences for these arrangements were studied in college courses in communications by McCroskey and McVetta (1978). They found that students' choices depended on the type of course (elective or required) and the students' *communication apprehension,* their fear of speaking out in class. The preference for the straight-row pattern went up for required courses, where students presumably wanted less involvement, and down for elective courses, where more students preferred the horseshoe arrangement. Communication apprehension was associated with a preference for the straight-row arrangement, where presumably less communication would be necessary.

Within each of the three arrangements, some seats had been found through previous research to be high-, moderate-, or low-interaction locations, as shown in Figure 9.7. Although the students were not told these findings, their preferences for seating location were related to their communication apprehension scores: Students with high communication apprehension tended to choose the low-interaction seats within each arrangement.

You may want to note students' choices of seats as clues to their willingness to participate in discussion. It is also important to remember that different structures give rise to a feeling among students of being more or less important (Schmuck & Schmuck, 1971). In general, the decentralized structures, which increase eye contact among students, help foster discussion. They prevent teachers and certain assertive students from completely taking over group discussions.

During the Meeting

Well, you have settled the questions of objectives, common ground, and physical setting. The discussion is about to begin. What do you do now? How should you behave during the meeting? How do you want your students to behave? When should you intervene?

The Teacher's Role

If you want, you can do almost all of the talking. Or you can just remain silent. Or you can interject comments here and there. The choice is yours because your role as teacher gives you authority.

Teacher participation

The more you talk, of course, the less students talk, and the less they benefit—a good reason to minimize your participation. Once you get the discussion started, you should become a listener, observer, and perhaps chairperson in the sense of giving students the floor by calling their names or pointing or nodding at them. Some teachers delegate chairmanship in order to be freer to listen and also to prevent students from directing their remarks at the teacher instead of at one another.

Ideally, with the teacher simply listening, the students will proceed to the topic—explaining it, agreeing on definitions and assumptions, questioning the adequacy of statements or the relevance of examples and analogies, and gradually arriving at a consensus on a noncontroversial topic or sharpening the issue in a controversial one. The teacher, although silent, is working hard: making notes and following, analyzing, and evaluating the discussion, its logic and relevance, and its factual basis. Sharing these thoughts with the students is important, but such feedback should not contain personal criticisms or take much of the group's time.

Student resistance to teacher silence

Often students resist a teacher's silence by addressing questions to the teacher. The teacher then faces the problem of whether to answer. Lawrence Shulman (1970) says no: "If [the teacher] gives in and responds, he will find the work will become a ritualized 'ask the expert' process in which the notion of mutual aid is totally lost."

• *One way to improve the teacher's role is to give students an explicit understanding of what their own role should be. (© Billy E. Barnes)*

Early in the history of a group, when the first questions come to the teacher, a technique must be devised to get students to help answer one another's questions. You may well have some good ideas on the discussion, but save them; you will have time to get them in later. As a discussion group gets under way, students infer your role more from what you do and don't do than from what you say about it.

To help you judge how well students are interacting with one another as well as with you, observe eye-contact patterns. When students are talking or when they finish a statement, do they look to you for approval? When no one is talking, do all eyes turn in your direction? If the answer is yes, you are probably in control of the group process even though you are not very talkative.

Group control

After a while, particularly if the discussion begins to bog down in confusion, repetitiveness, or irrelevance, you may want to step in. With a minimum of words, try to get the discussion back on track. Offer a distinction, a fact, or a perspective. Or offer just a part of one of these so that the students can have the pleasure of finishing it. Then, sit back, listen, and watch.

The Students' Role

One way to improve your teaching role is to give the students an explicit understanding of what their own role should be. In a discussion group, students should be able to state their own solution to a problem and be led by you and other students to elaborate on it, to defend it against attack, to relate it to other ideas, and to modify it, if necessary, in light of those other ideas (J. Axelrod et al., 1949).

Students' comments should, if possible, be evaluated by their fellow students, and every student should participate in evaluating the comments of others. And the students themselves should see to it that communication has been adequate by asking a fellow student to clarify a point and by asking questions of one another when necessary. When the teacher has to assume these responsibilities because the students do not, the teacher should point out that students are expected to ask their own questions. Unless students are told that these roles are proper, they may not develop them.

Define students' roles

Guided Reciprocal Peer Questioning

Another way to improve what students learn in small groups is to arrange guided reciprocal peer questioning (King, 1990). Students in small groups of two or three are taught to use a set of generic questions to be used in discussing a topic recently heard or read. The questions, shown in Table 9.4, are designed to get at the high levels of the Bloom Taxonomy (see Chapter 2). Each student in the groups asks such a question of another student, listens to the answer, and then in turn receives and answers such a question from another member of the group. This process continues for the time available or until the students feel satisfied with their understanding. When King (1990) experimented with this technique, she found that the experimental group, as compared with a control group that received no training, gave more explanations, gave fewer low-level (simple recall) elaborations, asked more questions calling for critical thinking and slightly fewer calling for recall, and had a substantially higher score on a comprehension test.

How would you use . . . to . . . ?
What is a new example of . . . ?
Explain why . . .
What do you think would happen if . . . ?
What is the difference between . . . and . . . ?
How are . . . and . . . similar?
What is a possible solution to the problem of . . . ?
What conclusion can you draw about . . . ?
How does . . . affect . . . ?
In your opinion, which is best, . . . or . . . ? Why?
What are the strengths and weaknesses of . . . ?

TABLE 9.4

Generic Questions Used in Experiments on Guided Reciprocal Peer Questioning

---

Source: King (1990).

To determine whether the *guided* reciprocal peer questioning was superior, King (1989) conducted another experiment in which the control group engaged in unguided reciprocal peer questioning. This experiment showed that the guidance (via training in using the generic questions shown in Table 9.4) again produced superior results along the same lines as those in the first experiment. Apparently, the guidance provided by these questions served to "generate critical thinking questions which elicit elaborated explanations" for which students "must think extensively about the material, organize it, . . . and this in turn promotes comprehension" (King, 1990, p. 676).

Generating critical thinking questions

When Should the Teacher Intervene?

There is a fine balance here. Too much teacher participation can limit the effectiveness of small-group discussion. And so can too little. It may be argued that everything students do has educational value. But a discussion that's gotten side-tracked lowers students' motivation for learning. The teacher needs to judge correctly and quickly when intervention is necessary. If it comes too soon and too often, students may be deprived of the opportunity to learn how to get themselves out of a blind alley. If it comes too late, students are frustrated.

How do you decide when to intervene? Here are some suggestions:

Digressions

- Notice whether a *digression* it taking too much time. If several contributions in a row are too far afield, insert a brief reminder of the topic and the part of it being discussed.

Pauses

- Notice whether *pauses* between contributions are becoming too long. Lengthy pauses may mean that participants are too bewildered to speak or hesitate to speak in the face of mounting confusion. If pauses grow too long, intervene to find out why.

Errors of fact

- Notice whether an outright *error of fact* is being accepted. If so, and if the error is having a serious effect on the validity of the discussion, step in and correct it. It is better, of course, if a student corrects the error. But you should not let the error do great damage before putting the discussion back on a valid factual basis. One problem here is that teachers themselves may not know the differences between values and facts. Zeigler (1967) found that 42 percent of 803 high school teachers agreed that the following statement was factual: "The American form of government may not be perfect, but it is the best type of government yet devised by man."

Distinguishing values from facts

Logical fallacies

- Notice whether serious *logical fallacies* are going undetected. These fallacies may be subtle and hard to detect, but they can damage the validity of a discussion in even the most mature groups. Piaget pointed out that at early ages students can be expected to be only moderately logical (see Chapter 4). But the teacher can do a great service to students—one with lasting and general value— by pointing out instances of the kinds of errors in logic that have been known to philosophers for many centuries.

What are *logical fallacies*? For a full explanation, you should take a look at a textbook in logic or a good encyclopedia. But it is possible to list some of them briefly in recognizable form:

- Confusing what is accidental (that is, incidental) with what is essential. Example: Thinking all mammals are land animals.
- Arguing from a general rule to a particular case, or vice versa, without noting special circumstances. Example: If it is wrong to kill, then capital punishment is necessarily wrong.
- Diverting attention to an extraneous fact instead of proving the fact in dispute. Example: Attacking the speaker personally instead of his or her ideas; or appealing to fear or sentiment, not logic.
- Begging the question—for instance, demonstrating a conclusion by means of premises that presuppose the conclusion. Example: Condemning a proposed new social policy on the grounds that it is "un-American," and anything un-American is bad.
- Arguing that a result is caused by any prior condition. Example: A man is industrious, and he becomes productive; therefore, if he is productive, he must be industrious.
- Basing a conclusion on an insufficient or erroneous reason. Example: If a woman is wealthy, she must have worked hard.
- Combining several questions into one in a way that conceals the fact that more than one question is involved. Example: Do you still cheat on tests? Here two questions—Did you ever cheat on tests? and Do you cheat on tests nowadays?—are combined, so that a yes or a no is an admission of having at one time cheated on tests.

These kinds of logical errors occur frequently in class discussions. So it is good policy for you to keep them in mind and use them as the focal point of a discussion at least once in a while. By pointing them out, you are modeling logical analysis for your students. And you'll know you've done so successfully when you yourself are stopped by a student for faulty reasoning.

After the Meeting

The teacher's activity after the discussion consists of making notes, keeping records, and evaluating the discussion.

Notes and Records

After the meeting, the teacher (or student!) should make notes about anything unanticipated that emerged in the discussion. Such things might be used as part of the discussion of that topic by other students in subsequent years. For

Unanticipated events

example, suppose in a discussion of classical conditioning, a teacher offers, without having planned to do so, an example of operant conditioning. That the teacher did so should be entered into the postmeeting notes. Or suppose in a discussion of *Finnegans Wake,* a student suggests that certain aspects of James Joyce's style are similar to Gertrude Stein's or Ernest Hemingway's. Again, this idea should be written down.

Difficult points

The teacher should also make note of points, issues, definitions, or logical fallacies that gave difficulty during the discussion. Calling these to the attention of the students at the beginning of the next session can help them see the intellectual continuity in their work and become more aware of discussion as a process.

Evaluations

Reaction sheet

Evaluation is another postmeeting procedure. You may decide to hand out a simple *reaction sheet,* which gives the students a rating scale like this one:

How valuable did you find today's meeting?

☐	☐	☐	☐	☐	☐
A complete waste of time	Somewhat valuable, but not much	Valuable, but often weak	Valuable, but sometimes weak	Valuable almost all the time	Completely valuable all the time
(0)	(1)	(2)	(3)	(4)	(5)

When you collect the ratings, make sure the students realize they are to remain anonymous. Then compute the average rating for the session. By charting the averages from one session to the next, you can check your own impressions, relating the cues you have observed during a discussion to the students' mean rating. Over time, you can learn to predict ratings and, as you are learning, can begin to govern your own behavior to improve ratings. Low ratings may turn out to be associated with too much participation on your part or that of a particular student, or with too much or too little insistence on sticking to the topic. Students' opinions should not be the sole criterion of the value of a discussion. But they can give you insight into how much your values are shared by the students.

Students' comments

Students' anonymous comments on the postmeeting rating sheet are another source of information. Here students can note the reason for their high or low ratings. Don't expect all the comments to be the same. Usually they deal with many different matters. And often one student condemns what another praises.

One obstacle to collecting and using students' ratings and comments is the teacher's understandable reluctance to be exposed to criticism. But teachers can't choose whether they or their discussion sessions are going to be evaluated. Their only choice is whether they want to know those evaluations.

Intellectual Pitfalls

Broadly speaking, the pitfalls in teaching by the discussion method are of two kinds—intellectual, and social and emotional. We talk first about the intellectual pitfalls, which include biasing the discussion, encouraging yielding, withholding crucial information, and sticking to a dead topic. To avoid these pitfalls, a teacher should occasionally tape-record discussions. Listening to them later helps to identify problem areas.

Listening back

Biasing the Discussion

Biasing the discussion means giving the students cues that tend to subvert their objectivity. Bias is often the end product of a teacher's expressing opinions in ways that close discussion or force students to conform. Students cannot discuss the problem of population control sensibly if the teacher gives them a set of fixed assumptions about how food production can be improved. And students cannot discuss the dramatic value of Hamlet's soliloquy honestly if they know that their teacher thinks everything Shakespeare wrote is perfect. The anthropologist Jules Henry (1957) studied the way some elementary school teachers influence their classes and how students docilely accept those biases:

Student docility

Second Grade.   The children have been shown movies of birds. The
    first film ended with a picture of a baby bluebird.
Teacher: Did the last bird ever look as if he would be blue?

The children did not seem to understand the "slant" of the question, and
answered somewhat hesitantly, yes.

Teacher: I think he looked more like a robin, didn't he?
Children (in chorus):   Yes.

Fourth Grade.   An art lesson. Teacher holds up a picture.
Teacher: Isn't Bob getting a nice effect of moss and trees?

Ecstatic ohs and ahs from the children . . .
The art lesson is over.

Teacher: How many enjoyed this?

Many hands go up.

Teacher: How many learned something?

Quite a number of hands go down.

Teacher: How many will do better next time?

Many hands go up.

Teacher power

Teachers at all grade levels must be constantly aware of their enormous power in the classroom. With the reward and coercive power of grades, even teachers' casual mention of their own opinions, attitudes, and beliefs can influence some class members. Students are very perceptive; they are very quick to zero in on what they think their teacher wants.

Of course a teacher's biases do not always limit student behaviors. They can enliven discussions if students feel free to challenge the teacher. Most of us have values and biases—strong convictions about rationality, about people's obligations to others. We don't have to conceal them. We can try *in rational ways,* never using grades or ridicule, to guide our students' beliefs.

In deciding on which of your values to share with your students, you have to rely on judgment about your proper role in relation to students at a certain grade level, in a certain subject matter. You need to know what is accepted as ethical teaching in your profession and community. You need to know the law concerning the teaching of controversial issues—evolution, for example, which is still controversial is some states, or "secular humanism"—and also to have worked out your own values in relation to the law. If you are teaching, say, chemistry, you may be unjustified in raising questions about the Bill of Rights, unless the freedom of a scientist to publicize controversial findings becomes germane. There can be no substitute for the teacher's best judgment as a citizen of a democracy and a responsible member of a profession.

Encouraging Yielding

Group power

Standard

A B C

Yielding to group pressure

When a group of people agree about an issue, fact, or opinion, and you go along with them, even though you think they are wrong, you are yielding. Groups exert an inordinate amount of power over the individual, some of it quite subtle. Asch (1956) studied this effect by having subjects individually join groups of seven other people—confederates who were working with the experimenter. On certain trials of what was supposed to a perceptual test, the groups were shown the two cards pictured in the left margin. The seven "confederates" unanimously agreed that line A was the same length as the standard line. In these test trials, where the subjects had to decide whether to go along with the majority consensus or to be independent, Asch found that about 37 percent of the subjects yielded. In postexperimental interviews, the subjects described the intense discomfort and stress they had felt in the situation.

In another study, the power of the group to influence the judgment of college students was noted. The students were subjected to group pressure and ended up agreeing that the following "facts" are correct:

1. The United States is populated by elderly people, with 60–70 percent of the population over 65 years old.
2. The average American eats six meals per day.
3. Americans average four to five hours sleep per night.
4. The average number of children in a family is between five and six.

5. The country is large, stretching 6,000 miles from San Francisco to New York. (Tuddenham & McBride, 1959).

Not every student agreed to every statement of this kind, but some did, particularly when they believed they were the only group member who differed.

Of the important findings in studies of conformity, two stand out for teachers. First, the phenomenon is widespread. The teacher and a group of students, or any coalition of people, may agree to something and "force" a minority opinion into conformity with the rest of the group. School groups usually have well-established mechanisms for dealing with deviants—ignoring them, physically attacking them, keeping them from games by not choosing them, and so on.

Yielding is widespread

The second important finding is that if just one other person supports the minority opinion, yielding is markedly reduced. So teachers must see to it that diverse positions are heard and that alliances are formed. A minority position is not likely to change a majority opinion, but at least it preserves the minority opinion.

Support from one other reduces yielding

Withholding Crucial Information

Sometimes teachers withhold crucial information in trying to maximize the amount of participation by students. But discussion can reach a point where it cries out for a fact, a definition, a distinction, a concept, or a principle. And the teacher, who has what is needed, does not provide it. There are no clear guidelines for teachers in this situation. Certainly it is not wrong to share expertise and experience when the discussion can profit from it. But it is wrong if the sharing stems merely from a teacher's need to establish competence in the eyes of the students.

Sticking to a Dead Topic

Sticking to a dead topic is a pitfall that also requires quick perceptiveness on the teacher's part. A *dead topic* is one whose value for promoting achievement of educational objectives has been exhausted. The signs that a topic has been exhausted are repetition of points already made, longer pauses between contributions, irrelevant contributions, and an air of boredom and inattention. Well before these signs appear, the topic should be changed, or a new facet of the topic should be introduced.

Signs of topic exhaustion

Social and Emotional Pitfalls

The social and emotional pitfalls of teaching by the discussion method arise from the attitudes of students toward themselves, other students, and the teacher. They can greatly reduce the value of the discussion method. These pitfalls include nonparticipation, the danger of hurting students' feelings, and mismatched participants.

Nonparticipation

When no one says anything

Sometimes nonparticipation is a problem. You finish your introductory remarks or question, and none of the students says anything. What should you do (Shulman, 1970)?

Wait the silence out.   Silence is acceptable. Of course, waiting too long may create an embarrassing or hostile situation. But allowing a reasonable period of silence—thirty seconds or even longer—indicates that taking time to think about what one wants to say is fine.

Ask what the silence means.   This question allows students to indicate their confusion, worries about seeming irrelevant or foolish, or need for time to think about the question at issue.

Guess out loud as to what the silence means.   By saying, "It's risky to be the first to talk," the teacher may free students to take that risk.

Break the total group into smaller groups.   By dividing a class of twenty into four groups of five each, the pressure on each student to participate may be increased somewhat, and the student's anxiety about speaking up may be decreased. (We return to this idea on page 439.)

"Going around the table."   The teacher can "require" everyone to speak up, without calling on and thus "threatening" an individual student, by asking for ideas, reactions, and the like, from everyone in the order in which the students are seated around the table (or circle). The next time this device is used, it can begin at the other end of the table so that the same students will not be first or last.

Uneven participation

Another aspect of the problem—found in almost all discussion groups—is uneven distribution of participation. Some students are almost always talking; others never do. In one survey, 20 percent of the students rarely if ever participated in class discussions (Andrews, 1965).

Uneven participation is not always a bad thing. On any given topic, students may differ greatly in knowledge and interest, and these differences should affect their participation. But if certain students participate a great deal whatever the topic, and other students fail to participate week after week, the teacher should suspect that social and emotional factors are at work.

Status and Participation.   Higher-status members of groups usually control the discussion, at least at the start. Males tend to dominate females, older children tend to dominate younger children, and white students tend to dominate minority-group members. For example, E. G. Cohen (1982) reviewed much evidence showing that African-American students participate less and have less influence in biracial groups. The differences showed up even when African-American and white participants had been matched on task-related competence. In playing a game requiring group decisions, fourteen of nineteen groups made up of two African-American and two white junior high school boys, matched on social class and attitude toward school, had African-American students participating less. Similar lower participation and influence rates have been observed for American Indian boys on a reservation, visibly distinctive Mexican-American boys, and Jews of Middle Eastern ancestry (as compared with Jews of Western background) in Israel.

What can we do to increase the participation and influence of minority-group students? The question is really one of status—of raising the status of these students in their own eyes and the eyes of others. There are several ways to go about this task:

Status and participation

- Assign *new roles* that lead to more positive expectations for the competence of low-status students. Let the low-status student be the "teacher," instructing higher-status students on a new task.
- Introduce a *referent actor,* someone from outside the group who belongs to the low-status minority and is highly competent in a task. In schools, minority-group members in positions of authority (principals, teachers) can serve as referent actors. Or show a videotape of minority-group members taking the lead in a game.
- Act as a *high-status evaluator,* raising the expectations of both minority- and majority-group members. Praise the competence, performance, and contributions of minority-group students.
- Create *equal-status norms* for the group, expectations that call for equal participation by all members. Tell the group that everyone should be listened to and that everyone should have a chance to talk.

Reducing differences in participation

These four approaches promise to improve the achievement of equality of opportunity in desegregated schools. In these schools, education can remain unequal despite physical proximity unless steps of this kind are taken to bring about greater social and psychological equality and togetherness. The approaches also have been successful in reducing gender and age differences in participation rates.

Group Size and Participation.

Group size can also affect participation. Hare (1962) concluded from his review of the research that groups of about five students each provide opportunity for participation to all, with enough participants for variety. Applegate (1969), using questionnaires, found that students feel they can participate in discussions more readily in groups of fifteen or less.

Make groups smaller

What about those students who do not participate whatever the size of the group? They usually give one of two reasons: "Not being able to say what they mean" and "The possibility of being wrong." Therefore, the remedy here is threefold:

1. Make discussion groups smaller.
2. Help students carefully and unobtrusively to say what they mean.
3. Create a climate of trust so that there is no penalty (ridicule) for being wrong.

●*Breaking larger groups into smaller ones can increase student participation.*
(© Elizabeth Crews)

Using Reinforcement.   For individual students, we can modify the rate of responding, like many other behaviors, by reinforcement procedures. But we can't reinforce a response until it's made. How do we get a student to respond in the first place? One relatively unobtrusive procedure is to announce at the beginning of the discussion, and repeatedly thereafter, "We'll now go around the table and let everyone take a minute or two to comment on the topic." This procedure does not call attention to any single student and has the obvious justification of getting all opinions stated before the discussion continues. One problem with this kind of procedure is the "next-in-line phenomenon," whereby the student who is to speak next concentrates so hard on what he is going to say that he pays no attention to the previous speaker (Tzeng, 1974).

**Next-in-line
phenomenon**

Once a student responds, the teacher can immediately reinforce that contribution. How? By acknowledging the student's ideas, thanking the student, or praising the student's insights. Also tying a student's ideas to other ideas and referring to them can be a kind of positive reinforcement that has repeatedly been found to promote achievement.

Operant conditioning works. Provided often enough, reinforcement should increase the frequency of responding in children who tend not to participate.

Bavelas, Hastorf, Gross, and Kite (1965) designed a method for demonstrating behavior change of this type. In their experiment, nine four-man groups discussed human relations case histories while being observed through one-way windows. At the end of the first discussion, leadership rankings were obtained from the participants. The group member who ranked third became the target of the behavior-change strategy. During the second discussion, each group member received individual feedback in the form of a green light if the experts rated his contribution positively and a red light if they felt the contribution was not helpful. Small light panels in front of each participant were hidden from other group members. By literally giving the green light to the target person (that is, the previously third-ranked person) whenever he talked, and by giving the red light to the three others unless they agreed with the target person, the experimenters made some remarkable changes in only twenty minutes. A third discussion, without feedback, showed that the changes endured to some extent (Table 9.5). "This all seems to imply that in a very short period of time we can take a person of fairly low status and make him a leader, at least in the eyes of the members of his group" (Hastorf, 1965).

As most operant psychologists would predict, changing the reinforcement contingencies in the environment can turn a follower into a leader. These environmental changes consist of positive reinforcement of participation by the target person and mild punishment of the verbal output of high responders. The mild punishment needs to be used in order to give the target person "room" to contribute. Positive reinforcement alone is not likely to be effective. Verbal and nonverbal communication probably serve as well as a green light. Head nods and positive exclamations ("Good point!" "That's interesting!") reinforce the target person's contributions, while frowns and cuing remarks ("Let's hold it, Johnny, and hear again from Myra; she was making a lot of sense") suppress the responding of other group members. You can prevent a criticism from seeming like a personal attack by introducing the criticism with a positive note: "I'm glad you brought that up, but . . . ."

Turning followers into leaders

	Session		
	1	2	3
Sociometric rank	3.23	1.70	2.30
Percentage of time talking	13.40	35.50	24.60
Percentage of total utterances	17.20	31.20	25.40

TABLE 9.5
Behaviors of Target Persons in Group Discussions

Source: Adapted from Alex Bavelas, et al., "Experiments on the Alteration of Group Structure." *Journal of Experimental Social Psychology,* 1:55–70. Copyright 1965. Used by permission of Academic Press and Alex Bavelas.

Hurting Students' Feelings

Stories have been written about the charm, humor, and educational values that flowed from the biting style of George Lyman Kittredge, a professor at Harvard:

> He had a violent temper and an undisguised contempt for the average student. White-bearded, cigar-puffing, loud-voiced, he commanded their respect rather than attracted their affection. They laughed at him once when he strode too far and fell off his platform. He glared at them, and said: "This is the first time I have ever reduced myself to the level of my audience." (Highet, 1955, pp. 218–219)

Don't use sarcasm or ridicule

But teachers like Kittredge, and students who are secure enough not to be harmed by them, are rare. Sarcasm and ridicule are weapons that almost no teacher should use. And they are weapons that no teacher should allow students to use.

Learning not to take criticism personally

What do we do about a student whose arguments are shown in a discussion to be false, irrelevant, or illogical? We have to correct the statements without attacking the student. There is a difference between saying, "Ariel, you're wrong" and saying, "Ariel, I don't agree with your statement." Furthermore, learning to receive criticism or correction without taking it "personally" is a major goal of the discussion method. Students should learn that their primary concern is the solution of the problem or task, not the protection of their self-esteem.

Teacher modeling task orientation

This goal may be hard to achieve, however. Teachers can help by reacting rationally and unemotionally to challenges to their own ideas. Here again we see the importance of teachers' opening their ideas to criticism.

Cooperative Learning

We've been talking so far about the discussion method, a method often used for teaching groups of about two to twenty students. But there are other methods for teaching small groups. Here we turn to one of the most important, cooperative learning.

Working together reduces prejudices

Getting students to work together rather than to compete may reduce interstudent and intergroup (including interethnic) prejudice and hostility. Suppose a teacher gives assignments and projects to groups of four to six students. The students divide the labor among themselves, help one another (especially the weaker members), and praise or criticize one another's efforts and contributions. Will liking and respect develop among group members? If the groups are ethnically mixed, the cooperative experience should reduce prejudice among students and even produce favorable attitudes. "Furthermore . . . given sufficient exposure to the cross-ethnic cooperative experience, stimulus generalization [see Chapter 6] will lead to the extension of favorable attitudes from ethnically different groupmates to members of other ethnic groups in general" (Weigel, Wiser, & Cook, 1975, p. 223).

TABLE 9.6

Types of Cooperative Learning Schemes

		Reward Structure	
		(a) Group rewards based on individual performance	**(b) No group reward or reward not based on individual performance**
Task Structure	**(d) Task specialization**	A. Student team learning 　　Teams-games- 　　　tournaments 　　Student teams and 　　　achievement divisions 　　Team-assisted 　　　individualization	B. Learning Together
	(c) Group study: no task specialization	C. Jigsaw II	D. Jigsaw 　　Group-Investigation

Source: Adapted from Bossert (1988, p. 229).

Types of Cooperative Learning Schemes

At least seven schemes for cooperative learning have been developed. They can be classified using two dimensions as shown in Table 9.6 (Bossert, 1988). The "reward structure" of the scheme indicates whether the cooperating group of students (a) gets rewarded on the basis of how well the individual members perform or (b) gets no reward as a group or, if it does get a reward, it does not depend on how well individual members perform. The "task structure" of the scheme shows whether the group of cooperating students (c) study the same material or task or (d) specialize in different materials or tasks. With these two distinctions, there are, of course, four cells: A, B, C, and D, shown in Table 9.6.

Of these combinations, we shall describe only the schemes in cell A, in which the group studies the same thing (with no task specialization), and the group receives rewards based on how well its individual members perform. The Learning Together (D. Johnson, R. Johnson, Holubec, & Roy, 1984), Jigsaw (Aronson, Blaney, Stephan, Sikes, & Snapp, 1978), Group-Investigation (Sharan et al., 1984), and Jigsaw II (Slavin, 1983) schemes are also worth considering but are omitted in the present brief treatment.

Student Teams and Achievement Divisions

One cooperative learning method is the *student teams and achievement divisions (STAD),* developed by Slavin (1983). In this method, the teacher assigns four or five students to each learning team. Each team should have high- and low-achieving students, boys and girls, and if possible, both minority- and

Reward structure

Task structure

Goal is understanding

nonminority-group members. After the teacher introduces a new unit of content, the team members study worksheets or other printed matter on the content. They work together a good part of the time—in pairs, trading roles (tutor and tutee, "quizzer" and "quizzee") and using other forms of problem solving. The students have free access to the answers to the problems, so they realize that their goal is understanding, not just getting the answers right. They continue to work until all of them feel that they grasp the concepts.

After this team-learning effort, students are tested on the unit. Here they work alone, independently. The teacher or a student scores the tests (percent of correct answers) as soon as possible, then derives the team scores. At this point, the method takes an unusual turn:

Scoring system

> The amount each student contributes to his or her team is determined by the amount the student's quiz score exceeds the student's own past average. A base score is set five points below each student's average, and students earn points, up to a maximum of ten, for each point by which they exceed their base scores. Students with perfect papers always receive the ten-point maximum, regardless of their base scores. This individual improvement score system gives every student a good chance to contribute maximum points to the team if (and only if) the student does his or her best, and thereby shows substantial improvement or gets a perfect paper. This improvement point system has been shown to increase academic performance even without teams . . . , but it is especially important as a component of STAD since it avoids the possibility that low performing students will not be fully accepted as group members because they do not contribute many points. (Slavin, 1983, p. 24)

Rewards

Rewards are given on a team basis. Each week the teams with the highest scores are listed in a weekly newsletter. Individual improvement is also recognized in the newsletter.

Teams-Games-Tournaments

Homogeneous grouping

Another small-group teaching method developed by Slavin and his co-workers is called *teams-games-tournaments (TGT)* (Slavin, 1983). Here groups of three students, all from the same achievement level, play a game. Each group member serves in turn as Reader, Challenger 1, or Challenger 2. The Reader chooses a numbered card from a deck of cards, finds the problem or question with the same number as that on the card, reads the problem or question out loud, and finally tries to solve or answer it. Challenger 1 then chooses either to challenge, by giving a different answer, or to pass. Then Challenger 2 looks up the correct answer. Whoever (Reader, Challenger 1, or Challenger 2) was right keeps the card with that problem or question. If the Reader was wrong, there is no penalty; if Challenger 1 or 2 was wrong, he or she must return a previously won card, if any, to the deck.

Weekly tournaments of this kind get students competing against others with similar previous achievement records from the various STAD teams. The competing trios change every week, but their homogeneity is preserved. "The high scorer at each table is moved to the next higher table for the next tournament, and the low scorer at each table is moved to the next lower table" (Slavin, 1983, p. 26). Thus all students, regardless of their performance level, can conceivably win points for their teams. Team scores are again recognized in the weekly newsletter.

Team-Assisted Individualization

A third small-group teaching method developed by Slavin and his coworkers is *team-assisted individualization (TAI)* (Slavin, 1983). Used in teaching mathematics, TAI, like STAD, uses heterogeneous four- or five-member groups. Each student first studies with one other student of his or her choosing, using programmed instructional materials, doing the necessary reading and worksheets, then taking subunit tests and a final unit-mastery test. The two students working together exchange answer sheets for scoring; the unit-mastery test is scored by a student monitor. Team scores are derived by totaling the members' test scores and number of tests taken each week. If the team score exceeds a preset team standard, the team members are rewarded with a certificate. Here the teams do not compete against other teams, but against their own predetermined team standard. And the teacher, free of test scoring and monitoring, can tutor and give individualized help to single students or groups of students as necessary.

Team standards

TAI uses individualization, rather than group instruction. It is especially useful, then, for extremely heterogeneous classes, particularly those with handicapped children.

The Effectiveness of Cooperative Learning

How effective is cooperative learning? Our answer comes from experiments in which children taught by cooperative learning methods have been compared with children taught by conventional methods. Comparisons have been made on achievement, intergroup relationships (friendships among African-American, white, Hispanic, and other students), and relationships between academically handicapped students (with learning disabilities or mental retardation) and their nonhandicapped classmates. On all these bases, cooperative learning has fared well. About two-thirds of several dozen experiments have found positive effects that are statistically significant, that is, probably greater than could be accounted for by chance.

The proportion is somewhat higher for race relations and somewhat lower for liking of class outcomes, but the two-to-one ratio of studies that find significantly positive effects to those that find no differences (negative effects are very rare) holds for most of the principal measures, including student achievement. (Slavin, 1983, p. 121)

Slavin's review also included "component analyses," that is, attempts to identify which part of the cooperative learning method has good effects. Among the components examined for effects on achievement have been (1) group incentives that motivate students to urge fellow students to perform well; (2) group study; (3) task specialization, which gives each member of a group a specified part of the group task, say, getting a certain piece of information that is necessary to attain the group's goal; (4) equal-opportunity test scoring, or scoring for improvement, so that all students, regardless of previous achievement, have a chance to earn high scores; and (5) competition among groups. Of these, it was component 1, group rewards dependent on the total learning scores of the group members, that seemed to be the single most effective component for improving achievement outcomes (Slavin, 1983).

Group rewards

SUMMARY

The lecture method has been the target of criticism for several centuries. Critics have called it an anachronism; they've blamed it for imposing an undesirably passive role on students and for being unadaptive to the individual student's needs. Those who believe the lecture method is of value point to its flexibility, the reinforcement it offers both lecturers and students, and the administrative benefits of the method. And research indicates that it can be an effective teaching method under certain conditions.

Preparing a lecture calls for making decisions about audiovisual media. It also requires taking a look at your own motivation and how much time you can devote to preparation.

The three distinct parts of a lecture (the introduction, the body, and the conclusion) serve different functions. The introduction motivates through students' interests and by providing motivational cues. The introduction should also expose essential content and help students structure that content with advance organizers and questions that help them remember related ideas they already know.

In the body of the lecture, the lecturer covers content; creates order, using one or more organizational forms and explanations; makes the organization clear, using explicit phrasing, the rule-example-rule technique, explaining links, verbal markers of importance, and structural support; clarifies content by giving examples and avoiding vagueness terms; and maintains attention by varying stimuli, changing communication channels, introducing physical activity, using humor, showing enthusiasm, and asking questions. The lecturer can help students take notes by pointing out what is important or by providing handouts of the structure and major points of the lecture.

The conclusion also serves several functions, allowing us to interact with students at a social level, to ask and answer questions that help clarify learning, and to review key points. This is also where we relate this lecture to the ones that come before and after it.

Some words of caution are provided: Don't overuse the lecture method if a better alternative is available. And don't use the method at all if your personality is simply unsuited to its demands.

The most widely used small-group method is discussion. Its primary objectives are to promote critical thinking ability, skills of democratic participation, and other cognitive abilities and skills. It is most effective for low-consensus fields, for changing students' attitudes, for teachers who can tolerate a low degree of structure, for teaching problem-solving skills, and for fostering speaking ability. It is less efficient for communicating information.

Before a discussion begins, you must choose a topic. The factors here are different for noncontroversial and controversial topics. Then you and your students need to establish some common ground—a book, a television program, a visit to a museum—a background from which to work on the topic. It is also important to let students know the specific problem or question around which the discussion will center. Finally, you have to choose a physical setting, how to arrange the classroom to make interaction easier.

During the meeting, your role must be clearly defined. Although too much teacher participation can limit the effectiveness of discussion for students, too little can be frustrating for them. Knowing when and how to intervene—watching for digressions, pauses, errors of fact, and logical fallacies, and adjusting for them—is critical to the success of a discussion. Teaching students their roles—such as reciprocal peer questioning, ways to evaluate the comments of other students, and how to attack and defend positions—is also important.

After the meeting, you should make notes about unanticipated ideas that emerged and difficulties that arose. Keep a record for future years. You may also find it helpful to evaluate discussion, combining your thoughts with students' ratings and comments.

Discussion-group teaching is not without pitfalls, both intellectual and social and emotional. To avoid the intellectual pitfalls, try not to bias the discussion in ways that lower its educational value. Don't encourage students to yield to group pressure. Don't withhold crucial information when it is needed. And be sensitive to signals that a topic has been exhausted.

Nonparticipation is a primary symptom of the social and emotional pitfalls. Often participation is linked to students' status—their gender or ethnic group. Group size can also be a factor. Reinforcement techniques are effective for correcting uneven participation. Another problem here is hurting students' feelings. Don't use sarcasm or ridicule to correct students. Although learning to accept criticism is a key part of discussion, that criticism should not come in the form of a personal attack by the teacher or other students.

Cooperative learning is another important method for small-group instruction. The method uses learning teams and group reinforcement procedures to motivate students' learning. In addition to academic achievement, the method has proved to be effective in combating status differences and prejudice among students.

10 ≡ Individual Instruction and Humanistic Education

OVERVIEW

How involved should we be in our students' learning? Are there times when students learn best working individually with a teacher? Are there times when they learn best working alone? If one of the primary objectives of teaching is for students to go on learning when formal schooling is over, don't we have to give our students opportunities to be independent, to learn alone? *Individual instruction* involves both one-on-one teaching and independent study. It allows, but does not ensure, *individualized* instruction. That is, individual instruction—its goals, materials, subject matter, and methods—may or may not be adapted to a single student. Individualized—or maybe *adaptive* is a better term—instruction may be carried out with one individual at a time or with groups of students at the same time. In this chapter, we talk about individual instruction, some of which is adaptive.

We begin by looking at the forms of individual instruction that require the least additional material or rearrangement of the classroom: homework, study skills, and independent and self-directed study. Next we turn to methods of individual instruction that require some changes in the way we organize our classrooms: mastery learning, personalized systems of instruction, and contracting systems. Then we discuss the components of the tutoring process and its effectiveness. The last of the individual instruction methods that we examine is programmed learning, including the use of computers in instruction.

Then we look at a very different form of teaching—humanistic education—that may or may not use individual instruction. Beginning about 1960, with the publication of A. S. Neill's

Summerhill, a movement aimed at changing the fundamental thinking about education got under way. In fact the movement was a rebirth of the progressivism that had its roots in the writings of Jean Jacques Rousseau in the 1700s and John Dewey in the early 1900s. The movement appealed to thousands of college students who had been unhappy with their own schooling. It seemed to respond to their resentment of what they had considered the regimentation, pressure, competition, and irrelevance they had vaguely sensed and finally found expressed by Neill, John Holt, Jonathan Kozol, Paul Goodman, and other writers. The movement has gone by several names: "the new romanticism" and "alternative educational systems" among others. We use the terms *open education* and *humanistic education.*

We begin our examination of humanistic education by discussing its objectives. Then we turn to the principles that underlie the movement. We go on to discuss humanistic, that is, open-education methods. We end with an analysis of open education and a look at its viability.

Objectives of Individual Instruction

Lecturing, explaining, and small-group methods are appropriate for certain educational purposes, but not for all. There are times when students ought to work by themselves. Why? Because individual instruction allows us to cope with our students' individual differences and helps students learn to be independent.

Coping with Individual Differences

In recent years educators have become increasingly dissatisfied with the conventional classroom, its basic assumptions, and its effectiveness. This dissatisfaction has arisen in part from efforts to take into account students' individual differences, a major concern in education at least since the 1920s. It was then that the testing movement revealed large differences in intelligence and achievement among students in a typical classroom. Studies showed that the brightest students in the usual classroom were capable of learning much more, at a much faster pace, than were the least able students. These differences complicated the teacher's task. Assignments appropriate for some students were inappropriate for others. And so were learning materials, explanations, topics, discussions, and many other ingredients of classroom work.

The problem obviously called into question the lecture method. Even classroom discussion, in which students could participate in different ways, centered on a single topic, the same topic for all students whatever their individual differences. Despite small-group methods, some students were bored, frustrated, and resentful. It seemed that any attempt to teach students in a group was likely to miss the mark for certain students.

The obvious solution was to individualize instruction: to set each student to work on tasks appropriate to his or her particular abilities and interests; to use

Individualized instruction

techniques and styles of learning appropriate to the student's temperament; and to move each individual ahead at his or her own rate.

Ability grouping

An intermediate step toward individualized instruction was ability grouping, which puts students together with others of about the same ability or level of achievement. Groups may be formed within a single class, or as separate classes for slower and faster learners. The idea behind this kind of grouping is that teaching is more effective with students of similar ability. Surprisingly this has not always been the case. The many studies of the effects of homogeneous grouping have yielded far from unanimous results. We have conflicting data on the effects of grouping on achievement, self-concept, attitudes toward others, and behavior (Rosenbaum, 1980). Also, ability grouping has been suspected,

Discrimination by social class

and often found guilty, of fostering social-class discrimination: Lower-income students wind up in one group; higher-income students in another (Oakes, 1985, 1991).

Other approaches to the problem of individual differences have taken the form of supplementary classes and tutoring, nongraded schools, retention (holding students back in the same grade another year) and acceleration (skipping grades), frequent promotion plans, and special activities and assignments for groups and individuals within the class.

Stable vs. momentary individual differences

All of these individualization techniques are plausible ways of coping with individual differences in *stable* characteristics. But they do not help us deal with individual differences in the *momentary* ways in which students differ at any given point in their learning. Students differ not only in relatively stable characteristics (scholastic abilities, interests), but at a given moment in the degree to which they understand an explanation, are ready to move on to another problem or topic, or need more practice on a particular concept or skill.

In short, teachers feel a need to custom-tailor teaching to students' stable and momentary individual differences, while working with large numbers of students. Meeting that need has always been a source of tension for teachers.

Promoting Independence

Learning how to learn

Apart from helping students meet educational objectives in general, individual instruction can also teach students to work and learn independently. "Learning how to learn" is regarded as a major objective in its own right. Students should be able to continue to learn after they have left school. This ideal was recognized as long ago as 1873, when the British philosopher Herbert Spencer wrote that

> in education, the process of self-development should be encouraged to
> the fullest extent. Children should be led to make their own investigations,
> and to draw their own inferences. They should be *told* as little as possible
> and induced to *discover* as much as possible. Humanity has progressed
> solely by self-instruction; and . . . to achieve the best results, each mind
> must progress somewhat after the same fashion. (quoted in E. Dale, 1967,
> p. 41)

We can help the students become independent learners, to take more responsibility for their own education, through programs of *independent study*. Independent study has always been performed by mature scholars and scientists, journalists, and creative workers. These programs put teacher and student in a one-to-one relationship. Fewer classes are held, and the teacher exerts less control over the time and thinking of each student. The student pursues an individual course of study or research.

In *self-directed study,* the formal course structure is preserved, and the teacher has many students, provides suggested objectives and materials, and gives tests. The major change consists of reducing the number of formal classes attended by the student. Advocated especially for adult education, self-directed study can proceed with the students' using only their own "frameworks of thought and action" or with the instructor "offering value systems, ideologies, behavioral codes, or images of the future" (Brookfield, 1985, p. 6). Much self-directed learning takes place by word of mouth, the interaction of students with their peers and teacher, rather than by use of libraries, cassettes, and self-instruction programs. In something of a paradox, then, successful self-directed learners may be highly dependent on other people, not really independent or inner directed.

Independent study

Self-directed study

Study Habits

Usually teacher and student alike expect much learning to go on while the student is working alone at home or in the classroom. The teacher assigns chapters in a history book, problems in a mathematics text, or pages of a novel, and the student works on the assignment. Whether the student is working at home or in class, certain study skills make the learning easier and more effective.

Homework

Homework consists of work assigned to students by teachers to be done outside of school. By this definition, Cooper (1989a, 1989b) excluded in-school guided study, home study courses, and extracurricular activities. Cooper found that some educators have argued against homework on the grounds that it can satiate and fatigue students, reduce leisure-time activities, bring about parental interference in how things are taught and parental pressure on students, encourage cheating, and increase differences between high and low achievers. These arguments may be justified some of the time. But the fundamental question—on which people want scientific evidence—is whether homework in general improves achievement.

Does homework improve achievement? Wolf (1979) found that, in the surveys done in various countries by the International Association for the Evaluation of Educational Achievement (IEA), "the number of hours of homework per

Homework and achievement

•Teacher and student alike expect learning to go on while working alone.
(© 1986 Peter Menzel)

week is substantially related to achievement" (p. 321). In another large-scale study, Keith (1982) controlled statistically for ethnicity, family background, general mental ability, and field of study (general-vocational or academic) of twenty thousand high school seniors. Homework time was measured as ranging from "no homework is ever assigned" or "I have homework but I don't do it" to "more than ten hours a week." By itself, with other variables uncontrolled, homework time correlated .32 with grades; when the other four variables were controlled, it still correlated .19 with grades. Cooper (1989b) found that of fifty such correlational studies, forty-three showed positive relationships between homework and achievement, and seven revealed negative relationships.

But all these were, after all, only correlational studies. They leave open the possibility that students who get higher grades are influenced by their rewards to do more homework, as well as the possibility that doing homework causes the higher grades.

To determine the *causal* influence of homework, experiments are less ambiguous. Cooper (1989a) found twenty experiments done since 1962—studies comparing the achievement of students given homework with that of no-homework students. Fourteen of these yielded positive effects of homework, and six yielded negative effects. But grade level made a big difference. In high schools, the homework tended to raise an average student's achievement to a level exceeding that of 69 percent of the no-homework students. The advantage produced by homework was smaller in junior high schools and nonexistent in elementary schools. Not surprisingly, the benefits of homework were smaller when compared not to the no-homework case, but to in-class supervised study.

Homework on the high school level

Cooper's careful review of homework experiments led him to conclude that there are no subject-matter differences in how effective homework would be as long as the work isn't too difficult or doesn't require skills that are new to the student. The desirable upper-limit amount in the junior high school is one to two hours, but it is higher at the senior high school level, where judgment should determine how much is too much. Even though homework does not improve achievement in elementary schools, it can have good effects on study habits, especially if it is easy enough to let pupils feel successful with it. At the junior high school level, Cooper recommended a mixture of required and interesting voluntary homework.

Guidelines for homework

- Be sure that assignments are related to what you're teaching. If not, it's unlikely you'll affect achievement in the curriculum.
- Plan homework assignments carefully, discuss them with students, and revise them if necessary in the light of that discussion.
- Be sure assignments are not routine; they should require thinking, planning, and problem solving appropriate to the students and the subject.
- Hold your students accountable for doing homework correctly, or their homework will be less effective. This advice means you should "count" homework in grading but homework itself should not be graded. Instead it should be used to diagnose individual pupils' problems with the subject matter.
- Comment on completed assignments, orally or in writing.
- If necessary, ask parents for their help in seeing to it that students do their homework. But, in Cooper's view, parents should not have a formal instructional role.
- If students from very low-income families have no suitable place to do homework, you and the school administration should try to provide such a place for them.

Study Skills

Doing homework means spending time outside of class on assignments. But how students spend that time depends on their study skills and habits.

Teachers can help students learn on their own by suggesting better study skills. Suggestions should be based on research findings—not intuition or common sense. Remember, the "obvious" isn't always true. For example, many people think that underlining and taking notes improve our understanding when we read. But do they?

A careful investigation of spontaneous study strategies was performed by getting 67 college students to report on how they were studying at eight points in their learning of a fairly technical 16-page article (Wade, Trathen, & Schraw, 1990). From tape recordings of the students' reports, the authors derived the fourteen study tactics shown in Table 10.1. Then they applied sophisticated

| TABLE 10.1 | Fourteen Study Tactics Identified (by Category) and Scoring Criteria |

Study Tactic	Scoring Criteria

Study Methods That Produce Artifacts

Text-Noting Tactics

1. Highlighting, underlining, circling	
2. Copying key words, phrases, or sentences	Verbatim copying.
3. Paraphrasing in notes	Rewrites in the subject's own words.
4. Outlining	May be as informal as showing a hierarchical arrangement of ideas.
5. Diagraming	Keyword diagrams, graphic organizers, any spatial array of information.

Study Methods That Do Not Produce Artifacts

Mental-Learning Tactics

6. Rote learning of specific information	Reciting material mentally, concentrating on specific information, memorizing, reading aloud, reviewing notes, or underlining, etc.
7. Mental integration	Stopping to get the whole picture, to mentally summarize, to draw connections between ideas in the text. Involves a transformation of information and occurs after reading the relevant segment of text.
8. Relating information to background knowledge or experience	May also include creating associations between a known idea and a new idea.
9. Imaging, visualizing	Generating mental pictures; imagining oneself in a scene.
10. Self-questioning/self-testing	Generating questions and answering them; testing one's comprehension and/or knowledge using notes or underlining.

Reading Tactics

11. Reading only	Reading at an average rate. No adjustment of reading rate to different types of information in the text is indicated.
12. Skimming	A very fast type of reading. May involve reading only for the gist or searching for the main point, creating an advanced organizer, or moving very quickly over unimportant information.
13. Reading slowly	Slowing down reading rate for particular types of information, often for better concentration.
14. Rereading selected portions of the text	Regressing to an earlier point in the text.

Source: Wade, Trathen, and Schraw (1990). Reprinted with permission of Suzanne E. Wade and the International Reading Association.

"Good Strategy Users"

statistical techniques to cluster the students into groups that tended to use the same tactics but differed from other groups. For example, in Cluster 1, the "Good Strategy Users," all the students used highlighting/underlining, verbatim copying, and rereading; almost all of them used mental integration, reading slowly, and skimming. These students, more than other students, used many different tactics. In fact, every one of the fourteen tactics listed in Table 10.1 was used by the students in Cluster 1. The students in the other clusters—called the information organizers, the text noters, the mental integrators, and so on—used fewer tactics in their studying.

After their studying and then some unrelated activity, all 67 students took a test measuring their ability to remember the information they had studied. Cluster 1, the Good Strategy Users, had a substantially higher average score than did the students in the other clusters, but the difference was not statistically significant because the number of students in each group was small, ranging from 6 to 21. Because of the design of this study, we cannot say the Cluster 1 activities *caused* their higher achievement. But it appears plausible that possessing and using a broad range of tactics during study will result in higher achievement.

Learning strategies that *had* been tested experimentally were brought together by Pressley, Johnson, Symons, McGoldrick, and Kurita (1989; see also Chapter 7). Their list included only strategies that students could learn to use themselves without a lot of time or effort on the teacher's part:

Strategies for students

1. *Summarization* consists of deleting trivial information, deleting redundant information, substituting overall terms for lists of items, using an overall action term to cover a series of events, and selecting a topic sentence or inventing a topic sentence if none was given. In addition, students can use headings, subheadings, and paragraphs to guide their summaries. These things can be done first for paragraphs and then for longer passages of text. Spatial devices (outlines, "maps" with boxes) can help.

2. *Mental imagery* can be representational (literal images of the prose) or mnemonic (substitute images). In either case, the student tries to imagine a picture of what the prose is saying. This strategy includes the *keyword* method whereby a well-known word is selected to stand for an image useful in remembering, such as "tailor" for Taylor or "scales" for justice. (See page 296.)

3. *Story-grammar training* gives students a structure (e.g., when? where? who?) for a story's beginning, then its beginning event, then the goal or problem, then the steps taken to solve the problem, then how the main character felt. Children taught this structure remembered much more than those not so taught about the stories they read.

4. *Question generation* calls for formulating broad overall questions while reading. Then, of course, the learner tries to answer them. In doing so, one finds out how well one understands the material and whether something needs to be done to improve comprehension. Pupils may need to be taught how to generate broad questions.

5. *Question answering*, or answering questions presented at the end of the reading matter, improves learning by adults but less so for children, perhaps because the adults reread the material after finding themselves unable to answer a question while children tend not to do so. But when children were taught how to find such answers, the children did improve in their ability to recall the information.

These relatively easy-to-teach learning strategies can be supplemented by one that takes more time and effort to teach:

6. *Prior knowledge activation* means using what one already knows to help one comprehend and remember new material. When children were trained in relating the text material to their own knowledge and experience, they remembered more of the story than children not given such training. They were also better able to answer questions requiring inferences from what they had read. But when the text material contradicted their prior knowledge, they tended to misremember the related text passages.

Strategies for various grade levels

Thus we have presented study strategies suitable for college (and, presumably, high school) students (Wade et al., 1990) and others usable in elementary school grades 3–8 (Pressley et al., 1989). Helping students acquire these broad, general strategies is likely to improve student achievement in all school and college subjects.

Independent and Self-Directed Study

We said earlier that promoting independence is a primary objective of individual instruction. Among the methods we use for this purpose are independent and self-directed study. In both of these forms, the teacher usually gives a student *an assignment that lasts over several days or weeks,* and frees the student from attending formal classes during that period. A survey of 150 examples identified several common behaviors among students involved in independent and self-directed study (Griffin, 1965). The students

- believe the goals and activities are worthwhile.
- make their learning personally significant.
- discipline themselves to do the work.
- use human and material resources.
- produce an outcome or product better than what they were originally capable of producing.

Obviously these are good behaviors. How do we go about developing them in our students?

Contracts with students

Contracting is one method of organizing independent study. The teacher and the student together write a contract that specifies (1) what is to be learned, (2) the way in which the student will demonstrate achievement, (3) the resources the student should use in carrying out the contract, (4) the steps or tasks to be carried out, (5) the intermediate points at which progress will be judged, (6) a schedule, and (7) the new activities to be undertaken. We talk more about contracts later in this chapter.

In independent study, students can identify and select their own problems, plan their own activities, and turn in a finished product at the end. (© 1987 Susan Lapides)

Choosing an appropriate degree of independence is critical to the success of independent study. The teacher can supervise and guide the student fairly closely. Or the teacher and student can plan the student's work cooperatively, with the student receiving less supervision and criticism. Or the students can work almost entirely on their own, identifying and selecting problems, planning activities, and turning in a finished product.

Degree of independence

The right degree of independence depends, of course, on the student's maturity and the objectives that are suitable for the student. Even children in the earliest grades should have experience at some level of independent study. And even the most mature students should at times learn from lectures, tutoring, and other "nonindependent" methods. That is, independent study ought to be mixed into school activities at all stages of a student's education. Under the labels "the integrated day" and "open education," which we discuss later in this chapter, many features of independent study have been introduced in the primary grades.

In England, the Open University (a system of correspondence and television courses at the college level) offers many independent study courses. Brew and McCormick (1979) investigated the way students approached one of these courses—how they organized their time, how they read (in detail or skimming), how they used learning aids (lectures, films). Some students thought lectures were simply a framework for further reading and thinking; others thought of them as the main part of the course. What researchers found is that students in independent study need guidelines about how to study and what kinds of learning (e.g., facts or structures of ideas) are desirable. Because independent study is

How students approach an Open University course

Helping students write

often aimed at the student's producing a term paper, we should look at the teacher's role in helping students write. Sperling (1988) looked at how a successful ninth-grade English teacher helped six college-bound students over a seven-week period. She analyzed video- and audiotape recordings and all the writing by each student along with the teacher's comments and two of the teacher's interviews with each student. "Results indicated that the students need to participate in conferences of different lengths, with different purposes, and with different tasks." As the tasks vary, shifts take place in patterns of dominance in the conference. Thus, "the teacher's initiations can be springboards for the student's active participation in conference talk" (p. 30). Although the study examined only one teacher, it suggests that teachers' conferences with students engaging in independent study should be flexible, not rigidly scheduled, and concerned with getting the student to speak up about ideas and problems.

Flexible conferences with students

Contracting in the Elementary Grades

One common form of individual instruction uses contracts for learning. A contract here is an agreement between a teacher and a student specifying particular activities or products by the student for which the teacher will provide specified rewards. You will recognize the similarity of contracting to the operant conditioning described in Chapter 6. We gave examples of contracts in Chapter 8. Such contracts make explicit what is often tacitly understood. Even at the doctoral level in graduate schools, dissertation proposals lay out what the candidate plans and agrees to do in order to meet the requirements for the Ph.D. thesis. Similarly, research proposals tell what the grantee will do if given funds by the supporting agency. So, although some contracts are childish, because they are intended to help a child, the same principle can help adolescents and adults do what they want to do.

The amount of time and work covered by a contract can vary greatly, of course, from a day's homework to a semester's term paper to a three-year research program. For motivating elementary and secondary school students, the amounts of time and work should probably increase as students mature.

Murphy's review (1988) found that contracts had been effective in improving academic productivity, performance accuracy, study skills, school attendance, and social behavior. Experience has revealed that many disaffected elementary and secondary school students develop increased motivation for school when they have a voice in determining their course of study (see Chapter 8). Not every student thrives under independent study, but not every student does well under traditional instruction either.

Independent study

How do we tell the level of independent study that a student will profit from? One way is to estimate how well the student can perform these four tasks:

- Identify the topic or project for independent study
- Outline what is to be done

- Identify resources to be used in the project
- Set deadlines

In a conference with the student, the teacher probes the student's ability to formulate an independent study project. Ward (1973) recommended a formal rating scheme like the one shown in Figure 10.1. Notice that under each area of independent study—identifying a topic, outlining a project, identifying resources, and setting deadlines—there are three levels of independence: guided study, cooperative planning, and individual pursuit. Students at the level of *guided study* show little ability to direct their own work or to be self-disciplined. We would have to spend considerable time helping these students define problems, outline a plan, find resources, and meet deadlines. Students at the *cooperative planning* level can direct their own activities but need help at a number of points during the project. We would need to monitor their progress, offering help when needed, and withdrawing as students become more self-sufficient. Those students who can already define topics, make decisions, locate resources, and hold to deadlines are operating at the level of *individual pursuit*—they have the ability to work independently in academically productive ways. Our role here is that of facilitator, critic, audience, guide, and colleague. We try to help students move from guided study to cooperative planning, and from cooperative planning to individual pursuit.

Independent study requires more resources than are needed in the traditional classroom. You may have to set up resource centers for science, mathematics, social studies, art, and the like. Ideally you might want to break down a

Guided study

Cooperative planning

Individual pursuit

Resource centers

FIGURE 10.1 *A System for Estimating Students' Level of Independence*

Area of Independent Study

Overall estimate of level of independence for students	Identifying a study topic			Outlining what is to be done			Identifying resources			Setting deadlines		
	Guided Study	Cooperative Planning	Individual Pursuit	Guided Study	Cooperative Planning	Individual Pursuit	Guided Study	Cooperative Planning	Individual Pursuit	Guided Study	Cooperative Planning	Individual Pursuit
Alexander S. 2		X			X		X					X
Manuel B. 3			X			X		X				X

Source: Adapted from Ward (1973).

Note: Numbers under names are overall estimates of students' level of independence. 3 = high; 2 = medium; 1 = low.

wall or build a small alcove in the classroom. But you may be able to get by with less drastic measures. You could band together with other teachers, pooling your instructional resources and creating resource centers in closets, hallways, storerooms, and the backs of classrooms. A resource center can contain programmed instructional materials, books, audio- and videotapes, reference works, films and filmstrips, workbooks, and lists of community volunteers who are willing to work with students on a given project (see Bechtol, 1973; Ward, Kelly, & Stenning, 1971).

Although many teachers and students enjoy and benefit from contracting for independent study, some do not. Both teachers and students need to find comfortable and personally meaningful techniques for teaching and learning. Sometimes a program simply takes getting used to. Give yourself a few weeks or even months to get a program running smoothly. Some surprisingly good things can happen once these systems have been functioning for a while.

Mastery Learning and Personalized Systems of Instruction

In 1968 two influential articles on individualized teaching appeared: B. S. Bloom brought forth his mastery approach, and Keller laid out his personalized system of instruction (PSI). Although the two plans were derived from different theoretical perspectives, they are alike in many ways.

Theoretical Background

Time-based learning

Mastery learning came from a model of school learning developed by Carroll (1963). That model defines some major factors in learning in terms of time:

Student aptitude: The amount of *time* required by the student for learning, other things being equal

Student motivation: The amount of *time* the student is willing to spend on learning, other things being equal

Task difficulty: The amount of *time* needed to learn a task, other things being equal

Other factors are instructional quality and time allowed for learning. Bloom's major insight was that, if students do not master a unit of the curriculum on their first attempt, they should be given additional time and a variety of instructional aids until they do master it. He insisted that, using this program, between 80 and 90 percent of the students could achieve at the A or B levels traditionally achieved by less than half the students.

Influence of operant conditioning

Keller arrived at his plan from Skinner's operant-conditioning principles (see Chapter 6). He argued that conventional teaching does not elicit enough responses or provide enough reinforcers. His solution was to break up the subject matter into units, so that students can study at their own rate, moving on to a new unit only after they have mastered the current one. (Mastery is indicated by a score of at least 80 or 90 percent of perfect on a unit test.) Again, those students who do not master the unit the first time around should receive more time, tutoring, instructional help, and testing until they do.

The Approaches at Work

The mastery approach has been used primarily in grades 1 through 12; PSI, at the college level. Both approaches are based on three fundamental conditions: that initial instruction be given, that instruction be mastery oriented, and that help be available when it's needed.

Initial instruction.   In the mastery approach, initial instruction is group-based, whole-class, more or less conventional classroom teaching. The initial instruction in PSI is through independent study of the text materials.

Mastery orientation.   In both systems, until students demonstrate mastery of a particular area of instruction, they do not go on to new material. There is no penalty for failure. Both systems require that parallel forms of short tests be designed in advance. Then, after a first failure and a new effort at studying, students are tested again. Students continue the cycle of studying and testing until the criterion for acceptable work—usually 80 or 90 percent correct responses— has been reached.

Supplementary help as necessary.   In the mastery approach, the class-room teacher usually provides remedial instruction. In PSI, more advanced students are available to the novice. They help with problems, talk about the subject matter, explore the implications of particular points, go over missed items, and, of course, provide encouragement and support.

Effectiveness of Mastery Learning Approaches

The effectiveness of the mastery approach depends on the duration of the experiment and the kind of achievement test used (i.e., whether it was made by the experimenter or is instead a standardized, commercially available test). Slavin (1987) found that longer-term experiments (lasting four weeks to a full school year) yielded much lower estimates of effectiveness than did briefer experiments. He also found, as did others (J. A. Kulik, C. C. Kulik, & Bangert-Drowns, 1990), that standardized achievement tests showed less effectiveness for the approach than did experimenter-made tests. Perhaps the latter tests emphasize the material in the mastery-approach curriculum more than that in the control, or conventionally taught, curriculum. Also, "even when the curriculum is held constant, it seems likely that the mastery learning procedures hold teachers more narrowly to the mastery objectives, whereas control teachers

Experiment duration and type of test

● *More advanced students can be available to help less advanced students. (© 1986 Jonathan A. Meyers)*

may be teaching material that is useful or important but is not assessed on the final test" (Slavin, 1990, p. 301).

Grade level and effectiveness

Slavin focused exclusively on *cognitive* achievement in *precollege* experiments. It is useful to look also at the affective outcomes and the college-level experiments as brought together by C. C. Kulik, J. A. Kulik, and Bangert-Drowns (1990). They concluded that mastery learning improves achievement fairly substantially at the college level and also improves attitudes toward the subject matter. Also, the mastery learning approach increased the amount of time students spent on the course (a "good" outcome) and decreased the

Attitude outcomes

percentages of college students who completed the course (a "bad" outcome).

Slavin (1987) considered the shorter-than-four-week experiments to be irrelevant to the *practical* value of mastery learning. He agreed with earlier critics that the mastery approach may have a "Robin Hood effect": helping

Robin Hood effect

slower-learning students at the expense of faster-learning students. Remember it is the classroom teacher who provides supplementary help in mastery learning. While the teacher is helping slower learners, faster learners may have to do "busy" work, rather than go on to new units of the curriculum. Just as the legendary Robin Hood stole from the rich to help the poor, so mastery learning may take educational resources (teacher's time and attention) from faster learners to benefit slower ones. As Slavin noted, the Robin Hood effect would not occur in PSI, where students work independently, at their own rate, from the very beginning of their study of each unit, rather than in the large-group setting used for initial instruction in the mastery approach.

One particular benefit of the mastery approach, its developer claims, is reinforcement. Once students realize they can achieve at the same level as anyone else in class, even if it takes them more time, they are motivated by their success experiences.

> Subject mastery affects the student's self- concept. . . . Mastery and its public recognition provide the necessary reassurance and reinforcement. This writer believes that one of the more positive aids to mental health is frequent and objective indications of self-development. Mastery learning, therefore, can be one of the more powerful sources of mental health. (B. S. Bloom, 1968)

Mastery learning and self-concept

Effectiveness of Personalized Systems of Instruction

A meta-analysis (quantitative synthesis) of the results of comparisons within sixty-seven college courses taught both conventionally and by PSI showed that PSI raised examination scores by an average of about 20 percentile ranks. PSI students would, on the average, achieve at the 70th percentile rank, while conventionally taught students achieved, on the average, at the 50th percentile rank (C. C. Kulik, J. A. Kulik, & Bangert-Drowns, 1990, p. 285). The PSI advantages for achievement were greater (1) in the social sciences than in mathematics, the natural sciences, or the humanities, (2) when locally developed rather than nationally standardized tests were used, (3) when the students had to follow the teacher's pace rather than go at their own rate, (4) when the mastery level required for proceeding to the next unit was higher, and (5) when the amount of feedback to students on quizzes was greater. Low-aptitude students seem to gain more from PSI than do high-aptitude students (the Robin Hood effect?).

PSI → superior student achievement

The feature students most often like in PSI courses is the self-pacing, which frees them to study where and when they please, but also, as noted earlier, tends to lower achievement. Personal interaction with a tutor rates as the second most frequently mentioned reason for preferring PSI courses. Students may spend more time studying in these courses, but in at least one study that time was matched by the amount of time lecture students spent attending lectures. So "total preparation time was about the same" (Born & Davis, 1974, p. 365).

Self-pacing

Some students delay starting PSI courses, put off taking tests, and generally flounder in the system. A recommended schedule, along with letters and phone calls to those who delay too much, can reduce this problem. Reiser (1984) compared two approaches—a penalty approach, whereby students lost two

Combating student procrastination

points for each instructional unit they failed to master by the suggested deadline, and a reward approach, whereby students gained two points for meeting the deadline. He found that the penalty approach was more effective in reducing procrastination and had no effects on achievement, self-concept, or withdrawal rate. Instructor-imposed deadlines, deadlines plus bonus credits for early completion, and individual contracting were compared by Lamwers and Jazwinski (1989), who found individual contracting most effective in speeding student progress.

Which of the components of PSI lead to higher achievement? Some studies have found that all of them—self-pacing, the use of proctors, the mastery requirement, immediate feedback, and frequent testing over relatively small units—contribute to the system's effectiveness (see, for example, Calhoun, 1973). But Block and Burns (1976) concluded from their review that "the unit mastery requirement has consistently produced the strongest effects" (p. 35). The effectiveness of the frequent testing feature of PSI (Abbott & Falstrom, 1977) has a history going back at least to the 1950s (Fitch, Drucker, & Norton, 1951).

Remedial instruction

Both mastery learning and PSI try to ensure remedial instruction of high quality. Small-group remediation allows greater adaptation to individual needs and gives teachers the opportunity to teach the same part of the curriculum in a different way. Alternative textbooks, workbooks, programmed instruction, games, and of course the interaction with a tutor may help a particular student to understand what he or she is learning.

Criticisms of mastery approaches

Both approaches have been criticized. Mueller (1976) and Cox and Dunn (1979) believe that mastery learning

- takes much of the responsibility for learning away from students, who may end up not knowing how to learn independently.
- requires nonfixed-time instructional units or greatly liberalized time allocations.
- makes faster learners "wait around" while slower learners catch up, unless the faster learners are motivated to spend their time achieving objectives beyond the prespecified ones.
- commits a major part of finite instructional resources—corrective effort, teacher aides, peer tutoring, and alternative learning materials—to slower students.
- assumes that everything in an instructional unit must be learned equally well by almost all students, although beyond basic skills and hierarchical subjects (such as mathematics) this assumption is hard to defend.

Mastery learning for basic skills and slow learners

Accordingly, Mueller claims the approach is most useful in the elementary grades with basic skills and for slow learners at all levels. He also claims that it is less effective in maximizing learning for fast learners, especially in subject areas where there are no prespecifiable objectives, and in the higher grades.

The inherently admirable philosophy of mastery learning must be balanced with practical realities to suggest that not everyone will equally achieve the desired objectives. The results of this ultimate confrontation of philosophy and reality should not in any way be considered a weakness of mastery learning. Rather, it should serve to strengthen the mastery learning approach by indicating some natural, possibly temporary, limitations. (Cox & Dunn, 1979, p. 29)

Where is the teacher in the mastery and PSI approaches? Besides preparing or selecting the reading assignments and the unit quizzes and supervising the course, does the teacher bow out? Keller's pronouncement in introducing PSI was "Goodbye Teacher." For Keller, the remedial teaching was to be done by proctors or student assistants. For Bloom, such "feedback and correctives" were to be provided by the teacher. But little research attention has been paid to alternative ways of doing these parts of the PSI and mastery approaches. The added paperwork needed for grading the frequent quizzes used in both approaches calls for teacher commitment to such work—as against the explaining, discussing, and demonstrating that teachers might value. Martinez and Martinez (1988) found that teacher differences of some unidentified kinds influenced the effectiveness of mastery learning approaches and recommended that future research should unmask these factors. "It is time to welcome the teacher back into the mastery learning classroom, not just as a paper-pusher or student-tutor or sitter, but as an active creator of learning" (p. 29).

Teacher's role in mastery and PSI

One shortcoming of PSI was noted by a student:

My main concern with the class, which was shared by many other students, was the lack of interaction among the students. The exchange of information and perspectives by students is crucial to the learning process. . . . With the Keller plan, I was forced to swim troubled waters by myself. Consequently, my perspective tended to be narrow. One remedy, of course, would be to initiate discussion groups and distribute phone numbers of students interested in such activity. (Gasper, 1980, p. 471)

What about interaction?

Our discussion of mastery learning and PSI would not be complete without recognition of the kinds of questions raised by Jaynes (1975):

I can see it in chemistry, mathematics, cooking, physics, engineering, harmony, law, auto repairing. But what of the subject where there is a huge variety of ways of teaching, of materials to be taught . . . ? Literature, history, philosophy—these subjects, if they are anything, are intercommunications between human beings. No one should learn [them] by rote. . . . One is not taught by the Keller Method. I object to the too arrogant standardization that it imposes upon the mind. . . . What the Keller Method in complex subjects does is to grind down the individual

Arrogant standardization?

student's particular style of going over things. It rebukes his wish to insert his own importances. (p. 631)

Tutoring

Another method of individual instruction is tutoring. This method can be used to help students at any age level. In most tutoring programs, the tutors have been nonprofessional teachers. They may be students of the same age as, or just a few years older than, those being tutored. Or they may be adults with no special training in education beyond that received as part of the tutoring program. At times the purpose of the tutoring is as much or more to help the tutor as it is to help the tutee. That is, tutoring is often used to increase the tutor's self-esteem and competence as much as to help the tutee. Many different tutor-tutee combinations have been tried.

Helping tutors and tutees

Components of the Process

Although content determines the particulars of the process, certain general components are widely recognized: The tutor should *diagnose,* then *remedy,* all the while providing *encouragement and support.*

Diagnosis.   Diagnostic processes are aimed at finding out as specifically as possible what is blocking the tutee's progress. Diagnosis can take the form of casual conversation, in which the tutee tries to describe his or her problem. Or the tutee can be asked to do a sample of work—for example, read aloud or try to solve an arithmetic problem—so that the tutor can observe where the tutee seems to be going wrong. Or for some kinds of tutoring, a diagnostic test can be given—one that reveals objectively what kinds of errors the tutee is making and where help is needed. The tutor can also consult the tutee's regular teacher for information on the nature of the problem, suggestions on how it can be solved, and materials with which to work.

Conversation, tryouts, and tests

Remedial Work.   The tutor, having formed some ideas as to the causes of the student's problems, proceeds to give the tutee opportunities to practice correctly the skills found to be deficient. The tutor asks questions, waits for answers, and praises correct responses or furnishes them if it is appropriate to do so. A correct response cues the tutor to stay at the same level or skill for additional practice or, if the evidence of learning is already adequate, to go on to the next skill or problem. An incorrect response often means that the tutor should give the right answer (not a cue or a prompt). It also means that the tutor needs to vary the instruction, offering the explanation in new words, with new examples. Then the tutor repeats the question, problem, or practice exercise. Della-Piana, Jensen, and Murdock (1970) have provided a sample of the kind of training a teacher might undergo in learning how to carry out a diagnosis-pre-

Handling correct and incorrect responses

•*The tutor should diagnose and then remedy while providing encouragement.* (© Elizabeth Crews)

scription cycle. A small part of such a cycle is shown in Figure 10.2. From this detailed program for tutor training, you can see how to make up your own set of procedures for handling tutoring. These procedures can help you train paraprofessionals and teaching aides as well.

Positive Reinforcement.   Most tutors should furnish lots of positive reinforcement. Many tutees have a history of what they perceive as failure, and their schooling is on the verge of becoming an aversive experience. For the tutee, the relationship to a respected and valued tutor can give the learning situation a saving warmth. Here are some guidelines to remember:

A saving warmth

- Compare the student's performance only with his or her own past performance.
- Report progress, however slight by other standards, in positive, encouraging terms.
- Keep tutoring sessions short enough so that they don't tire out or bore the tutee.
- Use a style that's appropriate to your age and status and to the tutee's. If you're tutoring a child, make a game of it and season that game with comfortable humor.
- Don't encourage the tutee by saying that a task is easy. In fact, we recommend you say the task is fairly difficult. If the tutee succeeds, the reward is greater; and if the tutee fails, you've salvaged the youngster's self-esteem.

Say "the task is hard"

FIGURE 10.2

Programmed Instructional Material for Training Teachers in a Diagnosis-Prescription Cycle

You will now be taken through one diagnosis and prescription cycle that simulates the role of the teacher we have just illustrated. Complete each step of this cycle precisely as directed before proceeding to the next step.

1. On three separate occasions a child looks at the word blank, then sounds out the letters and reads as follows:

   /b/ /l/ /a/ /nk/, black

   What is the child's reading problem? (Determine your answer before proceeding to the next step.)

   _____

   _____

2. Match your description of the child's reading problem against the following alternatives. Then go to the next step indicated. The child reads /b/ /l/ /a/ /nk/, black because

   a. He is a careless reader, or doesn't look carefully, or doesn't think. (Go to 3a).
   b. He knows the phonemic sounds, but for some reason does not blend them properly. Probably because "black" has a higher frequency rate than "blank" in the child's vocabulary. (Go to 3b.)
   c. Child doesn't know the sound of "n". (Go to 3c.)
   d. It is a configuration substitution. (Go to 3d.)

   3a. You said the child was "a careless reader . . ." This is a rather vague statement which does not provide enough information which can be used in prescribing diagnostic procedures or treatment. (Go back to 2b.)

   3b. Very good! The child does know the sounds corresponding to the letters. He simply did not blend

   them for the probable reason given. Now how would you check that diagnosis? (Determine your procedure for validating the diagnosis and then go to 4.)

   _____

   _____

   3c. The child did give the correct sound for each individual grapheme, but he didn't blend them correctly. So his problem was not inability to sound "n". (Go back to 2b.)

   3d. The words do look alike. But the child correctly sounded each element in "blank" and thus was "perceiving" each element and not likely using a configuration approach. The problem occurs in the next step of blending. (Go back to 2b.)

4. You suggested a procedure or procedures for checking the validity of your diagnosis. Match your suggestion against the three alternatives given here and follow the directions given.

   a. Have the child read the following paired words:

   back sack sick thick pink clack
   bank sank sink think pick clank

   b. Check to see if the error type occurs in context. Have the child read the following two sentences:
   Fill in the blank. The cat is black.

   c. Is the higher frequency rate for the word black built into the reading program? Check to see.
   (Regardless of your choice(s) above, move to 5a.)[1]

Source: Adapted from Della-Piana, Jensen, and Murdock (1970). Reprinted with permission of the authors and the International Reading Association.

Note: This figure presents only part of a diagnosis and prescription cycle.

Effectiveness

The research on tutoring usually shows positive results. A meta-analysis of 52 independent studies showed that being tutored typically raised achievement in elementary and secondary school classrooms from about the 50th percentile rank to about the 66th, and attitudes toward the subject matter were also improved (P. Cohen, Kulik, & Kulik, 1982). Furthermore,

> tutoring effects were larger in more structured programs, . . . in tutoring programs of shorter duration, . . . when lower level skills were taught and tested in examinations, . . . and when mathematics rather than reading was the subject of the tutoring . . . [and] on locally developed tests [than] on nationally standardized tests. (P. Cohen, Kulik, & Kulik, 1982, p. 243)

Effects of tutoring on attitude toward the subject matter were almost always positive in the eight studies of this effect, but the effect was small. Effects on self-concept were positive in 7 of 9 studies of this effect, but again the effect was small.

What about effects on the tutors? In 33 of 38 studies, tutors did better than nontutors on examinations in the subject taught. On the average they scored about thirteen percentile ranks higher. The effect on tutor achievement tended to be higher for mathematics tutors than for reading tutors. In 12 of 16 studies, the tutors' self-concept became higher than that of nontutors. And in 4 out of 5 studies, attitude toward the subject matter was more favorable for tutoring students than the control group.

Effects of tutoring on tutors

The desirability of any method of improving educational results depends not only on its effectiveness but also on its costs. For this reason, educators have studied the cost-effectiveness of educational changes. One such analysis (Levin, Glass, & Meister, 1984) compared the cost-effectiveness of four interventions in improving the mathematics and reading achievement of elementary school children: reducing class size, increasing the length of the school day, computer-assisted instruction, and peer and adult tutoring. The authors concluded that the most cost-effective approach was peer (not adult) tutoring, followed in turn by computer-assisted instruction, with reducing class size and lengthening the school day being the least cost-effective. The fact that the elementary school student tutors were assumed to cost nothing was *not* responsible for this result. Rather, it was the greater effectiveness of the tutoring.

Cost-effectiveness of peer tutoring

An ingenious experiment by Annis (1983) showed the effects of tutoring on both tutors and tutees. She randomly assigned 120 college women to five groups:

Read: This group read the material for a test.
Read to teach: This group read the material in preparation for tutoring it but did not actually teach it.
Read and teach: This group read the material in preparation for teaching it, then actually taught a tutee.
Taught: This group was taught the material by a tutor.
Read and taught: This group read the material, then was taught it by a tutor.

The material consisted of a three-page article on the Lisbon earthquake of 1755, introduced into a college course in world history. The posttest a week later was made up of forty-eight multiple-choice and essay questions evenly divided over the six main levels of the Cognitive Taxonomy (see Chapter 2).

For the comprehension and evaluation subtests, the five groups did not differ more than chance might allow. But the differences on the knowledge, application, analysis, and synthesis questions were statistically significant. On these subtests, "the students who were taught only scored lower than the students in the teaching conditions"; there was "a definite advantage for the tutor" (Annis, 1983, p. 45). Moreover, "cognitive benefits of teaching result from the preparation stage of teaching in itself. Students who Read to Teach scored higher than students who Read only in both the content-specific gains . . . and also in the more generalized achievement measured by Application and Analysis" (Annis, 1983, p. 45). Also the read-and-teach students scored higher than the Read to Teach students, so that the actual teaching had value beyond that of preparing to teach. "Peer tutoring thus appears to be a potentially powerful technique for increasing all levels of student learning" (Annis, 1983, p. 46).

Read-and-teach is most effective treatment for tutors

Programmed Instruction

Skinner's diagnosis

In 1954 there burst on the education scene a radically new and promising approach—programmed instruction. In a historic paper, "The Science of Learning and the Art of Teaching," Skinner (1954) diagnosed the ills of teaching and learning in our schools, then prescribed a cure. He wrote from his position as originator and leader of the operant-conditioning approach, developed in research on the behavior of rats and pigeons. He saw the main problem in education as a drastic inadequacy in the number and organization of the reinforcement contingencies available to students (see Chapter 6). In the ordinary classroom, Skinner claimed, students have altogether too few opportunities to respond to discriminative cues. Any one student can recite, or respond, only infrequently. Then, too, the cues themselves are sequenced too haphazardly. And often, when a student does have an opportunity to respond, say on a test, reinforcement or punishment comes too late to be effective.

Skinner's remedy

Skinner's remedy was *programmed instruction*—a system whereby each student is (a) presented with content (relatively brief presentations of about a sentence or a paragraph of instructional material), (b) required to respond actively (correctly answer a question or solve a problem), and (c) immediately given information about the correctness of the response.

Frames and Programs

Each a-b-c combination makes up a *frame* in the program. An example of a frame is shown in Figure 10.3. (Look at the figure and see whether you can identify the *a, b,* and *c* parts of the frame.) Each frame is followed by another that builds on its predecessors. The frames are arranged in a sequence that leads the student from the entering level (which could be called "ignorance") to what Skinner would call the wanted "behavior repertoire" and what nonbehaviorists would call

FIGURE 10.3

A Frame from a Programmed Textbook

THE FIRST PRINCIPLE: ACTIVE RESPONDING

1. In an early article, Skinner (1958) noted a similarity between an instructional program and a private tutor:

> "There is a constant interchange between program and student. Unlike lectures, textbooks, and the usual audiovisual aids, the machine induces sustained activity. Like a good tutor, the machine insists that a given point be thoroughly understood . . . before the student moves on. Lectures, textbooks, and their mechanized equivalents, on the other hand, proceed without making sure that the student understands and easily leave him behind."

Sounds good, doesn't it? While it is easy to make such claims for the ideal program, it is much more difficult to embody such wonders in real instructional materials. Does student activity — *any* sort of doing — really indicate "understanding"? Consider the following frames and their *un*mechanized equivalent (e.g., a lecture):

---

1. To *positively reinforce* an animal, you make a reinforcer, such as a bit of food, contingent on the animal emitting an appropriate response. When you make food contingent on a response, you p_____ly r_____ an animal's response.

2. Giving an animal a bit of food when it emits an appropriate response is called P_____ R_____ment.

A lecturer, of course, would not leave blanks in the statements — it sounds odd! Check any of these statements that *you feel* may be true of such teaching:

_____ In the frames, a student who fills in the blanks is engaging in *"activity"* (in other words, *doing* something).

_____ The student who correctly fills in those blanks thoroughly *understands* the given point.

_____ If a lecturer gave the same definition orally, the student who takes it down in written notes is engaging in *"activity"*.

_____ A student who accurately copies down the lecturer's definition thoroughly *understands* the given point.

The question asked for your opinion. We need to come to some agreement on what is meant by "active response." My concept of "activity" includes *both* filling in those blanks *and* taking notes during a lecture. The student *is* doing something, whether or not that something is going to lead to adequate learning. Scholars concerned with behavioral objectives (Mager, 1962; Popham and Baker, 1970; Vargas, 1972) tell us not to use the term "understand" because there is no consensus on what activities indicate understanding. However, I do find consensus on what does NOT — most people will agree that neither of our students above "understands" if that is *all* the activity each student performed.

Source: From Susan Meyer Markle, *Designs for Instructional Designers,* 2d ed. (Champaign, Ill: Stipes Publishing Company). © 1983 Susan M. Markle. Used by permission.

(or question as to its adequacy) "full knowledge and understanding of the subject matter," at the end of the program.

Create positive reinforcement

Some programmers believe that a program should be written so that most students (say, 90 percent) are be able to respond correctly to most frames (say, 90 percent). In this way, students are highly likely to experience only positive reinforcement as they proceed through the program. The positive reinforcement that goes along with each correct response makes it highly probable that students will make correct responses in the future and also strengthens their motivation or desire to learn.

The Contributions of Programmed Instruction

Research tells us that programmed instruction seems to have real value for learning a particular skill (how to use an oscilloscope, how to use a hand-held calculator, how to compute a correlation coefficient) and for remedial and enrichment purposes, but not for taking over a major part of the instruction in a given subject. The initial enthusiasm for programmed instruction has been dampened. It has not revolutionized schooling in America. One writer summed up its history as follows:

> Research on PI generally indicated that it worked and was based on sound learning principles. However, it never achieved a high degree of popularity. For all its soundness as an instructional technique, PI had one great failing. It was boring. Most learners found it tedious and dull. Also, PI did not generally fit well into the group-oriented, fixed-schedule school settings. Critics also pointed out that it was . . . of little value where attitudes and values were concerned. After a brief flirtation with the technique, educators generally turned their backs on PI and considered it just another of the passing fads that come and go on the educational scene. (Price, 1989, pp. 146–147)

Improved instructional materials

But programmed instruction has increased attention to what operant conditioning theory suggests for improving classroom management and school organization. And it has led to the development of improved instructional materials.

More effort to individualize

In the classroom, programmed instruction has led to renewed efforts to achieve the ideals of individualization—of treating students according to their unique abilities, rates of learning, and interests. Students now have more opportunity to work at their own speed—to go ahead more quickly or to review and work more slowly, with the help of a tutor if necessary.

Active participation

Another by-product of programmed instruction is that students have often become more active participants in the learning process; they are doing something beyond reading, listening, and looking. They have been given tasks that require relatively frequent responses—answering questions, taking tests, going places to find out things, working with books and puzzles, games, audio- and videotapes, and simple laboratory materials (magnets, paper clips).

And students are receiving feedback more frequently—both affective and cognitive. Affective feedback takes the form of praise and approval for appropriate behaviors and responses. Cognitive feedback is the knowledge that what one is doing is correct, or, if it's wrong, that with a certain change it can be made correct. Today's teachers have learned that students should not go too long without some idea of how they are doing.

More feedback

Computer-Assisted Instruction

The teaching machines that often went with programmed instructional materials have virtually disappeared. But computer-assisted instruction (CAI) makes possible programmed instruction with certain advantages:

- Information about students' *individual* and *group* responses can be stored, retrieved, and processed statistically, for review by the teacher almost immediately and at the end of each lesson.

Information-processing capabilities

- A computer program can be written so that it has "branches," providing instructional support appropriate for students of different ability.

Branching

- Computers allow us to collect information on the speed with which students respond to a stimulus or problem.

Response speed

- By means of earphones and television screens, it is possible to present material to students in nonverbal form (pictures, diagrams, motion pictures) and in auditory form (for example, a language teacher pronouncing French words or sentences, a music teacher presenting musical phrases). By means of a "light pen," it also is possible for students to respond simply by touching the television screen to identify, say, the part of a picture that shows the isosceles triangle or a rococo statue.

Light pen

- With the widespread popularity of desk-top computers, millions of individuals have CAI available to them at home and in school.

CAI makes individualized treatment of students easier in some instances. The computer can review a student's most recent response to a series of drill problems in reading or arithmetic and decide instantly whether the student needs much more practice or can skip to the next kind of problem. This saves the teacher the boring task of reviewing and scoring students' work. Besides, the teacher is much slower and less aware of the changes in students' performance. CAI can teach logic, Russian, business strategy, and any other subject that can be programmed.

Computer decision-making

CAI does have limitations, however. Suppes (1966) identified three levels of CAI: dialogue, tutoring, and drill-and-practice. CAI cannot yet respond adequately to the student's spoken language or to the student's written sentences, paragraphs, or essays; that is, it cannot engage in much dialogue with the student. But that is changing rapidly. For example, new writing programs

Dialogue, tutoring, and drill-and-practice

● *Computer-assisted instruction continues to be the basis of a vigorous research and development movement.*
(© Michael Siluk/ The Image Works)

conduct dialogues with students learning to write essays (Zellermayer, Salomon, Globerson, & Given, 1991). Dialogue is also a role uniquely suited to a teacher using CAI. It is the basis for the "HOTS" (Higher Order Thinking Skills) program now used in several hundred schools with apparent success. Teachers using the HOTS program learn to engage students working on computer programs in instructional dialogues. Thus HOTS lets the computer do what it does best, for example, create a microworld in which to make decisions. And it reserves for teachers what they can do best: ask the right question at the right time of a particular student (Pogrow, 1991). It is also true that only with much effort can CAI be made capable of tutoring, branching from the main program in ways that take account of the student's response history. But, as with other aspects of CAI, this limitation is changing, and intelligent tutors may be on the way. At the simplest level of instruction (that is, drill-and-practice), CAI presents and corrects a series of problems in spelling, addition, or foreign language vocabulary, for example, in the same way for all students. An example of a simple drill program in learning foreign language vocabulary is given in Figure 10.4. Notice that the computer can respond much like a person, with a

FIGURE 10.4

*An Example of a
Drill-and-Practice
Session in Foreign
Language*

Pupil (P) types in an identification number: 012

Computer (C) responds by writing: Good afternoon, David. This will be German-English lesson number four. If you are ready to start at once, please type *S*. If you would like to review the procedure, please type *P*.

P: S

C: *Reichen*

P: To hand

C: Good!
    Kochen

P: To boil

C: Very good!
    Öffnen

P: To offer

C: No, that is incorrect.
    Do you want to try again?

P: To open

C: OK.
    Arbeiten

P: To arbitrate

C: No, that is incorrect.
    Do you want to try again?

P: To look

C: No, that is incorrect. *Arbeiten* = to work. Dummkopf!
    Machen

P: To make

C: Correct, keep it up.

Source: Based on J. C. R. Licklider, *Programmed Learning and Computer Instruction.* © 1962 John Wiley & Sons, Inc.

touch of humor, when the student misses a word for the second time. (This is a 30-year-old drill-and-practice program. Newer CAI programs have colors, attractive graphics, and even sound effects. But the same question-answer-feedback system still characterizes drill-and-practice programs.)

Effectiveness

How effective is computer-assisted instruction? The results of scores of studies have been pulled together quantitatively by Kulik (1985). His overall conclusions, based mostly on drill-and-practice CAI, rather than tutoring or dialogue programs, were that

- students' average scores on final examinations improved from the 50th percentile rank without computers to the 61st percentile rank with computers.

- students' average retention of what they learned improved from the 50th percentile without computers to the 57th percentile with computers.
- students with computers used about 32 percent less time in learning their lessons.
- students' attitudes toward their classes improved to about the 61st percentile.
- students' attitudes toward computers were more favorable than those of about 63 percent of students who learned without computers. Thus experience in using CAI made students like computers more.
- students' attitudes toward the subject matter were unchanged.

Because the studies reviewed by Kulik ranged from elementary and secondary school to college and adult levels, over many uses of computers, and over many subject matters, his conclusions are broad generalizations. They indicate that the use of computers in instruction tends to have moderately favorable effects on achievement and attitudes.

Cost-effectiveness These gains do not come at low cost, however, either financially or organizationally (that is, in terms of disruptions of established ways of running schools and classrooms). Levin (1986) has studied the cost-effectiveness of computer-assisted instruction. In a preliminary survey and analysis, he concluded that CAI was less cost-effective (improved achievement less per dollar spent) than peer tutoring, but more so than extending the school day or reducing class size. While schools everywhere are increasing their purchases of computers, peer tutoring proved more cost-effective because it was much more effective in improving achievement.

These findings on the effectiveness and relative cost-effectiveness of CAI indicate some of the complexities facing the computer revolution in education or any other innovation in ways of teaching. The revolution is moving more slowly than was predicted in the 1960s. In the meantime, the role of the human teacher continues to predominate in the ways we describe throughout this book.

Intelligent Tutoring Systems

Intelligent tutoring systems (ITS) are in the forefront of current research on CAI. These systems

> attempt to mimic the capabilities of human tutors . . . the ability to meaningfully analyze each student's responses (not just determine whether they are correct by matching pre-defined answers) and the ability to interact with the student—give advice when a mistake is made and answer students' questions. (Rosenberg, 1987, p. 7)

The research for ITSs ultimately aims at doing what human tutors would do, including the social and emotional parts of tutoring. The critique by Rosenberg

(1987) indicates the inadequacies of the research thus far and points to the need for closer study by computer scientists of what actually goes on in tutor-student interactions.

Individual Instruction in the Service of Humanistic Ideals

Some of the individual methods of instruction noted above are prized by a group of educators whose ideas can be tied together under the term *humanistic*. These educators, discussed below, value the self-directed aspects of learning inherent in contract and project methods. They like the self-instruction and self-pacing found in the mastery and PSI approaches, because these systems are designed to minimize competition with others and eliminate lock-step instruction that punishes both the slowest and the fastest learners. The helping and responsibility for another inherent in tutoring also impress such educators as outcomes equal in value to achievement. And the self-pacing and imaginative microworlds provided by CAI are also seen as serving humanistic purposes. Let us look now at this style of teaching, the roots of which can be found in several fields, including psychology.

Objectives of Humanistic Approaches

It's easy to agree with the basic objectives of humanistic teaching:

- To increase learners' self-direction and independence
- To help students take more responsibility for determining what they are learning
- To increase learners' creativity
- To develop an interest in the arts
- To foster curiosity

Many humanistic educators believe there should be less emphasis on, or even complete abolition of, grades, standard curricula, lesson plans, tests, censorship, teacher certification, and compulsory attendance.

As practiced in classrooms humanistic teaching methods resemble a combination of small-group and individual instruction methods. But humanistic approaches change some of the roles of teachers and students. For example, teachers and students are on an equal footing. And students, not teachers or state curriculum planners, have the right to choose subject matter. At the foundation of humanistic teaching is the belief that students have a need for self-actualization and that teachers should build on this need, organizing their classes so that students are put in touch with meaningful events. When this happens, students will "wish to learn, want to grow, seek to find out, hope to master, desire to create" (Rogers, 1959).

New roles for teachers and students

• *Students, not teachers or state curriculum planners, have the right to choose subject matter. (© Jean-Claude Lejeune)*

Social and emotional outcomes vs. academic outcomes

Humanistic classrooms want to nourish free growth, to protect children from excessive societal and familial pressures. The academic outcomes of instruction take second place to the social and emotional outcomes. Yet under the right conditions, humanistic educators insist, academic outcomes are far superior to those ordinarily attained. Why? Because most learning under humanistic teaching is self-directed, and this characteristic makes it highly meaningful to students.

Roots of the Humanistic Movement

The goals and practices of humanistic teaching resemble those of the progressive movement during the first half of the 1900s. John Dewey was reacting to schooling that was irrelevant to an industrialized society (Goodman, 1970). He opposed the puritanism of the time, the denial of the ideas of modern psychology, the pervasive use of drill as a method of instruction, and the many decorative, nonutilitarian aspects of education. Today's humanistic educators are also reformers. They believe that contemporary urban society is heading toward a kind of mindless, 1984-like existence or, even worse, the end of the human species.

Summerhill

In founding Summerhill, a radically different school in England, A. S. Neill (1960) was perhaps the first of the recent humanistic educators. Carl Rogers, using guidelines for a school derived from his nondirective psychotherapy (in which psychotherapists avoid diagnosing and advising in favor of accepting and reflecting back to the client what he or she has said), and Abraham Maslow, using his conception of motivation, provided the psychological underpinnings of the movement. Although holding very different views in many areas, almost all humanistic theorists and practitioners share a belief that "a child is innately wise and realistic. If left to himself, without adult suggestion of any kind, he will develop as far as he is capable of developing" (Neill, 1960, p. 4).

Wise children

This is the idea of the "noble savage," set forth by Rousseau in reaction to eighteenth-century society. The same notion appears in John Holt's charge (1964, 1967) that our society and schools turn lively, inquiring three-year-olds into bored, fearful fifth-graders.

Intended Outcomes

Humanistic methods should enable students to become what Maslow (1954) called "self-actualized" (see Chapter 8). The creativity of the self-actualized person is within all of us. For its development and support, it requires no special talents or abilities, just the right environment. It shows up in everyday life, whenever people are perceptive, spontaneous, expressive, genuine, happy, and unafraid. Only a special kind of freedom in school can produce self-actualized people—people who have come to accept themselves, their feelings, and others more fully. These people are self-directed, confident, mature, realistic about their goals, and flexible. They've gotten rid of maladjustive behaviors. They became more like the people they wanted to be. A teacher who can create the right kind of climate in a classroom should have students who display some of these characteristics.

Self-actualization

As we noted in Chapter 2, some writers believe that many important objectives of education are difficult to specify in behavioral terms, and their achievement is even harder to measure. This difficulty certainly holds for the intended outcomes of humanistic teaching. Here knowledge and skills are less important than feelings and personal growth. Rogers' (1969) research and understanding of the conditions for meaningful learning led him to observe:

> I have come to realize, as I have considered these studies, and puzzled over the design of better studies which should be more informative and conclusive, that findings from such research will never answer our questions. For all such findings must be evaluated in terms of the goals we have for education. If we value primarily the learning of knowledge, then we may discard the conditions I have described as useless, since there is no evidence that they lead to a greater rate or amount of factual knowledge. . . . If we value independence, if we are disturbed by the growing conformity of knowledge, of values, of attitudes, which our present system induces, then we may wish to set up conditions of learning which make for uniqueness, for self- direction, and for self-initiated learning. (pp. 239–240)

Independence and uniqueness

• *Let students initiate an activity that interests them, and simply provide the necessary information and equipment. (© Barrera/Texas Stock)*

Principles of Humanistic Education

A few assumptions are basic to humanistic education. First, students learn what they need and want to know. Second, wanting to learn and knowing how to learn are more important than acquiring factual knowledge. Third, the students' own evaluation is the only meaningful judgment of their work. Fourth, feelings are as important as facts, and learning how to feel is as important as learning how to think. And finally, learning takes place only when students do not feel threatened.

Self-Direction

Responsibility for determining what is learned

The first principle in humanistic teaching is that students should choose what they should learn. Goodman (1964) argued that nothing is really learned unless it satisfies some need, want, curiosity, or fantasy; all other kinds of learning are promptly forgotten. Why should teachers and other educators determine what students should know, then worry about ways to motivate them? Why not let students initiate an activity that interests them and ask teachers simply to provide the necessary information and equipment? Certainly this approach would fit in with the idea of students' intrinsic motivation, exploratory drive, and curiosity (see Berlyne, 1965).

Traditional educators insist that the leadership of an older and wiser person (that is, a teacher) can help youngsters avoid painful and time-wasting experiences. Humanistic educators would reply:

> Every time we show Tommy how his engine works, we are stealing from that child the joy of life—the joy of discovery—the joy of overcoming an obstacle. Worse! We make the child come to believe that he is inferior, and must depend on help. (Neill, 1960, p. 25)

What does research tell us? Is self-direction a waste of time? Of course, few schools go to the extremes advocated in this first principle. But when Campbell (1964) compared self-directed learning with regular classroom learning of units in geography, history, mathematics, and other subject areas, each lasting a few weeks, he found no significant differences. For the students, this brief self-directing experience came after years of being told what to do. So the fact that they did not fall behind provides impressive evidence that self-direction in learning at least is not harmful. Moreover, Campbell and others who have tried similar programs have noted positive motivational effects from self-directed learning (Youngs, Farmer, & Damm, 1970). These effects were also noted by inspectors from the British Ministry of Education who examined Neill's famous school, Summerhill. They reported that the school operated under a principle of freedom of choice, that children were never obliged to attend any lessons. "The children are full of life and zest. Of boredom and apathy there was no sign. . . . Initiative, responsibility and integrity are all encouraged by the system" (Ministry of Education, 1949).

Achievement unharmed

But it is noteworthy that graduates of Summerhill acknowledged a lack of academic preparation after ages 10 or 12. Many parents of students at Summerhill, who themselves had attended the school, removed their children after age 13 because they lacked confidence in the academic aspects of the school (E. Bernstein, 1968). This impressionistic study of fifty former students of Summerhill did report some benefits: a healthy attitude toward sex and toward members of the opposite sex, confidence and ease in dealing with authority, continuing personal growth, and a better understanding of their own children.

What alumni have to say

Wanting and Knowing How to Learn

A second principle of humanistic education is that schools, especially schools for young people, should produce students who want to continue to learn and who know how to learn. Knowledge—what is learned—makes no real difference so long as children want to go on learning. The school's task is to make wanting to learn an explicit objective.

What is learned is unimportant

Humanistic educators would agree with J. W. Gardner (1963) that "the ultimate goal of the educational system is to shift to the individual the burden of pursuing his own education." We want students to want to learn on their own, to be self-motivated. And our job is to help them learn how to learn.

> All too often we are giving our young people cut flowers when we should be teaching them to grow their own plants. We are stuffing their heads with the products of earlier innovation rather than teaching them to innovate. We think of the mind as a storehouse to be filled when we should be thinking of it as an instrument to be used. (J. W. Gardner, 1963, pp. 21–22)

Self-renewal

One who knows how to learn about an area of knowledge, including oneself, will realize that new learning is always needed and be better able to meet the need for what Gardner called "self-renewal" (J. W. Gardner, 1963; Rogers, 1969).

Humanistic educators hardly have a monopoly on these ideas. Many recent reforms in mathematics and science education are based on the same principle. Criticism of unjustified rote and factual learning in the schools has a long history, attesting to the capacity for survival of this kind of learning (see Silberman, 1970). Most educators, whatever their philosophy, would agree that learning to learn or, in its more general form, learning to think is the essence of what schooling is all about.

What about practice?

In Chapter 7 we noted that learning is transferred only after extensive practice on particular types of problems. If in learning a series of problems, children stop practicing too soon, they are unable to transfer learning to a set of similar problems. Basic skills, then, must be mastered before transfer to more complex behavior is possible. This point is similar to the idea that some simple learning must precede more complex learning—a theory Gagné derived from his analysis of learning hierarchies in instructional settings (see Chapter 7).

These empirical studies, along with persuasive arguments in defense of drill (Ausubel, 1963), force us to consider again the role of rote and factual learning. Nothing can be more meaningless than learning by rote that A is a symbol called "a." Yet this knowledge is a basic requirement in mastering any learning hierarchy that uses written materials; it is a fundamental step toward literacy. *Unjustified rote learning does not belong in any curriculum.* But we cannot just dismiss rote learning that is basic to learning how to learn. The task for humanistic educators, for all responsible educators, is to separate the unjustified rote learning from the necessary.

Unjustified vs. necessary rote learning

Self-Evaluation

A third principle of humanistic education is that self-evaluation is the only meaningful kind of evaluation. Humanistic educators would argue that evaluations by schools and teachers, in the form of grades, marks, and report cards, interfere with learning; that standardized tests and other evaluation instruments are irrelevant. One of these educators, Glasser (1969), attacked objective tests because they imply that questions have a single correct answer and because

Grades, marks, report cards, and tests: Are they harmful?

they require that students do an inordinate amount of memorizing. He argued that students should be evaluated against their own standards, without comparison to other students and without grades.

Closed-book tests have also come under fire, because they too encourage memorization. If the purpose of a test is to provide feedback and guidance to students and teachers, not to evaluate, these reformers say, the books should stay open.

Closed- vs. open-book tests

Holt (1964) argued that comparisons and grades humiliate children. He believed that many children seem to forget things in school, not because of bad memories, but because they have come to distrust their memories. These children have been graded and corrected so often that they no longer chance a response because of its possible negative consequences. They have come to believe they are or will be wrong, and, victims of a self-fulfilling prophecy, they often act accordingly.

Assigning a grade, in this view, is at best irrelevant and at worst an indication that outsiders have the right to label other people or their products. Moreover, humanistic educators insist that grading initiates a process in which children work for grades rather than for personal satisfaction. They claim that grading is simply a way to make students feel inferior. And they say that when grades are made public, as they often are, failing students are likely to carry a stigma that affects their social identity. Some humanistic educators require that student files be open only to the student and people of the student's choosing. The files are the students' property and are given to them when they leave a class or school.

Files open only to students

If students are going to choose what to learn and develop skills in how to learn—the first two principles—they must have practice in self-evaluation. "It is when the individual has to take the responsibility for deciding what criteria are important to him, what goals he has been trying to achieve, and the extent to which he has achieved those goals, that he truly learns to take responsibility for himself and his directions" (Rogers, 1969, pp. 142–143). Humanistic educators would have teacher and student meet regularly to work out plans and contracts for learning activities. In these conferences, they would also set criteria for evaluation, giving the student an opportunity to practice and master self-evaluation.

The Importance of Feelings

Humanistic educators make no distinction between the cognitive and affective domains. They insist that both knowledge and feelings are a part of the learning process. They study love, pain, friendship, and joy, and react against what they believe to be an unfeeling, impersonal, computerized world that limits emotions and consequently dehumanizes human beings. Mood (1970), writing about the profound influence of teachers on the lives of their students, talked about psychological violence:

Importance of knowledge *and* feelings

Psychological violence

A whole new conception is developing of what constitutes civilized behavior. It is a substantially lovelier and kinder concept than we have been

● *Humanistic educators insist that both knowledge and feelings are part of the learning process. (© Elizabeth Hamlin/Stock Boston)*

accustomed to but it is somewhat difficult to recognize because it is usually advanced by nonestablishment young people whose behavior appears to be atrocious. . . .

The main ingredient of the new standard of civilized behavior is the decree that psychological violence is as abhorrent as physical violence. (p. 17)

Psychological violence is committed whenever an insensitive teacher, in order to promote "knowledge," turns away from those human acts that call forth feelings, emotions, and fantasy.

Developing personal meanings

Traditional education has tended to concentrate on the cognitive domain, ignoring affective areas. From the standpoint of humanistic teaching, learning is acquiring new information or experience *and* personally discovering its meaning. Our schools fail not because they don't provide information; they do that well. They fail because they don't allow students to develop personal meanings and feelings about objects, events, and knowledge (Combs, 1967).

Some writers have tried to tie together affective and cognitive material. Others value the affective experience in itself and advocate units or full courses in expressing feelings or understanding emotions. These programs often include exercises. For example, to develop and understand *trust* as a feeling, a common exercise is the "blind walk": Partners take turns leading each other, blindfolded, for a period of time. Schutz (1967) cataloged exercises for training people in interpersonal communication. Among these exercises are touching games, ostracizing and rewelcoming experiences, and games in which people practice putting their feelings into words. Although they may disagree on the ways to use affective experiences in schools, all humanistic educators recognize a need to stop what they see as an overemphasis on cognitive education.

Affective exercises

A Nonthreatening Environment

The final principle of humanistic education is that learning is easiest, most meaningful, and most effective when it takes place in a nonthreatening situation. This principle goes beyond grading or not grading; it implies that school for many students is a place that humiliates, ridicules, devalues, scorns, and treats with contempt. "These are threats to the person himself, to the perception he has of himself, and as such interfere strongly with learning" (Rogers, 1969, p. 162).

The child who reads poorly and is asked to read aloud; the child who cannot add who is sent to the chalkboard to work problems; the clumsy student who is forced to compete in athletics; the student who has poor parents or is homely or handicapped or slow—all are threatened by school. And when these youngsters feel threatened by the teacher, classroom structure, or school, they cannot learn well.

Teachers can create a threatening environment without ever intending to. After observing one teacher's system for promoting democratic responsibility in the classroom, Henry (1963) described how, in practice, the system served as "vigilantism" for the very opposite. Children ganged up on one another, he observed, and verbally attacked others in the class. In this kind of environment children are motivated more by a fear of failure than a desire to succeed. And children who are motivated by a fear of failure usually behave maladaptively. They withdraw, stop trying, "play it safe," take no chances. Or they may strike out against their teacher or classmates, disrupt, break the rules.

Vigilantism in the classroom

Fear of failure vs. desire to succeed

In a nonthreatening environment, children and adults feel secure, and that security frees them to learn. School takes on new significance as students, young and old, begin to venture into new areas, willing to learn because they are sure that their self-esteem will not be threatened.

Certain teaching methods are especially associated with humanistic education. We have noted that self-paced programs are preferable to lock-step methods and that projects and contracts fit the humanistic agenda. In addition, there is the major form of humanistic education called "open education."

Open-Education Programs

The Plowden report called attention to a revolution in British primary school education (Plowden et al., 1967). Journalists praised the British programs (for example, Silberman, 1970; Featherstone, 1971), and other writers presented

Integrated-day plans

their philosophy, practice, psychological underpinnings, and presumed effects (see Barth, 1970; Bussis & Chittenden, 1970; Cazden, 1969; Rathbone, 1972). These programs—called *open education, integrated-day plans, Leicestershire models,* or *informal education*—have in common a highly individualized approach to early education (see Walberg & Thomas, 1971). They also resemble fairly closely the progressive education movement that was active in the United States from the 1920s to the mid-1950s. In fact some writers see open education running into the same problems that led to the demise of progressive education (T. C. Hunt, 1976; Westbury, 1973).

In brief, open classrooms had a special approach to learning, the setting, student activities, evaluation of the learner, the use of time, and the teacher's roles (Rothenberg, 1989):

Integrated materials cutting across subjects

1. *Learning* proceeded with integrated materials cutting across reading, writing, mathematics, social studies, and science. It followed students' interests as stimulated by the teacher. It fostered learners' discovery and research. It allowed different learners to proceed at different rates, used games, sometimes supplemented with textbooks and packaged learning materials.
2. The *setting* was a classroom "divided into learning areas, each with its own topic or subject" (Rothenberg, 1989, p. 73).
3. *Student activities* consisted of working in small groups, which divided the labor and permitted learners to choose their own tasks and procedures, with the students permitted to move around freely and cooperate with other learners.
4. *Evaluation* was used by the teacher to give learners feedback based on comparisons with the learners themselves rather than their classmates or students elsewhere. It used the teacher's observations and deemphasized formal testing.
5. The *use of time* was flexible, often permitting long, uninterrupted work sessions whose duration was largely determined by the learners.
6. The *teacher's role* was to organize, provide resources, help learners in their planning, work with single learners or groups, and keep records of learner activities and use of time.

Demands of open education on teachers

For teachers, open-education programs are far more demanding than traditional methods of instruction.

Teaching in an open classroom, even in the best of circumstances is very demanding, perhaps far more so than in a traditional classroom. [It] requires constant planning, continuous innovation, a sensitive system of monitoring students' performance, and well-developed skills in maintaining order without being authoritarian. Maintaining the energy and commitment to do all this well is difficult for trained and experienced teachers. (Rothenberg, 1989, p. 78)

• *Open educators and teachers of informal classrooms insist on the right of children to pursue whatever interests them.* *(© Elizabeth Crews)*

Informal methods are also said to be far more rewarding for both teachers and children if the methods can be made to work. Primers on how to begin have been written by M. Brown and N. Precious (1973) and Silberman (1973).

There are still many questions to be answered about open-education programs. Are the programs ineffective or even harmful for children from low-income homes—sometimes considered unable to take the responsibility necessary for effective learning under these conditions? Does the method over-emphasize the experiential (messing about) aspects of the integrated day? Aren't some things learned and retained better when children are instructed directly? Does the open classroom, with its encouragement of free choice, produce students who have great competence in just one area and very little competence in other areas? Can open education be continued through the secondary grades? Or is it appropriate only for primary education?

And there is another fundamental question for researchers to answer: What is the nature and quality of learning under an open-education system? At pres-

Research questions on open education

Hard-to-measure outcomes

ent, methods for measuring creativity, responsibility, autonomy, ability to work without distraction, altruism, and other outcomes claimed for open education are poor. Still, the evaluation that follows suggests that although academic achievement suffers only slightly on average under open education, the probability is fairly good that creativity and attitudes toward self and school improve.

An Evaluation and Analysis of Open Education

Open education is highly controversial. For every argument in support of the concept there are others that oppose it. Skinner (1973), an ardent critic of humanistic education, wrote as follows:

> His name is Emile. He was born in the middle of the eighteenth century in the first flush of the modern concern for personal freedom. His father was Jean-Jacques Rousseau, but he had many foster parents, among them Pestalozzi, Froebel, and Montessori, down to A. S. Neill and Ivan Illich. He is an ideal student. Full of goodwill toward his teachers and his peers, he needs no discipline. He studies because he is naturally curious. He learns things because they interest him.
>
> Unfortunately, he is imaginary. He was quite explicitly so with Rousseau, who put his own children in an orphanage and preferred to say how he would teach his fictional hero; but the modern version of the free and happy student to be found in books by Paul Goodman, John Holt, Jonathan Kozol, or Charles Silberman is also imaginary. Occasionally a real example seems to turn up. There are teachers who would be successful anywhere—as statesmen, therapists, businessmen, or friends—and there are students who scarcely need to be taught, and together they sometimes seem to bring Emile to life. And unfortunately they do so often enough to sustain the old dream. But Emile is a will-o'-the-wisp, who has led many teachers into a conception of their role which could prove disastrous. (p. 13)

An imaginary child?

What Skinner would substitute for open education is not punishment—the kind of control students want to get away from. It is positive reinforcement: "responding to the student's success rather than his failures" (Skinner, 1973, p. 15).

Some of the critics of open education, like Skinner, base their arguments on general philosophical and psychological theory. Others find support in experiments that compare the results of open education with those of traditional education.

Definition and measurement problems

These comparisons are hampered by two basic problems: first, the lack of a clear-cut definition of open education; second, the difficulty of measuring its implementation.

In studying an assortment of open-education programs, researchers were able to identify a set of characteristics that appear in varying degrees in different programs (Giaconia & Hedges, 1982; H. Marshall, 1981):

- Free choice by students of the activities in which they participate
- Flexible space
- A rich variety of learning materials
- Integration of various subject areas in the curriculum
- Emphasis on individual and small-group, as against large-group, instruction
- Teachers serving as facilitators of learning
- Students learning to take responsibility for their own learning
- Genuine mutual respect between teachers and students
- Diagnostic evaluation to help improve student learning
- Multiage grouping of children
- Team teaching

Characteristics of open education

Advocates of open education do not agree on the importance of these characteristics. Nor do they agree on ways of measuring the degree of their use in the programs. Ratings by administrators, questionnaires for teachers, observations by trained outsiders—all have been used, and all have reported different results. The degree of implementation—of actually putting the methods into practice—varied greatly from one teacher, class, school, or school district to another. The same is true of reports on the same teacher, class, school, or school district. For example, many teachers who claimed to be "open" on questionnaires were described by observers as much less so. And classrooms considered equally open in terms of a total score for openness were found to differ markedly on the various components of openness. One class might be high on freedom of choice for students and low on flexible space; another class, equal in total openness, might be low on freedom of choice and high on flexible space. Obviously this variability made comparisons difficult and interpretation difficult.

Implementation variability

These problems led H. Marshall (1981) to advocate that open education be evaluated in terms of its components (and combinations of them) rather than as a single, whole, distinct pattern. This kind of evaluation would tell more about what parts of the concept might make a difference in how pupils learn.

Exactly this type of evaluation of components was provided by Giaconia and Hedges (1982). They performed a thorough meta-analysis of approximately 150 studies. After applying sophisticated statistical and analytical devices, Giaconia and Hedges reported the results of dozens of comparisons of open and traditional classrooms on each of four academic and twelve nonacademic outcomes. Table 10.2 shows their overall results before open education was broken down into its components. These results, combining the findings of dozens of studies, suggest that open education

A meta-analysis: traditional vs. open classrooms

- usually lowers language achievement (but only by an almost negligible amount) and achievement motivation (moderately).
- has almost no consistency of effect on math, reading, and other kinds of academic achievement.
- usually improves cooperativeness, creativity, and independence to a moderate degree.

TABLE 10.2   *Summary of Results of a Meta-Analysis of Studies Comparing Open and Traditional Classrooms*

Outcome	Number of Studies	Number of Comparisons	Mean Effect Size*	Percentage of Comparisons Favoring		
				Open	Traditional	Neither
Academic Achievement						
Language	33	34	−.069	33	63	4
Math	57	64	−.037	43	52	5
Reading	63	73	−.083	42	54	4
Miscellaneous	25	23	−.153	38	55	7
Nonacademic Outcomes						
Achievement motivation	8	10	−.262	29	57	14
Adjustment	9	19	.170	58	42	0
Anxiety	19	29	−.010	49	51	0
Attitude toward school	50	68	.169	68	31	1
Attitude toward teacher	17	20	.199	67	25	8
Cooperativeness	8	7	.229	80	10	10
Creativity	22	21	.286	69	19	12
Curiosity	7	5	.165	57	29	14
General mental ability	16	13	.183	59	36	5
Independence	22	26	.278	68	30	2
Locus of control	16	19	.007	46	50	4
Self-concept	60	84	.071	53	41	6

Source: Adapted from R. M. Giaconia and L. V. Hedges, "Identifying Features of Effective Open Education," *Review of Educational Research, 52*: 579–602. Copyright 1982 American Educational Research Association, Washington, D.C.

*Positive effect sizes indicate superiority for open education; negative, for traditional education. Effect sizes of .000 to .200 are small; those higher than .200 are moderate.

- has almost no consistency of effect on adjustment, anxiety, locus of control, or self-concept.
- usually improves, but only slightly, the students' attitudes toward school and teacher, creativity, and general mental ability.

Effectiveness of separate features of education

The results in Table 10.2 show what happens when open education is accepted as an undifferentiated whole. Giaconia and Hedges (1982) went beyond this global analysis. They compared studies on the basis of the *number* of separate features of open education used in the studies in order to determine which features were associated with a larger or smaller effect in favor of open education. The features they considered included the following:

- Role of the child (degree of activity in learning).
- Diagnostic evaluation (use of work samples and observations, but seldom tests, to guide instruction).

- Materials to manipulate.
- Individualized instruction (adjusting rate, methods, and materials; using small-group methods).
- Multiage grouping of students (two or more grades housed in the same area).
- Open space (flexible use of areas and activity centers; no interior walls; flexible seating).
- Team teaching (two or more teachers sharing planning and instruction of the same students; use of parents as teaching aides).

For the nonacademic outcomes, all the features except open space and team teaching were present more often in the studies that showed large effects. These results mean that the role of the child, the use of diagnostic evaluation, the presence of many materials to manipulate, the use of individual instruction, and multiage grouping were associated with larger effects on self-concept, creativity, and attitude toward school. *For the academic outcomes, materials to manipulate and team teaching were present more often in the studies that showed large effects.* These features, then, were associated with higher achievement. Multiage grouping, on the other hand, was present less often and hence was associated with lower achievement.

These results provide the most substantial and detailed analysis of what makes what kind of difference in the effects of open education. The picture is not black and white. For certain purposes, certain features of open education seem to help; for other purposes, other features seem to hinder. Educators need to weigh their ends and means carefully. They need to search for new methods and practices that will allow fuller realization of all the goals without sacrificing either academic or nonacademic outcomes.

In sum, open education seems to have good average effects on nonacademic outcomes, namely, self-concept, creativity, and attitude toward school. It seems to have only slightly negative effects, or no consistent effects, on achievement in reading, mathematics, and language. A reasonable conclusion: Overall, open education usually does some good for attitudes without adversely affecting achievement.

The Viability of Open Education

How viable is open education? How well does it survive in the real world of schooling? Does it take hold among teachers? Once it is tried, does it last?

Cuban (1984) looked at the history of how teachers taught during the years from 1890 to 1980. He was interested in the degree to which teacher-centered or student-centered instruction prevailed. In the *teacher-centered* classrooms, teachers do more of the talking, teach the whole class at one time, and determine the use of time, and students' desks are arranged in rows facing the chalkboard. In the *student-centered* classroom, students talk as much or more

Teacher-centered classrooms

Student-centered classrooms

than the teacher, are usually taught individually or in small groups, have a voice in choosing and organizing learning and the rules of classroom conduct, and have available a variety of materials and often a voice in determining how the materials are used. Also the classroom is arranged to allow students to move around and work together. Cuban's teacher-centered instruction looks a lot like what we call traditional, or conventional, classroom teaching. And his student-centered instruction bears a close resemblance to what we call open education.

In writing his history, Cuban could not refer to systematic observational research on what went on in classrooms from 1890 to 1980 because this kind of research was extremely rare until about 1960. Instead he used an ingenious array of evidence:

- Photographs of teachers and students in class
- Textbooks and tests teachers used
- Student recollections of their experiences in classrooms
- Teacher reports of how they taught
- Reports from persons who visited classrooms, for example, journalists, parents, and administrators
- Student writings in school newspapers and yearbooks
- Research studies of teacher behavior in classrooms
- Descriptions of classroom architecture, size of rooms, desk design and placement, building plans, etc. (Cuban, 1984, pp. 7–8)

Historical viability of teacher-centered instruction

Cuban found that teacher-centered instruction predominated during the period from 1890 to 1980. And this predominance held despite major reform efforts on the part of progressive and open educators.

Cuban's findings indicate that teacher-centered instruction has been extremely viable, for better or worse. They suggest that open education was seldom adopted, and that when it was, it was usually replaced by the traditional teaching that reformers had struggled to change.

What went wrong with open education

Rothenberg (1989) tried to understand "what went wrong" with open education. Apart from being "very demanding" (see page 486), he said, open education did not seem to improve achievement (on the average), was often inadequately prepared, was used without integrating its elements into a unified approach, was inadequately monitored and so allowed students to neglect important parts of the curriculum, especially the basic skills. Perhaps the movement promised more than it could deliver. It was often opposed in schools with many low-income and minority-group students, where parents saw it as neglecting basic skills, fostering chaos, and experimenting on their children.

This historical analysis gives us an appropriate transition to the next chapter, which deals with what we call classroom teaching. Such teaching is traditional: It centers more on the teacher than the student. But it has one important advantage—viability. It is the kind of teaching toward which teachers gravitate and to which they return. But it is not an all-or-nothing proposition. Traditional teaching can be done in ways that are good for student achievement and attitudes.

SUMMARY

Individual instruction helps us cope with students' individual differences and teach them to learn independently. There are study methods—study habits— that can make independent learning more efficient. There are also teaching methods that use a mastery orientation to make learning more effective. Both mastery learning and personalized instruction systems rely on this kind of orientation to improve students' achievement and attitudes.

Schools can also use contracting and tutoring for independent learning. In general these methods of individual instruction are highly adaptive to the individual student; they allow for greater individualization of instruction.

Programmed instruction and computer-assisted instruction are other forms of individual instruction. Although programmed instruction was originally conceived for use in the major part of schoolwork, after some two decades it has become instead a way of supplementing instruction on special topics. Research on computer-assisted instruction shows moderately positive results in student achievement and attitudes, although the method's cost-effectiveness is still in question. Dialogue programs and intelligent tutoring systems that will mimic human tutors are being developed. These are likely to have strong effects on student achievement. Drill-and-practice, truly helpful at times, still remains the most prevalent form of CAI.

A couple of things to think about: First, because teachers and students are individuals, no single method works for all of us all the time. For this reason, innovation is valuable. It can give us new ways to handle problems, to reach a student who is not responding to traditional methods. Second, innovation is also difficult. Implementation (putting innovations into effect) can be demanding, and success slow, if it comes at all. A commitment to something new, then, means a commitment in time and patience—for teachers and their students.

The primary objectives of humanistic education are to increase students' self-direction and to foster their creativity, interests in the arts, and curiosity. These stem from humanistic educators' strong belief that traditional education impairs the innate creativity of children. The basic principles that underlie humanistic teaching are that students should be allowed to determine what they should learn; that students need more opportunity to learn how to learn rather than to learn any body of subject matter; that self-evaluation is more meaningful than the evaluations of others; that learning to express, communicate, understand, and cope with feelings is as important as intellectual learning; and, finally, that living and learning are best done in an atmosphere free of threats, pressures, competition, and externally imposed standards.

Open-education programs have made promising beginnings, but evaluations show that there is much room for improvement. To avoid the fate of earlier reform movements, humanistic education must buttress its claims with empirical evidence, which has been hard to obtain. History shows that teachers and schools have been slow to adopt student-centered methods of teaching and quick to replace them with traditional methods. We turn now to an examination of that traditional method, which we call classroom teaching.

11 ≡ Classroom Teaching

OVERVIEW

What can we tell you about classroom teaching that you don't already know? After all, you've been surrounded by the process for at least twenty hours a week, forty weeks a year, for more than twelve years.

What we hope to do in this chapter is introduce you to the process from two new points of view: the teacher's and the educational psychologist's. From the teacher's point of view, you'll be looking at classroom teaching as an activity in which you have the power to shape the process. You probably had little of that power when you were in the student's role. Then you did pretty much what your teacher wanted you to do. Now, as the teacher, you have the determining role and the responsibility that goes with it.

From the educational psychologist's point of view, you will be examining classroom teaching through the concepts and principles we've talked about throughout this book. You will also come across some new concepts developed expressly for the purposes of understanding and improving classroom teaching and for fostering student outcomes.

We emphasize the kind of teaching that has received the most attention from research workers—the interactive aspects of teaching in the classroom. This is what most of us think of as typical teaching because it is what we have most often experienced. We will introduce you to a diverse set of teaching behaviors that can help you plan and actually be more effective whatever the subject or grade. For the most part these behaviors have been shown to be effective through research. In a look at recitation, we talk about how the teacher's use of structuring and question-asking and probing skills help students learn in the classroom. The effects on achievement of praise, the use of students' ideas, and high rates of teacher criticism and disapproval are also noted. We finish up with an examination of seatwork, presenting the relationship between academic learning time and student achievement and suggesting how academic learning time can be improved.

Compared with the large-group (lecture), small-group (discussion), and individual teaching methods we looked at in Chapters 9 and 10, the interactive phase of classroom teaching has been overwhelmingly predominant at the elementary and secondary school levels throughout the world, including the United States. Even today, when education is changing so rapidly, classroom teaching of the type we describe in this chapter strongly prevails.

The Pattern of Classroom Teaching

Classroom teaching is what many people mean by the word *teaching*. It is the prototypical teaching method, and for that reason it has been the subject of more research than have any other major teaching methods.

At times classroom teaching combines elements of the lecture, discussion, and independent-study methods. Occasionally short, five- to fifteen-minute *lectures* are part of the program. Usually, however, the teacher allows more interruption by students' questions than is possible in a large lecture hall. If the interruptions become frequent enough and take the form of questions and responses to statements the teacher or other students have made, this kind of lecturing shades off into *discussion*. But typically classroom teaching, with students seated in rows all facing in the same direction (rather than seated around a table), is dominated far more by the teacher—the teacher does most of the talking. Finally, *independent study* may go on, especially in elementary and secondary school classrooms where teachers frequently assign *seatwork*—assignments for students to work on by themselves or with one or two other students.

But classroom teaching is more than a combination of other teaching methods. What distinguishes it is recitation—"an instructional segment in which the teacher calls on individual children to answer questions, to read in turn, or to give answers to homework. A recitation usually involves relatively short exchanges between students and teachers" (Stodolsky, Ferguson, & Wimpelberg, 1981, p. 123). Recitation took up about a third of the instructional time in mathematics and social studies observed by Stodolsky and her associates (1981).

Researchers have found evidence that recitation has persisted in somewhat the same form since at least the beginning of the twentieth century (Cuban, 1984; Hoetker & Ahlbrand, 1969). Hoetker and Ahlbrand found that nine teachers of junior high school English in St. Louis behaved in ways similar to those of the fifteen teachers of eleventh-grade economics in New York observed by Bellack, Kliebard, Hyman, and Smith (1966). That is, both groups adhered to what Bellack and his associates called the "rules of the classroom-language

Combining elements of other methods

The classroom-language game

game." Teachers in both samples did much more than half of the talking (Table 11.1). The talk was distributed similarly in the two studies, among four categories of behavior:

1. *Structuring:* Setting the context for classroom behavior by starting or ending an interaction and indicating its nature
2. *Soliciting:* Seeking a response
3. *Responding:* Fulfilling the expectation set by the soliciting behavior
4. *Reacting:* Modifying or evaluating a previous response

The ubiquitous recitation: similar across subjects, grades, countries, and decades

In Table 11.1, it is clear that teachers did most of the structuring, soliciting, and reacting. It is equally clear that pupils did most of the responding. The consistency between the two studies is impressive, and the results agree with what most of us have experienced. Further, Bellack and his associates reported that teachers tend to be highly similar in their patterns of behavior from one class session to another. And Bellack (1976) reported that the structuring-soliciting-responding-reacting formulation of recitation had been used in about thirty-five studies describing teaching at all grade levels; in subjects as varied as reading, English, mathematics, business, science, teaching, and nursing; in seven countries (Australia, Canada, Finland, West Germany, Japan, Sweden, and the United States); and in individualized instruction, in open elementary school classrooms, and in early education programs. More recently the same kinds of results were obtained in fourth-grade Finnish classes (Komulainen, Kansanen, Karma, Martikainen, & Uusikylä; 1981) and in San Diego, California, where the investigator called the pattern "initiation-reply-evaluation" (Mehan, 1979). In the United States, Goodlad and Klein (1970) and their co-workers found the recitation pattern clearly predominant across the country when they observed teaching in 260 classrooms ranging from kindergarten to grade 3 in the late 1960s. Much the same pattern emerged in a later report on another large-scale study by Goodlad (1984).

Variations within the uniformities

Within these uniformities, there are variations. Stodolsky and her co-workers (1981) found differences according to the socioeconomic status (SES) of the school district. Recitation was more frequent in lower-SES schools both in social studies and mathematics. The functions of recitation also varied in different classes. It was used for review, introducing new material, checking answers, practice, and checking understanding of materials and ideas. Often more than one purpose was served in a single recitation session. And along with these different functions came differences in students' opportunity to participate.

Stodolsky and her colleagues (1981) found that recitation had positive features. Children paid relatively good attention, they seemed to learn more easily by recitation than by seatwork, they were not highly anxious, and they did receive some attention from the teacher. The researchers also found that recitation can be boring and dull, for example, when children spend significant amounts of time taking turns reading aloud. This finding may explain why high-expenditure (high-SES) districts did not use recitations so much in social studies classes: They had other curricula and materials available.

TABLE 11.1

Comparisons Between Selected Mean Measures of Classroom Behavior in Two Studies

	Percentage of Talking			
	Bellack et al.		Hoetker & Ahlbrand	
	Teacher	Student	Teacher	Student
Structuring	14.5	3.0	22.4	3.4
Soliciting	20.3	2.5	20.6	1.2
Responding	5.0	15.6	4.3	13.1
Reacting	24.8	5.1	31.4	0.6
Total	64.6	26.2	78.7	18.3
Totals	90.8		97.0	

Source: Adapted from J. Hoetker and W. P. Ahlbrand, "The Persistence of the Recitation," *American Educational Research Journal*, 6, pp. 145–167 and 589–592. Copyright 1969 American Educational Research Association, Washington, D.C. Used by permission.

Note: Percentages within studies add to less than 100 because some talking fell into other categories of classroom behavior.

Finally, a major study, the Beginning Teacher Evaluation Study (BTES), showed that the amount of recitation was even more important than the amount of group work in which the class engaged. The amount of group work that was done correlated .31 with overall time on task. But the amount of recitation, or "the substantive interaction which took place—explanations, questions and answers, and feedback," correlated .45 with overall time on task (Rosenshine, 1980, p. 121). We will talk more about time on task later in this chapter.

Reasons for the Prevalence of the Recitation in Classroom Teaching

Why has classroom recitation been so prevalent for so long? The open-education advocates, and before them the progressive educators, argued against the teacher-centeredness of recitation. More recently (for example, Goodlad, 1984), criticisms of recitation as limiting and unimaginative have received much attention. Most recently, in advocating the revival of the open classroom, Rothenberg (1989) criticized the traditional classroom as follows:

> Recitation is a large-group activity during which all members of the class do the same task at the same time. Teachers have a high degree of control. Evaluation [of student performance] is public and comparative. . . . Students develop competitive norms and form rigid, unchanging cliques that are hierarchically ordered based on achievement. Class-task activities are ones in which students work individually or in small groups, but all students work on the same task at the same time (for example, all do the same page in a math workbook). (p. 74)

Yet recitation shows little sign of disappearing, and it has been open education that has waned.

> The studies that have been reviewed show a remarkable stability of class-room verbal behavior patterns over the past half-century, despite the fact that each successive generation of educational thinkers, no matter how else they differ, has condemned the rapid-fire, question-answer pattern of instruction. What is there about the recitation . . . that makes it so singularly successful in the evolutionary struggle with other, more highly recommended methods? (Hoetker & Ahlbrand, 1969, p. 163)

Let us look at some answers to this question about survival. As we do so, examine the excerpt from a recitation given in Figure 11.1. This example of a good recitation may explain in part why the method flourishes.

Adaptability.   First, classroom recitation, despite its apparent uniformity from one grade level and subject matter to another, is highly adaptable. If the objective is knowledge or understanding of facts, concepts, and principles, the classroom teacher can *lecture,* more or less formally, for a few minutes or more depending on the students' maturity. If the objective is the ability to examine ideas critically, the teacher can promote *discussion* in which the students' own points of view and values can be expressed. And if the objective is that students be able to work by themselves, at their own rate, on tasks suited to their own needs, the teacher can allow them to practice *independent ways of learning.*

Classroom teaching can include other methods

Just how much lecturing, discussion, and individual study actually go on in classrooms can be estimated from the findings of Stodolsky and her co-workers (1981), which are summarized in Table 11.2. The table is based on extensive observation in eighteen mathematics and seventeen social studies classes in the fifth grade, in schools in twenty-two school districts in the Chicago area. The data show that

- lectures were used infrequently, as we would expect at this grade level.
- recitation tended to be more frequent in mathematics than in social studies, and in low-SES classes than in high-SES classes.
- seatwork was more frequent in mathematics and in low-SES classes.
- small-group work was much more frequent in social studies classes, especially in high-SES classes.

The nature of the subject matter makes the differences between mathematics and social studies classes easier to understand. But what about the differences among SES groups? These differences may reflect teachers' adaptations to their perceptions of their students' ability levels, which are correlated with SES. They may also reflect the variations in richness of the curriculum materials available in schools with different levels of financial support.

FIGURE 11.1

**Example of Recitation
in a Ninth-Grade Class**

Setting

Discussion of the book *Roll of Thunder, Hear My Cry*. John (a student) has summarized chapter four, while the teacher has tried to write his key points on the chalkboard.

Transcript

Teacher [to the class as a whole]:   Wow! What do you think about that?

Student: It was very thorough.

Teacher: Yeah, pretty thorough. I had a lot of trouble getting everything down [on the board], and I think I missed the part about trying to boycott. [Reads from the board]: ". . . and tries to organize a boycott." Did I get everything down, John, that you said?

John: What about the guy who didn't really think these kids were a pest?

Teacher: Yeah, okay. What's his name? Do you remember?

John: [indicates he can't remember]

Another student: Wasn't it Turner?

Teacher: Was it Turner?

Students: Yes.

Teacher: Okay, so Mr. Turner resisted white help. Why? Why would he want to keep shopping at that terrible store?

John: There was only one store to buy from because all the other ones were white.

Teacher: Well, the Wall Store was white too.

Another student   [addressed to John]: Is it Mr. Holling's store? Is that it?

John: No. Here's the reason. They don't get paid till the cotton comes in. But throughout the year they still have to buy stuff—food, clothes, seed, and stuff like that. So the owner of the plantation will sign for what they buy at the store so that throughout the year they can still buy stuff on credit.

Teacher [writing on board]:   So "he has to have credit in order to buy things, and this store is the only one that will give it to him."

John: [continues to explain]

Teacher: [continues to write on board]

Another student: I was just going to say, "It was the closest store."

(continues)

FIGURE 11.1

Continued

Teacher [writing on board]:   Okay—it's the closest store; it seems to be in the middle of the area; a lot of sharecroppers who don't get paid cash—they get credit at that store—and it's very hard to get credit at other stores. So it's going to be very hard for her to organize that boycott; she needs to exist on credit. Yeah? [nods to another student]
[Discussion continues]

Analysis by Nystrand and Gamolan

Noteworthy is the seriousness with which the teacher treats the students ideas. She summarizes his points and notes for clarifications. She shows meticulous interest in John's thinking. She is genuine in her interest. She models the kinds of questions and issues germane to a realistic discussion of literature. Her questions are authentic—not "test" questions. [We return to this kind of recitation later in this chapter.]

Source: Adapted from Nystrand and Gamolan (1991, pp. 264–265).

Teacher variability around averages

Also the data here are only average percentages. They do not tell us about the variability among teachers around these averages. (Some teachers were far above and some were below these percentages.) This variability would suggest that classroom teaching is used for lectures, discussions, and individual study in just the ways that might help us understand the widespread use of the method. Classroom teaching allows teachers to take advantage of all of the other major approaches to teaching in proportions suited to the students' abilities, the teacher's temperament and training, and the requirements of the subject matter and educational objectives.

Reinforcement Value.   A second reason for the prevalence of classroom recitation is that it may be reinforcing to the teacher (White, 1974). The teacher has several ways of finding out whether students are learning: checking their homework, using teacher-made or standardized tests, and asking questions in class. Of these, the last is by far the easiest, the fastest, and the most interesting. In addition, it is usually more relevant to what has been taught than are standardized tests. The other methods are not nearly as reinforcing because recitation also provides social reinforcement. That is, the pupils provide not only correct answers but, through the attention they pay the teacher, social reinforcement.

Social reinforcement

The correct answers come forth, however, only if the questions can readily be answered, if they are not too complex for the class. White (1974) suggested that only simple "fact questions" are reinforcing. But teachers can also learn to

TABLE 11.2

Average Percentages of Segments* Used for Various Instructional Formats in Grade 5

Format Type	Mathematics			Social Studies		
	Low SES	Middle SES	High SES	Low SES	Middle SES	High SES
Seatwork	42.6	19.5	21.9	17.2	15.0	4.9
Diverse seatwork	0.6	2.1	7.8	1.5	2.8	6.2
Individualized seatwork	1.2	13.6	20.3	—	—	—
Recitation	37.7	27.1	18.8	29.1	17.7	5.6
Discussion	—	—	3.1	3.7	3.3	3.1
Lecture	2.5	1.7	—	—	1.1	—
Demonstration	—	0.4	1.6	0.7	1.7	0.6
Checking work	6.2	7.6	1.6	3.0	3.9	—
Test	3.7	3.8	1.6	1.5	2.2	1.2
Group work	—	2.1	4.7	26.9	28.9	58.0
Film/audiovisual	—	—	—	3.7	2.8	5.6
Contest	0.6	14.0	1.6	0.7	3.3	—
Student reports	—	—	—	0.7	2.8	4.9
Giving instructions	4.3	5.9	6.2	7.5	10.6	8.6
Preparation	—	1.7	1.6	0.7	3.3	1.2
Tutorial	—	0.4	9.4	—	—	—
Other	0.6	—	—	2.2	0.6	—
Total instructional segments	100%	100%	100%	100%	100%	100%

Source: Adapted from S. S. Stodolsky et al., "The Recitation Persists But What Does It Look Like," *Journal of Curriculum Studies, 13*:121–130. Copyright 1981. Used by permission.

*"A segment is defined as a unique time-block in a lesson which possesses one instructional format, a specified curriculum content and student participants, and occurs in a fixed physical setting" (p. 122).

be reinforced by answers that reflect high-level cognitive processes at work and show that students are struggling with more complex answers. Whatever the nature of the questions, recitation may be prevalent because it provides teachers with reinforcement that is relatively easy to obtain. This reinforcement need not sacrifice student achievement if classroom recitation is used with the kinds of variety, flexibility, and skill we talk about in this chapter.

Lack of Knowledge of Alternatives.   Third, teachers may use the recitation and other features of classroom teaching simply because they don't know any other way to teach. If their training has not been influential, teachers tend to teach as they themselves were taught. So the classroom-teaching process is handed down from one generation of teachers to the next.

Class Size.   Fourth, class size can promote the use of classroom recitation. The vast majority of public schools in the United States are organized into

Advantages of smaller class size

classes of approximately thirty students (plus or minus fifteen). This structure was supported by research that has generally been interpreted to show that class size, within the range from about fifteen to forty-five students, makes no difference in academic achievement. Yet teachers have long insisted that they can do a better job with smaller classes. And meta-analyses back up that claim. Cahen, Filby, McCutcheon, and Kyle (1983) reviewed dozens of class size and achievement studies. They concluded that if a student at the 50th percentile rank on a nationally standardized test was to be placed in a class of forty for an academic year, that student would probably score at under the 40th percentile rank at the end of the year. But if that same student was placed in a class of fifteen, he or she would be likely to achieve at over the 60th percentile rank. Why? Probably because teachers in smaller classes can more readily spend time on writing assignments, monitor students' time on task, create individualized programs, and provide feedback.

High cost of class-size reduction

Knowing that smaller classes are more effective and creating them are two different things. A major problem is cost. In a large-population state a reduction in class size of one student throughout the state would cost millions of dollars each year. The arithmetic is simple. Divide 1,000,000 by 30 to get the number of teachers needed for 1,000,000 pupils in classes of 30; the answer is 33,333. Now divide 1,000,000 by 29; the answer is 34,483. Another 1,150 teachers would be needed for classes of 29. If the annual pay for teachers averages $30,000, we would need $34.5 million to reduce class size by just one student, from 30 to 29, and that would not cover the cost of facilities, because an additional 1,150 classrooms would be needed. Of course, large states have not one million but several million pupils. And reducing class size at all grades from 30 to 15, to obtain a substantial improvement in education, would increase the cost much much more.

Physical Arrangements of Classrooms.   A fifth problem is that until recently schools have been built and staffed in ways that encourage traditional classroom teaching. The rigid physical arrangement of traditional classrooms fosters classroom recitation. Fixed seats facing in the same direction make discussions harder to conduct than do circular seating arrangements, where students can see one another (see Chapter 9). And even where movable seats

Immovable movable seats

are provided, teachers often arrange them in rows facing forward, as though the seats were immovable. Immovable movable seats!

Fitness for Basic Tasks.   Sixth, classroom teaching allows teachers to perform three basic tasks: presenting what they want to teach, giving students opportunities to practice the material, and setting up conditions for ensuring that their students are prepared for and interested in learning (Westbury, 1973). Classroom teaching can be used to promote all of the various kinds of achievement. It makes possible mixing the other three approaches (lecturing, discussion, individual study) with recitation in various proportions.

Classroom Teaching: An Orchestration of Methods

Classroom teaching, with a large component of recitation and seatwork, consists in large part of a synthesis of lecturing and explaining (Chapter 9), the discussion method (Chapter 9), individual instruction (Chapter 10), and what we call humanistic teaching (Chapter 10). Classroom teaching uses different forms of these methods at certain times, for certain purposes, for all or certain students in the class. This combination makes sense. Teachers and students have more than one objective in any unit of instruction. And for any objective, and for any group of students, some methods are more effective than others.

A combination makes sense

But classroom teaching is more than a combination of other teaching methods. Think for a minute about *orchestration,* the way music is arranged for an orchestra. The composer weaves musical themes and sections of the orchestra together to achieve artistic effects. The composition is more than the separate themes and the instrument designations. It is also the connections, relationships, and transitions between them. It is this sequencing that determines the effect of the whole. It is the relationship between notes, not the individual notes themselves, that determines the melody. That's why a change in key does not change the melody.

Importance of connections and sequences

In classroom teaching the relationships among methods are just as important as the teaching methods themselves. The time we give to each method—and the sequences, rates, structures, and variations we use—all determine the character of our teaching. It is not enough to study the component parts of the method; we have to look at the "symphony" as a whole.

The Planning and Interactive Phases of Classroom Teaching

The classroom teacher's work goes on in two phases: planning and interactive. In the interactive phase, the teacher is actually face to face with the students, interacting with them in the give-and-take of learning. This is social interaction: two or more people stimulating and responding to one another. We deal with the interactive phase of teaching later in this chapter.

In the planning phase, teachers work alone (or, in team teaching, with other teachers) preparing their teaching. They think about objectives and about their students. They organize course materials and schedules. They plan assignments, exercises, learning experiences, field trips, demonstrations, visual aids, audiotapes, discussion outlines, and tests of achievement. They consider the class as a whole, its interests and ability level, and the individual students, their achievements and problems.

Planning goes on both before and after the interactive phase. *Preinteractive* reflection and planning come before a course or term begins and before each

Preinteractive planning

● *In the planning phase, teachers work alone or in teams. (© Alan Carey/The Image Works)*

Postinteractive reflection

class meeting. *Postinteractive* reflection and planning take place after each class meeting and after a course is over.

In earlier chapters we've talked about objectives, about the purposes of your teaching. We've talked about student characteristics and how intelligence, personality, gender, and culture affect the ways students learn and are motivated. And we've talked about several distinct teaching methods—the kinds of objectives and students for which each is most suitable and the ways in which they should be carried out. All of this has been designed to prepare you for the planning phase of classroom teaching. It is here that you synthesize all these concepts and principles, that you make decisions about the way you will teach.

Decision-making

Decision-making is a critical part of planning. You are going to spend a good deal of time deciding on textbooks and other curricular materials; on schedules for rates of progress, examinations, report cards, and the like; and on out-of-class assignments and activities (homework, field trips). And you are going to spend a good deal of time modifying those decisions. Most educators believe that teachers should organize their teaching as much as possible before they meet their students, at the same time staying ready to revise their plans once they meet their students and learn about their students' abilities, interests, previous learning, and experience.

How Teachers Plan

The importance of planning cannot be overestimated. Decisions made by teachers while planning instruction have a profound influence on their classroom behavior and on the nature and outcomes of the education children receive. Teachers' instructional plans serve as "scripts" for carrying out interactive teaching. (Shavelson, 1987, p. 483)

In Chapter 2 we described a model of the instructional process. This model identifies five primary teaching tasks: (1) choosing objectives, (2) determining student characteristics, (3) understanding and using ideas about the nature of learning and motivation, (4) selecting and using methods of teaching, and (5) evaluating student learning. The model is a rational one in that the first step is deciding where you want to go before you choose a means of getting there.

We know the model is prescriptive: It defines the ways teachers *should* begin to plan. But is it also descriptive? Does it tell us how teachers actively go about planning teaching?

While this prescriptive model of planning may be one of the most consistently taught features of the curriculum of teacher education programs, the model is consistently *not* used in teachers' planning in schools. Obviously there is a mismatch between the demands of classroom instruction and the prescriptive planning model. The mismatch arises because teachers must maintain the flow of activity during a lesson or face behavioral management problems. (Shavelson & Stern, 1981, p. 447)

Mismatch between teaching demands and prescriptive planning model

Another possible reason for the mismatch between the model and what teachers do may be that teachers do formulate objectives, as the model prescribes, but only implicitly, almost unconsciously. It may be that research techniques for describing what teachers do have not been subtle and searching enough to reveal the objectives that teachers have in mind without being able to talk about them.

Implicit planning?

What do teachers actually do? They focus on activities and tasks: what they want their students to do and how to get them to do it. Shavelson (1987) notes that these tasks are made up of

- content, often in a textbook.
- materials, including things to manipulate.
- activities—the things to be done in the lesson, in sequence, with a given pace and timing.
- goals, or general aims, which are less specific than objectives.
- references to students whose characteristic needs must be considered, especially early in the year.
- references to the class as a whole, including groups of students within it.

What teachers' planning focuses on

• Decisions made by teachers while planning instruction have a profound influence on students. (© Jean-Claude Lejeune)

A Finnish study of teacher planning

The same general picture emerged from a study in Finland. Kansanen (1981) interviewed six teachers about their "ways of thinking during the preinteractive phase of teaching" (p. 34). Table 11.3 summarizes the activities in which teachers engaged regularly or quite regularly, sometimes, or not at all. Kansanen noted that "the teachers did not think on the basis of objectives. None of them ever mentioned the objectives as guidelines in their thinking" (p. 35).

Notice the variety of activities in the table and how the teachers used them. All six regularly made mental outlines, used the textbook and its guide, and planned the forms of activities. All made short-term plans and used background material, at least sometimes. And most never wrote an outline in detail (or any outline!), consulted with their colleagues, or planned homework in detail. Otherwise they had little in common. Teachers A, C, and F performed many of these activities; teachers B, D, and E, relatively few.

The different ways of planning Kansanen described probably could be found among teachers everywhere, and what Kansanen had to say about the teacher's role also applies outside Finland:

> The curriculum is written in such a way—at least in Finland—that all goals do not emerge in the teaching material. The general aims . . . won't be realized if the teachers do not know the curriculum and the goals. It is easy to see how important a person the teacher in the teaching process really is. (1981, p. 37)

TABLE 11.3

*Finnish Teachers'
Activities During the
Planning Phase*

Activity	Teacher					
	A	B	C	D	E	F
Long-term planning	R	N	R	S	N	R
Short-term planning	R	S	R	S	S	R
Form of the plan						
Mental outline	R	R	R	R	R	R
Following the textbook	R	R	R	S	R	R
Written outline	R	N	S	N	N	N
Written outline in detail	S	N	N	N	N	N
Facilities in planning						
Nationwide curriculum	R	N	S	N	N	R
Local curriculum	R	N	R	N	N	R
Textbook	R	R	R	R	R	R
Teacher's guide for the textbook	R	R	R	R	R	R
Colleagues	N	N	S	N	N	N
Background material	S	S	S	S	S	R
Content of the plan						
Forms of activities	R	R	R	R	R	R
Audiovisual material	R	S	S	N	S	R
Homework	S	N	N	N	N	N
Evaluation	S	N	R	N	N	R

Source: Adapted from P. Kansanen, "The Way Thinking Is: How Do Teachers Think and
Decide," from E. Komulainen and P. Kansanen (Eds.), *Classroom Analysis: Concepts, Findings,
Applications.* Helsinki: Institute of Education, University of Helsinki, 1981.

Note: R = regularly or quite regularly; S = sometimes; N = never.

Humanistic educators have a special problem with planning and objectives.
Remember, one primary goal of open education is to allow students a greater
voice in their learning, to give them the freedom to choose what and how they
learn. This means they must have input into the objective-setting process. One
model that allows for that input is the *integrated ends-means model* (Zahorik,
1975, 1976a). The model assumes that ends do not necessarily need to be
specified before means are selected; but that ends should "emerge from activity
to redirect the activity and add meaning to it. Learning activity becomes a
primary consideration from this perspective rather than a secondary consideration" (Zahorik, 1976a, p. 489). This perspective means that the activities
students choose are as important as the objectives. And the objectives should
be determined by the students with a teacher's guidance.

**Integrated ends-
means model**

Yinger (1980) observed and recorded one first-and-second-grade teacher's
behavior for forty days during the first twelve weeks of the school year. He also
recorded the teacher's thinking aloud during planning sessions. Later he observed the teacher's planning behavior in a simulated planning task. He found
that the teacher's planning dealt with instructional *activities* (the basic units in

Activities

Routines

which the planning went on), which had seven elements: location, structure and sequence, duration, participants, criteria of acceptable student behavior, instructional moves or routines, and content and materials. Planning also focused on four teaching *routines:* activity, instruction, management, and executive planning. These routines simplified classroom activities and make them predictable. (Note that activities are performed by students, while routines are carried out by teachers.)

Levels of planning

From the study Yinger identified five levels of planning: yearly, term, unit, weekly, and daily. At any given level, the teacher plans goals, uses information sources, and uses criteria for judging the plan's effectiveness. Yinger also concluded that planning entails problem finding (formulation) as well as problem solving.

Problem-finding

Problem-finding is the process by which one becomes aware of a problem that needs to be solved. In teacher planning, problem-finding is the discovery of a potential instructional idea that requires further planning and elaboration. (1980, p. 115)

Problem solving goes on through the "progressive elaboration of plans." Finally, the plan is put into effect and evaluated. If it works, it becomes part of the teacher's routine.

Nested planning

A similar study of six middle-school teachers (D. S. Brown, 1988) also found that planning was "nested": planning for days took place within weeks; planning for weeks was determined by plans for units of subject matter; planning for units, within planning for the semester and the year. The amount of detail increased in going from the larger "nests" to the smaller ones. Teachers revised plans at each level, each revision being based on the previous day's or year's experience. The teachers used unit notebooks containing notes, handouts, worksheets, audiovisual aids, quizzes, and tests—all based on previous experience and revised to fit the current year's students and schedule. Textbooks, the school calendar, the district curriculum guide, and less often, the state's statement of objectives were taken into account. Plans took the form of sketchy outlines of content and activities, lists, notes, homework assignments, textbook exercises, and reminders about things to tell students about procedures.

A beginning teacher's planning

The fantasy stage

If teachers' planning relies heavily on their previous experience with the same content, activities, and units, how do teachers plan when they have no previous experience to rely on? Here we have only the results of one case study (Bullough, 1987) of a single beginning seventh-grade teacher of English, social studies, and reading, who was observed and interviewed repeatedly during her first year of teaching. She paid little attention to district objectives and guidelines. During the year she went through three stages: fantasy, survival, and mastery. In the *fantasy* stage, she relied on her imagination, on her experience with her own children, and on other teachers to select materials and organize activities. She feared having problems in controlling her class, made guesses about how long each activity would take, then experienced real classroom-control problems.

After three weeks, she moved into the *survival* state, where she realized she needed to plan for control and order. She developed policies for dealing with students who did not finish their work, handed assignments in late, or misbehaved. Similarly, she developed ways of moving students from one activity to another. She discovered by chance the school's policy of "assertive discipline." She realized she should have established these policies at the beginning of the school year. She encountered students of kinds that were new to her: low in ability, altogether uninterested and unmotivated, unpredictable in behavior, or prone to violence against classmates. Control became her main concern, even for instructional matters. She gave up her language arts activity centers, scheduled a quiet activity after lunch to calm students down, and avoided unusual kinds of activity. In identifying activities and routines, she began to realize that other teachers' ideas often did not fit her values or her students. By trial and error she found activities that worked, or went the way she'd planned. Sometimes her actions were erratic and confused her class.

In the *mastery* stage, she had developed her own teaching style. She knew herself and her students more accurately and so acquired more appropriate expectations—about how long assignments would take and how the students would behave. She also made more accurate comparisons of herself with other teachers, and her confidence improved. So did her pacing and transitions, her feeling of control, her ability to plan effective activities and an appropriate curriculum. She planned in more detail. Control became a less central concern, as compared with student learning. Her behavior became smoother, more consistent, less impulsive. Her planning "became a part of life, something she was continually doing even while teaching" (Bullough, 1987, p. 244). To become better organized, she wrote notes to herself as reminders. She monitored the relationship between content and activity more closely. As a result, less class time was wasted.

This teacher's experiences during her first year may tell as much about the inadequacies of her training as about how planning should proceed. But the transition from fantasy to survival to mastery seems natural and typical. It suggests what we discuss next.

A Hierarchy of Planning Needs

Think back to our discussion of motivation in Chapter 8. We talked about a hierarchy of personal needs. Hunger and thirst must be satisfied before we attend to other needs, which in turn must be met before we can achieve the highest level of motivation, self-actualization. In the same way, classroom needs fall into a rough order of priority.

We must establish classroom *discipline, control,* and *management.* Without some kind of order in the classroom, nothing much of educational value can be done. Second, we have to *control our biases* and deal with all students fairly. Third, we need to use our *pedagogical content* knowledge. Fourth, we must plan to provide *scaffolding* for our students—instructional supports that help them learn in the less structured areas of curriculum. Finally, when all these kinds of planning have been done and the corresponding needs of the classroom have been taken into account, we are ready to plan for *variety and flexibility*. There is more to this last kind of planning than simply making a class more fun. Variety and flexibility are found more often in classes where students learn more.

Planning for Classroom Discipline and Management

Discipline: prime cause of teacher failure

We turn now to an issue that many teachers and principals believe is the most important cause of teacher failure—the problems of discipline, of classroom control and management. "The most common type of failure is weakness in maintaining discipline. This particular form of failure is the leading cause for dismissal in studies of teacher failure which have been conducted over the past seventy years" (Bridges, 1986, p. 5). When students misbehave or disrupt activities in any of a hundred different ways, the teacher has failed to create the environment necessary for classroom teaching and learning. That failure can also be reflected in a classroom that is too quiet.

Factors Beyond the Teacher's Control

The mass media tell us that problem behavior in the schools is widespread. Teachers in many schools know from their own experience the problems of tardiness, truancy, insubordination, profanity, vandalism, and violence. Although the problems are serious today, there is a question about whether they are worse than they used to be. Doyle (1978) compared the 1890s and the 1970s and concluded that "students today are behaving no worse than they used to behave" (p. 14). On the other hand, Check (1979) concluded from responses by 634 teachers in Wisconsin and Iowa that most teachers (about 62 percent) felt that "their discipline problems were more extensive now than five years ago" (p. 135); this feeling was much more prevalent among elementary and middle school teachers (79 percent) than among senior high school teachers.

Is discipline worse nowadays?

Societal factors

Teachers are affected by violence and vandalism, but they are not solely responsible for causing or reducing it. Some causes reside in the same societal factors that produce crime outside the schools—parental rejection of children, poverty, violence on television, the frustration of low scholastic aptitude or achievement (correlations between achievement and aggression are −.39 for boys and −.36 for girls), and peer and gang influences (Feldhusen, 1979).

School factors

Still beyond the control of the typical teacher are the causes of behavior problems that stem from the way schools are organized. Sometimes school structure forces students to take courses that are inappropriate for them, that do not allow for their individual needs or level of achievement. This kind of structure breeds failure and threatens self-esteem. And delinquent behavior is one way of escaping that failure and threat. Several researchers have concluded that the family plays a much larger role than the school in causing delinquency (Feldhusen, Thurston, & Benning, 1973; McPartland & McDill, 1977). Yet the schools do play a significant role (Edmonds, 1981; Purkey & Smith, 1983; Rutter, Maughan, Mortimore, & Ouston, 1979). Schools that are impersonal and overcrowded, and that have weak administrative leadership, low expectations concerning student achievement, little emphasis on basic skills, large classes that prevent teachers from helping or even identifying students who need special attention, poor communication between school and home—schools that operate under these conditions contribute to the crime, delinquency, and problem behavior that exist in them.

By and large these problems lie beyond the scope of educational psychology operating alone. These are problems that need the attention of all the social and behavioral sciences—in particular, economics, political science, sociology, and social psychology. Political and economic forces operating at levels far beyond the local community create conditions that cause poverty, alienation, and profit-seeking commercialism. It is this commercialism, for example, that leads television to emphasize the seductive, degrading violence that many researchers believe is a cause of aggression in our youngsters (for example, Leifer, Gordon, & Graves, 1974; Liebert, 1974).

Political and economic forces

The Teacher's Role: Two Categories of Problem Behavior

Of course there are things the individual teacher can do when students misbehave in the classroom. The strategies we use to cope with problem behavior depend on the kind of problem behavior we run into: too many unwanted behaviors or too few wanted ones. The first category includes physical aggression, moving around the room at inappropriate times, making too much noise, challenging authority at the wrong time or in the wrong way, and making unjust or destructive criticisms and complaints. The second category includes failing to pay attention, to show interest in work, to interact appropriately with other students, to attend school, to be prompt, and to be sufficiently independent. In one study, elementary school teachers were asked to rank problem behaviors on the basis of how tolerable they were (Safran & Safran, 1984). The researchers identified two clusters of behaviors that the teachers found most intolerable:

Too much unwanted vs. too little wanted behavior

- Negative aggression (pokes, torments, or teases classmates; destroys others' property; verbally belittles others; breaks classroom rules)
- Poor peer cooperation (works poorly with peers; will not cooperate with other children by sharing equipment or materials)

Intolerable behaviors

The least tolerable behaviors, then, were outer directed or disruptive, having an effect on other pupils. Irrelevant thinking, need for direction, or failure anxiety—considered self- or teacher-directed—were thought to be less intolerable by the teachers.

The difference between these two kinds of problem behaviors is reflected in how we plan to handle them. The "too much" kind calls for extinction or punishment—two ways of weakening or eliminating unwanted behavior that we

Least tolerable behaviors affect others

described in Chapter 6. The "too little" kind calls for reinforcement, which strengthens behavior.

Strategies for Too Much Unwanted Behavior

In general, our strategies for dealing with too much of an unwanted behavior are to prevent it, to extinguish it, to elicit incompatible behavior, or to punish it.

Prevention.   Certain managerial skills of teachers were considered to prevent unwanted behavior. Kounin (1970) identified several of these skills:

Withitness
- *Withitness,* the knack of seeming to know what is going on all over the room, of having "eyes in the back of your head." A teacher's awareness, and the students' awareness of it, make a difference. Teachers with high withitness make few mistakes in identifying which student is misbehaving, in determining which of two misbehaviors is the more serious, or in timing an effort to stop a misbehavior.

Overlappingness
- *Overlappingness*—attending to two or more behavior problems at the same time—without getting confused or losing awareness of all of the problems.

Momentum
- Maintaining *momentum;* effective teachers don't allow their classes to slow down.

Smoothness
- *Smoothness;* effective teachers are able to maintain a continuous flow of activities without being distracted or distracting students during changes in activities.

Group alerting
- *Group-alerting* skill, the ability to manage recitations in ways that keep students involved, attentive, and alert, perhaps by maintaining suspense about the kinds of questions that are going to be asked next or who is going to be called on.

These carefully derived measures of teacher's sensitivity and behavior are based on Kounin's analysis of videotape recordings. They correlate positively with students' involvement in their work and with the absence of misbehavior in the classroom. Also, in studies by Brophy and Evertson (1974), the degree to which teachers were observed behaving in these ways was positively associated with students' achievement in reading in the early elementary school grades.

Having managerial skills is obviously an important part of the prevention process. And so is knowing when to use them. The beginning of the school year is an especially important time in terms of classroom management. In the first **Setting a pattern** few weeks, you set the pattern that determines how well your classes will be organized and managed during the rest of the school year. Emmer, Evertson, and Anderson (1980), in a study of third-grade teachers, observed that more effective classroom managers achieved certain conditions in the first three weeks of the year:

- more workable systems of rules.
- a greater degree of being in touch with their students' needs and problems.
- a tendency to give clear directions and instructions.

Similar practices characterized more effective junior high school teachers observed during the first three weeks of the school year (Evertson & Emmer, 1982). At this grade level, however, there was less emphasis on the teaching of rules and procedures. Rather, these teachers became more effective by communicating more clearly what they expected of their students, checking up on whether students did what was expected, providing students with information to help correct deviant behavior, and giving students responsibility for getting their own work done.

Clear instructions and expectations

Extinction.   One way of stopping misbehavior is to extinguish it, to withhold reinforcement. This usually means not paying attention to it—a strategy that seems paradoxical but has been found repeatedly to work (see O'Leary & O'Leary, 1977). Where it is feasible, simply ignore the student. Turn your back, pay attention to a student who is behaving properly, walk away. Don't give the student who is misbehaving the attention that has often been found to result in unintentional reinforcement of unwanted behavior. Teachers have for centuries been undermining their own purposes by scolding, threatening, shaming, and even physically punishing students who have misbehaved. And many of those students, reacting to the teacher's attention, even unfavorable attention, have repeated the same offense or found some new one.

Withholding attention

What if a student's misbehavior is being reinforced by other students' amusement or admiration? You can ask the other students to ignore the behavior too. Model the ignoring behavior for them, and keep them occupied with interesting tasks so that ignoring their classmate is that much easier. If the other students call your attention to their classmate's misbehavior, simply change the subject and continue with whatever you were doing or talking about before the misbehavior occurred.

Have students withhold attention

Extinction takes time. It may be a while before a child's misbehavior begins to decrease. But be careful. Even an occasional unintentional reinforcement on your part can undo the whole process. In Chapter 6 we talked about reinforcement schedules. By changing from a continuous nonreinforcement schedule to a variable schedule, you can make it extremely difficult to extinguish behavior. So you and your students must ignore the unwanted behavior consistently. (Your own behavior—ignoring the disruptive student—will be reinforced by the gradual extinction of the problem behavior!)

Brophy and Putnam (1979) saw the need for exceptions to the extinction approach:

Certain misbehaviors are too disruptive or dangerous to be ignored. Some students interpret lack of overt disapproval as approval. . . . More generally, it is contrary to common and accepted practice to ignore open defiance, obscenity, or hostility directed specifically at the teacher. . . . Attempts to ignore here will confuse students and leave them with the impression that the teacher is not consistently aware of what is going on or is completely unable to cope with it. (p. 206)

When to intervene

When to intervene was discussed by Doyle (1986). The decision to do so depends on which pupil is misbehaving and the nature and timing of the misbehavior. If the student is a frequent misbehaver, intervention is more appropriate. Intervention becomes even more suitable if the misbehavior is serious and highly inappropriate. When misbehavior takes place during an important instructional sequence or learning activity, teachers are more likely to intervene.

Strengthening Incompatible Behavior.   The idea here is to strengthen (reinforce) a wanted behavior that is incompatible with the unwanted behavior. For example, if a student has been blurting out, without raising his hand and getting permission before he speaks, you can call on him *before* he talks without permission, and you can call on him whenever he does raise his hand and praise him for doing so. If a student has been fighting with others who have been calling her names on the playground, you can ask her to make a competing response, to write down the name-caller's name on a slip of paper and ignore the name calling (Clarizio, 1971). The writing is incompatible with the fighting. Or

Remove controlling stimulus

you can replace stimuli that have come to trigger unwanted behavior with stimuli that bring forth acceptable behavior. If fighting breaks out primarily during certain games, substitute other games. If fighting breaks out whenever two students get together, put each of them with another student with whom they get along.

Punishment.   Use punishment as a last resort—only when you've tried everything else and have not been able to reduce the unwanted behavior to a level that permits effective teaching. But if punishment is necessary, don't be afraid to use it. If the education of other students suffers too much because of the misbehavior of one or two, your responsibility is to do what is needed, including punishing, to make effective teaching possible.

Punishment can take the form of (1) soft reprimands, (2) reprimands coupled with praise and prompts to behave appropriately, (3) social isolation, (4) response cost or point loss (O'Leary & O'Leary, 1977), and (5) corporal punishment. The soft reprimand is one heard only by the student concerned and is often (but not always) more effective than one that other students can hear (O'Leary, Kaufman, Kass, & Drabman, 1970).

Negative attention

Also teachers whose classes are excessively disruptive can use *negative attention.* This means responding quickly to unwanted behavior with words (an emphatic "Wait your turn," "That's enough," or "Not now") or with facial expressions, tone of voice, movements, and gestures that indicate the student is misbehaving. Important here too are quick positive attention and reinforcement when the student begins behaving appropriately. Time-out, depriving the student of time for having fun (see Chapter 6), can also be used. Using role-playing, researchers trained teachers in these behaviors (F. H. Jones & Miller, 1974). They found that these new behaviors reduced disruptiveness and that the trained teachers were still using these skills when observed three months later.

Corporal punishment is a controversial idea. Recall what was said in Chapter 6 about the justifiable use of mild electric shocks to eliminate dangerous and harmful head-banging in autistic children. But in regular classrooms, most psychologists (American Psychological Association, 1975) and educators (Cryan, 1981) oppose corporal punishment. Still it has been widespread in American (Hyman & Lally, 1981) and British education (Starr, 1978; Whittaker, 1979). Apart from ethical, legal, and medical considerations (see Wessel, 1981, for a pediatrician's view), the psychological aspects are best summarized in the 1975 resolution of the American Psychological Association:

Corporal punishment

> WHEREAS: The resort to *corporal* punishment tends to reduce the likelihood of employing more effective, humane, and creative ways of interacting with children;
>
> WHEREAS: It is evident that socially acceptable goals of education, training, and socialization can be achieved without the use of physical violence against children, and that children so raised, grow to moral and competent adulthood;
>
> WHEREAS: *Corporal* punishment intended to influence "undesirable responses" may create in the child the impression that he or she is an "undesirable person"; and an impression that lowers self-esteem and may have chronic consequences;
>
> WHEREAS: Research has shown that to a considerable extent children learn by imitating the behavior of adults, especially those they are dependent upon; and the use of *corporal* punishment by adults having authority over children is likely to train children to use physical violence to control behavior rather than rational persuasion, education, and intelligent forms of both positive and negative reinforcement;
>
> WHEREAS: Research has shown that the effective use of punishment in eliminating undesirable behavior requires precision in timing, duration, intensity, and specificity, as well as considerable sophistication in controlling a variety of relevant environmental and cognitive factors, such that punishment administered in institutional settings, without attention to all these factors, is likely to instill hostility, rage, and a sense of powerlessness without reducing the undesirable behavior;
>
> THEREFORE BE IT RESOLVED: That the American Psychological Association opposes the use of *corporal* punishment in schools, juvenile facilities, child care nurseries, and all other institutions, public or private, where children are cared for or educated. (American Psychological Association, 1975, p. 632)

RECAP

You can reduce or eliminate unwanted behavior by

- preventing it.
- extinguishing it (ignoring it consistently and getting other students to ignore it consistently).
- strengthening a wanted behavior that is incompatible with the unwanted behavior (through reinforcement or by removing the stimuli—the settings or occasions—that seem to trigger the unwanted behavior).
- punishing it.

Strategies for Too Little Wanted Behavior

Many behavior problems take the form of a student's doing too little of something good—too little volunteering to recite, standing up for his or her own opinion, paying attention to what is being explained or discussed in class, being involved and active in individual or group projects. These unobtrusive kinds of behavior, in the opinion of psychiatrists and clinical psychologists, can be symptomatic of something more seriously wrong than are obvious kinds of misbehavior. A child who is excessively shy, withdrawn, and inattentive may need referral to someone in the helping professions—a psychiatric social worker, a school or clinical psychologist, or a psychiatrist—who can decide whether you ought to continue to work on the problem alone or whether the student needs some kind of specialized professional help.

Seriousness of withdrawal

One way to decide whether the problem is too serious for you to handle is to see whether your techniques do any good. Those techniques are eliciting, modeling, reinforcing, and shaping wanted behaviors (see Chapter 6).

Eliciting

We *elicit* wanted behavior by calling on the student, providing opportunities for engagement or involvement in interesting school tasks, and giving assignments that require the wanted activity. *Modeling* can be provided by showing a film, a videotape of a television program, or otherwise depicting appropriate behavior (Henderson, Swanson, & Zimmerman, 1975; O'Connor, 1972).

Modeling

Reinforcing

When the student responds to being called on, *reinforce* immediately (but not too obviously) with praise. When the student volunteers, call on him. When the student shows signs of interest or involvement, give her your attention by talking to her, accepting her ideas, falling in with her plans. When the student expresses an opinion, agree if you can do so honestly, or at least take the opinion seriously and treat it respectfully. We deal with praise again later in this chapter, when we discuss ways of improving the interactive part of classroom teaching.

One eighth-grade teacher of social studies increased on-task behavior by providing (1) contingent positive verbal feedback ("You read well, John," "I like your poster") and (2) free time during the time remaining after academic work was completed (Fontenelle & Holliman, 1983). The teacher's initial positive feedback rate was 17 percent; it increased to 94 percent after she received three one-hour training sessions. Average on-task behavior of her students increased substantially after use of the two reinforcers increased.

Here too change takes time. You cannot expect a new behavior to show up immediately or in complete form. So remember and apply the principle of *shaping* successive approximations (see Chapter 6). When the student *almost* volunteers, reinforce the tentative behavior. When the student shows a fleeting spark of interest, seize the opportunity to reinforce again with attention and praise. When the student offers a hesitant, tentative opinion, immediately accept the offer and use the idea in your next remark. As these kinds of wanted behaviors grow a little stronger, you begin—but not too quickly!—to demand a little more before you reinforce. Gradually, as much experience has shown, your patience will be rewarded. Moreover, your own strategy for shaping student behavior will be shaped by the increasingly close approximations of the student's behavior to that of an active, involved, participating, attentive, and self-respecting youngster.

Shaping

One aid in this process, for which the student may be ready, is the kind of *contracting* we discussed in Chapters 6 and 10. You can, for example, agree that the student will volunteer once each day for a week. If the contract is met, the reward will be something (within reason) that the student wants—perhaps five minutes alone with the teacher, perhaps time with a computer game, or, for an older student, perhaps a chance to use the school's new microscope. After that contract expires, make a new one, for, say, volunteering twice a day for three days in a row. Again, when the student completes the contract, give the agreed-on reward. Soon the contract becomes unnecessary as the intrinsic rewards of volunteering—being an accepted and active member of the classroom group—begin to provide the reinforcement that maintains the student's volunteering.

Contracting

RECAP

You can increase the amount of a wanted behavior by

- modeling it.
- reinforcing it.
- eliciting it.
- applying the principle of shaping successive approximations (possibly using contracts).

Whenever a student shows any bit of the wanted behavior, be ready with praise. Call on the student or provide other opportunities (assignments, student partnerships) for the student to behave in wanted ways. Accept and reward gradual approximations to the wanted behavior until they are shaped into an adequate performance.

Do such techniques for improving student behavior work? Borg and Ascione (1982) trained an experimental group of seventeen teachers in grades 3 through

An experiment demonstrating feasibility and effectiveness of teacher change

6 to use all of a set of these teaching skills. At the same time, they gave a randomly equivalent control group, made up of another seventeen teachers, an irrelevant (self-concept) training program. The nine-week training program provided pamphlets describing the skills. The teachers studied the pamphlets, applied the skills in simulated situations, practiced them in their own classrooms, and checked on their performance with partners by discussing tape recordings. Observers looked for the set of seventeen specific classroom behaviors in the classrooms of both the experimental-group teachers and the control-group teachers before and after the training. They found that the training resulted in the wanted changes in teaching behavior on fourteen of the seventeen teaching behavior variables; it was by and large effective. The students in the classes of the experimental-group teachers did better in showing on-task behavior and in avoiding both mildly and seriously deviant behavior.

If you plan and use procedures for maintaining order in your classroom, you will have the opportunity to teach. But you also need to control your biases—common human failings that are especially important in teaching. We turn now to such control.

Planning for Control of Bias

We once gave a group of new teachers, as an observation exercise, the task of classifying the students involved in the teacher-student interactions of experienced teachers. They were asked to use the following categories:

- Seated in the front half of the class versus seated in the rear half of the class
- Seated on the left-hand side of the class versus seated on the right-hand side of the class
- Minority-group members versus nonminority-group members
- Nice-looking students versus average-looking students
- Girls versus boys
- More able students versus less able students (based on IQ scores)

By simple calculations, we were able to determine the distribution of interactions expected by chance. For example, if teacher and students had one hundred interchanges, we would expect half to be with students on the left-hand side of the class and half with students on the right-hand side. If a class had ten minority-group students and twenty nonminority-group students, we would expect the distribution of the one hundred interactions to be approximately thirty-three to the minority students and sixty-seven to the nonminority students.

Teacher interactive biases

From observation, we were able to determine the actual distribution of interactions. We found that every observed teacher showed some bias. Some worked mainly with students in the front of the room. Some worked predominantly with girls; others, with boys. Some worked almost exclusively with the more able students. Not all these biases are harmful, but some certainly are.

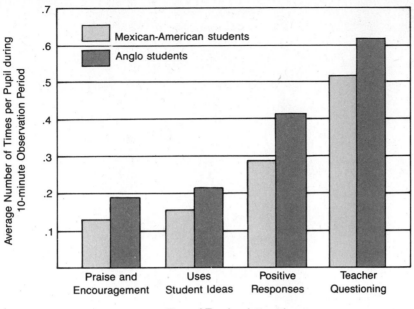

FIGURE 11.2

Teacher Interactions with Mexican-American and Anglo Students

Source: Civil Rights Commission (1973).

Bias with minorities

Bias in teacher-student interaction with minority-group members is particularly harmful. Yet the Civil Rights Commission (1973) report on Mexican-American and Anglo students' interactions with their teachers (observed in 429 classrooms throughout the Southwest) clearly revealed this kind of bias (Figure 11.2). Such bias probably still exists in many communities, and it affects achievement, attendance, school completion, and rate of college entrance among minority-group students (Valencia, 1991).

Attractiveness bias

Even the facial attractiveness of students is related to how some teachers judge or interact with them. In one study, when photographs of attractive and unattractive pupils were attached to reports and teachers were asked to make judgments about the pupils, the teachers made more favorable judgments about the attractive children (Clifford & Walster, 1973). M. Ross and J. Salvia (1975) found similar bias in teachers' predictions of students' academic achievement and need for special education. In another study, teachers in grades 4 and 5 in one school were observed in their interactions with eighty boys and girls. The interactions were classified as positive, negative, or neutral. After the observations had been made, the teachers categorized the students in several ways, including most and least attractive. The attractive boys and girls were involved in more positive interactions than were the unattractive boys and girls. Unattractive girls received more negative interactions, but there was no difference related to the attractiveness of the boys (Algozzine, 1977). These differences occurred despite the fact that there were no differences in social class (father's

• *Teachers sometimes show bias in their treatment of students. (© 1986 Susan Lapides)*

occupation) between the groups. Similar biases have been found in student-student interaction. Attractive children are more often chosen by other children for activities reflecting acceptance (Gronlund, 1959; Salvia, Sheare, & Algozzine, 1975).

Dogmatism and bias

Teachers differ in their susceptibility to bias. Babad (1979) found that some teachers differentiated much more than others in evaluating two equivalent drawings when one drawing was attributed to a high-status child and the other to a low-status child. The high-bias teachers also saw themselves as more reasonable and less emotional—tendencies that Babad attributed to their dogmatism. The same interpretation of these kinds of bias differences was made by Babad, Inbar, and Rosenthal (1982).

Overcoming your biases

Human beings simply do not act randomly; we act in ways that agree with our habits, attitudes, and expectations. Unconscious or unintentional biases are a part of those habits, attitudes, and expectations. To overcome them requires planning. If you've been short-changing a student because, say, he's Hispanic or she's not pretty, you have to make a conscious effort to interact with that student. You must plan to ask him to work on a report or to call on her to answer some questions. Try pairing your favorite student with the one you find most difficult to work with, so that interaction includes them both. Make coded notes to yourself and place them around the room. Every time you see "B > G" on your desk, it's a reminder to call on a few more boys to offset your bias. Or a sign in the back of the room with a B on it (back of room) or an R (right side) or an L (lower-income status) is a reminder to counteract your biases. More than other people, teachers have to face and compensate for their biases to avoid harming their students.

Compensating for bias

Planning for Use of Your Pedagogical Content Knowledge

Everyone agrees that teachers ought to know the subject matter of their teaching. Recently, however, we have realized that this knowledge should take a special form: *pedagogical content knowledge* (Shulman, 1986). Such knowledge consists of that which anyone trained in the subject matter possesses plus the ways in which that content can and should be taught. It would thus include ways of representing for students the structure of the field, the relative importance for students of different parts of that structure, the most useful sequence of topics for promoting student comprehension, and the strengths and weaknesses of different conceptions or emphases within the field. These "large" concerns are accompanied by "small" ones, such as the best *analogy* for explaining a given concept, the best *diagram* for illustrating a certain relationship, the best *example* of a given phenomenon, knowing the areas of the content that create *puzzlements* for most students and the best way of coping with it, and so on.

Structures, sequences, emphases

Analogies, metaphors, examples, puzzles

Some uses of your pedagogical content knowledge will be displayed on the run, as occasions arise in the course of teaching. But some can be planned: analogies, metaphors, examples, the structure of the subject or topic, and the relative importance of various topics.

Mere content knowledge itself makes a difference. For example, teachers who know a lot of math present the subject as one permitting flexibility in ways of solving problems and comprehend why different approaches succeed or fail. But teachers who know little math present the subject as something that is fixed and that has to be accepted, not necessarily understood. In history, more knowledgeable teachers tend to emphasize its uncertainty and interpretiveness, whereas those less knowledgeable tend to stress its facts, dates, and settled character.

Low content knowledge → inflexibility in teaching

Although teachers tend to avoid teaching content about which their own knowledge is weak, their knowledge level can also affect how they teach the subject. In one study, science teachers who knew the subject well used whole-group teaching more often, and less knowledgeable teachers used small-group approaches more often. Nonetheless, the former group permitted more student talk, except that, when the teachers felt less secure with the topic, they "tended to dominate the discussions" (P. Grossman, 1991, p. 207). Similar relationships were found between the teachers' knowledge level and their questions (less knowledge went with more lower-order questions).

Thus, knowledge of the subject alone is not enough for the teacher. You'll need to know your students—their typical abilities and backgrounds at their age. You'll need to know how they learn—from conditioning, from observing models (such as you, the teacher), from cognitive information processing. You need to know how your subject is formulated in the curriculum you're using and how it fits into your school system. Combined and integrated, these kinds of knowledge constitute your pedagogical content knowledge. We call attention to it here because it has only recently begun to be recognized as a kind of knowledge peculiar to teachers, as against all the other people (e.g., users, researchers) who may have something to do with a field of subject matter.

Pedagogical content knowledge builds slowly

As you might guess, pedagogical content knowledge builds slowly. It is the rare teacher who, during the first year of teaching, has the proper metaphor at her fingertips or can provide just the right example for a student unlike herself. Postinteractive reflection is the time for deciding what should be kept and what should be changed the next time that particular topic is taught.

Although pedagogical content knowledge seems important in its own right, we want to know in the long run how it connects with student learning. So, "The next step in research on teachers' subject matter knowledge will be to investigate the connection between teachers' knowledge and students' learning" (P. Grossman, 1991, p. 213).

Planning for Teaching Scaffolds, or Instructional Supports

Relatively unstructured skills

Teachers often want to help students acquire relatively unstructured skills, such as summarizing a story, taking notes, or writing a term paper. So researchers have done experiments to try out and evaluate ways of helping students along these lines. Rosenshine (1991) tracked down forty such studies and extracted tentative lessons for teachers from the ways in which the successful experiments helped students acquire such skills as reading expository and narrative text or ability to generate questions, summarize, and take tests. These "scaffolds," instructional supports, were taught to students as ways of helping them improve their abilities in these less-structured tasks. The student progresses toward increasing independence, from being a spectator to a novice, to an increasingly responsible participant, to an initiator and independent worker for

Scaffolds are temporary and adjustable

whom the teacher becomes merely an audience. The scaffolds are considered temporary and adjustable, to be abandoned after a skill (e.g., expository essay writing, writing laboratory reports, producing a news story) is acquired.

The teachers who used scaffolds in these experiments engaged in modeling, thinking aloud (while students listened), and giving prompts, aids, suggestions, and guidance. Later in the teaching, other students provided supports. Giving students examples of finished work by experts, to compare with their own work, also was used. Checklists for use by students in evaluating their own work were sometimes provided.

Rosenshine organized the findings from successful studies under four headings:

1. Assessment of students' readiness levels. This step calls for assessing the student's "zone of proximal development" (see Chapter 4), that is, the tasks that the student cannot perform by herself but could perform when guided by a teacher. The "zone" can be identified with tests, observations, and discussions with the student.
2. Presentation of new skills
   a. Development of "procedural facilitators" consists of giving students such aids as "question words" (*who, what, when,* etc.) or summarizing strategies (identify the topic, write a few words to describe the topic, and then identify the main idea). **Procedural facilitators**
   b. Modeling the strategy using the facilitator consists of the teacher's going through the steps to show how the various aids could be used to carry out the relatively unstructured task, thinking aloud as she does so.
   c. Anticipating student difficulties calls for telling students just what pitfalls they should watch for and also of selecting initial tasks that are unlikely to give the students much trouble.
   d. Increasing gradually the task's complexity means giving students problems that are still challenging but not too much so, as the students begin to acquire some skill at the task. The teacher can first give finished examples (of summarizing, for example), then half-finished examples, then even skimpier ones. Or the teacher can provide cue cards (e.g., for elements of a story: leading character, goal, obstacles, outcomes, theme). **Increasing task competency**
   e. The teacher can arrange reciprocal teaching in which a student teaches the teacher or the class or group. The students can be required to tell why they are using certain procedures. **Arrange reciprocal teaching**
   f. Similarly, the teacher can arrange for students to practice the task in small groups.
3. Provision for feedback to students and student self-checking can take various forms: giving students checklists with which to evaluate their own work, such as the completeness, nonrepetitiveness, and relevance of their summaries. Similarly, the teacher can give students models of expert work against which to compare their own.
4. Provision for students to engage in independent practice with new examples means giving students opportunities to pull the various parts of the strategy together, with less and less use of the aids and "scaffolds" provided earlier.

Although Rosenshine's review dealt only with the teaching of less-structured skills in reading and study tasks, he was able to find similar scaffolds being used in helping students increase the quantity of their writing and their ability to solve problems in mechanics in college physics and mathematics. Remember that the scaffolds do not reduce the student's need for background knowledge and understanding of relevant concepts.

TABLE 11.4	*Ways of Applying Three Types of Planning Skills to Eight Different Features of Instruction*

	Three Types of Essential Planning Skills		
Features of Instruction	Generating Alternative Instructional Procedures	Recognizing Alternative Value Assumptions	Altering the Existing Circumstances of Instruction
Diagnosing student attainment	Use teacher-constructed pretest, *or* analyze previous written assignments.	The teacher can value performance on multiple-choice tests *or* on performance tests.	If standardized tests are the required means of diagnosis, the teacher can use portfolios as additional data.
Subgrouping students for instruction	Have high-achiever work with low-achiever, *or* group all low-achievers together.	The teacher can value social learning *or* cognitive learning.	If pupils are grouped homogeneously for reading instruction, the teacher can form temporary subgroups for study of literature on the basis of varying interests.
Learning outcomes (behavioral objectives)	Given several examples, pupils will discover an appropriate rule, *or* given a rule, pupils will generate examples of it.	The teacher can value independent thinking *or* knowledge.	If behavioral objectives are required in planning instruction, the teacher can state some additional long-term goals.
Instructional resources	Use manipulative materials, *or* use a filmstrip to teach a mathematics principle.	The teacher can value concrete learning *or* abstract learning.	If a social studies film is available, the teacher can adapt it to use in a language arts lesson.
Instructional strategies	Use a structured discussion, *or* use an open-ended discussion to analyze a film.	The teacher can value an authoritarian relationship *or* a nonauthoritarian relationship with students.	If individualized instruction is the norm, the teacher can provide group instruction by making the group participation optional.
Classroom arrangements	Seat children in several small clusters for buzz sessions [brief discussions] *or* seat them in a large semicircle around the teacher to discuss contents of a film.	The teacher can value pupil-pupil interaction *or* pupil-teacher interaction.	If standard desks and chairs are provided, the teacher can move them out of the room and have students construct their own tables.
Acquiring feedback from students	Have children write answers on small individual chalkboards, *or* have them give verbal (oral) answers to questions in a grammar lesson.	The teacher can value a noncompetitive atmosphere *or* competition.	If worksheets and workbooks are the normal methods of acquiring feedback on pupil achievement, the teacher can introduce learning contracts as a new method.

TABLE 11.4	*Continued*

Features of Instruction	Three Types of Essential Planning Skills		
	Generating Alternative Instructional Procedures	Recognizing Alternative Value Assumptions	Altering the Existing Circumstances of Instruction
Providing feedback to students	Ask other pupils to evaluate a generalization stated by one pupil, *or* provide new data so pupils can test their own generalization.	The teacher can value external evaluation *or* self-evaluation.	If grading students' work is the accepted means of providing feedback to them, the teacher can begin to utilize individual conferences.

Source: Copyright by the American Association of Colleges for Teacher Education, G. Morine, "Planning Skills: Paradox and Parodies," *Journal of Teacher Education,* Volume 34, 1973, 135–143.

Planning for Variety and Flexibility

Once you've created an environment for learning, planned to control your biases, thought about your pedagogical content knowledge, and considered the scaffolding needed for the content you wish to teach, you're ready to plan for variety and flexibility in your teaching. You can create variety by changing instructional procedures, value assumptions (what is important in the learning), and the circumstances of learning. Morine (1973) integrated these three elements in three essential planning skills:

Planning skills

1. Generating alternative instructional procedures
2. Recognizing alternative value assumptions
3. Altering the existing circumstances of instruction

These skills can be applied to various features of instruction (see Table 11.4).

Suppose you are planning to diagnose student attainment of objectives. You have several ways to achieve this goal. You could use a teacher-constructed pretest, or you could analyze previous written assignments. Either of these procedures would diagnose pupil attainment. As part of your planning, you can recognize alternative value assumptions, say, testing with multiple-choice items or a performance test. And you can plan to alter the existing circumstances by analyzing the student's regular written work in addition to using standardized tests.

Alternative ways of instruction

Or suppose you want to place students in small unstructured groups. Here you might plan to have a high-achiever work with a low-achiever, or you could group low-achievers together. These alternatives place different emphases on cognitive and social learning. Altering the circumstances could take the form of grouping students according to ability for reading instruction and grouping them according to interests for teaching literature.

Table 11.4 shows how the same kind of alternative procedures, values, and circumstances can be applied to six additional areas that require planning:

- Formulating learning objectives
- Choosing instructional resources
- Choosing instructional strategies
- Arranging classrooms
- Acquiring feedback from students
- Providing feedback to students

Teaching is choosing

Teaching should involve choices. Teachers who are not prepared to make these choices tend to do what comes most readily—and this can turn into a deadly monotony.

Size of the segments varied

In thinking about variety, we need to be clear about the segments of behavior or teaching that can vary. (A segment is a piece of teaching—a piece into which any of the features of teaching, such as diagnosing student attainment, can be broken up.) The length of segments can vary. Relatively short segments would be parts of teaching that take only a minute or two, such as asking a question, gesturing, giving an explanation, using an intonation, or speaking loudly. Relatively long segments would take an hour, a day, or a week. They could take the form of a field trip, a film, a debate, a role-playing or tutoring session, or a lecture.

Style variations

Variation in classroom teaching can also refer to style and method. *Style* is the way the teacher expresses himself or herself; it is reflected in the teacher's gestures, movement about the room, tone and volume of voice, warmth, humor, and enthusiasm. *Method* refers to the more formal and self-conscious aspects of teaching; the ways in which the teacher interacts with students; the kinds of questions asked (lower or higher order); how questions are addressed to students (to individuals or groups, with responses elicited from individuals or groups); the sequence of questions (from lower to higher order or vice versa); the pacing or tempo of the lesson; the social arrangement (competition or cooperation between students); the activities students are required or allowed to take part in (reading silently, reading aloud, looking at films or television or slides, listening to tapes or records, working in a laboratory in science or a foreign language, working alone or in a group); and the amount and kind of decision making that the teacher allows the students.

Method variations

Materials and facilities variations

Variation can also refer to *teaching materials and facilities*. Different themes—political, seasonal, geographic, national, cultural, and others—can be used as bases for changes in materials of instruction, that is, books, films, projects, bulletin boards, and so on. Facilities outside the classroom—parks, observatories, factories, museums—can be used to vary the learning environment. Classroom seating can be varied by arranging students in circles or small clusters.

• *Facilities outside the classroom can be used to vary the learning environment. (© 1981 Jerry Howard 1981/ Positive Images)*

In the preinteractive stage of teaching, the teacher can and should plan for variation in all of these aspects of short and long segments of teaching: (1) style, (2) method, and (3) teaching materials and facilities.

Does Variety Help?

Does variety in teaching help? We could argue that regularity and uniformity in teaching are good things because they allow students to concentrate more on the substance of what is being learned and do not require students to use time and energy adjusting to new ways of teaching and learning. On the other hand, we could argue that variety is a good thing because it recaptures students' attention, arouses curiosity, prevents boredom, and gives students new ways to learn where old ones may have failed. What does research suggest?

Variety vs. regularity and uniformity

Several studies have yielded positive correlations between the amount of short-segment variation and students' attention to their learning tasks. Kounin (1970), for example, reported that variety in the overt behavior patterns of the teacher and variety in the pacing of materials correlated positively (.83 and .52) with students' work involvement in eleven first-grade and forty-nine second-grade classrooms. In measuring variety, Kounin divided the classroom events into "activities," each of which was coded for content, covert behavior mode, teacher's lesson presentation pattern, and five other dimensions. The score for variety consisted of the number of these eight dimensions that changed from one activity to the next. Thus, a teacher could vary by engaging in many slightly

Short-segment variation and attention

different activities or in a few highly different ones. Work involvement was measured by noting for individual students every twelve seconds whether they were "definitely in," "probably in," or "definitely out of" the assigned work. Although achievement itself was not measured, we can infer from other research that greater achievement goes along with greater work involvement (Berliner, 1990).

Variation and achievement

Studies of relationships between variations in short or long segments of teaching and either student achievement or student work involvement have been brought together by Rosenshine (1971b). The correlations tend to be positive but low and (because the number of teachers in a given study is usually small) not greater than chance would allow. Of eight studies in which measures of teacher flexibility were obtained by counting teacher behaviors in the classroom, six yielded positive correlation coefficients (.46, .43, .37, .25, .19, .02), one yielded a negative coefficient (−.07), and one could not be interpreted. Flexibility was measured by how often the teacher changed from one behavior, such as discussion, to another, such as administrative routine.

Variety in materials and techniques

To illustrate what we mean by *variety,* let's look briefly at three studies. In one, variety in instructional materials and techniques was measured by interviewing twenty-one fifth-grade teachers and observing their classrooms. A composite measure of this kind of variety, combined with variety in praise and testing methods, correlated .48 with student achievement adjusted for pretest differences among classrooms in student aptitude or achievement. In a second study, similarly positive correlations were obtained by measuring the variety of the cognitive processes used by fifteen teachers in tenth- and twelfth-grade social studies classes. Here the measure of variety consisted of the ratio of the most frequently used process (that is, "empirical," or fact stating and explaining) to the least frequently used processes (that is, analytic, or defining and evaluating). The lower the ratio, the greater the teacher's variation. The three teachers whose students learned most had significantly higher cognitive variation scores than did the other twelve teachers. In a third study, fifteen fourth-grade teachers were classified as high, medium, and low in their ratios of "convergent" (one-right-answer) to "divergent" (many-right-answers) questions. The medium, or most variable, group of teachers had the students who gained most in vocabulary and (although not significantly) in social studies.

Variety in cognitive processes used

Variety in questions asked

Finally, Rosenshine (1971b) brought together eight studies in which teachers' variability was measured by observers' or students' *ratings* or *reports,* rather than by observers' counts of behaviors. The ratings in these studies were made on several dimensions: variety versus nonvariety; the number of books and the amount of equipment, displays, and space in the classroom; the number of kinds of reading materials, audiovisual activities, different research materials, maps and globes, and class activities employed each day over twenty consecutive school days; and teacher flexibility. In all but one of the eight studies, the measure of variety and flexibility was positively (but not always significantly) related to student achievement.

RECAP

The weight of the evidence suggests that greater variety and flexibility in teaching go along with greater student achievement or attention. Because these studies used correlational, not experimental, methods, a causal relationship has not been demonstrated. Even so, you probably would do well to plan for variety and flexibility in your teaching as a way to improve your students' involvement with their learning tasks and their achievement of cognitive objectives.

How to Plan and Organize for Variety and Flexibility

All of your plans for variety and flexibility are limited by the constraints on teachers. American school systems do not give teachers a free hand in determining curriculum. The whole society takes a part in deciding what is taught and how it is taught in the public schools. As Kirst and Walker (1973) showed, curriculum policy is made at many levels for the public schools of the United States. At the national level, Congress and its committees on education, as well as the executive branch's Department of Education, Office of Educational Research and Improvement, and National Science Foundation, exert great influence. They support curriculum development and dissemination programs in the natural sciences, mathematics, foreign languages, and early childhood education, among other fields. Textbook publishers and national testing agencies influence curriculum in obvious ways. Foundations and business corporations support or oppose trends in curriculum. The Association for Supervision and Curriculum Development and other national professional organizations influence the curriculum. In the states, legislatures, departments of education, accrediting associations, and subject-matter associations affect the curriculum. Within cities and counties, the school board, the superintendent, the principal, and sometimes the department chairpersons, along with various city or county associations of educators, have an effect. And the American political system encourages local organizations, conservative and liberal, through their influence on elected and appointed officials, to shape what is taught in the classroom. Still,

Constraints on teachers

teachers have autonomy with regard to the mode of presentation of material within their own classroom. The teacher regulates her own schedule and methods of instruction. But studies dealing with curriculum innovation at the classroom level find "teachers seldom suggest distinctly new types of working patterns for themselves." (Kirst & Walker, 1973, p. 503)

Teachers control their methods of presentation

How, then, should you plan and organize for variety and flexibility?

Alternatives to Recitation

There are several ways to increase variety in the classroom, to move away from question-and-answer recitation. First, remember the alternatives we've discussed about lectures, small-group instruction, individual instruction, and open education (Chapters 9 and 10). In addition, within the framework of classroom teaching, think about the following kinds of adaptations.

Large-Group Alternatives.   ($N \geq 40$) These include

- demonstrations by the teacher or students.
- oral reports to the whole class by individual students or committees of students.
- slides, movies, or television viewing.
- radio or record listening.
- field trips.

Small-Group Alternatives.   ($N = 2$ to 20) These include

- debates (usually not more than twenty or thirty minutes) between pairs of students or student teams.
- role-playing sessions or dramatizations.
- panel discussions.
- project construction activities.
- discussions of right and wrong answers in tests already taken.
- class response in unison to drill exercises on skills the students have been taught.
- instructional conversations (discussed in the next section of this chapter).
- reading circles, in which a small group of students read orally, usually in turn, and discuss the content under the direction of a teacher.
- games, in which the student "plays" a gamelike instructional activity according to a set of rules.

Individual-Instruction Alternatives.   ($N = 1$) These include

- examination of posters, maps, charts, photographs, and the like, on a bulletin board.
- consulting reference books and other library materials (encyclopedias, newspaper and magazine files, *Who's Who,* atlases).
- supervised study.
- seatwork, in which students respond in writing to a variety of materials while working independently.

- silent reading, in which students read without having to respond at the time.
- construction, in which a student makes a product from a set of materials.
- play, in which the students have fun for no obvious academic purpose.

Administering Classroom Variation

You can plan these kinds of variations around traditional classroom recitation. But to implement them you must develop administrative skills. You are going to have to schedule and budget your time; anticipate needs for materials, equipment, transportation, and other resources; and have a supply of alternatives and supplements on hand to meet unforeseeable turns of events, either in the logic of the discussion or in the equipment or materials. Only experience and practice can help you improve your skills in the administrative parts of planning and organizing for variety. Educational psychologists can only point to the theory and research underlying the idea that variety improves classroom teaching. Acting on that idea is your responsibility.

Administrative skills

Classroom Teaching: The Interactive Phase

After you have planned your teaching, interactive teaching—the heart of it all—occurs. Despite the fact that hundreds of thousands of classrooms are operating every school day, remarkable similarities are found in the way instruction is carried out in those classrooms. Traditional, interactive classroom teaching, for better or worse, is part of the American, indeed, the worldwide experience. Of course, custom and tradition are not in themselves sufficient reasons for using a teaching method. But they are a strong force for the status quo. Change would have to be gradual and would come only in response to overwhelming evidence that other teaching methods are more effective in helping students achieve educational objectives. So far evidence of this sort has not been found. Moreover, many of the advantages of other teaching methods can be realized within the framework of interactive classroom teaching. So we turn now to our knowledge about what constitutes effective interactive classroom teaching.

Classroom teaching—custom and tradition

Interaction in the Classroom Recitation

Recitation is used increasingly in place of seatwork as one moves into the upper elementary and secondary school grades. As described by Bellack and his colleagues (1966), it is the continually repeated chain of events in which:

Repeated chain of events

1. *The teacher provides structuring,* briefly formulating the topic or issue to be discussed.
2. *The teacher solicits a response or asks a question* of one or more students.
3. *A student responds to the question.*
4. *The teacher reacts* to the student's answer.

At times one or two of the four links in the chain are omitted. For instance, structuring and reacting may occur only occasionally. But the teacher questioning and student responding are almost always present. They are the essential parts of classroom recitation. Let us look at three of these parts in more detail. The variables we talk about here have to do with structuring, soliciting, and reacting—the three tasks in classroom recitation that are predominantly the teacher's responsibility.

Teacher Structuring

- "All right, now let's turn away from the facts about Nazism and try to see what may have been its causes. No such movement as deep and all-embracing as Nazism could come from nowhere. It had to have causes in the history—the previous economic, political, and social phenomena and processes— of Germany. Let's see what we can find if we look for the reasons why the Nazis came to power."
- "Another kind of triangle is the isosceles. It has two angles that are equal. It also has some other interesting properties. Let's look at them."
- "Please put your reading material away. It's time for music."

All of these are examples of teacher structuring.

Structuring defined

Structuring moves serve the pedagogical function of setting the context for subsequent behavior by either launching or halting-excluding interaction between students and teachers. For example, teachers frequently launch a class period with a structuring move in which they focus attention on the problem or topic to be discussed during that session. (Bellack et al., 1966, p. 4)

We find that studies of teacher structuring deal with the following topics:

- The rate of teacher initiation and structuring
- Signal giving
- Organization
- Teacher talk

Rate of Teacher Initiation and Structuring.   How much teacher initiation and structuring is necessary? A lot or a little? We can't give you a quantita-

● *In recitation, the teacher provides structuring, briefly formulating the topic or issue to be discussed. (© 1983 Susan Lapides)*

tive answer, but we can offer some generalizations from research. "A moderate use of teacher initiation and structuring is (weakly) associated with high pupil achievement" (Dunkin & Biddle, 1974, p. 334). The term *moderate,* of course, is vague. We can only note that during a fifty-minute lesson, very high and very low rates of teacher initiation and structuring were not as beneficial for students as were more moderate rates.

Signal Giving.   One kind of structuring takes the form of signal giving, particularly to indicate *transition,* that one part of a lesson has ended and another has begun ("All right, that's enough about the effects of inflation. Now, let's look at its causes"). Arlin (1979) found a much lower number of student disruptions during transitions from one classroom activity to another when the teachers used structured rather than unstructured transitions. He defined *structured transitions* as those in which the teacher used "definite rules or procedures for making a transition," such as "OK, we're going to start math in five minutes, you should begin cleaning up your art projects now" (p. 48). Apparently, this

Signal starts and endings

kind of signal giving can relate to achievement in very short lessons (ten minutes) and in longer ones (forty-five minutes). In one study of two ten-minute lessons in the sixth and twelfth grades, with six and thirty-five teachers, respectively, signals of transition were positively related to achievement (Crosson & Olson, 1969). This study also found a positive relationship between the teacher's tendency to *emphasize concepts to be learned* and achievement ("Remember the term *selective migration*. It stands for an important kind of argument"). Similarly, Pinney (1969) counted the frequency with which beginning teachers used another kind of signal giving, *verbal markers of importance* ("Now note this . . ."), in the teaching of two forty-five-minute social studies lessons at the eighth- and ninth-grade levels. The frequency of these markers was positively related to achievement.

Finally, L. M. Anderson, C. M. Evertson, and J. E. Brophy (1979), in a successful experiment with first-grade teachers, included as one of their effective teaching practices the use of a well-recognized signal (snapping fingers, "Attention class!") for gaining pupil attention.

Organization.   Another kind of structuring can be measured by obtaining ratings of organization. Ratings by students of the degree to which brief (ten- to fifteen-minute) teaching exercises were organized were found to be positively correlated with student achievement (Belgard, Rosenshine, & Gage, 1971). Similarly, students' ratings of disorganization, in a large sample of high school physics classes, were consistently found to be negatively related to measures of student achievement and interest in science (G. J. Andersonn & Walberg, 1968; Walberg, 1969a, 1969b; Walberg & Anderson, 1968). So, being perceived by students as being organized is likely to be associated with higher student achievement.

How can you make students feel that a lesson is organized? The perception should not be a false one; it should be based on their seeing and hearing evidence that the lesson has a direction—is going somewhere—and that the steps in that direction have been given some thought. Structuring moves—including signal giving, emphasizing words (concepts) to be learned, and providing verbal markers of importance—can help. It probably also helps to give students evidence of planning, by having materials and demonstrations well arranged before class and by being able to tell them in advance about the structures of the ideas they are going to be learning.

Finally, a lesson is better organized if the teacher uses the self-discipline necessary to avoid digressions or *discontinuities*. This term was used by L. R. Smith and M. L. Cotten (1980) to refer to disorderly transitions *within* a lesson or a topic from one point to another. They are "digressions or irrelevant interjections of subject matter," and they were found, as noted in Chapter 9, to reduce not only student achievement but students' favorable responses on such items as "The teacher stayed on the main subject very well" and "The teacher really knew what he was talking about."

Emphasize important concepts and terms

Verbally marking important ideas

Perceived organization

Discontinuities

Teacher Talk. We turn now to a dimension of teacher behavior—teacher talk—that has been the subject of many studies. *Teacher talk* is the amount of time during which the teacher speaks, or the number of lines or words spoken by the teacher in a given amount of time. Teacher talk sets the context for student behavior. It is made up in good part of lecturing and giving directions. Much of educational doctrine in recent decades has put a low value on teacher talk, urging teachers not only to reduce the amount of their own talk but to increase the amount of student talk.

Teacher talk has entered into nine correlational studies brought together by Rosenshine (1971b) and by Dunkin and Biddle (1974). The correlations were consistently low but positive.

In another study, Soar (1966) counted the number of seconds during which the teacher lectured before asking a question. He was unable to distinguish whether the comments referred to the previous discussion or to the forthcoming questions. Still, this measure correlated positively (.28) with general achievement over two semesters in the classes of fifty-five teachers in grades 3 through 6. Later Soar (1973) correlated "extended" teacher talk with adjusted reading achievement in the second grade and obtained a correlation of .44. Thus there tends to be a low positive relationship between teacher talk and student achievement.

Teacher talk: low positive relationship with achievement

If we assume that teacher talk consists largely of the teacher-structuring component of classroom recitation, we can infer that higher degrees of teacher structuring are associated with higher student achievement. Of course, there probably is an optimum point above which teacher structuring and talk inhibit student growth in some areas. But the low positive correlations between teacher talk and achievement suggest that teachers who talked more than the average teacher in these studies tended slightly to have higher student achievement. Similarly, the correlations suggest that teachers can talk too little to foster maximum achievement.

The quality of teacher talk is, of course, more important than its quantity. Here we are supported by the consistently positive and substantial correlations between rated clarity of teacher talk and student achievement (Rosenshine, 1971b). But ratings of clarity do not tell us how to be clear, only that it is important. (We talked about specific ways to be clear in Chapter 9.)

Rated clarity

Experiments on Structuring. Several types of structuring were manipulated together in an experiment on teaching a sixth-grade unit on ecology over a nine-day period (C. M. Clark et al., 1979). Four teachers were carefully trained to teach eight classes each, providing sixteen classes with high structuring and sixteen randomly equivalent classes with low structuring. In the high-structuring classes, the teachers

- reviewed the main ideas and facts covered in a lesson, both at the end of the lesson and at the beginning of the next lesson.

- stated objectives at the beginning of the lesson.
- outlined the lesson content.
- signaled transitions between parts of the lesson.
- indicated important points in the lesson.
- summarized the parts of the lesson as the lesson proceeded.

In the low-structuring classes the teachers did not use any of these structuring behaviors.

Structuring improves achievement

The average score on an ecology achievement test was higher for the high-structuring classes. The difference was sufficient to make the average high-structuring class rank above about three-fourths of the low-structuring classes. The difference appeared, however, only on the lower-order (knowledge) questions, not on the higher-order (reasoning) questions of the achievement test.

In another experiment, Borg (1975) trained teachers in voice modulation, cuing (calling attention to important points), terminal structuring (adding information not previously covered, near the end of a lesson), opening review, and summary review. He found that cuing, terminal structuring, and opening review—structuring behaviors of one sort or another—showed substantial positive relationships to achievement.

Inconsistencies in effects of structuring

But the research, as reviewed by Doenau (1987b), shows enough inconsistencies and complexities in its findings to raise questions about whether we have learned all we should about structuring. This important component of teaching ought to be something we understand well and are ready to use if we expect it to have consistently good effects on achievement. It may be that how students *perceive* the structuring is at least as important as the structuring itself (Stayrook, Corno, & Winne, 1978). If so, we need to learn to use structuring in ways that students can recognize.

Teacher Soliciting

Having structured a teacher-student exchange in a recitation, the teacher solicits a response or requests a contribution, verbal or nonverbal, from one or more students:

- "Now, class, let's begin with some of the facts about Nazism. When did the Nazis come to power in Germany? What was the situation of the middle class in Germany at that time? What was the big fear of the German industrialists at that time? How did Hitler take advantage of the various aspects of the German situation in 1933?"
- "What else is true about an isosceles triangle besides its having two equal angles?"
- "What is a sonata?"

Studies of teacher soliciting or questioning behavior deal with these topics:

- The frequency of questions
- The cognitive level of questions
- Wait-time I
- Directing questions
- Redirecting questions and probing

The Frequency of Questions.   The average frequency of teachers' oral questions has been estimated in various studies to be very high—ranging around 150 questions per hour for primary-grade science and social studies teachers, and around several hundred per day for both elementary and secondary school teachers (reviewed by Gall, 1970). Do students learn more as the number of questions increases? As reviewed by Doenau (1987a), the evidence on frequency of questioning in relation to achievement seems inconsistent. But when the frequencies of academic and nonacademic questions were studied separately, the former correlated positively (.32) and the latter negatively (−.29) with achievement in reading in the third grade (Stallings & Kaskowitz, 1974). Walberg's meta-analysis (1991) suggests a moderate, but still substantial, positive effect of frequency of questioning, particularly in the teaching of science.

Frequent questioning may not be effective if a teacher wants to foster discussion, not recitation. Dillon (1985) found evidence in five classrooms in five

High frequency of questions

Questioning and discussion

Questions foil discussion

big-city high schools that "questions foil discussion," while "nonquestions foster discussion" (p. 109). When a teacher in one case study urged students to participate, discussion did not result. Why? Because the teacher had been asking questions.

> Students speak briefly, for three to four seconds on average. They do not ask questions, they do not comment on their classmates' contributions, they do not speak to or about one another. All they do is answer questions, because the teacher is asking questions. The questions are asked to get a discussion going, but they work to keep it from getting started. (Dillon, 1985, p. 111)

And when a discussion does get started, questions frustrate it: "They turn it away and gradually diminish it" (p. 111).

If the teacher wants to foster discussion and thus decides to reduce or avoid the asking of questions, what should he do? He can

Nonquestion alternatives

1. make a *statement* of his selected thought in relation to what the student has just said; or
2. provide for a *student question* related to the speaker's contribution; or
3. give some *signal* of receiving what the speaker has said, without himself taking and holding the floor; or yet
4. say nothing at all but maintain a deliberate, appreciative *silence*. (Dillon, 1988, p. 132)

Also, as E. D. Wong (1991) has pointed out, the teacher can *summarize* what a student has just said or make a *short comment* ("Right," "Okay"). These types of responses may work best after a question has been asked to start the discussion.

But, as E. D. Wong (1991) has insisted, it is not merely the question or nonquestion form of what the teacher says that affects how long students talk. What also matters is the type of question. Yes-no or nonyes-no questions call for, or encourage, shorter and longer student responses, respectively. So, if you ask a question beginning with "Is," or "Was," or "Did," and so on, and the student can logically answer yes or no, the student is likely to do so, and a discussion is stymied. But if you ask, "How would you explain . . . ?" or ". . . analyze?" or ". . . evaluate?" or ". . . apply?" you are likely to get a longer answer.

Yes-no questions → Yes-no answers

Similarly, as E. D. Wong (1991) pointed out, asking factual questions is likely to bring forth shorter answers than asking opinion questions. And asking questions on topics that students know more about, and are more interested in, is likely to produce longer student answers.

Nonetheless, as Dillon (1991) emphasized, student responses to nonquestions are longer than those to questions, regardless of the type of question—opinion or fact, yes-no or nonyes-no—and regardless of the topic and the average length of the student utterances for that topic. Dillon also contended that students not only talk more but show more complex thought, initiative, participation, questioning, student-student exchanges, and student-student references when the teacher uses nonquestion alternatives. Student initiative here refers to elaborate responses, voluntary contributions, ideas, and student questions. In every case among nineteen discussions analyzed, "not only was student initiative greater overall when teachers questioned less, but also the initiative in every case was greater in response to alternatives than to questions—2 and 3 times greater" (Dillon, 1991, p. 164). The results were the same for students aged from 2 to 12.

Student initiative and questioning

Remember, though, that if the teacher's purpose is something other than fostering a discussion, teacher questions remain a valuable tool.

The Cognitive Level of Questions.

The cognitive level of questions, or interchanges, also matters. One basis for classifying the cognitive level of questions is the taxonomy we described in Chapter 2: knowledge, . . . , analysis, . . . , evaluation. Questions can also be used for purposes other than promoting the intellectual processes set forth in the taxonomy (Gall, 1970). These other purposes include

- asking students to improve on their first attempts ("Go on. Can you elaborate?").
- arousing curiosity and motivating inquiry ("Why would anyone want to spend $20 billion on getting people to the moon when so many people are starving here on earth?" "Why do you think those prehistoric people built Stonehenge?").
- guiding students' efforts at acquiring a cognitive or social skill ("What do you think would happen if you applied the Pythagorean theorem at this point?" "Why do you think Sue lost her temper?").

The cognitive level of a question depends on the students' previous experience. No matter how complex the answer, if students have previously read or heard it, the question simply requires recall (knowledge). Some questions seem to call for a higher mental process, say, analysis ("What are the main causes of the increase in pornographic films in recent years?") or synthesis ("How did the invention of long-playing records and tape recorders influence American music-listening habits?"). But if the students have read or heard the answers to these questions, all they have to do is simply remember the responses.

Cognitive level of questioning and student experience

Similarly, some questions that seem to call for simple recall ("When did television come into wide use?" "Which party controlled Congress in 1929?") may actually call for deductive reasoning if students have never read or heard the answers. Students may arrive at one answer by reasoning from the facts that President Franklin Roosevelt gave his famous fireside chats over the radio while President Eisenhower addressed the nation over television. Or they may put together the facts that Congress passed the high-tariff Smoot-Hawley Act in

1929 and that Republicans traditionally favored high tariffs. In short, students' previous learning determines which cognitive processes they must use to develop the right answer.

Types of questions and achievement

This relationship to previous experience may in part explain the relationships between types of questions and achievement, which are low and only moderately consistent. This research has tried to determine whether teachers who tend to ask high-level questions have students who achieve objectives to a greater degree. The research has been motivated in part by repeated findings that most (up to 80 percent) of the questions teachers ask just require only recall, or knowledge, of what was in the textbook or what has been read or heard elsewhere; only about 20 percent call for mental processes higher on the cognitive scale (Gall, 1970). The high percentage of recall questions may be justified, because these kinds of questions bring out the raw information on which higher mental processes (analysis, synthesis, and evaluation) can operate. Yet individual teachers have varied around those average percentages; some teachers ask much higher percentages of high-level questions than others do. So we have an intriguing question: Do variations in student achievement go along with variations in the level of questions asked by their teachers?

Question difficulty and cognitive level

Lower-order questions tend to be less difficult than higher-order questions. So it is noteworthy that, in the early grades, the percentage of time spent on low-difficulty material (as determined in the studies of how much time students actively engage in academic tasks at a low level of difficulty [Fisher et al., 1980]) was positively correlated with achievement, whereas the percentage of time spent on high-difficulty material was negatively correlated with achievement. This finding argues for the greater value of lower-order questions for fostering certain kinds of achievement.

When the difficulty of questions is in general low, so that correct answers are given 80 to 90 percent of the time, lower-achieving students seem to achieve more (Brophy & Evertson, 1974). For such students in the third grade, the percentage of right answers in the class correlated positively (.51) with achievement. But for high-achieving, more academically oriented students, the percentage of correct answers correlated negatively (−.31) with achievement. We should not misinterpret the latter finding, however; it means only that the percentage of correct answers should be lower—but still quite high.

Higher-order questions foster achievement

It could be argued then that, because questions should be at a low level of difficulty, and because questions at lower cognitive levels tend to be less difficult, teachers are right in asking more questions at lower cognitive levels. Yet experiments show the opposite. When brought together in a meta-analysis by Redfield and Rousseau (1981), the results of fourteen relevant experiments showed "that predominant use of higher level questions during instruction has a positive effect on achievement" (p. 241). Furthermore, the effect is fairly large: "The average student in a no treatment group [a student in a class whose teacher asked low-cognitive-level questions for the most part] could be expected to achieve at the 77th percentile following treatment [that is, if taught in a class whose teacher asked high-cognitive-level questions for the most part]" (p. 243).

How can we explain the apparent contradiction between the effectiveness of low-difficulty-level questions and the effectiveness of higher-cognitive-level questions? The answer may lie in the fact that the findings favoring low-difficulty were obtained in grades 1 through 5, whereas the findings favoring high-cognitive-level were obtained in higher grade levels. As Winne (1979) pointed out, citing Piaget (see Chapter 4), children's cognitive development at lower grade levels may not have reached the stage at which they can deal effectively with questions calling for higher mental processes.

Apart from its effects on achievement, higher-level questioning can also be defended because it influences what students say in class. The research on this question has been reviewed by Winne (1979) and Dillon (1982). All in all, the "votes" from five correlational studies are unanimous: Teachers who ask relatively more questions at higher, more complex levels (requiring application, analysis, synthesis, and evaluation) also tend to elicit student *behavior* at relatively higher levels. That is, students' responses to a teacher's questions—or statements (see Dillon, 1982)—tend to be at about the same level of cognitive complexity as the teacher's questions or statements. The correspondence is definitely present (Giaconia, 1987). "Cognitive correspondence between teacher intervention and student response occurs about half the time" (Dillon, 1982, p. 548). Asking higher-level questions works in the sense of making students behave at relatively higher levels of cognitive processing. Higher-order questions tend to make students go through higher-order mental processes—processes that require more than simple recall. Higher-order questions may be justified on this basis alone.

Higher-order questions and student behavior

Higher-level questions elicit higher-level mental processes

Wait-Time I.   After the teacher asks a question, the interval *before* the student responds is called *wait-time I* (Rowe, 1974). Wait-time II, which we discuss later in this chapter, is the interval *after* a student's response until the teacher speaks. Rowe (1974) found that both kinds of wait time averaged about one second. But Giaconia (1987) found that the average wait-time of her nine elementary school teachers ranged from 1.5 to 3.9 seconds and average wait-time II ranged from .63 to 2.15 seconds for the teachers she studied.

Rowe (1974) suggests that increasing either kind of wait-time from an average of one second to an average of more than three seconds has several beneficial effects on students' responses:

- The length of response increases.
- The number of unsolicited but appropriate responses increases.
- Failures to respond decrease.
- Confidence, as reflected in decrease of inflected responses [questionlike tones of voice], increases.
- Incidence of speculative responses increases.
- Incidence of child-child comparisons of data increases.
- Incidence of evidence-inference statements increases.
- The frequency of student questions increases.

- Incidence of responses from students rated by teachers as relatively slow increases.
- The variety in type of moves made by students increases. (p. 81)

Give students time to think

If you ask a higher-level question, you need to give your students more time to think about the answer. But Giaconia (1987) found that teachers did not tend to do so. Students need time to process information. Don't rush to get a response. Rowe (1974) found that teachers tend to wait longer for an answer from the students they think of as more able than from students they think of as less able (one of the common biases we mentioned above), but no such tendency was found by Giaconia (1987).

There have been experiments in which *both* wait-time (high and low) and the cognitive level of questions (high and low) were manipulated by training teachers. Fagan, Hassler, and Szabo (1981) worked with twenty teachers of language arts in grades 3, 4, and 5 as they led discussions of literature. Each of four groups of five teachers received training in both wait-time and higher-order questioning, or in only one of them, or in neither. The length of students' responses was greater for the teachers who used longer wait-time. Higher-

Higher-order questioning + longer wait-time → success

order questioning resulted in more alternative student explanations and a greater number of higher-level student responses, but the longer wait-time plus higher-level questioning combination yielded even stronger results. The teachers who received wait-time training asked more higher-level questions but a smaller total number of questions—a finding that makes sense when we realize that longer wait-time means that fewer questions can fit into a class period.

A similar experiment was performed by Tobin and Capie (1982) with thirteen teachers conducting eight science lessons in grades 6, 7, and 8. They also found that longer wait-time (up to three seconds, but not beyond) improved student attending and that wait-time correlated .69 with the mean achievement scores of the thirteen classes. Further the effect of three-second wait-time was greatest when it occurred together with questions of higher quality—that is, higher cognitive level, higher clarity, and higher relevance to objectives.

Effects of longer wait-time on achievement are generally positive. Tobin (1987) found such effects in five of the six experiments he reviewed. In short, you should guard against any tendency to rush students. Allowing substantial wait-time after a question is asked is good teaching practice. But the generally positive effects of longer (about three seconds) wait-time do not mean longer wait-time is *always* a good thing:

There are many classroom contexts in which shorter pauses between speakers can be justified. For example, when rote memorization or recall of facts is required, drill and practice activities might be conducted at a brisk pace using a shorter wait-time. (Tobin, 1987, p. 91)

Name or question first?

Directing Questions. The data suggest that, at least in the early grades, when directing a question at a specific student, the teacher should call on the child by name *before* asking the question. This recommendation goes contrary to the argument that asking a question and then calling a child's name is more effective because it gets all the children thinking about the question. Yet it was found that choosing respondents before asking questions correlated positively (.55) with reading achievement in third-grade classes (Brophy & Evertson, 1974). Similarly, the "percent of all interactions that were selected by ordered turns" correlated positively with reading achievement in the first grade (L. M. Anderson, Evertson, & Brophy, 1979, p. 203).

It appears to be better to call on young students in a patterned, predictable (nonrandom) order. Perhaps this patterned order is more effective because it reduces anxiety. Of course, a little anxiety helps maintain students' attention. What is more of a problem with random order is that teachers then tend to favor the more able pupils, depriving less able students of an equal opportunity to respond (Brophy & Evertson, 1976).

Random vs. predictable order

From all this it follows that teachers should call on volunteers less than 10 to 15 percent of the time, increasing the likelihood of all students' getting a fair share of chances to respond. In two studies, calling on volunteers correlated negatively with reading achievement (L. M. Anderson, Evertson, & Brophy, 1979; Brophy & Evertson, 1974).

Calling on volunteers

The same was true for the practice of accepting or permitting *call-outs*— answers given by students without waiting for the teacher's permission to respond. The frequency of call-outs correlated negatively with average class achievement in reading in two studies (L. M. Anderson, Evertson, & Brophy, 1979; Brophy & Evertson, 1974). But additional evidence in both studies indicated that call-outs should be permitted for low-SES (less confident?) children, who often tend to withdraw from opportunities to respond during recitation. Accepting call-outs from these pupils correlated positively with achievement in reading. The idea is to control recitation so that all students have an equal chance to respond and so that activity focuses on the academic goals.

Call-outs

Redirecting Questions and Probing.   Suppose you ask a question and a student gives an incorrect or inadequate answer. What should you do? Two alternatives are redirecting and probing.

Redirecting is asking the same question of another student:

Redirecting defined

T: Charles, how many degrees are there in an isosceles triangle?
Charles: 360.
T: Margaret, can you tell us how many degrees there are in an isosceles triangle?

It forces the class to continue thinking about the question. On the face of it, redirecting ought to correlate positively with achievement. Wright and Nuthall (1970) studied the behavior of seventeen third-grade teachers and their students in three nature study lessons. The content of the lessons was standardized. The frequency of the teacher's redirection of nonanswered or incorrectly answered questions correlated positively (.54) with student achievement on a test of knowledge. This variable was also found to correlate positively (.54) with student achievement for middle-class pupils in one study (Brophy & Evertson, 1974) but did not correlate with achievement in another (L. M. Anderson, Evertson, & Brophy, 1979). It correlated negatively (−.65) with achievement in classes in which low-income pupils were predominant (Brophy & Evertson, 1974). It seems better, then, with lower-income pupils to "stay with the original respondent and get an answer if possible" (p. 47).

Probing defined

Probing, on the other hand, is the teacher's continued questioning of the same student. If an answer is incorrect, the teacher repeats the question using different words. If an answer is correct, the teacher asks another question, pursuing the implications of the first answer; then perhaps another and another.

T: Sam, after Hitler had made his promise to Chamberlain at Munich, what did he do next?

Sam: Well, he took over Czechoslovakia anyway, in a few months, even though he had promised not to.

T: Okay, Sam, then what happened?

Sam: Well, the Allies saw that nothing would satisfy Hitler. Like they couldn't stop him. Like he was insatiable. War seemed inevitable, and they began to realize that.

Probing can be used to get some kind of creditable response from even low-achieving, less academically oriented pupils. This kind of probing tends to reduce the frequency of no response—a frequency that correlates negatively (−.63) with achievement in low-income classes (Brophy & Evertson, 1974).

Probe gently

Probing to reduce the no-response frequency must be done gently. It can take the form of rephrasing the question, giving clues, or asking a new question. The frequency of each of these procedures correlates positively (about .45) with the average reading achievement of both low-income classes and middle-income classes (Brophy & Evertson, 1974; L. M. Anderson, Evertson, & Brophy, 1979).

Probing can also be used to get extended higher-level responses from higher-achieving pupils. Probing of this kind was studied by Soar (1966). He found that asking for the development of interrelationships, generalizations, and problem solutions was one of a group of behaviors that correlated positively with arithmetic and other kinds of achievement.

Probing can also take the form of the teacher's trying, in a nonthreatening way, to get students to clarify their answers. This kind of behavior was found to be one of a set of related behaviors that correlated positively with student achievement in mathematics and reading (Spaulding, 1965).

In the study by Wright and Nuthall (1970) we described earlier, the teacher's directing another question on the same level to the same student and asking questions at a higher level were not correlated with student achievement. But Abraham, Nelson, and Reynolds (1971) studied two teachers trained to conduct discussions in both probing and nonprobing styles. The two teachers then led discussions in eight sixth-grade classes, using one style in half of the classes and the other style in the other half. Achievement was measured in terms of ability to (1) observe, or gather data; (2) infer, or project ideas into new areas; (3) verify, or validate an inference; and (4) classify, or form groups with specified common properties. The probing lessons resulted in greater ability to verify inferences on the part of students in both more and less academically oriented schools. The probing lessons also resulted in greater ability to observe in more academically oriented schools, but the nonprobing lessons yielded greater ability to observe in the less academically oriented schools. These findings are consistent with the more general finding that low-difficulty questions and tasks resulted in better achievement for less academically oriented pupils.

One additional concept, called *simple reciprocation* involves teaching *cycles* made up of either (1) soliciting, responding, and reacting or (2) soliciting and reacting (Dunkin & Biddle, 1974). In the study by Wright and Nuthall, the frequency of this simple-reciprocation teaching cycle (where *soliciting* means questioning or probing or redirecting) was found to be positively correlated with student achievement.

Simple reciprocation

It appears, then, that both redirection and probing are associated with higher student achievement. But this statement is based on a small number of "votes." That is, relatively few studies have been done in too few contexts to allow great confidence in the conclusion. If for no other reason, redirecting and probing of both kinds—to get any acceptable answer and to get a better answer—are recommended because they keep students involved in the lesson. Active student involvement always allows for the possibility of a positive effect on achievement.

Redirecting and probing probably effective

Teacher Reacting

In any classroom recitation, after the teacher has perhaps done some structuring and then some soliciting, typically a student responds. Then comes the teacher's reacting. These behaviors "serve to modify (by clarifying, synthesizing, or expanding) and/or rate (positively or negatively) what has been said previously" (Bellack et al., 1966, p. 4). Teacher's reactions can be classified according to how quickly they occur (wait-time II) and whether they are positive, negative, or structuring.

Reacting defined

Wait-Time II.   The second kind of wait-time comes after a student has answered a question. As we noted, Rowe (1974) found benefits in teachers' waiting longer than they customarily wait after asking a question, or before they repeat a question, call on another student, or say anything.

As already noted, teachers typically react very quickly (within one or two seconds) to students' responses. By increasing this wait-time (to at least three seconds), they can change the nature of recitations, making them less "inquisitional" and more "conversational" (Rowe, 1974). These changes can improve students' attending and achievement. That is, as the teacher waited longer, the students tended to elaborate and otherwise raise the level of their

Conversational recitation

● *Pedagogically, reacting moves serve to modify and/or rate what has been said previously. (© Michael Weisbrot)*

response. But Giaconia (1987) found that the cognitive level of questions was even more important than wait-time II as a correlate of the cognitive level of students' responses.

Positive Reactions.   Positive reactions can take the form of giving verbal praise, accepting students' ideas, and using tokens. All of these are kinds of positive reinforcers. Offhand we would expect their frequency to associate positively with higher student achievement and a more favorable attitude toward school, teacher, or subject matter. What does research show?

Praise

Praise needs no clarification. When a teacher says, "Good!" "Correct," or "That's fine," we can assume that the message is intended, and often is received, as a positive reinforcer. According to operant-conditioning theory, this kind of reinforcer should strengthen whatever student behavior it follows.

How often do teachers praise their students' responses? Dunkin and Biddle (1974), summarizing ten studies, stated that "teachers use praise no more than 6 percent of the total time on the average. . . . It appears that teachers use praise sparingly in standard classrooms" (p. 121). Similarly Brophy (1981), summarizing six later studies, concluded that "praise of good answers or good work occurred less than five times per hour. Praise of good conduct was rare, appearing only once every 2–10 hours in the early grades and virtually dropping out of sight thereafter" (p. 10). But negative reactions are also rare (Brophy, 1981; Dunkin & Biddle, 1974). Most reactions by the teacher are neutral.

Do teachers who praise their students more often have students who achieve at higher levels? The evidence, as brought together by Rosenshine (1971b) and by Dunkin and Biddle (1974), consists of thirteen interpretable correlational studies. Of these, eight yielded positive coefficients of correlation; and five yielded negative relationships. No consistent relationship between praise and achievement is apparent. Brophy (1981) cited evidence that "in the early elementary grades, praise rates correlate weakly with student achievement in low-SES or low-ability classes . . . but do not correlate at all or correlate weakly but negatively in high-SES or high-ability classes" (p. 16).

Praise-
achievement
relationship
inconsistent

How do we explain these results? If praise is reinforcing, it should improve achievement. But apparently praise as used by teachers often is not reinforcing. Brophy (1981) made a detailed analysis based on several observational studies and discussions. He found that, rather than being used as a reinforcer, teacher praise was often (1) a "spontaneous expression of surprise or admiration," (2) a "balance for criticism" or a justification of the teacher's earlier reproof, (3) "attempted vicarious reinforcement" (when the teacher praises one student in an effort to control the behavior of others), (4) positive guidance in trying to foster warmth, (5) an "ice breaker or peace offering," (6) "student-elicited stroking," (7) a "transition ritual," or (8) a "consolation prize or encouragement" (pp. 17–18). For praise to be effective, it should follow the guidelines in Table 8.6. Look again at that table on page 370 to see what it means in context here.

The effect of praise depends on what students attribute it to—what they see as the cause of the praise. If they believe that praise is something received only by students of low ability, that is, as a kind of "overpraise," then praise loses its effectiveness. If praise is given too often, it loses its value, particularly in upper grades.

Effective praise

Teachers should probably have an intrinsically favorable attitude toward people of all sorts, including students. In questionnaires, well-regarded teachers have expressed warm, accepting, sympathetic attitudes toward others (Ryans, 1960). These teachers should have little difficulty finding reasons to praise students, seeking out what is laudable in even the "poorest" student's performance.

We do not mean that a teacher should be oversweet. The teacher should also communicate high expectations. When an answer is wrong, the teacher can indicate that fact by redirecting the question to another student or by providing the correct answer, reactions that correlate positively (.61) with reading achievement in high-SES classes (Brophy & Evertson, 1974).

Accepting students' ideas means using students' contributions in subsequent discussion. The use may consist of acknowledging, modifying, applying, comparing, or summarizing what has been said or suggested by a student. This kind of reacting is included in the Flanders Interaction Analysis Categories (Flanders, 1970). Acceptance of an idea is a favorable reaction because it indicates to the

Accepting
students' ideas

● *Real life pressures and problems can provide meaningful topics for classroom activities. (© Jean-Claude Lejeune)*

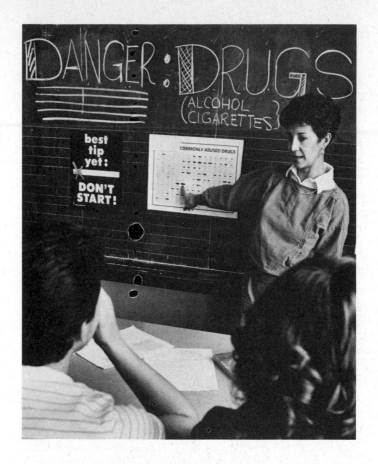

student that the teacher considers that idea worth taking seriously. Praise may be perfunctory or courteous; acceptance of a student's ideas is less likely to be. So acceptance presumably has reinforcing, or motivating, effects in addition to the cognitive value of repeating and reprocessing an idea.

T: Bill, what else is true of an isosceles triangle?

Bill: A line drawn from the apex between the two equal angles to the midpoint of the opposite side will be perpendicular to that side.

T: Good. Let's put that on the board. Notice how what Bill said turns out to be true. If we draw a line from this point, where the two sides intersect, to the midpoint of the opposite side, that line is always perpendicular to that side.

T: After the Nazis had come to power, what did they do? Katie?

Katie: They began a program of putting down the opposition. They went after everybody in Germany who had raised any questions about them.

T: Right, Katie. They installed one of the most efficient, thorough, and ruthless systems of suppression in human history. They used scientific methods to seek out and wipe out their opposition.

What does research show about the relationship of "accepting students' ideas" to student achievement? Rosenshine (1971b) and Dunkin and Biddle (1974) identified nine easily interpretable studies bearing on this question. Of these, eight yielded positive correlations, averaging .19. It seems likely that using student ideas during teaching is associated with higher achievement and more positive student attitudes toward the teacher. It is also possible that higher-achieving students have ideas that are more easily accepted. But it seems safe, in the absence of experiments that would settle the question, to act on the assumption that the teacher's acceptance causes the higher achievement. Of course, students' ideas should be accepted only if they are related to the academic focus of the recitation.

Accepting students' ideas related to achievement

In Chapter 8, we noted the effectiveness of tokens when they are part of an extensive system, such as a token economy. But tokens can also be used more casually as reinforcers for appropriate behavior. In the primary grades they can be exchanged for things normally found in classrooms, such as freedom to read for pleasure, to watch a videotape or film, or to play computer games.

Tokens

As brought together by Dunkin and Biddle (1974), the research on the use of tokens in classrooms has dealt mostly with student behavior, especially problem behavior in the primary grades. Tokens for wanted behavior (and their withdrawal for unwanted behavior) have been found useful in reducing unwanted behavior. Further, in three experiments in special classes the teacher's use of extrinsic tokens (those not ordinarily found in the classroom) succeeded in increasing both the proportion of correct responses and student achievement (Birnbrauer, Wolf, Kidder, & Tague, 1965; Hewett, Taylor, & Artuso, 1969; Wolf, Giles, & Hall, 1968). So a token system can be used to react to students in a way that shows approval of their response.

Negative Reactions.   When students respond or behave incorrectly, some teachers tend to disapprove, reprove, criticize, and rebuke:

- "That's not right."
- "Wrong!"
- "Stop that!"
- "You didn't do that very well."
- "You will simply have to stop behaving that way: I'm not going to put up with it."
- "Your answer indicates that you haven't read the assignment."
- "Your facts and your logic are both wrong."

According to Dunkin and Biddle (1974), "Teachers use criticism less than 6 percent of the total time on the average" (p. 125). Brophy (1981) also found a low rate (from 0.25 to 2.19 times per teacher per hour) of criticism of poor

Criticism infrequent

answers, poor work, and poor conduct in six studies using the Brophy-Good Dyadic Interaction Coding System. Many of the studies of this variable have used the Flanders Interaction Analysis Categories. Item 7 of these categories is

> *Criticizing or justifying authority.*
> Statements intended to change pupil behavior from nonacceptable to acceptable pattern; bawling someone out; stating why the teacher is doing what he is doing; extreme self-reference. (Flanders, 1970, p. 34)

Criticism and disapproval negatively related to achievement

Of the sixteen interpretable studies of the relationship between a teacher's use of criticism and disapproval and student achievement, thirteen yielded a negative relationship and three yielded a positive relationship. The median of the negative correlations was –.32, and they ranged from –.22 to –.61. The preponderance of evidence indicates that teachers who more frequently criticize their students tend to have students who do less well on achievement tests.

Does gender make a difference?

Which is cause and which is effect? Does more frequent criticism cause lower achievement? Or does lower achievement cause the teacher to criticize more? Statistical adjustments do not completely rule out the possibility of a vicious circle. According to Dunkin and Biddle (1974), "boys receive more criticism from teachers than girls" (nine out of ten studies show this), and "lower (prior) pupil achievement is associated with greater teachers' use of criticism" (p. 125). Because boys do less well than girls in the elementary school grades, where all of these studies of teacher criticism were conducted, the negative correlation between teacher criticism and student achievement may arise from the association of both variables with the gender of the student. That is, classes with more boys may tend to achieve less well and to receive more teacher criticism and disapproval.

Experiments needed

To settle the question of whether disapproval causes lower achievement, or vice versa, we need experiments in which teacher criticism is manipulated. That kind of evidence is hard to get. Meanwhile, it seems safe to say that teachers should be careful about using criticism and disapproval too freely. In fact, too much criticism and disapproval indicate that something is wrong—with the teacher's attitudes or methods, the curriculum, the organization, the schedule, or any of the other factors that we have talked about *except* the student. To say that the cause of excessive disapproval of the student is fruitless, because it is the teacher's responsibility to do what is needed to see that criticism isn't necessary.

Alternatives to criticism and disapproval

Structuring Reactions.   But what do we do when students respond incorrectly? According to Wright and Nuthall (1970), our alternatives to criticism and disapproval include

- redirecting the question to another student.
- structuring at the end of an episode (a section of recitation that begins with a solicitation and ends with the next solicitation).

Both of these amount to the kind of mild criticism that communicates higher expectations. With high-achieving students, they correlate positively with achievement.

Redirecting and terminal structuring were found by Wright and Nuthall to be positively related to student achievement (.54 and .67). Their study dealt with the behavior of seventeen third-grade teachers who were teaching a unit on nature study extending over three lessons of about ten minutes each. Studies of these kinds of structuring-reaction variables have not been repeated. So the evidence is merely suggestive. It means that a sequence like the following—the teacher's structuring behavior is indicated in italics—is probably associated with higher achievement:

T: Name a country where it is colder in August than in December, John.
John: Sweden.
T: (*redirecting the question*) Hal? Where is it colder in August?
Hal: Australia
T: (*giving praise and thanks*) Good. Thank you Hal. (*Structures the terminal episode*) So, class, in August, when it's hot here in the United States in the Northern Hemisphere, it's cold in Australia and New Zealand and other countries in the Southern Hemisphere.

These structuring reactions make sense. The teacher makes no traumatic criticism and does not humiliate the student who has answered incorrectly. The teacher implicitly corrects John's error by accepting and praising Hal's answer. Praise is given only for correct responding, which is as it should be. And by terminal structuring, the teacher repeats the correct response rather than proceeding with a class that has had one correct and one incorrect response presented. Without the repetition of Hal's correct response, some members of the class would probably learn John's incorrect response.

The evidence on *academic feedback* (informing students about the correctness of their answers or statements) as a form of structuring reaction is unusually clear. Academic feedback improves achievement. The "feedback that reacting behavior provides is consistently related to increases in student achievement in basic skills at the elementary-school level" (Zahorik, 1987, p. 421). In other grade levels and subject matters, the evidence is somewhat more complex but still positive on the whole.

Responses to low-achieving students need special attention. What happens when students repeatedly answer incorrectly, so that any honest response by the teacher becomes a sign of student failure? This problem raises the whole question of the ways in which teachers should deal with low-achieving students. We noted earlier that teachers should ask easier questions of these students— questions that will almost certainly be answered correctly. But obviously a consistent policy of this kind may doom the students considered to be low

Structuring reactions help avoid criticism

Keeping students from learning incorrect responses

Academic feedback improves achievement

Reactions to low-achieving students

Don't communicate low expectations

achievers to a school experience that must result in low achievement. Here we are concerned about reacting to such students. Brophy and Good (1974) have made several suggestions to help teachers avoid communicating low expectations to low-achieving students:

- Wait just as long for low-achieving students to answer as for high-achieving students.
- Be just as willing to repeat the question, provide a clue, or ask a new question for low-achieving as for high-achieving students.
- Withhold praise for unacceptable answers just as often for low-achieving as for high-achieving students.
- Avoid criticizing low-achieving students more frequently than high-achieving students.
- Praise correct answers from low-achieving students just as often as you praise correct answers from high-achieving students.
- Confirm correct answers by low-achieving students as often as those given by high-achieving students.

And here are some others:

- Pay as much attention to low-achieving students as to high-achieving students.
- Call on low-achieving students as often as on high-achieving students.
- Seat low-achieving students just as close to you as high-achieving students.

Many studies have shown that teachers often unwittingly discriminate against low-achievers (Brophy & Good, 1974). It is your responsibility to keep track of your interactions with low- and high-achieving students and to reduce or eliminate as much of this unintentional bias as possible.

The Flexibility of the Recitation in Principle

The preceding pages show that the recitation can take almost innumerable forms. Structuring has various components, which may or may not be present in any single recitation sequence. The same is true of soliciting and reacting. Just to illustrate, suppose we say that each of these parts of a recitational sequence can take five forms: five ways of structuring, five ways of soliciting, five ways of reacting. Then there would be 125 (i.e., $5 \times 5 \times 5$) possible combinations, each one representing a different form of the recitational sequence. Surely, with 125 possibilities in any one sequence, and the many sequences that constitute a single recitation lesson, this kind of teaching can go on in many different ways and should be considered extremely flexible.

Shortcomings of the Recitation in Practice

But this great flexibility does not apparently show up in practice, because the recitation as observed in many classrooms has been widely condemned. Tharp and Gallimore (1988) brought together a series of references in which the recitation was characterized undesirably as

> a series of unrelated teacher questions that require convergent factual answers and student display of (presumably) known information. Recitation questioning seeks predictable, correct answers. It includes up to 20 % yes/no questions. Only rarely in recitation are teacher questions responsive to student productions. Only rarely are they used to develop more complete or elaborated ideas. (p. 14)

Similarly,

> This unresponsive, "automatic" teaching seems devoted to creating and maintaining activity and assessing pupil progress. . . . For the most part, teachers controlled what transpired, and the focus was on the total group of students rather than small groups or individuals. Teachers emphasized rote learning and immediate responses, a pattern rather like television game shows. On the average, only 7 of 150 min [*sic*] of the school day involved a teacher responding to a student's work. Most of the time, teachers lectured and explained. Almost never were there opportunities for give-and-take between a challenging teacher and learning students. The student role was passive, and few teachers made any effort to adapt instruction to individual differences. (pp. 14–15)

Clearly, this kind of recitation fails to exhibit the great variety of forms that can be seen in the research literature that we have reviewed. Too many teachers apparently use only a restricted and narrow version of the recitation. Their structuring does not, for example, relate the text to the students' background knowledge. Their soliciting does not include enough higher-level questions requiring more than recall. Their reacting does not build on what students have contributed. They try to conduct their lessons with the whole class, so that individual students get too little attention. They work with groups of students who may differ greatly in their previous achievement and current readiness for a particular topic.

The Instructional Conversation

To remedy the deficiencies of the recitation as they describe it, Tharp and Gallimore (1988) have developed an approach to teaching that they call the *instructional conversation*. This approach has been derived from theory (especially Vygotsky's zone of proximal development, as described in Chapter 4) and experience in the Kamehameha Early Education Program (KEEP) in Hawaii. It has been developed primarily for language and literacy instruction in the early grades and to provide teacher in-service education aimed at helping teachers use the approach.

Small-group instruction

In the early grades, the instructional conversation is used with groups of three to six children at a time, while their classmates are engaged (and being monitored by the teacher) in other activities at centers elsewhere in the classroom. Each small group is made up of children fairly similar (homogeneous) in ability.

The conversation has an order following

The E-T-R sequence

a pattern of repeated thematic routines, labeled "E-T-R sequences." . . . The teacher introduces content drawn from the child's experience (E), followed by text (T) material, followed by establishing relationships (R) between the two. These sequences may last from a few sentences up to several minutes. (Tharp & Gallimore, 1988, p. 122)

The teacher's questions range across various levels of cognitive complexity—from recall to inference and extrapolation. The participation of the pupils is informal and self-initiated, and it receives quick feedback from the teachers, with no penalty for "wrong" answers. The teacher tries to use, recognize, and build upon the pupils' contributions, while keeping the conversation on course, using her judgment as to when the "script" for the lesson should be abandoned in favor of even better ways of attaining its goals. The conversation typically lasts for about twenty minutes for each group of children, and then the next group of children joins the teacher for such a conversation. At higher grade levels, the conversational periods are longer.

The "text" may not be a textbook or even something printed. It can be student written matter, a movie, a historical document, or a student project. Whatever it is, the teacher tries to get the students to understand it by talking about what it means to them and relating their experience to it. The conversation can be aimed at a product—ranging from worksheets to a mural to a bulletin board or some other application of the acquired knowledge. In any case, the instructional conversation makes demands on the teacher:

Finely tuned attention to students' utterances

Conducting this conversation requires of teachers a finely tuned attention to the utterances of students. Too much distraction, or too many students, and the crucial opportunities to assist performance are lost, because responsive teaching in this context means that teacher assistance and instruction are contingent on student productions, rather than being preplanned, scripted, or didactic. Because student productions are not predictable, responsive teaching involves thoughtful, reflective tailoring of assistance to learners as instructional opportunity and need arise. (Tharp & Gallimore, 1988, p. 135)

Responsive teaching

This brief account of the instructional-conversation approach to teaching necessarily omits many of its elaborations. Whether it represents something fundamentally different from the recitation depends on how one defines the recitation. As we have seen, the recitation need not be the simple, repetitive, low-level, boring procedure that Tharp and Gallimore describe. (For example, see Figure 11.1, pages 499–500.) It can in principle be extremely varied and flexible. But the instructional conversation does represent a carefully formulated approach to teaching—one with many of the essential components (structuring, soliciting, responding, reacting) of the recitation but given a pattern (the experience-text-relationship sequence) that may improve the recitation's instructional value.

The heavy emphasis on questioning in both the recitation and the instructional conversation should, however, be challenged in the light of Dillon's conclusion that "questions foil discussions" (Dillon, 1991). If the teacher wants students to talk more, at greater length, on their own initiative, to other students, with more complexity, the teacher should use more nonquestion alternatives. This approach follows from the abundant research in many fields that Dillon (1990) has brought together to support the dictum that "nonquestions foster discussion."

Use or avoid questions?

Seatwork

Reasonable estimates suggest that elementary school students in the early grades work alone about 50 to 70 percent of the time and participate in recitations only about 10 to 15 percent of the time (Rosenshine, 1980). These figures indicate that the variables in seatwork may be quite important as correlates, and presumably causes, of achievement. Why are we seeing so much seatwork in the elementary school grades? Probably because today's teachers make such frequent use of small-group teaching. While teachers are working with small groups of, say, five to eight students in oral reading or mathematics instruction, the rest of the students are assigned seatwork—preferably academically relevant and appropriate to a high success rate for each student (Rosenshine, 1980).

Seatwork time > recitation time

Some teachers misuse seatwork for mindless, inappropriate purposes, as a way to keep students busy at any cost. Like any other teaching practice, seatwork can be overused, abused, and subverted. But it can also be put to good purposes: drill and practice on skills (e.g., arithmetic) in which students should become fluent, test-taking skills, problem-solving without the teacher's immediate assistance, writing on lively subjects, and so on.

Variables in Seatwork: Academic Learning Time

The variables in seatwork take the form of content covered, task orientation, academic focus, and engaged time. Classes differ greatly on measures of these variables (Berliner, 1979). As is shown in the bottom line of Table 11.5, in four

• *Elementary school students in the early grades work alone about 50 to 70 percent of the time. (© David S. Strickler)*

Computing academic learning time

second-grade classes, the number of hours devoted to academic learning time on mathematics per 150-day school year (row 9) were estimated to be 33, 30, 50, and 58, respectively. Similarly, in four fifth-grade classes in reading, the estimates were 60, 78, 140, 148.

The method of obtaining these estimates clarifies what we mean by *academic learning time*. Look at column 1 in the table. Row 1 shows that the total time devoted to mathematics in this second-grade class over all the days of observation and log-keeping was 2,530 minutes. The number of days in which data were collected is shown in row 2. If we divide 2,530 by 93, we get 27 minutes as the average time per day given to mathematics (row 3). "Percentage of engaged time" (row 4) is defined as the percentage of time during which pupils are seen by trained observers to be actually working on the curriculum materials and activities. This percentage times row 3 gives us row 5. This time is considered to lead to greater achievement when the students can handle the tasks readily, that is, (a) when the time spent results in a high success rate (80 percent or more) for the students' responses to workbook pages, tests, or classroom exercises, or (b) when the observer estimates the difficulty level of the task to be low. Thus the percentage of time students are engaged with material with

TABLE 11.5	*Pupil Time Measures for Four Second-Grade and Four Fifth-Grade Classes*

		Grade Level and Subject							
		Second-Grade Mathematics Classes				Fifth-Grade Reading Classes			
Row	Variable	(1)	(2)	(3)	(4)	(5)	(6)	(7)	(8)
1	Allocated total time in minutes	2,530	2,687	4,736	5,127	5,749	6,344	12,383	9,965
2	Number of days data collected	93	83	94	96	97	96	87	74
3	Average allocated time per day in minutes (row 1 ÷ row 2)	27	32	50	53	59	66	142	135
4	Percent of time students are engaged	71	62	61	78	82	77	84	75
5	Engaged minutes per day (row 3 × row 4)	19	20	31	41	48	51	119	101
6	Percent of time students are engaged in material that yields high success	67	59	65	55	51	61	47	58
7	Academic learning time per day in minutes (row 5 × row 6)	13	12	20	23	24	31	56	59
8*	Engaged hours per 150-day school year (row 5 × 150 ÷ 60)	48	50	78	103	120	128	298	283
9*	Academic learning time in hours per 150-day school year (row 7 × 150 ÷ 60)	33	30	50	58	60	78	140	148

Source: Adapted from D. C. Berliner, "Tempus Educare," from Penelope L. Peterson and Herbert J. Walberg (Eds.), *Research on Teaching: Concepts, Findings, and Implications.* Copyright 1979 by McCutchan Publishing Corporation. Used by permission of the publisher.

*Although many school districts throughout the country have about 180 school days per year, a number of other factors are at work. The fall and spring statewide testing, the week before the Christmas holiday, the week before school ends, the Halloween party, field trips, and the like, all reduce the instructional time available so that the 180-day school year may yield 150 or fewer instructional days.

which they succeed is obtained (row 6). The product of rows 5 and 6 yields "academic learning time per day in minutes" (row 7). To estimate the number of "engaged hours per 150-day school year" (row 8), we multiply row 5 by 150, then divide by 60 to convert minutes to hours. To estimate the "academic learning time in hours per 150-day school year" (row 9), we multiply row 7 by 150 and divide by 60.

The evidence that academic learning time is positively related to achievement comes from studies in second- and fifth-grade classes (Fisher et al.,

1980). These studies—together called the Beginning Teacher Evaluation Study (BTES)—showed that allocated time and engagement rate did predict achievement in reading and mathematics to an important degree. Because postteaching achievement is highly correlated with preteaching achievement, it is necessary in evaluating *teaching* behavior to remove statistically, or control for, preteaching achievement. When preteaching achievement was controlled, the adjusted postteaching achievement of the students still varied. And about 10 percent of that variation was attributable to the differences among the students in academic learning time, which was in turn influenced by their teachers. The findings from this and other studies strongly suggest that changing teaching in ways that affect academic learning time causes changes in achievement (Fisher et al., 1980; Berliner, 1990).

Academic learning time influences achievement

Improving Academic Learning Time

Allocate more time to academic activities

How can teachers improve the academic learning of their students? One answer is simply to allocate more time to academic activities. In planning their daily schedules, teachers can set aside forty-five minutes instead of thirty minutes for reading or mathematics. It may be possible to do so without sacrificing something that, on careful examination, is truly valuable. It turns out that teachers differ greatly in the efficiency with which they use class time. And it also turns out that more efficient ways of using time—or avoiding waste of time—are associated with higher pupil achievement.

Efficient ways of using teaching time

What are these more efficient ways of using teaching time? Several of them were identified through an examination of four studies of the teaching behaviors found to correlate with class achievement in reading in the early grades (Crawford et al., 1978). The four studies yielded hundreds of correlations (Brophy & Evertson, 1974; McDonald & Elias, 1976; Soar, 1973; Stallings & Kaskowitz, 1974). Additional ideas came from the BTES (Fisher et al., 1980). When these were examined, along with the averages and variabilities of the measures of teaching behavior, it was possible to identify behaviors that seemed effective because they reduced wasted time and increased academic learning time.

1. *Teachers should have a system of rules* that allows students to attend to their personal and procedural needs *without* having to obtain the teacher's permission (Brophy & Evertson, 1974; Stallings & Kaskowitz, 1974).
2. *Teachers should move around the room to monitor students' seatwork* and communicate to the students an awareness of their behavior (McDonald & Elias, 1976; Stallings & Kaskowitz, 1974). The same point was made by the authors of the BTES, which was conducted over a six-year period in California:

The term monitoring can . . . be used to refer to the teacher behavior of circulating around the room during seatwork, checking on

how students are doing. We found that a teacher rarely stops to observe a student's work without making some comment, providing
feedback or explanation. When a student receives this kind of attention from an instructor during seatwork, s/he pays attention more.
. . . Descriptions of high-achieving classes suggest that good teachers do this not only to keep students on task, but also to find out as
much as they can about how students are doing so they can plan further instruction. (Fisher et al., 1980, pp. 26–27)

3. *Teachers should see to it that assignments are interesting and worthwhile* and still easy enough to be completed by each student working without teacher direction (McDonald & Elias, 1976; Stallings &
   Kaskowitz, 1974).
4. *Teachers should be sure to provide but keep to a minimum such activities as giving directions and organizing* the class for instruction; they
   can do this by writing the daily schedule on the board, ensuring that
   students know where to go and what to do (McDonald & Elias,
   1976; Soar, 1973). Yet evidence in the BTES also indicates that

   Some nonengaged activities seem inevitable. Most teachers were
   fairly similar in the amount of time spent on noninstructional activities such as transitions before and after breaks, housekeeping
   tasks, and waiting between activities. . . .
       The teachers with the highest engaged minutes were able to re-
   duce student offtask time (day-dreaming, socializing) from the average of 8 minutes per hour to 4 minutes per hour, but they were
   similar to the average teachers in all the above noninstructional and
   nonengaged activities. (Rosenshine, 1980, p. 109)

5. *Teachers should make abundant use of textbooks, workbooks,* and
   other paper-and-pencil activities. Using these materials has been
   found to be associated with higher pupil achievement, while the
   use of nonacademic games, toys, and machines has been found
   to be associated with lower student achievement (Brophy &
   Evertson, 1976; McDonald & Elias, 1976; Stallings & Kaskowitz,
   1974).
6. *Teachers should avoid "timing errors";* that is, they should prevent misbehavior from continuing long enough to increase in severity or spread to and affect other children (Brophy & Evertson,
   1974).
7. *Teachers should avoid "target errors";* that is, they should attempt to
   direct disciplinary action accurately—at the student who is the primary cause of a disruption (Brophy & Evertson, 1974).

    All of these teaching practices for seatwork are recommended on the basis
of the findings of the correlational studies cited. They make good sense as well.

• *Teachers should move around the room to monitor students' seatwork and communicate to students an awareness of their behavior. (© David S. Strickler/The Picture Cube)*

Obvious? Perhaps, but still . . .

Perhaps reduce seatwork

Are they obvious? Perhaps. But even if they were obvious, it would not mean that teachers do not need this information or that teachers are already behaving in these ways. These teacher-behavior variables could not have survived the research test if they did not correlate with student achievement. And they could not correlate with student achievement if teachers did not vary substantially on these dimensions. Yet all of these ways of improving seatwork may not be as effective as simply reducing (not eliminating) the amount of seatwork. This idea makes sense not because seatwork is trivial or without value; but because students were found in the BTES and other studies to be engaged less often during seatwork (about 70 percent of the time) than during teacher-led group work (about 84 percent of the time) (Rosenshine, 1980).

Cross-Cultural Differences in Academic Learning Time

The importance and meaning of some of the ideas about academic learning time can be seen in the ways time is spent in mathematics classes in three countries: Japan (J), Taiwan (T), and the United States (U.S.) (Stigler, Lee, & Stevenson, 1987). The two Asian countries have significantly higher average mathematics

Class organization, total class	J,T > U.S.	
Leader of activity, teacher	T > J > U.S.	*Observed Differences*
		Between Mathematics
On-task behaviors: attending	T > J > U.S.	*Classrooms in Grades*
Ask academic question	T > J > U.S.	*1 and 5 in Japan (J),*
Seatwork	U.S. > T, J	*Taiwan (T), and the*
		United States (U.S.)
Off-task behaviors		
Out of seat	U.S. > T, J	
Out of seat and off-task	U.S. > T, J	
Inappropriate peer interaction	U.S. > T, J	
Other inappropriate action	U.S. > T, J	
Total inappropriate	U.S. > T, J	
Who teacher works with		
Class	J,T > U.S	
Group	U.S. > J,T	
Individual	U.S. > J,T	
No one	U.S. > J,T	
Teaching behaviors		
Imparting information	T > J > U.S.	
Ask academic question (individual)	U.S. > J,T	
Ask academic question (group)	J,T > U.S.	
Ask nonacademic question	U.S. > J,T	
Giving directions	U.S., J > T	
Academic feedback		
Praise	U.S. > J,T	
Correct	U.S., J > T	
Behavior feedback		
Physical correction	T > U.S., J	
Punishment	T, J > U.S.	
Use of audiovisual	U.S.,T > J	

Source: Adapted from Stigler, Lee, and Stevenson (1987). © The Society for Research in Child Development, Inc. Adapted by permission.

achievement than the United States at all levels from kindergarten through high school. When twenty classes at the first-grade and also at the fifth-grade levels in similar cities in each of these countries were observed, the differences shown in Table 11.6 appeared.

It is certainly not only what teachers do that makes for differences between nations in student achievement. Yet it also seems highly likely that teaching-practice differences between nations are among the causes of between-nation differences in achievement. In Table 11.6 we see a much greater effectiveness in fostering academic learning time among teachers in Japan and Taiwan. Note that the United States is consistently higher (worse) than Japan and Taiwan in the various indices of off-task behavior. Note, similarly, that Japan and Taiwan are consistently higher in the on-task behaviors. Given what we know about the relationship between academic learning time and achievement, we should not be

Differences between classes in Japan, Taiwan, and the United States

surprised that the two Asian countries do better in mathematics than the United States.

***Causal* relations between teaching practices and student achievement**

We also have evidence within the United States that the relationship between teaching practices and achievement is a causal one. Fifteen experiments were cited by Gage and Needels (1989; see also Needels & Gage, 1991) to show that training teachers in behaviors that seem effective correlationally makes those teachers' students do better on measures of achievement, attitude, and behavior. At least a part of the U.S. inferiority in mathematics achievement could be overcome by educating teachers in practices of the kinds described in this chapter.

The Importance of the Melody in Classroom Teaching

Much of what we present in this chapter may give you the wrong impression. By dealing with the research on one teacher-behavior variable at a time, we may seem to be saying that the frequency of a single kind of teacher behavior is the important thing in teaching. But it isn't.

Just as in music, it is not the frequency of single kinds of behaviors (notes) that determines the whole effect (the melody). It is the combinations, sequences, rhythms, and paces of what the teacher does (and hence what the students do) that also accounts for some of the difference between effective and ineffective teaching. At least this is a plausible, commonsense idea. Unfortunately researchers are only beginning to invent methods of getting at teaching in these subtle, sophisticated ways. In the meantime, we are forced by the research that is available to deal with teaching as if one dimension of teaching behavior could make a difference. And, you have seen in this chapter, that approach is not completely fruitless. We have strongly suggestive evidence that some single kinds of behaviors are effective and others are not. Certainly it makes sense to use the evidence we do have to guide your planning and interaction with students in classroom teaching.

Thus, we agree with Joyce (1975):

At times . . . I feel that the teacher is being conceived almost as a swordsman who lays about the learner with his repertory of sharp-pointed skills, each of which will have a mechanical effect on learning outcomes. The expectation seems to be that if he pushes on the learner with a certain kind of question, then a certain kind of learning will pop out and we will be able to see it quickly and clearly. Such is not the nature of the interaction between learning environments and learners. It is very rare that any one skill (any single sword thrust) or any stylistic characteristic will stand out as the cause of the learning. Even where we find that increased learning is associated with the presence of a certain kind of skill or style in teaching, it is very likely that the reason is because that skill or aspect of style is an index of a much larger complex of behaviors that signals the presence of a certain kind of environment. (p. 81)

It now appears that one way to identify the environment that yields higher achievement on the part of students, at all grade levels, is to examine the clarity of the goals of the episode, class period, weekly unit, or term, and the time on task. Behaviors that help students know what to do or what we expect of them contribute to achievement. Monitoring, questioning, and other teacher behaviors that increase time on task are also likely to result in increased achievement. If we let students know what we expect of them in the task and give them enough time on that task, we should be able to improve learning outcomes.

Time on task and clarity of goals

SUMMARY

Classroom teaching, the most common kind of teaching, combines lecture, discussion, individual instruction, and recitation. Classroom teaching has planning and interactive phases. Planning deals with what goes on before the teaching and before the assessment of achievement.

Planning follows a hierarchy of planning needs. Teachers plan for (1) discipline, control, and management; (2) controlling biases in dealing with individual students; (3) using pedagogical content knowledge; (4) providing scaffolding; and (5) variety and flexibility in classroom teaching.

1. In planning for classroom discipline and control, you should deal with behavior problems of two kinds: too much unwanted behavior and too little wanted behavior. For the "too much" kind, prevention is the best plan. If that doesn't work, you can withdraw attention (your own and your students'), strengthen incompatible behavior, or use punishment. The "too little" kind, although less disruptive, can actually be more serious. Don't hesitate to refer a child who is very shy or withdrawn to a mental health professional. To increase wanted behaviors, you can elicit the behaviors, provide positive models, and use reinforcement and shaping techniques (contracts can help here).

2. Research has shown that bias is rampant in classroom teaching. To control it, you must compensate for your tendencies to treat students differently, and often unfairly, according to their gender, social class, achievement, intelligence, race, ethnic background, physical attractiveness, or even location in the room. Everything you do in the classroom—choosing a student to call on, waiting for a student to answer, reacting to the student's answer—is affected by your biases. You may find giving yourself cues helpful here.

3. Planning to teach the main ideas and the structure of the field and to use the right analogies and examples for the content being taught in the context of the classroom and your students' abilities is part of planning to use your pedagogical content knowledge.

4. Working on ways to provide scaffolds to help student learn what they should in less structured areas of the curriculum is also a part of planning.

5. Because variety and flexibility have been found to be associated with higher student achievement, you should learn to plan for them in your teaching. So your planning ought to be aimed at developing and choosing among alternative ways of carrying out instructional tasks. You can use many alternatives to recitation, for example, large-group, small-group, and individual-instruction settings. Only experience and practice can help a teacher develop the skills necessary for arranging these kinds of alternatives.

Recent major reviews of studies on and experiments with classroom recitation have made possible a research-based examination of the kinds of teacher behaviors that are effective and those that are not. Our groupings of these behaviors—structuring, soliciting, and reacting behaviors—are based on the three links in the classroom recitation chain that the teacher controls.

Structuring behaviors include the rate of teacher initiation and structuring, signal giving, organization, and teacher talk. The research evidence suggests that teacher initiation and structuring should be at moderate or intermediate levels, that signal giving is effective, that at least the perception of organization is probably associated with student achievement, and that teacher talk relates positively to high achievement.

The frequency of teachers' soliciting behaviors (typically, asking questions) has no consistent relationship to student achievement. The cognitive level of teachers' questions is positively related to the cognitive level of students' answers, or inferred thought processes, and, somewhat, to student achievement. Waiting about three seconds after you ask a question (wait-time I) helps. So does reducing the frequency of your questions if you want to foster a discussion. It seems, too, that less academically oriented students should be asked *slightly* less difficult questions. Research on the targeting of questions to particular students—predictable or random—shows a positive association between predictable targeting and higher achievement, at least in the lower grades. Redirecting questions and probing also seem, on the basis of a few studies, to be associated with higher achievement.

Reacting behaviors can be quick or less quick, positive or negative. Increasing wait-time II—the time between the student's response and the teacher's reaction—to about three seconds has beneficial effects. Of the positive reactions, the frequency of praise in itself has inconsistent relationships with achievement; but some evidence suggests that contingent, or appropriate, praise is associated with higher achievement, especially for less academically oriented students. Accepting and using students' ideas goes along fairly consistently with higher achievement, as does the reinforcing use of tokens for appropriate behavior. Of the negative reactions, criticism is consistently associated with lower achievement, but the question of which of the two variables causes the other is much in doubt. Structuring reactions—redirecting questions and terminal structuring—seem, on slight evidence, to be associated with achievement. Responses to low-achieving students need to be monitored carefully. Many teachers have been found to discriminate against low-achievers unintentionally in a variety of subtle ways.

The "instructional conversation" consists of dialogue with pupils arranged to follow an E-T-R sequence: relating the topic to the pupils' own *Experience* and referring to the *Text* material in *Relation* to that experience. Such conversations have been advocated as an improvement on the typical recitation.

Seatwork is effective to the degree that it fosters academic learning time— the time spent on academic tasks. The ways to increase this time include using systems of rules and schedules, teacher monitoring, making use of academic materials (not toys and games), and avoiding disciplinary errors.

Experiments in which some teachers have been trained to use these and similar practices have resulted in improved class achievement as compared with that of teachers who did not receive the training. These experiments support the *causal* value of these practices in improving achievement.

Finally, although in this chapter we've examined one behavior variable at a time, it is likely that the total pattern of teacher behavior is most important. But the lack of research evidence prevents our being clear and specific about this pattern. The one-variable-at-a-time approach does have some value, but you should recognize that in looking at single behaviors we are not examining the relationships that together make up the environment in which we teach.

V Assessment

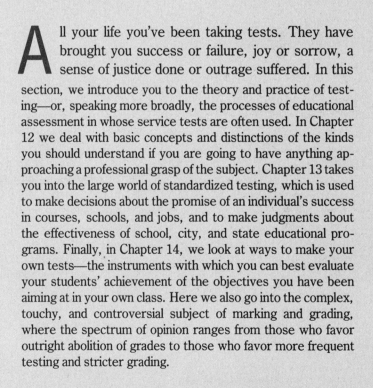

All your life you've been taking tests. They have brought you success or failure, joy or sorrow, a sense of justice done or outrage suffered. In this section, we introduce you to the theory and practice of testing—or, speaking more broadly, the processes of educational assessment in whose service tests are often used. In Chapter 12 we deal with basic concepts and distinctions of the kinds you should understand if you are going to have anything approaching a professional grasp of the subject. Chapter 13 takes you into the large world of standardized testing, which is used to make decisions about the promise of an individual's success in courses, schools, and jobs, and to make judgments about the effectiveness of school, city, and state educational programs. Finally, in Chapter 14, we look at ways to make your own tests—the instruments with which you can best evaluate your students' achievement of the objectives you have been aiming at in your own class. Here we also go into the complex, touchy, and controversial subject of marking and grading, where the spectrum of opinion ranges from those who favor outright abolition of grades to those who favor more frequent testing and stricter grading.

12 ≡ Basic Concepts in Assessment

OVERVIEW

Assessment is the process of collecting, interpreting, and synthesizing information in order to make decisions. Teachers make decisions about their students virtually every few minutes of the day. They may be concerned about whether their class understands a particular concept or not. Or whether Sandra can complete the assignment within the time limits allowed. They ask questions like these: "Is Jeffrey adjusting to the front row?" "Am I going too fast or too slow?" Assessment of student characteristics or achievement can be informal, to obtain general information about a student. In such cases few records are kept. Most of that information is stored in the teacher's mind. Assessment can also be formal, usually involving assignments, quizzes, reports, and tests. Sometimes the formal evaluations are used for official purposes, such as giving grades or placing students in special programs. Formal evaluations are mainly assessments of cognitive achievement, and records are kept of such assessments.

The basic concepts of assessment are discussed in this chapter: the nature of tests, how standards and norms are created for judging test performance, how tests are linked to those norms or to criteria set in advance, and how tests must show reliability and validity. We note also the ways in which educational evaluation takes place, both to improve curriculum, instructional methods, or projects, and to judge their usefulness and cost-effectiveness. Included in this chapter are the basic concepts you will need as you engage in the everyday, anxiety-provoking process of educational assessment.

Assessment with Tests

A test is a *systematic procedure* for *measuring a sample* of a person's *behavior* in order to *evaluate* that behavior against *standards and norms*. Tests generally come in two forms: *norm-referenced* and *criterion-referenced*. Good tests of either type must be *reliable* and *valid*. Let's take a closer look at some of the concepts used in these three sentences about tests.

Systematic Procedures

We're all observers, constantly watching the world around us. But most of our observations are unsystematic—and what they tell us may well turn out to be untrue or only partially true. Suppose you're watching some young children playing on swings. Yes, you can see what they are doing, but you can't judge their psychomotor skills. To do that, you would have to hold constant the kind of swing, the chain or rope holding the swing, how the children get started (with a push or by themselves). Your observations would have to follow some standardized procedures, rules and schedules—a system—so that all the children have an equal chance to show their psychomotor ability.

Standardized procedures

In the same way, you can't judge problem-solving ability by just watching. Suppose your brother and his friend are both trying to figure out a way to get a raise in their allowances. If your brother manages to get a raise and his friend doesn't, does this mean his friend has less problem-solving ability? Without systematic procedures, you can't tell. Maybe he does, or maybe your parents are more influential than the friend's parents.

The point is that casual, unsystematic observation is not enough for teachers. For feedback to students and their parents, and for examining the effectiveness of their own teaching, irregular, unsystematic observation is much too fallible. Too much is at stake! When we want estimates of a student's achievement, as we surely do a great many times each school year, we have to use systematic procedures to obtain those estimates. A test is a method for obtaining trustworthy estimates of achievement. A test, when designed correctly, provides the same stimuli (e.g., questions) for all students. Tests are not substitutes for observations. They are themselves observations of behavior— observations that are more efficient, more refined, and less biased than other ways of observing. Tests are also easier to summarize and interpret than most other kinds of observation. Perhaps it is for this reason that, in surveys of test use, about 90 percent of elementary school teachers and 99 percent of high school teachers said they used tests as part of their assessment of students. In fact, 16 percent of the teachers reported using tests daily, 95 percent used them weekly, and 98 percent reported at least biweekly use of tests (Gullickson, 1990). A reasonable estimate is that teachers spend 20–30 percent of their time in assessment, and that time is often connected to testing activities. So it is important to learn about testing procedures.

Tests are observations

• *How does measurement and evaluation in educational psychology resemble—and differ from—the kind of measurement shown here? (© Jean-Marie Simon/Taurus Photos)*

Measuring

Quantitative estimates

One reason for the popularity of tests is that they give us a quantitative estimate of ability or achievement; they tell us how much. In education the attributes that interest us emphasize the abilities and achievements of students—such things as intelligence, creativity, spelling ability, science knowledge, and interest in art. When we quantify a student's social studies achievement, academic aptitude, or appreciation of poetry, we are measuring.

Objective vs. subjective tests

Some tests are *objective* in that it is easy to get different judges to agree about the score or measure yielded by the test. Objective tests can be scored by clerks or machines. Other tests require expert judgment, and it is harder to get the experts to agree closely or exactly because the criteria each expert uses when scoring the tests either are not described or cannot be described; these tests are called *subjective* tests. The objectivity or subjectivity of a test depends on the scoring—not on the test's content.

Sample

We must remember that a test samples behavior. We do not test all of a student's mathematics knowledge or ability to understand French. We use only a small number of many possible tasks or problems to determine whether the student knows how to add or knows the meaning of certain French words. From that sample, we estimate how well the student can use information or apply ideas. We generalize from a small sample of behavior to the larger domain of behavior we are really interested in—from items about such things as World War I to knowledge of history. Thus the sample of behavior should be as unbiased as possible, should cover important areas of the curriculum, and should provide many ways for the student to demonstrate competence. When certain students perform poorly on a test, the fault may lie with our sampling procedure, not their ability. Every one of us has at some time or other felt ready to take a test—only to find we knew the answers to a lot of questions the teacher never asked. Some methods of seeing to it that a test is a fair sampling of behavior or achievement are discussed in Chapter 14.

Sampling behavior

Behavior

Tests are designed to elicit behavior from students. We cannot deal with what students are thinking when they solve problems unless we can observe their thinking through their thinking aloud, their writing, or their solutions to problems. We cannot study students' creativity unless we can see its processes and its products. What we examine are what people say or do and their solutions to problems or their productions in music, writing, or art; that is, we examine creative behavior. That we must rely on what is observable is an important point. When we don't, our judgments may not be accurate. That silent little boy in the back row may not be thoughtful and reflective; he may just be quiet. The young woman nodding her head in the second row may understand the point you just made, or she may just be socially acquiescent. When you want to measure thoughtfulness, physical prowess, or understanding, you must convert these dimensions into observable behaviors.

Eliciting behavior

Evaluation

Evaluation is the process by which we attach value to something. Measuring a sample of a student's observable behavior allows us to estimate how much of a given attribute that student has. Evaluating the measurement is an altogether separate issue. For example, suppose a student scores 40 points on a reading comprehension test. What does this measurement tell us about the student's reading comprehension? Is it good enough or weak, commendable or regrettable? In the process of evaluating, we determine how well a student has mastered the material. Or an evaluation can tell us whether a student should be recommended for advanced training or whether a class is doing poorly or whether a school is achieving at an excellent level. Measurement gives us

How good something is

● **When we want estimates of a student's achievement, we have to use systematic procedures to obtain those estimates.** (© Mimi Forsyth/ Monkmeyer Press Photo Service)

numbers. Human judgment, concern, and interpretation turn those numbers into evaluations.

Standards and Norms

Standards and norms are both means of comparison. When we talk about *standards* we mean that people have made a judgment about what is acceptable and reasonable performance for an individual or a group of individuals on a specific test. A student's numerical score is evaluated differently depending on the standards we use to interpret the score. We might want to know whether a score of 40 points on a reading comprehension test is above or below the *established criterion for acceptable competence* in reading.

Established criterion

A standard is different from a *norm,* which is used to interpret a student's score in relation to the scores of other students. Norms require comparisons among students. Some norms, such as those based on students in the same class or in the same school district, are called *local norms.* Other norms, such as

Local norms

those derived from a sample of students representing the whole country, are called *national norms.* Both of these kinds of norms are used to interpret the scores obtained in norm-referenced testing. Standards, on the other hand, are used in criterion-referenced testing. Let us look at these two markedly different forms of testing now.

National norms

Norm-Referenced Testing

Norm-referenced tests are those that use the test performance of other people on the same measuring instrument as a basis for interpreting an individual's test performance. A norm-referenced measure allows us to compare one individual with other individuals.

Using a Local Norm Group

Suppose Lisa received the highest score, an A, on her test in auto mechanics class (her peer group). Gloria, with a B, was seventh in the class. In this norm-referenced situation, using the scores of their immediate peer group as our norms, we can say that Lisa knows more about auto mechanics than Gloria knows, at least as measured by this test. But unfortunately the scores by themselves tell us nothing about what the two girls really know.

No information on what students really know

Suppose the test they took was used as a basis for admission to an advanced class in auto mechanics. If only six openings were available, Lisa would get into the class and Gloria would not. It may be that even Lisa does not know enough to be able to benefit from the advanced class, but we could not determine this fact from the norm-referenced test because it does not necessarily tell us what Lisa knows about how cars work. It tells us only where she ranks in comparison with others who took the same test. Norm-referenced tests give us a way to pick the higher achieving from the lower achieving students in a particular subject matter area. When the norm group is a student's own class or fellow students in the same grade at school or within the district, the local peer group provides the norms by which we judge performance.

Using a National Norm Group

Let's say that Lisa and Perry both take a national test on knowledge of auto mechanics. Perry scores at the 74th percentile in comparison with thousands of others who have taken the same test. That is, his knowledge of auto mechanics is equal to or better than 74 percent of the students who took this test. We could also say that only 26 percent of the other students know more about auto mechanics than Perry does. The other students, a representative norm group against which Perry's score can be judged, are like a distant, somewhat invisible peer group. To the degree that the distant peer group is meaningful—that is, appropriate as a basis for comparison—we can interpret Perry's score in light of the group's scores.

Distant, somewhat invisible, peers

Now suppose Lisa receives a score that places her at the 54th percentile rank on the national norms. Although Lisa's knowledge when compared with that of her local peer group was at the 99th percentile rank, she seems clearly less knowledgeable when compared with the distant peer group that made up the national norming group. If we learn, however, that the national norm group—the norm group for the test—contains mostly males, we can evaluate Lisa's score differently. In many cultures, males tend to know more about the workings of cars than do females. So the comparison may not be a fair one. This is the same problem that many African-Americans, Chicanos, and Native Americans face with norm-referenced testing when the norms are based on distant, but supposedly representative, peer groups. Minority-group students who show excellent performance relative to their local peers often seem to perform poorly on nationally standardized tests. Why? Because the norm group used to judge their scores is not really representative; it does not include enough members of minority groups. For certain purposes, then, the norm group is biased. A biased norm group can unfairly penalize a minority-group student who has a different cultural background. In the case of Lisa, if the test is being used as a basis for admission to an auto mechanics course, perhaps her performance should be compared only with that of other women. That is, we might want to use different norms to evaluate performance on a test if we are concerned about equal opportunity, as we are in an admissions test. Here social class, gender, race, and ethnicity can be relevant considerations. But if the test Lisa took was an evaluation of course work and we want highly competent rather than mediocre auto mechanics, then social class, gender, race, and ethnicity are probably irrelevant.

Biased norm group

Equal opportunity and admissions

Criterion-Referenced Testing

Recommendation: use criterion-referenced achievement tests

If we really want to determine the content of what Lisa knows about cars, we would have to abandon the norm-referenced approach and turn to a criterion-referenced approach. No matter what we learn about a person's standing relative to his or her peers, in the norm-referenced approach we can never learn whether the person knows a certain thing, such as how to diagnose problems with automobile transmissions. Except when the purpose of testing is to select a fraction of students for scarce positions (for example, at a highly competitive college or for a small honors class), a student's achievement should be assessed through criterion-referenced, not norm-referenced, approaches. For most school purposes, criterion-referenced testing markedly improves assessment and evaluation.

Criterion-referenced tests measure an individual's ability with respect to some content-based standard. The standard, or criterion, is determined in advance by knowledgeable people in the field. Automobile driving tests are not norm referenced (who wants the best of a group of bad drivers?); they are criterion referenced, based on standards of content or performance. Comparison among students is not a factor here. The criterion-referenced measure is used when we want to know what students know or can do, rather than how they compare with immediate or distant peer groups (Popham & Husek, 1969; Airasian, 1991). The criterion-referenced test is deliberately constructed to give information that is directly interpretable in terms of an absolute criterion of performance (Glaser & Nitko, 1971).

What students can do

The absolute criterion is usually based on a teacher's experience with students, on the particular curriculum area, on records of past performance, and also on the teacher's intuition and values. Suppose a teacher decides that students must be able to solve eight out of ten questions of the following kind:

- Which word is the name for something worn on the head?
  (HAT/FAT/CAT)

In this case the teacher would read the question, and the students would pick answers that demonstrate reading skills. If a student can do eight, nine, or ten questions correctly, the teacher concludes that reading skills of the type tested have been mastered. Failure to reach the teacher-set criterion is defined as seven or fewer items correct.

In this kind of testing, we learn that a student can or cannot read. Comparing Henry's test score with Ann's test score does not meet a big part of a parent's or a teacher's need for information. It is too bad that parents do not always recognize this. They often want information about how their child compares to others rather than information about the actual knowledge and skills their child has learned. Teachers need to educate parents that the criterion-referenced approach is often more in tune with classroom needs than is the norm-referenced approach.

Pass-fail grading

Usually criterion-referenced tests are graded with a pass-fail system. An example is your state's test of your knowledge of auto-driving laws; you either pass or fail, and in principle, everyone taking the test might pass or fail. You don't get a score comparing you with other people. Our concern here is whether each student has mastered the material, not how much each student knows in relation to what other students know. One student may do more work in an area than another. One student may be quicker to finish work than another. But when it comes to judging proficiency in certain curricular areas, criterion-referenced tests allow us to determine how well students are meeting the criterion. Perhaps all the students will pass a test; perhaps none of them will. If there are several standards for different letter grades, perhaps all students will receive a C, or none will.

Set criteria before giving the test

It is important that the criteria of performance be set *before* students take a test. Then the criteria cannot be influenced by how well the students do on the test. And then it is impossible for the teacher to adjust standards so that some predetermined percentages of the students receive grades of A, B, and so on. The choice of either norm-referenced or criterion-referenced testing, then, has important consequences for your classroom and school. Table 12.1 lists some pros and cons of each type of testing (Clift & Imrie, 1981; see also L. A. Shepard, 1979).

TABLE 12.1

Pros and Cons of Criterion- and Norm-Referenced Measurement

Criterion-Referenced Measurement (CRM)

Description

A criterion-referenced test measures whether a student has or has not reached a criterion or specified level of achievement. Test scores depend on specifying an *absolute standard of quality*. This standard is independent of the scores achieved by other students taking the same test and completing the same course.

Applications

Criterion-referenced measurement is useful

- for evaluating individualized learning programs.
- for diagnosing student difficulties.
- for estimating a student's ability in a particular area.
- for measuring what a student has learned.
- for certification of competence.
- for controlling entry to successive units of instruction.
- whenever mastery of a subject or skill is of prime concern.
- wherever quota-free selection is being used.
- whenever we want to encourage students to cooperate rather than to compete with one another.

Criticisms

Educators tend to disagree about the value of CRM. The following arguments are those that commonly appear in the literature:

- Criterion-referenced measurement tells us what a student knows or can do but does not tell us the degree of excellence or deficiency of the student's performance in relation to peers. So CRM provides only part of the information required to judge a student's performance.
- It is unrealistic to expect a teacher to provide the degree of detail necessary to write instructional objectives so that reliable criterion-referenced measures can be obtained.
- Knowledge and understanding do not lend themselves to clear definition. It is extremely difficult, then, to establish adequate criteria of achievement.
- Criterion-referenced measurements discourage the use of problem-solving questions and encourage the use of questions with right and wrong answers. Here responding is not problem solving; it is simply choosing from among another person's solutions.

TABLE 12.1

Continued

Norm-Referenced Measurement (NRM)

Description

A norm-referenced score measures the student's performance against the scores achieved by others completing the same test.

Applications

Norm-referenced measurements are particularly useful for

- classifying students.
- selecting students for fixed quota requirements.
- making decisions as to *how much* (more or less) a student has learned in comparison to others.

Criticisms

The following criticisms of NRM have been drawn from those that commonly appear in the literature:

- If NRM is used in a classroom—say, a large freshman psychology class—the final grade received by a student in the subject conceals the student's misunderstandings, inadequate study skills, and potential limitations in the subject. For any interpretation to have meaning, each individual's score needs to be related to the content of the test.
- Any given mark does not signify a definite amount of knowledge and so has little relevance to content or meaning for those who try to have absolute standards.
- Over a period of time, some students who are continually exposed to NRM suffer a diminishing level of motivation. Although they master everything they are supposed to, if they are not among the very highest scorers in the class, they may never get the A's.
- With everyone out for the top marks, students are pitted against one another. They do not tend to cooperate with others.
- Tests constructed to provide NRM sample only a small number of the course objectives.
- The use of NRM in classroom tests hides the fact that some courses are very good while others are very bad, or that teachers set different standards.
- The setting of frequency limits in failure and pass rates (that is, "grading on the curve," an activity associated with NRM that is impossible with CRM) can become an administrative necessity that overrides individual, educational, and even statistical considerations.

Reliability

There are two major criteria for judging the quality of the tests we use: reliability and validity. A good test is both reliable and valid. Here we examine test reliability; in the next section, we look at test validity.

Suppose we are interested in the academic performance of a student named Carmine. She has just finished a test of knowledge about botany. The test had 40 items, each worth 1 point. Carmine received a score of 24. To interpret Carmine's test performance in terms of norms, we would find it useful to know that the mean or average score of the class was 29. To interpret her test performance in terms of criteria, we would have to know that the teacher had set 80 percent or more items correct as the criterion of competence. So 32 (.80 × 40) was the cut-off score to determine who has or has not mastered botany. Given this information and either a norm-referenced or criterion-referenced perspective, we could say that Carmine's performance is somewhat below average, or that she has not reached the mastery criterion.

But the issue is not this simple. With any test, we must ask whether we would make the same decisions about Carmine's performance if she took the same or a similar test again within a short period of time. We must consider how dependable, consistent, or stable the test performance of a student is. To do so, we need to know his performance over different testings and time spans. The dependability, consistency, and stability of a score are different aspects of what we call *test reliability,* one of the fundamental characteristics of tests. If we believe that the decisions we make about people on the basis of a test will be the same from time to time, we are assuming that the test is reliable.

Precision, consistency, stability

Test-Retest Reliability

How do we know whether a test gives us reliable information about a student? One way is to retest Carmine (with the same test or a parallel test, at a later time) and see whether her score is about 24 on the retest. If it is, our evaluation that Carmine is slightly below average in knowledge of botany or has not mastered botany seems to hold. The test appears to be a reliable instrument. Moving from one student to a class of thirty, we see that reliability refers to the degree to which the scores received by students on one test occasion are about the same as the scores they would receive if tested again on a different occasion.

When we are interested in norm-referenced interpretations of scores, the reliability question becomes a question of the degree to which the rank ordering of individuals will be the same from one time to the next. Insofar as students' ranks according to their scores are about the same from one test occasion to another, the test may be considered reliable in the sense that it is highly stable.

Reliability in the sense of stability

One estimate of reliability for norm-referenced tests that we might use is the correlation between the ranks obtained on the first testing occasion and the ranks obtained on the second testing occasion. Remember that a correlation tells us the degree of relationship between two things. Suppose we had five

TABLE 12.2

Hypothetical Student Rankings on Two Tests

Student	Rank on First Testing	(A) Rank on Second Testing	or	(B) Rank on Second Testing
Jeana	1	2		4
Thu	2	1		3
Alison	3	4		1
Bobby	4	3		5
Henry	5	5		2

students take a test and then retake it, with the results of the second testing described in columns A or B of Table 12.2.

If we obtained the results in column A, we would not be too surprised. There have been some changes in ranks: For example, the first- and second-ranked students switched ranks, and so did the third- and fourth-ranked students. But the least able student on the first test remained fifth ranked on the second test. The test has some stability in terms of how it orders people from lowest to highest in ability, although it clearly is *not* perfect. (The rank-difference coefficient of correlation for this case is +.80.) But if the results were like those in column B (where the ranks correlate −.20 with those on the first testing), there are too many changes in rank to feel the test is stable or dependable. In this case the test probably is not reliable. (A correlation that is near zero, or negative, indicates no reliability from one testing occasion to another. The correlation in this case is now negative, indicating undependable data.)

Rank-difference coefficient of correlation

The coefficient of correlation between the ranks (on the same test given twice or on two parallel tests) obtained by students in a class can be used to estimate stability, dependability, or reliability, giving us a numerical value to use for interpreting a test's reliability. If two rank orderings of test scores were exactly the same, the correlation would equal 1.00, which would mean the test was perfectly reliable. If the correlation equals .90 or .84, the reliability is high because the rank orderings are pretty much the same on the two testing occasions; that is, the information we get from a score, which we then use to make decisions, stays relatively constant from one testing occasion to another.

Generally, we need reliability coefficients above .80 to make important decisions about students from norm-referenced tests. Lower reliabilities generally are not acceptable. But if a student scores extremely high or low on a test, some decisions become safe even if the reliability is lower than .80. That is, even with low test reliability, say about .60, we would not expect the top- and bottom-scorers to switch places completely. Perhaps the low-scorers move up a bit and the high-scorers move down a bit, but those at the extremes of a distribution move around a lot only if reliability is down near .00.

Reliability in the sense of precision

When we deal with criterion-referenced tests, reliability has a different meaning. The precision of the score is less important to us than the dependability of our *decision* about whether Carmine has or has not mastered the botany

Dependability of decision

unit. In a way, Carmine's exact score is not very important—all scores under 32 are grouped together as failures, and all scores at 32 or above are grouped together as passes. The interpretive decision, not the actual score, is what matters.

The test-retest method can also be used to estimate the reliability of our decision about Carmine. If she was retested and we found once again that she has not mastered the unit, the test shows some reliability. For a group of students, we would analyze the decisions made about them each time they were tested. We might ask how we classified Carmine, Henry, Phyllis, Herman, and the other members of the class on each test. Inspecting these data tells us whether or not the decisions are being confirmed.

Probability estimates

The numerical indices of test-retest reliability for criterion-referenced tests provide either correlational information, which is what we've been discussing, or probability estimates (Berk, 1980; Sweezy, 1981). If one criterion-referenced test has a probability of .82 for correctly classifying "masters" and "non-masters," it is more reliable than a test that has a probability of only .55. Both correlational and probability estimates of reliability can have numerical values between 0 and 1.00 and are interpreted in a similar way—the closer to 1.00, the higher the estimate of reliability.

Internal-Consistency Reliability

Determine reliability from one testing occasion

To determine test-retest reliability, we have to give students the same test (or a parallel form of the same test) on a second occasion. But most teachers do not have the time to retest students. They have to be able to determine reliability from a single administration. Internal-consistency reliability does not reflect stability over time; it indicates how precisely a single test measures whatever it measures, at a single time.

How does it work? What we do is estimate the correlation between the test we are giving and some hypothetical test that would be given at the same time. The statistical procedures for computing internal-consistency reliability are too complicated to discuss here. But an introductory textbook on testing or measurement can give you the information you need if you want to estimate the internal-consistency reliability for your own norm-referenced tests. Procedures for determining the reliability of criterion-referenced tests from a single administration are still too difficult for classroom teachers to use easily (see Hambleton, Swaminathan, Algina, & Coulson, 1978; Subkoviak, 1980). The reliability of teacher-made tests, in general, is usually low. These facts suggest that any one test, particularly a short one, provides a teacher with untrustworthy information. Only the sum of several teacher-made tests typically has substantial reliability.

Single teacher-made tests usually unreliable

The Standard Error of Measurement

More important than the ability to compute reliability estimates is the realization that scores from tests have less than perfect stability and internal consistency. Reliability estimates for tests in education are always less than 1.00 and often less than .80. Therefore, the scores for individuals will fluctuate a little (or a lot) from one occasion to the next. Be sure to remember, then, if you ever have to make decisions based on a single score for a student (say, assigning all those who have scored above 45 on a certain test to the gifted program, or giving D's to all those who have scored below 18 on a certain test), that the observed scores you are using to characterize each student are not all that precise. The lack of precision in scores—a lack that results from unreliability—is reflected in a statistic we call the *standard error of measurement*.

Any score on any test is made up of "error" as well as the "true" level of the attribute we are measuring. When we measure IQ, we measure an aptitude for performing certain intellectual tasks. But that measurement is affected on any given day by the person's health, emotional state, motivation, rapport with the examiner, recent practice in the area being tested, attention, coordination, memory, and fatigue. Of particular importance here is the individual's luck in guessing on a given test occasion.

True score ± error score = observed score

An observed score—say, Carmine's 24 points on the botany test—is made up of true score and error score. The estimated amount of the error in a person's score is what we want to know. After we estimate the error, we can estimate a *confidence band* around the observed score and be pretty sure that a person's true score is within that confidence band. The standard error of measurement (further described, with its formula, in almost all introductory testing and measurement texts) provides us with the information we need to develop a confidence band for observed scores. By tradition we usually talk of 68, 95, or 99 percent confidence in estimating true scores.

Confidence band

Suppose we learn from the use of the statistical formula that the standard error of measurement was 4 points for the botany test that Carmine took. Then we would know that Carmine's true score was probably somewhere in the range from 4 points below to 4 points above the score she received. That is, her true score would probably be between 20 and 28. This is the confidence band, and from our statistics we would have confidence that we were right 68 percent of the time.

There is an important point here for teachers to learn. Because of the errors in our measurement system, we must learn to think of Carmine's score, and those of our other students, as falling within ranges, not at precise points, on our tests. Knowing there is a standard error of measurement also keeps us on guard when we compare two or more students whose observed scores seem different. Suppose Henry's observed score on the botany test was 31. At first glance it would appear that Henry is slightly over and Carmine under the average for the class, and that Henry scored 7 points higher than Carmine. But when we use the standard error of measurement to determine confidence bands, we find a situation like the one shown in Figure 12.1. Thinking in terms of confidence bands, not precise scores, leads us to different interpretations. First, we notice that the two confidence bands overlap. So we probably do not want to conclude too quickly that Henry's true score is higher than Carmine's. If Henry's true score is at the low end of the confidence band determined for his observed score and Carmine's true score is at the high end of the confidence band around her

Think of confidence bands, not precise scores

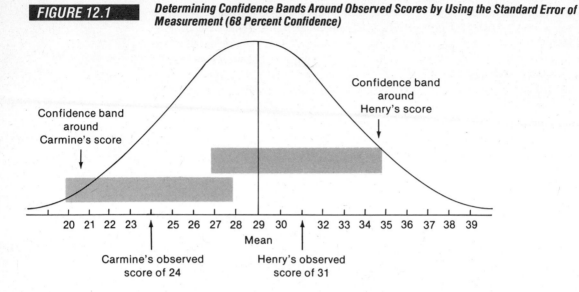

FIGURE 12.1 *Determining Confidence Bands Around Observed Scores by Using the Standard Error of Measurement (68 Percent Confidence)*

The "no decision" category

observed score, Carmine would actually be performing better on the botany test than Henry!

Because scores are not precise points, but rather indicators of bands, many people who use criterion-referenced tests add a third category to "mastery" and "nonmastery"—a category called "no decision." To reflect the acknowledged lack of precision in the scores on the botany examination, it might pay to designate 30 to 33 items correct as a band within which we need more information before classifying someone as showing "mastery" or "nonmastery." The size of the band we choose reflects our concern about the magnitude of the standard error of measurement.

All this discussion of unreliability and error of measurement is designed to keep you cautious. In any testing you are involved with, in any tests you interpret, in any selection or grading you do, remember that each score has associated with it a confidence band that defines the range of error for that particular score. If reliability is less than 1.00, the obtained score contains some error. Do not think of numerical scores as godgiven. They are fallible, as are the people who must interpret them.

Fallible scores, fallible people

Improving Reliability

Adding items

One way to improve test reliability, and thus reduce the standard error of measurement, is to increase the length of a test. This is true for both norm-referenced and criterion-referenced tests. You should remember that *all tests sample behavior.* Of the hundreds of test questions that could be asked in an area of arithmetic or about a novel, only a subset of items are used to make up a test. If a student has a momentary lapse in attention or makes a careless error on one question, he or she is sunk if the test is short. Or if a student doesn't remember one character or incident in a novel, and that is what all the questions on a test are about, again the student is in trouble. More items that sample widely from a domain of knowledge really work to a student's advantage when taking a test. Although students who take tests and teachers who construct tests both complain about the tedium of lengthy examinations, the relation between reliability and test length is clear. If you had a 5-item test with reliability of .20, adding 5 items of the same type would increase the estimated reliability coefficient to .33. If you add 15 items of the same type, the reliability estimate increases to .50. *When the reliability of a test is low, adding items of the same kind increases the reliability coefficient. When reliability is already high, adding items does not have much effect.*

Validity

Test validity is the degree to which testing procedures and interpretations help us assess what we want to assess. It is the single most important issue to consider when evaluating a test (Committee to Develop Standards for Educational and Psychological Testing, 1985). This is because so many tests really do not function as they should. A highly reliable test of verbal ability may not identify the most creative students in art, only those who have learned art terms. Or the test may identify students for an art program who are really no better at art than the ones who were not picked. Reliability is important, but ultimately what we most want in a test is validity. We want the test to measure what we intend to measure—achievement of a certain kind, the promise of various candidates for scarce positions, the latent talent of students, and so forth. There are many different kinds of validity, but we concentrate here on just three: content validity, criterion validity, and construct validity—the three C's (see Cronbach, 1971; Messick, 1980, 1989).

Validity most important

The three C's

Content Validity

We must be sure when we put together, say, a geology test that we are really measuring geology knowledge and skills. We have to be sure that the questions pertain to what we've taught—either the entire curriculum or just the material in one class. We have to know that the questions are representative of the material and that there are enough of them to sample adequately the different kinds of knowledge and skill in that domain.

If a social studies test asks questions that could be answered on the basis of general intelligence, test wiseness, or regular newspaper reading, the course content in social studies is not being tested adequately. *The items on an achievement test should be tied to an instructional domain that students have had an opportunity to learn.* If independent experts agree that a test in eighth-grade social studies is measuring the common curriculum in that subject area, the test has content validity. As the social studies subject matter changes or as new

Test material that students have had an opportunity to learn

subtopics are stressed, the content sample for the eighth-grade social studies test must also change if it is to remain valid.

Test content should match course content

Content validation is a logical procedure; it is based on good sense. (In Chapter 14 we describe how to define a domain and sample from it.) If we don't rely on sensible sampling procedures, we probably cannot interpret our tests in the way we intended to. That is, a test is not a valid test of geology or social studies or whatever unless its content is appropriately matched with the defined domain of content in geology or social studies or whatever. Content validity is a special problem for norm-referenced tests; it is less of a problem with criterion-referenced tests, in which instructional objectives are tied directly to test items.

Criterion Validity

Correlation of test scores with criteria of success

If you are using a test for selecting students for admission to a school, curriculum, or course, you must make sure that it is valid for the purpose. Suppose in your district you have a program for academically gifted students and are using a creativity test for selection. Does the test actually select students who are more likely than others to profit from the program? To estimate the criterion validity, we need to test a group of students and then let all of them, whatever their scores, into the program. We would then correlate scores on the selection test with scores on some criterion measure that reflects success in the instructional program. This correlational procedure allows us to see the degree to which the high-scorers on the selection test profit more from the program than the low-scorers on the selection test. If they do profit more from instruction, and if in the future we want to choose students who will get the most from the special program, we can use the test for selection. The test is valid for predicting who will do well on the criterion. (What we are calling criterion validity is sometimes called *concurrent* or *predictive* validity.) College testing offices want applicants to take the SAT or the ACT tests and supply a transcript of high school grades because, over the years, it has been established that these tests and grades have predictive validity. When the criterion is first-semester grades in college, the SAT or ACT and high school grades predict with well-above-chance accuracy levels how well students are likely to do.

Predictive validity

Validity holds only for kinds of students with whom test was validated

Once again, a warning: Criterion validity coefficients provide us with a useful basis for selecting and counseling students in various curriculum areas, but *only* when a particular student is like the students who were in the sample on which the validity coefficient was determined. Teachers, sometimes with school psychologists, curriculum specialists, or special educators, may be part of committees that make important decisions about students. When tests are used as a way of getting information to help them make decisions, teachers should ask whether a particular test has a substantial criterion-validity coefficient. Then they must check whether the group used to determine that coefficient is like the group to which the information is now being applied. Selection for special programs can be helped by valid tests, but selection should also take into account the unique circumstances of a particular student, the student's motivation, and the meaning of wrong decisions.

Construct Validity

Our third C is construct validity, and it may be the most difficult kind of validity to understand. In fact, it may also be the most important. Construct validity deals with the question of whether a test measures the attribute or characteristic it claims to measure; whether our interpretations of the test are sensible; and whether the consequences of using the test are acceptable. These are extremely complex issues, and they tie test validity to issues within the culture of which the test is a part.

Does the test measure what it is intended to measure?

We call certain abstract characteristics or attributes of people *constructs*. Intelligence is a construct. So are creativity, anxiety, and many other things. We cannot measure these attributes, characteristics, traits, or constructs directly, the way we do arithmetic achievement or spelling ability. So we invent the idea of intelligence or creativity or anxiety to talk about a complex set of behaviors that, all together, seem to indicate that a person can or will act intelligently, creatively, or anxiously. How do we tell if a test we are using to measure, say, scientific aptitude is really measuring the construct of scientific aptitude? Maybe it is measuring only knowledge of science, general intelligence, reading comprehension, or all of these. This is a tricky question. Too many tests pass as tests of creativity, art aptitude, or mechanical knowledge when they do *not* measure the attribute they claim to measure.

How do we check for construct validity? One way is to use correlations. If we have a test of art aptitude and a rating of how well students did in art, the two measures ought to be related. The same would be true for a test of mechanical aptitude and performance in auto mechanics, or any other aptitude test and a criterion measure of the corresponding kind of performance. Even a moderate correlation would be reassuring. We can also correlate one test of, say, IQ with another. For example, a new short IQ test had better correlate substantially with the Stanford-Binet and Wechsler IQ tests, both well-accepted tests of the construct of IQ. If the new measure of IQ does not have much in common with these tests, then what it measures is *not* what we usually mean by intelligence, regardless of what the test is intended to measure.

Correlational evidence on construct validity

Another way to check a test for construct validity is to test hypotheses about how high-scorers and low-scorers should act. When we test leadership, self-concept, attitude toward mathematics, or other constructs, high-scorers and low-scorers on these tests should act differently. If they do in fact behave the way we expect them to, the tests have a claim to construct validity.

Hypothesis-testing evidence

One particular aspect of construct validity is often overlooked. This is the interpretation associated with the test. A test of career interests may validly identify students who will or will not enjoy engineering as a field. But if that test is used to counsel students out of a drafting course in high school, it is being used inappropriately. The construct of "drafting achievement" was never examined. The test only purports to be a test of "interest in engineering." Erroneous interpretation of the test destroys its construct validity. It is being used in ways it was never intended to be used and therefore is not measuring the things it claims to measure. A test's consequences must be thought about if we are to

Erroneous interpretation destroys construct validity

Social consequences and construct validity

judge the test as possessing construct validity. If the "interest in engineering" construct is more often associated with males or middle-class white students and the construct results in counseling women and minority-group members away from courses that are precursors to engineering careers, such as high school drafting, then the test is having unacceptable social consequences. The test may not be having the effects we desire and thus may be failing society in general. In each case, when we are determining whether the test measures what it is supposed to, whether it is interpreted correctly, or whether it is having unanticipated consequences, we must ask about the construct validity of the test. What does it mean to use the Jones test of career interest? What does it mean in terms of teachers, students, and society, when I use my midterm test of language arts achievement? Issues of construct validity are issues about the use, interpretation, and consequences of tests. These are tough and controversial issues in present-day society.

No public regulation of tests

Claims about how drugs affect people are carefully checked by federal and state agencies, and physicians' use of drugs is monitored, even if only casually. But there is no such regulation of test development. The claims associated with tests, including their interpretation and their consequences, are not monitored. Education is filled with people who make up tests and advocate their use without looking carefully at their test's validity, and they disclaim any responsibility for the interpretations made or consequences associated with using the test. This is unethical behavior. Teachers, then, have to be careful about the tests they use and the interpretations and consequences associated with their use. Teachers, more than anyone else in education, must be advocates for children and keep them away from tests that are inappropriately used or interpreted. To do so will require that you learn more about test and measurement issues, as your career progresses, than we can give you here.

Advocates for children

RECAP

Good tests are *reliable.* This means that we can trust the information they give us about a student, believing it to be precise, consistent, and stable. The reliability coefficient and the standard error of measurement tell us how much faith we can have in these aspects of a particular test score. We need to think about test scores as having confidence bands around them. Errors of measurement and true scores are always mixed together.

Most important, good tests are *valid:* They measure what we intend them to measure. Achievement tests should have content validity—a logical match between a test and the domain it is intended to sample. The criterion validity of tests used for counseling and selecting students should also be known, for it tells the degree to which tests used in selection and counseling predict some criterion (or accepted measure) of performance in courses or jobs. All tests should have construct validity. They should measure the constructs (attributes, traits, tendencies) that they claim to measure, be interpreted cautiously, and not have undesirable consequences. Valid tests measure what they are supposed to measure, nothing more, nothing less. Consequences of test use must accord with the goals of the society in which their use occurs.

Evaluation

Evaluation has become a specialized activity in education. People now are trained to be evaluators. Agencies that fund educational projects are specifying that the projects be evaluated. Teachers and administrators are being asked more and more for evidence that what they do is working. Evaluation is a part of educational accountability (holding educators accountable for the success of their efforts), product development, and curriculum development.

Evaluation is a form of assessment concerned with the collection and use of information for making decisions about programs, curricula, teaching methods, and other school activities (see McLaughlin & Phillips, 1991). Evaluators address these kinds of questions:

- How have the new attendance boundaries in the district affected segregation?
- How can I change the reading program to help students learn more?
- How do students like the food since we hired the new cafeteria manager?
- Should this teacher get a merit raise?
- Is the new curriculum on patriotism doing what it should?

Evaluators are educators helping members of a policy-shaping community to recognize their own interests, weigh the consequences of alternative approaches, and discover new ways to perform their tasks (Cronbach & associates, 1980). Evaluators are detectives: They look for evidence to shed light on some problem. They must collect evidence to help others make decisions. The evidence may include measures of student achievement by means of teacher-made and standardized tests, observations of teacher and student behavior, attitude measurements, surveys of parental opinion, interviews with school-board members, financial costs, and a variety of other things.

Evidence for decision making

Whatever is being evaluated—a reading unit or an entire science curriculum—two kinds of evaluation go on: *formative* evaluation, which is used to change a program so that it operates as it was intended to operate, and *summative* evaluation, which is used to judge a program on the basis of how well and at what cost it brings about wanted outcomes.

Formative Evaluation

Formative evaluation is what we use as a basis for revising materials or programs. It is the responsibility, not only of the developers of the materials or programs, but of teachers and administrators too. Is the new film on mitosis effective the way it is, or do we need more instructional time? Are the inductive

Evaluation as a basis for revisions

• *In formative evaluation, whenever you try out new teaching methods or programs, you must implement a system for monitoring the innovation.*
(© *Jean-Claude Lejeune*)

methods you are using to teach the concept of "peninsula" working as you want? Are the instructional games for use with Native American youngsters in the Southwest doing what we intended? Whenever you try out new materials, teaching methods, or programs, you must put into use a system for monitoring the innovation. You can work alone or with other teachers. Your evaluation is the basis for improving the program or abandoning it.

Of course an innovation should be used in a way that gives it a fair chance to work in your unique classroom circumstances. If it is a new product, say, a teacher-training module or a logic game for students, it might have to be modified many times by yourself or the developer before you are satisfied with it. Formative evaluation is concerned with making activities or materials work the way they are supposed to.

Summative Evaluation

Evaluation of the final product

After a product, program, or activity has been refined, modified, and used, a summative evaluation may be called for. A good summative evaluation examines competing methods or programs too, to see whether they can produce the same or better results for less money or in less time. The usual summative evaluation is like a horse race: Curriculum A is pitted against curriculum B; textbook C is pitted against textbook D.

The horse-race approach is narrow, but it seems to be valued. From experience with these kinds of comparisons, educational psychologists now know enough to expect that in any comparison of educational programs or products, each will have better effects in those curriculum areas that are deliberately stressed by the materials, and each will do about as well as the others in those areas of the curriculum that are not especially emphasized (see Walker & Schaffarzick, 1974).

The horse-race approach

The evaluation of materials or activities must also take into account factors other than educational effects, namely, cost-effectiveness (see Levin, 1983), time required, ease of use, needs met by the program, attitudes of students, preferences of teachers, judgments of specialists, and so on. Summative evaluation is complex because many sources are used to obtain information for making decisions about keeping or abandoning the materials or activities.

Teachers are rarely involved in summative evaluation. This is a job for unbiased evaluators from outside the school system. These evaluators must be skilled in measuring achievement, attitudes, opinions, and interests and in examining the economics, management, and politics of education. Cronbach and his associates (1980) called these evaluators "public scientists"—people who use systematic inquiry techniques to affect social systems.

Outside experts

Public scientists

Teachers have a right and a responsibility to demand summative evaluation reports. When consumers want information about washing machines, automobiles, or cameras, they can get that information from local consumers groups, agencies of the federal government, or *Consumer Reports,* a magazine that offers summative evaluations of many products each year.

What do we do? Where do we get the information we need about the effectiveness of textbooks, curricula, audiovisual aids, workbooks, educational games, computer programs, and other educational products. We have to begin to ask product developers to answer questions like these:

- Which of my students will profit from these materials—the brightest only, middle-class students only, or others as well?
- What skills and knowledge will my students have after using the materials? Can you show me what a final test would look like?
- What is the cost per student? Are the materials reusable? Will the books last? Can I make copies?
- How much of my time will be needed? Of students' time? What are the prerequisites for students and teachers who want to use these materials?
- How does this product compare with the one I have been using? How do you know?
- Can you give me the name of someone in the area who is using these materials?

Questions for educational product developers

Teachers have a responsibility for helping improve educational quality as much and as quickly as possible. One way to meet that responsibility is to demand summative evaluations of new teaching programs and materials—in short, to be a good consumer.

SUMMARY

A primary function of teachers is the assessment of students, materials, and programs. Often we use tests in the evaluation process. A good test relies on systematic procedures for observing student performance and quantifies that performance. A test samples only a small amount of what students have learned. But that small amount can provide a meaningful indicator of what has been learned. We use the measurement of observable behavior—the student's score—to evaluate learning.

Norms allow us to interpret a student's score in relation to the scores of other students—in the local area or for the nation as a whole. Norm-referenced testing tells us how a student's knowledge compares with that of other students; it does not tell us what the student actually knows. For this kind of interpretation, we have to use criterion-referenced testing—tests that allow us to compare student behavior with some preset standard of performance.

A good test must be both reliable and valid. Reliability has to do with stability. No test is ever perfectly reliable. As a result, we must take account of the standard error of measurement; we have to think of a student's score, not as a precise point, but as a range—a confidence band around the observed score.

Validity—that a test measures what we want it to measure—is the most important element in the assessment process. An achievement test has content validity when it tests material that students have had an opportunity to learn. Criterion validity tells us how well a test predicts success in an instructional program or a job. Construct validity is more difficult to determine because it deals with the degree to which a test measures an abstraction. Here the question is whether a test in fact measures the construct (ability, trait, or tendency) it is intended to measure. And we add to this the notions that a test must be interpreted sensibly and that the consequences of its use are anticipated and acceptable. A test fails to achieve sufficient construct validity if we are not comfortable about its meaning in the educational context in which it is used.

We've been talking about testing as a means of measuring and evaluating learning. But teachers are also responsible for evaluating the programs and materials they are using or plan to use. That is, we use evaluation to make decisions not only about students' learning but also about the programs and materials we use to teach them.

Formative evaluation gives teachers and others the information they need to improve programs or curricular materials. Summative evaluation, which is usually conducted by outside experts, tells us whether programs and products are producing what they were intended to produce at reasonable costs in money, effort, and time. Teachers should demand more information about evaluation from curriculum developers and those who sell educational materials.

Popham (1981) dramatically summed up the need for educators to understand assessment:

> We live in an era when everybody adores *evidence*. We want evidence that patent sleeping pills do indeed send us off to the land of Nod. We want evidence that food additives are not carcinogenic . . . we want evidence that the nation's schools are effective.
>
> There is no doubt that we are living smack in the middle of an evidence-oriented era. That evidence orientation having intruded most dramatically on the educational enterprise, should force educators to consider a fundamental truth. *In an evidence-oriented enterprise, those who control the evidence-gathering mechanisms control the entire enterprise.* Since, in education, tests constitute our chief evidence-gathering mechanisms, it is apparent that all educators should become knowledgeable regarding the fundamentals of educational measurement. (pp. 5–6)

Assessment and Standardized Tests

OVERVIEW

All through your schooling you have been dealing with standardized testing. But you have always been on the student's side in this aspect of assessment. In this chapter we talk about the other side—the teacher's and, more generally, the educator's. Both standardized tests and teacher-made tests rest on the basic concepts we looked at in Chapter 12, but they offer different advantages and serve different purposes. Let's look at these before we go on to the ways in which we select, administer, and interpret standardized tests, in order to enhance assessment.

Advantages and Special Uses of Standardized Tests

A standardized test is one that has been given to a large representative sample of some population so that scores on the test can be compared with those of the people in that sample. That is, norm-referenced standardized tests provide norms that make possible the comparison of any student's score with those of many other students. Whenever you want to evaluate a student against criteria that go beyond a single teacher's classroom and that teacher's conception of what should be taught, you need a standardized test. A comparison of standardized and teacher-made achievement tests (discussed in the next chapter) is shown in Table 13.1.

In addition to having norms—that is, bases for interpreting scores in terms of other students' scores—standardized tests

Norms

| TABLE 13.1 | Comparison of Standardized and Teacher-Made Tests of Achievement |

Criterion	Standardized Tests	Teacher-Made Tests
Reliability	Reliabilities usually high, often around .90 for norm-referenced tests.	Reliabilities rarely estimated; when estimated, average about .60.
Validity	Criterion validity generally determined; construct validity discussed.	Construct and criterion validity unknown.
	Content validity generally high for criterion-referenced tests; difficult to assess in the case of norm-referenced tests, but can be estimated.	Content validity generally high if systematic procedures used to construct the test.
Measurement of content taught	Measures content common to a majority of American schools but may not always reflect local curriculum.	Measures content unique to local curriculum.
		Continual adaptation of test possible.
	Measurement of basic skills and complex outcomes adaptable to many local situations.	Tests adaptable to changes in emphases; can rapidly reflect new curriculum.
		Tend to stress knowledge rather than higher-order outcomes.
Student preparation	Studying usually does not help a student obtain a better score unless the test is tied closely to the local curriculum.	Studying usually helps a student obtain a better score.
Quality of test items	Quality generally very high; items written by test experts, tried out, and revised before included in test.	Quality unknown, varied; test item files of variable quality often available from publishers of texts in use.
Item type	Usually multiple-choice.	Various kinds of items used.
Administration and scoring of test	Procedure standardized and constant from class to class.	Procedures for testing are flexible.
	Specific instructions given.	Teacher scored.
	Machine scored.	
Interpretation of scores	Scores usually compared with state or national norms.	Scores interpretable on basis of immediate peer group, or local norms.
	Scores often have confidence bands.	
	Test manuals provide help in interpreting information and making decisions.	

Careful construction

Background information

Administration

are usually more carefully constructed than teacher-made tests because they are constructed by experts, using the technical, statistical, and research knowledge of the testing field. Also standardized tests usually come with more or less detailed background information about the test—its rationale, its purposes, and the ways in which its content and items were chosen. This information includes evidence about the test's reliability and validity (see Chapter 12). And standardized tests usually have detailed instructions about how the test should be administered—the exact directions to be given the students, the time limits (if any), and the ways in which the teacher should handle any special problems that may arise.

Criterion-referenced standardized tests

Criterion-referenced standardized tests are becoming more popular, particularly for tests mandated by a state. These tests yield direct information about how well a student has performed in relation to some specific criterion, rather than in relation to the performance of other students. Some tests of reading disabilities, the Red Cross lifesavers' tests, the requirements for merit badges in the Boy Scouts—all are criterion-referenced standardized tests that are being used today in educational programs. And criterion-referenced tests are rapidly being developed to measure achievement in many other areas of the curriculum. Examples of the information a teacher receives from a well-known norm-referenced standardized test and a criterion-referenced test are given in Figures 13.1 and 13.2.

Types of Standardized Tests Used in Schools

The two main kinds of standardized tests used in schools are aptitude tests and achievement tests.

Aptitude Tests

General vs. special ability tests

When tests cover broad areas of intellectual functioning, they are called intelligence tests, scholastic aptitude tests, academic aptitude tests, or general ability tests. When they are aimed at more specific kinds of intellectual ability, they are called special ability or special aptitude tests. The most frequently used tests of this kind are verbal, mathematical, spatial, mechanical, and clerical aptitude tests.

Uses and misuses of aptitude tests

In general, aptitude tests are norm-referenced and provide information for student guidance and counseling. In colleges, business, and industry they are used for selection and placement. Students have been put into special classes, or treated differently within regular classes, on the basis of their scores on aptitude tests. As we saw in Chapter 3, controversies rage over whether aptitude tests (in the form of intelligence tests) in the schools do more harm than good. Certainly when Spanish-speaking children are classified and treated as mentally retarded because they do poorly on scholastic aptitude tests printed in English, the conclusion that these tests are harmful is easy to defend. Some writers think that the tests do harm by influencing teachers' expectations of their students. They argue that teachers act on their expectations, treating some of their students inappropriately—calling on them less often, "staying with" them

STANFORD

ACHIEVEMENT TEST SERIES, EIGHTH EDITION
WITH OTIS-LENNON SCHOOL ABILITY TEST, SIXTH EDITION

STUDENT SKILLS ANALYSIS
FOR
JOHN A SNYDER

TEACHER:	CESTERO	1988 STANFORD OLSAT
		NORMS: GRADE 04 GRADE 04
SCHOOL:	NEWTOWN ELEM	GRADE: 04 PERIOD 12 NATIONAL NATIONAL
		TEST DATE: LEVEL: INTERMED 1 E
DISTRICT:	NEWTOWN	05/89 FORM: J 1

TESTS	NO. OF ITEMS	RAW SCORE	SCALED SCORE	NATL PR-S	NATL NCE	GRADE EQUIV	AAC RANGE	NATIONAL GRADE PERCENTILE BANDS 1 10 30 50 70 90 99
Total Reading	94	64	630	57-5	53.7	5.0	HIGH	
Vocabulary	40	33	661	81-7	68.5	7.2	HIGH	
Reading Comp.	54	31	611	41-5	45.2	4.0	MIDDLE	
Total Math	118	37	569	13-3	26.3	3.1	LOW	
Concepts of No.	34	15	595	30-4	39.0	3.8	MIDDLE	
Computation	44	8	537	4-2	13.1	2.4	LOW	
Applications	40	14	575	20-3	32.3	3.2	MIDDLE	
Total Language	60	42	628	53-5	51.6	4.7	HIGH	
Lang Mechanics	30	20	616	40-5	44.7	4.1	MIDDLE	
Lang Expression	30	22	640	61-6	55.9	5.6	HIGH	
Spelling	40	19	603	31-4	39.6	3.6	MIDDLE	
Study Skills	30	15	601	30-4	39.0	3.1	MIDDLE	
Science	50	38	650	87-7	73.7	8.2	HIGH	
Social Science	50	35	631	71-6	61.7	5.8	HIGH	
Listening	45	35	654	88-7	74.7	7.8	HIGH	
Using Information	70	46	627	54-5	52.1	4.8	HIGH	
Thinking Skills	101	55	607	45-5	47.4	4.4	MIDDLE	
Basic Battery	387	212	605	35-4	41.9	3.9	MIDDLE	
Complete Battery	487	285	614	45-5	47.4	4.4	MIDDLE	

OTIS-LENNON SCHOOL ABILITY TEST	RAW SCORE	SAI	AGE PR-S	AGE NCE	SCALED SCORE	NATL GRADE PR-S	NATL GRADE NCE	1 10 30 50 70 90 99
Total	72	25	81	12-3	25.3	574	27-4	37.1	
Verbal	36	14	87	21-3	33.0	583	36-4	42.5	
Nonverbal	36	11	80	11-3	24.2	565	21-3	33.0	

AGE 11 YRS 6 MOS

READING GROUP Comprehension	LANGUAGE ARTS GROUP Study Skills	MATHEMATICS GROUP Computation	COMMUNICATIONS GROUP Average

CONTENT CLUSTERS	RAW SCORE/ NUMBER OF ITEMS	BELOW AVERAGE	AVERAGE	ABOVE AVERAGE
Reading Vocabulary	33/ 40			✓
Synonyms	20/ 24			✓
Context	6/ 8		✓	
Multiple Meanings	7/ 8			✓
Reading Comprehension	31/ 54		✓	
Recreational	11/ 18		✓	
Textual	9/ 18		✓	
Functional	11/ 18		✓	
Literal	10/ 21		✓	
Inferential	16/ 26		✓	
Critical	5/ 7		✓	
Concepts of Number	15/ 34		✓	
Whole Numbers	7/ 16		✓	
Fractions	1/ 4		✓	
Decimals	2/ 3		✓	
Operations and Properties	5/ 11		✓	
Mathematics Computation	8/ 44	✓		
Add and Subtract/Whole Nos	3/ 12		✓	
Multiplication/Whole Numbers	3/ 12		✓	
Division/Whole Numbers	1/ 10		✓	
Add and Subtract/Decimals	1/ 6		✓	
Add and Subtract/Fractions	0/ 4		✓	
Mathematics Applications	14/ 40		✓	
Problem Solving	5/ 22		✓	
Graphs and Charts	5/ 6			✓
Geometry/Measurement	4/ 12		✓	

CONTENT CLUSTERS	RAW SCORE/ NUMBER OF ITEMS	BELOW AVERAGE	AVERAGE	ABOVE AVERAGE
Language Mechanics	20/ 30		✓	
Capitalization	6/ 7			✓
Punctuation	6/ 11		✓	
Applied Grammar	8/ 12			✓
Language Expression	22/ 30		✓	
Sentence Correctness	14/ 20		✓	
Sentence Effectiveness	8/ 10		✓	
Spelling	19/ 40		✓	
Study Skills	15/ 30		✓	
Library/Reference Skills	8/ 17		✓	
Information Skills	7/ 13		✓	
Science	38/ 50			✓
Physical Science	12/ 16			✓
Biological Science	14/ 20			✓
Earth/Space Science	12/ 14			✓
Social Science	35/ 50		✓	
Geography	8/ 13		✓	
History	8/ 8			✓
Political Science	8/ 10			✓
Economics	6/ 10		✓	
Psych/Sociol/Anthro	5/ 9		✓	
Listening	35/ 45			✓
Vocabulary	11/ 15			✓
Listening Comprehension	24/ 30			✓
Using Information	46/ 70		✓	
Thinking Skills	55/101		✓	

COPY 02

PROCESS NO. 18904271-8909-03356-2

Abbreviations used: GR = Grade Equivalent, PR = Percentile, S = Stanine, RS/NP = Raw Score/National Percentile.

FIGURE 13.2 Information from a Criterion-Referenced Test

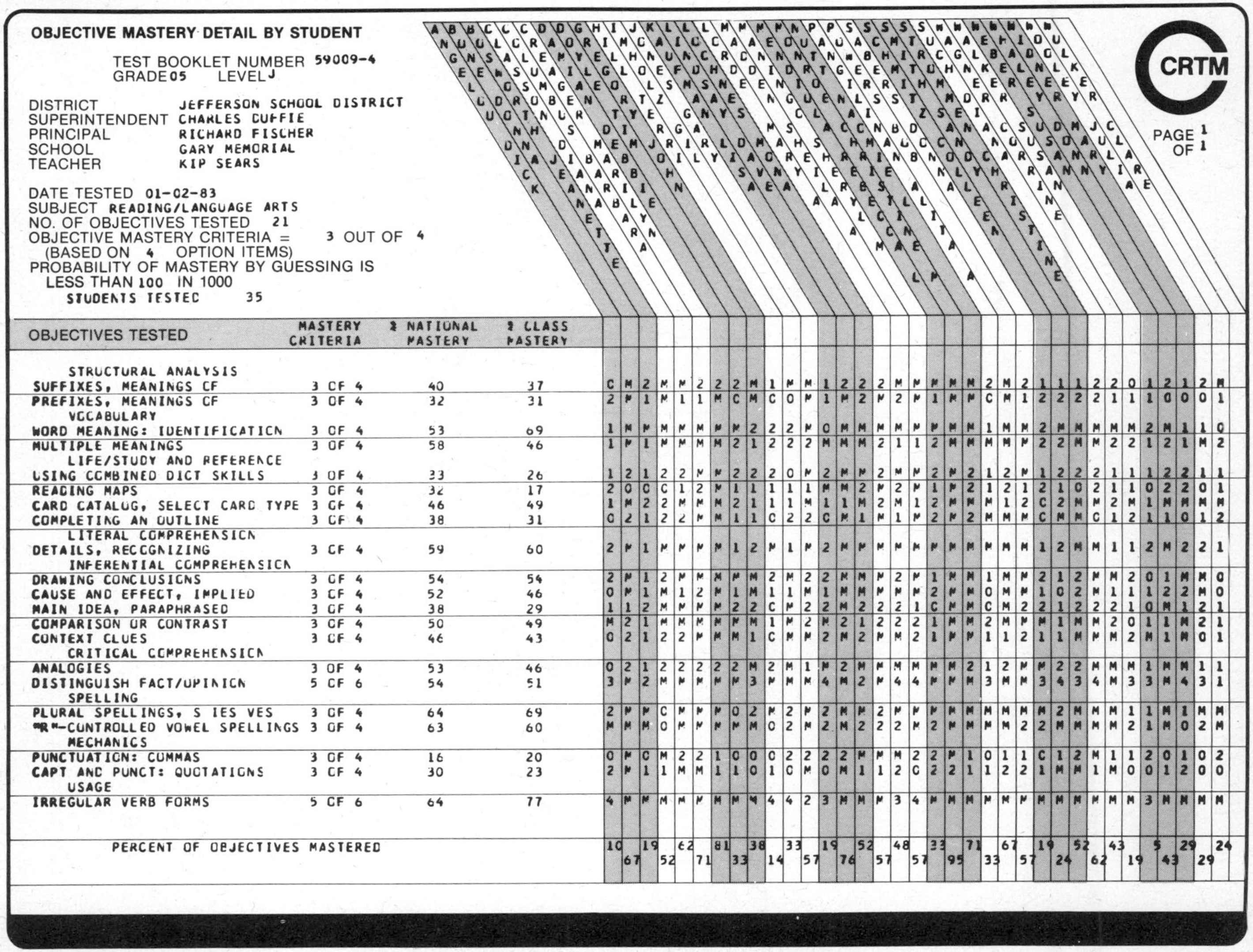

OBJECTIVE MASTERY DETAIL BY STUDENT

TEST BOOKLET NUMBER 59009-4
GRADE 05 LEVEL J

CRTM
PAGE 1 OF 1

DISTRICT JEFFERSON SCHOOL DISTRICT
SUPERINTENDENT CHARLES CUFFIE
PRINCIPAL RICHARD FISCHER
SCHOOL GARY MEMORIAL
TEACHER KIP SEARS

DATE TESTED 01-02-83
SUBJECT READING/LANGUAGE ARTS
NO. OF OBJECTIVES TESTED 21
OBJECTIVE MASTERY CRITERIA = 3 OUT OF 4
(BASED ON 4 OPTION ITEMS)
PROBABILITY OF MASTERY BY GUESSING IS
LESS THAN 100 IN 1000
STUDENTS TESTED 35

OBJECTIVES TESTED	MASTERY CRITERIA	% NATIONAL MASTERY	% CLASS MASTERY
STRUCTURAL ANALYSIS			
SUFFIXES, MEANINGS OF	3 OF 4	40	37
PREFIXES, MEANINGS OF	3 OF 4	32	31
VOCABULARY			
WORD MEANING: IDENTIFICATION	3 OF 4	53	69
MULTIPLE MEANINGS	3 OF 4	58	46
LIFE/STUDY AND REFERENCE			
USING COMBINED DICT SKILLS	3 OF 4	33	26
READING MAPS	3 OF 4	34	17
CARD CATALOG, SELECT CARD TYPE	3 OF 4	46	49
COMPLETING AN OUTLINE	3 OF 4	38	31
LITERAL COMPREHENSION			
DETAILS, RECOGNIZING	3 OF 4	59	60
INFERENTIAL COMPREHENSION			
DRAWING CONCLUSIONS	3 OF 4	54	54
CAUSE AND EFFECT, IMPLIED	3 OF 4	52	46
MAIN IDEA, PARAPHRASED	3 OF 4	38	29
COMPARISON OR CONTRAST	3 OF 4	50	49
CONTEXT CLUES	3 OF 4	46	43
CRITICAL COMPREHENSION			
ANALOGIES	3 OF 4	53	46
DISTINGUISH FACT/OPINION	5 OF 6	54	51
SPELLING			
PLURAL SPELLINGS, S IES VES	3 OF 4	64	69
*R-CONTROLLED VOWEL SPELLINGS	3 OF 4	63	60
MECHANICS			
PUNCTUATION: COMMAS	3 OF 4	16	20
CAPT AND PUNCT: QUOTATIONS	3 OF 4	30	23
USAGE			
IRREGULAR VERB FORMS	5 OF 6	64	77
PERCENT OF OBJECTIVES MASTERED			

Source: Reprinted from *Curriculum Referenced Tests of Mastery Reports Catalog* by permission of Psychological Corporation. Notice that for every objective either a number or a letter indicates how many items each student got right or whether the student has mastered (M) the area.
A printout like this is a source of valuable diagnostic information for teachers, students, and parents.

in classroom recitations less often, giving them enriched assignments less often, and so on (see Good, 1983). It is argued that any measurement of any student characteristic that is thought of as an aptitude measure—a prediction of future learning or performance—is in effect a prophecy that teachers may then unconsciously fulfill, to the detriment of the students who have done poorly on this kind of test. Others argue that teacher knowledge of a student's general or special ability can help the teacher adjust teaching, explanations, assignments, and overall treatment so as to challenge the more able and avoid frustrating and discouraging the less able. So far research has only revealed the possibilities; it has not shown how to make sure students benefit. It is also clear that teachers can form fairly accurate impressions of student aptitude just from student performance in class, without using aptitude tests. These impressions, however, can have the same dangers or advantages as those based on aptitude tests—and the same uses.

Achievement Tests

Standardized achievement tests are used to measure students' achievement of the objectives of instruction in a given course or other curriculum unit. We have

In colleges, business, and industry, norm-referenced aptitude tests are used for selection and placement. (© 1986 Susan Lapides)

standardized achievement tests in, say, third-grade reading, fifth-grade arithmetic, seventh-grade social studies, ninth-grade algebra, and eleventh-grade chemistry. The tests have been constructed by specialists in the curriculum areas and have been administered to large samples of students in the appropriate grade levels and courses. They tell us how well any particular student, class, school, school district, county, or state has done in comparison with the norm group.

Comparisons possible

Thus you often see newspaper articles reporting that the students of a certain city have fallen above (or below) the norm for the state as a whole in reading achievement. Or an article may conclude that, within a given city, certain schools do better and others do worse than the citywide average in achievement in sixth-grade arithmetic. Comparisons of this kind are possible only with standardized, as against teacher-made, tests of achievement and, as we said in Chapter 12, only if the group being compared is like the norm group.

Concerns About Achievement Tests.

Presentation of uninterpretable data

Twenty million days per year taking tests

We always feel frustrated when the newspapers publish test results with no explanation of poverty rates in the various schools, language difficulties, social-class differences, and expenditures per pupil in each district. It is not fair to present uninterpretable data. We also wonder why newspapers do not also foolishly print the unexplained annual death rates per thousand admissions to hospitals in the region. Perhaps editors feel it is acceptable to attack teachers, but not physicians. People worry also that about 20 million school days per year are spent by schoolchildren in the United States taking standardized and teacher-made achievement tests (National Commission on Testing and Public Policy, 1990). It is likely that an *additional* 200–300 million school days are spent in preparation for achievement tests, and about 0.7 to 0.9 billion dollars are spent annually on purchasing, administering, and scoring such tests (S. G. Paris, Lawton, Turner, & Roth, 1991).

But *amounts per pupil* per year make more sense. With about 45 million K–12 students, we get one-half day of testing time, 4.4 to 6.7 days of preparation, and $15–$20 of cost. These less alarming numbers suggest the problem is *not* the amount of testing.

The Differences Between Aptitude and Achievement Tests.

Future vs. past orientation

How do aptitude tests differ from achievement tests? They differ primarily in function: Aptitude tests are used to *predict* achievement, or the outcomes of *future* learning experiences; achievement tests are used to measure and *evaluate* achievement, or the outcomes of *past* learning experiences. But achievement tests often predict future achievement as well as, if not better than, aptitude tests do. So the distinction between the two kinds of tests in terms of function does not always hold up well.

"Taughtness"

We can also make a distinction in terms of content. In an achievement test, the content should, and usually does, deal with what is taught directly and intentionally in schools. Here we ask questions about the content of what has been read in textbooks, discussed in class, practiced in homework and at the chalkboard, and explained by the teacher. Achievement test content should always be high in what we might call "taughtness"; aptitude test content need not be. We would not usually ask questions about the geography of a state or

French vocabulary on an aptitude test, and we would not usually include questions that measure spatial ability (which is not taught in most schools) on an achievement test. But such questions are sometimes included, and, when they are, confusion reigns.

Experts also have trouble with the distinction between aptitude and achievement (Anastasi, 1980; Ebel, 1980; D. R. Green, 1974). For your purposes, it is enough to remember that aptitude tests should have validity for selection and prediction, and that achievement tests should be high in "taughtness" and content validity. Remember too that aptitude tests, which predict future performance, cannot be criterion-referenced. We do not expect a *future* astronomer or jet engine mechanic to meet the criteria for acceptable performance in those fields now. We only want to find the best candidates for training programs in astronomy or engine repair. Achievement tests, however, can be either norm- or criterion-referenced.

Noncognitive Tests. In addition to ability and achievement, teachers and schools sometimes use standardized tests to measure other human characteristics. These kinds of tests are often called *noncognitive,* but you should realize that it is virtually impossible to have a truly "noncognitive" test (see Weiss, 1980). Messick (1979) has proposed a classification of the noncognitive variables of interest to teachers. He identified twelve areas, among them attitudes, interests, motives, temperament, social sensitivity, cognitive styles, and values. Because the use of the instruments to assess these characteristics lies beyond the scope of this book, we do not discuss them further here. You should plan to work closely with school psychologists and counseling psychologists when measures of temperament, cognitive style, attitudes, and values are needed.

Selecting Standardized Tests

Hundreds of standardized tests have been published. How should we decide which to use? How shall we interpret them? Let us first address the issue of selection. Actually there are two kinds of problems here: deciding which criteria to use in making a choice, and getting the necessary information about standardized tests to use in applying the criteria. These problems usually are solved by committees of teachers who have been appointed to recommend standardized tests for use throughout the district or the state. Sometimes the teachers are helped by school psychologists or curriculum personnel who are relatively well versed in the technicalities of test construction. In any case, teachers themselves can do a better job of interpreting and selecting standardized tests if they know more about them.

Criteria and information

The Questions to Ask When Helping to Select Tests

Test selection is not a simple matter. The criteria for selecting standardized tests have been the subject of scores of textbooks and monographs over the last several decades. Our list is presented in checklist form in Figure 13.3. Briefly, you might ask the following thirteen questions about standardized tests.

FIGURE 13.3

A Simple Form for Rating Standardized Tests

| Test _____ | Date _____ |
| Reviewer _____ | |

Criteria			Rating	
	Very Good	Good	Fair	Poor
1. View of learners and learning	_____	_____	_____	_____
2. Descriptions of behavior measured	_____	_____	_____	_____
3. Items per measured behavior	_____	_____	_____	_____
4. Validity	_____	_____	_____	_____
5. Reliability	_____	_____	_____	_____
6. Teaching feedback	_____	_____	_____	_____
7. Student feedback	_____	_____	_____	_____
8. Examinee appropriateness	_____	_____	_____	_____
9. Freedom from bias	_____	_____	_____	_____
10. Ease of administration	_____	_____	_____	_____
11. Ethical propriety	_____	_____	_____	_____
12. Retest potential	_____	_____	_____	_____
13. Cost	_____	_____	_____	_____

Source: W. James Popham, *Modern Educational Measurement,* p. 63. Copyright 1981. Adapted by permission of Allyn & Bacon.

Behavioral view of learning

Learning out of context

Portfolios

1. What Sort of Learning Theory Is Implicit in the Test?   The developers of most standardized tests have a behavioral view of learning; that is, learning is seen as a sequence of small steps, where basic skills are the prerequisites for later learning. Complex learning is believed to come about *after* prerequisites are mastered. Both criterion-referenced and norm-referenced tests often have this quality. They all assume cognition can be decomposed into isolated skills and that information can be taken out of the context of the situations in which it was learned. These underlying assumptions are now seriously questioned in the light of contemporary learning theories. Resnick and Resnick (1990) and Shepard (in press) caution us not to buy tests that treat learners and learning in this way. We may actually have to scrap almost all current tests, and we should do so if they do not measure up. Perhaps more authentic tests can be developed, or portfolios of achievement (collections of student work, such as essays, stories, math problems solved, drawings) can be built up, that will reflect with greater validity *what* students learn and *how* they learn. But a good first question to ask, when participating with other educators in selecting an achievement test, is, What view of learners and learning is reflected in this test? And if you do not like the answer, you have a professional obligation to question the selection and use of that test.

• *Teachers can pool their judgment in arriving at decisions about the content validity and overall suitability of standardized achievement tests. (© 1985 Walter S. Silver)*

2. Is the Behavior That Is Measured Adequately Described?   The developers of commercial, statewide, or districtwide standardized tests always note in the test manual some description of what they think they are measuring. It could be a brief statement of an objective or a detailed statement of the behavior-content matrix used to develop test items. You are likely to find that the manuals for norm-referenced standardized tests provide more general statements about the attributes they are measuring and the procedures for choosing items than do the manuals that accompany criterion-referenced tests. Your job is to decide whether the description gives you confidence that you know what the test claims to measure and whether that is worthwhile.

3. How Many Items per Measured Behavior Are There?   It is customary in criterion-referenced tests to have only a small number of items per objective. Perhaps three items of two-column addition may be enough to satisfy some people that a student's ability in two-column addition has been adequately measured. But would three items be enough to satisfy you? What if we had a three-item test of vocabulary? Almost everyone would agree that you cannot measure vocabulary with a three-item test. So part of the decision about whether or not the test has a sufficient number of items depends on the subject matter we are teaching. Norm-referenced tests face a similar problem. If you have a sixty-item elementary reading and language arts test, there may be one item on prefixes, one item on syllabication, four items on comprehension, two items on grammar, and so on. To cover the broad range of curricula in use in some countries, a nationally normed standardized test may have only an item or two for each area in your language arts program. Is this enough? Obviously there can be only subjective answers to this kind of question. But you are going to have to make informed subjective judgments if you are going to be an intelligent user of standardized tests.

4. Is the Test Valid for Your Use?   In Chapter 12 we noted that criterion-referenced test developers generally do a good job on *content validity*. But this can be a problem for norm-referenced test developers. A careful comparison of three leading textbooks in fourth-grade mathematics with five frequently used norm-referenced standardized tests had startling results. As you can see in Figure 13.4, in the *best* match between what a textbook taught and what a test measured, only 71 percent of the topics tested actually were taught! In the worst case, only 47 percent of the topics tested were covered in the curriculum.

Underestimating student learning

Such mismatches between curriculum and tests cause gross underestimates of what students learn in school. A teacher or committee can judge content validity by studying the test's questions and asking, for each question, Is this something I (we) teach? Is the topic dealt with the way I teach it? The answers to such questions lead to decisions about content validity.

If a test is going to be used to predict something important—say, performance in a special school—it must have high enough *criterion validity* to make you comfortable with your decisions. How high is high? There is no simple answer. You must think through how you are going to use the information from the test and what the costs of a wrong decision are.

Construct validity can be evaluated quantitatively by examining the correlations of a test's scores with other indicators of the construct it supposedly measures. A group IQ test ought to show a moderate to high correlation with an individual test of intelligence such as the Stanford-Binet. And an achievement test ought to correlate at least moderately with teachers' ratings of student achievement in that curricular area. You must also ask if the test will be interpreted reasonably by the school board, parents, and newspapers, and whether it has unanticipated consequences (e.g., forces some teachers to cheat). Remember, the full meaning of using a test must be explored and discussed to ensure that the construct validity of a test will be adequate.

5. How Reliable Is the Test?   To what degree do two or more testings with the same or parallel instruments give the same information for decisions? How large is the standard error of measurement? You must ask whether there

FIGURE 13.4 *Percent of Tested Topics Actually Covered in Each Fourth-Grade Mathematics Textbook*

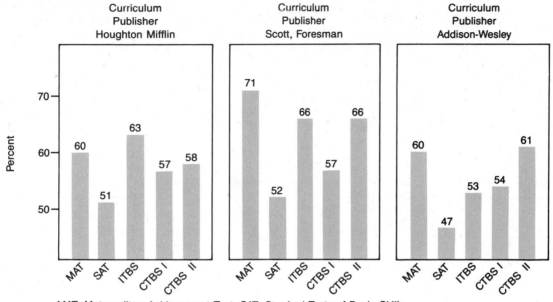

MAT: Metropolitan Achievement Test SAT: Stanford Tests of Basic Skills
ITBS: Iowa Test of Basic Skills CTBS I, CTBS II: Comprehensive Tests of Basic Skills

Source: Institute for Research on Teaching, Michigan State University (1980). Adapted by permission.

is too much error associated with scores or with decision making for the test to be useful for the purposes you have in mind.

6. Does the Test Provide Sufficient and Timely Feedback to the Teacher?

Tests that give us clear, simple information, that can be used by relatively untrained people for making decisions, rate high on "teaching feedback." For norm-referenced tests this has a lot to do with the norm group because feedback to a teacher about a student's or a class's performance depends, in part, on how easily the norms enable you to interpret the performance. Thus the value of feedback to a teacher may depend on the breadth of the age, ability, and educational levels covered by the test's norms. It may also depend on how representative the norm group is—the geographic areas, ages, cultural groups, and types of schools and school districts it was drawn from and the recency of its testing. Remember that the interpretation of a single individual's score on a norm-referenced test depends on how closely that individual resembles the norm group. The question you must ask is whether the individual is being compared against an appropriate set of norms. The feedback has little value for teachers, parents, and students if the student comes from a rural or minority-group home and the norms are heavily wieghted with suburban, majority-group members. Another consideration is how easily the raw scores yielded by the test can be converted into the kinds of scores (percentile ranks, standard scores, or whatever) used in the table of norms.

For criterion-referenced tests, we might assess achievements like "Ability to comprehend literally stated written materials." We could be told through the wonders of computer analysis and printouts who passed, who failed, and whom we need more information about. This feedback is crucial for the teacher who wants to improve instruction. But feedback must be timely, as well. It is silly to test in April and give high-quality feedback to teachers about their students only two weeks before school is out in the spring. That kind of schedule allows us to judge only how schools and districts are doing in helping students achieve. But testing so late in the year provides little or no diagnostic information for teachers.

Timeliness of feedback

7. Does the Test Provide Student Feedback?   How well can students and their parents understand the test results? Most test publishers today supply every student and parent with a printout like the one in Figure 13.5. This is the kind of feedback to students and parents you should look for in a standardized test.

8. Does the Test Show Examinee Appropriateness?   Examinee appropriateness is the suitability of the test for the people to be tested. This criterion refers to the level of comprehension required by the test, its physical format, and the way in which students make their responses. The age or grade range of the test should not be too large; otherwise, the students at the lower part of the range will find the test too hard, and those at the upper levels will find it childish. Appropriateness means the right level of difficulty for people of a given age, grade, sex, or cultural background. The directions for taking the test or making the observations should be clear and appropriate. The visual layout of the questions, the typography, and the use of white space and color should make for clarity. The same kinds of factors apply to tests designed to be presented by sound rather than in print. Here you must think about the test's timing, pacing, and ways of recording answers (speaking, writing, marking, or performing), as well as the necessary equipment.

9. Is the Test Free of Obvious Bias?   Despite many noble attempts, it turns out to be hard to create a test that is fair to every group. Hidden biases permeate standardized and teacher-made tests. But some obvious sources of bias can be eliminated by checking that the publisher has had the test reviewed by members of various cultural and ethnic groups and by people from different regions of the country. You should also examine the test items to see whether they are (1) relevant to the life experiences of the examinees, (2) direct rather than wordy, and (3) moderately stimulating. For example, in an attempt to be relevant, one test writer referred to acne, which is such an extremely sensitive subject for many American teenagers that it may have distracted some of them while taking the test (Popham, 1981).

PARENT / STUDENT REPORT FOR DAVID WILLIAMS

DEAR PARENT AND STUDENT

BELOW YOU WILL FIND THE RESULTS OF THE ACADEMIC ACHIEVEMENT TESTS ADMINISTERED TO ALL THIRD GRADE STUDENTS IN THE BARRINGTON SCHOOLS JUST A FEW WEEKS AGO. THE TESTS HELP TO SHOW YOU AND ALL OF US IN THE BARRINGTON SCHOOLS THE PROGRESS WE HAVE MADE DURING THE LAST EIGHT MONTHS.

THESE TESTS PROVIDE VALUABLE INFORMATION ON THE SPECIFIC SKILLS TAUGHT AND LEARNED IN READING AND LANGUAGE ARTS. THE SCORES BELOW ARE EXPLAINED IN DETAIL ON THE REVERSE SIDE OF THIS REPORT.

STUDENT'S INDIVIDUAL ACCOMPLISHMENTS ARE REPORTED UNDER THE HEADING "STUDENT'S SCORES." TO SEE HOW THESE ACCOMPLISHMENTS COMPARE TO THOSE OF OTHER THIRD GRADERS, COMPARE THE STUDENT'S SCORES TO THE DISTRICT AVERAGES FOR THIRD GRADES UNDER THE HEADING "COMPARISON SCORES."

THESE TESTS PROVIDE MORE THAN SCORES. THEY PROVIDE SPECIFIC DETAILED INFORMATION ABOUT THOSE SKILLS WHICH WE MUST EMPHASIZE

IN TEACHING OUR STUDENTS IN THE REMAINDER OF THIS SCHOOL YEAR AND IN THE COMING YEAR. THESE ARE THE SKILLS WHICH WE CONSIDER MOST IMPORTANT FOR STUDENTS TO HAVE MASTERED FOR SUCCESS IN SCHOOL. AND I CAN ASSURE YOU THAT THEY WILL RECEIVE OUR CONCERTED EFFORTS. WE WELCOME YOUR COOPERATION IN HELPING OUR STUDENTS MASTER THESE IMPORTANT SKILLS.

IF YOU HAVE ANY QUESTIONS ABOUT THESE RESULTS, PLEASE ASK YOUR CHILD'S TEACHER AT THE NEXT PARENT-TEACHER CONFERENCE. THE TEACHER WILL SHARE WITH YOU OTHER OBSERVATIONS AND RECOMMEN- DATIONS BASED ON THEIR EXPERIENCE IN WORKING WITH YOUR SON OR DAUGHTER DURING THE LAST SEVERAL MONTHS.

THANK YOU FOR YOUR CONTINUED SUPPORT OF THE BARRINGTON SCHOOLS.

PAUL BEACHER, SUPERINTENDENT

------- DESCRIPTION OF TEST -------

SUBJECT: READING/LANGUAGE ARTS	
NUMBER OF SKILLS TESTED	19
AVERAGE NO. QUESTIONS PER SKILL	4
MASTERY STANDARD	
(REQUIRED NO. CORRECT PER SKILL)	3
TOTAL QUESTIONS IN TEST	80

------- STUDENT'S SCORES -------

PERFORMANCE SCORE	574
NUMBER OF OBJECTIVES MASTERED	14
NUMBER OF CORRECT ANSWERS	60

------- COMPARISON SCORES -------

STUDENT'S PERCENTILE RANK:	
IN DISTRICT	62
IN NATION	58
AVERAGE NO. OBJECTIVES MASTERED:	
IN DISTRICT	11.0

-----THESE SPECIFIC SKILLS WERE MASTERED:

SELECT THE PHRASE THAT BEST DESCRIBES THE MEANING OF A PREFIXED WORD
SELECT THE MEANING OF A GIVEN WORD USED IN A PHRASE
SELECT THE MEANING FOR MULTIPLE-MEANING WORD FROM CONTEXT OF SENTENCE
SELECT INFORMATION FROM A TABLE OF SIX ROWS UNDER FIVE CATEGORIES
SELECT DEFIN. STRESSED SYLL, WORD IN PRONKEY, AND GUIDE WORDS FOR DICTENTRIES
SELECT PAGE NUMBERS CONTAINING REQUESTED INFORMATION IN AN INDEX WITH CROSS-REFS
SELECT THE CONCLUSION THAT CAN BEST BE INFERRED FROM INFO STATED IN PASSAGE
SELECT IMPLIED CAUSE OF A CAUSE-EFFECT RELATIONSHIP OCCURRING IN THE PASSAGE
INDICATE THE INFERRED MEANING OF AN UNFAMILIAR WORD FROM CONTEXT OF THE PASSAGE
SELECT WD PART REPRESENTING CORRECT SPELLING OF VARIANT CONSONANT IN DICTATED WD
SELECT WD PART REPRESENTING CORRECT SPELLING OF THE LONG VOWEL IN DICTATED WORD
SELECT WD PART REPRESENTING CORR SPELL OF VOWEL COMBINATION IN DICTATED WORD
SELECT THE SENTENCE WITH CORRECT CAPITALIZATION
INDICATE WHETHER SENTENCE IS A COMMAND, QUESTION, STATEMENT, OR EXCLAMATION

-----THESE SPECIFIC SKILLS HAVE NOT YET BEEN MASTERED:

SELECT THE PHRASE THAT BEST DESCRIBES THE MEANING OF A SUFFIXED WORD
SELECT DIRECTION, DISTANCE, OR LOCATION ON POLITICAL MAP W/KEY, SCALE, COMPASS
IDENTIFY A DETAIL STATED IN A FIFTH-GRADE PASSAGE
SELECT THE SENTENCE THAT BEST PARAPHRASES MAIN IDEA OF FIFTH-GRADE PASSAGE
SELECT PAST OR PAST PARTICIPLE FORM OF IRREGULAR VERB THAT COMPLETES SENTENCE

Source: Reprinted from *Curriculum Referenced Tests of Mastery.* Copyright © 1983 by the Psychological Corporation. Reproduced by permission. All rights reserved.

10. Is the Test Easy to Administer?   Tests that can be given to large groups are much easier to use than those that can be given only to small groups or to individuals. Tests that require less time but still give reliable information are also easier to use. And you should consider how clearly the purposes and limitations of the test and the directions for administering it are stated. How much training is required to give the test? How long does it take to get ready to give the test? Can students take the test on their own, or does it have to be administered by a trained psychometrist?

11. Does the Test Show Ethical Propriety?   The ethics of testing can apply to the way in which the test is administered, the content of the test, or the kinds of recommendations that can be based on the tests. Does the test involve more than a normal amount of stress (for example, very short time limits that prevent anyone from finishing it)? If the content could be offensive, insulting, or embarrassing, the test is questionable on ethical grounds. Or if it leads to recommendations, including feedback to the student, that are possibly offensive or insulting, again it rates low in ethical propriety.

12. Does the Test Have Retest Potential?   Are equivalent forms of the test available so that students can be retested with them if necessary? Is there adequate evidence that the forms are truly equivalent? This consideration is particularly important for criterion-referenced tests. When this issue arises for norm-referenced tests, it is appropriate to ask if each of the alternate forms has norms.

13. Is the Cost of the Test Acceptable?   Educational testing is expensive. Do you really want to spend the students' time and the district's money for the information the test scores give you? If the district intends to use tests, can you get the information it needs by some other method and use the money for another educational purpose? The cost of a test should be commensurate with the benefits derived from it. Contemporary thinking is that most standardized tests cost far more than they yield in benefits. Although school boards, legislators, and real estate agents talk a lot about the performance of students in different schools, administrators and teachers in those schools are sometimes barely affected by the information they receive.

Sources of Information

Where can you get the information you need to evaluate a set of standardized tests? The sources take the three forms discussed in the following paragraphs.

The Test, Its Manual, Scoring Keys, and Norms.   You can write to the test's publisher and ask for a catalog. If the publisher has the kind of test you are looking for (for example, a test of third-grade reading achievement), you can

Specimen sets   write or call for a sample, or specimen, set of the test materials by following the directions given in the catalog. Most reputable test publishers require that purchasers furnish some evidence of their qualifications for using the particular kind of test they want to buy.

Once you have the test and its manual, scoring key, tables of norms, and other information, you can apply the criteria that we have discussed to evaluate the test. The choice requires some judgment and insight, as well as experience in teaching the subject, knowledge of the curriculum, and (sometimes) psychological training relevant to the test. In choosing tests, however, there really is no satisfactory substitute for your own investigation and common sense. A good strategy to use is to *take the test yourself* and, as you do so, make judgments item by item as to content validity and other criteria. Then score your test and interpret your score, using the norms and other materials provided. If the test requires timing and reading directions aloud to students, have another teacher administer the test to you. This procedure, along with a careful reading of the test manual on how the test was developed and what evidence is available regarding its validity, should help you make an intelligent decision.

Take the test yourself

Be sure to check whether the norms are current. If the norm group was tested eight or ten or more years ago, you might want to question its appropriateness for interpreting present-day performance. Teachers tell us that students do not differ much year to year, but when they look back after five to ten years they see great shifts in their students and their curriculum. So norms need to be somewhat current to interpret current performance. There is, however, a great problem associated with current norms. Invariably students appear to have better performance on older norms. As teachers learn what is on a test, they teach those things. Students, naturally, do better. So a student, a school, or a state at the 65th percentile rank on a set of norms ten years old may end up at the 40th percentile rank on a set of new norms. In fact, today's students perform better than did those of a decade ago, but we have raised the performance level needed to score at the 50th percentile rank on these norm-referenced tests (Linn, Graue, & Sanders, 1990).

The age of norms

Better performance on older norms

So we have a problem. If we use out-of-date norms, we look better as teachers and schools, but we really do not know how our students are performing against similar students *at this time*. If we use new norms, teachers and schools will surely not look as good, but we'll have comparative information about our students that is interpretable at present. Because of these problems with norms, many educators are advocating criterion-referenced systems of assessment. These problems evaporate if criterion-referenced tests are used.

Problems with old norms and new norms

The Literature Concerning the Test.   For many tests there is considerable research literature. It can often be located through the bibliography in the test manual. In addition, the many volumes of the *Mental Measurements Yearbook,* described in the next subsection, contain exhaustive bibliographies on many tests. A four-volume reference work, *Test Critiques,* is also a good source of information (Keyser & Sweetland, 1984–1985). Two useful documents that describe and analyze tests for children from birth through middle elementary school are those by Goodwin and Driscoll (1980) and H. W. Johnson (1979).

Journals for teachers

Journals for teachers in the various subject matter fields—such as the *Journal of Research in Science Teaching, The Mathematics Teacher,* and the *Elementary School Journal*—carry articles reporting research on tests. Various bibliographic aids—ERIC's CIJE and RIE (the *Current Index to Journals in Education* and *Research in Education* of the Educational Resources Information Center), the *Education Index,* and *Psychological Abstracts*—also can lead you to testing literature. One journal, *Educational and Psychological Measurement,* has a section called "Validity Studies of Academic Achievement," in which evidence on the validity of tests is reported.

The Mental Measurements Yearbooks. This series of volumes, originally under the editorship of Oscar K. Buros, has been appearing about every five years since the 1930s. Each volume contains experts' reviews of many standardized tests of educational achievement, general and special aptitude, temperament, and personality. Like its predecessors, the tenth yearbook, contains reviews of hundreds of tests (Conoley & Kramer, 1989). The reviews tend to be searching and critical. For example, Buros (1972) warned that "at least half of the tests currently on the market should never have been published." Broad reading in these volumes on the kind of test you are considering will tell you about the strengths and weaknesses of tests in the field. As noted earlier, the bibliographies of research on many of the tests are exhaustive, running to more than a thousand items for some of the older and more widely used tests. Carefully edited, the Buros yearbooks have become a major resource of the testing function in the United States.

Administering Standardized Tests

The term *standardized* refers in part to the way the tests are given. Unless directions are followed carefully, the results are meaningless. You should prepare the students as necessary, depending on their age and the kind of test. Motivate them, but don't make them anxious about the test. And watch for signs **Test anxiety** of parent-induced anxiety. A survey of teachers in one state reported many cases of children crying, misbehaving, vomiting, and soiling themselves during standardized testing (Haas, Haladyna, & Nolen, 1989). Older students who know more about what the tests mean will motivate themselves to the extent that they want to do well in school. But they too can feel debilitating anxiety or a sense of meaninglessness. In fact, there are many reports of older students making random designs on their answer sheets because they believed that standardized test results have no impact on their grades, are unrelated to what they are learning, and are of no interest to their parents or teachers. One survey indicated that, compared to elementary students, adolescents were more likely to cheat, to become nervous, to have difficulty concentrating, to guess, and to **Adolescent anomie** look for answers that matched the questions, without really reading them for comprehension. Such strategies, note the researchers, are designed to avoid personal effort and responsibility (Paris, Lawton, Turner, & Roth, 1991). Teachers have a tough job if they want valid test data. They must alleviate anxiety in the young, and build motivation to achieve among their older students.

You must also see to it that students know how to take the test. Some youngsters may not be familiar with the format of a test. Others may not be used to working alone. Still others may not understand that they shouldn't move ahead in a test when each section is timed. Many children, particularly poor children and youngsters from different cultures, may need special coaching in the skills of test taking. New students in a district may also need coaching, especially if other students in the group have taken a similar test before.

It's a good idea to teach students to understand test-item formats that are strange to them. ("Baker is to bread as _____ is to poem"; "There are men (who, whom) many say cannot be trusted.") It was only a few years ago that most people believed that scores on the Graduate Record Examination, the Scholastic Aptitude Test, and other standardized tests could not be improved by preparation. It is now clear that an allocation of study time for developing familiarity with item types and test formats does improve student performance on standardized tests. The best estimate we have is a correlation of over .70 between the time spent coaching students and the students' improvement on the Scholastic Aptitude Test, with a great deal of that improvement coming from just small amounts of coaching time (Messick, 1982). One commercial course for preparing students for the Scholastic Aptitude Test takes about eighteen hours and costs $500. Students who are motivated and can afford to take the course have reported as much as a 200-point gain in SAT scores (Owen, 1985). If the reports are true, there is a moral question for American society to consider: Should this kind of advantage be available primarily for the wealthy? That wealth is the issue here is evident from research that shows coaching of minority-group and low-income students can lead to dramatic test score improvements (Anastasi, 1981; Messick, 1982).

Coaching works

A moral question

If a test has time limits for the test as a whole or for various parts, observe them exactly. If a test has unusual kinds of answer sheets, you should become familiar with them in advance so that you can warn students about them and help students handle them (but only in keeping with the directions for administration!). If students need special supplies (scratch paper, calculators, special pencils), make sure they are on hand ahead of time.

Giving a standardized test is not particularly difficult for teachers who are prepared. But it can be a nightmare for teachers (and their students) who discover too late that they are not prepared. Confusion, unclear directions, unobserved time limits, the inability to answer questions about what is (and is not) permissible can make students do much more poorly (or meaninglessly better) than they should.

Preparation for giving tests

So, prepare yourself. Read a copy of the test, the manual, and the directions for administering the test at least a few days in advance. You might even try a trial run with another teacher acting as a student to help you do justice to your students and to the standardized test itself.

Trial run

Interpreting Standardized Tests

Although you have taken many standardized tests, you may have only a partial understanding of their interpretation. As a teacher you need to be able to make sense out of test data presented as raw scores, stanines, grade-equivalents, and so forth, so that you, your students, and their parents can benefit from the information they provide. We shall present this material briefly as a set of questions, as if asked by parents when presented with their child's norm-referenced, standardized achievement score.

Q 1:   What is the raw score?

A 1:   The raw score is the number of right answers. But that turns out not to be very useful. If a student gets a 36 or a 56 as a raw score, we cannot tell much about that student's performance vis-à-vis others. If we learn that the test had 60 items, it might seem that 36 was a marginally acceptable score and 56 was terrific. But if the test was hard, 36 might really indicate very good performance, and if the test was easy, then 56 no longer seems as good a score. Thus raw scores are not easy to interpret.

Q 2:   What is the percentile rank?

A 2:   The percentile rank is a way to judge the raw score with respect to local, state, or national norms. It is the most commonly used score in standardized achievement tests. If Tommie got a score of 36, we would find out what percent of the students in the norm group (the district, state, or nation) scored below that score. On a difficult 60-item test of mathematics, the score of 36 might be at the 86th percentile. Tommie then would have scored better than 86 percent of the norm group, and his percentile rank would be 86. If the test was easy, the raw score of 36 might be equivalent to the 12th percentile rank. Then Tommie's performance was only better than 12 percent of those in the norm group, and he was exceeded in performance on the test by about 88 percent of the students in the norm group. Percentiles allow us to judge relative performance—at least if the norm group is like the student whose score is being interpreted.

Q 3:   What is the stanine score?

A 3:   Stanines (from "standard nine") are scores on a nine-point scale, from 1 (the lowest) to 9 (the highest). They are matched to percentile ranks—but cover broader ranges. A stanine of 5 covers the percentile ranks of 41–60, approximately the middle 20 percent of the distribution of the raw scores that occurred in the norm group. Table 13.2 presents the stanine scores and the percentile ranks with which they are associated. A stanine of 3 for a raw score of 56 would indicate performances at about the 17th percentile rank, that is, below-average achievement in comparison to a particular norm group. Generally teachers regard stanines 1, 2, and 3 as low; 4, 5, and 6 as average; and 7, 8, and 9 as above average in achievement. While stanines are quite imprecise, they are handy to use to get a rough estimate of performance relative to the norm group.

Q 4:   What is the NCE, or Normal Curve Equivalent?

A 4:   This also is geared to percentile ranks. It is designed to spread out the scores in the middle of the percentile rank distribution, where so many of the students are located, so that performance of the students in the middle can be compared more readily with one another and with the norm group. An NCE score of 47 should be read as a score that exceeds 47 percent of those in the norm group, just as you might read a percentile rank.

Q 5:   What is a standard score?

A 5:   Many times a score on one test is not comparable to a score on another test. We then try to transform the scores so that they will be in a similar measuring scale, sometimes called standard scores. Some of the various standard scores are called T scores, transformed scores, or z scores. All of these transformations respond to the same need: How do we compare Jennifer's raw score of 26 in

Raw scores hard to interpret

TABLE 13.2

Stanines and Their Equivalent Percentile Ranks

Stanine	Percentile Ranks
1	0–4
2	5–11
3	12–23
4	24–40
5	41–60
6	61–77
7	78–89
8	90–96
9	97–100

Transformed scores

language arts with her raw score of 47 in mathematics and her raw score of 12 in math skills. One way is to convert them all to percentile ranks. Another way is to get them into the same standard score, such as z scores with a mean of 0.00, and scores generally running from $+3.0$ to -3.0. So a score of $+.50$ would be a little above average, and -1.00 would be somewhat below average. In contrast, the standard scores called T scores have a mean of 50. A T score of 65 is well above average, and 47 is a little below average. You may have taken the Scholastic Aptitude Test (SAT) to apply for admission to college. In that case your verbal raw score was transformed to have a mean of 500 (50th percentile) and to range between 200 and 800. So 400 is below average, actually at about the 35th percentile rank, and 700 is terrific, at about the 95th percentile rank, in comparison to the norm group for that test. The advantage of the various standard scores is that you can add them together and average them. But fundamentally, they are interpretable as percentile ranks, and thus for teachers are not nearly as sensible to use.

Advantages of standard scores

Q 6:   What is a grade equivalent score?

A 6:   Grade equivalents are a widely used way of reporting scores and one that teachers and parents have much trouble with. Suppose Leticia, a fifth-grader, received a grade equivalent score on a mathematics achievement test of 8.6. What does it mean? Airasian (1991) believes 95 out of 100 teachers would answer as follows:

- Leticia does as well in mathematics as an eighth-grade student in the sixth month of school.
- Leticia can do the mathematics expected of an eighth-grader.
- Leticia's score indicates she could succeed in an eighth-grade mathematics curriculum.
- Leticia could be placed in an eighth-grade mathematics class and succeed.

Grade equivalents often misinterpreted

In fact, *every one of these interpretations is wrong!* Leticia took a fifth-grade achievement test. It covered fifth-grade material. The fact that she answered as many items as an eighth-grader in the sixth month might answer indicates that she really has a great grasp of *fifth-grade mathematics. It does not mean that she has mastered eighth-grade material!* She has not yet had sixth-grade mathematics, or seventh-grade mathematics, or any of eighth-grade mathematics. If Leticia had to take an eighth-grade mathematics test, she would probably perform poorly in comparison to eighth-graders. Leticia has mathematics skills—of that there is no doubt. She has mastered fifth-grade mathematics at a level equivalent to the *estimated* performance of the average child in the sixth month of the eighth grade.

This distinction is subtle, but you need to understand it so that you know how to communicate with parents who want their child skipped because her performance is at the eighth-grade level, and she is only in fifth grade. What we *really* know about Leticia is that when we compare her to the fifth-graders for whom the test was intended, and on whom the test was normed, she performs quite a bit above the average.

The Consequences of High-Stakes Testing

The stakes are high when tests are used to judge teachers, schools, districts, the curriculum in use, or even whole states. Corporations may not relocate to a particular area because of their perception that schools are not good in that area. Real estate prices in a neighborhood can change because of schools' test scores. And people move into and out of geographic areas because of their beliefs about the performance of schools in that area. So a lot of decisions rest on test scores, and there have been some unexpected consequences for teachers. Smith (1991), through interviews with teachers, has documented a number of unanticipated effects of high-stakes testing:

- The publication of *average and low standardized achievement* test scores produces feelings of shame, embarrassment, guilt, and anger in teachers. They do whatever is necessary to avoid such feelings. Thus they teach items on the test, break standardization procedures, send their least able students on field trips during testing times, or change answers on answer sheets. Cheating, fudging, bending rules, and the like have become widespread. And why not cheat, some teachers say, if the scores are to be used as hammers against them by principals, superintendents, and the public who do not understand the effects on test performance of the "curriculum" in the students' homes, malnutrition, lead poisoning, child abuse and neglect, and repeated moving from school to school? When a well functioning bilingual school—for example, one filled with Asians or Haitians or Nicaraguans—shows up in the newspapers as having students with low English verbal scores on the state-mandated achievement test, some excellent bilingual teachers are disparaged unfairly. The test never revealed the fact that the children spoke no English at all three years earlier. So the teachers may feel shame, and they may take steps to improve the scores in the future by dishonest methods. This is *not* the effect the tests were intended for.

  Dishonesty occurs

- Teachers believe test scores to be invalid, and so feel alienated from the system of which the tests are a part. As one teacher put it, "Why worry about test scores when we all know they are worthless?" This teacher may have seen the mismatch between what she taught and what was tested (a content validity issue). Or the diagnostic information about performance came too late to use. Or, if

  Teacher alienation fostered

the diagnostic information was timely and revealed that the child was performing below the norm group on identifying initial consonants, it still may be inadequate because in norm-referenced tests such a diagnosis may be based on only one test item. Or the diagnosis may be of no interest to a teacher who shuns tests and expects that particular problem to take care of itself as the child reads more and more genuine literature.

- Teachers feel guilty and anxious because the tests have harmful effects on their students. Though not all teachers and administrators believe this is the case, enough reports exist to indicate that standardized testing disturbs teachers who see how the tests cause stress in young children, or alienation among older students.

Instructional time lost

- Teachers resent the instructional time lost. State-mandated achievement testing and preparation for the tests in the schools Smith studied resulted in the loss of about 100 hours of instructional time. School weeks are about 30 hours. Thus more than three weeks of instructional time are lost through yearly standardized achievement tests—nearly 10 percent of the entire school year!

- The tests narrow a teacher's range of curriculum choices. Smith (1991) presents the following exchange to document this narrowing:

Interviewer: Do the [standardized test] scores ever get used against you?

Teacher: Well, the first year I used Math Their Way [a program designed for conceptual understanding of math concepts through the manipulation of concrete materials], I was teaching a second grade class and they scored at grade level. But other second grades in that school scored higher than grade level, and I had to do an awful lot of talking before they allowed me to use that program again.

Interviewer: So they were willing to throw out the program on the basis of the scores. How did you feel?

Teacher: I was angry. I was really angry because so many of the things I had taught those children about math were not on the test—were not tested by the test. And, indeed, the following year they did extremely well in the third grade. I had no children who were in any of the low math classes and a great many of my children were in the advanced classes doing better than some of the children who had scored higher than they had on the [test]. . . . But it's very hard to start a new program knowing that the [test] may be used against you. (p. 8)

Smith witnessed a class that went from 40 minutes of writing a day before January to no writing after January, as "the test" became of paramount importance. The time allocated for social studies and health disappeared as "the test" drew nearer. Drill and practice, a lack of critical inquiry, came to dominate the curriculum as "the test" came closer. In another school a hands-on science program was abandoned in favor of a test-based program—so that students could score higher. Note that the reason given was not that they could learn more or learn science by actually doing it. The reason given for abandoning the program was to have students score higher on the test, a much less worthy educational goal by far.

Learning vs. scoring higher

- The good news is that some teachers, though a minority, resisted such pressures. One primary teacher said: "My contract doesn't say that I'm here to raise test scores, and if it ever does, I'm out of teaching. So we're going to keep doing what we're doing. They're going to keep writing in their journals and doing math manipulations and we're going to keep reading stories every day."

- Because multiple-choice standardized testing leads to multiple-choice teaching, the methods teachers use are narrowed, and the profession of teaching can become a deskilled one. Teaching has become more testlike, with many more short questions, worksheets, problems, and drill-and-practice activities. In districts where pressure to do well on the tests is heavy, what goes out of the curriculum is problem solving, math with manipulatives, science as a process approach, free reading time, social studies discussions, extended art, music, or physical education, and anything else that requires time or creative thought. The pressure to answer multiple-choice items has made teachers in some districts more like technicians than professional educators. And this trend is dangerous. Smith (1991, p. 11) says it well: "A teacher who is able to teach only that which is determined from above and can teach only by worksheets is an unskilled worker." Thus the high-stakes standardized achievement testing movement has some consequences for teachers that are not pleasant to contemplate.

Teachers becoming unskilled workers

We are in a time of transition. The problems caused by the use of standardized tests are being weighed against their benefits. It is hard to read the future, but the use of multiple-choice standardized tests has been found to have so many negative side effects that their use in education will probably decrease. New tests or new ways of using such tests need to be found.

Whither Standardized Testing?

At least two major issues concerning standardized testing can be seen: (1) Should present-day standardized multiple-choice tests be replaced by other kinds of standardized tests? (2) Should *any* standardized tests be used, even those that would measure achievement of instructional objectives much more directly and with greater validity?

Should standardized tests become "authentic"?

Current thinking on the first question seems to be crystallizing. Multiple-choice tests are typically biased against the higher-level, "thinking" kinds of educational objectives. They seldom require in any genuine way the kinds of writing, reading, mathematical problem-solving, extended analysis and synthesis of ideas, creation of curriculum-relevant products, and so on, that educators are increasingly emphasizing (Fredericksen, 1984; Resnick & Resnick, 1990). Even if multiple-choice tests of ability to edit prose, for example, correlated substantially with assessments of students' writing ability, the multiple-choice tests are undesirable because of their side effects on teaching and learning. "You

You get what you assess

get what you assess, you do not get what you do not assess," and you should "build assessments toward which you want educators to teach" (Resnick & Resnick, 1990, p. 66). So, if we want teachers to aim at their students' ability to write, read, do mathematics, understand history, think about political issues, and grasp the nature of science and its methods, we should assess these kinds of achievement directly. Assessing them indirectly, as is now typically attempted through multiple-choice tests, misses the mark too widely and pulls teachers toward "multiple-choice teaching" rather than the real-life forms of these kinds of achievement.

So it now seems clear that American education, after the movement toward multiple-choice testing that began in the 1920s, is ready to move to a system more like that coming in England, where one educator noted that "we do not have much of a history of multiple-choice testing" (Burstall, 1991, p. 1). What Burstall described as well underway in England and Wales resembles the direct and authentic testing of achievement in real-life forms urged by Resnick and Resnick. (We discuss in Chapter 14 the ways in which such tests can be made and scored.)

Should even improved standardized testing be done?

On the question of whether *any* standardized testing should be done, the opinions seem more sharply divided. Here standardized testing means tests given to the classes of all, or a sample of, the teachers of a given grade level in a school district, state, or nation. Would much of the distress teachers feel in the present-day standardized testing situations disappear if the teachers had high respect for what was being measured by the tests? Or would teachers still feel anxious and resentful because the tests still *evaluated* the achievement of their students in ways that inevitably made possible comparisons with other teachers. As we know, teachers of students from low-income homes will very often have classes with lower average scores on achievement tests. These teachers will then seem to be ineffective to individuals unfamiliar with the nonteacher factors, especially those in the home background, that affect achievement.

Can we assume that even authentic evaluations of student achievement with measures that are the same for many teachers are desirable? Some teachers might say, "No," because they believe any such evaluation must inevitably measure achievement in a way inappropriate for the emphases, styles, and approaches unique to their own teaching and thus different from those of any other teacher.

Other teachers, however, might recognize the value of such authentic standardized testing. It could reveal schools and teachers who are helping students overcome the obstacles faced by students from minority-group, non-English-speaking, low-income homes. Such identifications of effective schooling might carry important lessons for other teachers and schools.

Nonetheless, such testing might also identify teachers and schools with, say, relatively advantaged, middle-class students who are not doing as well as might be expected on the authentic achievement tests. It is seemingly negative evaluations of this kind that understandably arouse teacher anxiety.

In short, any kind of evaluation, even the most direct, valid, and authentic, creates the possibility of comparisons that—even when adjusted and corrected for the nonteacher factors affecting achievement—seem to imply ineffectiveness in a teacher or school or both. Thus far, the opponents of present-day standardized multiple-choice testing have not considered the possible benefits of standardized testing that evaluated the kinds of achievement teachers agreed upon.

Our own position is that standardized testing will be desirable when it:

1. Uses tests that most teachers consider to be valid, authentic approaches to the kinds of knowledge, thinking, reasoning, problem-solving, and creativity they value.
2. Uses tests that representative groups of teachers have had genuine involvement in creating.
3. Is accompanied by education of the public concerning the factors, other than those controlled by teachers and schools, that affect achievement, so that the public will not make unjustifiable judgments concerning teacher and school effectiveness.
4. Is accompanied by thoughtful, considerate efforts to understand and remedy the low performance of any teachers and schools that cannot reasonably be attributed to factors outside the control of the teacher or school involved.
5. Is accompanied by sufficient financial resources to meet the much higher costs of authentic assessment, as compared with those of standardized multiple-choice testing, just as those costs are being met in England and other countries that have never used multiple-choice testing.

Five features of desirable standardized testing

SUMMARY

Norm-referenced tests—the most commonly used—allow us to compare the performance of any individual student with that of other students. Because they are constructed by experts, they are usually more carefully designed than are teacher-made tests. They also come with important information—on test reliability and validity and on administration procedures and problems. Standardized tests should not, however, be used for grading students or for evaluating a teacher's performance.

Schools use two kinds of standardized tests: aptitude and achievement tests. Aptitude tests give us information for student guidance and counseling. They are used to predict achievement—a source of controversy among educators, some of whom believe that teachers accept predictions as fact and act accordingly with students. Achievement tests, which may actually be better than aptitude tests as predictors of future learning, are used primarily to measure past learning.

There are many hundreds of standardized tests available. Learning about them or choosing among them means asking critical questions about the kinds of learners and learning implicit in the construction of the test, and about their validity, reliability, and appropriateness, among other things. It also means locating the information necessary to evaluate different tests.

Administration is a critical part of the standardized-testing process. Preparation is twofold here. Talk to students about how to take the test—about the rules, format, item types, and time requirements. Try to reduce anxiety among your students and increase their motivation to do well. And prepare yourself: Read the test and the directions, do a trial run, and collect any necessary materials ahead of time.

Your work isn't finished with administration. You have to be able to interpret the results. Test results are usually reported as raw scores, percentile ranks, stanines, normal curve equivalents, standard scores, or grade equivalents. The grade equivalents are easily misunderstood. They are not indicative of the grade level a student can perform at. Whatever the form the score is reported in, remember that scores are not perfectly reliable.

The reliance on standardized tests in industrialized societies has had some negative side effects. Teachers may be embarrassed about performance, be anxious for their students, falsify the data, resent the time lost in testing, and be unnecessarily restricted in what they teach and how they teach. Standardized achievement testing may contribute to the deskilling of teachers. Unanticipated problems with standardized testing now have become obvious.

Two major issues in standardized testing are evident. The first is whether present-day multiple-choice tests should and can be replaced by more authentic, direct, and valid kinds of achievement tests. The second is whether even the latter kinds of standardized testing are defensible. On the first issue, we say yes. On the second, we also say yes provided five conditions are met: teachers respect the test, teachers have helped compose the test, the public is helped to make appropriate interpretations of the test, teachers are helped to deal with low achievement, and funds are provided to meet the higher costs of authentic testing.

This chapter on standardized tests and the next chapter on teacher-made tests can give you only the briefest glimpse of a highly technical field. We urge you to take a specialized course on testing and to read some of the recent literature on the subject.

14 ≡ The Teacher's Assessment and Grades

OVERVIEW

We turn now to one of your most important functions as a teacher: evaluating your students' achievement of your instructional objectives. Standardized tests measure achievement of objectives that are common to many classes, teachers, and schools. They are not tailored to your class.

Informal and formal assessments are made by you to evaluate students against the objectives you hold. You decide what it is important to learn, and you decide what and how to assess that, during and after instruction. Most assessment actually takes place during instruction, though these are informal assessments. Formal assessment, usually by means of tests, often takes place after instruction has occurred.

Formal assessment in the classroom by teachers is designed to measure important and relevant kinds of achievement—and only those kinds of achievement. Differentiating among students is altogether beside the point. The students' test scores and grades should reveal how well they have achieved objectives, not how well they have performed as compared with their fellow students. If every student does perfectly on a test, that's wonderful. We shouldn't worry that a test was too easy or ineffective because it failed to differentiate among students. If every student fails the test, we conclude that they have not been taught adequately and have not learned well enough, not that the test was too difficult. Formal assessment of this kind relies on criterion-referenced achievement tests.

To meet the goals of teacher-made criterion-referenced achievement tests, you need to know (1) how to determine what kinds of achievement are important, (2) how to elicit student performance or behavior that reveals those kinds of achievement, and (3) how to interpret that performance or behavior in ways that can help you do a better job with your students. In this chapter we go into each of these areas in turn.

We also talk about some of the pros and cons of evaluation systems, the ways we gather and combine information about students, and the kinds of standards on which grading systems are based. We end with a brief look at two critical components of evaluation—good sense and kindness—and urge an awareness that grades are a serious matter and that our own biases and those of our testing instruments demand a special generosity toward our students.

Informal Assessment

There are two kinds of informal assessment to which teachers devote a lot of time each year. These are *sizing-up* and *instructional* assessments. Both are considered informal in that records are not usually kept of these assessments. Rather, the information is stored in teachers' heads and influences their actions and opinions as the year progresses. They are also considered informal because teachers use subjective criteria for these assessments, though their judgments are based on experience and should be made carefully.

Sizing-up Assessments

Sizing-up assessments provide teachers with practical knowledge of the students' cognitive, affective, and psychomotor skills. Such assessment occurs primarily during the first two weeks of the school term, when teachers naturally begin to understand their students as helpful, highly motivated, athletic, bright, shy, sassy, sad, emotionally needy, or tricky. In fact, such assessments may start even before school begins, as when one teacher says to another, "I hear you have Jimmie Scott next year—boy that one's a handful!" It is worth noting that expert teachers tend not to pay attention to such comments, nor do they check the school records at the start of the year to learn about their students. They want all children to have a chance to behave differently in their classes than they might have behaved in other classes. The experts recognize that every student acts differently in different environments. Accordingly, experts tend to hold off using records or other information about students longer than do beginning teachers (Carter, Sabers, Cushing, Pinnegar, & Berliner, 1987). Perhaps that is a good policy for all teachers to follow.

Students act differently in different classes

One problem to beware of in making sizing-up assessments is that early impressions can become permanent, leading to self-fulfilling prophesies. Teachers can hold on to beliefs that a child is unmotivated, or very bright, long after his classroom behavior indicates otherwise. Another problem concerns the validity of the impressions. Teachers tend to be good judges of cognitive ability and much poorer judges of things like interest, self-concept, and emotional stability. Also, these attributes of children are far less stable than are the

Permanence of early impressions

cognitive characteristics they display. Furthermore, sizing-up assessments, because they are unspoken and subjective, are subject to all the cultural stereotyping that teachers naturally bring to their classrooms. This stereotyping occurs subtly, for example, by interpreting Carolyn's low mathematics score on a review test as due to the fact that Carolyn can't do math—she's a girl—rather than to the fact that Carolyn forgot her math over the summer. Or it shows up when you see Rodney (an African-American boy) hit Henry (an Asian boy) and decide that Rodney is aggressive and will need extra watching, when what really happened is that Henry stole Rodney's watch just before their dispute caught your attention. So the validity and reliability of sizing-up assessments in the personality or affective domain must be questioned, and teachers must learn to be careful about the permanence of their sizing-up assessments of their students.

Stereotypes in "sizing up" assessments

Assessment During Interactive Teaching

The second kind of informal assessment, taking up much time throughout the school year, is assessment during interactive teaching, or *instructional assessment*. During interactive teaching, teachers, like other performers such as actors, dancers, and musicians, must "read" their audience. They must constantly assess their performance. (Should I give more examples? Am I beating a dead horse? Should I write that out on the board?) It has been found that during interactive instruction the greatest proportion of a teacher's thoughts deal with how well instruction is being received by students (Clark & Peterson, 1986). Experienced teachers seem to be adept at reading cues about the comprehension of instruction from their own students, in their own classrooms, but the skill may not be generalizable. Accurate interpretation of cues about the comprehension of a lesson may depend upon a teacher's knowing the subject matter being taught, the ability of the students, the events that preceded instruction, and so forth (Stader, Colyar, & Berliner, 1990). With experience, then, comes a "feel" for how instruction is going in the classroom—but perhaps only one's own classroom.

"Reading" the audience

A "feel" for how instruction is going

The problems with informal assessment during instruction are the basic problems of all assessment: reliability and validity. Problems with reliability have to do with the rapidly changing nature of instruction in classrooms, such that dependable estimates of instructional effectiveness and student involvement are not easy to get. And teachers may not "read" the cues from all the students. Some students not monitored by the teachers may or may not be learning and enjoying the lesson in the same way as the few who are monitored by the teachers. Teachers often are found to have steering groups, about four or five students they monitor carefully, to gauge the effectiveness and motivational aspects of their instruction. Thus they may have too small a sample (like too few test items) to get a reliable reading of what is going on in the classroom.

Steering groups

Validity in informal assessment during instruction is questionable, since most teachers are biased—they are seeking ways to confirm that their marvelous instruction is working well and fully appreciated by their students. Because of

Problems of validity in instructional assessment

this all-too-human need to feel competent, teachers sometimes give away the answers to questions by tipping off the students, by skipping hard topics, or by attributing wrong answers to the inadequate sleep or motivation of their students, instead of attributing wrong answers to faulty instruction. Problems of validity also rise in the judgments made about how a lesson is being received when a student is nodding at appropriate times, has his eyes on the teacher, is taking notes, and has a thoughtful expression on his face. With all that, the student could still be on Mars! It is hard to know what students—particularly older students—are thinking.

Airasian (1991) offers three suggestions to improve the validity and reliability of assessment during interactive instruction:

Ways to improve instructional assessments

1. Include a broad sample of students when gathering information about instructional success. (For example, don't just call on volunteers when asking questions.)
2. Try to assess the progress of learning, not just whether or not students are paying attention. (For example, ask many higher-order questions as you proceed; don't just monitor whether the students are participating actively.)
3. Supplement informal assessment with more formal means. (For example, you can use homework assignments and the review exercises and worksheets that accompany a text, so that you can obtain some written records to analyze how instruction is progressing.)

In summary, then, you will make two major kinds of informal assessments: sizing-up assessments and instructional assessments. Each is regularly engaged in by teachers, and each is important. Sizing-up assessments, though, can be improved by delaying your evaluations of students and ensuring that those evaluations are subject to change. Instructional assessments need to be monitored to ensure adequate sampling of students, and they must also be focused on instructional progress, rather than just participation in activities, as gratifying as that might be. You must also be on your guard not to let your own needs—wanting to see everything go well—bias your observations. Experience and thoughtfulness will help you get better at this very complex kind of minute-to-minute assessment of the state of your classroom as a learning environment.

Formal Assessment: Determining What Kinds of Achievement Are Important

Formal assessment occurs periodically throughout the school year. The performance of students has some permanence—a test, an essay, homework, a project—and the assessment itself is made permanent by recording it in record books or storing it in portfolios or files. Formal assessments, unlike sizing-up assessments, are mostly cognitive. They provide records for placing or grouping students, or—very important to teachers—grading students. Formal assessment requires much more forethought than does informal assessment. You must decide what it is you want your students to know and to do. Formal assessment is not subject to the idiosyncrasies inherent in informal assessments. First, you must decide what kinds of achievement are important for your students. This issue is basically the same one we dealt with in Chapter 2. It is the question of educational objectives: how they should be determined, what form they should be expressed in, what structure they should have, what categories they should fall into.

Domain-Referenced Testing

In certain fields it is possible to map the whole domain of achievement with some confidence. The multiplication of one- and two-digit numbers up to 12—the multiplication tables that all of us learned as children—is a prime example. Homework assignments, review exercises, or an achievement test could be based on a large representative sample of the 144 possible combinations. (Let us concentrate here on test development, but the procedures to be described hold for homework, review exercises, projects, and any other assignment you give. You must *always* think about what it is your students need to know and do. Otherwise, homework, tests, projects, and the like are time fillers with little educational significance.)

The kind of sample of multiplication items we would develop from the multiplication table would give us a domain-referenced as well as a criterion-referenced test. If a student does the multiplications in this sample correctly, we can infer that he or she can do the whole domain correctly, and we would evaluate the student's achievement positively. Whether the student's classmates did as well or much less well is irrelevant to our evaluation of this particular student's achievement.

The Table of Specifications

In other subject matters the domain of achievement is not finite; it cannot be laid out as objectively and neatly as can multiplication tables. Here we have to analyze and outline the content, say, of this book or any of its chapters. That outline of topics acts as one dimension of a table. The other dimension would set forth what students should be able to do with each topic. Do we want them simply to *know* the facts, definitions, concepts, and conventions? Or do we also want students to *comprehend* them? Or should they be able to *apply, analyze, synthesize,* or *evaluate* material within each of the topics? You may recognize these italicized terms as major headings of the taxonomy of the cognitive domain we described in Chapter 2. They help us define what students should be able to do with any given part of the content.

Crossing the two dimensions—content and types of cognitive performance—yields a *table of specifications* for an achievement test—much like the

Analysis and outline of content

The behavior dimension

Behavior-content matrix

behavior-content matrix we talked about in Chapter 2. Into each cell of the table, where a given behavior intersects with a given topic, we can put the percentage of questions that, in our judgment, should deal with that behavior-content combination.

Two examples of tables of specifications are shown in Table 14.1: one for a test on four novels by two American authors and one on educational assessment and evaluation. Notice how these tables organize the test material. They help us avoid asking too many questions about some topics and too few about others, or too many "memory" questions and too few "thought" questions.

A table of specifications is useful not only in designing a test but also in analyzing the scores obtained with it. We can score the questions in the various cells separately to see whether students have mastered a particular topic or type of cognitive performance. If these part scores are reliable enough—if they are based on adequate samples of items on the topic or the behavior—they can serve a diagnostic function, helping teacher and student pinpoint specific areas that call for further instruction.

Diagnostic function

It is also possible to design a test for just one cell in a table of specifications— say, "skill in the solution of mathematical problems dealing with chemical energy and changes." Obviously a student's score on this kind of focused criterion-referenced test could be used to determine whether the student has mastered this part of the course.

Tell students about the table of specifications

We think it is important to share the objectives of instruction with students. In our opinion, it is also a good idea, when students are old enough, to share the table of specifications with them. It can help them understand what they should be learning. It can also help parents, taxpayers, school board members, and others understand what you are trying to help your students achieve. And it can do so with greater specificity and directness than many other ways of communicating objectives.

How do you decide on the number of questions for each cell? How do you determine the relative emphasis on each behavior-content combination? Your decision should reflect the relative amount of effort, time spent in class and out, and the importance of each cell in the total array of objectives. Educational values are involved here, and your judgment, influenced by what you read and learn from experts, is usually more useful than any scientific data.

Judgment

How many questions?

How many questions should you ask? Other things being equal, more questions mean greater reliability, and thus greater assurance that the decisions you make about a student are accurate. But other things are not always equal, and sometimes you will have to compromise. You may choose to use essay and short-answer questions in formal assessment. Then only a small number of items can be used at each testing occasion. You may choose a performance as an assessment device, such as requiring the students to conduct a simple science experiment, or having the student do a series of exercises on the parallel bars. Generally, performance assessments take a long time and may consist of one item only—the experiment or the exercises to perform. Students' ages and abilities, the difficulty of questions, and the available time also limit the number of questions you can ask. If you use multiple-choice items, as so many teachers

TABLE 14.1	**Tables of Specifications for Two Teacher-Made Tests**

Behavioral Competence	**Novels Studied**				**Total**
	A Farewell to Arms	*The Sun Also Rises*	*The Great Gatsby*	*Tender Is the Night*	
Knowledge of facts about characters and plot	5%	5%	5%	5%	20%
Ability to identify various literary devices	5	5	5	5	20
Ability to relate novel to social history of its time	5	5	5	5	20
Ability to apply criteria to evaluations of novel as a whole	10	10	10	10	40
Total	25%	25%	25%	25%	100%

Subject Matter Category	**Educational Assessment and Evaluation**			**Total**
	Knowledge of Facts, Definitions, and Principles	Understanding of Basic Concepts and Considerations	Ability to Apply Principles and Rules to Practical Problems	
Basic concepts in assessment and evaluation	10%	10%	10%	30%
The teacher and standardized testing	5	5	5	15
The teacher's assessments and grades	10	10	35	55
Total	25%	25%	50%	100%

do, experience will tell you how many items of a certain kind your students can handle per minute. The range is probably from 15 seconds per item for able older students and easy items to 100 seconds per item for less able younger students and harder items. Younger students can sometimes sustain attention to test taking for only about 15 minutes, whereas twelfth-graders, if motivated, can handle up to 120 minutes of test-taking at a time. What you can do is use frequent short tests, written to objectives, and add the scores together to give you the reliability of longer tests. But keep in mind that critics argue, perhaps correctly,

Use frequent testing to get reliability of longer tests

Testing time vs. instructional time

Tests "speak louder" than words

that in contemporary classrooms too much time is spent in testing and too little on actual instruction.

Something to think about before we go on: Your tests are deeds that speak louder than your words about your educational values. You may claim proudly that you want your students to learn to think about the subject—to learn how to learn or to solve problems or to acquire a sense of what is important. But if your tests turn out to measure verbatim knowledge of what is in the textbook or what has been said in class, your students will learn what your deeds—not your words—have told them. You probably remember with some bitterness teachers who tested your rote knowledge after you had been told, and had tried, to learn to evaluate significant concepts and principles. As a teacher, you will have the challenge of making up tests that really measure student achievement. And the place to start is with the table of specifications.

Choosing Among Types of Test Questions

After you have made a table of specifications, you have to choose the kinds of test items you want to use. There are three major categories: performance tests, long-answer (essay) questions, and short-answer questions. The short-answer questions can in turn be divided into "supply" and "select" types—the types of short-answer questions in which students supply the answer (a word, phrase, sentence) or select it from a set of alternatives. Select types can be further divided into multiple-choice, true-false, and matching questions. Figure 14.1 presents this taxonomy in a visual form.

Questions determine the processes students use to answer them

Performance and long-answer questions easier for complex objectives

Your choice of question types determines in large part the kinds of cognitive processes that students will need to use in answering the questions. As we saw in Chapter 2, those processes can range from knowledge and comprehension to application, analysis, synthesis, and evaluation—from lower-level to higher-level processes. In general, performance tests, long-answer questions, and supply questions are easier to compose so that they tap higher-level cognitive processes. Although experts are capable of writing multiple-choice questions that measure processes more complex than knowledge (recall), even they find it difficult to do so. Most teachers do better in measuring various kinds of reasoning and problem-solving achievement when they use essay questions or short-answer supply questions. Besides, a multiple-choice item reflects the fact that you believe knowledge is fragmented into little pieces, and you probably will not want to teach that way. Nor do you want knowledge to be decontextualized, that is, seen as isolated chunks of information, as is often the case when short-answer select-type items are presented. For example, for the true-false item "Eisenhower was the president at the end of World War II," a proper answer might be, who cares? It is important to know about the Roosevelt presidency, the Truman presidency, the beginning of the cold war, the war in Korea, Eisenhower's presidency, and other events of the 1944–1952 time period. But is it sensible to pick out little bits of information about that time period, without their surrounding meanings? There are views of education and

FIGURE 14.1 **Types and Examples of Questions for the Design of Tests by Teachers**

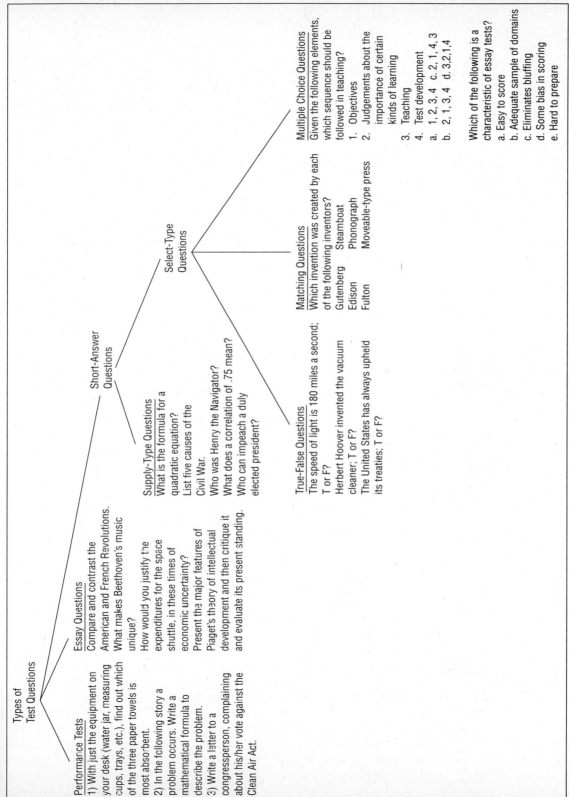

Types of
Test Questions

Performance Tests
1) With just the equipment on
your desk (water jar, measuring
cups, trays, etc.), find out which
of the three paper towels is
most absorbent.
2) In the following story a
problem occurs. Write a
mathematical formula to
describe the problem.
3) Write a letter to a
congressperson, complaining
about his/her vote against the
Clean Air Act.

Essay Questions
Compare and contrast the
American and French Revolutions.
What makes Beethoven's music
unique?
How would you justify the
expenditures for the space
shuttle, in these times of
economic uncertainty?
Present the major features of
Piaget's theory of intellectual
development and then critique it
and evaluate its present standing.

Short-Answer
Questions

Supply-Type Questions
What is the formula for a
quadratic equation?
List five causes of the
Civil War.
Who was Henry the Navigator?
What does a correlation of .75 mean?
Who can impeach a duly
elected president?

Select-Type
Questions

True-False Questions
The speed of light is 180 miles a second;
T or F?
Herbert Hoover invented the vacuum
cleaner; T or F?
The United States has always upheld
its treaties; T or F?

Matching Questions
Which invention was created by each
of the following inventors?
Gutenberg   Steamboat
Edison   Phonograph
Fulton   Moveable-type press

Multiple Choice Questions
Given the following elements,
which sequence should be
followed in teaching?
1. Objectives
2. Judgements about the
     importance of certain
     kinds of learning
3. Teaching
4. Test development
a. 1, 2, 3, 4 c. 2, 1, 4, 3
b. 2, 1, 3, 4 d. 3,2,1,4

Which of the following is a
characteristic of essay tests?
a. Easy to score
b. Adequate sample of domains
c. Eliminates bluffing
d. Some bias in scoring
e. Hard to prepare

627

knowledge that hold it is appropriate to just learn "the facts." But contemporary cognitive psychologists and educators believe that we have gone overboard in fragmenting and decontextualizing (taking out of context) the knowledge to be learned. And the tests we use to assess learning reflect that problem. We have little doubt that our students should know who was president at the end of World War II and when Eisenhower became our president. We worry if that is all they know and remember about that entire period of American history.

Testing for related ideas, integrated networks

Performance tests, long-answer questions, or supply questions are more likely to reinforce the concept that knowledge is made up of sets of related ideas, of large integrated networks of facts, opinions, and feelings. Also, in the real world, business people and professionals have to be able to solve problems and write descriptive reports, informative letters, and all kinds of communications. Performance tests, long-answer questions, and supply questions are a form of practice that can develop these kinds of abilities. Short-answer select questions do not do that.

The "real test bias"

Multiple-choice and the other kinds of select questions work best in measuring knowledge, the ability to recall what has been learned. The real test bias, notes Fredericksen (1984), is the influence of tests on teaching and learning and the tendency of multiple-choice tests to get at knowledge rather than the ability to reason. This bias has been present for a long time, but its pernicious effects have only recently been fully appreciated. It implies that American educators beginning in the 1920s may have made a mistake in moving so heavily toward short-answer select questions in their tests. We are already seeing a swing toward long-answer questions on achievement tests, and even more recently has come the rediscovery of performance tests for assessing higher levels of student achievement in an authentic way.

Performance Tests

If you received a license to drive a car, you have successfully passed a performance test. There is nothing new about such tests (see Remmers & Gage, 1943, Chapter 11, "Product and Procedure Evaluation"), but in recent years they have been brought back into education as an alternative to traditional testing, particularly multiple-choice testing. Rather than short-answer select-type items, a true test of intellectual achievement requires the performance of exemplary tasks (Wiggins, 1989). Assessments must be designed to present or simulate as closely as possible the kinds of tasks performed by individuals who write, conduct business, do science experiments, calculate numbers, and so forth. Such tasks are authentic. They match what is expected of us in life outside of school settings. Even if such authentic tasks are not easily judged, they represent the kind of tasks that should be done to be sure a person has the skills needed to be successful in the real world. Performance tests ensure that a person can translate his or her knowledge and understandings into action. Neither essay examinations nor multiple-choice exams can make that claim. Would you like to employ a reporter who knows how to find misspelled words in

Authentic and exemplary tasks

a paragraph and can tell you the meaning of the prefix "anti"; or, would you prefer to hire someone who can write a news story? Clearly, the latter is our goal if we are employers or faculty advisers to a school newspaper. Performance tests can be used to find the writer we want; multiple-choice tests are inherently inadequate for our purposes.

Why is it that in athletics, arts, and clubs, we accept performance tests as appropriate, but hold no such requirement for most academic subjects? The game, recital, play, debate, and science fair are performance measures of skill and ability that we all acknowledge to be appropriate. Moreover, for these performances we allow coaching and are told the criteria and standards for judgment in advance. These tests are transparent; that is, the test takers know what is coming and how to prepare for it. There are few surprises.

Transparent tests

> If we wish to design an authentic test we must first decide what are the actual performances that we want students to be good at. We must design those performances first and worry about . . . grading them later. Do we judge our students to be deficient in writing, speaking, listening, artistic creation, finding and citing evidence, and problem solving? Then let the tests ask them to write, speak, listen, create, do original research, and solve problems. Only then need we worry about scoring the performances, training the judges, . . . [and providing] useful feedback to students about results. (Wiggins, 1989, p. 705)

Traditional tests are like drills in athletics or exercises on the violin or piano. Performance tests, however, are like games and recitals; they are the real thing. If we break out of our mind-set about what a test is supposed to look like, we might start making academic tests more like public performances. For example, the advocates of performance tests believe that doing and presenting to a class or panel of judges one original piece of research, with all its ambiguities and unstructured aspects, is probably a better indicator of scientific knowledge than an efficient 50-item, multiple-choice, end-of-semester examination. Performance test advocates say that students need more sophisticated and genuine tests of ability to prepare for the real world and to stay interested in the evaluative process. Performance tests, however, need not be just end-of-semester tests. They can be an integral part of instruction, and not separate from it. Table 14.2 presents two examples of performance tests, in which one, the history examination, is integrated into classroom instruction, and the other, the economics examination, is an end-of-semester test, though it may require weeks to prepare for it.

Public performance

Shavelson and his colleagues (1991) have developed performance assessments in science, in which middle-school students are given, for example, three paper towels, trays of water, and other materials, and asked to determine which towel will absorb the most. Silver and his colleagues (1991) have developed performance tests of mathematics—tapping far more than whether the child can do calculations. Such states as Arizona, Connecticut, and California currently have large programs under way to develop performance measures to be admin-

TABLE 14.2   *Examples of Performance Tests in History and Economics at the High School Level*

Oral History Project, 9th Grade
(Developed in Hope High School,
Providence, Rhode Island)

You must complete an oral history based on interviews and written sources and present your findings orally in class. The choice of subject matter will be up to you. Some examples of possible topics include: your family, running a small business, substance abuse, a labor union, teenage parents, or recent immigrants. You are to create three workable hypotheses based on your preliminary investigations and come up with four questions you will ask to test each hypothesis.

To meet the criteria for evaluating the oral history project described above, you must:

- investigate three hypotheses;
- describe at least one change over time;
- demonstrate that you have done background research;
- interview four appropriate people as sources;
- prepare at least four questions related to each hypothesis;
- ask questions that are not leading or biased;
- ask follow-up questions when appropriate;
- note important differences between fact and opinion in answers that you receive;
- use evidence to support your choice of the best hypothesis; and
- organize your writing and your class presentation.

Economics Project
(Developed in Brighton High School,
Rochester, New York)

You are the chief executive officer of an established firm. Your firm has always captured a major share of the market, because of good use of technology, understanding of the natural laws of constraint, understanding of market systems, and the maintenance of a high standard for your product. However, in recent months your product has become part of a new trend in public tastes. Several new firms have entered the market and have captured part of your sales. Your product's proportional share of total aggregate demand is continuing to fall. When demand returns to normal, you will be controlling less of the market than before.

Your board of directors has given you less than a month to prepare a report that solves the problem in the short run and in the long run. In preparing the report, you should: 1) define the problem, 2) prepare data to illustrate the current situation, 3) prepare data to illustrate conditions one year in the future, 4) recommend action for today, 5) recommend action over the next year, and 6) discuss where your company will be in the market six months from today and one year from today.

The tasks that must be completed in the course of this project include:

- deriving formulas for supply, demand, elasticity, and equilibrium;
- preparing schedules for supply, demand, costs, and revenues;
- graphing all work;
- preparing a written evaluation of the current and future situation for the market in general and for your company in particular;
- preparing a written recommendation for your board of directors;
- showing aggregate demand today and predicting what it will be one year hence; and
- showing the demand for your firm's product today and predicting what it will be one year hence.

Source: Adapted from Wiggins (1989, p. 707).

istered as statewide assessments. Though these measures are expensive and time consuming, all the developers share a hope that more authentic performance tests will improve the nature of teaching in our schools.

Writing is one of the easiest arenas in which to develop performance assessments. A scale to judge writing is not hard to develop. Scales of oral reading are also easy to develop. Levels of performance—say, excellent, good, average, and poor—can be described with examples from previous performances used to illustrate the categories. Checklists can also be used to judge performance (as in driving examinations), or rating scales of key elements can be used, just as judges do when rating diving or ice skating at the Olympics. The remarks of Stiggins (1987), however, must be kept in mind: "If you do not have a clear sense of the key dimensions of sound performance—a vision of poor and outstanding performance—you can neither teach students to perform nor evaluate their performance" (p. 37).

Clear visions of poor and outstanding performance

Performances in art, writing, mathematics, science projects, and so forth can be stored in portfolios—repositories of the student's achievements over a span of time. These allow teachers, at grading time and at parent conferences, to examine and assess an entire body of work and to document growth over time. Portfolios will be described later as a way of improving grading. But they are a natural accompaniment of performance assessments. They constitute the archives for documenting growth in areas representing genuine achievement.

Portfolios and performance tests

In many performance assessments, prompts are provided by a tester to see if only a momentary lapse of memory or judgment is involved, or whether genuine lack of understanding is the root of a problem. (Remember the discussion, in Chapter 4, of Vygotsky's zone of proximal development? In traditional testing it is ignored; in performance assessment it can be integrated into the assessment process.) The British have had mathematics performance assessment for years, and when a student has difficulty, the assessor is asked to prompt the student: "Is there a way to check your answer?" "Would it help you here to measure the diameter of the circle?" The student's responses are scored using categories like

Zone of proximal development

1. Success without aid
2. Success after one prompt
3. Success after a series of prompts
4. Success after teaching by the tester; prompts did not work
5. Unsuccessful response even after prompting and teaching by the tester

Such testing seems more humane and insightful than a multiple-choice test of whether the student can tell which term is missing in determining the circumference of a circle, where

$$C = \Box \, d$$

and five choices are provided to fill in the blank: (a) r, (b) $2r$, (c) r^2, (d) pi, (e) pi square.

Identifying new talent

Although performance testing is still being explored, one interesting fact has emerged: The student who does well on a traditional test may not do well on a performance measure. Because of the difference in the nature of the tasks and the requirements for success, other people are often identified as talented by a performance test than by a traditional test (Shavelson, 1991). It is not yet clear that performance tests will be more equitable than traditional tests for minorities and students living in poverty. But they could be. We all know unlicensed contractors, landscape architects, auto mechanics, plumbers, and electricians who cannot pass the state multiple-choice examinations but who perform impressively on the job. Perhaps more low-income, minority, and linguistically and culturally different students will be able to show their talents through performance assessment than would be able to do so with traditional tests.

The building of performance assessments is an exciting new movement in education. Four characteristics will distinguish such assessments: Students will demonstrate what they have been taught or learned; the nature of what is to be demonstrated will be specified in advance (that is, the test will be transparent); the demonstration will have a public component (that is, it will be observable); and the performance will be assessed by experienced, well-trained judges with clear perceptions of standards for performance at different levels of accomplishment (cf. Stiggins, Backland, & Bridgeford, 1985). One advantage of performance assessment is that—after you work hard on developing scales, checklists, or descriptions for holistic scoring of oral presentations, written products such as book reports, science or social studies projects, and the like—you need not hide them. You can give them to students and their parents.

Making standards clear

You thus make clear what the standards are. And you can even remove yourself from being judge, since you can evaluate students' performances in another class or school, and other teachers can evaluate your students' performance.

The construction and use of performance assessments are *not* beyond the ability of most classroom teachers (Airasian, 1991). And as criticisms of the traditional means of assessment continue, teachers will be asked, singly and in teams, to develop more authentic ways of assessing students. This stimulating movement promises to revolutionize educational assessment. Meanwhile, we will now discuss in more detail the forms of tests that are now in greatest use—the long-answer (essay) test and the short-answer test.

Essay Versus Short-Answer Questions

An essay question is useful when you want to evaluate a student's ability to organize and carry out an attack on a fairly complex problem. The problem may demand all the cognitive processes of the taxonomy: knowing, comprehending, applying, analyzing, synthesizing, and evaluating. Obviously an essay question can call for just a paragraph or many pages of student writing.

Essay question structure

Some experts argue that an essay question should be highly structured. They would have you say, "Discuss the Articles of Confederation in terms of *a, b,* and *c.*" Others claim you learn more about what your students know and how

| TABLE 14.3 | Assigned Percentage Grade and Estimated Grade Level of Same Composition Submitted to 100 English Teachers |

Percentage Grade Assigned	Estimated Grade Level of Paper										
	Elementary				High School				College		
	5th	6th	7th	8th	9th	10th	11th	12th	13th	14th	15th
95–99		1		3	3	1	2	3	2		2
90–94			1	4	4	7	5	2	1		
85–89		1	2	3	4	4	6				
80–84		1	2	2	8	8		1			
75–79				2	2	1	3				
70–74				2	1	1	2				
65–69											
60–64	1	1			1						

they think if you leave the question unstructured and simply say, "Discuss the Articles of Confederation." Then the students must supply their own *a, b,* and *c.*

The main advantage of essay questions is the complex response they require of the student. This is also their major fault. Because answers are so complex, they are hard to score reliably. Here *reliability* means agreement among teachers scoring the same tests. We have known since about 1910 that reliable scoring is a problem with essay tests. To see how large a problem, look at Table 14.3. The table shows how 100 different English teachers scored the same composition. Percentage grades ranged from the low 60s to the high 90s, that is, from roughly a D– to an A+. And when the teachers were asked to guess the grade level of the student who wrote the paper, their estimates ran from the fifth grade to the junior year in college! The same teacher's grading over time has also been studied. A teacher re-marked the same ten essay examinations after two months, and the correlation between grades assigned the first time and grades assigned the second time was only about .45. Clearly reliability is a problem if even the same teacher's grades do not agree from one scoring to another. To get high reliability in grading essay tests requires careful and question-specific training of the grader.

Essays and reliable scoring

Irrelevant variables, among them the physical attractiveness and the penmanship of the writer, also appear to have some effect on grading (Bull & Stevens, 1979). Even a student's first name can influence the grader (Erwin & Caler, 1984). Essay questions, because they are inherently open to interpretation, are subject to more bias in grading than are select questions, whose answers are objectively right or wrong. Nevertheless, we have learned techniques for scoring such tests reasonably well, and these will be described later.

Irrelevant variables affect essay grades

Another problem with essay questions, which also stems from their complexity, is inadequate coverage, or sampling, of the domain of achievement. Because each question is relatively time consuming, only a few can be asked.

Inadequate coverage in essay testing

Therefore, a test may cover too little, neglecting important parts of the subject matter.

Combining essay and short-answer questions

Finally, although essay questions are relatively quick and easy to make up, they take much more time and are much more difficult to grade. So the question of whether you should use essay tests boils down to a trade-off between the advantages of getting at complex kinds of achievement and the ease of preparation, and the disadvantages of lower reliability, the possibility of more bias, a limited sampling of the subject matter, and time-consuming scoring. Many teachers get the advantages of both types of questions by using both essay and short-answer select questions. In this way they get the advantages of essay questions, which motivate students to do a different kind of studying, to look at the subject as a whole so that they can discuss it intelligently in their own terms; and they get the advantages of short-answer questions in broader coverage and motivating students to focus more on details and specifics. If you think both kinds of learning are good, you should use both kinds of questions.

Objectively scorable questions

Short-answer questions have the advantage of enabling you to pinpoint the particular fact, concept, or principle that you want to test your students on. They also have the advantage of being relatively easy to score, because you need to pay attention to only a limited range of ideas—a word, a phrase, or at most a few sentences. So your judgment of an answer's correctness can be made more simply and reliably. Teachers agree with themselves and with one another much more closely in scoring short-answer questions than in scoring essay questions. That is why short-answer questions are often called *objectively scorable questions*.

But don't misunderstand. Short-answer questions, if good, can test more than knowledge or memory. Given enough ingenuity and command of your subject matter, you can devise short-answer questions that call for higher-order cognitive processes, as we see in a later section.

Table 14.4 summarizes the relative advantages and disadvantages of performance, essay, and short-answer testing, and displays their key characteristics as well.

Supply Versus Select Questions

Supply types

If you decide to use some short-answer questions, you need to choose between the supply and select types. In supply types the student supplies the answer; in select types the student selects the answer from given alternatives. Supply types take the form of direct questions:

- Who discovered America?
- What is the definition of a sonnet?

or incomplete statements:

- America was discovered by _____.
- A sonnet may be defined as _____.

	Type of Test Having the Advantage			TABLE 14.4
Consideration	Performance	Essay	Short Answer	**Relative Advantages of Performance, Essay, and Short-Answer Tests**
Integrative	+			
Closest to the real-world skills that are wanted	+			
Potentially most valid	+			
Potentially most interesting to take	+			
Tasks to be performed and standards of performance known in advance	+			
Capable of calling for higher levels of cognitive processes	+	+		
Eliminates effects of guessing	+	+		
Easier and quicker to prepare		+		
Useful for testing writing ability		+		
Adequately samples the whole domain of achievement			+	
Reliable scoring or grading			+	
Easier and quicker to score			+	
Eliminates effects of bluffing by writing or talking "around" the topic	+		+	
Eliminates effects of writing ability, quality of handwriting, quality of speech, and the appearance of the testee			+	

Select types can be in *multiple-choice* form:

Multiple-choice items

America was discovered by
  a. Magellan.
  b. da Gama.
  c. Vespucci.
  d. Columbus.
  e. Eric the Red.

A sonnet is a verse form consisting of
  a. six lines.
  b. eight lines.
  c. ten lines.
  d. twelve lines.
  e. fourteen lines.

True-false items

Or they can take the form of *true-false* statements:

T   F   America was discovered by Amerigo Vespucci.
T   F   A sonnet is a verse form consisting of six lines.

Matching items

Finally, select questions can be put in *matching* form:

1. Magellan
2. da Gama
3. Columbus

a.   was a great Portuguese navigator.
b.   discovered America.
c.   landed in Newfoundland.
d.   discovered Greenland.
e.   was first to sail around the world.

1. Limerick
2. Sestina
3. Sonnet

a.   five lines
b.   seven lines
c.   fourteen lines
d.   sixteen lines
e.   thirty-nine lines

Difficulty of scoring supply-type questions

The advantage of the supply type is that it requires the student to be able to recall or create the correct answer. The select type requires the student simply to recognize the correct answer or distinguish correct from incorrect alternatives. The disadvantage of the supply type is that, unless the correct answer can take one and only one form, the teacher may have trouble in deciding whether a student's answer is correct. A bewildering array of synonyms, arguable alternatives, and debatable misinterpretations of the correct answer is bound to show up. Also, supply questions tend to make the teacher resort to asking for the *one* correct word, term, or name that fits the question. This kind of knowledge can be important. But if teachers use only short-answer supply questions, their tests tend to neglect the abilities to make important distinctions and to do subtle reasoning—abilities for which these questions are not suited.

Multiple-Choice, True-False, and Matching Questions

Multiple-choice form flexible

To measure the ability to make important distinctions and do subtle reasoning, you should use well-constructed multiple-choice questions. (We talk about writing multiple-choice questions in the next section.) Indeed, of all the select-type forms, the multiple-choice question is probably the most flexible. In expert hands, multiple-choice questions can be written so that students must use higher-order mental processes to answer them. Writing these questions can be intellectual fun, but it is also time consuming. Just the opposite of essay questions, multiple-choice questions take a lot of time to make up and little time to score. The task of writing good multiple-choice items is demanding enough that major test-construction organizations expect their item writers to produce no more than perhaps ten items in an eight-hour workday.

There are several problems with true-false questions. First, they tend to be misused. Many teachers pick sentences out of a textbook and use them as they are (for true statements) or insert *not* (for false statements), or in other ways use these questions to measure verbatim knowledge rather than understanding. Second, people have a tendency, in differing degrees, to say "true" when they are in doubt. This variability in acquiescence tendency clouds the meaning of scores on true-false tests.

Acquiescence tendency

The usefulness of matching items tends to be limited. They are usually appropriate only for measuring ability to match up relatively discrete facts; they do not lend themselves to the measurement of more complex and subtle kinds of knowledge or comprehension.

Writing Essay and Multiple-Choice Test Questions

Because of the limitations of true-false and matching questions, we deal here only with essay questions and multiple-choice questions. Between them, they can demand a great range of intellectual processes from students. We suggest you use *both* kinds of questions whenever possible, to gain the advantages of each kind and to reduce the disadvantages of either kind used alone.

Writing and Grading Essay Tests

First, essay tests should be used primarily to measure the kinds of achievement that cannot readily be tested with multiple-choice items. These include application, analysis, synthesis, and evaluation. Essay tests are much less effective for getting at simpler kinds of knowledge and comprehension.

Essay testing for complex achievement

Second, having decided to use essay testing for what is uniquely appropriate to it, you should use it with all the flexibility needed to aim at exactly the kind of higher-order cognitive processes you want to measure. In other words, you should realize that essay questions can range widely in the kinds of complex responses they call for. At one extreme, you can ask that your students write on "How your thinking about _____ has changed as a result of your recent learning experiences." You can fill in the blank with broad subjects (botany, rock music, civil liberties, for example) or specific ones (rhododendrons, the Soviet Union, the right to hand out leaflets on street corners). The broad topics are harder to evaluate reliably, but they require students to provide their own structure and focus. The length of the answer required is related to the breadth of the topic. Longer answers can call for greater complexity, but they are again harder to evaluate consistently.

Broad vs. specific topics

The verbs you use in your questions are important. Explain them to your students. Tell them that when you say "compare and contrast," you are asking

Choose verbs carefully

them to point out the likenesses and unlikenesses of two or more things. When you say "identify," you are not usually looking for a long answer, just information about a person, place, or thing. When you say "analyze," you want students to break some subject down into parts. And when you say "argue," you are asking for advocacy, as a lawyer might do when defending or prosecuting. *Discuss, define, justify, explain, summarize*—all imply more or less specific tasks. Choose among them carefully, and be sure your students understand them.

Disallowing choice among questions

Although giving students a choice among questions usually makes them feel better, it gives you the problem of seeing to it that achievement is expressed just about as well in answering one alternative question as in answering another. This is usually impossible to do. So it is probably best to have all students answer all essay questions.

Length of answer asked for

You may want to get at the students' ability to write fairly long (more than one or two pages) essays under test conditions (which might be at home as well as in the classroom). But you gain certain advantages if you ask for relatively short (say, five lines to a half-page) answers. First, you can ask more of these shorter questions per unit of time and thus broaden your sample of student achievement. Second, you can probably evaluate shorter answers more reliably, because they are less complex and offer less room for compensating virtues and defects that you then have to weigh before evaluating the total answer.

Writing a model answer

In any case, you might write out a model answer to guide yourself in grading the students' answers. Unless the question was intentionally vague to force students to do the structuring, you can then indicate to yourself in advance (and later to your students) what you intend the question to call for. The technique used for these broad questions is *holistic scoring,* in which a single score is provided based on an overall reading of the essay as a whole. This is quick and amazingly reliable *if* model answers are available for broad categories of scores (for example, unacceptable, marginally acceptable, good, exceptional) and the essay readers have had practice in scoring with these models. Holistic scoring does not provide fine gradations between evaluations, but it can provide good classifying information.

Holistic scoring

Analytic scoring

If your model answer can be analyzed into separate points (for example, one for pointing out that civil liberties are provided in the Bill of Rights, one for pointing out that the First Amendment provides for freedom of speech and press, one for pointing out a recent news story that involved the First Amendment, and so on), you can use this list of points in grading the answers. These different points allow you to do *analytic scoring,* which is much more useful for providing feedback to students. It is more time consuming, as well, because essays may need to be read more than once. Whether you engage in holistic or analytic scoring, you should take one crucial step before you give an essay to your class. You should write a model answer *in advance.* Doing so will help ensure that your question can be answered in the terms you intend. (It should also be noted that much of the advice about holistic and analytic scoring essays, having levels of performance specified in advance, and having model answers in advance is the same kind of advice that should be heeded in preparation for scoring performance tests. An essay examination is in some ways like a performance test; thus it is not surprising that these guidelines for scoring essays are also useful for scoring performance tests.)

Biases in scoring essay tests are common. Research has shown that teachers cannot easily separate out of their ratings of social studies essays such factors as spelling, punctuation, and grammar. Other studies have shown the effects of handwriting on scoring. Incidentally, you can have students write their names on the back page of their essays, or use random code numbers to hide students' identities. We find that scores can be biased on the basis of teachers' expectations for particular students. Human beings always seem to have a hard time being objective. You also should score answers to each question separately if there are two or more questions on a test. That is, do all the scoring of answers to one essay question before you do the others. And, although very time consuming, the best way to ensure fairness in judging the essays is to read them a second time and check your two independent assessments of their worth.

After you do your best to score an essay test objectively, you must remember that your feedback to students should always contain positive elements—no matter how poor the performance. The most frequently committed sin of language arts teachers, English teachers, and others who grade essay questions is their failure to say something good about a student's answers. Students are sensitive about their writing, especially their term papers and other essay projects. If students never receive anything but criticism and faultfinding, they develop a crippling anxiety about writing and, as soon as possible, stop writing altogether. Use well-placed, sincere praise, along with moderate amounts of corrective criticism, in grading essay tests.

You should realize that essay tests allow you to "get into" your students' minds in a way otherwise impossible. What they say orally is one thing, and what they say in writing is another. Both are important, and students who are effective in one medium are not necessarily good in the other. Properly used, essay tests can give you a basis for excellent understanding of and feedback to your students—about their knowledge, reasoning, biases, and creativity.

Writing Multiple-Choice Items

Multiple-choice items have two main parts: (1) the *stem*, either a question or an incomplete statement that comes first and states the topic or problem with which the item is concerned; and (2) the *alternatives*, which require students to demonstrate their achievement by choosing the best or correct one and thus rejecting the others, called distractors. The effectiveness of a multiple-choice item depends on how we deal with each of these parts individually and together. Over time, some rules have grown out of experience in writing multiple-choice items. Let's look at them.

Margin notes:

Biases in scoring essay tests

Score all answers to a given question before going to the next question

Say something favorable

Essay tests get into students' minds

The stem and the alternatives

Stem should state a problem

1. *The stem should focus on and state a meaningful problem rather than simply lead into a collection of unrelated true-false statements.* For example:

Poor: The United States
   a. has more than 300 million people.
   b. grows large amounts of rubber.
   c. has few good harbors.
   d. produces most of the world's automobiles.

Better: The population of the United States is characterized by
   a. stable birthrate.
   b. people of varied national backgrounds.
   c. its even distribution over the area of the country.
   d. an increasing movement from suburbs into cities.

Still better: The birthrate of the United States during the 1990s could be characterized as
   a. rising.
   b. staying fairly stable.
   c. falling.

Use plausible distractors

2. *The distractors (incorrect alternative responses) should be plausible so that students who do not have the achievement being evaluated (knowledge, comprehension, and so on) will tend to select them rather than the correct answer.* You can get plausibility by making the distractors familiar, reasonable, and relevant.

3. *Use as many distractors, up to four, as can be logically created.* But don't just fill the page and waste the students' valuable reading time.

4. *Don't hesitate to change the number of distractors from item to item.* Where it is sensible you might want to use four distractors; for another item, only two may be appropriate.

Use direct questions when appropriate

5. *Use direct questions rather than incomplete statements in the stem when it seems appropriate to do so.* Questions are not as likely to lead to your shifting the point of view in the middle of an item or its response alternatives. Usually direct questions make it easier to express ideas because incomplete statements make the alternatives come at the end of the statement, where they may not fit as well.

Poor: In analyzing the cost of living in the United States, we find that its largest component is
   a. food.
   b. housing.
   c. clothing.
   d. health care.
   e. recreation.

Better: Which of the following is the largest component of the cost of living in the United States?
- **a.** Food
- **b.** Housing
- **c.** Clothing
- **d.** Health care
- **e.** Recreation

6. *When possible, avoid repeating words in the alternatives; put them in the stem.*

Poor: Which of the following is the best brief description of this novelist's writing?
- **a.** A flowery approach to characterization
- **b.** A psychiatric approach to characterization
- **c.** An inner-feeling approach to characterization
- **d.** An overt-action approach to characterization

Better: Which of the following is the best brief description of this novelist's approach to characterization?
- **a.** Flowery
- **b.** Psychiatric
- **c.** Inner feeling
- **d.** Overt action

7. *The length and precision of the choices should not vary systematically with their correctness.* Careless item writers tend to make the correct choice the longest one.

8. *The correct response alternative should vary from item to item.* Careless writers tend to build a bias into their tests by favoring, say, the *a* option and rarely using, say, the *d* option.

9. *All choices should be grammatically consistent with the stem and one another.*

Grammatical consistency

Poor: The Judiciary Committee's impeachment deliberations resulted in a resolution in favor of
- **a.** no impeachment.
- **b.** the majority voted for three articles.
- **c.** a sharp division between the two parties.
- **d.** one article cited obstruction of justice.

Better: The Judiciary Committee's impeachment deliberations resulted in resolutions in favor of how many articles of impeachment?
- **a.** None
- **b.** One
- **c.** Two
- **d.** Three
- **e.** Four

Check the scoring key

10. *There should be one and only one choice that experts would consider best.* Otherwise, students will question the scoring of the item and the fairness of the test. One way to observe this rule is to have other teachers check your test and scoring key, preferably *before* you give the test.

11. *It is probably best to avoid using "none of these" as an alternative.* Some experts accept its use, but only with qualifications: an absolutely correct answer to the stem should be possible. In mathematics or science tests, where answers can sometimes be absolutely right or wrong, a response alternative such as "none of these" may be acceptable. But in tests of aesthetic judgment, where answers are only "best," this kind of alternative is confusing.

Power vs. speed

12. *Do not make tests so long that they become speed rather than power tests.* A multiple-choice test that requires a lot of thinking can easily exceed the time originally allotted for the test. We usually want students to show their power—by having time to attempt all the items. We rarely want to judge students' cognitive achievement by their speed. You should remember that some very able students (among them, Albert Einstein) have been very slow test takers.

Paraphrase to measure comprehension

An approach to the writing of multiple-choice achievement test items that measure comprehension rather than rote memory has been offered by R. C. Anderson (1972). In this systematic approach, *comprehension* is defined as the student's ability to answer a question based on a *paraphrase* of a statement that appeared in the learning materials. A paraphrase is related to the original material with respect to meaning but not related with respect to the sounds of words or shapes of letters or any other dimension that provides cues for rote memory. A statement is a paraphrase of another if none of the substantive words (modifiers, verbs, nouns) is common to both statements and the statements are equivalent in meaning.

For example, a paraphrase for the statement, "The private single-handedly blew up the ammo dump," might be:

The soldier who ignited the enemy's supply of shells was
   a. on patrol.
   b. working alone.
   c. with a team of frogmen.

If the text reads, "Punishment results in a decrease in responding," the paraphrase might be

An activity may slow down or stop after
   a. a negatively valued event.
   b. the removal of a negatively valued stimulus.
   c. a contingent reinforcer.
   d. a secondary reinforcer.

If you've said that "rising air cools and releases water" in a lecture, the test item might be

When ocean winds go over the coastal mountains, they are likely to
  a. pick up moisture.
  b. increase in velocity.
  c. bring rain.

In this item, we have not only paraphrased but also used an example of the phenomenon we are interested in. This is always a good way to measure comprehension of principles, because items with specific examples of principles are usually easy to answer if the principle is understood and hard to answer if the principle was simply memorized.

Use examples of principles to measure comprehension

Another approach to writing multiple-choice items was developed by J. S. Brown and R. R. Burton (1979). They saw the choice of distractors in multiple-choice items as rich sources of information if the test items were designed with diagnosis in mind, not just as ways to assess knowledge. A good example of diagnostic testing comes from mathematics, but this kind of test can also be built in other areas, such as reading comprehension, physics, and music. To construct a diagnostic test, a teacher must know the subject matter well and keep in mind all the tasks and subtasks necessary to solve particular kinds of problems. For example, to test subtraction we might build an item like this: $327 - 48 = ?$ The response alternatives could be (a) 389, (b) 321, (c) 279, and (d) 189. Response (c) is correct. If a student chose response (a), we would hypothesize that he correctly "borrowed" 10 from the appropriate number on top but forgot to reduce the number in the column he borrowed from by 1, a common and easily corrected error. If he chose (b), we would infer that the student subtracted the smaller number from the larger number regardless of whether it was on top or on the bottom. And if the student chose (d), we would assume that the student borrowed twice from the left-most digit on top, and never from the adjoining column. We can learn much about a student's difficulties if we construct a diagnostic test where the errors tell us the nature of the student's problem. Piaget and others have reminded teachers that they should not always try to judge student responses as right or wrong. Instead they should use responses as pieces of information that reveal what a child is thinking—a philosophy that allows for much better diagnosis of problems.

Diagnostic items

Types of Multiple-Choice Items

Multiple-choice items can require higher-order thinking. Making up these items takes time, but the process is challenging and can be fun, and the collection of items can be built up over a number of years, not done all at once. Here are some examples of items at each level of the taxonomy of cognitive objectives. Your tests should measure higher levels of cognitive processing even when you use multiple-choice items. (Asterisks indicate correct choice.)

Knowledge (memory):   Which of the following books is most likely to provide information that could help you choose a standardized test?

*a. Mental Measurements Yearbook
   b. Handbook of Research on Teaching
   c. Achievement in California Schools
   d. Annual Review of Psychology

Comprehension: Which of the following is used to measure content validity?

   a. Correlations between the test and a criterion
*b. Inspection of test items and the curriculum
   c. Correlations between the test and other similar tests
   d. Inspection of the test manual and test reviews

Application: On the basis of a series of observations in school, and multiple-choice tests and essays in class, Tyrone was judged aggressive, extremely knowledgeable, and creative. Which one of these judgments is likely to be the most valid?

   a. Aggressive
*b. Knowledgeable
   c. Creative

Analysis: Without any other information, which of the following standardized tests of spelling would you choose to see how well your fifth-grade class was doing in relation to a national sample?

   a. The Smith test of medical terminology: test-retest reliability, .92; correlation with general intelligence, .35; test time, 72 minutes.
   b. The Jones test of frequently used words: test-retest reliability, .63; norms from a representative set of urban schools; correlation with the Brown reading test, .41; test time, 60 minutes.
   c. The Michigan test of spelling ability: test-retest reliability, .79; complete state norms; correlation with spelling grades, .35; test time, 35 minutes.
*d. The Hardy test of spelling: parallel-form reliability, .89; words selected from a sample of newspapers; norming group, a 5 percent random sample of all elementary schoolchildren in the United States; test time, 40 minutes.

Synthesis: Given the following elements:

   1. Construct a table of specifications for an achievement test.
   2. Determine whether essay or short answers are called for.

3. Determine whether supply or select items are called for.
4. Assign weights to reflect the importance of different content areas.
5. List objectives.

What would be the appropriate sequence to use in developing a classroom test?

*a. 5, 1, 4, 2, 3
 b. 2, 3, 4, 1, 5
 c. 5, 3, 2, 4, 1
 d. 4, 5, 1, 2, 3

Evaluation: Using everything you have learned about the ways in
    which the following things would affect the environment, rank them
    in order of their danger to the world's future.

1. Overpopulation
2. Leakage from nuclear energy power plants
3. The disappearance of the grizzly bear, the bald eagle, and other en-
    dangered species

*a. 1, 2, 3
 b. 1, 3, 2
 c. 2, 1, 3
 d. 2, 3, 1
 e. 3, 1, 2
 f. 3, 2, 1

Item writing as an art form

In general, writing multiple-choice items is a kind of art form. It can be learned, but some people have more talent for the task than others. In courses in educational measurement, students can practice this art form and receive criticism from their instructors and fellow students. Properly used, multiple-choice testing allows you to measure your students' knowledge and understanding over a broader range of ideas than can essay testing. And only your own ingenuity and subtlety limit the searching character of your questions. If you want to go more deeply into this art form, look at Wesman (1971) and Millman and Greene (1988). For more examples of questions of all kinds that tap achievement at all levels of the taxonomy of the cognitive domain, go to the *Taxonomy of Educational Objectives* (Bloom et al., 1956).

After Multiple-Choice Testing, What?

After a multiple-choice test is completed, you can use the students' responses as feedback for revising the test. This is the process of *item analysis*. It is beyond this introductory text to teach you the many item-analysis procedures available. Some further coursework or independent reading is needed to learn those. When item-analysis methods are applied, you can determine which items to keep, which to modify, and which to throw out, based on your students' performance. You can learn which distractors draw low-achieving students' responses, and which do not. You can learn which items are most sensitive to instruction, and which hardly show instructional effects at all. You can learn which items are too difficult and which are too easy to be useful. And you can learn which items really discriminate well (that is, pick out the high scorers), and which items do not discriminate well (that is, are answered in the same way by the highest and lower scorers). When a teacher, a district, or a state keeps refining the items in the test pool of items, a technically sound test can be built

Test security

after a few administrations. And that is why test security is maintained on many tests. When you have spent a few years refining the test items to get a short, reliable, and valid multiple-choice test, you don't want students to have access to the items, forcing you to start again.

The Microcomputer and the Teacher's Assessments

It won't be long until every teacher in every classroom has access to a micro-computer or to a terminal hooked up to a larger computer somewhere else in the building or district. You know about computer-assisted instruction; you should also know that computers are excellent aids for test developers. They allow us

Item banking

to store items by objectives, a process called *item banking*. Anytime we call up an objective, we can get a printout of the multiple-choice items and the essay questions that have been used to assess learning of that objective in the past. Item analyses, including difficulty level, are available for each item, and the data are updated each time the item is administered. Software allows us to estimate the reliability of a test before we administer it and to compute total reliability after we administer it. More and more optical scanning systems (which count the black pencil marks located in the correct places on special answer sheets) are within reach in terms of cost and reliability, removing even the drudgery of scoring select-type items.

For entire academic departments—English, history, sciences, music, mathematics—where substantially the same curriculum is taught to many students year after year, this technology can easily be used to improve testing. But even the individual teacher can build, over a few years, an item bank that eventually saves time and increases test quality. Dozens of item bank programs are already available for all kinds of computers, and dozens more are on the way. The most comprehensive of these programs also do complete item analyses as well as store student information in separate files for each student, and then they even prepare report cards.

Simulations and testing on computers

Increasingly we are seeing simulations and testing on computers, particularly in science, where it is expensive to set up real performance tests. With a computer the test problem can be simulated. For example, a series of fluids representing certain chemicals can appear on the screen, and the student is asked to do certain things with them. Then, on the basis of what gets done, the student is asked to identify the chemicals. This process could be very time consuming, messy, and costly if done in a laboratory as a genuine performance test of inquiry in chemistry. Once the test has been programmed and the simulation made to appear real, the cost per pupil to assess knowledge is low, it is not messy, and less time is taken to assess chemical knowledge. But such tests depend for their validity upon their realism, and not all of them appear realistic. Furthermore, we do not yet know whether the student who does well in a simulation of this kind will do well on traditional tests or genuine performance tests. The current evidence (Shavelson, 1991) is that the students who do well on these tests are different from those who do well on traditional or performance tests. Right now it appears that if you tested knowledge and understanding of the chemistry concepts with multiple-choice items, computer simulations, and genuine performance tests, different students would appear to have mastered the concepts. Thus we do not yet know how to choose among the available alternative approaches to assessment.

Disagreement among alternative approaches to assessment

From Assessment to Grading: A Difficult Transition

Grading students is one of the teacher's hardest tasks. Many teachers think of their students as friends, and shrink from the job of standing in judgment of them. The two roles, friend and judge, seem incompatible.

But, however painful the process, formal evaluation is a necessary part of education. Schools are designed to transmit the values of a society. Because classroom teachers are agents of the society, their value judgments about students' school behavior and achievement must in some degree represent what is considered important and good by the society. This is why schools set up regular procedures for communicating teachers' value judgments to students, parents, and others, who use these judgments in making decisions about past performance and future courses of action.

Teachers as agents of society

Grading is a kind of summary evaluation; it helps identify students' strengths and weaknesses. We can use this evaluation to make immediate decisions (say, counseling one student to skip general mathematics or advising another to take remedial writing), long-term plans (helping a student decide whether to choose or reject a college preparatory program or a particular curriculum area), and vocational plans (suggesting career possibilities that seem to fit students' aptitudes and interests).

Evaluation and decision making

Summary evaluations also give students and their families information about the students' progress toward educational goals. They are also a source of information for other teachers and even employers. For instance, a person who judges applicants for admission to medical school or for a job as a laboratory technician has a need to know the candidates' achievement in chemistry.

Information for students, parents, teachers, and employers

We also use summary evaluations for administrative purposes, where teachers' grades and marks serve as a basis for honors, promotion, graduation, probation, and other selection, retention, and sorting functions. Sometimes grading is done simply to provide an incentive for greater effort by students.

In short, with all the purposes that grades and marks serve, it does not make sense to abolish them. Despite the stress and anxiety that grades may cause, too many people and too many functions need what they provide.

Some Common Questions About Testing, Grading, and Marking

You can find interesting attacks on traditional testing and grading in Holt (1969), Glasser (1969), Hoffman (1962), and Eisner (1991). A good defense of evaluation is offered by Ebel (1974). We have tried to present the most common arguments as we most often hear them, in the form of questions beginning teachers ask us. Some of the questions and answers are matters of logic and values, but some are directly addressed by empirical research.

Isn't grading something of a farce because there is so much error in the measures used to evaluate students and so much variability from one teacher to another in grading? We think that low reliability and unknown validity force teachers to be tentative in their judgments about students. This observation does not mean, however, that marks should not be used. It means we have to give them more carefully, combine them more thoughtfully, and help students, parents, and other family members interpret them more realistically.

Reducing grading variability among teachers

The issue of variability in grading practices from teacher to teacher is real. But two changes in marking systems can reduce this variability. First, teachers in a school or a school system can profit from a discussion of grading standards. By discussing and sharing their views, teachers can arrive at a common policy. Such discussion can lead to greater similarity among teachers in their definitions of grades. Second, moving from norm-referenced to criterion-referenced evaluations, where possible, also helps. Teacher variability in grading is reduced in criterion-referenced approaches, where only the pass–no pass cutoff point is determined arbitrarily.

Do grading and testing practices interfere with or help learning? If students see the whole assessment and grading system as threatening and arbitrary, they might work more for the grade than for any learning. Teachers need to watch carefully that their marking and grading methods do not simply force students to learn what they would otherwise shun. Unfair testing and grading programs can reduce students to a frenzied search for what the tester wants. Even a casual observer can see this situation in many schools today.

Some critics argue that school testing and grading is much like wages for labor (Bowles & Gintis, 1976). They claim that classrooms are economic systems where student performance is exchanged for grades—where students are earners, not learners. These critics are not surprised to find that students forget what they've learned once they've been tested. This kind of learning would not be intrinsically driven (Krale, 1981). One proposal that has been made to remedy this problem is for teachers to act as critics, not markers, of student work (Mull, 1984), particularly if more performance measures of achievement

● *Evaluating students is one of a teacher's hardest tasks. (© 1983 Susan Lapides)*

are used. Personal oral or written criticism communicates serious concern for the quality of a student's work. Marks, like wages, may not be as personally meaningful to many students. That is, genuine criticism may motivate; marks may not.

On the other hand, if the marks earned in a subject matter area indicate progress toward mastery of that area, then working for marks actually furthers the purposes of education. This condition clearly holds for criterion-referenced programs. The mark or symbol P (for pass) stands for the mastery of some educational material. Working for mastery and working for marks become the same thing. It's not a problem here if students are working for a mark because the mark means that the material has been learned. Even in norm-referenced programs, a mark should be a valid indication of important educational outcomes. An A in a course in educational psychology should signify a student's ability to state objectives, describe the concept of intelligence, list several motivational techniques, and so forth.

Marks can symbolize genuine achievement

Testing and grading practices can also improve learning and performance. For example, Nungester and Duchastel (1982) had high school students study a history text. One group, the control group, simply read the text; a second group was given time for review after reading the text; a third group was tested after reading the text, with the test taking about the same amount of time as the review. All students were tested (or retested) one week later. The review group scored 10 percent higher than the control group. The tested group, however, scored 25 percent higher than the control group! The effect held for both supply- and select-type items. So a test can facilitate retention. Moreover, the simple knowledge that a test is going to be given affects study habits and the time students spend studying (Halpin & Halpin, 1982). From this information we might predict that a course with frequent quizzes would produce greater amounts of learning than a course with no quizzes. This relationship has in fact been shown many times (for example, Fitch, Drucker, & Norton, 1951). The evidence is clear that testing and grading affect student achievement in a positive way. But there is a side effect: Students sometimes rate instructors who test them lower than those who do not test them (Halpin & Halpin, 1982).

**Frequent tests →
higher
performance and
lower attitudes**

In a study of grading practices, D. C. Clark (1969) compared two classes of graduate students in education. One class ($N = 49$) was graded on research papers but not on an examination. The other class ($N = 59$) received no grades on either the research papers or the examination. The term paper performances were judged on fairly objective indexes of motivation: number of studies read, number of times the paper was discussed with the instructor, number of hours spent preparing and writing the paper, the percentage of the class handing in papers, and the grades given the papers by the instructor. The first class performed at a significantly higher level than did the second on the research papers. On the examination, where neither class expected grades, both classes performed at the same level. The performance of these graduate students was significantly higher when they expected grades despite the often-made claim of many graduate students that their motivation is already so high that they do not need extrinsic incentives!

**Expectation of
grading improves
performance**

Does leniency or strictness in grading affect the attitudes and motivation of students? Goldberg (1965) compared lenient and strict grading approaches with a number of other ways to grade. Results showed that the different grading policies had no effect on the students' subsequent test performance.

Strict grading, however, has other consequences. Sometimes it determines whether a student will choose a particular course or curriculum area. Bridgham (1972a, 1972b) examined how secondary school science enrollments were influenced by ease of grading. He noted that students in science courses are usually graded more severely than they are in other courses. From this he developed an index of ease of grading: the discrepancy between the students' grades in the science course and their grades in other academic subjects, averaged across the students in the course. He found that for female students, ease of grading in one science course markedly affected enrollment in another science course. The data showed that making ease of grading equal to zero (so that grades in chemistry and physics are as high as those in other academic courses) for girls taking chemistry would increase the proportion of girls going on to physics from chemistry from 18 percent to 32 percent. So the enrollment of girls in science can probably be increased by reducing the severity of grading in science courses. This kind of reduction would not lower grading "standards" beneath

**Effects of grades
on science
enrollments**

	Courses							
	Within Major Field				Outside Major Field			
Mean grades in previous courses	3.68	3.19	2.69	2.25	3.68	3.23	2.73	2.25
Mean grades that would have been assigned if the pass-fail option had not been exercised	2.90	2.24	1.88	1.68	2.82	2.12	1.94	1.42

TABLE 14.5

Comparison of Grades Obtained Under Conventional and Pass–No Credit Grading

Source: Based on Hales, Bain, & Rand (1971).

those maintained in other academic subjects. Instead it would increase the numbers of people finding positive reinforcement in their attempt to master this subject matter area.

Effects of pass–no credit grading

Another aspect of grading severity is seen in the problem of whether pass–no credit or pass-fail grading affects classroom performance. It turns out, in some studies at least (for example, Hales, Bain, & Rand, 1971), that motivation, or the performance of students from which we infer motivation, is somewhat lower when pass–no credit grading is used instead of conventional letter grades (A, B, C, D, F). Table 14.5 presents the mean grades received by 50 students in each of four strata based on previous grades: 3.50–4.00, 3.00–3.49, 2.50–2.99, and 2.00–2.49. The students were also classified according to whether they were taking courses within or outside their declared major field. All in all, 400 seniors—50 students per stratum × 4 grade strata × 2 course locations (within or outside major)—at Ohio State University made up the sample. In the table the previous mean grade point averages for each stratum, within and outside the major field, are listed first in each column. These were assumed to be the grades that would have been received had the pass–no credit options not been exercised. In this study the instructors always gave letter grades that were automatically converted to pass or no credit if the student chose that option. This system allows us to compare the letter grades previously earned and the grades earned (but not reported) by the pass–no credit students. In every stratum, students performed less well under the pass–no credit option than they had when taking courses in which regular grading systems were used.

These results confirm what most teachers have long believed: that students do not work as hard or as well with pass–no credit grading. Students too have observed the same effect. One campus survey of faculty and students on the pass–no credit option pointed it out (Main & Gallagher, 1972). As you can see in Table 14.6, 31 percent of the students noted doing less work as an effect of pass-fail grading. But students and faculty even more frequently mentioned the positive consequences of this kind of grading system: less pressure on students, healthy experimentation in new areas, and healthier attitudes toward the course. These benefits may outweigh the lower amount and quality of student

Reducing tensions about marks

What Positive or Negative Consequences of the Pass-Fail Option Did You Note This Year?	Students Mentioning (Percent)	Faculty Mentioning (Percent)
Relieves pressure in students	29	16
Fostered healthy experimentation in new or challenging areas	21	15
Fostered healthier attitudes toward the course	21	8
Students do less work—learn less	31	28

Source: Main and Gallagher (1972).

achievement under pass–no credit grading. In any case, the data show the motivational importance of grades and grading systems.

Don't most grading and testing systems cause student tension and anxiety, often leading to cheating? We think that assessment systems can be honestly administered and can provide important feedback to students and those concerned with the students' performance without becoming so punitive that cheating results.

Reducing student tension

There are many ways to cut down the tension students feel about marks and grades. You can decide not to fail anyone. You can see to it that all marks are kept private. These steps should reduce fear of ridicule and parental punishment, and the tension that could lead to cheating. You can decide to negotiate grades, letting students contribute to the process. Or you can choose to drop students' poorest test performances, not including them in the sum or average of all of a student's performances on a series of tests. A poor performance in, say, long division early in a mathematics unit would not be averaged in with that student's perfect score in a long division test later in the unit. According to Holt (1974), averaging that includes all of a student's grades

Dropping poorest test performances

> is idiotic, unfair, outrageous. The aim of the class is to learn long division, not to have a contest to see who can learn it in the fewest number of tries. Anyone who learns it, however long it takes, however many times he fails along the way, should get a perfect mark for that part of the course. (p. 572)

Obviously, a criterion-referenced approach to assessment in long division or some other subject area would eliminate some major problems. In a criterion-referenced system, students simply continue to study and take tests until they demonstrate mastery. The impetus to cheat that exists in a one-shot try to show what you know is removed when students understand that they will have many opportunities to demonstrate achievement. Cheating is a sign that the teacher's system of student assessment needs change.

Anxiety and performance

Another aspect of the anxiety must be addressed: Moderate amounts of anxiety improve student performance. This relationship is schematized in

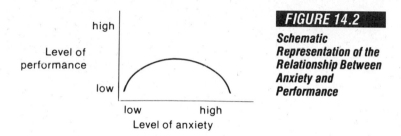

FIGURE 14.2

Schematic Representation of the Relationship Between Anxiety and Performance

Figure 14.2. When anxiety is very high or very low, performance decreases. The problem is finding a balance, to bring the motivational levels down in the case of highly anxious students and up in the case of students who show too little anxiety. Anxiety can be reduced by lengthening instructions and giving pretest practice in responding. The teacher can use such devices to achieve a moderate level of anxiety.

Goals of a Student Assessment System

We have evaluated several pros and cons, and we still think grading has a valuable role. But you should remember that every student assessment system should have the improvement of students as its goal. Everything else is secondary. When we assess, we should give information that individual students and those concerned with their well-being can use. We must devise systems that give feedback on important dimensions of students' behavior. The students can then use the assessments in deciding whether to continue or modify their behavior. **Student improvement is primary goal**

As an integral part of effective teaching, the assessment experience should lead to feelings of success. If our objectives are sound and our teaching methods are appropriate, we should always be able to find and praise positive aspects in each student's performance. Any comments about students' weaknesses should go hand in hand with suggestions about how the students might improve. **Say something positive**

If you give tests, you should announce them in advance, clearly specify the areas you will be testing, and indicate how much the tests will count in some summary marking system. You should also provide for individual student's problems—say, absences and makeup tests. If you have students who did not understand instructions, who studied the wrong material, who were nervous or tired, arrange to give them special or individual attention.

Always keep private your collection of students' tests and written papers, and your observations and notes about them. Share them only with the student or, sometimes, with parents, guidance counselors, or medical personnel. But only students or their parents should be able to authorize access to these reports. By maintaining privacy, you reduce the competition among students or among parents—competition that can penalize slower or less able students. Maintaining privacy also keeps you in compliance with federal laws that prohibit anyone but students and their families from obtaining school records. **Privacy**

Separate relevant from irrelevant factors

When grading student achievement, use only relevant information. Don't include students' tardiness records in your evaluation of their English compositions. Try to provide feedback to a student on each area of concern to you and the student, independent of his behavior in any other area of concern. Separate effort from achievement. Achievement is achievement; attendance, effort, and what the student's father wants are separate issues. Don't ignore them; just keep them separate.

Sources of Evidence

Use a wide range of evidence

When grading a student in any curriculum area, you should use a wide range of relevant and appropriate sources of information. Why? Because each source of evidence is fallible, each has different weaknesses and strengths. Your sources might include performance, multiple-choice, and essay tests, and special student projects. And they might include careful observations of the student's participation in large-group, small-group, and individual activities. Any one source of information is likely to provide a less valid estimate of a student's achievement than is some combination of sources.

How do you go about combining data gathered from numerous sources? As you try to integrate all you know about a student's performance in some area, you can interpret some observational data informally. But information from tests must be combined systematically.

Formal Assessments

During a semester or a year, students are usually evaluated several times in several ways—multiple-choice tests, essay tests, projects, oral reports, homework assignments, and performance tests. Most of these assessments result in a score, grade, or summary mark. That mark could be a letter grade (A, B–, D +), a percentage grade (78 percent), a proportion (8/13), the number right (+43), the number wrong (–7), or simply information about whether the performance is passing or failing (P or F).

Don't combine criterion-referenced scores

When criterion-referenced testing is used, you don't need to combine the scores or marks. Each score is itself an example of some definable achievement. It makes no sense to combine achievement on a test of multiplication of two-digit numbers with achievement on a test of multiplication of decimals. All we want to know is whether the student has achieved each objective. But parents often want letter grades, not a report of objectives achieved, so you may need to provide summary grades as well.

Combining norm-referenced data

When norm-referenced testing is used, or when trying to get a summary grade of criterion-referenced assignments and tests, you may need to combine scores in various tests to obtain an overall grade. For example, a final grade in biology may be the average of sixteen weekly tests. Or you may have to combine scores on a midterm, a term paper, and a final examination to determine a student's grade in social studies.

Merging information from many diverse sources is a problem. You might have scores on essays, multiple-choice tests, class presentations, and projects—all of which had very different mean scores and altogether different measures of variability. How do you combine data from these different sources?

Combining Data. Some advanced coursework in assessment can teach you the most technically sound procedures for doing this. But if your district has no guidelines, and you need a simple and reasonably sound way to get started, we offer some advice. Think of putting all student products you receive into a pass/fail system equivalent to the following: pass = 60–100 percent; fail = less than 60 percent. Or you might assign letter grades to student products as follows (cf. Airasian, 1991):

A = 94 or higher	C = 74–76
A– = 90–93	C– = 70–73
B+ = 87–89	D+ = 67–69
B = 84–86	D = 64–66
B– = 80–83	D– = 60–63
C+ = 77–79	F = less than 60

Or, if you do not like so many gradations, you might use: A = 90–100, B = 80–89, C = 70–79, and so forth. If you put all the assessment information that you collect throughout the semester or marking period into percentages, you can average and weight the evidence at the time you must assign grades. Otherwise, you will have trouble combining information from several sources. For example, how would you make sense out of your assessments in, say, social studies if, during the school term, you gave an essay exam of three questions, four homework assignments, three short-answer multiple-choice tests, and an exercise calling for an oral report? If the essays were holistically scored A–F, then a B grade would be translatable into something in the 80–89 range of percentages, say 85. Or a B– would be worth 81 or 82 percent. The homework assignments you required of your students could have been given grades too— Excellent (worth 95), Good (worth 85), Acceptable (worth 75), Failure (worth nothing, must be redone until acceptable). The short-answer multiple-choice tests could be graded in percentages right from the start, and if the test was criterion-referenced, then you might specify right from the start what percentage is equivalent to excellent, good, acceptable, and unacceptable performance. Perhaps you could consider excellent performance to be 90–100, good to be 80–89, and acceptable, which is the minimum mastery level that you choose, to be 70–79. If some performance was deemed unacceptable, which is the non-mastery level, it would be worth no points until the performance was tried again and became at least acceptable. In this case everyone in the class would eventually have a score of between 70 and 100, though some may have initially scored below the minimally acceptable level. This kind of system, of course, calls for more work by teachers. But wouldn't it be nice never to fail a student? For the vast majority of students, more time to study and more opportunities to

Average and weight the evidence

Never needing to fail a student

take tests that they initially failed will result in acceptable (or better) levels of performance. And that really is what everyone wants.

Oral reports or term projects, holistically scored, could also be given letter grades corresponding to some percentage system. Then, at the end of the grading period you might have records such as those displayed in Table 14.7. This simple percentage system for combining scores allows you to average different pieces of information and provide a letter grade for the marking period.

Weighting scores

The system allows for weighting of scores as well. For example, suppose you want to weight the oral presentation 50 percent higher than the other evidence you collected, and you wanted to weight the fourth homework assignment three times more than other sources of evidence because it covered more material, took a long time to finish, and was more complex. You would then multiply the percentage given to the oral examination by 1.5 and the percentage given on the fourth homework assignment by 3. Using Tyrone Adams as an example, we see that his unweighted semester average percentage score was 90, equivalent in this grading scheme to an A–. Recalculating his oral presentation to be worth 1.5 × 88, or 122, and his fourth homework assignment to be worth 3 × 75, or 225, we get a higher sum of the 9 scores than before. But now, instead of dividing that sum by 9 we divide it by 11.5 (the weights of 3 + 1.5 are added to the other 7 scores). Now Tyrone's semester average is 86, and his semester grade would drop from an A– to a B. Weighting may result in grades different from those resulting from equal weights, but that is appropriate if your sources of evidence about a student are not all of equal value to you.

Despite the technical problems in this and virtually all grading systems we have examined, this system has some decided advantages. None of its technical flaws are so serious as to require us to abandon it. The system is simple and flexible, it allows weighting and combining, and it is understandable to students, their parents, and employers. You might do well to start your teaching career with this kind of system.

Informal Assessments

Much of the information you need in order to know a student well can be obtained from simple observations. By watching youngsters playing in the playground or working with counting blocks or learning to use a dictionary, by observing adolescents in the laboratory or on the dance floor or in a discussion group, you can get considerable insight into their academic and social behavior. When you see students tackling a problem, you are seeing intelligence in use!

Going beyond test scores

Of course, seeing isn't enough. You also have to remember Mary's brilliant analysis of Robert Frost's poetry in front of the class, John's kindness to Margaret, Alice's achievements in three-dimensional tic-tac-toe. And since informal assessments are not usually written down, you may not remember all the incidents that helped you size up Mary, John, and Alice. Perhaps you need to write little notes about salient events you have witnessed and put them into the files or portfolios for each student. Notes will help you remember the incidents much later, because at some time you can expect to be called on to help

TABLE 14.7 Example of a Simple Combination of Percentages for Grading

Names	Homework Assignment #1	Homework Assignment #2	Multiple-Choice Test #1	Homework Assignment #3	Multiple-Choice Test #2	Homework Assignment #4	Multiple-Choice Test #3	Essay Test	Oral Presentation	Semester Average	Semester Grade
Adams, Tyrone	Exc. 95	Good 85	Exc. 95	Good 85	Exc. 95	Accept. 75	Exc. 95	A 97	B+ 88	90	A−
Bestor, Edwina	Accept. 75	Accept. 75	Unaccept. Accept. 75	Good 85	Accept. 75	Good 85	Unaccept. Accept. 75	B 85	C 75	78	C+
Corleone, Thomas	Accept. 75	Accept. 75	Good 85	Unaccept. Accept. 75	Accept. 75	Good 85	Accept. 75	C− 72	C+ 78	77	C+
· · ·	· · ·	· · ·	· · ·	· · ·	· · ·	· · ·	· · ·	· · ·	· · ·	· · ·	· · ·
Zandejas, Zulin	Good 85	Exc. 95	Good 85	Good 85	Good 85	Exc. 95	Good 85	B+ 88	B− 82	87	B+

students plan their future or to recommend students for some school, club, or honor. Your informal observations can give you more insight into a student than can test scores alone. And your notes will help you recall those insights. So take the time to watch some of your students playing, studying, solving problems, flirting, or debating. You will probably have opinions about them in more than the cognitive areas. And in elementary and middle schools you may often be asked to record your perceptions of the noncognitive aspects of behavior, say, motivation or the ability to get along with others, on student report cards.

The Teacher's Thoughts During Grading

What exactly are the rules by which teachers make judgments from all the data they have? Whitmer (1982) studied teachers' thoughts while grading and found that they make heavy use of their grade book—the record of achievement, number of tasks completed, absences, behavior problems, and so forth. The most important variable in that book was rate of task completion—the speed with which students move through the curriculum. This was a disappointing finding. Certainly the rate of task completion should not be given the greatest weight in assigning grades to elementary school students. The study also showed that when a student's grade was not clear, teachers marked up or down depending on their own ratings of the student's ability and effort. Furthermore, they also used their own ratings of home support, classroom behavior, physical maturity, and difficulty of the task to be learned. Sometimes, outside-the-class-

Outside-the-classroom factors

room factors enter into a teacher's grading decisions. For example, in a study by Di Gangi, Faykus, Powell, Wallin, and Berliner (1991), teachers claimed they did not allow information about parental involvement in school activities influence their grades. Nevertheless, it was found that a big factor in grading was

Effects on grades of parent involvement in school

whether parents participated in school activities as a teacher's aide, member of the parent-teacher group, member of the community board for the school or district, and so forth. Students who would have received a C or C + grade for their work received a B or B + if their parents were active; they received a D or D + if their parents were thought to be unconcerned about school activities. Obviously, poor children receive poor grades in part because they have no wealthy mother who can come to school and participate in the life of the school. This tendency is obviously unfair.

Although out-of-classroom factors can influence grading, Whitmer's study concluded that most grading is classroom bound. That is, most grading is based on classroom events, not judgments about children's out-of-class behavior. This is as it should be. But it does not mean that teachers are free of the biases they bring with them to the classroom.

Bias in evaluation

Whatever we do—grading essay tests or observing students in a discussion group—we bring to it certain biases. Zillig (1928) was one of the first to demonstrate how our biases affect grading. Notebooks containing assignments from students judged to be bright by their teachers were examined and compared with notebooks of students judged to be much less competent by their teachers. The number of errors that had *not* been noted by the teachers was found to be

• *Watching children play can give you insight into their academic and social behavior. (© Paul Conklin/Monkmeyer Press Photo Service)*

higher for the students judged to be brighter. Teachers seemed to expect, then actually found, more errors in the notebooks of the students they judged less competent. Errors made by the brightest students were less likely to be caught. The teachers misperceived reality because they believed that the brighter students were less likely to make errors.

Expectations influence perceptions

Students have learned how to play the schooling game and take advantage of the teachers' biases. In extensive studies of grading, Stiggins, Conklin, Bridgeford, and Green (in press) noted that

> there appears to be a stereotypic personality type among high school students that teachers respond favorably to. These are the students who *appear* attentive and aggressive during class and who therefore receive higher grades than others, not because they've learned more of the material but because they've learned to act like they are learning more. The implicit message communicated to these students seems to be, "You don't have to learn as much if you *look like* you're trying." Once they read the message, they may learn that they can manipulate classroom affective assessment to advantage. This is dangerous because it may be that white, male students are more prepared culturally to fit this stereotype than females or members of minority groups. This may lead to sex and ethnic inequities in assessment and grading systems.

We have talked about bias many times in this book. We raise the issue again because it comes up in all kinds of teaching activities—including evaluation. The grades you give can greatly influence your students' future. You must be acutely aware of your own frailties when you sit in judgment on the strengths and weaknesses of others.

The Toughest Grade of All: A Recommendation for Nonpromotion

In these times of public demands that schools uphold academic standards, pressure to retain students in grade has increased. Because of students' failure or emotional immaturity, teachers in the United States will probably recommend that around 2 million students not be promoted this year. Principals and superintendents will point to increased rates of nonpromotion as evidence of "tougher" schools. The cost to the nation of these recommendations is in the neighborhood of $10 billion (see Nikleson, 1984). While all this is happening, research has been accumulating to suggest that this education trend goes against the best interests of the vast majority of students who are left back.

Nonpromotion vs. promotion

A meta-analysis of forty-four independent studies of retained or promoted students showed great consistency (Holmes & Matthews, 1984). The studies covered elementary and junior high school grade levels, comparing in total 4,208 students who were not promoted with 6,924 similar students who were promoted. The meta-analysis showed that, if we had two students of comparable achievement, the academic achievement of the one who was left back would measure next year 17 percentile ranks below that of the one who was promoted. The nonpromoted student would lag behind the promoted student by about 15 percentile ranks in language arts, 18 percentile ranks in reading, and 22 percentile ranks in grade-point average. On measures of adjustment, the nonpromoted student would be about 11 percentile ranks lower in social adjustment, 14 percentile ranks lower in emotional adjustment, and 12 percentile ranks lower in behavioral ratings. In attitude toward school, the nonpromoted student would measure 6 percentile ranks lower and would be absent from school more frequently by 5 percentile ranks.

Those who recommend retaining students in grade without recommending special programs for those students are simply asking students to repeat an experience in which they have already done poorly. Those who recommend retaining students in grade because of special programs for them would do better to think about promoting the students and still providing special programs. This way students can stay with their age-mates. There are also economic factors here. The students would not lose a year of employability by remaining in school a year longer, and society would not have to bear the costs of an extra year of schooling. Of course, we don't recommend "social promotion"—a policy that might let students reach high school without being able to read. But where possible it makes good sense to promote students and offer special services to bring them up to grade level.

We know teachers and administrators who would argue with us that there are good reasons for retaining certain students in grade. And there is research that finds that nonpromotion can have a positive effect on some retained children (Sandoval & Hughes, 1981). But most do not thrive when retained in grade. Teachers forget that they cannot compare the growth they see in the child that was retained with the growth that they might have seen if the child had been promoted. The evidence is clear that the growth would have been greater if the child had been promoted.

Smith and Shepard (1988) collected evidence indicating that the reason some teachers leave children back is that they believe that knowledge is accumulated in a linear fashion and that IQ is fixed at birth. Teachers who believed that IQ was not fixed but molded by the environment, and who believed that if you miss learning something you'll learn it later on, or that it would not be a great tragedy if you missed something, rarely left a child back. So it appears that the teachers', as well as the principals' and school boards' beliefs about childrens' intelligence and curriculum sometimes result in high levels of retention in grade, despite the scientific evidence of its harmfulness. Moreover, it's hard to understand why a treatment that costs between $3,000–5,000 per year per child (the costs of an extra year of schooling in a typical state) and produces about the same (or worse) results as promotion should be considered effective. For the low-achieving student, retention in grade is seldom the answer.

Teachers' beliefs and retention decisions

Referencing a Reporting System

The purpose of grading, marking, observing, and other assessment activities is to provide information to students, their parents, and school officials about performance and achievement. Reporting evaluations is therefore necessary— even if you only report your judgments privately to a student. Before reporting, you need a frame of reference for your value judgments. For this purpose, you can use either absolute or relative standards.

Absolute Standards

When you decide to use absolute standards to interpret a student's performance you imply that you know what is and what is not an acceptable level of performance. Any student's performance can be judged in relation to the standard you have chosen. Criterion-referenced standards are absolute standards.

Criterion-Referenced Standards. One criterion-referenced test of concept attainment for young students uses 10 pictures of pairs of pencils, houses, shadows, blocks, and ladders to see whether students can tell which of the two objects in each picture is longer or shorter. If a child answers all of the items correctly, we can agree that the child has mastered the concepts "longer" and "shorter." But if a child gets even one answer wrong, we might doubt that the child has mastered the concepts. In this case, then, the child must answer all

**Recognizing
absolute
standards**

items correctly to pass. A criterion of 8 out of 10 right can also be an absolute standard. Whenever our expectations of performance are clear, whenever we are willing to give all A's or all F's, we are using absolute standards as a reference for judging student performance.

Pseudoabsolute Standards.   In many instances grades or percentage letter grades are used as absolute standards when they are really relative standards. For example, if a teacher always gives A's to just 10 percent of a class or has a record of never failing anyone, this teacher's grading system is probably

**Juggling to obtain
a distribution**

not based on preset standards of performance. He or she will juggle the composite scores until they "fit" some wanted distribution (see Millman, 1970). Percentage grades that are not tied explicitly to achievement are also misleading. For example, a 75 percent in reading comprehension implies that some total amount of reading comprehension exists at this age level and that this student has only three-fourths of it. But such a 75 percent grade is often only a global rating on a scale from 60 to 100. Teachers often talk about percentage scores as if they were absolute standards, by stating that a score of 60 percent or better is needed to pass the course. Then the teacher adjusts the distributions and scoring standards of particular tests to fit the cutoff point and get most students over that point (see Terwilliger, 1971). Thus the apparently absolute system is really a relative system in which overall ratings are adjusted to fit loosely into a preconceived distribution with so many 90s, 80s, 70s, and 60s. The students are actually being compared with one another rather than with absolute standards of excellent-to-poor performance. This is the kind of system that is prevalent in the United States. We urge, instead, that teachers think about the ways to make the pseudoabsolute standards they use truly absolute, by more criterion-referenced tests, projects, and assignments. Percentage systems of the type we describe on pages 655–656 need not be used with predetermined numbers of students getting certain grades. They can be designed to be more like absolute standards than relative standards, which we discuss next.

Relative Standards

Relative standards are more commonly used than are absolute standards. Here individual students are evaluated on the basis of how well they are doing relative to other students in the class, grade, age group, or ability level. If a student ranks high, he or she is likely to get an A or B letter grade. If a student ranks low, he or she may receive a C, a D, or even an F. Relative standards do not necessarily mean that a teacher is marking "on the curve." (To do that, you would take a distribution of student scores and assign, say, 7 percent A's, 24 percent B's, 38 percent C's, 24 percent D's, and 7 percent F's.) Relative standards simply mean that students are being evaluated in relation to other students. The difficulties inherent in this system are most noticeable in selective colleges, where the freshman class represents the best high school students in the country. These freshman find themselves getting some D's and F's or no credit for courses because they are being evaluated in relation to their brilliant classmates. The use of relative standards for these students inevitably and often unjustifiably lowers the self-esteem of many of them.

> **Inevitable lowering of self-esteem**

Another problem with relative standards is one we noted in our discussion of norm-referenced tests. These standards do not really tell us what students know, just how much they know in relation to other students. A student may be the best mathematician in the fifth grade, but still may not be doing very well in multiplication. The top test-taker in American history may be doing better than his or her peers and still not know much about this country's past.

Still, norm-referenced standards have their place. They are particularly helpful where criterion-referenced standards are hard to define (as they are in social studies courses, for example) and where complex learning outcomes are expected. They are easy to use, have a long tradition, are understood by most people, and serve well when admission and selection criteria are needed. The norm-referenced performance of elementary and secondary school students has always been a consistent predictor of school performance.

> **Why norms are used**

A Portfolio System of Reporting: A Little Bit of Everything

We do not yet know what should go into portfolios, or how to assess them. But they still seem to make sense, and we'll never find out how to use them intelligently if we don't just start working with them. They have great potential as a way to report achievement.

> **Potential of portfolios**

Our models of what a portfolio system might look like can come from writing and language arts classrooms in Pittsburgh (Camp, 1990). Teachers there collect many samples of classroom writing over a long period, and the writing samples show the drafts and rewriting of students so the improvement in particular pieces may be seen. The students also can select which pieces to put into the portfolio as examples of their best works and of works that show how they improved over time. If they feel they can comment about what was inadequate in a piece, they willingly put those in without embarrassment. They have learned that they have control of their portfolio and that it is appropriate to show poor work *if* they know how it can be improved.

> **Showing improvement**

The portfolio also allows students to reflect on what they have learned, to remember the writing strategies they tried out. In reflection, they "make explicit much that is ordinarily hidden from student writers and their teachers. [Reflection on portfolios] makes visible certain aspects of students' perceptions and purposes that are not accessible from their written products alone" (Camp, 1990, p. 13). It is hoped that by reflecting on their portfolios students will learn to be more self-evaluative, a skill everyone needs to develop. Some evidence for

> **Portfolios can make reflection possible**

that is apparent in the writing of a ninth grader working on writing dialogues, who looked at his work and wrote:

I feel like my writing formed two hills, like this

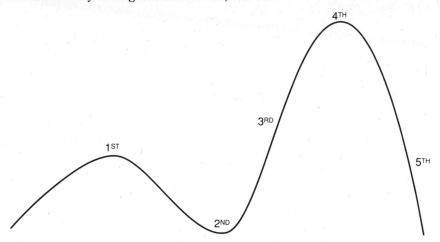

I was writing good, to my standards, then it started lacking what I thought made it good. Then I started climbing again, this time greater than my first one. Finally, my last dialogue was terrible. (Camp, 1990, p. 27)

Developing personal standards

This student sees the evolution of his work. He is fully aware of his writing. Even though not a fluent writer himself, he has developed standards by which to judge his own work. This kind of self-assessment, over time, will not happen without portfolios to work with.

The teachers in Pittsburgh have learned that negotiating with students about what should be in the portfolio is a good way to understand what students think they have learned, what they think is important, and why portfolios are useful to teachers in making instructional decisions and in individualizing those decisions as well. A body of work is always more revealing to the teacher than any single performance, test, assignment, project, or piece of volunteered work can ever be.

In science, history, mathematics, and other areas of the curriculum, portfolios can also be developed. Performances, tests, projects, reports, homework, and so forth can be collected, and the material can be used by the students for reflection about what was learned and can be used by the teachers for discussion of a student's progress with that student's parents. It can serve also for narrative feedback to the students from the teacher. Instead of giving a letter grade,

Narrative feedback

which hides so much that was done, a teacher can write a narrative report about what the student accomplished over the long haul. This report can be a more complete and satisfying form of assessment for both teachers and students. For all these reasons it is expected that portfolios are likely to become common in assessment.

• *When you are unsure about a grade, give students the benefit of the doubt.*
(© 1981 Susan Lapides)

Sensibility and Humaneness

Efforts are constantly being made to improve marking and reporting practices through cooperation among teachers, students, parents, and school administrators. In elementary schools, parent conferences are being used more and more to supplement the information on report cards, and portfolios can become the basis for fruitful parent-teacher conferences. And report cards themselves are being designed for each grade level, using objectives as a framework for each curriculum area.

There is ongoing debate in educational circles about how to improve marking and reporting. Clearly, the information we give students should be helpful to them and their parents. Because our society places so much emphasis on grades, teachers must take the process of grading seriously. When you are unsure about a grade, be lenient. Students deserve the benefit of the doubt, given our imprecise instruments and the importance of the decision. Kindness is likely to do more good than harm, particularly in norm-referenced grading. Fewer moral dilemmas arise when we use criterion-referenced standards for traditional tests and performance tests because the criteria for success—acceptability and passing—are clear-cut.

Grading, marking, and reporting systems should not be abolished. If we think about them carefully and apply them humanely, these systems work well.

Take grading seriously

What do we do when grades are used punitively, when they give rise to anxiety and stressful competition? The answer is not to abolish them but to change the system. What we need is to apply grades humanely and tie them to defined levels of achievement.

SUMMARY

Informal assessment is done to size up students and to monitor learning and motivation during instruction. Formal assessment of your classroom usually requires tests of some sort, and these must be constructed by you. A standardized test will not do. The first step in creating a test is preparing a table of specifications, which lists the number of questions that should deal with each behavior-content combination at which instruction has been aimed. The next step is choosing among types of questions. Here you should take into account the advantages of performance tests, particularly their authenticity and transparency. You need also to consider essay tests for getting at complex kinds of achievement and the advantages of short-answer tests in enabling greater breadth of coverage and higher reliability in scoring. In choosing between supply-and-select-type questions, you should again be aware of the advantages of each type: Supply questions force students to recall or create answers; select questions offer flexibility and the opportunity for students to do subtle reasoning. Overall, the best solution for most teachers is probably a combination of performance test, essay, and multiple-choice questions, with an emphasis on the first two forms of testing.

In writing test questions, you will do well at first to check your work against the suggestions we've made in this chapter. These have been developed over many years out of the experience of teachers and test authors who have learned the pitfalls and tricks of the trade. Sometimes they are easy to follow; sometimes they are difficult. But they are always worthwhile.

Assessment is not an easy process. Why do we do it? Our responsibility to society is one reason. Another is that the information is so necessary for a host of educational, vocational, and administrative decisions. Because the role grades play in our students' lives is so important, we have a special responsibility to make the system work as effectively as possible. This means reducing errors and variability in marking systems, making marks reflect actual achievement, and finding a balance between maintaining standards and minimizing anxiety levels created by grading. Grades should not be dropped from an educational program simply because they do not work to everyone's satisfaction. Rather they need to be improved.

Joined to effective teaching, grading systems should lead to feelings of success and should provide students with suggestions for improving performance. Also important is understanding a student's special circumstances, keeping student information confidential, and separating irrelevant influences from your judgment of a student's achievement.

Assessment should rest on a wide range of sources of information. Scores from tests and other formal evaluations (papers, projects) need to be supplemented by careful observations of students in social and academic settings. Unhappily, another element enters into the grading decision—teacher bias. It is very important to watch for your biases, to see that they don't influence your judgment of student achievements.

The most difficult decision many teachers have to make is to retain a student in grade. Despite a trend toward more nonpromotions each year, research tells us that retention is usually not beneficial for the student. Beyond the academic and social costs of nonpromotion are the economic costs to the student and society.

When it is time to report evaluations, you must choose between absolute and relative standards. Criterion-referenced programs use absolute standards—standards based on a predetermined level of performance. Pseudoabsolute standards are often part of the letter grade and percentage grading systems that are used by many schools. Relative standards are used when each student's performance is judged in relation to every other student's performance. They are particularly helpful where criterion-referenced standards are hard to define and where complex learning outcomes are expected.

Grading and reporting student performance is serious business and is likely to be improved if portfolio systems have been set up to keep track of student achievements over the marking period. We have to work hard to create fair, easy-to-use assessment systems. Another responsibility here is to give students the benefit of the doubt—in recognition of the fact that we and the instruments we use are fallible.

Appendix: Standard Deviation

The scores on a test can spread over a considerable range, or their distribution can be narrow, with most scores near the mean, or average. Figure A.1 presents examples of these two kinds of distributions. The preferred measure of this kind of variability or dispersion in scores is the *standard deviation*. It has special meaning for certain distributions called *normal curves*. Such distributions have the bell shape shown in Figure A.1. They are mathematically defined abstractions that approximate the actual distribution of many variables, such as the height of adult white females in the United States. Often test scores have distributions that are fairly normal.

The standard deviation is a statistic that, for curves that are normal or approximately normal, marks off the distribution of scores into intervals that contain a known percentage of the cases. In both distributions shown in Figure A.1, the interval between the mean and 1 standard deviation above the mean contains 34 percent of the cases. Similarly, the interval between the mean and 1 standard deviation below the mean contains 34 percent of the cases. When a particular score falls anywhere within 1 standard deviation of the mean, we know it is grouped with about 68 percent of the other scores in that normal distribution. If a score falls 2 standard deviations below the mean, it is exceeded by about 98 percent of the scores in that normal distribution. If a score falls 1 standard deviation above the mean, it is exceeded by about 16 percent of the scores and exceeds 84 percent of the scores. All this information is known because of the mathematical properties of normal distributions. The percentage of cases associated with various standard-deviation distances from the mean, as determined by mathematicians, is given in Figure A.1.

Here is a numerical example. Suppose a student receives a score of 33 points on the test whose distribution is displayed on the left in Figure A.1. Since we know that the mean is 29 and the standard deviation is 2, we know that this student is 2 standard deviations above the mean. Because the standard deviation marks off interpretable percentages of cases in the distribution, we can estimate that this student's score falls at about the 98th percentile, exceeded by only

Two Distributions of Test Scores with the Same Mean and Different Standard Deviations

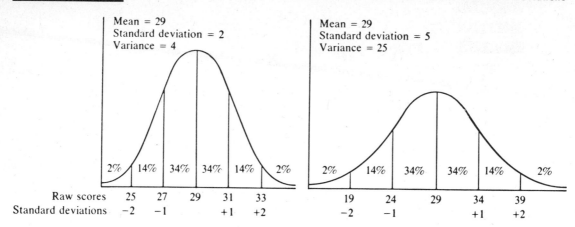

about 2 percent of the scores in that distribution. Now, suppose that the same score is received by a student whose test comes from the distribution presented on the right in Figure A.1. The mean is the same as in the first distribution, but the variability of scores is more than twice as great. The test score does not quite reach the point that is 1 standard deviation above the mean. This score certainly falls lower than the 84th percentile, and we can estimate that it is at about the 80th percentile, exceeded by about 20 percent of the scores. Thus we see that, even when the mean is the same, the same score has very different meanings, depending upon the dispersion of scores in the distribution in which it occurs. In one case the score of 33 is practically the best score one could obtain; in another case it is above average, but hardly exceptional.

The standard deviation, along with the mean, provides some of the most important information you can obtain about a test. The mean tells you about the central tendency of the distribution, and the standard deviation tells you about the variability of the scores. The smaller the standard deviation, the more closely the scores are clustered around the mean. Knowing the standard deviation and the mean, and assuming that the scores are approximately normally distributed, you can tell almost immediately the percentile rank of a score. You can accurately estimate (or use tables provided in most testing and statistics books) how this score compares with other scores in the distribution. For example, suppose you learn that a friend received a score of 390 on the verbal part of the Graduate Record Examination. Since the Graduate Record Examination has a mean of 500 and a standard deviation of 100, we know immediately that the person's score is more than 1 standard deviation below the mean. Therefore, the score of 390 is almost at the 16th percentile, exceeded by over 84 percent of the scores received by other students.

Although information of this kind is often important, it still tells us nothing about what that particular test taker knows or what he or she can do. The interpretation of score by reference to the mean and standard deviation is a norm-referenced approach to evaluation.

Glossary

Ability grouping The practice of putting students of roughly similar levels of ability together, either within groups in a classroom, sometimes called homogeneous grouping, or in separate classrooms, sometimes called tracking.

Academic engaged time The time a student attends to learning tasks relevant to academic objectives.

Academic learning time (ALT) The time that students are engaged, have high success at what they are doing, and do things related to desired outcomes. Example: A student who is attending to his worksheet in two-column addition and getting mostly right answers is accruing ALT in arithmetic.

Acceleration Moving students ahead faster than is normal or customary because they are presumably capable of learning faster. Example: letting students skip a grade.

Accommodation As used by Piaget, the modification of an already existing cognitive structure to permit understanding of a new concept or experience. A change in *schema*. Compare *assimilation*.

Accountability Being responsible for something. Example: holding administrators and teachers responsible for the quality of instruction and student achievement.

Achievement motivation A desire for or interest in success in general or in a specific field of activity. A need to excel at something.

Achievement test A test that measures a student's achievement of educational objectives, usually in the *cognitive domain* and in a specific subject matter.

Adaptation As used by Piaget, describes both *accommodation* and *assimilation,* which are related processes.

Adaptive behavior The social and cognitive skills needed to get along in a particular environment. Often used to judge retardation because IQ scores alone can be misleading.

Advance organizer As used by Ausubel, a beginning section, usually verbal and abstract, about the structure of a body of subject matter, intended to facilitate its comprehension and retention.

Affective domain That part of human behavior characterized by attitudes, emotions, feelings, interests, and values. See also *cognitive domain* and *psychomotor domain. Educational objectives* are written in this domain These may be called *affective outcomes.*

Affective outcomes Those outcomes of instruction dealing with the *affective domain.* Examples: appreciating music, enjoying reading, caring about others.

Aggression Behavior intended to express hostility or do harm to another, symbolically or physically.

Allocated time The time set aside by the state, district, or teacher for instruction in a particular area. Example: a second-grade teacher sets aside 40 minutes per day for mathematics.

Alterable variables A variable under the teacher's control, such as choice of content or allocated time. Unalterable variables from the teacher's perspective include social class and academic slowness.

Analogy items Test items in which the student is asked to infer the relationship between two initial concepts and then apply that relationship to the selection of a fourth concept that has the same relationship to a given third concept. Example: Hand is to glove as foot is to _____.

Analysis   Breaking down a subject into its components. A part of the cognitive domain of the *Taxonomy of Educational Objectives*.

Anxiety   A sense of vague or specific fear that may be either a *state* or a *trait*.

Application   The ability to use concepts and principles in the solution of problems or in new situations.

Appreciation   A tendency to see value in, and understand the subtleties of something, often in the arts.

Aptitude   Primarily used to refer to an ability to acquire skills given an opportunity to learn, often measured with an aptitude test. Example: identifying a student for a special course in auto mechanics because she has an *aptitude* for mechanical objects. Also used to refer to any *individual differences* among people—ability, anxiety, motivational level, visual acuity—as in *aptitude-treatment interaction*.

Aptitude test   See *aptitude*.

Aptitude-treatment interaction (ATI)   The phenomenon whereby a given treatment (typically an instructional method or practice) has different effects on a dependent variable (typically achievement or attitude) for students at different points on the scale of some characteristic (ability, aptitude, gender, social class, etc.). Example: Girls may perform better than boys in mathematics when cooperative learning is used; boys may perform better than girls when competitive learning structures are used.

Aspiration   What one wants to achieve.

Assessment   The process of determining, estimating, and evaluating a broad range of evidence concerning student achievement and other characteristics.

Assimilation   As used by Piaget, the process of fitting concepts or experiences into already existing cognitive structures. Compare *accomodation*.

Attention   The focusing of the mind on one thing.

Attitude   A feeling for or against something, having both cognitive and affective aspects and being more or less long-lasting.

Attribution   Assigning responsibility for one's success or failure to oneself (typically ability or effort) or something outside oneself (typically task difficulty or luck).

Authentic assessment   Assessment procedures and tools that come close to the way in which educational achievement would be manifested under real-life conditions. Example: using tasks requiring extended written matter rather than multiple-choice tests.

Autonomy versus doubt   As used by Erikson, the second stage of development during which children begin exploring the environment.

Aversive stimulus or situation   One that an organism finds unpleasant and avoids.

Avoidance learning   See *escape learning*.

Baseline   The frequency of a behavior before any systematic *behavior modification* begins.

Behavior   The activity of an organism. Usually refers to the overt or visible but also can refer to covert, invisible, or internal processes, such as thinking.

Behavior modification   The application of the principles of learning theory, particularly operant conditioning and social learning theory, to the changing of behavior. Example: using a *token economy* to improve student performance.

Behavior-content matrix   A two-dimensional table, with one dimension consisting of categories of the subject matter being taught or learned and the other dimension consisting of types of cognitive, affective, or psychomotor process to be applied to the types of subject matter. Used in formulating objectives and the structure of achievement tests. The cells of the table, where the dimensions intersect, define specific ways of processing specific kinds of content.

Behavioral objective   An *educational objective* stated in terms of observable (visible or audible) behavior.

Behaviorism   A philosophical and scientific orientation toward psychology, one that restricts scientific effort to the study of observable events and that excludes mental phenomena.

Behaviorists   Psychologists who believe in *behaviorism*.

Bias   The tendency to interact with others with a frequency or an attitude that differs from what would be expected on the basis of statistical probability or the concept of fairness to all.

Bloom's taxonomy   See *Taxonomy of Educational Objectives*.

Bottom-up processing   Constructing meaning primarily from external stimuli. Example: making sense of prose primarily from what is read, not from past experience. Compare *top-down processing*.

CAI See *computer-assisted instruction.*

Causal relationship A relationship between two variables such that different values of one bring about, determine, or cause different values of the other.

Classical conditioning The type of conditioning, formulated by Pavlov, whereby previously *neutral stimuli* become capable of eliciting responses similar to *unconditioned responses.* The *conditioned stimulus* acquires this capability by being paired with, or presented frequently just prior to, the *unconditioned stimulus.*

Classification As used by Piaget, the process of grouping objects into various categories, especially during the concrete operational stage. Involves ability to classify entities according to one or more characteristics.

Classroom management The process of ensuring that, in classroom teaching, sufficient order and freedom from disruption are maintained.

Classroom teaching The predominant approach to teaching in which the teacher works with a group of students, usually about fifteen to forty in number, and sequentially or simultaneously uses such methods as large-group lecturing, small-group discussion and cooperative learning, recitation, and seatwork.

Coefficient of correlation The numerical value of a *correlation.* May run from -1.00 through 0 to $+1.00$. High correlation coefficients (e.g., .83, $-.75$) indicate close relations between two variables. Low correlation coefficients ($-.07$, .15) indicate very little relationship between variables.

Cognition The process whereby the mind comes to know facts, concepts, principles, etc. In general, all the ways in which people think.

Cognitive development The process whereby individuals acquire more complex and adaptive ways of thinking and problem solving as they grow from infancy to adulthood.

Cognitive domain Those aspects of behavior that call primarily on cognitive processes. Distinguished from *affective domain* and *psychomotor domain. Educational objectives* are written in this domain. They are concerned with *cognitive outcomes.*

Cognitive objectives Used to refer to the intellectual processes that a learner uses, say, in translating a mathematics word problem into mathematical symbols in appropriate ways and in carrying out the appropriate intellectual subtasks to reach a solution.

Cognitive outcomes Those outcomes of instruction dealing with the *cognitive domain.* Examples: spelling, mathematics, reading skill.

Cognitive psychology A philosophical and scientific conception of psychology that deals with cognition. It focuses on the internal, not directly observable, mental processes by which human beings acquire, remember, and use information about their internal and external environments. Contrasted with the psychological position of *behaviorism,* which denies the scientific validity of references to unobservable mental processes.

Cohort A specified set of individuals. Examples: All first-graders or all mainstreamed children in one year are Cohort 1; the first-graders or mainstreamed children studied in the next year are Cohort II, etc.

College Board score A standard score on a scale with a mean of 500 and a standard deviation of 100. Used by the College Entrance Examination Board for its Scholastic Aptitude Test (SAT).

Co-membership Membership in the same group or culture as that in which another person is a member, so that cultural norms and values are shared.

Comprehension The ability to understand without necessarily being able to analyze or apply information. The lowest level of understanding in the *Taxonomy of Educational Objectives.*

Computer-assisted instruction Instruction mediated by a computer, either mainframe or desktop, which presents content, asks questions, and records and reacts to responses. May provide drill and practice, tutoring, a simulation, or a game.

Concept An idea that embodies what is common to a whole set of things that have one or more properties in common. May be concrete or abstract. Examples: dog, reinforcer, development.

Conceptual model The words or diagrams used in instruction to help learners build mental models of subject matter.

Concrete operations As used by Piaget, the third major stage of *cognitive development* covering approximately the elementary school years. Refers to the nature of children's thought, which is concrete and logical but not abstract.

Conditioned response A response elicited by an originally ineffective or *neutral stimulus* that has become effective through being presented repeatedly just prior to the presentation of an originally effective *unconditioned stimulus.* A conditioned response is a learned response.

Conditioned stimulus   An originally ineffective or *neutral stimulus* that has become effective in eliciting a response by being repeatedly paired with, or presented just prior to, an originally effective or *unconditioned stimulus*.

Conditioning   Changed relationships between stimuli and responses, between responses, or between stimuli, resulting from practice, contiguity, or *reinforcement*. Includes *classical conditioning* and *operant conditioning*.

Confidence interval   A student's test score plus and minus the standard error of measurement, providing a band, not a point, for thinking about scores.

Consequence   The stimulus or event that follows a response and that controls the strength or frequency of the response. Example: Getting a gold star or having a sad face drawn on your worksheet by a teacher is the consequence associated with doing worksheets in class.

Conservation   As used by Piaget, the process whereby a person considers the mass, weight, or volume of some matter, solid or liquid, to stay the same despite changes in its shape, configuration, or placement.

Construct validity   The degree to which a test measures the construct, or psychological concept or variable, at which it is aimed (e.g., intelligence, anxiety). Inferred from all of the logical arguments and empirical evidence available.

Content validity   The degree to which an achievement test's content contains a representative and appropriate sample of the content (subject matter) contained in the instructional objectives whose attainment the test is intended to measure.

Contextualization   Understanding an idea, word, skill, event, etc., in the context, or setting, in which it occurs. Example: understanding percentages in the context of baseball batting averages.

Contiguity learning   The learning that results from the presentation of two or more stimuli very close together in time or space, so that subsequently the presentation of one of the stimuli calls forth, as a response, the other stimulus. Association of the events in mind is considered a natural process. *Reinforcement* is not needed to explain *learning*.

Contingency   The dependence of a reinforcement on the occurrence of a specific response.

Contingency contract   A commitment that is mutually agreed on, often in writing, such that on completion of certain tasks or on achieving certain levels of proficiency a specific *reward* is given.

Contingency management   The systematic use of *contingencies* and the development of *contingency contracts* to achieve particular goals.

Continuous reinforcement   A schedule whereby every response of a certain kind is reinforced.

Control   The capability of bringing about change in a *dependent variable* by manipulating the causally related *independent variable*.

Control group   The subjects in an *experiment* who either receive no treatment or receive their usual treatment, not the experimental treatment. It is used to measure the level of the *dependent variable* in the absence of the experimental treatment. Example: In an experiment to see if a "new" music curriculum is associated with outcomes different from those of an "old" music curriculum, the group receiving the "old" curriculum is the control group.

Conventional level of morality   After Kohlberg, the middle of three stages, focused on maintaining rules and order and pleasing others.

Convergent questions   Questions for which there is a single right answer.

Convergent thinking   Thinking that leads to a single correct or customary answer to a question or problem.

Cooperative learning   An approach to learning, arranged by the teacher, that requires two, or a small group of, students to work together to achieve an educational objective.

Correlation   A statistical description of the closeness and direction of the relationship between variables. May be positive, where being low or high on one variable means being low or high on another. (Example: The correlation between high school GPA and number of hours spent studying.) May also be negative, indicating that being low or high on one variable means being the opposite on the other variable. (Example: high school GPA and number of hours spent watching television.)

Creativity   The process or ability that results in the formulation or production of new ideas, approaches, or products that have some artistic or scientific merit.

Criterion   A basis or means for judging something, such as the validity of an intelligence test.

Criterion validity   The degree to which the score on a test predicts the individual's score or performance in some other area. Example: If correlated, a test of scholastic achievement can be used to predict job success.

Criterion-referenced evaluation   The process of determining the degree to which a performance or achievement fits prespecified standards or criteria. Distinguished from *norm-referenced evaluation.*

Criterion-referenced tests Tests with a prespecified standard, so that students succeed when they exceed the standard. No comparison with other students, as with *norm-referenced tests,* is required.

Crystallized intelligence The kind of intelligence, after R. B. Cattell, that is expressed in well-structured forms by a given culture, e.g., school achievement, vocational skills. Distinguished from *fluid intelligence.*

Cue A stimulus that, through previous experience, indicates a situation where, if a correct response is made, a reinforcer will or will not follow.

Culture The information, ideas, ways of thinking and behaving of a social group, large (e.g., Navajos) or small (e.g., the Jones family).

Culture-free test A test that calls for skills or attitudes that have been minimally, or not at all, influenced by the culture in which the individual being tested has grown up. Sometimes called a culture-fair test. An ideal that may not be achievable.

Decay The fading or disappearance of information from *short-term memory.*

Declarative knowledge Knowledge or memory of factual things; includes *episodic memory* and *semantic memory.*

Decontextualization Understanding an idea, word, event, etc., in any context or at least outside of any single context or field or environment. Example: understanding words (e.g., percentage) in more than one, or in any, context (e.g., baseball batting average, interest on a loan, etc.).

Deficit model of education An approach to education for poor minority-group children based on the assumption that they are "disadvantaged" and need education that will compensate for their disadvantage.

Dependent variable The variable in a research investigation that is considered to be influenced by one or more other variables that are either being manipulated or are varying freely, within the context of the study.

Desensitization A conditioning procedure whereby strong emotional responses are progressively weakened by pairing stimuli that elicit those responses with pleasant events. Example: For a person scared of algebra, you develop a hierarchy of fearful stimuli and pick the weakest of them to pair with an antagonistic response to anxiety (say, pairing thoughts about two-

column addition with relaxation responses). Then you move up the hierarchy, progressively removing or weakening fear responses.

Development Physical or psychological change over time, as from infancy to old age.

Developmental crises After Erikson, referring to the struggles individuals have at various points in the life cycle. Example: Learning how to live with and share life with another, versus maintaining autonomy and living alone, are crises every young adult faces in our society.

Differential reinforcement Used in conditioning, refers to a process of reinforcing some responses and not others.

Direct instruction A set of instructional practices in which the teacher controls student behavior fairly closely by presenting the material to be learned, soliciting and reacting to students' responses, and generally keeping instruction tied to objectives.

Disadvantaged A term applied to children who have economic and social handicaps. Usually refers to low-income minority children who have experiences different from those of middle-class suburban white children.

Discipline Refers both to the control of a class by teachers and the dispensing of punishment by teachers.

Discovery learning A kind of learning in which the student must induce concepts or principles fairly independently of *direct instruction,* i.e., by observation and analysis of events and processes. Usually entails relatively free exploration by the student but may be guided by the teacher.

Disequilibrium After Piaget, the process that occurs when events cannot be handled by existing knowledge and skill, requiring *adaptation* by the organism. When cognitions are characterized by disequilibrium, new learning takes place, so cognitive *equilibrium* can be reestablished.

Disinhibition The appearance of behavior that had been suppressed or inhibited. Example: the violence of ordinary people in a lynch mob.

Distractor An incorrect response alternative in a multiple-choice test item.

Divergent questions Questions for which many answers or unique answers are acceptable.

Divergent thinking Thinking that leads to a variety of desirable or relevant responses or to unusual responses to a particular problem situation. Regarded as a form of *creativity*.

Domain   As used in the *Taxonomy of Educational Objectives,* a major category of educational objectives: cognitive, affective, or psychomotor. Can also refer to a clearly defined body of knowledge or skill. Examples: two-column addition, the Federalist papers, stick handling in hockey.

Domain-specific knowledge   Knowledge about a particular area, such as an occupation, a unit of instruction, or a sport (e.g., soccer). Can correlate more highly than IQ with achievement in that area.

Dual-coding   The coding of information in long-term storage in a verbal or symbolic form and a pictorial or iconic form.

Educational objectives   The goals and outcomes of education. Can be broad, as in specifying that all children should become good citizens; or narrow, as in a *behavioral objective,* such as specifying that all children can recognize the Bill of Rights.

Educational psychology   The study of learning, teaching, and schooling, and related areas, using the concepts and methods of the discipline of psychology.

Egocentrism   An inability to take the view of others, characteristic of children's thinking. Also, a belief that others experience events the same way as oneself.

Elicited response   A response brought about by a stimulus. Example: salivation after sight of food, feelings of hunger. See *classical conditioning*.

Emitted response   A response made by an organism, for which the eliciting factors are unknown. See *operant conditioning*.

Emotional stimuli   Stimuli that elicit an emotional reaction. Examples: words like "blood" or "pizza" or "danger."

Empathy   The ability to put oneself in the psychological place ("shoes") of another person or group.

Empirical   Relying on experience, as in observation or experimentation. Compare *logical*.

Enactive stage   After Bruner, the first stage of *cognitive development,* characterized by motor responses—touching, grasping, feeling, chewing, etc.—through which the child comes to know the objective world. Followed by *iconic* stage and *symbolic* stage.

Encoding   Transforming verbal, visual, musical, and other forms of sensory information into some system for processing and storing that information.

Engaged time   That part of allocated time during which students are actually paying attention to, or involved in, an activity.

Enrichment   Offering additional learning opportunities in some area to gifted students. Often used instead of *acceleration*.

Episodic memory   Storage of personal, dated, autobiographical memories.

Equalization effect   A characteristic of students to use all available resources when studying for a test, thus making it difficult to evaluate the effects of different teaching methods. Example: The effects of teaching one class via small groups and the other as a large group may be wiped out if the two classes have the same textbook.

Equilibrium   After Piaget, a balance between *accommodation* and *assimilation*. Maintaining equilibrium is the force behind cognitive growth.

Escape learning   The avoidance of *aversive stimuli* by leaving or escaping from an aversive situation before the aversive stimuli appear (called *avoidance learning*) or right after the aversive stimuli occur.

Essay tests   Achievement tests that call on the student to write a relatively lengthy response typically based on comprehension, application, analysis, synthesis, or evaluation.

Esteem needs   From the hierarchy of motives, after Maslow, the need to belong to and be accorded status in some group. If not fulfilled, one will not reach higher levels of the hierarchy.

E-T-R sequence   See *instructional conversation*.

Evaluation   A cognitive process calling for judgments of either the goodness or correctness (i.e., the valuing) of something. Also, a procedure whereby observations and measurements are compared with norms or criteria in order to arrive at a recommendation concerning a decision or policy. Examples: calling a score of twenty-four superb; using all available data to determine whether a citizenship program is having its intended effect.

Exceptional children   Children who are not in the typical range on some characteristic. Physically handicapped, learning disabled, mathematically precocious, and artistically gifted are all exceptional children.

Expectancy   A prediction or prophesy about performance, sometimes coming true, as in the *self-fulfilling prophesy*.

Experiment   A method of investigation or research in which one variable, the independent or experimental variable, is manipulated and the subsequent value of another, or dependent, variable is measured to determine whether changes in the independent variable cause changes in the dependent variable.

Explaining links   Linkages between clauses, sentences, or paragraphs that help tie them together and make their implications clear. Words like "because," "therefore," "thus," and others clarify a message.

Explanation   Accounting for a relationship between variables by showing that it is logical.

Expository teaching   Teaching that sets forth, presents, and explains the material to be received, as against discovered, by the student.

External   See *locus of control.*

Extinction   The disappearance, more or less rapid, of a previously conditioned response. In classical conditioning, it results from presentation of the conditioned stimulus without subsequent presentation of the unconditioned stimulus. In operant conditioning, it results from unreinforced occurrences of the operant behavior.

Extrinsic motivation   Motivation that results from reinforcers that are not inherent in the activity.

Extrinsic reinforcement   Reinforcement that is external to an activity, not from within, as in the difference between grades versus self-satisfaction for finishing a term project

Face validity   The extent to which a test appears to laypersons to measure what it is supposed to measure. Example: A test of first-aid ability would be judged to have some face validity if it has items on setting splints and tying tourniquets. It would have less face validity if it has items on arthritis—a chronic disease.

Factor analysis   A statistical method for identifying the common dimensions underlying a set of variables that correlate more or less highly with one another. Used in identifying primary abilities, or types of intelligence, such as verbal, numerical, spatial. Also applicable to attitudes and other types of variables.

Fear of failure   Anxiousness about undertaking certain kinds of tasks, often leading to choices of tasks that are too easy or too difficult, so as to maximize success or avoid personal responsibility for failure.

Fear of success   Apprehensiveness about losses of friendship and love relationships owing to high levels of achievement.

Feedback   Information about performance. Examples: Teachers receive feedback about their teaching by watching students and *assessing* their test performance; students receive feedback from their teachers in the form of grades and personal comments.

Fixed-interval schedule   A *schedule of reinforcement* whereby reinforcers occur at points equally separated in time from one another.

Fixed-ratio schedule   A *schedule of reinforcement* whereby reinforcers occur after equal numbers of specified responses have been made since the preceding reinforcement.

Flexibility   In creativity, the ability to use many different procedures, concepts, or strategies in solving problems.

Fluency   In creativity, the ability to rapidly and steadily come up with alternative views or solutions.

Fluid intelligence   A kind of intelligence, after R. B. Cattell, which has not been closely shaped by cultural forces, or learned in formal educational settings, but rather has developed through free and unstructured interaction with the environment. Distinguished from *crystallized intelligence.*

Formal operations   As used by Piaget, the stage of *cognitive development* in which the adolescent becomes capable of dealing with and manipulating abstractions and logical relationships.

Formative evaluation   A kind of *evaluation* intended to provide information for the improvement of teaching, curricula, or instructional materials. Compare *summative evaluation.*

Frame   A segment of programmed instructional material in which content is presented and a question or problem calls on the student to respond.

Fraternal twins   Twins resulting from simultaneous fertilization of two ova by two sperms and hence no more similar genetically than ordinary siblings. Compare *identical twins.*

Frequency distribution   A table in which, for each value or group of values of a variable, the number of persons or entities possessing that value is indicated.

Frustration   An emotional response, leading to aggressiveness or regression, stemming from an inability to obtain reinforcement.

g   See *general factor.*

Gatekeeper   A person who influences or determines the entrance of other persons into an occupation, organization, opportunity, etc.

General or *g* factor   The common factor running through all tests of mental ability.

Generative learning   After Wittrock, the idea that students learn through generating, or developing more or less on their own, the meanings inherent in what they are studying.

Generativity versus self-absorption   As used by Erikson, the stage of development in which the individual reaches out beyond personal concerns toward broader societal problems as against being preoccupied with one's own interests.

Grade-equivalent score   A way of interpreting test scores such that a given raw score is translated into the grade level of the average student who has received that raw score in a specified norm group. For example, a grade equivalent score of 4.3 means that the student's raw score equals the average score expected from students in the third month of the fourth grade.

Group tests   Tests that can be given to more than one person at a time, as against *individual tests.*

Heritability index   The proportion of the variation in a characteristic that is accounted for by variation in heredity; i.e., the genetic contribution to the characteristic.

Heterogeneous grouping   The practice of grouping students without regard for ability, gender, or the like.

Hidden curriculum   The portion of the schooling process not easily noticed but part of what is learned. Examples: the ways schools sort children by achievement scores and social class; how society's gender expectations become part of the school culture; or the fact that the history of nonwhite people is rarely presented.

Hierarchical structure   After Gagné, the arrangement of learning tasks so that early tasks are prerequisites to, or facilitative of, learning the next task, and so on.

High-consensus field   Subject matter areas where there is a great deal of agreement about the facts, concepts, principles, and methods that should be taught to students. Examples: mathematics in the elementary grades, introductory biology in high school.

High-inference variables   Variables in teaching that can be judged only by using a high degree of inference, interpretation, or extrapolation from cues. Examples: clarity, warmth.

High-stakes testing   Standardized testing whose results, as interpreted by school administrators, political officials, business enterprises, and others, can have important effects on the status of students and their teachers.

Higher-level questions   Questions that call for thinking, or cognitive processing of ideas. Often refers to levels above knowledge when using the *cognitive domain* of the *Taxonomy of Educational Objectives.*

Holophrastic language   Language in which single words are used to express complete thoughts, typically in infancy, when, for example, "Go" means "I want to go now."

Homogeneous grouping   See *ability grouping.*

Humanistic   An orientation toward those characteristics that are the essence of being human—love, grief, laughter, caring, sharing, embarrassment, self-worth, and so forth. Humanistic psychologists and humanistic education emphasize these aspects of the human condition.

Hypothesis   A statement of the relationship between two or more variables, awaiting validation on the basis of research.

Iconic representation   Mentally coding information in pictorial or diagrammatic form, or as icons, characteristic of an intermediate stage of maturity in learning. Contrasted with *enactive* and *symbolic* learning.

Ideational scaffolding   Providing or calling forth a cognitive structure within which to fit new experience. Used to account for the effectiveness of *advance organizers.*

Identical elements   The theory that transfer depends on the degree to which the new situation resembles, or has identical elements with, the original situation in which a skill was acquired.

Identical twins   Twins resulting from fertilization of a single ovum by a single sperm and hence carrying the same genes. Compare *fraternal twins.*

Identity   After Piaget, the idea that the quantity of something stays the same unless some amount is added or subtracted. Also, more generally used to refer to the sense of self, a particularly important concern of adolescents who may suffer an "identity crisis."

Identity versus role diffusion   After Erikson, the stage of development in which adolescents deal with their roles in society and the nature of their own self.

Imagery   A mental representation of information in pictorial, diagrammatic, or iconic form. An aid to memory.

Imitation   To behave in the same way as a *model*. To copy another's behavior. An important part of *social learning theory*.

Incentive   Something that can satisfy a motive. Example: Money is an incentive for those who want to be rich; they can be motivated by the promise of money.

Incidental learning   Learning that takes place unintentionally, while doing other things. Examples: learning a good deal about driving a car, while a passenger; learning probability while playing poker.

Independent variable   The variable in a relationship that freely takes on different values or is manipulated so that subsequent values of another variable, the *dependent variable,* can be studied to see if they are a function of the independent variable.

Individual differences   Variations among individuals that have psychological significance. Examples: *intelligence,* personality, learning rate, *anxiety,* etc.

Individual instruction   Teaching one student at a time. May or may not be *individualized instruction.* Examples: tutoring, computer-assisted instruction.

Individual tests   Tests that can be given to only one person at a time, as against *group tests.* Example: Stanford-Binet Intelligence Scale.

Individualized education program (IEP)   A program of educational experiences specifying objectives and means for achieving them. Required by law for handicapped students.

Individualized instruction   Instruction that has been adjusted to be appropriate to the abilities, interests, and needs of specific students.

Industry versus inferiority   After Erikson, the stage of development in which children learn to obtain satisfaction from doing productive work independently.

Information processing   A cognitive conception of learning describing how individuals attend to, store, code, and retrieve information.

Inhibition   In conditioning, the blocking of a response.

Initiative versus guilt   After Erikson, the stage of development in which children first try to see how well they can handle adult problems and roles.

Instructional assessments   Informal assessments that are made during interactive teaching so that teachers can assess their own performance.

Instructional conversation   An approach to teaching based on E-T-R sequences: content from the child's *experience* is introduced, then *text* material, and finally *relationships* between them are established.

Instructional objectives   The ways of behaving, thinking, feeling, and moving that are set forth as the goals of teaching.

Instrumental conditioning   See *operant conditioning.*

Integrated ends-means model   Used to describe teacher planning where ends are not always specified before means are picked. Ends can rise from activities (means).

Integrity versus despair   After Erikson, the stage of development in which old persons look back on and evaluate their careers, with more or less satisfaction.

Intelligence   The ability of an organism to solve problems, usually involving abstractions and general knowledge of the kind acquired through informal interaction with the environment as against formal educational processes. Often regarded as a single *general factor,* but also considered as a set of *special abilities* (verbal, mathematical, spacial, etc.), or multiple intelligences, after Howard Gardner, or made up of trainable components, after Robert Sternberg.

Intelligence quotient (IQ)   Originally the ratio of mental age to chronological age × 100. Now typically measured differently but still a scale with a *mean* of 100 and a *standard deviation* of about 16, for quantifying general intelligence or mental ability.

Interactive stage of instruction   The time in which teachers and students are working together for instructional purposes. Examples: lecturing, recitation, small-group work. Contrast with *preactive stage of instruction.*

Interests   The things a person likes to pay attention to or have in consciousness, thus motivating the person in certain ways. Examples: academic interests, outdoor interests.

Interference   In studying memory, the problem that new learning sometimes prevents the recall of old learning, a blocking of the information already in storage.

Interlecture structure   Tying a lecture to the preceding and subsequent lectures in a series.

Intermittent reinforcement   The process whereby responses are sometimes but not always reinforced.

Internal   See *locus of control.*

Internal consistency reliability   A measure of the dependability or consistency of a test based on the average intercorrelation of the items of the test.

Interpretive research   The study of some phenomena, usually using qualitative, ethnographic, or naturalistic methods of investigation, and relying on the interpretive powers of the investigator. Describes events and the meanings of those events to the participants involved.

Interval schedule   A schedule of reinforcement based on time; may be a *fixed interval* or *variable interval*.

Intimacy versus isolation   After Erikson, the stage of development in young adulthood in which attempts to form an intimate relationship with another person take on great importance.

Intrinsic motivation   Motivation due to reinforcers that are inherent in the activity being performed.

Item stem   See *stem*.

Keller plan   A system of personalized instruction in which the subject matter is broken up into one- or two-week units. The student studies the material independently and takes a test of her mastery of the subject matter. If she passes the test, she goes on to the next unit. If not, she is given assistance through tutors and supplementary material. The process continues until all of the units have been mastered. Developed by Fred Keller.

Keyword method   A mnemonic method in which students can use visual imagery of a word to think of another word. Example: "Vin" ("wine" in French) is associated with a "van," with a bottle of wine in it. When hearing "Vin," the key word and visual image appear and a translation is possible.

Knowledge   The ability to recall or recognize something: a fact, definition, concept, principle, custom, etc. The lowest level of achievement in the *Taxonomy of Educational Objectives, cognitive domain*. Requires little cognitive processing of information.

Knowledge of results   Information, preferably given immediately, about the correctness or incorrectness of a person's responses.

Large-group instruction   Ways of teaching fifteen to twenty or more students at a time. Example: lecturing.

Law   A principle so strongly supported by logic and evidence that it cannot be doubted without much new evidence.

Learned helplessness   A chronic condition of failure to deal effectively and energetically with the inevitable challenges one faces. Giving up quickly in mathematics problem solving, perseverance at inane tasks, low levels of aspiration, etc., characterize the child with learned helplessness.

Learning   A change in behavior as a result of experience. The change is not attributable to physiological forces, such as fatigue or drugs, or to mechanical forces, such as stumbling. It occurs in all of life's settings, including schools and classrooms. Although an internal change, learning is inferred from changes in observable behaviors.

Learning strategy   One of a family of procedures with which a student can improve her comprehension of a body of content. Includes self-questioning, summarizing, reviewing, and underlining.

Least restrictive environment   The requirement that handicapped children be placed in environments as close to normal as possible. Thus many physically, mentally, and emotionally handicapped children have been removed from special schools and classes, where they were segregated, and returned to regular classrooms, a process called *mainstreaming*.

Level of aspiration   The level of achievement or performance that an individual wants and expects to attain.

Libido   After Freud, the life force, springing from a person's sexual energy.

Loci   See *method of loci*.

Locus of control   The *attribution* for behavior. May be internal, as when one attributes success or failure to ability or effort. May be external, as when one attributes success or failure to luck or the nature of the task. Persons with internal or external locus of control differ in many ways, particularly in taking responsibility for their own actions.

Logical   Relying on consistency in reasoning. Compare *empirical*.

Logical fallacies   The subtle, hard-to-detect but logically erroneous arguments that can mislead a participant in a discussion.

Long-term memory (LTM)   The hypothetical repository of information that has been coded so that it can be retrieved after months or years.

Longitudinal study   An investigation in which the same individuals are observed, interviewed, questioned, or tested at several points in time, usually separated by one or more years.

Lookback strategy   A learning strategy by which students look back in text when they have questions.

Low-consensus field   Subjects where there is a wide range of acceptable ideas about what should be taught to students. Examples: literature, art, social studies.

Low-inference variables   Variables in teaching that can be judged without much inference, interpretation, or extrapolation from cues. Examples: frequencies of smiles, chalkboard diagrams.

Mainstreaming   The practice of putting handicapped children in regular classrooms, whenever possible, so that they will experience the *least restrictive environment* for their development.

Mastery learning   An approach to learning through instruction that divides the subject matter into many units of one or a few weeks' duration, gives students tests of their mastery after each unit, provides supplementary instruction through tutors and varied materials to students who do not attain mastery on the first attempt, and continues this process until all students have achieved mastery, usually defined as getting between 80 or 90 percent of the total possible achievement score. The initial instruction usually takes place in a regular classroom, rather than through independent study, as in the *Keller plan,* but subsequent and supplementary instruction is conducted individually or in small groups. Developed by Benjamin S. Bloom.

Matching items   A type of objectively scorable test item requiring the student to match a set of, say, three items with the appropriate member of a class of, say, five alternatives.

Maturation   The process of change in an individual's physical, physiological, and behavioral characteristics as a result of normal processes of aging, rather than through learning. Examples: development of breasts and beards, acquisition of language, and according to Piaget, formal operational thought.

Mean   The arithmetic mean, popularly called the average, equal to the sum of scores divided by the number of scores. Affected by extremely high or low scores.

Measurement   The process of determining the amount or quantity of something, such as height or, in education, ability, achievement, or attitude.

Median   The middle score when all of the scores are arranged in rank order from high to low; used as a measure of central tendency or the point around which scores tend to fall. Unaffected by a few extremely high or low scores.

Mediation   Mental processes that occur between a stimulus and a response. Also, a way to increase meaningfulness by associating items to be learned with each other. Example: To remember that Sacramento is the capital of California, you might remember that Sacramento is where the Gold Rush began and that was in California. The information about the Gold Rush is a mediator.

Mental age   A measure of mental ability determined by the chronological age of the persons who are able to answer correctly a set of intelligence test items. Thus, if a ten-year-old boy can answer questions typically answerable only by twelve-year-olds, the ten-year-old would be said to have a mental age of twelve.

Mentoring   A relationship between a person who is an experienced and excellent performer and a relative newcomer in the same field. Examples: seasoned baseball players for rookies; established scientists for graduate students; experienced teachers for new teachers.

Meta-analysis   The quantitative synthesis of the results of two or more studies of roughly the same relationships or phenomena. Originated by Gene V Glass and applied to large bodies of research results in the behavioral sciences.

Metacognition   The mental processes whereby one monitors one's cognitive processes in thinking, learning, and remembering. Thus metacognition allows one to be aware of whether one has understood a paragraph after reading it.

Metalinguistic awareness   Knowing and being able to talk about language and its rules and customs.

Method of loci   A *mnemonic* device based on putting information to be remembered in familiar locations, such as in different pockets of your suit, or in different places around your home; retrieving the information, then, requires mental trips to the right locations.

Microcomputer   A computer small enough to fit on a desk and be used in a classroom or home for personal word processing, computation, problem solving, and learning.

Misperceptions   In *cognitive psychology,* the kind of intractable naive beliefs people hold, in spite of what they learn in school. Example: belief that light travels farther at night than during the day.

Mnemonics   Memory devices that make the task of remembering easier, particularly when the to-be-remembered information has little intrinsic structure or meaning.

Model   In *social learning theory,* someone or something that one can *imitate.* A person, a videotape, a prose description can all serve as models for new learning.

Modular theory   After Howard Gardner, the conception that different forms of intelligence—musical, spatial, verbal, etc.—are semi-independent, neurologically distinct systems, using different coding systems as well.

Moral dilemmas   Descriptions of situations where the proper or right moral course of action is unclear. Used to study moral development.

Moral judgment   Beliefs about proper and improper behavior when faced with a *moral dilemma*.

Motivation   The hypothetical internal process that energizes and directs behavior.

Multiple intelligences   After Howard Gardner, the conception that intelligence takes perhaps six highly distinct forms (verbal, spatial, musical, etc.) identified on neurological, pathological, and other bases, in addition to the traditional psychometric, factor-analytic research.

Multiple-choice tests   Tests of ability, achievement, aptitude, or attitude in which the individual is required to choose a correct, best, or preferred response from two or more presented alternatives.

Nature-nurture   The argument about the contributions to variations in intelligence of variations in heredity (nature) or environment (nurture).

Needs   What an individual requires, subjectively or objectively, for physical or psychological comfort.

Negative reinforcement   The process of reinforcing behavior by the withdrawal of an aversive stimulus. Example: discontinuing criticism after a student begins to behave properly.

Neutral stimulus   A stimulus that is ineffective in producing an *elicited response*. A stimulus to which the organism pays no particular attention.

Noncognitive tests   Tests of interests, attitudes, values, and so forth. Tests classified outside the *cognitive domain*.

Nonquestion alternative   Something, other than a question, a teacher can do or say during a discussion. Includes making a statement, acknowledging a student statement, building on a student remark, or nonverbally inviting a student to speak.

Norm-referenced evaluation   Any system of testing, grading, rating, or evaluation in which an individual's or group's measure is judged by comparisons with that of other individuals or groups, who constitute the norm group.

Norm-referenced tests (NRT)   Tests with no pre-specified standards. Comparisons are made between a student and other students who constitute a comparison or norm group.

Normal curve   See *normal distribution*.

Normal distribution   A mathematically defined bell-shaped frequency distribution. Approximated by actual data when the values, or scores, are determined by many independently operating factors, each with only a small influence.

Object permanence   A child's awareness that objects exist even when out of sight.

Objective   Desired outcome, goal, aim, purpose. Choosing objectives is often considered the first step in the educational process.

Objective tests   Tests that can be graded or scored objectively, even by machine, such as multiple-choice or true-false tests.

Observational learning   Learning resulting from the observation of another individual (a *model*).

Obvious reaction   A tendency to regard the findings of social and educational research as obvious, regardless of whether they are the actual findings or the opposite of the actual findings.

Operant   See *emitted response*.

Operant behavior   Behavior controlled by its consequences.

Operant conditioning   The learning resulting from the reinforcement or nonreinforcement of an *emitted response*.

Operation   After Piaget, a logical thought process, carried out mentally, without need of physical manipulations. Example: learning $3 + 2 = 2 + 3$ without having to check each time that this is true.

Operational thought   After Piaget, logical, scientific rational thought. A characteristic of children from about early elementary school is *concrete operational* thought. Older children become capable of *formal operational* thought.

Opportunity to learn   A powerful predictor of learning. Related to *allocated time,* exposure to content, pace of instruction, practice, and many other terms referring to whether or not students have had a sufficient chance to learn what it is we want them to learn.

Organism   A term used in psychology to refer to living animals, such as rats, pigeons, babies, and adults, among others.

Orienting response   Attention or arousal to changes in the stimulus situation.

Originality   The infrequency or rarity of a response. Used as a measure of creativity.

Origins   After Richard DeCharms, persons who feel that they control their own success or failure. See also *locus of control.*

Overachiever   A student whose classroom performance or achievement test scores are quite a bit higher than would be expected given his or her aptitude or intelligence test scores.

Overlapping distributions   Frequency distributions in which some of the members of the distribution with the lower mean have measures (e.g., scores) higher than some members of the other distribution.

Overlearning   The continuation of practice or rehearsal beyond the point at which a perfect performance first occurs.

Overregularization   In language learning, the application of a rule to cases where it is inappropriate. Example: "He gived me candy."

Participant structure   The rules that govern turn-taking in a discussion, conversation, classroom recitation, and other settings.

Pawns   After Richard DeCharms, persons who feel their success or failure is out of their own control. See *locus of control.*

Pegword method   A *mnemonic* device for associating new items to be learned. Example: learning one is a bun, two is a shoe, etc., then learning the presidents' names by association, e.g., Washington is on a bun, Adams is tying a shoe, etc.

Percentile   The raw score that has a given *percentile rank.* Example: On the Blank Test, the 50th percentile is 39; so a score of 39 has a percentile rank of 50.

Percentile rank   The percentage of persons in a norm group whose scores are exceeded by any specific raw score, which then is assigned that percentile rank. Often (and inappropriately) called percentile.

Perception   The process of assigning meaning to a sensation, something seen, heard, touched, etc.

Performance   Another term for *behavior.* Changes in performance are the basis for judging that *learning* has taken place.

Personalized system of instruction (PSI)   See *Keller plan.*

Pivot words   Words used by children in combination with other words to express a number of complex items. Examples: "No eat" and "No car" meaning "I do not want to eat now" and "The car is gone."

Population   All members of a group or groups about whom it is desired to make a generalization. Examples: all fifth-graders in the United States, all third-grade classes in City C.

Portfolio assessment   Assessment based on a collection of the student's or candidate's work over a period of, perhaps, a school term or year—work in whatever forms are authentic for the kinds of achievement or ability being assessed. Compare *authentic assessment.*

Positive reinforcement   The process of strengthening a response through the presentation of a stimulus that has that effect, as when food is presented to a hungry organism or when information that a response is correct is presented to a student.

Postconventional stage of morality   After Kohlberg, to describe the highest two levels of moral development where ethical principles, the welfare of society in general, and other complexities are taken into account when making *moral judgments.*

Poverty circle   The process in which parents who are low in income and educational level produce children low in income and educational level, who then grow up and, as parents, repeat the process with their own children. A form of "vicious circle."

Preactive stage of instruction   The planning, choosing, thinking, analyzing kinds of activities of teachers that occur before they meet their students during the *interactive stage of instruction.*

Preconventional stage of morality   After Kohlberg, to describe the lowest two levels of moral development characterized by concerns for authority or rewards and punishment when *moral judgments* are made.

Prediction   Foretelling the subsequent values of a variable with better than chance accuracy on the basis of knowledge of the earlier values of the same or some other variable.

Predictive validity   The *validity* of a test that is used to predict performance in some other area. See *criterion validity.*

Predictor   A *variable* that can be used to foretell values of another variable. Example: The number of hours spent in paid work can predict, to some extent, high school grade-point average.

Premack principle   The idea that behaviors that occur more frequently under natural conditions can be used as reinforcers for behaviors that occur less frequently. Example: using computer games to reinforce computer drill-and-practice programs.

Preoperational   After Piaget, the stage of development in childhood in which the child cannot do *operations*. The child is learning language and gaining experience but is still incapable of understanding relational terms, multiple classifications, and in the intuitive phase, from about ages four to seven, relies on vague impressions and unverbalized perceptual judgments.

Primary reinforcers   Stimuli that act as *positive reinforcers* for an organism without having been learned. Examples: food, drink, and sexual activity.

Principle   A relationship between two or more *concepts* established through scientific methods of observation, correlation, and experimentation.

Prior knowledge   What a student already knows about a topic or subject to be learned. Regarded by some as the most important factor influencing new learning. Synonym: prerequisite capability.

Probing   Continuing to question a student after an initial response to get out more knowledge or clarify points that the student made.

Problem solving   The application of principles to the solution of a problem that is new to the student.

Procedural knowledge   Knowledge about how to perform a physical or cognitive activity.

Processing   The general term applied to the many cognitive activities concerned with receiving information, including rehearsing, storing, and retrieving the information.

Programmed instruction   Instruction that proceeds by presenting the learner with an organized series of *frames,* each presenting information, a question calling for a response, and immediate knowledge of the correctness of the response. Permits self-pacing.

Projective tests   Tests consisting of unstructured stimuli that, when interpreted by the individual, yield information useful in understanding the individual's personality, including needs. Example: Thematic Apperception Test, used in measuring need for achievement.

Psychomotor   Behavior consisting of bodily movements, from fine finger movement to whole-body activity, governed by the individual's awareness of his own position or movements and evaluation, given what is intended. Examples: typewriting, violin playing, high diving, ice skating, sewing, dancing.

Psychomotor domain   Those aspects of human behavior characterized by *psychomotor* behavior, and one of three domains in which educational objectives are often written. See also *affective domain* and *cognitive domain.*

Punishment 1   The presentation to an organism of an aversive ("unpleasant") stimulus resulting in a decrease in the strength or frequency of responses that preceded the punishment. Example: sharp criticism of a student's behavior.

Punishment 2   The withdrawal from an organism of a pleasant or wanted stimulus resulting in a decrease in the strength or frequency of the responses that preceded the punishment. Example: removal of a child from the playground. See also *response cost* and *time-out.*

Qualitative research   Forms of research in which the observational and interpretive skills of the researcher play an important role and the assignment of numerical values to variables is less frequent.

Quantitative research   Forms of research in which measurement and statistics play an important role.

Random assignment   The assigning of individuals or groups in an *experiment* to the experimental or *control group* on the basis of chance alone, thus maximizing the likelihood of the equivalence of the experimental and control groups of subjects.

Random selection   In research studies, the selection of respondents in such a way that all individuals in a population have an equal probability of being included in the sample, thus maximizing the degree to which the *sample* is representative of the *population.*

Ratio schedule   A schedule of *reinforcement* based on the proportion of correct responses that are made, as when one out of twenty correct responses is reinforced. May be a *fixed ratio* or *variable ratio* schedule.

Raw score   The original or actual score obtained on a test before it has been transformed to a more interpretable form. Example: A raw score of twenty-two on a mathematics test may equal a *College Board score* of 500 or a *stanine* of five.

Reciprocal teaching   A form of instruction in which students learn to ask questions of other students and the teacher in order to learn what comprehension questions might be asked on tests and what comprehension monitoring they must engage in if they are to show they understand the material.

Recitation A component of classroom teaching in which the teacher *structures* (introduces or presents a topic), solicits (presents a question and seeks a response from a student), a student responds, and the teacher reacts to the student's response.

Recognition test A testing format where the correct answer is presented and must be recognized, as in multiple-choice or matching tests. Distinguished from test formats where recall of information (as in fill-in-the-blank) is required or memory and production is required (as in essay examinations).

Redirection Channeling a question that has been unanswered or partially answered by one student to another student, and so on, until all the requisite information is brought out.

Rehearsal Continued practice. Example: repeating a phone number over and over to remember it.

Reinforcement The process of presenting a reinforcing stimulus to an organism after the organism has made a response. Result: increasing the strength of that class of responses.

Reinforcer An event or stimulus that strengthens a class of responses.

Reliability The degree to which a test or other measurement device yields consistent, dependable, stable measures across time, test administrations, forms of the test, items of the test, judges, or raters.

Replication The repetition of an investigation—observational, correlational, or experimental—to determine the consistency of findings or to confirm previously obtained results.

Respondent conditioning See *classical conditioning.*

Response Originally a behavior either *elicited* by a stimulus (as in *respondent conditioning*) or *emitted* by an organism to no known stimulus (as in *operant conditioning*). The behavior involved the action of either muscles or glands. More recently, with the growth of *cognitive psychology,* we talk of cognitive responses, where covert not overt processes are at work. Thus, today, a response is any behavioral or cognitive change.

Response cost A version of *punishment 2,* where reinforcers are taken away when unacceptable behavior is demonstrated. Example: speeding tickets—the taking away of money for violation of traffic laws; the 15-yard penalty in football for unnecessary roughness.

Retention Used to describe delayed recall of knowledge, as in a retention test, and to be differentiated from an immediate test of learning. A synonym for memory.

Retrieval Bringing forth information from memory.

Reversibility After Piaget, an *operation* that allows a child to work backward and forward, rotate objects in mind, work from either direction on a problem, and undo activities that have been completed in actuality or in thought.

Reward An outcome or event that is perceived by the organism as enjoyable and thus acts as a *positive reinforcer.* Examples: food pellets for rats, gold stars for children, money, candy, etc.

Rhetoric The study of the elements used in composition or lecturing, including hyperbole, irony, and the like.

Role The set of behaviors expected of a person occupying a position in a social group or organization. Examples: the teacher's role, the student's role, women's roles in the family.

Rote learning Memorization without attempting to make the material meaningful.

Routines Well-rehearsed, virtually automatic patterns of behavior. Examples: doing figure eights in ice skating, driving a car almost automatically. In classrooms routines are used to hand in papers, take roll, check homework, etc. Routines may be one of the important differences between expert and novice teachers.

Rule-eg-rule pattern In lecturing or writing, the presentation of a principle or generalization, followed by positive examples of it, and then, the repetition of the principle or generalization.

Sample A portion of a total *population,* perhaps representative of the population. Example: 500 children randomly selected for a study of reading habits in a Chicago suburb are a sample of the total population of children living in that suburb.

Scatterplot A graphic representation of cases, each with two values, plotted on a two-dimensional graph to show the relationship of two variables. Used to portray a correlation—high or low, positive or negative. Example: a scatterplot in which each "dot" represents a student and the two scores obtained by that student on two tests.

Schedule of reinforcement The way in which reinforcement is presented to an organism, such as in the form of *ratio schedules* and *interval schedules* of reinforcement.

Schema (plural: schemata) The abstract but organized set of ideas that reflect an individual's understanding of a phenomenon, situation, or event. Example: All the ideas one possesses about Africa, or dining out, are in separate schemata. Schemata intersect as in understanding dining out in an Ethiopian restaurant.

Seatwork In classroom teaching, the setting in which students work at their seats on problems or assignments received from the teacher.

Secondary reinforcers Stimuli that through learning act as *positive reinforcers*. Contrast: *primary reinforcers*. Examples: kind words, money, hugs.

Selective migration (or selective immigration) The hypothesis used to account for the fact that urban or suburban people have higher IQs than rural people, or that northern African-Americans have higher IQs than southern African-Americans. Refers to the best and brightest of some group leaving, such that the remaining group is less talented.

Selective placement Placing adoptive children in families whose socioeconomic status is similar to that of the children's biological parents. A hypothesis offered as a partial or complete explanation of the correlation between IQs of children and those of their adoptive parents.

Self-actualization After Maslow, the stage of motivational development at which the individual fulfills his or her potential for personal achievement. A central goal for *humanistic* educators and psychologists.

Self-concept A person's definition of his or her own characteristics and worth in general and in specific contexts (mathematics, dating, field hockey).

Self-fulfilling prophecy A prediction that, if believed, tends to make itself come true. Example: The teacher's overt or covert communication of a prediction that a pupil will succeed tends to make the pupil try harder and thus succeed. Works, as well, in the opposite manner, promoting failure.

Self-regulation The ability to keep track of one's own behavior and to control it.

Semantic maps Visual and verbal maps of *declarative knowledge* and *procedural knowledge* created as an aid to organization for the purpose of learning and remembering.

Semantic memory Storage of concepts, principles, and characteristics of objects without personal involvement.

Sensorimotor stage After Piaget, the stage of development in which the infant is learning to use its sense organs and muscles.

Shaping The process of reinforcing *successive approximations* to a desired complex behavior.

Short-term memory (STM) The component of *information processing* models in which information from the *short-term sensory store* is either forgotten or coded and transferred to *long-term memory*. Sometimes called *working memory*.

Short-term sensory store (STSS) Also called the sensory register. A component of models of *information processing* in which sensations are stored very briefly before being either forgotten or transferred to the *short-term memory* for further processing.

Significance In statistics, the probability that the results of an *experiment* or of a correlational study are not due to chance. Thus, to say the results were significant is to say that the probability is very small that the results obtained are just due to unsystematic events; therefore, the results can probably (but not certainly) be accepted as not due to chance.

Sizing-up assessments Informal assessments providing teachers with practical knowledge of students' cognitive, affective, and motor skills, primarily during the first two weeks of schooling.

Small-group instruction Ways of teaching appropriate for two to twenty, or so, students at a time. Examples: discussion, cooperative learning methods.

Social climate The beliefs held by members of a school or classroom about the fairness, humor, academic orientation, permissiveness, opportunities for personal choice, and other social dimensions that characterize that place.

Social learning theory The theory concerning the process by which individuals learn from the observation of other individuals.

Socioeconomic status (SES) The status of an individual or group that is determined by educational level, financial wealth, place of residence, material possessions, occupational level, general prestige, and the like.

Special abilities The group factors that are found when factor analyzing *intelligence*—verbal ability, spatial ability, mathematical ability, etc. These abilities show low correlations with each other but are positively related, indicating a *general* or *g factor* as well for intelligence.

Standard deviation A measure of the variability of a set of measures around the average (arithmetic mean) of the measures.

Standard error of measurement   A statistical and psychometric quantity, determined by the reliability and standard deviation of test scores, which tells how much a score would be expected to vary if a very large number of repeated measurements were made with the same instrument under the same conditions; the higher the reliability, the smaller the standard error of measurement; the larger the standard deviation or variability of the test scores, the larger the standard error of measurement. Used in determining the *confidence interval*.

Standardized tests   Tests of ability, achievement, attitude, or interest that are commercially available, intended for widespread use, equipped with directions for administration and interpretation, presumably constructed by experts, and usually *norm-referenced*, although *criterion-referenced* standardized tests are increasingly available.

Stanine   A standard score on a scale ranging from one to nine, with a mean of five and a standard deviation of approximately two.

State   A condition of an individual that is relatively temporary and specific to a given situation. Example: Anxiety over a particular test is state anxiety. If anxiety appears for almost every test, that is *trait* anxiety.

Stem   The component of a multiple-choice test item that states the task, either as a question or as an incomplete statement.

Stimulus   (plural: stimuli) Anything in the environment that activates a sense organ.

Stimulus generalization   Responding in the same way to stimuli that differ more or less widely.

Stimulus-response (S-R) learning   Refers to *classical* and *instrumental conditioning* and *contiguity learning*.

Story grammar   The way in which stories are organized. Learning is enhanced if students are aware that stories are organized in certain recurring ways.

Structure   The organization, or set of relationships, that underlies something, such as a subject matter, an intellectual discipline. Also, as a verb, the statements by the teacher in introducing and laying out a new topic.

Student teams and achievement divisions (STAD)   Developed by Slavin, whereby heterogeneous small groups cooperate to achieve and compete against other groups to obtain group rewards.

Subjects   The people or animals that are studied in a research project. Also, the content studied in schools.

Successive approximations   Responses that come closer and closer to the desired complex response. *Shaping* results from reinforcing successive approximations as they occur.

Summarization   A learning strategy that involves identifying the main information, deleting trivial and redundant information, and relating main and supporting information.

Summative evaluation   Evaluation at the end of a program or project to determine the degree to which it has achieved its purposes. Compare *formative evaluation*.

Supply-type items   Test items that require furnishing the correct response, such as short-answer completion or essay-test items.

Symbolic stage   After Bruner, the third and final stage of development, which begins with the systematic use of language and is characterized by use of symbol systems, such as in language, mathematics, and science. See *enactive stage* or *iconic representation*.

Synthesis   One of the higher levels of the *Taxonomy of Educational Objectives*, referring to cognitive processes that require putting pieces of things together to form a whole. Example: synthesizing the causes of the Civil War.

T-score   A standardized score scale, with a mean of 50 and a standard deviation of 10, derived from *z-scores*. $T = 50 + 10z$ eliminates the negative values and decimals that characterize z-scores.

Targeting error   Identifying or disciplining the wrong person when calling attention to student misbehavior.

Task analysis   The process used for identifying the step-by-step procedures needed to accomplish something. Example: The precise steps, skills needed, and prerequisite knowledge to multiply three-digit numbers by three-digit numbers.

Taxonomy   A system of classification. Often applied to educational objectives, such as the *Taxonomy of Educational Objectives*.

Taxonomy of Educational Objectives   Developed by Benjamin Bloom and his colleagues, sometimes referred to as Bloom's taxonomy, classifies objectives of education from the lowest levels of cognition (knowledge, rote memory) through to the higher levels of cognitive activity (analysis, synthesis, evaluation).

Teaching method   A recurrent pattern of teaching behavior, applicable to various subject matters, characteristic of more than one teacher, and relevant to learning.

Teaching practice   A component of a *teaching method*. Examples: questioning during recitation, using overheads during lectures.

Team-assisted individualization (TAI)   Developed by Slavin, whereby students in heterogeneous small groups study together and test each other, freeing the teacher from many monitoring and testing duties. Scores for teams and students are evaluated against preset standards.

Teams-games-tournaments (TGT)   Developed by Slavin, an achievement game whereby teams of three students, matched on ability, compete against each other for rewards that go to their teams.

Terminal behavior   Behavior indicating that an educational objective has been achieved. It is the end at which an instructional effort is aimed. Examples: reciting the alphabet, solving a quadratic equation.

Test   One or more questions or problems used for estimating a person's ability, achievement, or aptitude and calling on the person to perform at the highest level of which he or she is capable.

Test bias   The degree to which a test contains content or requires behavior that is more frequently found in one cultural group than another. Often considered as a possible explanation of group differences in average test scores.

Test-retest reliability   One method of estimating the *reliability* of a test, obtained by administering the same test to the same individuals two or more times. The *coefficient of correlation* obtained is the estimate of reliability.

Thematic Apperception Test (TAT)   A projective test developed by Henry A. Murray for the measurement of psychological needs, e.g., need for achievement, affiliation, power. Consists of ambiguous pictures about which the person being tested is asked to create stories.

Theory   A set of organized ideas—concepts and their relationships, or principles—used to describe systematically a set of phenomena or to provide an explanation of those phenomena. Examples: attribution theory, operant conditioning theory, measurement theory.

Theory of identical elements   See *identical elements*.

Time-out   A form of *punishment 2* consisting of keeping an organism from access to desirable things or activities for a specified time.

Time-on-task   (time-on-target) The amount of time a student is actually attending to the tasks that were assigned or are appropriate for that subject matter. More than *engaged time*. This is engaged time on the appropriate task.

Timing error   Intervening in student misbehavior at the wrong time. Examples: intervening too soon, when misbehavior might have stopped by itself; intervening too late, after the misbehavior is out of hand and affecting others.

Token economy   An economic system (wages for work) using *tokens* to strengthen the display of appropriate behavior.

Token reinforcement   Reinforcement by means of physical or symbolic things, such as coins, discs, or stars, which the students can exchange for other desired things or activities, such as toys or free time.

Top-down processing   A way of cognitive functioning that imposes organization by examining information with a broad and inclusive schema and then uses more specific and less inclusive ideas to comprehend events. In reading, it emphasizes that what the reader brings to the text is at least as important as what is in the text for making sense of what is there. Contrast *bottom-up processing*.

Tracking   See *ability grouping*.

Trait   A stable and general way of behaving that manifests itself in a wide variety of situations. Trait anxiety is anxiety that the individual experiences more or less continuously regardless of the situation.

Transfer   The process whereby previous learning in one situation influences subsequent behavior in a more or less different situation. Substantive transfer refers to the number of identical elements present in each situation (driving a car, driving a truck). Procedural transfer refers to the principles that are present in each situation (playing hockey, playing soccer). Transfer may be positive, facilitating learning or desirable behavior, or negative, interfering with learning or desirable behavior.

True score   The hypothetical mean of the scores that an individual would receive if he or she took a test an infinite number of times under the same conditions.

True-false items   Test items in the form of statements to which the individual responds "true" or "false."

Trust versus mistrust   After Erikson, the crisis in infancy in which one learns the degree to which other persons can be counted on.

Tutoring Teaching one student at a time. Tutor may be a teacher, aide, older student, or peer.

Unalterable variable Variables such as gender, *intelligence, socioeconomic status,* motor coordination, that are not easily if at all alterable by teachers or schools. Contrast *alterable variables.*

Unconditioned response (UR) The response, muscular or glandular, that an individual makes when presented with an *unconditioned stimulus* (US). The US-UR connection is built into the individual's nervous system. Example: pupillary contraction when the eye is stimulated by light. The concept of UR is used in *classical conditioning* theory.

Unconditioned stimulus (US) A stimulus event that naturally elicits an *unconditioned response (UR).* The US-UR connection is built into the organism's nervous system. Example: Food in the mouth (US) increases salivation (UR). See *classical conditioning.*

Underachiever A student whose classroom performances or achievement test scores are quite a bit lower than would be expected given his or her aptitude or intelligence test scores.

Validity The degree to which a test measures what it is intended to measure (see *construct validity, content validity,* and *criterion validity).*

Variability The degree to which the measures, scores, or values of a variable cluster or spread widely around the average, or central tendency, of the measures. Examples of variability measures: range, standard deviation.

Variable A concept that can take on different qualitative or quantitative values. Examples: gender (male, female), IQ.

Variable-interval schedule A system of reinforcement whereby the amount of time between reinforcers varies. Example: one reinforcer for a correct response every thirty seconds, then one reinforcer for a correct response every sixty seconds, then one every twenty-five seconds, etc.

Variable-ratio schedule A system of reinforcement whereby the ratio of reinforcers to desired responses changes from one set of responses to another. Example: one reinforcer for each response, one reinforcer for every five responses, then one reinforcer for every three responses.

Variance The standard deviation squared. A measure of variability. Compare *standard deviation, variability.* (Has advantages over the standard deviation for some statistical purposes. Sometime used as a synonym for variability.)

Verbal ability That cluster of abilities, separate from mathematical, musical, spatial, or other group factors, having to do with the use of language. Vocabulary, analogy use, composition writing, reading comprehension, anagram solutions, etc., all make up this ability.

Verbal markers of importance In lectures, indicating which points are important and should be attended to in more depth. Example: "Now this a key factor . . ."

Vicarious reinforcement Effects on behavior from observing the *reinforcement* contingencies of another person. An important concept in *social learning theory.*

Wait time I The time between the end of a teacher's thought-provoking question and a student's being called on to answer the question.

Wait time II The time between the end of a student's response and the beginning of the teacher's commenting on that response.

Withitness After Kunin, a characteristic of teacher behavior whereby the teacher exhibits awareness of what is going on in the classroom even when not obviously looking at or listening to the students being attended to.

Working memory (WM) Used in information processing models of memory to describe the focus of attention. Sometimes viewed as identical to *short-term memory (STM),* sometimes distinguished from STM.

Yielding Going along with a group even though you believe them to be wrong.

z-score A standardized score, with a mean of zero and a standard deviation of one. $z = (X - M)/SD$, where X = raw score, M = arithmetic mean, and SD = standard deviation.

Zone of proximal development From Vygotsky, the difference between what children can do on their own and what they can do under adult guidance and tutelage.

Author-Reference Index

Number following dash indicates page on which work is cited. Some major entries are annotated.

Abbott, R. D., & Falstrom, P. (1977). Frequent testing and personalized systems of instruction. *Contemporary Educational Psychology, 2,* 251–257.—464

Abraham, E. C., Nelson, M. A., & Reynolds, W. W., Jr. (1971). *Discussion strategies and student cognitive skills.* Paper presented at the annual meeting of the American Educational Research Association, New York.—544–545

Abrami, P. C., Leventhal, L., & Perry, R. P. (1982). Educational seduction. *Review of Educational Research, 52,* 446–464.—397

Adelson, J. (1979). Adolescence and the generation gap. *Psychology Today, 12*(9) 33–37.—140

Airasian, P. W. (1991). *Classroom assessment.* New York: McGraw-Hill.—575, 622, 632

Alber, M. B. (Ed.) (1978). *Listening: A curriculum guide for teachers of visually impaired students.* Springfield, IL: Specialized Educational Services. State Board of Education.—215

Algozzine, R. F. (1977). Perceived attractiveness and classroom interactions. *Journal of Experimental Education, 46,* 63–66.—519

Allen, W. H. (1957). Research on film-use: Student participation. *AV Communication Review, 5,* 423–450.—413

Allen, W. H. (1960). Audio-visual communication. In C. W. Harris (Ed.), *Encyclopedia of educational research* (3d ed., pp. 115–137). New York: Macmillan.—413

Allison, S. G., & Ash, P. (1951). *Relationship of anxiety to learning from films* (Tech. Rep. SDC269–7–24, Instructional Film Research Program, Pennsylvania State University). Port Washington, NY: Special Devices Center.—394

Alloway, N. (1984). *Teacher expectations.* Paper presented at the meetings of the Australian Association for Research in Education, Perth.—74

Allport, G. W., & Odbert, H. S. (1936). Trait-names: A psycholexical study. *Psychological Monographs, 47*(211).—147

Alschuler, A. S. (1967). *The Achievement Motivation Development Project: A summary and review* (Occasional Paper No. 3). Cambridge: Center for Research and Development on Educational Differences, Harvard University. (Cooperative Research Project of the Office of Education, Department of Health, Education, and Welfare, Contract No. OE5–10–239)—358

Alschuler, A. S. (1968). *How to increase motivation through climate and structure* (Working Paper No. 8). Cambridge: Achievement Motivation Development Project, Graduate School of Education, Harvard University.—364–366

Alschuler, A. S. (1973). *Developing achievement motivation in adolescents.* Englewood Cliffs, NJ: Educational Technology Publications.—358

American Psychological Association. (1975). Proceedings . . . for the year 1974: Minutes of the annual meeting of the Council of Representatives. *American Psychologist, 30,* 620–651.—515

Ames, C., & Ames, R. (1984). Goal structures and motivation. *Elementary School Journal, 85,* 39–52.—343

Ames, R. (1982). Teachers' attributions for their own teaching. In J. M. Levine & M. C. Wang (Eds.), *Teacher and student perceptions.* Hillsdale, NJ: Erlbaum.—341

Anastasi, A. (1958). *Differential psychology* (3d ed.). New York: Macmillan. *A comprehensive, lucidly written textbook on differences (gender, race, class, and the like) between individuals and groups in intelligence and many other dimensions.*—23, 84, 87, 187

Anastasi, A. (1980). Abilities and the measurement of achievement. In W. B. Schrader (Ed.), *New directions for testing and measurement* (No. 5). San Francisco: Jossey-Bass.—599

Anastasi, A. (1981). Coaching, test sophistication and developed abilities. *American Psychologist, 36,* 1086–1093.—609

Anastasi, A. (1986). Intelligence as a quality of behavior. In R. J. Sternberg & D. K. Detterman (Eds.), *What is intelligence?* Norwood, NJ: Ablex.—52

Anastasiow, N. J., Hanes, M. P., & Hanes, M. L. (1982). *Language and reading strategies for poverty children.* Baltimore: University Book Press.—128, 136

Andersen, M. (1970). *The intelligent use of intelligence tests.* San Jose, CA: Author, Psychology Department, San Jose State University.—87

Anderson, G. J., & Walberg, H. J. (1968). Classroom climate and group learning. *International Journal of Educational Sciences, 2,* 175–180.—534

Anderson, J. R. (1985). *Cognitive psychology and its implications* (2d ed.). New York: Freeman.—280

Anderson, L. M., Evertson, C. M., & Brophy, J. E. (1979). An experimental study of effective teaching in first-grade reading groups. *The Elementary School Journal, 79,* 193–223. *A carefully performed experiment, with real teachers, showing that teachers can be trained to help students improve achievement.*—8, 534, 543, 544

Anderson, R. C. (1972). How to construct achievement tests to assess comprehension. *Review of Educational Research, 42,* 145–170. *Provides a method for changing memory questions into higher-order questions.*—197, 642

Anderson, R. C. (1974). Concretization and sentence learning. *Journal of Educational Psychology, 66,* 179–183.—294

Anderson, R. C., & Pearson, P. D. (1985). A schema theoretic view of basic processes in reading comprehension. In P. D. Pearson, R. Barr, M. Kamil, & P. Mosenthel (Eds.), *Handbook of reading research.* White Plains, NY: Longman.—301

Anderson, R. C., & Pichert, J. W. (1978). Recall of previously unrecallable information following a shift in perspective. *Journal of Verbal Learning and Verbal Behavior, 17,* 1–12.—287

Anderson, R. C., Reynolds, R. E. Schallert, D. L., & Goetz, E. T. (1977). Frameworks for comprehending discourse. *American Educational Research Journal, 14,* 367–381.—287

Anderson, R. C., Spiro, R. J., & Anderson, M. C. (1978). Schemata as scaffolding for the representation of information in connected discourse. *American Educational Research Journal, 15,* 433–440.—286

Anderson, T., & Boyer, M. (1970). *Bilingual schooling in the United States* (Vols. 1 & 2). Washington, DC: Government Printing Office.—133

Andrews, G. R., & Debus, R. L. (1978). Persistence and the causal perception of failure: Modifying cognitive attributions. *Journal of Educational Psychology, 70,* 154–166.—360

Andrews, J. D. (1965). *The effect of group model-reinforcement counseling on increasing voluntary verbal participation in classroom discussion.* Unpublished manuscript, Stanford University, Stanford, CA.—438

Angoff, W. H. (1988). The nature-nurture debate, aptitudes, and group differences. *American Psychologist, 43,* 713–720. *Points out that high heritability is compatible with the high alterability of a human characteristic.*—68

Annis, L. F. (1983). The processes and effects of peer tutoring. *Human Learning, 2,* 39–47.—469–470

Anonymous. (1968). *Physicists continue to laugh.* Moscow: MIR.—415

Applebee, A. (1981). *Writing in the secondary schools: English and the content areas.* Urbana, IL: National Council of Teachers of English.—303

Applegate, J. R. (1969). Why don't pupils talk in class discussions? *The Clearing House, 44,* 78–81.—439

Arlin, M. (1979). Teacher transitions can disrupt time flow in classrooms. *American Educational Research Journal, 16,* 42–56.—533

Aronoff, J., Raymond, N., & Warmoth, A. (1965). *The Kennedy-Jefferson school district: A report of neighborhood study in progress.* Unpublished manuscript, Harvard University, Graduate School of Education, Cambridge, MA.—358

Aronson, E., Blaney, N., Stephen, C., Sikes, J., & Snapp, M. (1978). *The jigsaw classroom.* Beverly Hills, CA: Sage.—443

Asch, S. E. (1956). Studies of independence and conformity. A minority of one against a unanimous majority. *Psychological Monographs, 70* (9, Whole No. 416). *A seminal study demonstrating the powerful effect of group opinion on personal judgment.*—436

Asimov, I. (1971). *Treasury of humor.* London: Woburn Press. —415

Atkinson, J. W. (1980). Motivational effects on so-called tests of ability and educational achievement. In L. J. Fyans, Jr. (Ed.), *Achievement motivation.* New York: Plenum Press.—330

Audley, R. J., & Rawles, R. E. (1990). Review of Joynson's *The Burt affair. The Psychologist, 3*(8), 360–361.—68

Ausubel, D. P. (1963). Is drill necessary? The mythology of incidental learning. *Bulletin, National Association of Secondary School Principals, 47,* 44–50.—482

Ausubel, D. P. (1968). *Educational psychology: A cognitive view.* New York: Holt, Rinehart & Winston.—282, 395, 396

Ausubel, D. P. (1978). In defense of advance organizers: A reply to the critics. *Review of Educational Research, 48,* 251–257.—282, 395

Axelrod, J., et al. (1949). *Teaching by discussion in the college program.* Chicago: College of the University of Chicago.—431

Axelrod, S., Hall, R. V., & Tooms, A. (1979). Comparison of two common classroom seating arrangements. *Academic Therapy, 15,* 29–36.—427

Azrin, N. H., & Holz, W. C. (1966). Punishment. In W. K. Honig (Ed.), *Operant behavior: Areas of research and application* (pp. 380–447). New York: Appleton-Century-Crofts.—247

Babad, E. (1979). Personality correlates of susceptibility to biasing information. *Journal of Personality and Social Psychology, 37,* 195–202.—520

Babad, E., Inbar, J., & Rosenthal, R. (1982). Teacher judgment of students' potential as a function of teachers' susceptibility to biasing information. *Journal of Personality and Social Psychology, 42,* 541–547.—520

Baller, W. R., Charles, D. C., & Miller, E. (1967). *Mid-life attainment of the mentally retarded: A longitudinal study.* Lincoln: University of Nebraska Press.—210

Bandura, A. (1963). The role of imitation in personality development. *Journal of Nursery Education, 18,* 207–215.—255 (fig.)

Bandura A. (1969). *Principles of behavior modification.* New York: Holt, Rinehart & Winston. *An authoritative development of operant conditioning, observation, and other theories of learning and their application to a variety of practical problems.*—157, 252, 258

Bandura, A. (1977). *Social learning theory.* Englewood Cliffs, NJ: Prentice-Hall.—225, 259 (fig.)

Bandura, A. (1978). The self system in reciprocal determinism. *American Psychologist, 33,* 344–358.—264, 265, 327

Bandura, A. (1986a). From thought to action: Mechanisms of personal agency. *New Zealand Journal of Psychology, 15,* 1–17.—263

Bandura, A. (1986b). *Social foundations of thought and action: A social-cognitive theory.* Englewood Cliffs, NJ: Prentice-Hall. *The melding of social learning theory with cognitive psychological concerns to provide, among other things, a picture of how competence and efficiency are learned.*—263

Bandura, A., & Schunk, D. H. (1981). Cultivating competence, self-efficacy, and intrinsic interest through proximal self-motivation. *Journal of Personality and Social Psychology, 41,* 586–598.—368

Baratz, D. (1983). *How justified is the "obvious reaction"?* Unpublished doctoral dissertation, Stanford University, Stanford, CA.—11

Baratz, S. S., & Baratz, S. C. (1982). Early childhood intervention: The social base of institutional racism. In N. R. Yetman (Ed.), *Majority and minority: The dynamics of race and ethnicity in American life* (3d ed.). Boston: Allyn & Bacon.—171

Barker, R. G., Dembo, T., & Lewin, K. (1943). Frustration and regression: An experiment with young children. In R. G. Barker, J. S. Kounin, & H. F. Wright (Eds.), *Child behavior and development.* New York: McGraw-Hill.—356

Barnett, W. S. (1985). Benefit-cost analysis of the Perry Preschool Program and its policy implications. *Educational Evaluation and Policy Analysis, 7,* 333–342.—98

Bar-Tal, D. (1978). Attributional analysis of achievement-related behavior. *Review of Educational Research, 48,* 259–271.—341

Bar-Tal, D. (1979). Interactions of teachers and pupils. In I. H. Frieze, D. Bar-Tal, & J. S. Carroll (Eds.), *New approaches to social problems: Applications of attribution theory.* San Francisco: Jossey-Bass.—339, 341

Bar-Tal, D. (1982). The effects of teachers' behavior on pupil's attributions: A review. In C. Antaki & C. Brieson (Eds.), *Attribution and psychological change:*

A guide to the use of attribution theory in the clinic and the classroom. London: Academic Press.—361

Bar-Tal, D., & Darom, E. (1979). Pupils' attributions of success and failure. *Child Development, 50,* 264–267.—339

Bar-Tal, D., Raviv, A., & Bar-Tal, Y. (1982). Consistency of pupils' attributions regarding success and failure. *Journal of Educational Psychology, 74,* 104–110.—340

Barth, R. S. (1970). *Open education: Assumptions about learning and knowledge.* Unpublished doctoral dissertation, Harvard University, Cambridge.—486

Battle, E. S. (1965). Motivational determinants of academic task persistence. *Journal of Personality and Social Psychology, 2,* 209–219.—187

Battle, E. S. (1966). Motivational determinants of academic competence. *Journal of Personality and Social Psychology, 4,* 634–642.—187

Bavelas, A., Hastorf, A. H., Gross, A. E., & Kite, W. R. (1965). Experiments on the alteration of group structure. *Journal of Experimental Social Psychology, 1,* 55–70.—441, 442t

Baxter, J. (1987). *Teacher explanations in computer programming: A study of knowledge transformation.* Unpublished doctoral dissertation, Stanford University, Stanford, CA.—392

Bechtol, W. M. (1973). *Individualizing instruction and keeping your sanity.* Chicago: Follett.—460

Beck, I. L., & Carpenter, P. A. (1986). Cognitive approaches to understanding reading. *American Psychologist, 41,* 1098–1105.—301

Beilin, H. (1980). Piaget's theory: Refinement, revision, or rejection? In R. H. Kluwe & H. Spada (Eds.), *Developmental models of thinking.* New York: Academic Press.—119

Belgard, M., Rosenshine, B., & Gage, N. L. (1971). Effectiveness in explaining: Evidence on its generality and correlation with pupil ratings. In I. Westbury & A. A. Bellack (Eds.), *Research into classroom processes: Recent developments and next steps* (pp. 182–191). New York: Teachers College Press.—395, 534

Bellack, A. A. (1976, May 25). *Studies in the language of the classroom.* Paper presented at the First Invitational Conference on Research on Teaching, Memorial University of Newfoundland, St. John's.—496

Bellack, A. A., Kliebard, H. M., Hyman, R. T., & Smith, F. L. (1966). *The language of the classroom.* New York: Teachers College Press. *The classroom "game" described on the basis of thorough analyses of what was said by teachers and students in fifteen tenth- and twelfth-grade economics classes.*—495, 531–532, 545

Bellezza, F. S. (1981). Mnemonic devices: Classification, characteristics and criteria. *Review of Educational Research, 51,* 247–275.—296

Belmont, J. M., Butterfield, E. C., & Ferretti, R. P. (1982). To secure transfer of training instruct self-management skills. In D. K. Detterman & R. J. Sternberg (Eds.), *How and how much can intelligence be increased* (pp. 147–154). Norwood, NJ: Ablex.—318

Benbow, C. P., & Stanley, J. C. (1980). Sex differences in mathematical ability: Fact or artifact? *Science, 210,* 1262–1264. *Sets forth the tentative and controversial idea that gender differences in mathematical ability are determined in substantial part by hereditary factors.*—183

Berdine, W. H., & Cegelka, P. T. (1980). *Teaching the trainable retarded.* Columbus, OH: Merrill.—209

Berelson, B., & Steiner, G. A. (1964). *Human behavior: An inventory of scientific findings.* New York: Harcourt, Brace & World. *A storehouse of verified knowledge from psychology, sociology, and anthropology—selected, condensed, organized, and translated—covering the individual, family, small group, organization, institution, stratum, public, society, and culture.*—290

Berk, R. A. (1980). *Criterion-referenced measurement: The state of the art.* Baltimore: Johns Hopkins University Press.—580

Berliner, D. C. (1968). *The effects of test-like events and note-taking on learning from lecture instruction.* Unpublished doctoral dissertation, Stanford University, Stanford, CA.—416, 417t

Berliner, D. C. (1979). Tempus educare. In P. L. Peterson & H. J. Walberg (Eds.), *Research on teaching: Concepts, findings, and implications.* Berkeley, CA: McCutchan.—555–557

Berliner, D. C. (1982). Instructional variables. In D. E. Orlosky (Ed.), *Introduction to education.* Columbus, OH: Merrill.—368

Berliner, D. C. (1990). What's all the fuss about instructional time? In M. Ben-Peretz & R. Bromme (Eds.), *The nature of time in schools* (pp. 3–35). New York: Teachers College Press.—16, 330, 528, 558

Berlyne, D. E. (1965). Curiosity and education. In J. D. Krumboltz (Ed.), *Learning and the educational process* (pp. 67–89). Chicago: Rand McNally.—372, 425, 481

Bernard, J. (1973). *Sex differences: An overview* (Module 26). New York: MSS Modular Publications. 182

Bernstein, E. (1968). What does a Summerhill old school tie look like? *Psychology Today, 2*(5), 37–41, 70. *On the retrospections of former students at Summerhill, a school designed to be "humanistic."*—481

Bergquist, W. H., & Phillips, S. R. (1989). Classroom structures which encourage student participation. In. R. A. Neff & M. Weiner (Eds.), *Classroom communication: Collected readings for effective discussion and questioning* (pp. 19–23). Madison, WI: Magna.—431

Berrueta-Clement, J. R., Schweinhart, L. J., Barnett, W. S., Epstein, A. S., & Weikart, D. P. (1984). Changed lives: Effects of the Perry Preschool Program through age 19. *Monographs of the High/Scope Educational Research Foundation, 8.*—98

Bierly, M. M. (1978). *The need for including the topic of developmental psycholinguistics in educational psychology courses.* Paper presented at the meetings of the American Psychological Association, Toronto.—132

Bigge, J. L. (1982). *Teaching individuals with physical and multiple disabilities* (2d ed.). Columbus, OH: Merrill.—214

Birnbrauer, J. S., Wolf, M. M., Kidder, J. D., & Tague, C. E. (1965). Classroom behavior of retarded pupils with token reinforcement. *Journal of Experimental Child Psychology, 2,* 219–235.—549

Blatt, M. M. (1969). *The effects of classroom discussion on the development of moral judgment.* Unpublished doctoral dissertation, University of Chicago.—146

Bligh, D. A. (1972). *What's the use of lectures?* (2d ed.). Harmondsworth, England: Penguin.—390, 399

Block, J. H., & Burns, R. B. (1976). Mastery learning. In L. S. Shulman (Ed.), *Review of research in education* (Vol. 4). Itasca, IL: F. E. Peacock.—464

Bloom, B. S. (1953). Thought processes in lectures and discussions. *Journal of General Education, 7,* 160–169.—389

Bloom, B. S. (1964). *Stability and change in human characteristics.* New York: Wiley. *Puts forth the thesis that most of what we call intelligence is determined by age 8; a technical report that provides a rationale for early childhood education programs.*—57, 93

Bloom, B. S. (1968). Learning for mastery. *Evaluation Comment, 1*(2). (University of California Center for the Study of Evaluation, Los Angeles)—460, 463, 465

Bloom, B. S. (1980). The new direction in educational research: Alterable variables. In *The state of research on selected alterable variables in education* (Mesa Seminar, 1980). Chicago: Department of Education, University of Chicago. *The provocative statement by a ranking scholar concerning advantages of research on variables that we can do something about.*—14

Bloom, B. S. (Ed.). (1985). *Developing talent in young people.* New York: Ballantine. *Case studies of high-achieving people in very different fields, and the commonalities in their education and training.*—156

Bloom, B. S., Engelhart, M. D., Furst, E. J., Hill, W. H., & Krathwohl, D. R. (1956). *Taxonomy of educational objectives. The classification of educational goals: Handbook 1. Cognitive domain.* New York: Longmans, Green. *"Bloom's taxonomy," the classic attempt to bring order into the welter of what teachers say they want their students to learn.*—43, 645

Bloom, S. (n.d.). *Peer and cross-age tutoring in schools: An individualized supplement to group instruction.* Chicago: Author, Chicago Board of Education, District 10.—465

Blumenfeld, P. C., Pintrich, P. R., & Hamilton, V. L. (1986). Children's concepts of ability, effort, and conduct. *American Educational Research Journal, 23,* 95–104.—342

Boden, M. A. (1980). *Jean Piaget.* New York: Viking.—117

Borg, W. R. (1975). Protocol materials as related to teacher performance and pupil achievement. *Journal of Educational Research, 69,* 23–30.—536

Borg, W. R., & Ascione, F. R. (1982). Classroom management in elementary mainstreaming classrooms. *Journal of Educational Psychology, 74,* 85–95. *A nice demonstration of the possibility and value of significant experiments in real classrooms.*—201, 517–518

Boring, E. G. (1923). Intelligence as the tests see it. *New Republic, 35,* 35–36.—51

Born, D. G., & Davis, M. L. (1974). Amount and distribution of study in a personalized instruction course and in a lecture course. *Journal of Applied Behavior Analysis, 7,* 365–375.—463

Bornstein, R. (1982). Sexism in education. In M. P. Sadker & D. M. Sadker (Eds.), *Sex equity workbook for schools.* White Plains, NY: Longman.—195

Bossert, S. T. (1988). Cooperative activities in the classroom. In E. Z. Rothkopf (Ed.), *Review of Research in Education, 15,* 225–250.—443

Boswell, J. (1953). *Life of Johnson.* London: Oxford University Press. (Original work published 1799)—386

Bouchard, T. J., Jr., Lykken, D. T., McGue, M., Segal, N. L., & Tellegen, A. (1990). Sources of human psychological differences: The Minnesota study of twins reared apart. *Science, 250,* 223–228.—65, 66, 68

Bower, G. H. (1970a). Analysis of a mnemonic device. *American Scientist, 58,* 496–510.—294

Bower, G. H. (1970b). Organizational factors in memory. *Journal of Cognitive Psychology, 1,* 18–46.—283

Bower, G. H., Clark, M., Winzenz, S., & Lesgold, A. (1969). Hierarchical retrieval schemes in recall of categorized word lists. *Journal of Verbal Learning and Verbal Behavior, 8,* 323–343.—283, 284 (fig.)

Bower, G. H., Karlin, M. B., & Dueck, A. (1975). Comprehension and memory for pictures. *Memory and Cognition, 3,* 216–220.—279

Bowles, S., & Gintis, M. (1976). *Schooling in capitalist America.* London: Routledge & Kegan Paul.—648

Brainard, C. J. (1978a). *Piaget's theory of intelligence.* Englewood Cliffs, NJ: Prentice-Hall.—117

Brainard, C. J. (1978b). The stage question in cognitive-developmental theory. *The Behavioral and Brain Sciences, 2,* 173–213.—118

Bransford, J. D., Arbitman-Smith, R., Stein, B. S., & Vye, N. J. (1985). Improving thinking and learning skills: An analysis of three approaches. In J. W. Segal, S. F. Chipman, & R. Glaser (Eds.), *Thinking and learning skills* (Vol. 1). Hillsdale, NJ: Erlbaum.—100

Bransford, J. D., & Johnson, M. K. (1972). Contextual prerequisites for understanding. Some investigations of comprehension and recall. *Journal of Verbal learning and Verbal Behavior, 11,* 717–726.—287

Bransford, J. D., Sherwood, R., Vye, N., & Rieser, J. (1986). Teaching thinking and problem solving. *American Psychologist, 41,* 1078–1089.—305

Bransford, J. D., & Stein, B. S. (1984). *The IDEAL problem solver.* New York: Freeman.—305

Brew, A., & McCormick, B. (1979). Student learning and an independent study course. *Higher Education, 8,* 429–441.—457

Brickey, M., Browning, L., & Campbell, K. (1982). Vocational histories of sheltered workshop employees placed in projects with industry and competitive jobs. *Mental Retardation, 20,* 52–57.—210

Bridgeman, B., & Shipman, V. C. (1978). Preschool measures of self-esteem and achievement motivation as predictors of third-grade achievement. *Journal of Educational Psychology, 70,* 17–28.—159

Bridges, E. M. (1986). *The incompetent teacher: The challenge and the response.* Philadelphia: Palmer Press. *An approach to the problem of how a school administration can cope with an incompetent teacher.*—510

Bridgham, R. G. (1972a). Ease of grading and enrollments in secondary school science: Pt. 1. A model and its possible tests. *Journal of Research in Science Teaching, 9,* 323–329.—650

Bridgham, R. G. (1972b). Ease of grading and enrollments in secondary school science: Pt. 2. A test of the model. *Journal of Research in Science Teaching, 9,* 331–343.—650

Broden, M., Hall, R. V., & Mitts, B. (1971). The effect of self-recording on the classroom behavior of two eighth-grade students. *Journal of Applied Behavior Analysis, 4,* 191–199.—264

Brolyer, C. R., Thorndike, E. L., & Woodyard, E. R. (1927). A second study of mental discipline in high school studies. *Journal of Educational Psychology, 18,* 377–404. *One of Thorndike's famous, massive, and ingenious studies—one that undermined the idea that some subject matter improves the general power of the mind.*—308

Bronfenbrenner, U. (1961). Some familial antecedents of responsibility and leadership in adolescents. In L. Petrullo & B. M. Bass (Eds.), *Leadership and interpersonal behavior.* New York: Holt, Rinehart & Winston.—188

Brookfield, S. (1985). Self-directed learning: A critical review of research. In S. Brookfield (Ed.), *Self-directed learning: From theory to practice.* San Francisco: Jossey-Bass.—451

Brophy, J. E. (1981). Teacher praise: A functional analysis. *Review of Educational Research, 51,* 5–32. *The most comprehensive and circumspect analysis of an age-old topic, based on careful observation and research to an unprecedented degree.*—369, 546–547, 549–550

Brophy, J. E. (1987). On motivating students. In D. C. Berliner & B. V. Rosenshine (Eds.), *Talks to teachers* (pp. 201–245). New York: Random House.—368

Brophy, J. E., & Evertson, C. M. (1974). *Process-product correlations in the Texas teacher effectiveness study: Final report* (Research Rep. No. 74–4). Austin: Research and Development Center for Teacher Education, University of Texas.—540, 543, 544, 547, 558, 559

Brophy, J. E., & Evertson, C. M. (1976). *Learning from teaching: A developmental perspective.* Boston: Allyn & Bacon.—373, 512, 543, 559

Brophy, J. E., & Good, T. L. (1974). *Teacher-student relationships: Causes and consequences.* New York: Holt, Rinehart & Winston. *A valuable collation and review of studies of intraclassroom differences in teacher-student interaction, showing biases against certain kinds of students.*—552

Brophy, J. E., & Putnam, J. G. (1979). Classroom management in the elementary grades. In D. L. Duke (Ed.), *Classroom management: Seventy-eighth yearbook of the National Society for the Study of Education.* Chicago: University of Chicago Press. *Based on research findings to a greater degree than most previous treatments of the subject.*—513–514

Brophy, J. E., Rohrkemper, M. M., Rashad, H., & Goldberger, M. (1983). Relationships between teachers' presentations of classroom tasks and students' engagement in those tasks. *Journal of Educational Psychology, 75,* 544–552.—368

Broudy, H. S. (1963). Historic exemplars of teaching method. In N. L. Gage (Ed.), *Handbook of research on teaching* (pp. 1–43). Chicago: Rand McNally. *A brief but scholarly introduction to great thinkers about teaching from the Sophists (5th century B.C.) to Herbaert (1893).*—411

Broverman, I. K., Broverman, D. M., Clarkson, F. E., Rosenkrantz, P., & Vogel, S. R. (1970). Sex-role stereotypes and clinical judgments of mental health. *Journal of Consulting Psychology, 34,* 1–7.—187, 191

Brown, A. L. (1978). Knowing when, where, and how to remember: A problem of metacognition. In R. Glaser (Ed.), *Advances in instructional psychology.* Hillsdale, NJ: Erlbaum.—310

Brown, A. L. (1980). Metacognitive development and reading. In R. J. Spiro, B. C. Bruce, & W. F. Brewer (Eds.), *Theoretical issues in reading comprehension.* Hillsdale, NJ: Erlbaum.—313

Brown, A. L., Armbruster, B. B., & Baker, L. (1985). The role of metacognition in reading and studying. In J. Orasanu (Ed.), *Reading comprehension: From research to practice.* Hillsdale, NJ: Erlbaum.—312

Brown, A. L., Bransford, J. D., Ferrara, R. A., & Campione, J. C. (1983). Learning, remembering and understanding. In J. H. Flavell & E. M. Markman (Eds.), *Handbook of child psychology: Vol. 3. Cognitive development* (4th ed.). New York: Wiley.—312

Brown, A. L., & Campione, J. C. (1986). Psychological theory and the study of learning disabilities. *American Psychologist, 41,* 1059–1068.—301

Brown, A. L., & Palincsar, A. S. (1982). Inducing strategic learning from texts by means of informal, self-control training. *Topics in Learning and Learning Disabilities, 2*(1), 1–16.—311

Brown, D. S. (1988). Twelve middle school teachers' planning. *Elementary School Journal, 89,* 69–87.—508

Brown, J. S., & Burton, R. R. (1979). Diagnostic models for procedural bugs in basic mathematical skills. In R. W. Tyler & S. H. White (Eds.), *Testing, teaching and learning.* Washington, DC: National Institute of Education.—643

Brown, J. S., Collins, A., & Duguid, P. (1989). Situated cognition and the culture of learning. *Educational Researcher, 18,* 32–41.—321

Brown, J. W., & Thornton, J. W., Jr. (1963). *College teaching: Perspectives and guidelines.* New York: McGraw-Hill.—415

Brown, M., & Precious, N. (1973). *The integrated day in the primary schools.* New York: Ballantine.—487

Brown, R. (1965). *Social psychology.* New York: Free Press. *Each chapter presents a sprightly, yet searching and critical, analysis of a topic in social psychology; fascinating.*—186

Brown, R. (1973) *A first language.* Cambridge: Harvard University Press.—128

Brown, R., Cazden, C. B., & Bellugi, U. (1969). The child's grammar from I to III. In J. P. Hill (Ed.), *Minnesota symposium on child psychology* (Vol. 2). Minneapolis: University of Minnesota Press.—131

Bruner, J. S. (1966). *Toward a theory of instruction.* Cambridge: Harvard University Press. *Insightful comments about teaching by a developmental psychologist of great learning.*—119–122, 124, 125

Bryant, J., Comisky, P. W., Crane, J. S., & Zillman, D. (1980). Relationship between college teachers' use of humor in the classroom and students' evaluations of their teachers. *Journal of Educational Psychology, 72,* 511–519.—414

Bull, R., & Stevens, J. (1979). The effects of attractiveness of writer and penmanship on essay grades. *Journal of Occupational Psychology, 52,* 53–59.—633

Bullough, R., Jr. (1987). Planning and the first year of teaching. *Journal of Education for Teaching, 13,* 231–250.—508, 509

Buros, O. K. (1972). *The seventh mental measurements yearbook.* Highland Park, NJ: Gryphon Press.—608

Burstall, C. (1991). *The British experience with national educational goals and assessment.* Slough, England: The Author, The National Foundation for Educational Research in England and Wales.—616

Burt, C. L. (1966). The genetic determination of differences in intelligence: A study of monozygotic twins reared together and apart. *British Journal of Psychology, 57,* 137–153. *One of the five major studies of identical twins reared apart. Subsequently alleged to be untrustworthy (See Hearnshaw, 1979; Kamin, 1975; Joynson, 1989; Fletcher, 1991).*—65, 68

Burton, R. V. (1963). Generality of honesty reconsidered. *Psychological Review, 70,* 481–499.—149

Bushway, A., & Nash, W. R. (1977). School cheating behavior. *Review of Educational Research, 47,* 623–632.—149

Bussis, A. M., & Chittenden, E. A. (1970). *Analysis of an approach to open education.* Princeton, NJ: Educational Testing Service.—486

Butler, R., & Nisan, M. (1986). Effects of no feedback, task-related comments, and grades on intrinsic motivation and performance. *Journal of Educational Psychology, 78,* 210–216.—353

Buxton, C. E. (1956). *College teaching: A psychologist's view.* New York: Harcourt, Brace.—398

Bybee, R. W., & Sund, R. B. (1982). *Piaget for educators* (2d ed.). Columbus, OH: Merrill.—104

Byrne, B. M. (1984). The general/academic self-concept nomological network: A review of construct validation research. *Review of Educational Research, 54,* 427–456.—159

Cahen, L., Filby, N., McCutcheon, G., & Kyle, D. (1983). *Class size and instruction.* White Plains, NY: Longman.—502

Calder, B. J., & Straw, B. M. (1975). Self-perception of intrinsic and extrinsic motivation. *Journal of Personality and Social Psychology, 31,* 599–605.—352

Calhoun, J. F. (1973). *Elemental analysis of the Keller method of instruction.* Paper presented at the annual meeting of the American Psychological Association, Montreal.—464

Campbell, V. N. (1964). Self-direction and programmed instruction for five different types of learning objectives. *Psychology in the Schools, 1,* 348–359.—481

Campione, J. C., & Armbruster, B. B. (1985). Acquiring information from texts: An analysis of four approaches. In J. W. Segal, S. F. Chipman, & R. Glaser (Eds.), *Thinking and learning skills,* Vol. 1: *Relating instruction to research* (pp. 317–359). Hillsdale, NJ: Erlbaum.—122

Campione, J. C., Brown, A. L., & Ferrara, R. A. (1982). Mental retardation and intelligence. In R. J. Sternberg (Ed.), *Handbook of human intelligence* (pp. 392–490). New York: Cambridge University Press.—100–101

Caproni, V., Levine, D., O'Neal, E., McDonald, P., & Garwood, G. (1977). Seating position, instructor's eye contact availability, and student participation in a small seminar. *Journal of Social Psychology, 103,* 315–316.—427

Carey, S. (1985). Are children fundamentally different kinds of thinkers and learners than adults? In S. F. Chipman, J. W. Segal, & R. Glaser (Eds.), *Thinking and learning skills* (Vol. 2). Hillsdale, NJ: Erlbaum.—118

Carey, S. (1986). Cognitive science and science education. *American Psychologist, 41,* 1123–1130.—301

Carpenter, T. C., Fennema, E., Peterson, P. L., Chiang, C., & Loef, M. (1989). Using knowledge of children's mathematics thinking in classroom teaching: An experimental study. *American Educational Research Journal, 26,* 499–532.—300

Carroll, J. B. (1963). A model of school learning. *Teachers College Record, 64,* 723–733. *An early statement of the model of learning that underlies the mastery approach in instruction.*—460

Carroll, J. B. (1965). School learning over the long haul. In J. D. Krumboltz (Ed.), *Learning and the educational process* (pp. 249–269). Chicago: Rand McNally.—330

Carroll, J. B. (1971). *Learning from verbal discourse in educational media: A review of the literature* (Research Bulletin RB 71–61). Princeton, NJ: Educational Testing Service.—413

Carter, K., Sabers, D., Cushing, K., Pinnegar, S., & Berliner, D. C. (1987). Processing and using information about students: A study of expert, novice, and postulant teachers. *Teaching and Teacher Education, 3,* 147–157.—150, 620

Case, R. (1978). A developmentally based theory and technology of instruction. *Review of Educational Research, 48,* 439–463.—118

Case, R. (1985). A developmentally based approach to the problem of instructional design. In S. F. Chipman, J. W. Segal, & R. Glaser (Ed.), *Thinking and learning skills* (Vol. 2). Hillsdale, NJ: Erlbaum.—118

Case, R. (Ed.). (1991). *The mind's staircase: Stages in the development of human intelligence.* Hillsdale, NJ: Erlbaum.—118

Case, R., & Griffin, S. (1990). Child cognitive development: The role of central conceptual structures in the development of scientific and social thought. In C. A. Havert (Ed.), *Developmental psychology: Cognitive, perceptual, motor, and neuropsychological perspectives.* Amsterdam: Elsevier/North Holland.—118–119

Cattell, R. B. (1963). Theory of fluid and crystallized intelligence: A critical experiment. *Journal of Educational Psychology, 54,* 1–22.—71

Cazden, C. B. (1966). On individual differences in language competence and performance. *Journal of Special Education, 1,* 135–150.—129

Cazden, C. B. (1969). *Infant school.* Newton, MA: Education Development Center.—486

Cazden, C. B. (1972). *Child language and education.* New York: Holt, Rinehart & Winston.—135

Center for the Study of Evaluation—Research for Better Schools (1976). *CSE-RBS test evaluations: Tests of higher-order cognitive, affective, and interpersonal skills.* Los Angeles: Dissemination Office, Center for the Study of Evaluation, University of California.—600 (fig.)

Charters, W. W., Jr. (1963). Social class and intelligence tests. In W. W. Charters, Jr., & N. L. Gage (Eds.), *Readings in the social psychology of education* (pp. 12–21). Boston: Allyn & Bacon. *Describes attempts to develop tests that would not discriminate against lower-class children and how the tests failed.*— 90

Chastain, K. D. (1970). A methodology study comparing the audio-lingual habit theory and the cognitive code-learning theory—a continuation. - *Modern Language Journal, 54,* 257–266.—218– 219

Check, J. F. (1979). Classroom discipline—where are we now? *Education, 100,* 134–137.—510

Cheong. See **Lau Kam Cheong.**

Chi, M. T. H. (1985). Interactive roles of knowledge and strategies in the development of organized sorting and recall. In S. F. Chipman, J. W. Segal, & R. Glaser (Eds.), *Thinking and learning skills* (Vol. 2). Hillsdale, NJ: Erlbaum.—118

Chi, M. T. H., Glaser, R., & Rees, E. (1982). Expertise in problem solving. In R. Sternberg (Ed.), *Advances in the psychology of human intelligence.* Hillsdale, NJ: Erlbaum.—317

Chipman, S. F., Segal, J. W., & Glaser, R. (Eds.). (1985). *Thinking and learning skills* (Vol. 2). Hillsdale, NJ: Erlbaum.—304, 310

Chomsky, N. (1957). *Syntactic structures.* The Hague: Mouton.—128

Chomsky, N. (1968). *Language and mind.* New York: Harcourt Brace Jovanovich. *One of the most important books on language.*—128

Christmas, J. J. (1973). Self-concept and attitudes. In K. S. Miller & R. M. Dreger (Eds.), *Comparative studies of blacks and whites in the United States.* New York: Seminar Press.—158

Chukovsky, K. (1968). *From two to five* (M. Morton, Trans.). Berkeley: University of California Press.— 130–131

Civil Rights Commission. (1973). *Teachers and students,* Rep. 5: *Differences in teacher interaction with Mexican-American and Anglo students.* Washington, DC: Government Printing Office.—519

Clarizio, H. F. (1971). *Toward positive classroom discipline.* New York: Wiley.—514

Clark, B. (1979). *Growing up gifted.* Columbus, OH: Merrill.—217

Clark, C. M., Gage, N. L., Marx, R. W., Peterson, P. L., Stayrook, N. G., & Winne, P. H. (1979). A factorial experiment on teacher structuring, soliciting, and reacting. *Journal of Educational Psychology, 71,* 534–552.—535

Clark, D. C. (1969). Competition for grades and graduate-student performance. *Journal of Educational Research, 62,* 351–354.—650

Clark, H. H., & Clark, E. V. (1977). *Psychology and language.* New York: Harcourt Brace Jovanovich.— 131

Clark, R. (1982). *Family interaction, community opportunity structure, and children's cognitive development.* Unpublished manuscript, Claremont Graduate School of Education, Claremont, CA.—180

Clarke, A., & Clarke, A. (1990). Review of R. B. Joynson's *The Burt affair. British Journal of Educational Psychology, 60*(1), 122–124.—68

Clement, J. (1982). Students' preconceptions in introductory mechanics. *American Journal of Physics, 50*(1), 66–71.—301

Clevenger, T., Jr. (1955). A definition of stagefright. *Central States Speech Journal, 7,* 26–30.—392

Clifford, M., & Walster, E. (1973). The effect of physical attractiveness on teacher expectations. *Sociology of Education, 46,* 248–258.—519

Clift, J. C., & Imrie, B. W. (1981). *Assessing students, appraising teaching.* New York: Wiley.—575– 577

Cognition and Technology Group at Vanderbilt. (1990). Anchored instruction and its relationship to situated cognition. *Educational Researcher, 19,* 2– 10.—321

Cohen, E. G. (1982). Expectation states and interracial interaction in school settings. *Annual Review of Sociology, 8,* 209–235. *A comprehensive and critical review of theory and research on what it takes to foster genuinely integrated, not simply desegregated, classrooms.*—438

Cohen, H. L. (1973). Behavior modification and socially deviant youth. In C. E. Thoresen (Ed.), *Behavior modification in education: Seventy-second yearbook of the National Society for the Study of Education* (Pt. 1). Chicago: University of Chicago Press. *Shows powerful effects of a behavior modification program.*— 361–362, 364, 367

Cohen, P., Kulik, J. A., & Kulik, C. C. (1982). Educational outcomes of tutoring. *American Educational Research Journal, 19,* 237–248.—469

Cohen, R. L. (1989). Memory for action events: The power of enactment. *Educational Psychology Review, 1,* 57–80.—291

Cole, M., Gay, J., Glick, J., & Sharp, D. W. (1971). *The cultural context of learning and thinking.* New York: Basic Books.—54

Cole, M., & Means, B. (1981). *Comparative studies of how people think.* Cambridge: Harvard University Press.—176

Cole, M., & Scribner, S. (1974). *Culture and thought: A psychological introduction.* New York: Wiley.—176

Cole, N. (1990). Conceptions of educational achievement. *Educational Researcher, 19*(3), 2–7.—44

Coleman, J. S. (1960). The adolescent subculture and academic achievement. *American Journal of Sociology, 65,* 337–347.—377–378

Coleman, J. S., Campbell, E. Q., Hobson, C. J., McPartland, J., Mood, A. M., Weinfeld, F. D., & York, R. L. (1966). *Equality of educational opportunity.* Washington, DC: Government Printing Office. *The well-known Coleman report that led to questions about the efficacy of schools in reducing inequalities of educational achievement. Much reanalyzed, defended, and challenged.*—81, 85, 90, 342

Coleman, W., & Cureton, E. E. (1954). Intelligence and achievement: The "jangle fallacy" again. *Educational and Psychological Measurement, 14,* 347–351. *Why giving variables different names, such as "intelligence" and "achievement," does not necessarily make them different.*—71

Combs, A. W. (Ed.). (1967). *Humanizing education: The person in the process.* Washington, DC: Association for Supervision and Curriculum Development, National Education Association.—484

Committee to Develop Standards for Educational and Psychological Testing. (1985). *Standards for educational and psychological testing.* Washington, DC: American Psychological Association. *The recommended criteria for testing, test development, using information, and rights of test-takers, as developed by three professional associations.*—583

Conoley, J. C., & Kramer, J. J. (1989). *The tenth mental measurements yearbook.* Lincoln, NE: Buros Institute of Mental Measurement.—608

Cooper, H. M. (1979). Statistically combining independent studies: A meta-analysis of sex differences in conformity research. *Journal of Personality and Social Psychology, 37,* 131–146. *A demonstration of the power of meta-analysis—a new way of bringing together research results on a given issue.*—186

Cooper, H. M. (1989a). *Homework.* White Plains, NY: Longman. *A meta-analysis of many experiments.*—451, 452

Cooper, H. M. (1989b). Synthesis of research on homework. *Educational Leadership, 47*(3), 85–91.—451, 452

Cooper, H. M., & Good, T. L. (1983). *Pygmalion grows up: Studies in the expectations communication process.* White Plains, NY: Longman.—73

Corno, L., Mitman, A., & Hedges, L. (1981). The influence of direct instruction on student self-appraisals: A hierarchical analysis of treatment and aptitude-treatment interaction effects. *American Educational Research Journal, 18,* 39–61.—159, 160

Covington, M. V. (1984). The self-worth theory of achievement motivation: Findings and implications. *Elementary School Journal, 85,* 5–20.—343, 345

Covington, M. V., Crutchfield, R. S., Davies, L., & Olton, R. M. (1974). *The Productive Thinking Program: A course in learning to think.* Columbus, OH: Merrill.—153

Covington, M. V., & Omelich, C. L. (1979). Effort: The double-edged sword in school achievement. *Journal of Educational Psychology, 71,* 169–182.—342

Covington, M. V., & Omelich, C. L. (1981). As fortunes mount: Affective and cognitive consequences of ability demotion in class. *Journal of Educational Psychology, 73,* 796–808.—342

Cox, W. F., Jr., & Dunn, T. G. (1979). Mastery learning: A psychological trap? *Educational Psychologist, 14,* 24–29.—464–465

Cramond, B., & Martin, C. E. (1985, April). *In-service and preservice teachers' attitudes toward the academically brilliant.* Paper presented at the annual meeting of the American Educational Research Association, Chicago.—156

Crandall, V. J. (1963). Achievement. In H. W. Stevenson (Ed.), *Child psychology: Sixty-second yearbook of the National Society for the Study of Education* (Pt. 1). Chicago: University of Chicago Press.—369

Crawford, J., Gage, N. L., Corno, L., Stayrook, N. G., Mitman, A., Schunk, D., & Stallings, J. (1978). *An experiment in teacher effectiveness and parent-assisted instruction in the third grade* (Vols. 1–3). Stanford, CA: Center for Educational Research, Stanford University. (ERIC Document Reproduction Service No. ED 160 648)—159, 558

Cronbach, L. J. (1980). Evaluation for course improvement. *Teachers College Record, 64,* 672–683.—587

Cronbach, L. J. (1971). Test validation. In R. L. Thorndike (Ed.), *Educational measurement* (2d ed., pp. 443–507). Washington, DC: American Council on Education.—583

Cronbach, L. J. (1990). *Essentials of psychological testing* (5th ed.). New York: Harper & Row. *A widely used, comprehensive, and thoughtful book.*—22

Cronbach, L. J., & Associates. (1980). *The reform of program evauation.* San Francisco: Jossey-Bass.—587, 589

Cronbach, L. J., & Snow, R. E. (1977). *Aptitudes and instructional methods: A handbook on interactions.* New York: Irvington/Erlbaum. *An authoritative source on aptitude-treatment interaction research; includes excellent critiques, discussions, and methodological advice.*—218

Crosson, D., & Olson, D. R. (1969, February). *Encoding ability in teacher-student communication games.* Paper presented at the meeting of the American Educational Research Association, Los Angeles.—534

Crovitz, H. F. (1970). *Galton's walk.* New York: Harper & Row.—295 (fig.)

Crowne, D. P., & Marlowe, D. (1964). *The approval motive: Studies in evaluative dependence.* New York: Wiley.—349

Crutchfield, R. S. (1966). Sensitization and activation of cognitive skills. In J. S. Bruner (Ed.), *Learning about learning.* Washington, DC: Department of Health, Education, and Welfare, U.S. Office of Education.—153

Cruttenden, A. (1979). *Language in infancy and childhood.* New York: St. Martin's Press.—130

Cryan, J. (Ed.). (1981). Corporal punishment in the schools: Its use is abuse. *Educational Comment/1981.* (College of Education and Allied Professions, University of Toledo, Toledo, OH) *A comprehensive treatment of a practice now outlawed in most of Western Europe but still permitted, even if not prevalent, in England.*—515

Cuban, L. (1984). *How teachers taught: Constancy and change in American classrooms: 1890–1980.* White Plains, NY: Longman.—491–492, 495

Cullinan, D., Epstein, M. H., & Lloyd, J. (1982). *Behavior disorders.* Englewood Cliffs, NJ: Prentice Hall.—211

Cummins, J. J. (1986). Empowering minority students: A framework for intervention. *Harvard Educational Review, 56*(1), 18–36.—179

Dale, E. (1967). Historical setting of programmed instruction. In P.C. Lange (Ed.), *Programmed instruction: Sixty-sixth yearbook of the National Society for the Study of Education* (Pt. 2, pp. 28–54). Chicago: University of Chicago Press.—50

Dale, P. S. (1976). *Language development* (2d ed.). New York: Holt, Rinehart & Winston.—128

Davey, B., & McBride, S. (1986). The effects of question generation training on reading comprehension. *Journal of Educational Psychology, 78,* 256–282.—302

Davidson, H. H., & Lang, G. (1960). Children's perceptions of their teachers' feelings toward them related to self-perception, school achievement, and behavior. *Journal of Experimental Education, 29,* 107–118.—158

Davis, A., & Eells, K. W. (1953). *Davis-Eells tests of general intelligence or problem-solving ability.* New York: World Book. *A major but unsuccessful attempt to develop an intelligence test on which lower-class children would do as well as middle-class children.*—90

DeCharms, R. (1970). *Motivation change in low-income black children.* Paper presented at the meetings of the American Educational Research Association, Minneapolis.—359 (fig.)

DeCharms, R. (1976). *Enhancing motivation.* New York: Irvington Press/Wiley.—358

DeCharms, R. (1980). The origins of competence and achievement motivation in personal causation. In L. J. Fyans, Jr. (Ed.), *Achievement motivation.* New York: Plenum Press.—358

DeCharms, R., & Moeller, G. H. (1962). Values expressed in American children's readers. *Journal of Abnormal and Social Psychology, 64,* 136–142.—337

Deci, E. L. (1975). *Intrinsic motivation.* New York: Plenum Press.—353

Deci, E. L., & Ryan, R. (1985). *Intrinsic motivation and self-determination in human behavior.* New York: Plenum Press.—353

DeCrow, K. (1972). "Look, Jane, look! See Dick run and jump! Admire him!" In S. B. Anderson (Ed.), *Sex differences and discrimination in education.* Worthington, OH: Charles A. Jones.—192–193

DeFries, J. C., & Decker, S. N. (1981). Genetic aspects of reading disability. In P. G. Aaron & M. Halatesha (Eds.), *Neuropsychological and neuropsycholinguistic aspects of reading disabilities.* New York: Academic Press.—205

de Groot, A. (1965). *Thought and choice in chess.* The Hague: Mouton.—317

Delain, M. T., Pearson, D. P., & Anderson, R. C. (1985). Reading comprehension and creativity in black language use: You stand to gain by playing the sounding game! *American Educational Research Journal, 22*(2), 155–173.—179

De Landsheere, V. (1977). On defining educational objectives. *Evaluation in Education, 1,* 73–150.—45

Delguardi, J., Greenwood, C. R., Wharton, D., Carter, J. J., & Hall, R. V. (1986). Classwide peer tutoring. *Exceptional Children, 52,* 535–542.—202–203

Della-Piana, G. M., Jensen, J., & Murdock, E. (1970).   New directions for informal reading assessment. In W. K. Durr (Ed.), *Reading difficulties: Diagnosis, correction, and remediation* (pp. 127–132). Newark, DE: International Reading Association.—466, 468 (fig.)

Deshler, D. D., & Schumaker, J. B. (1986).   *Strategies instruction: A new way to teach.* Salt Lake City: Worldwide Media.—202

Deshler, D. D., & Schumaker, J. B. (1988).   An instructional model for teaching students how to learn. In J. L. Graden, J. E. Zinns, & M. J. Curtis (Eds.), *Alternative educational delivery systems: Enhancing instructional options for all students.* Washington, DC: National Association of School Psychologists.—304

Dew, N. (1984).   The exceptional bilingual child: Demography. In P. C. Chinn (Ed.), *Education of culturally and linguistically different exceptional children.* Reston, VA: Council for Exceptional Children.—178

Dewey, J. (1933).   *How we think: A restatement of the relation of reflective thinking to the educative process* (rev. ed.) New York: Heath.—153

Diaz, R. M. (1983).   Thought and two languages: The impact of bilingualism. In E. W. Gordon (Ed.), *Review of research in education* (Vol. 10). Washington, DC: American Educational Research Association.—136

Diaz, S., Moll, L. C., & Mehan, H. (1986).   Sociocultural resources in instruction: A context-specific approach. In *Beyond language: Social and cultural factors in schooling language minority students.* Los Angeles: California State University at Los Angeles.—178

Dickinson, D. (1974).   But what happens when you take the reinforcement away? *Psychology in the Schools, 11,* 158–160.—367

Diener, C., & Dweck, C. (1978).   An analysis of learned helplessness: Continuous changes in performance, strategy, and achievement cognitions following failure. *Journal of Personality and Social Psychology, 36,* 351–362.—360

Di Gangi, S. A., Faykus, S. P., Powell, J. H., Wallin, M., and Berliner, D. C. (1991).   *Novice and experienced teachers' decisions about grading.* Paper presented at the meetings of the American Psychological Association, San Francisco.

Dillon, J. T. (1982).   Cognitive correspondence between question/statement and response. *American Educational Research Journal, 19,* 540–551.—541

Dillon, J. T. (1985).   Using questions to foil discussion. *Teaching and Teacher Education, 1,* 109–121.—537–538

Dillon, J. T. (1988).   *Questioning and teaching.* New York: Teachers College Press.—538

Dillon, J. T. (1990).   *The practice of questioning.* New York: Routledge. *A synthesis of research on questioning in many different contexts, including teaching.*—555

Dillon, J. T. (1991).   Questioning the use of questions. *Journal of Educational Psychology, 83,* 163–164.—538–539, 555

Doenau, S. J. (1987a).   Soliciting. In M. J. Dunkin (Ed.), *International encyclopedia of teaching and teacher education.* Oxford: Pergamon Press.—537

Doenau, S. J. (1987b).   Structuring. In M. J. Dunkin (Ed.), *International encyclopedia of teaching and teacher education* (pp. 398–407). Oxford: Pergamon Press.—536

Dowaliby, F. J., & Schumer, H. (1973).   Teacher-centered versus student-centered mode of college classroom instruction is related to manifest anxiety. *Journal of Educational Psychology, 64,* 125–132.—161, 218

Doyle, W. (1978).   Are students behaving worse than they used to behave? *Journal of Research and Development in Education, 11,* 3–16.—510

Doyle, W. (1986).   Classroom organization and management. In M. C. Wittrock (Ed.), *Handbook of research on teaching* (3d ed., pp. 392–431). New York: Macmillan.—514

Dreger, R. M., & Miller, K. S. (1968).   Comparative psychological studies of Negroes and whites in the United States: 1959–1965. *Psychological Bulletin Monograph Supplement, 70*(3, Pt. 2).—80

Dressel, P. L. (1977).   The nature and role of objectives in instruction. *Educational Technology, 17*(5), 7–15.—40

Dubin, R., & Taveggia, T. C. (1968).   *The teaching-learning paradox: A comparative analysis of college teaching methods.* Eugene: Center for the Advanced Study of Educational Administration, University of Oregon. *Concludes that college instructional methods have equal effects on final examination scores, but is based on outmoded methods of synthesizing research.*—388

Duffy, G. G., Roehler, L. R., Meloth, M. S., & Vavrus, L. G. (1986).   Conceptualizing instructional explanation. *Teaching and Teacher Education, 2,* 197–214.—403, 406

Duin, A. H., & Graves, M. F. (1987).   Intensive vocabulary instruction as a prewriting technique. *Reading Research Quarterly, 22,* 311–330.—300

Duncker, K. (1945).   On problem-solving. *Psychological Monographs, 58*(5, Whole No. 270). *A classic description of a series of studies about how humans solve complex problems.*—372

Dunkin, M. J., & Biddle, B. J. (1974). *The study of teaching.* New York: Holt, Rinehart & Winston. *No longer useful as a summary of research on teacher behavior and its correlates, but still a comprehensive introduction to research approaches and issues.*—533, 535, 545, 546, 547, 549, 550

Durkin, D. (1979). What classroom observations reveal about reading comprehension instruction. *Reading Research Quarterly, 14,* 481–538.—303

Dweck, C. (1975). The role of expectations and attributions in the alleviation of learned helplessness. *Journal of Personality and Social Psychology, 31,* 674–685.—360

Eagly, A. H., & Carli, L. L. (1981). Sex of researchers and sex-typed communications as determinants of sex differences in influenceability: A meta-analysis of social influence studies. *Psychological bulletin, 90,* 1–20.—186–187

Ebel, R. L. (1974). Should we get rid of grades? *Measurement in Education, 5*(4), 1–5.—648

Ebel, R. L. (1980). Achievement tests as measures of developed abilities. In W. B. Schrader (Ed.), *New directions for testing and measurement* (No. 5). San Francisco: Jossey-Bass.—599

Edgington, D. (1976). *The physically handicapped child in your classroom: A handbook for teachers.* Springfield, IL: Charles C Thomas.—214

Edman, I. (1938). *Philosopher's holiday.* New York: Viking.—398

Edmonds, R. R. (1981). Making public schools effective. *Social Policy, 12,* 56–60.—511

Edwards, J. R. (1979). *Language and disadvantage.* London: Wauld.—132

Effros, E. G. (1989, February 14). Give U.S. math students more rote learning. *New York Times* (editorial page).—43

Eisner, E. W. (1991). *The enlightened age.* New York: Macmillan. *A reminder that psychological science is only one way to know or make sense of the world or to obtain a basis for important decisions. Explains the value of qualitative methods and ways of knowing.*—648

Elashoff, J. D., & Snow, R. E. (1971). *Pygmalion reconsidered.* Worthington, OH: Charles A. Jones. *A technically sophisticated reanalysis of the original Pygmalion data. Teachers' expectations have many effects but not, as originally claimed, on measured intelligence.*—73

Elawar, M. C., & Corno, L. (1985). A factorial experiment in teachers' written feedback on student homework: Changing teacher behavior a little rather than a lot. *Journal of Educational Psychology 77,* 162–173.—369

Elkind, D. (1976). *Child development and education.* New York: Oxford University Press.—124, 126

Ellis, H. P., & Jones, A. D. (1974, Winter). Anxiety about lecturing. *Universities Quarterly,* pp. 91–95.—392

Elsen, A. (1969). The pleasures of teaching. In *The study of education at Stanford: Report to the university,* Part 8: *Teaching, research, and the faculty* (pp. 21–23). Stanford, CA: Stanford University.—388

Emmer, E., Evertson, C., & Anderson, L. (1980). Effective classroom management at the beginning of the school year. *The Elementary School Journal, 80,* 219–231.—512

Epstein, J. L. (1984). *Effects of teacher practices on parent involvement and change in student achievement in reading and math.* Paper presented at the annual meetings of the American Educational Research Association, New Orleans.—180

Erickson, F. (1975). Gatekeeping in the melting pot: Interaction in counseling encounters. *Harvard Educational Review, 45,* 44–70.—178

Erickson, F. (1986). Qualitative methods in research on teaching. In M. C. Wittrock (Ed.), *Handbook of research on teaching* (3d ed.), pp. 119–161. New York: Macmillan.—13, 25

Erickson, F., & Mohatt, G. (1982). Cultural organization of participant structures in two classrooms of Indian students. In G. Spindler (Ed.), *Doing the ethnography of schooling: Educational anthropology in action.* New York: Holt, Rinehart & Winston.—170

Erickson, E. (1963). *Childhood and society* (2d ed.). New York: Norton. *One of the finest psychoanalysts of our time literately describes the development of children.*—138

Erickson, E. (1968). *Identity, youth and crisis.* New York: Norton.—139

Erlenmeyer-Kimling, L., & Jarvik, L. F. (1963). Genetics and intelligence: A review. *Science, 142,* 1477–1479.—138

Erwin, P. G., & Caler, A. (1984). The influence of Christian name stereotypes on the marking of children's essays. *British Journal of Educational Psychology, 54,* 223–227.—633

Estes, W. K. (1982). Learning, memory, and intelligence. In R. J. Sternberg (Ed.), *Handbook of human intelligence.* New York: Cambridge University Press.—52

Evans, W. E., & Guyman, R. E. (1978). *Clarity of explanation: A powerful indicator of teacher effectiveness.*

Paper presented at the annual meeting of the American Educational Research Association, Toronto.—410

Evertson, C. M., & Emmer, E. T. (1982). Effective management at the beginning of the school year in junior high classes. *Journal of Educational Research, 74,* 485–498.—513

Eysenck, H. J. (1979). *The structure and measurement of intelligence.* Berlin, West Germany: Springer-Verlag.—62

Eysenck, H. J. (1980). *The causes and effects of smoking.* Beverly hills, CA: Sage. *Builds a research-based, but still highly questionable, case against the causal character of the relationship between smoking and health.*—20

Fagan, E. R., Hassler, D. M., & Szabo, M. (1981). Evaluation of questioning strategies in language arts instruction. *Research in the Teaching of English, 15,* 267–273.—542

Fagot, B. I. (1981). Male and female teachers: Do they treat boys and girls differently? *Sex Roles, 7,* 263–271.—190

Fagot, B. I., and Patterson, G. R. (1969). An in vivo analysis of reinforcing contingencies for sex-role behaviors in the pre-school child. *Developmental Psychology, 1,* 563–568.—190

Featherstone, J. (1971). *Schools where children learn.* New York: Liveright.—485

Feld, S., Ruhland, D., & Gold, M. (1979). Developmental changes in achievement motivation. *Merrill-Palmer Quarterly, 25,* 43–60.—337

Feldhusen, J. F. (1979). Student behavior problems in secondary schools. In D. L. Duke (Ed.), *Classroom management: Seventy-eighth yearbook of the National Society for the Study of Education.* Chicago: University of Chicago Press.—510

Feldhusen, J. F., Thurston, J. R., & Benning, J. J. (1973). A longitudinal study of delinquency and other aspects of children's behavior. *International Journal of Criminology and Penology, 1,* 341–351.—510

Fennema, E. (1981). Woman and mathematics: Does research matter? *Journal for Research in Mathematics Education, 12,* 380–385.—184

Fennema, E. (1982). *Women and mathematics: A state of the art review.* Paper presented at the annual meetings of the American Association for the Advancement of Science, Washington, DC.—183

Fennema, E. (1987). Sex-related differences in education: Myths, realities, and intervention. In V. Koehler (Ed.), *Educational handbook: Research into practice* (pp. 329–347). White Plains, NY: Longman.—183

Fennema, E., & Peterson, P. L. (1987). Effective teaching for girls and boys: The same or different? In D. C. Berliner & B. V. Rosenshine (Eds.), *Talks to teachers* (pp. 111–125). New York: Random House.—183

Ferster, C. B., & Skinner, B. F. (1957). *Schedules of reinforcement.* New York: Appleton-Century-Crofts. *Portrays in detail the lawfulness of animal behavior under various reinforcement schedules.*—234–235

Feuerstein, R. (1980). *Instrumental enrichment: An intervention program for cognitive modifiability.* Baltimore: University Park Press. *The basis of much hope that complex cognitive skills can be taught and learned. Feuerstein's work with supposedly low-ability children has attracted international attention.*—122

Feuerstein, R., Jensen, N., Hoffman, N. B., & Rand, W. (1985). Instrumental enrichment, an intervention program for structural cognitive modifiability: Theory and practice. In J. W. Segal, S. F. Chipman, & R. Glaser (Eds.), *Thinking and learning skills* (Vol. 1). Hillsdale, NJ: Erlbaum.—100

Fillmer, H. T. (1974). Sexist teaching—what you can do. *Teacher, 91*(5), 30–32.—196

Finn, J. D. (1989). Withdrawing from school. *Review of Educational Research, 59,* 117–142. *A review of research on the drop-out problem, offering identification with and participation in the school's activities as a major factor.*—379

Finn, J. D., Dulberg, L., & Reis, J. (1979). Sex differences in educational attainment: A cross-national perspective. *Harvard Educational Review, 49,* 477–503.—183

Fisher, C. W., Berliner, D. C., Filby, N. N., Marliave, R., Cahen, L. S., & Dishaw, M. M. (1980). Teaching behaviors, academic learning time, and student achievement: An overview. In C. Denham & A. Lieberman (Eds.), *Time to learn.* Washington, DC: National Institute of Education.—540, 557–558, 559

Fitch, M. L., Drucker, A. J., & Norton, J. A. (1951). Frequent testing as a motivating factor in large lecture classes. *Journal of Educational Psychology, 42,* 1–20.—464, 650

Fitzgerald, J., & Markham, L. R. (1987). Teaching children about revision in writing. *Cognition and Instruction, 4,* 3–24.—303

Flanagan, J. C., Davis, F. B., Dailey, J. T., Shaycroft, M. F., Orr, D. B., Goldberg, I., & Neyman, C. A., Jr. (1964). *The American high school student* (Final Rep., Office of Education, Cooperative Research Project No. 635). Pittsburgh: Project TALENT, University of Pittsburgh. *Full of data from a major longitudinal study, beginning in 1960, of American high school students' abilities and interests.*—23

Flanders, N. A. (1970). *Analyzing teacher behavior.* Reading, MA: Addison-Wesley. *A full treatment of the author's well-known and once widely used approach to the observation and analysis of classroom verbal behavior.*—547, 550

Flavell, J. H. (1963). *The developmental psychology of Jean Piaget.* Princeton, NJ: Van Nostrand. *One of the major presentations of Piaget's thoughts about the development of cognitive processes; a technical but accurate interpretation.*—104

Flavell, J. H. (1976). Megacognitive aspects of problem solving. In L. B. Resnick (Ed.), *The nature of intelligence.* Hillsdale, NJ: Erlbaum.—310

Flesch, R. (1954). *How to make sense.* New York: Harper.—21

Fletcher, R. (1991). *Science, ideology, and the media: The Cyril Burt scandal.* New Brunswick, NJ: Transaction.—68

Flynn, J. R. (1987). Massive IQ gains in 14 nations: What IQ tests really measure. *Psychological Bulletin, 101,* 171–191. *A fascinating look at large increases in intelligence test scores in several industrial nations over the period of a generation. Questions whether those scores measure intelligence or only a "weak correlate" of intelligence.*—69

Fontenelle, S., & Holliman, W. (1983). Social management techniques for classroom teachers. *Psychological Reports, 52,* 815–818.—516

Foreman, G. (1972). *The five civilized tribes: Cherokee, Chickasaw, Choctaw, Creek, Seminole.* Norman, OK: University of Oklahoma Press. (Original work published 1934)—170

Forlano, G. (1936). School learning with various methods of practice and rewards. *Teachers College Contributions to Education, 688.*—290

Forman, G. E., & Kuschner, D. S. (1977). *The child's construction of knowledge.* Monterey, CA: Brooks/Cole.—127

Formanek, R., & Gurian, A. (1976). *Charting intellectual growth.* Springfield, IL: Charles C Thomas.—127

Fortune, J. C., Gage, N. L., & Shutes, R. E. (1966, February). *The generality of the ability to explain.* Paper presented to the American Educational Research Associations, Chicago.—395

Fosterling, F. (1985). Attributional retraining: A review. *Psychological Bulletin, 48,* 495–512.—360, 361

Fowler, J. W., & Peterson, P. L. (1981). Increasing reading persistence and altering attributional style of learned helplessness children. *Journal of Educational Psychology, 73,* 251–260.—360

Fox, L. H., Tobin, D., & Brady, L. (1979). Sex role socialization and achievement in mathematics. In M. A. Wittig & A. C. Peterson (Eds.), *Sex-related differences in cognitive functioning.* New York: Academic Press.—183

Frazier, N., & Sadker, M. (1973). *Sexism in school and society.* New York: Harper & Row.—193, 194, 196

Fredericksen, N. (1984). The real test bias: Influences on teaching and learning. *American Psychologist, 39,* 193–202.—628

Fremouw, W. J., & Harmatz, M. G. (1975). A helper model for behavioral treatment of speech anxiety. *Journal of Consulting and Clinical Psychology, 43,* 652–660.—392

French, E. G. (1956). Motivation as a variable in work partner selection. *Journal of Abnormal and Social Psychology, 55,* 96–99.—336

French, E. G., & Thomas, F. (1958). The relation of achievement motivation to problem-solving effectiveness. *Journal of Abnormal and Social Psychology, 56,* 45–48.—336

Frieze, I. H. (1980). Beliefs about success and failure in the classroom. In J. H. McMillan (Ed.), *The social psychology of school learning.* New York: Academic Press.—340

Frieze, I. H., & Snyder, H. N. (1980). Children's beliefs about the causes of success and failure in school settings. *Journal of Educational Psychology, 72,* 186–196.—339

Furth, H. G. (1981). *Piaget for teachers* (2d ed.). Englewood Cliffs, NJ: Prentice-Hall.—104

Furth, H. G., & Wachs, H. (1982). *Thinking goes to school: Piaget's theory in practice.* Oxford: Oxford University Press.—104

Fyans, L. J., Jr., & Maehr, M. L. (1980). Attributional style, task selection and achievement. In L. J. Fyans, Jr. (Ed.), *Achievement motivation.* New York: Plenum Press.—339

Gage, N. L. (1969). Teaching methods. In R. L. Ebel, V. H. Noll, & R. M. Bauer (Eds.), *Encyclopedia of educational research* (4th ed., pp. 1446–1458). New York: Macmillan.—383

Gage, N. L. (1972). I.Q. heritability, race differences, and educational research. *Phi Delta Kappan, 53,* 308–312.—68, 87

Gage, N. L. (1985). *Hard gains in the soft sciences: The case of pedagogy.* Bloomington, IN: CEDR, Phi Delta Kappa.—128

Gage, N. L. (1991). The obviousness of social and educational research results. *Educational Researcher, 20*(1), 10–16.—12, 400

Gage, N. L., & Berliner, D. C. (1989). Nurturing the critical, practical, and artistic thinking of teachers. *Phi Delta Kappan, 71,* 212–214.—27

Gage, N. L., & Cronbach, L. J. (1955). Conceptual and methodological problems in interpersonal perception. *Psychological Review, 62,* 411–422.—393

Gage, N. L., & Needels, M. C. (1989). Process-product research on teaching: A review of criticisms. *The Elementary School Journal, 89,* 253–300.—17, 562

Gagné, R. M. (1964). The implications of instructional objectives for learning. In C. M. Lindvall (Ed.), *Defining educational objectives* (pp. 37–46). Pittsburgh: University of Pittsburgh Press.—34

Gagné, R. M. (1970). Some new views of learning and instruction. *Phi Delta Kappan, 51,* 468–472.—396

Gagné, R. M. (1985). *The conditions of learning* (4th ed.). New York: Holt, Rinehart & Winston. *Especially noteworthy for the hierarchy of types of learning, by a leading theorist of instructional technology.*—46, 282

Gall, M. D. (1970). The use of questions in teaching. *Review of Educational Research, 40,* 707–721.—537, 539, 540

Gall, M. D., & Gall, J. P. (1976). The discussion method. In N. L. Gage (Ed.), *The psychology of teaching methods: Seventy-fifth yearbook of the National Society for the Study of Education* (Pt. 1, pp. 166–216). Chicago: University of Chicago Press.—423, 424

Gallagher, J. J. (1975). *Teaching the gifted child* (2d ed.). Boston: Allyn & Bacon.—217

Galton, F. (1952). *Hereditary genius: An inquiry into its laws and consequences.* New York: Horizon Press. (Original work published 1869) *The first and classic statement and supporting biographical evidence that genius results from genetic rather than environmental factors.*—216

Garai, J. E., & Scheinfeld, A. (1968). Sex differences in mental and behavioral traits. *Genetic Psychology Monographs, 77,* 169–299.—185

Gardner, H. (1983). *Frames of mind.* New York: Basic Books. *The evidence to provide backing for a theory of multiple semi-independent intelligences.*—53, 61, 76, 167

Gardner, H. (1985). *The mind's new science.* New York: Basic Books. *A tour de force by a gifted writer on the history, problems, achievements, and future of cognitive science.*—286, 297

Gardner, H., & Hatch, T. (1989). Multiple intelligences go to school: Educational implications of the theory of multiple intelligences. *Educational Researcher, 18*(8), 4–10.—79

Gardner, J. W. (1963). *Self-renewal.* New York: Harper & Row.—481

Garner, R., Hare, V. C., Alexander, P., Haynes, J., & Winograd, P. (1984). Successful use of a text look-back strategy among unsuccessful readers. *American Educational Research Journal, 21,* 789–798.—302

Garner, R., Macready, G. B., & Wagoner, S. (1984). Readers' acquisition of the components of the text-lookback strategy. *Journal of Educational Psychology, 76,* 300–309.—302

Gasper, K. L. (1980). The student perspective. *Teaching Political Science, 7,* 470–471.—465

Gates, A. I. (1917). Recitation as a function in memorizing. *Archives of Psychology, 6*(40).—289–290, 413

Gearheart, B. R., & Weishahn, M. W. (1976). *The handicapped child in the regular classroom.* St. Louis: Mosby.—209

Gearheart, B. R., & Weishahn, M. W. (1980). *The handicapped child in the regular classroom* (2d ed.). St. Louis: Mosby.—207, 208

Gearheart, B. R., & Weishahn, M. W. (1984). *The exceptional student in the regular classroom* (3d ed.). Columbus, OH: Merrill.—207, 208

Gelman, R. (1985). The developmental perspective on the problem of knowledge acquisition: A discussion. In S. F. Chipman, J. W. Segal, & R. Glaser (Eds.), *Thinking and learning skills* (Vol. 2). Hillsdale, NJ: Erlbaum.—117

Getzels, J. W., & Jackson, P. W. (1962). *Creativity and intelligence.* New York: Wiley.—151

Giaconia, R. (1987). *Teacher questioning and wait-time.* Unpublished doctoral dissertation, Stanford University, Stanford, CA.—541, 542, 546

Giaconia, R. M., & Hedges, L. V. (1982). Identifying features of effective open education. *Review of Educational Research, 52,* 579–602. *A demonstration of how meta-analysis can throw light on otherwise inaccessible issues; in this case, the aspects of open education that made a difference.*—27, 488, 489–490

Gilligan, C. (1982). *In a different voice.* Cambridge: Harvard University Press. *A feminist critique of a well-researched area: moral development.*—145, 185, 187, 348

Ginsburg, H., & Opper, S. (1988). *Piaget's theory of intellectual development* (3d ed.). Englewood Cliffs, NJ: Prentice-Hall.—104

Glaser, R., & Nitko, A. J. (1971). Measurement in learning and instruction. In R. L. Thorndike (Ed.), *Educational measurement* (2d ed.). Washington, DC: American Council of Education.—575

Glass, G. V. (1976). Primary, secondary and meta-analysis of research. *Educational Researcher, 5,* 3–8.—27

Glasser, W. L. (1969). *Schools without failure.* New York: Harper & Row. *Outlines plans for making schools more responsive to children's affective needs.*—482–483, 648

Gold, M. W., & Ryan, V. M. (1979). Vocational training for the mentally retarded. In I. H. Frieze, D. Bar-Tal, & J. S. Carroll (Eds.), *New approaches to social problems: Applications of attribution theory.* San Francisco: Jossey-Bass.—61

Goldberg, L. R. (1965). Grades as motivants. - *Psychology in the Schools, 2,* 17–24.—650

Goldenberg, C. N. (n.d.). *Low-income Hispanic parents' contributions to the reading achievement of their first-grade children.* Lennox, CA: Lennox School District.—180

Good, T. L. (1983). Research on classroom teaching. In L. S. Shulman & G. Sykes (Eds.), *Handbook of teaching and policy* (pp. 42–80). White Plains, NY: Longman.—595

Good, T. L. (1987). Teacher expectations. In D. C. Berliner & B. V. Rosenshine (Eds.), *Talks to teachers* (pp. 157–200). New York: Random House.—73, 177

Goodlad, J. I. (1984). *A place called school.* New York: McGraw-Hill.—496

Goodlad, J. I., & Klein, M. F. (1970). *Behind the classroom door.* Worthington, OH: Charles A. Jones.—496, 497

Goodman, P. (1964). *Compulsory miseducation.* New York: Horizon Press. *A polemic on the unsuitability of our schools for our society.*—480

Goodman, P. (1970). [Untitled essay]. In H. H. Hart (Ed.), *Summerhill: For and against.* New York: Hart.—478

Goodwin, W. L., & Driscoll, L. A. (1980). *Handbook for measurement and evaluation in early childhood education.* San Francisco: Jossey-Bass.—607

Goslin, D. A. (1967). *Teachers and testing.* New York: Russell Sage Foundation.—72

Goyer, R. S. (1966). *A test to measure the ability to organize ideas* (Special Rep. No. 9). Athens: Center for Communication Studies, Ohio University. (Mimeograph)—399

Graham, S. (1986). Teacher feelings and student thoughts: An attributional approach to affect in the classroom. *The Elementary School Journal, 85,* 91–104.—342

Graham, S., & Barker, G. P. (1990). The down side of help: An attributional-developmental analysis of helping behavior as a low-ability cue. *Journal of Educational Psychology, 82,* 7–14.—263

Graham, S., Doubleday, C., & Guarino, P. (1984). The development of relations between perceived controllability and the emotions of pity, anger, and guilt. *Child Development, 55,* 561–565.—342

Green, D. R. (Ed.). (1974). *The aptitude-achievement distinction.* Monterey, CA: CTB/McGraw-Hill.—599

Green, J. L. (1983). Research on teaching as a linguistic process: The state of the art. In E. W. Gordon (Ed.), *Review of research in education* (Vol. 10). Washington, DC: American Educational Research Association. *A real state-of-the-art paper describing a decade of research in areas that were not even thought about ten years earlier.*—37

Greeno, J. C. (1976). Cognitive objectives. In D. Klahr (Ed.), *Cognition and instruction.* Hillsdale, NJ: Erlbaum.—46

Gregory, I. D. (1975). A new look at the lecture method. *British Journal of Educational Technology, 6,* 55–62.—395

Gresham, F. M. (1981). Social skills training with handicapped children: A review. *Review of Educational Research, 51,* 139–176.—202

Griffin, W. M. (1965). Schedules, bells, groups, and independent study. In D. W. Beggs III & E. G. Buffie (Eds.), *Independent study: Bold new venture* (pp. 1–8). Bloomington: Indiana University Press.—456

Grimes, J. W., & Allinsmith, W. (1961). Compulsivity, anxiety and school achievement. *Merrill-Palmer Quarterly, 7,* 247–271.—61

Gronlund, N. E. (1959). *Sociometry in the classroom.* New York: Harper.—520

Grossman, H. (Ed.). (1977). *Manual on terminology and classification in mental retardation.* Washington, DC: American Association on Mental Deficiency.—209

Grossman, P. (1991). Mapping the terrain: Knowledge growth in teaching. In H. C. Waxman & H. J. Walberg (Eds.), *Effective teaching: Current research* (pp. 203–215). Berkeley, CA: McCutchan.—521, 522

Gruber, H. E., & Vonèche, J. J. (Eds.). (1977). *The essential Piaget: An interpretive reference and guide.* New York: Basic Books. *The difficulty of reading Piaget still exists, but these editors have chosen the most important passages and articles. Truly the essential Piaget.*—104

Guilford, J. P. (1952). *General psychology* (2d ed.). Princeton, NJ: Van Nostrand.—276

Gullickson, A. R. (1990). Teacher education and teacher perceived needs in educational measurement and evaluation. *Journal of Educational Measurement, 23,* 347–354.—569

Gumperz, J. J., & Gumperz, J. C. (1981). Ethnic differences in communicative style. In C. A. Ferguson &

S. B. Heath (Eds.), *Language in the USA*. Cambridge, England: Cambridge University Press.—174

Guthrie, L. F., & Hall, W. S. (1983). Continuity/discontinuity in the function and use of language. In E. W. Gordon (Ed.), *Review of research in education* (Vol. 10). Washington, DC: American Educational Research Association.—137

Haas, N., Haladyna, T. M., & Nolen, S. B. (1989). *Standardized testing in Arizona: Interviews and written comments from teachers and administrators* (Technical Report 89–3). Phoenix: The Authors, Arizona State University.—608

Hakuta, K. (1986). *Mirror of language: The debate on bilingualism*. New York: Basic Books. *A comprehensive and scientific look at the evidence for concluding that bilingual children are cognitively advantaged in comparison with monolingual children.*—136

Hales, L. W., Bain, P. T., & Rand, L. P. (1971, February). *An investigation of some aspects of the pass-fail grading system.* Paper presented at the meetings of the American Educational Research Association, New York.—651

Hall, C. S., & Lindzey, G. S. (1978). *Theories of personality* (3d ed.). New York: Wiley.—142

Hall, E. T. (1976). *Beyond culture.* Garden City, NY: Doubleday.—167

Hall, R. V., & Hall, M. C. (1980a). *How to select reinforcers.* Lawrence, KS: M & M Enterprises.—240

Hall, R. V., & Hall, M. C. (1980b). *How to use time out.* Lawrence, KS: M & M Enterprises.—249

Haller, E. J., & Davis, S. A. (1980). Does socioeconomic status bias the assignment of elementary school students to reading groups? *American Educational Research Journal, 17,* 409–418.—14

Halpin, G., & Halpin, G. (1982). Experimental investigation of the effects of study and testing on student learning, retention, and ratings of instruction. *Journal of Educational Psychology, 72,* 32–38.—650

Hamachek, D. E. (1978). *Encounters with the self* (2d ed). New York: Holt, Rinehart & Winston.—159

Hambleton, R. K., Swaminathan, H., Algina, J., & Coulson, D. B. (1978). Criterion-referenced testing and measurement: A review of technical issues and developments. *Review of Educational Research, 48,* 1–47.—580

Hamilton, R. J. (1985). A framework for the evaluation of the effectiveness of adjunct questions and objectives. *Review of Educational Research, 55,* 47–86.—42

Hare, A. P. (1962). *Handbook of small group research.* New York: Free Press.—439

Haring, N. G., & McCormick, L. (Eds.) (1986). *Exceptional children and youth.* Columbus, OH: Charles E. Merrill.—200 (fig.)

Harrow, A. J. (1972). *A taxonomy of the psychomotor domain.* New York: David McKay.—43

Hartley, J. (1976). Lecture handouts and student note-taking. *Programmed Learning and Educational Technology, 13,* 58–64.—418

Hartley, J., & Davies, I. K. (1972) Preinstructional strategies: The role of pretests, behavioral objectives, overviews, and advance organizers. *Review of Educational Research, 40,* 239–265.—396, 417

Hartley, J., & Davies, I. K. (1977). *Notetaking.* Unpublished manuscript, University of Keele, Keele, England.—417

Hartley, J., Goldie, M., & Steen, L. (1979). The role and position of summaries: Some issues and data. *Educational Review, 31,* 59–65.—419

Hartshorne, H., & May, M. A. (1928). *Studies in the nature of character,* Vol. 1: *Studies in deceit.* New York: Macmillan. *Classic experiments showing the relative specificity of honesty, deceit, and other traits.*—148, 149t, 150 (fig.)

Hastings, W. M. (1977). In praise of regurgitation. *Intellect, 105,* 349–350.—43

Hastorf, A. H. (1965). The reinforcement of individual actions in a group situation. In L. Krasner & L. P. Ullmann (Eds.), *Research in behavior modification.* New York: Holt, Rinehart & Winston.—441

Hattie, J., & Rogers, H. J. (1986). Factor models for assessing the relation between creativity and intelligence. *Journal of Educational Psychology, 78,* 482–485.—151–152

Haynes, M. C., & Jenkins, J. R. (1986). Reading instruction in special education resource rooms. *American Educational Research Journal, 23,* 161–190.—205

Heath, S. B. (1983). *Ways with words: Ethnography of communication, communities, and classrooms.* Cambridge, England: Cambridge University Press. *An insightful long-term study of children's acquisition of language and community norms.*—180

Heath, S. B. (1986). Sociocultural contexts of language development. In *Beyond language: Social and cultural factors in schooling language minority students.* Los Angeles: California State University at Los Angeles.—170, 171–172

Hebbeler, K. (1985). An old and a new question of the effects of early education for children from low-income families. *Educational Evaluation and Policy Analysis, 7,* 207–216.—98

Heckhausen, H. (1967). *The anatomy of achievement motivation.* New York: Academic Press.—336

Heckhausen, H., Schmalt, H. D., & Schneider, K. (1985). *Achievement motivation in perspective.* Orlando, FL: Academic Press.—336, 346 (fig.), 358

Hedges, L. V. (1987). How hard is hard science, how soft is soft science? The empirical cumulativeness of research. *American Psychologist, 42,* 443–455.—28

Henderson, J. E., & Burke, J. B. (1971). *Protocol material teaching strategies.* Unpublished manuscript, Michigan State University, College of Education, East Lansing.—228

Henderson, R. W., Swanson, R., & Zimmerman, B. J. (1975). Inquiry response induction in preschool children through televised modeling. *Developmental Psychology, 11,* 523–524.—516

Hendrickson, G., & Schroeder, W. H. (1941). Transfer of training in learning to hit a submerged target. *Journal of Educational Psychology, 32,* 205–213.—308

Henry, J. (1957). Attitude organization in elementary school classrooms. *American Journal of Orthopsychiatry, 27,* 117–133.—435

Henry, J. (1963). *Culture against man.* New York: Random House. *An important anthropological view of schools, including examples from ethnographies of the classroom.*—485

Hernandez, H. (1989). *Multicultural education.* Columbus, OH: Merrill.—177

Herrnstein, R. J. (1971). IQ. *Atlantic Monthly, 228,* 43–64. *A modern look at social Darwinism, suggesting how and why IQ is associated with higher social-class status.*—61

Hewett, F. M., Taylor, F. D., & Artuso, A. A. (1969). The Santa Monica Project: Evaluation of an engineered classroom design with emotionally disturbed children. *Exceptional Children, 35,* 523–529.—549

Heyns, R. W., & Lippitt, R. (1954). Systematic observational techniques. In G. Lindzey (Ed.), *Handbook of social psychology,* Vol. 1: *Theory and method* (pp. 370–404). Cambridge, MA: Addison-Wesley.—393

Highet, G. (1955). *The art of teaching.* New York: Vintage. *A beautifully written discussion of teaching by a classicist, with no use of, or reference to, the behavioral sciences.*—441

Hilgard, E. R., Atkinson, R. C., & Atkinson, R. L. (1971). *Introduction to psychology* (5th ed.). New York: Harcourt Brace Jovanovich.—67, 145 (fig.)

Hiller, J. E. (1968). *An experimental investigation of the effects of conceptual vagueness on speaking behavior.* Unpublished doctoral dissertation, University of Connecticut, Storrs. *Initiated a line of research on vagueness, subsequently applied by others in several studies of teaching.*—411

Hodgkinson, H. L. (1981). *All one system.* Washington, DC: Institute for Educational Leadership.—177

Hoetker, J., & Ahlbrand, W. P., Jr. (1969). The persistence of recitation. *American Educational Research Journal, 6,* 145–167. *Cites studies from 1908, 1912, 1966, and 1969 to show that the recitation has been around, much unchanged, for a long time.*—495–496, 497, 498

Hoffman, B. (1962). *The tyranny of testing.* New York: Crowell-Collier-Macmillan.—648

Holmes, C. T., & Matthews, K. M. (1984). The effects of nonpromotion on elementary and junior high school pupils: A meta-analysis. *Review of Educational Research, 54,* 225–236.—660

Holt, J. (1964). *How children fail.* New York: Pitman. *A blistering critique of the ways schools can destroy the minds and emotions of young children.*—479, 483

Holt, J. (1967). *How children learn.* New York: Pitman.—479

Holt, J. (1969). *On testing.* New York: Pitman.—648

Holt, J. (1974). Marking and grading. In M. D. Gall & B. A. Ward (Eds.), *Critical issues in educational psychology.* Boston: Little, Brown.—652

Homme, L. E. (1966). Human motivation and environment. *Kansas Studies in Education, 16,* 30–39.—241

Homme, L. E., Csanyi, A. P., Gonzales, M. A., & Rechs, J. R. (1970). *How to use contingency contracting in the classroom.* Champaign, IL: Research Press. *A first-rate guide to the use of behavior modification in the classroom.*—242

Homme, L. E., & Tosti, D. T. (1965). Contingency management and motivation. *National Society for Programmed Instruction Journal, 4*(7), 14–16.—240–241

Homme, L. E., & Tosti, D. T. (1971). *Behavior technology.* San Rafael, CA: Individual Learning Systems.—157

Hopkins, K. D., & Bracht, G. H. (1975). Ten-year stability of verbal and nonverbal IQ scores. *American Educational Research Journal, 12,* 469–477.—57

Horner, M. S. (1969). Fail: A bright woman is caught in a double bind. *Psychology Today, 3*(6), 36–38, 62.—187

Hovland, C. I., Lumsdaine, A. A., & Sheffield, F. D. (1949). *Experiments on mass communications,* Vol. 3: *Studies in social psychology in World War II.* Princeton, NJ: Princeton University Press.—394

Hudgins, B. B. (1977). *Learning and thinking.* Itasca, IL: F. E. Peacock.—319

Hunt, M. W. (1969). Tips for beginning teachers. In *Discipline in the classroom: Selected articles of continuing value to elementary and secondary school teachers.* Washington, DC: National Education Association. —153

Hunt, T. C. (1976). Open education: A comparison, an assessment, and a prediction. *Peabody Journal of Education, 53,* 110–114.—486

Hunter, J. E. (1986). Cognitive ability, cognitive aptitudes, job knowledge, and job performance. *Journal of Vocational Behavior, 29,* 340–362.—60

Hurt, H. T., Scott, M. D., & McCroskey, J. C. (1978). *Communication in the classroom.* Reading, MA: Addison-Wesley.—428

Husén, T. (Ed.) (1967). *International study of achievement in mathematics: A comparison of twelve countries* (Vol. 2). New York: Wiley.—397

Hyde, J. S. (1981). How large are cognitive gender differences? *American Psychologist, 36,* 892–901. *Makes clear that gender differences in cognition cannot be used for any kind of social policy because the differences are so very small.*—183–184

Hyde, J. S., Fennema, E., & Lamon, S. J. (1990). Gender differences in mathematics performance: A meta-analysis. *Psychological Bulletin, 107,* 139–155.—183

Hyde, J. S., & Linn, M. C. (1988). Gender differences in verbal activities: A meta-analysis. *Psychological Bulletin, 104,* 53–69.—182, 183

Hyman, I. A., & Lally, D. M. (1981). Corporal punishment in American education: A historical and contemporary dilemma. *Educational Comment/1981,* pp. 8–15. (College of Education and Allied Professions, University of Toledo, Toledo, OH)—515

Hymes, D. (1972). Introduction. In C. B. Cazden, V. P. John, & D. Hymes (Eds.), *Functions of language in the classroom.* New York: Teachers College Press.—174

Idol, L. (1987). Group story mapping: A comprehension strategy for both skilled and unskilled readers. *Journal of Learning Disabilities, 20,* 196–205.—303, 304 (fig.)

Inhelder, B., & Piaget, J. (1958). *The growth of logical thinking from childhood to adolescence.* New York: Basic Books. *A presentation of theory and supporting observations.*—104, 114

Inhelder, B., & Piaget, J. (1964). *The early growth of logic in the child.* New York: Harper & Row.—104

Institute for Research on Teaching. (1980, Winter). *Communication Quarterly.* (Michigan State University, East Lansing)—603 (fig.)

Jacklin, C. N., & Maccoby, E. E. (1972). *Sex differences in intellectual abilities: A reassessment and a look at some new explanations.* Paper presented at the meetings of the American Educational Research Association, Chicago.—182, 193

Janicki, T. C., & Peterson, P. L. (1981). Aptitude-treatment interaction effects of variations in direct instruction. *American Educational Research Journal, 18,* 63–82.—219

Jaynes, J. (1975). Hello, teacher . . . A review of Fred S. Keller, "The history of psychology: A personalized system of instruction" and Fred S. Keller, "Selected readings in the history of psychology: A PSI companion," *Contemporary Psychology, 20,* 629–631.—465–466

Jensen, A. R. (1967). Social class and verbal learning. In J. P. DeCecco (Ed.), *The psychology of language, thought, and instruction.* New York: Holt, Rinehart & Winston.—281

Jensen, A. R. (1969). How much can we boost IQ and scholastic achievement? *Harvard Educational Review, 39(1),* 1–123. *The blockbuster that revived the nature-nurture controversy about IQ, especially because of its pessimism about compensatory education and its hereditarianism on racial differences.*—84, 87, 99

Jensen, A. R. (1974). Kinship correlations reported by Sir Cyril Burt. *Behavior Genetics, 4,* 1–28.—68

Johnson, D. (1981). Naturally acquired learned helplessness: The relationship of school failure to achievement behavior, attributions, and self-concept. *Journal of Educational Psychology, 73,* 174–180.—341

Johnson, D. W., & Johnson, R. T. (1979). Conflict in the classroom: Controversy and learning. *Review of Educational Research, 49,* 51–70.—425–426

Johnson, D., Johnson, R., Holubec, E., & Roy, P. (1984). *Circles of learning.* Washington, DC: Association for Supervision and Curriculum Development.—443

Johnson, H. W. (1979). *Preschool test descriptions.* Springfield, IL: Charles C Thomas.—607

Johnston, J. M. (1972). Punishment of human behavior. *American Psychologist, 27,* 1033–1054.—248

Jones, E. E., & Nisbett, R. E. (1971). *The actor and the observer: Divergent perceptions of the causes of behavior.* Morristown, NJ: General Learning Press.—162

Jones, F. H., & Miller, W. H. (1974). The effective use of negative attention for reducing group disruption in special elementary school classrooms. *Psychological Record, 24,* 435–448.—515

Joyce, B. R. (1975). Listening to different drummers: Evaluating alternative instructional models. In

Competency assessment, research, and evaluation: A report of a national conference (pp. 61–81). Albany, NY: Multi-State Consortium on Performance-Based Teacher Education.—562–563

Joynson, R. B. (1989). *The Burt affair.* London: Routledge.—68

Judd, C. H. (1908). The relation of special training to general intelligence. *Educational Review, 36,* 28–43.—308

Juel-Nielsen, N. (1965). Individual and environment: A psychiatric-psychological investigation of monozygotic twins reared apart. *Acta Psychiatrica et Neurologica Scandinavica.* Monograph Supplement 183.—65

Kagan, S. (1986). Cooperative learning and sociocultural factors in schooling. In *Beyond language: Social and cultural factors in schooling language minority students.* Los Angeles: California State University at Los Angeles.—179

Kagan, S., Zahn, G. L., Widaman, K. F., Schwarzwald, J., & Tyrrell, G. (1985). Classroom structural bias: Impact of cooperative and competitive classroom structure on cooperative and competitive individuals and groups. In R. E. Slavin, S. Sharan, S. Kagan, R. Hertz-Lazarowitz, C. Webb, & R. Schmuck (Eds.), *Learning to cooperate, cooperating to learn.* New York: Plenum Press.—179, 180

Kansanen, P. (1981). The way thinking is: How do teachers think and decide? In E. Komulainen & P. Kansanen (Eds.), *Classroom analysis: Concepts, findings, applications.* Helsinki: Institute of Education, University of Helsinki.—506, 507t

Kaplan, R. M., & Pascoe, G. C. (1977). Humorous lectures and humorous examples: Some effects upon comprehension and retention. *Journal of Educational Psychology, 69,* 61–65.—414

Karoly, P. (1977). Behavioral self-management in children: Concepts, methods, issues and directions. In M. Hersen, R. M. Eisler, & P. M. Miller (Eds.), *Progress in behavior modification* (Vol. 5). New York: Academic Press.—265

Kazdin, A. E. (1989). *Behavior modification in applied settings* (4th ed.). Homewood, IL: Dorsey. *One of the best examples of the power of operant conditioning to change people's behavior.*—244, 246

Keller, F. S. (1968). Good-bye teacher! *Journal of Applied Behavioral Analysis, 1,* 79–84. *The paper that started the movement toward personalized systems of instruction.*—460, 465

Kelley, T. L. (1927). *Interpretations of educational measurements.* Yonkers, NY: World Book.—71

Kemer, B. J. (1965). *A study of the relationship between the sex of the student and the assignment of marks by secondary school teachers.* Unpublished doctoral dissertation. Michigan State University, East Lansing.—189, 192t

Kennedy, W. A., & Willcutt, H. C. (1964). Praise and blame as incentives. *Psychological Bulletin, 62,* 323–332.—369

Keyser, D. J., & Sweetland, R. C. (Eds.). (1984–1985). *Test critiques* (Vols. 1–4). Kansas City: Test Corporation of America.—607

Kibler, R. J., Barker, L. L., & Miles, D. T. (1970). *Behavioral objectives and instruction.* Boston: Allyn & Bacon.—36

Kifer, E. (1975). Relationships between academic achievement and personality characteristics: A quasi-longitudinal study. *American Educational Research Journal, 12,* 191–210.—159

King, A. (1990). Enhancing peer interaction and learning in the classroom through reciprocal questioning. *American Educational Research Journal, 27,* 664–687.—431–432

King, A. (1991, August). *Effects of students' self-questioning, summarizing, and note taking-review on immediate and delayed lecture comprehension.* Paper presented at the meeting of the American Psychological Association, San Francisco.—416

Kirk, S. A., & Gallagher, J. J. (1988). *Educating exceptional children* (6th ed.) Boston: Houghton Mifflin. *The latest edition of an authoritative textbook.*—197, 200, 205, 208

Kirst, M. W., & Walker, D. F. (1973). An analysis of curriculum policy-making. *Review of Educational Research, 41,* 479–509.—529

Klauer, K. J. (1984). Intentional and incidental learning with instructional texts: A meta-analysis for 1970–1980. *American Educational Research Journal, 21,* 323–339.—42

Klausmeier, H. J., Sorenson, J. S., & Ghatala, E. S. (1971). Individually guided motivation: Developing self-direction and prosocial behaviors. *The Elementary School Journal, 71,* 339–350.—366

Klineberg, O. (1935). *Negro intelligence and selective migration.* New York: Columbia University Press. *A classic, ingenious, and careful early study questioning the hereditarian position on racial differences in measured intelligence.*—82

Klineberg, O. (1963). Negro-white differences in intelligence test performances: A new look at an old problem. *American Psychologist, 18,* 198–203.—79–80

Knoblock, P. (1982). *Teaching emotionally disturbed children.* Boston: Houghton Mifflin.—200

Kohlberg, L. (1963).   The development of children's orientations toward moral order, Pt. 1: Sequence in the development of moral thought. *Vita Humana, 6,* 11–33.—142

Kohlberg, L. (1981).   *The philosophy of moral development.* San Francisco: Harper & Row.—142

Komarovsky, M. (1950).   Functional analysis of sex roles. *American Sociological Review, 15,* 508–516.—187

Komulainen, E., Kansanen, P., Karma, K., Martikainen, M., & Uusikylä, K. (1981).   Investigations into the instructional process. In E. Komulainen & P. Kansanen (Eds.), *Classroom analysis: Concepts, findings, applications.* Helsinki: Institute of Education, University of Helsinki.—496

Kounin, J. S. (1970).   *Discipline and group management in classrooms.* New York: Holt, Rinehart & Winston. *A sensible view of classroom management by one who sat, watched, recorded, and categorized what he saw.*—512, 527

Krale, S. (1981, October).   *What is learned by measuring learning in grades?* Paper presented at the NFPF Congress, Tampere, Finland.—648

Krathwohl, D. R., Bloom, B. S., & Masia, B. B. (1964).   *Taxonomy of educational objectives. The classification of educational goals,* Handbook 2: *Affective domain.* New York: McKay. *The affective counterpart of the well-known taxonomy of cognitive objectives.*—43

Krueger, W. C. F. (1929).   The effect of overlearning on retention. *Journal of Experimental Psychology, 12,* 71–78.—292

Kulik, J. A. (1985).   *Consistencies in findings on computer-based education.* Paper presented at the annual meetings of the American Educational Research Association, Chicago.—475–476

Kulik, C.-L. Kulik, J. A., & Bangert-Drowns, R. L. (1990a).   Effectiveness of mastery learning programs: A meta-analysis. *Review of Educational Research, 60,* 265–299.—461, 462, 463

Kulik, J. A., Kulik, C.-L., & Bangert-Drowns, R. L. (1990b).   Is there better evidence on mastery learning? A response to Slavin. *Review of Educational Research, 60,* 303–307.—461

Kulik, J. A., & Kulik, C-L. C. (1984).   Effects of accelerated instruction on students. *Review of Educational Research, 54,* 409–426.—217

Kunihira, S., & Asher, J. J. (1965).   The strategy of the total physical response: An application to learning Japanese. *International Review of Applied Linguistics, 3,* 277–289.—290–291, 413

Lambert, W. E., & Tucker, G. R. (1972).   *Bilingual education of children.* Rowley, MA: Newburg House.—133

Lambiotte, J. G., Dansereau, D. F., Cross, D. R., & Reynolds, S. B. (1989).   Multirelational semantic maps. *Educational Psychology Review, 1,* 331–368.—284, 285 (fig.)

Lamwers, L. L., & Jazwinski, C. H. (1989).   A comparison of three strategies to reduce student procrastination in PSI. *Teaching of Psychology, 16*(1), 8–12.—464

Larkin, J. H. (1985).   Understanding problem representations and skill in physics. In S. F. Chipman, J. W. Segal, & R. Glaser (Eds.), *Thinking and learning skills* (Vol. 2, pp. 141–159.). Hillsdale, NJ: Erlbaum.—305

Larkins, A. G., McKinney, C. W., Oldham-Buss, S., & Gilmore, A. C. (1985).   Teacher enthusiasm: A critical review. In H. S. Williams (Ed.), *Educational and psychological research monographs.* Hattiesburg, MS: University of Southern Mississippi.—415

Larrivée, B. (1989).   Effective strategies for academically handicapped students in the regular classroom. In R. E. Slavin, N. L.., Karweit, & N. A. Madden (Eds.), *Effective programs for students at risk.* Boston: Allyn & Bacon.—203

Lau Kam Cheong (1972).   *Augmenting lecture presentation with structural support.* Unpublished doctoral dissertation, University of Malaya, Kuala Lumpur.—410

Lawson, R. (1965).   *Frustration: The development of a scientific concept.* New York: Macmillan.—357

Lazar, I., & Darlington, R. (1982).   Lasting effects of early education: A report from the Consortium for Longitudinal Studies. *Monographs of the Society for Research in Child Development, 17*(2–3, Series No. 195). *An impressive collection of difficult-to-obtain long-term results of early education programs, with positive conclusions concerning long-range values.*—97, 98, 99*t*

Lazarsfeld, P. F. (1949).   The American soldier—an expository review. *Public Opinion Quarterly, 13,* 377–404.—11

Lee, E. S. (1951).   Negro intelligence and selective migration: A Philadelphia test of the Klineberg hypothesis. *American Sociological Review, 16,* 227–233.—82

Leifer, A. D., Gordon, N. J., & Graves, S. B. (1974).   Children's television: More than mere entertainment. *Harvard Educational Review, 44,* 213–245.—511

Lenneberg, E. H. (1967).   *Biological foundations of language.* New York: Wiley.—128

Lepper, M. R., & Chabay, R. W. (1985).   Intrinsic motivation and instruction: Conflicting views on the role of motivational processes in computer-based education. *Educational Psychologist, 20,* 217–230.— 375

Lepper, M. R., & Greene, D. (1975). Turning play into work: Effects of adult surveillance and extrinsic rewards on children's intrinsic motivation. *Journal of Personality and Social Psychology, 31,* 479–488.— 352

Lepper, M. R., Greene, D., & Nisbett, R. E. (1973). Undermining children's intrinsic interest with extrinsic rewards: A test of the overjustification hypothesis. *Journal of Personality and Social Psychology, 28,* 129– 137.—352, 367

Lepper, M. R., & Hodell, M. (1989). Intrinsic motivation in the classroom. In C. Ames & R. Ames (Eds.), *Research on motivation in education* (Vol. 3). San Diego: Academic Press.—353, 372

Levin, H. M. (1986). *Cost-effectiveness of computer-assisted instruction: Some insights.* Paper presented at the First International Conference on Courseware Design and Evaluation, Ramat Gan, Israel.—476

Levin, H. M., Glass, G. V., & Meister, G. R. (1984). *Cost-effectiveness of four educational interventions.* Stanford, CA: Institute for Research on Educational Finance and Governance (Project Report No. 84– A11).—469

Levin, J. R. (1976). What have we learned about maximizing what children learn? In J. R. Levin & V. L. Allen (Eds.), *Cognitive learning in children.* New York: Academic Press.—294

Levin, J. R. (1981). The mnemonic 80s: Keywords in the classroom. *Educational Psychologist, 16,* 65– 82.—296

Levin, M. E., & Levin, J. R. (1990). Scientific mnemonics: Methods for maximizing more than memory. *American Educational Research Journal, 27,* 301– 321.—297

Lewin, K. (1947). Group decision and social change. In T. M. Newcomb & E. L. Hartley (Eds.), *Readings in social psychology.* New York: Holt, Rinehart & Winston. *Classic experiments on the relative effectiveness of lectures and of group discussions and decisions in changing attitudes and behavior.*— 422

Licklider, J. C. R. (1962). Preliminary experiments in computer-aided teaching. In J. E. Coulson (Ed.), *Programmed learning and computer-based instruction.* New York: Wiley.—475 (fig.)

Liebert, R. M. (1974). Television and children's aggressive behavior: Another look. *American Journal of Psychoanalysis, 34,* 99–107.—511.

Linden, M., & Wittrock, M. C. (1981). The teaching of reading comprehension according to the model of

generative learning. *Reading Research Quarterly, 17,* 44–57.—288

Linn, M. C. (1986). Science. In R. F. Dillon & R. J. Sternberg (Eds.), *Cognition and instruction* (pp. 155– 204). New York: Academic Press.—301

Linn, M. C., & Hyde, J. S. (1989). Gender, mathematics, and science. *Educational Researcher, 18,* 17– 19, 22–27.—183

Linn, R. L., Graue, M. E., & Sanders, N. M. (1990). Comparing state and district test results to national norms: The validity of claims that "Everyone is above average." *Educational Measurement: Issues and Practice, 9,* 5–14.—607

Linscheid, T., Iwata, B., Ricketts, R., Williams, D., & Griffin, J. (1990). Clinical evaluation of the Self-Injurious Behavior Inhibiting System (SIBIS). *Journal of Applied Behavior Analysis, 23*(1), 53–78.—248

Linton, T. E., & Juul, K. D. (1980). Mainstreaming: Time for reassessment. *Educational Leadership, 37,* 433–437.—200–201

Lipe, D., & Jung, S. M. (1971). Manipulating incentives to enhance school learning. *Review of Educational Research, 41,* 249–280.—369

Lochhead, J. (1985). Teaching analytic reasoning skills through pair problem solving. In J. W. Segal, S. F. Chipman, & R. Glaser (Eds.), *Thinking and learning skills* (Vol. 1). Hillsdale, NJ: Erlbaum.– -305

Loehlin, J. C., Lindzey, G., & Spuhler, J. N. (1975). *Race differences in intelligence.* San Francisco: Freeman.—82–83

Long, N. J., Morse, W. E., & Newman, R. G. (Eds.). (1980). *Conflict in the classroom* (4th ed.). Belmont, CA: Wadsworth.—198 (fig.), 211

Lordahl, D. S. (1961). Concept identification using simultaneous auditory and visual signals. *Journal of Experimental Psychology, 62,* 283–290.—413

Luchins, A. S. (1942). Mechanization in problem-solving: The effect of Einstellung. *Psychological Monographs, 248. A classic demonstration of negative transfer—how learning one thing can prevent efficient problem solving.*—308

Luiten, J., Ames, W., & Ackerman, G. (1980). A meta-analysis of the effects of advance organizers on learning and retention. *American Educational Research Journal, 17,* 211–218.—282

Luria, A. R. (1968). *The mind of a mnemonist: A little book about a vast memory.* New York: Basic Books. *The case history of a person who never forgot anything!*—291–292, 293–294

Luria, A. R. (1979). Cultural differences in thinking. In M. Cole & S. Cole (Eds.), *The making of mind: A* *personal account of Soviet psychology.* Cambridge: Harvard University Press.—176

Lynn, D. B. (1972). Determinants of intellectual growth in women. *School Review, 80,* 241–260.—185

Maccoby, E. E. (1966). Sex differences in intellectual functioning. In E. E. Maccoby (Ed.), *The development of sex differences.* Stanford, CA: Stanford University Press.—183, 186, 188, 189, (fig.)

Maccoby, E. E., & Jacklin, C. N. (1974). *The psychology of sex differences.* Stanford, CA: Stanford University Press.—182, 185

Machado, L. A. (1981). The development of intelligence: A political outlook. *Intelligence, 5,* 2–4.—101

Macmillan, D. L., Keogh, B. K., & Jones, R. L. (1986). Special educational research on mildly handicapped learners. In M. C. Wittrock (Ed.), *Handbook of research on teaching* (3d ed., pp. 686–724). New York: Macmillan.—201

Madden, N. A., & Slavin, R. E. (1983). Mainstreaming students with mild handicaps: Academic and social outcomes. *Review of Educational Research, 53,* 519–569.—202

Maddox, H., & Hoole, E. (1975). Performance decrement in the lecture. *Educational Review, 28,* 17–30.—409

Maehr, M. L. (1976). Continuing motivation: An analysis of a seldom considered educational outcome. *Review of Educational Research, 46,* 443–462.—371

Mager, R. F. (1962). *Preparing instructional objectives.* Palo Alto, CA: Fearon. *The little book that became the bible for those who wanted to learn how to write behavioral objectives.*—36, 471 (fig.)

Maier, N. R. F. (1933). An aspect of human reasoning. *British Journal of Psychology, 24,* 144–165.—152

Main, S., & Gallagher, D. (1972). *Student and faculty evaluations of the new undergraduate grading system: A preliminary report.* Unpublished manuscript, Stanford University Planning Office, Stanford, CA.—651

Maker, J. (1987). Teaching the gifted and talented. In V. R. Koehler (Ed.), *Handbook for educators* (pp. 420–456). White Plains, NY: Longman.—217

Maltzman, I. M. (1960). On the training of originality. *Psychological Review, 67,* 229–242.—152

Mandler, G. (1969). Words, lists, and categories: An experimental view of organized memory. In J. L. Cowan (Ed.), *Thought and language.* Tucson: University of Arizona Press.—283

Mandler, G., & Sarason, S. B. (1952). A study of anxiety and learning. *Journal of Abnormal and Social Psychology, 47,* 166–173.—159

Mansfield, R. S., Busse, T. V., & Krepelka, E. J. (1978). The effectiveness of creativity training. *Review of Educational Research, 48,* 517–536. *Raises serious questions about the real-life payoff of creativity training.*—154

Markle, S. M. (1983). *Designs for instructional designers* (2d ed.). Champaign, IL: Stipes.—471

Marks, C. B., Doctorow, M. J., & Wittrock, M. C. (1974). Word frequency and reading comprehension. *Journal of Educational Research, 67,* 259–262.—288

Marliave, R., & Filby, N. N. (1985). Success rate: A measure of task appropriateness. In C. W. Fisher & D. C. Berliner (Eds.), *Perspectives on instructional time.* White Plains, NY: Longman.—355

Marshall, H. (1981). Open classroom: Has the term outlived its usefulness? *Review of Educational Research, 51,* 181–192.—488–489

Martinez, J. G. R., & Martinez, N. C. (1988). "Hello, teacher": An argument for reemphasizing the teacher's role in PSI and mastery learning. *American Journal of Education, 97,* 18–33.—465

Marx, M. H. (1960). Motivation. In C. W. Harris (Ed.), *Encyclopedia of educational research* (3d ed., pp. 888–901). New York: Macmillan.—372

Maslow, A. H. (1954). *Motivation and personality.* New York: Harper & Row.—332–334, 479

Maslow, A. H. (1971). *The farther reaches of human nature.* New York: Viking.—334

Mastropieri, M. A., & Scruggs, T. E. (1989). Constructing more meaningful relationships: Mnemonic instruction for special populations. *Educational Psychology Review, 1,* 83–112.—296

Matson, J. L., & DiLorenzo, T. M. (1984). *Punishment and its alternatives.* New York: Springer.—247

May, M. A. (1965a, July 10) *Enforcements and simplifications of motivational and stimulus variables in audio-visual instructional materials* (Working Paper, Office of Education Contract No. OE–5–16–006). Washington, DC: Department of Health, Education, and Welfare.—413

May, M. A. (1965b, July 20). *Word-picture relationships in audio-visual presentations* (Working Paper, Office of Education Contract No. OE–5–16–006), Washington, DC: Department of Health, Education, and Welfare.—413

Mayer, R. E. (1983). Can you repeat that? Qualitative effects of repetition and advance organizers on learning from science prose. *Journal of Educational Psychology, 75,* 40–49.—292

Mayer, R. E. (1986). Mathematics. In R. F. Dillon and R. J. Sternberg (Eds.), *Cognition and instruction.* New York: Academic Press.—299

Mayer, R. E. (1989). Models for understanding. *Review of Educational Research, 59,* 43–64. *Demonstrates through clever studies how visual models of complex processes help students transfer what they learn.*—314, 315 (fig.)

McCall, R. B. (1981). Early predictors of later IQ: The search continues. *Intelligence, 5,* 141–147.—57

McClelland, D. C., & Atkinson, J. W. (1948). The projective expression of needs, Pt. 2: The effect of different intensities of the hunger drive on thematic apperception. *Journal of Experimental Psychology, 38,* 643–658.—335

McClelland, D. C., Atkinson, J. W., Clark, R. A., & Lowell, E. L. (1953). *The achievement motive.* New York: Appleton-Century-Crofts. *One of the major works in the literature on achievement motivation.*—335

McConnell, F. (1973). Children with hearing disabilities. In L. M. Dunn (Ed.), *Exceptional children in the schools: Special education in transition* (2d ed.). New York: Holt, Rinehart & Winston.—212–213

McCroskey, J. C., & McVetta, R. W. (1978). Classroom seating arrangements: Instructional communication theory versus student preferences. *Communication Education, 27,* 99–111.—428

McDonald, F. J., & Elias, P. (1976). *The effects of teaching performance on pupil learning. Beginning Teacher Evaluation Study: Phase II, Final Report* (Vol. 1). Princeton, NJ: Educational Testing Service.—558, 559

McKeachie, W. J. (1961). Motivation, teaching methods, and college learning. In M. R. Jones (Ed.), *Nebraska symposium on motivation, 1961* (pp. 111–142). Lincoln: University of Nebraska Press.—346–347

McKeachie, W. J. (1967). Research in teaching: The gap between theory and practice. In C. B. T. Lee (Ed.), *Improving college teaching* (pp. 211–239). Washington, DC: American Council on Education.—390

McKeachie, W. J., & Kulik, J. A. (1975). Effective college teaching. In F. N. Kerlinger (Ed.), *Review of research in education* (Vol. 3). Washington, DC: American Educational Research Association.—389, 420

McKeachie, W. J., Lin, Y.-G., Milholland, J. E., & Isaacson, R. L. (1966). Student affiliation motives, teacher warmth, and academic achievement. *Journal of Personality and Social Psychology, 4,* 457–461.—348

McKinney, C. W., Larkins, A. G., Kazelskis, R., Ford, M. J., Allen, J. A., & Davis, J. C. (1983). Some effects of teacher enthusiasm on student achievement in fourth-grade social studies. *Journal of Educational Research, 76,* 249–253.—415

McLaughlin. T. F. (1975). The applicability of token reinforcement systems in public school systems. *Psychology in the Schools, 12,* 84–89.—362

McLeish, J. (1968). *The lecture method.* Cambridge, England: Cambridge Institute of Education.—279t

McLeish, J. (1976). The lecture method. In N. L. Gage (Ed.), *The psychology of teaching methods: Seventy-fifth yearbook of the National Society for the Study of Education.* Chicago: University of Chicago Press.—386, 389, 390

McLaughlin, M. W., & Phillips, D. C. (Eds.). (1991). *Evaluation and education: At quarter century. Ninetieth Yearbook of the National Society for the Study of Education,* (Part II). Chicago: University of Chicago Press.—587

McNeil, D. (1970). *The acquisition of language.* New York: Harper & Row.—128

McPartland, J. M., & McDill, E. L. (1977). *Violence in schools.* Lexington, MA: Lexington Books.—510

Mead, M. (1935). *Sex and temperament in three primitive societies.* New York: Morrow. *A highly acclaimed description of sex roles in different cultural groups.*—186

Meade, J. (1980). Mainstreaming: The big wind died out. *Children's World, 12.*—201

Mehan, H. (1979). *Learning lessons: Social organization in the classroom.* Cambridge: Harvard University Press.—137, 496

Mehan, H. (1982). The structure of classroom events and their consequences for student performance. In P. Gilmore & A. A. Glatthorn (Eds.), *Children in and out of school.* Washington, DC: Center for Applied Linguistics.—137

Meichenbaum, D. (1975). Enhancing creativity. *American Educational Research Journal, 12,* 129–145.—156

Meier, J. (1971). Prevalence and characteristics of learning disabilities found in second-grade children. *Journal of Learning Disabilities, 4,* 7–20.—205

Mental Retardation News. (1977). NARC on-the-job training project: How it placed 15,000 retarded persons in meaningful employment. *Mental Retardation News, 26,* 6.—210

Meredith, G. M. (1985). Intimacy as a variable in lecture-format courses. *Psychological Reports, 57,* 484–486.—417

Messick, S. (1979). Potential uses of noncognitive measurement in education. *Journal of Educational Psychology, 71,* 281–292.—599

Messick, S. (1980). Test validity and the ethics of assessment. *American Psychologist, 35,* 1012–1028.—583

Messick, S. (1982). Issues of effectiveness and equity in the coaching controversy: Implications for educational and testing practice. *Educational Psychologist, 17,* 67–91.—609

Messick, S. (1989). Validity. In R. L. Linn (Ed.), *Educational measurement* (3d ed., pp. 13–103). New York: American Council on Education/Macmillan.—583

Metfessel, N. S., Michael, W. B., & Kirsner, D. A. (1969). Instrumentation of Bloom's and Krathwohl's taxonomies for the writing of educational objectives. *Psychology in the Schools, 6,* 227–231.—39, 45

Miller, G. A. (1962). *Psychology.* New York: Harper & Row.—108–109

Miller, P. H. (1989). *Theories of developmental psychology* (2d ed.). New York: Freeman.—142

Millman, J. (1970). Reporting student progress: A case for a criterion-referenced marking system. *Phi Delta Kappan, 52,* 226–230.—662

Millman, J., & Greene, J. (1988). The specification and development of tests of achievement and ability. In R. Linn (Ed.), *Educational measurement* (3rd ed.) (pp. 335–366). New York: Macmillan—645

Miltz, R. J. (1971). *Development and evaluation of a manual for improving teachers' explanations.* Unpublished doctoral dissertation, Stanford University, Stanford, CA.—409, 408*t*

Ministry of Education. (1949). *Report by H. M. inspectors on the Summerhill School, July 20 and 21, 1949.* Leicester, Suffolk East, England: Author.—481

Mischel, W. (1973). Toward a cognitive social learning reconceptualization of personality. *Psychological Review, 80,* 252–283.—147, 148

Mitchell, J. J. (1975). Moral growth during adolescence. *Adolescence, 10,* 221–226.—147

Mitchell, R. R., & Piatkowska, O. E. (1974). Characteristics associated with underachievement: Targets for treatment. *Australian Psychologist, 9*(3), 19–41.—331

Moely, B. E., Hart, S. S., Santulli, K., Leal, L., Johnson-Barron, T., Rao, N., & Burney, L. (1986). How do teachers teach memory skills? *Educational Psychologist, 21,* 55–72.—292, 303

Moll, L. (Ed.).(1990). *Vygotsky and education.* Cambridge, England: Cambridge University Press.—123

Mood, A. M. (1970). Do teachers make a difference? In *Do teachers make a difference? A report on recent research on pupil achievement* (pp. 1–24). Washington, DC: Bureau of Educational Personnel Development, Office of Education, Department of Health, Education, and Welfare.—483–484

Moore, J. C. (1968). Cueing for selective note-taking. *Journal of Experimental Education, 36,* 69–72.—417

Moores, D. F. (1982). *Educating the deaf* (2d ed.). Boston: Houghton Mifflin.—212

Morgan, M. (1984). Reward-induced decrements and increments in intrinsic motivation. *Review of Educational Research, 54,* 5–30.—353

Morine, G. (1973). Planning skills: Paradox and parodies. *Journal of Teacher Education, 34,* 135–143.—525

Morine-Dershimer, G. (1987). Can we talk? In D. C. Berliner & B. V. Rosenshine (Eds.), *Talks to teachers* (pp. 37–53). New York: Random House.—138

Morine-Dershimer, G., & Tenenberg, M. (1981). *Participant perspectives of classroom discourse* (Final Rep., Executive Summary, NIE–G–78–0161). Washington, DC: National Institute of Education.—137, 138

Moss, H. A. (1967). Sex, age and state as determinants of mother-infant interaction. *Merrill-Palmer Quarterly, 13,* 19–36.—189

Mueller, D. J. (1976). Mastery learning: Partly boon, partly boondoggle. *Teachers College Record, 78,* 41–52.—464

Mull, C. (1984). Marking. A critical alternative. *Journal of Curriculum Studies, 16,* 155–164.—648

Murphy, J. J. (1988). Contingency contracting in schools: A review. *Education and Treatment of Children, 11,* 257–269.—10

Murray, H. et al. (1938). *Explorations in personality: A clinical and experimental study of fifty men of college age.* New York: Oxford University Press. *Raised the study of personality to a much higher level of sophistication, ingenuity, and insightfulness.*—332

Myklebust, H. R. (1960). *The psychology of deafness.* New York: Grune & Stratton.—213

Nagy, P., & Griffith, A. K. (1982). Limitations of recent research relating Piaget's theory to adolescent thought. *Review of Educational Research, 52,* 513–556.—117

National Coalition on Television Violence. (1981). *NCTV News, 2*(4).—262

National Commission on Testing and Public Policy. (1990). *Reforming assessment: From gatekeepers to gateway to education.* Chestnut Hill, MA: Boston College.—598

National Education Association. (1980). *Marking and reporting pupil progress* (Research Summary 1970–5–1). Washington, DC: NEA Research Division.—189

Needels, M., & Gage, N. L. (1991). Essence and accident in process-product research on teaching. In H. C. Waxman & H. J. Walberg (Eds.), *Effective teaching: Current research* (pp. 3–31). Berkeley, CA: McCutchan.—562

Neill, A. S. (1960). *Summerhill: A radical approach to child rearing.* New York: Hart. *The first of the wave of writings by the new humanistic educators of the 1960s.*—448–449, 478–479, 481

Neisser, U. (1976). General, academic, and artificial intelligence. In L. Resnick (Ed.), *The nature of intelligence.* Hillsdale, NJ: Erlbaum.—88

Nelson, K. (1973). Structure and strategy in learning to talk. *Monographs of the Society for Research in Child Development, 38*(149).—129

Nelson, R. D. (1977). Assessment and therapeutic functions of self-monitoring. In M. Hersen, R. M. Eisler, & P. M. Miller (Eds.), *Progress in behavior modification* (Vol. 5). New York: Academic Press.—264

Nesher, P. (1986). Learning mathematics. *American Psychologist, 41,* 1114–1122.—299

Newman, F. B., & Jones, H. E. (1946). The adolescent in social groups. *Applied Psychology Monographs, 9.*—23

Newman, H. H., Freeman, F. N., & Holzinger, K. J. (1937). *Twins: A study of heredity and environment.* Chicago: University of Chicago Press. *One of the few studies of identical twins reared apart, and hence important.*—65

Nickerson, R. S., & Adams, M. J. (1979). Long-term memory for a common object. *Cognitive Psychology, 11,* 287–307.—275–276

Nikleson, L. B. (1984). Nonpromotion, a pseudoscientific solution. *Psychology in the Schools, 21,* 485–495.—660

Nisan, M. (1990, September). *Motivation and school aims: Sense of ought and "identity" aims.* Paper presented at the Conference on Effective and Responsible Teaching, University of Fribourg, Fribourg, Switzerland.—379

Nisbet, R. A. (1967). Conflicting academic loyalties. In C. B. T. Lee (Ed.), *Improving college teaching* (pp. 12–34). Washington, DC: American Council on Education.—398

Nucci, L. P. (1982). Conceptual development in the moral and conventional domains: Implications for values education. *Review of Educational Research, 52,* 93–122.—146

Nungester, R. J., & Duchastel, P. C. (1982). Testing versus review: Effects on retention. *Journal of Educational Psychology, 74,* 18–22.—649

Nuthall, G., & Snook, I. (1973). Contemporary models of teaching. In R. M. W. Travers (Ed.), *Second handbook of research on teaching* (pp. 47–76). Chicago: Rand McNally.—251

Oakes, J. (1985). *Keeping track: How schools structure inequality.* New Haven, CT: Yale University Press.—450

Oakes, J. (1991). *Can tracking research influence school practice?* Paper presented at the meetings of the American Educational Research Association, Chicago.—450

O'Connor, R. D. (1972). Relative efficacy of modeling, shaping, and the combined procedures for modification of social withdrawal. *Journal of Abnormal Psychology, 79,* 327–334.—516

Office of the President. (1951). *A healthy personality for every child: A digest of the fact-finding report to the Midcentury White House Conference on Children and Youth.* Washington, DC: Government Printing Office.—140

Ogbu, J. Y., & Matute-Bianchi, M. E. (1986). Understanding sociocultural factors: Knowledge, identity and school adjustment. In *Beyond language: Social and cultural factors in schooling language minority students.* Los Angeles: California State University at Los Angeles.—82

O'Leary, K. D., & Drabman, R. S. (1971). Token reinforcement programs in the classroom: A review. *Psychological Bulletin, 75,* 379–398.—362

O'Leary, K. D., Kaufman, K. F., Kass, R. E., & Drabman, R. S. (1970). The effects of loud and soft reprimands on the behavior of disruptive students. *Exceptional Children, 37,* 145–155.—514

O'Leary, K. D., & O'Leary, S. G. (Eds.). (1977). *Classroom management: The successful use of behavior modification* (2d ed.). New York: Pergamon Press.—513, 514

O'Leary, S. G., & Dubey, D. R. (1979). Applications of self-control procedures by children: A review. *Journal of Applied Behavior Analysis, 12,* 449–465.—266

Olson, D. R. (1984). "See, jumping!" Some oral antecedents of literacy. In H. Goelman, A. A. Oberg, & F. Smith (Eds.), *Awakening to literacy.* London: Heinemann.—179

Ortiz, A. A., & Yates, J. R. (1983). Incidence of exceptionality among Hispanics: Implications for manpower planning. *National Association of Bilingual Education Journal, 7,* 41–54.—178

Ortony, A. (1975). Why metaphors are necessary and not just nice. *Educational Theory, 24,* 45–53.—287

Oser, F. (1986). Moral education and values education: The discourse perspective. In M. C. Wittrock (Ed.), *Handbook of research on teaching* (3d ed., pp. 917–943). New York: Macmillan.—146, 426

Owen, D. (1985). *None of the above: Behind the myth of scholastic aptitude.* Boston: Houghton Mifflin. *A scathing, populist attack on the Scholastic Aptitude Test, the concept of aptitude, and the process of testing.*—609

Page, E. B. (1958). Teacher comments and student performance: A seventy-four classroom experiment in school motivation. *Journal of Educational Psychology, 49,* 173–181.—369

Paivio, A. (1969). Mental imagery in associated learning and memory. *Psychological Review, 76,* 241–263.—294

Paivio, A. (1971). *Imagery and verbal processes.* New York: Holt, Rinehart & Winston.—279

Paivio, A. (1978). Dual coding: Theoretical issues and empirical evidence. In J. M. Scandura & C. J. Brainard (Eds.), *Structural/process models of complex human behavior.* Leyden, The Netherlands: Sijthoff, Nordhoff.—279

Palincsar, A. S. (1986). Metacognitive strategy instruction. *Exceptional Children, 53,* 118–124.—202

Palincsar, A. S., & Brown, A. L. (1981). *Training comprehension-monitoring skills in an interpretive learning game.* Unpublished manuscript, University of Illinois, Urbana.—311, 313 (fig.)

Paris, S. G., Lawton, T. A., Turner, J. C., & Roth, J. L. (1991). A developmental perspective on standardized achievement testing. *Educational Researcher, 20*(5), 12–20, 40.—598, 609

Paris, S. G., Wixson, K. K., & Palincsar, A. S. (1986). Instructional approaches to reading comprehension. In E. Z. Rothkopf (Ed.), *Review of research in education.* Washington, DC: American Educational Research Association.—301

Pastore, N. (1949). *The nature-nurture controversy.* New York: Kings Crown Press, Columbia University.—62–63

Peel, E. A. (1976). The thinking and education of the adolescent. In V. P. Varma & P. Williams (Eds.), *Piaget, psychology, and education.* Itasca, IL: F. E. Peacock.—116

Pegnato, W., & Birch, J. W. (1959). Locating gifted children in junior high. *Exceptional Children, 26,* 303–304.—216

Perfetti, C. A., & Curtis, M. E. (1986). Reading. In R. F. Dillon & R. J. Sternberg (Eds.), *Cognition and instruction.* New York: Academic Press.—301

Perl, E., & Lambert, W. E. (1962). The relation of bilingualism to intelligence. *Psychological Monographs, 76,* 1–23.—132

Peterson, L. R. (1966). Short-term memory. *Scientific American, 215*(1), 90–95.—275

Peterson, L. R., & Peterson, M. J. (1959). Short-term retention of individual verbal items. *Journal of Experimental Psychology, 58,* 193–198.—276 (fig.)

Peterson, P. L. (1976). Interactive effects of student anxiety, achievement orientation, and teacher behavior on student achievement and attitude. *Journal of Educational Psychology, 69,* 779–792.—218

Peterson, P. L., Clark, C. M., & Dickson, W. P. (1990). Educational psychology as a foundation in teacher education: Reforming an old notion. *Teachers College Record, 91,* 322–346.—289

Petrie, C. R., Jr. (1963). Informative speaking: A summary and bibliography of related research. *Speech Monographs, 30,* 79–91.—409

Petty, M. F., & Field, C. J. (1980). Fluctuations in mental test scores. *Educational Research, 22,* 198–202.—57, 58

Phillips, S. U. (1983). *The invisible culture: Communication in classroom and community on the Warm Springs Indian Reservation.* White Plains, NY: Longman. *Describes how the participant structures in two cultures can be different and clash, yet be practically invisible to the people in each culture.*—137, 170, 174

Piaget, J. (1926). *The language and thought of the child* (M. Worden, Trans.). New York: Harcourt, Brace.—104

Piaget, J. (1928). *Judgment and reasoning in the child* (M. Worden, Trans.). London: Routledge & Kegan Paul.—104

Piaget, J. (1932). *The moral judgment of the child* (M. Worden, Trans.). New York: Harcourt, Brace.—104

Piaget, J. (1951a). *The child's conception of physical causality* (M. Gabain, Trans.). New York: Humanities Press. (Original work published 1930)—104

Piaget, J. (1951b). *Play, dreams and imitation in childhood* (C. Gattegno & F. M. Hodgson, Trans.). London: Heinemann.—108

Piaget, J. (1952). *The origins of intelligence in children* (M. Cook, Trans.). New York: International Universities Press.—107

Pinney, R. H. (1969). *Presentational behaviors related to success in teaching.* Unpublished doctoral dissertation, Stanford University, Stanford, CA.—409, 534

Pittman, T. S., Boggiano, A. K., & Ruble, D. N. (1982). Intrinsic and extrinsic motivational orientations: Interactive effects of reward, competence, feedback, and task complexity. In J. M. Levine & M. C. Wang (Eds.), *Teacher and student perceptions.* Hillsdale, NJ: Erlbaum.—352

Plowden, Lady B., et al. (1967). *Children and their primary schools: A report of the Central Advisory Council for Education.* London: Her Majesty's Stationary Office. *The report that documented and helped spread the revolution in primary school education in England.*—485

Pogrow, F. (1990). *HOTS (higher order thinking skills): A validated thinking skills approach to using computers with students who are at risk.* New York: Scholastic.—474

Polya, G. (1954). *How to solve it.* Princeton, NJ: Princeton University Press. *A mathematician's sprightly attempt to give lay people an introduction to heuristics, or problem solving.*—153

Popham, W. J. (1990). *Modern education measurement.* Englewood Cliffs, NJ: Prentice-Hall.—591, 604

Popham, W. J., & Husek, T. R. (1969). Implications of criterion-referenced measurement. *Journal of Educational Measurement, 6,* 1–9.—575

Pottker, J., & Fishel, A. (Eds.). (1977). *Sex bias in the schools.* Cranburg, NJ: Associated University Presses.—189

Powell, J. P., & Andresen, L. W. (1985). Humour and teaching in higher education. *Studies in Higher Education, 10,* 79–90.—413, 414–415

Powell, R. R., Garcia, J., & Denton, J. J. (1985, March). *The portrayal of minorities and women in selected elementary science series.* Paper presented at the annual meeting of the American Educational Research Association, Chicago.—193

Prawat, R. S. (1989). Promoting access to knowledge, strategy, and disposition in students: A research synthesis. *Review of Educational Research, 59,* 1–41.—292

Premack, D. (1965). Reinforcement theory. In D. Levine (Ed.), *Nebraska Symposium on Motivation* (Vol. 13, pp. 123–180). Lincoln: University of Nebraska Press. –240

Pressey, S. L. (1963). A new look at acceleration. In *Acceleraton and the gifted.* Columbus: Ohio State Department of Education. *A forerunner of the work on mathematically gifted youth.*—217

Pressley, M., Burkell, J., Cariglia-Bull, T., Lysynchuck, L., McGoldrick, J. A., Schneider, B., Snyder, B. L., Symons, S., & Woloshyn, V. E. (1990). *Cognitive strategy instruction.* Cambridge, MA: Brookline. *A practical guide for teachers. Describes in detail the available strategies for increasing learning in reading, mathematics, writing, and other academic subjects.*—302, 303

Pressley, M., Johnson, C. J., Symons, S., McGoldrick, J. A., & Kurita, J. A. (1989). Strategies that improve children's memory and comprehension of text. *Elementary School Journal, 90,* 3–32.—455, 456

Pressley, M., Levin, J. R., & Delaney, H. D. (1982). The mnemonic keyword method. *Review of Educational Research, 52,* 61–91.—296

Pressley, M., Levin, J. R., & McDaniel, M. A. (1987). Remembering versus inferring what a word means: Mnemonic and contextual approaches. In M. McGeown & M. E. Curtis (Eds.), *The nature of vocabulary acquisition* (pp. 107–127). Hillsdale, NJ: Erlbaum.—296

Pressley, M., Woloshyn, V., Lysynchuck, L. M., Martin, V., Wood, E., & Willoughby, T. (1990). A primer of research on cognitive strategy instruction: The important issues and how to address them. *Educational Psychology Review, 2,* 1–58.—302

Price, R. (1989). An historical perspective on the design of computer-assisted instruction: Lessons from the past. *Computers in the Schools, 6,* 145–157.—472

Purkey, S. C., & Smith, M. S. (1983). Effective schools: A review. *The Elementary School Journal, 83,* 427–452. *A critical analysis of the factors that are associated with more and less effective schools.*—378, 511

Quinn, M. E., & Kessler, C. (1986). Bilingual children's cognition and language in science learning. In J. J. Gallagher & G. Dawson (Eds.), *Science education and cultural environments in the Americas* (pp. 32–39). Washington, D.C.: National Science Teachers Association.—136

Raphael, T. E., & Wonnacott, C. A. (1985). Metacognitive train in question-answering strategies: Implementation in a fourth-grade developmental reading program. *Reading Research Quarterly, 20,* 282–296.—301

Rappaport, M. D., Murphy, M. A., & Bailey, J. E. (1982). Ritalin vs. response cost in the control of hyperactive children: A within-subject comparison. *Journal of Applied Behavior Analysis, 15,* 205–216.—250

Rathbone, C. H. (1972). Examining the open education classroom. *School Review, 80,* 521–549.—486

Read, J. (1947). *Humour and humanism in chemistry*. London: Bell.—415

Redfield, D. L., & Rousseau, E. W. (1981). A meta-analysis of experimental research on teacher questioning behavior. *Review of Educational Research, 51*, 237–245.—28, 540

Reed, S. K. (1989). Estimating answers to algebra word problems. *Journal of Experimental Psychology: Learning, Memory, and Cognition, 10*, 778–790.—300

Reimanis, G. (1968). *Social approval and achievement striving in the kindergarten* (Research and Development Memorandum No. 35). Stanford, CA: Stanford Center for Research and Development in Teaching.—369

Reinert, H. R. (1976). *Children in conflict: Educational strategies*. St. Louis: Mosby.—211

Reiser, R. A. (1984). Reducing student procrastination in a personalized system of instruction course. *Educational Communication and Technology: A Journal of Theory, Research, and Development, 32*, 41–49.—463–464

Remmers, H. H., & Gage, N. L. (1943). *Educational measurement and evaluation*. New York: Harper.—628

Resnick, L. B., & Resnick, D. P. (1990). Tests as standards of achievement in schools. In *Proceedings of the 1989 ETS Invitational Conference: The uses of standardized tests in American education* (pp. 63–80). Princeton, NJ: Educational Testing Service. *A criticism of current practices in standardized achievement testing and a sketch of standardized testing approaches that would not have deleterious side effects on curriculum and instruction.*—600, 616

Rest, J., Thoma, S., Volker, J., Yong, L. M., Getz, I., Deemer, D., & Berndt, T. (1985, March). *Research on moral development*. Symposium presented at the meetings of the American Educational Research Association, Chicago.—144, 145

Riley, M. S., Greeno, J. G., & Heller, J. I. (1983). Development of children's problem-solving ability in mathematics. In H. P. Ginsburg (Ed.), *The development of mathematical thinking*. New York: Academic Press.—46, 299

Rimland, B. (1990). Personal communication to N. L. Gage, October 2.—248

Ringness, T. A. (1965). Affective differences between successful and non-successful bright ninth-grade boys. *Personnel and Guidance Journal, 43*, 600–606.—331

Ripple, R. E., & May, F. B. (1962). Caution in comparing creativity and IQ. *Psychological Reports, 10*, 229–230.—151

Rist, R. C. (1973). *The urban school: A factory for failure*. Cambridge; MIT Press. *An ethnography of school life over three years for some disadvantaged youth. Depressing descriptions of schooling!*—14

Rogers, C. (1959). Significant learning: In therapy and education. *Educational Leadership, 16*, 232–242.—477

Rogers, C. (1969). *Freedom to learn*. Columbus, OH: Merrill. *The major statement on education by one of the most articulate of the humanistic psychologists.*—479, 482, 483, 485

Rohrkemper, M. M. (1986). The functions of inner speech in elementary school students' problem-solving behavior. *American Educational Research Journal, 23*, 303–314.—360–361

Rohwer, W. D., Jr. (1972). Decisive research: A means for answering fundamental questions about instruction. *Educational Researcher, 1*(7), 5–11.—294

Romberg, T. A., & Collis, K. F. (1987). Different ways children have to add and subtract. *Journal for Research in Mathematics Education*, Monograph 2.—299

Root, A. A. (1970). What instructors say to the students makes a difference. *Engineering Education, 61* 722–725.—333

Rosenbaum, J. E. (1980). Social implications of educational grouping. In D. C. Berliner (Ed.), *Review of research in education* (Vol. 8). Itasca, IL: F. E. Peacock.—450

Rosenbaum, M. S., & Drabman, R. S. (1979). Self-control training in the classroom: A review and critique. *Journal of Applied Behavior Analysis, 12*, 467–485.—264, 266

Rosenberg, R. (1987). A critical analysis of research on intelligent tutoring systems. *Educational Technology, 27*(11), 7–13.—476

Rosenberg, M., & Simmons, R. G. (1973). *Black and white self-esteem: The urban school child*. Washington, DC: American Sociological Association.—158

Rosenholtz, S. J., & Simpson, C. (1984). Classroom organization and student stratification. *The Elementary School Journal, 85*, 21 38.—345

Rosenshine, B. V. (1971a). Objectively measured behavioral predictors of effectiveness in explaining. In I. D. Westbury & A. A. Bellack (Eds.), *Research into classroom processes* (pp. 51–98). New York: Teachers College Press.—408, 409, 412

Rosenshine, B. V. (1971b). *Teaching behaviours and student achievement*. London: National Foundation for Educational Research in England and Wales. *Brings together, clusters, and summarizes about fifty studies.*—415, 428, 535, 547, 549

Rosenshine, B. V. (1980). How time is spent in elementary classrooms. In C. Denham & A. Lieberman (Eds.), *Time to learn*. Washington, DC: National Institute of Education.—497, 555, 559, 560

Rosenshine, B. V. (1991). *The use of scaffolds for teaching higher-level cognitive strategies*. Urbana: Bureau of Educational Research, University of Illinois.—522–523

Rosenshine, B. V., & Stevens, R. (1986). Teaching functions. In M. C. Wittrock (Ed.), *Handbook of research on teaching* (3d ed., pp. 376–391). New York: Macmillan.—355

Rosenthal, R., & Jacobson, L. (1968). *Pygmalion in the classroom*. New York: Holt, Rinehart & Winston.—73

Ross, J., & Lawrence, K. A. (1968). Some observations on memory artifice. *Psychonomic Science, 13*, 107–108.—295–296

Ross, M., & Salvia, J. (1975). Attractiveness as a biasing factor in teacher judgments. *American Journal of Mental Deficiency, 80*, 96–98.—519

Roth, V. J., & Anderson, C. W. (1990). Promoting conceptual change learning from science textbooks. In P. Romsden (Ed.), *Improving learning: New perspectives*. New York: Nichols.—301

Rothenberg, J. (1989). The open classroom reconsidered. *Elementary School Journal, 90*, 69–86.—486, 492, 497

Rowe, M. B. (1974). Wait-time and rewards as instructional variables, their influence on language, logic, and fate control, Pt. 1: Wait-time. *Journal of Research in Science Teaching, 11*, 81–94.—541–542, 545

Royce, J. (1891). Is there a science of education? *Education Review, 1*, 15–25, 121–132.—28

Royer, J. M., Hambleton, R. K., & Cadorette, L. (1978). Individual differences in memory: Theory, data and educational implications. *Contemporary Educational Psychology, 3*, 182–203.—277

Ruble, D. N. (1980). A developmental perspective on theories of achievement motivation. In L. J. Fyans, Jr. (Ed.), *Achievement motivation*. New York: Plenum Press.—337

Rumelhart, D. E. (1980). Schemata: The building blocks of cognition. In R. J. Spiro, B. C. Bruce, & W. F. Brewer (Eds.), *Theoretical issues in reading comprehension*. Hillsdale, NJ: Erlbaum.—286

Rumelhart, D. E., & Ortony, A. (1977). The representation of knowledge in memory. In R. C. Anderson, R. J. Spiro, & W. E. Montague (Eds.), *Schooling and the acquisition of knowledge* (pp. 99–135). Hillsdale, NJ: Erlbaum.—284

Russell, W. A., & Storms, L. H. (1955). Implicit verbal chaining in paired-associate learning. *Journal of Experimental Psychology, 49*, 287–293.—281

Rutter, M., Maughan, B., Mortimore, P., & Ouston, J. (with A. Smith).(1979). *Fifteen thousand hours: Secondary schools and their effects on children*. London: Open Books. *A widely noted and influential multiyear study of London schools that yielded evidence suggesting how differences among schools are associated with differences in students' achievement and attitudes.*—378, 511

Ryans, D. G. (1960). *Characteristics of teachers*. Washington, DC: American Council on Education. *Factor analyses of ratings of teacher and student behavior; still one of the most comprehensive and careful studies of teaching.*—547

Sadker, M., Sadker, D., & Klein, S. (1991). The issue of gender in elementary and secondary education. In G. Grant (Ed.), *Review of Research in Education, 17*, 265–334.—182, 186, 193

Sadker, M. P., & Sadker, D. M. (1982). *Sex equality handbook for schools*. White Plains, NY: Longman.—193, 194, 195–196

Safran, S. P., & Safran, J. S. (1984). Elementary teachers' tolerance of problem behaviors. *The Elementary School Journal, 85*, 287–243.—511

Sailor, W., & Guess, D. (1983). *Severely handicapped students: An instructional design*. Boston: Houghton Mifflin.— 209, 210

St. John, N. (1975). *School desegregation outcomes for children*. New York: Wiley.—158

Salili, F., Maehr, M. L., Sorensen, R. L., & Fyans, L. J., Jr. (1976). A further consideration of the effects of evaluation on motivation. *American Educational Research Journal, 13*, 85–102.—371

Saloman, G., & Globerson, T. (1987). *Skill is not enough: The role of mindfulness in learning and transfer* (Rep. No. 11). Tel Aviv: Tel Aviv University, School of Education, Unit for Communication and Computer Research in Education.—321

Salomon, G., & Perkins, D. N. (1989). Rocky roads to transfer: Rethinking mechanisms of a neglected phenomenon. *Educational Researcher, 19*, 2–10.—321

Salvia, J., Sheare, J., & Algozzine, B. (1975). Facial attractiveness and personal-social development. *Journal of Abnormal Child Psychology, 3*, 171–178.—520

Sandoval, J., & Hughes, G. P. (1981). *Success in nonpromoted first-grade children*. Davis: Department of Education, University of California.—661

Sarason, S. B., Lighthall, F.F., Davidson, K. S., Waite, R. R., & Ruebush, B. K. (1960). *Anxiety* *in elementary school children.* New York: Wiley.— 159

Sato, I. (1982).   *Catalog of educational materials for gifted/talented.* Ventura, CA: National/State Leadership Training Institute on Gifted and Talented, Ventura County Superintendent of Schools Office.— 217

Saxe, G. (1988).   Candy selling and math learning. *Educational Researcher, 17,* 14–21.—300

Scandura, J. M., & Scandura, A. B. (1980).   *Structural learning and concrete operations.* New York: Praeger.—118

Scarr, S., & Weinberg, R. A. (1976).   IQ test performances of black children adopted by white families. *American Psychologist, 31,* 726–739.—91

Scheirer, M. A., & Kraut, R. E. (1979).   Increasing educational achievement via self-concept change. *Review of Educational Research, 49,* 131–150.—159

Schiff, M., Duymé, M., Dumaret, A., Stewart, J., Tomkiewicz, S., & Feingold, J. (1978).   Intellectual status of working-class children adopted early into upper-middle-class families. *Science, 200,* 1503–1504.—92

Schiff, M., Duymé, M., Dumaret, A., & Tomkiewicz, S. (1982).   How much could we boost scholastic achievement and IQ scores? A direct answer from a French adoption study. *Cognition, 12,* 165–196.— 92

Schlaefli, A., Rest, J. R., & Thoma, S. J. (1985). Does moral education improve moral judgment? A meta-analysis of intervention studies using the Defining Issues Test. *Review of Educational Research, 55,* 319–352.—146

Schmelkin, L. P. (1981).   Teachers' and nonteachers' attitudes toward mainstreaming. *Exceptional Children, 48,* 42–47.—201

Schmidt, G. W., & Ulrich, R. E. (1969).   Effects of group contingent events upon classroom noise. *Journal of Applied Behavior Analysis, 2,* 171–179.—245

Schmuck, R. A., & Schmuck, P. A. (1971).   *Group processes in the classroom.* Dubuque, IA: William C. Brown.—429

Schneider, W., Körkel, J., & Weinert, F. E. (1989). Domain-specific knowledge and memory performance: A comparison of high- and low-aptitude children. *Journal of Educational Psychology, 81,* 306–312.—61

Schultz, C. C., & Sherman, R. H. (1976).   Social class, development, and differences in reinforcer effectiveness. *Review of Educational Research, 46,* 25–59.—355

Schultz, J. J., Florio, S., & Erickson, F. (1982). Where's the floor? Aspects of cultural organization of social relationships in communication at home and in school. In P. Gilmore & A. A. Glatthorn (Eds.), *Children in and out of school.* Washington, DC: Center for Applied Linguistics.—137

Schunk, D. C. (1981).   Modeling and attributional effects on children's achievement: A self-efficacy analysis. *Journal of Educational Psychology, 73,* 93–105.— 260

Schutz, W. C. (1967).   *Joy: Expanding human awareness.* New York: Grove Press.—485

Schwarzer, R. (1982).   Worry and emotionality as separate components in test anxiety. *International Review of Applied Psychology, 33,* 205–220.—161

Scollon, R., & Scollon, S. B. K. (1981).   *Narrative, literacy, and face in interethnic communication.* Norwood, NJ: Ablex.—173, 174

Scott, K. P. (1980).   Sexist and non-sexist materials. What impact do they have? *Elementary School Journal, 81,* 47–52.—194

Segal, J. W., Chipman, S. F., & Glaser, R. (Eds.). (1985).   *Thinking and learning skills* (Vol. 1). Hillsdale, NJ: Erlbaum.—304

Seibert, L. C. (1932).   A series of experiments on the learning of French vocabulary. *Johns Hopkins University Studies in Education, 18.*—290

Semmel, M., Gottlieb, J., & Robinson, N. M. (1979). Mainstreaming: Perspective on educating handicapped children in the public schools. In D. C. Berliner (Ed.), *Review of research in education* (Vol. 7). Washington, DC: American Educational Research Association.—201

Serpell, R. (1979).   How specific are perceptual skills? A cross-cultural study of pattern reproduction. *British Journal of Psychology, 70,* 365–380.—175

Sexton, P. O. (1965).   Schools are emasculating our boys. *Saturday Review, 48,* 57.—192

Sharan, S., Russell, P., Hertz-Lazarowitz, R., Bejarano, Y., Raviv, S., & Sharan, Y. (1984).   *Cooperative learning in the classroom: Research in desegregated schools.* Hillsdale, NJ: Erlbaum.—443

Shavelson, R. J. (1987).   Teacher planning. In M. J. Dunkin (Ed.), *International encyclopedia of teaching and teacher education* (pp. 483–486). Oxford: Pergamon Press.—505

Shavelson, R. J., Hubner, J. J., & Stanton, G. C. (1976).   Self-concept: Validation of construct interpretations. *Review of Educational Research, 46,* 407–441.—158 (fig.)

Shavelson, R. J., & Stern, P. (1981).   Research on teachers' pedagogical thoughts, judgments, decisions, and behavior. *Review of Educational Research, 51,* 455–498.—505

Shepard, L. A. (1979). Norm-referenced and criterion-referenced tests. *Educational Horizons, 58,* 26–32.—575

Shepard, L. A., Smith, M. L., & Vojir, C. P. (1983). Characteristics of pupils identified as learning disabled. *American Educational Research Journal, 20,* 309–331.—205

Shepard, R. N. (1967). Recognition memory for words, sentences, and pictures. *Journal of Verbal Learning and Verbal Behavior, 6,* 156–163.—294

Shepard, L. A. (in press). Psychometricians' beliefs about learning. *Educational Researcher.*—600

Sherman, J. (1978). *Sex-related cognitive differences.* Springfield, IL: Charles C Thomas.—184

Sherwood, J. J., & Nataupsky, M. (1968). Predicting the conclusions of Negro-white intelligence research from biographical characteristics of the investigaor. *Journal of Personality and Social Psychology, 8*(1, Pt. 1), 53–58.—63

Shields, J. (1962). *Monozygotic twins brought up apart and brought up together.* London: Oxford University Press.—65

Shoenfeld, A. H. (1985). *Mathematical problem solving.* Orlando, FL: Academic Press.—300

Short, E. J., & Ryan, E. B. (1984). Metacognitive differences between skilled and less skilled readers: Remediating deficits through story grammar and attribution training. *Journal of Educational Psychology, 76,* 225–235.—303

Shuey, A. (1966). *The testing of Negro intelligence* (2d ed.). New York: Social Science Press.—79

Shulman, Lawrence (1970). The hidden group in the classroom. *Learning and Development, 2*(3), 1–6. (McGill University, Montreal)—429, 438

Shulman, Lee S. (1986). Those who understand: Knowledge growth in teaching. *Educational Researcher, 15,* 4–14.—521

Shulman, Lee S. (1987). Knowledge and teaching: Foundations for the new reform. *Harvard Educational Review, 57,* 1–22.—391

Shutes, R. E. (1969). *Verbal behaviors and instructional effectiveness.* Unpublished doctoral dissertation, Stanford University, Stanford, CA.—418

Siegel, L., Siegel, L. C., Capretta, P. J., Jones, R. L., & Berkowitz, H. (1963). Students' thoughts during class: A criterion for educational research. *Journal of Educational Psychology, 54,* 45–51.—390

Siegler, R. S. (1985). Encoding and the development of problem solving. In S. F. Chipman, J. W. Segal, & R. Glaser (Eds.), *Thinking and learning skills* (Vol. 2). Hillsdale, NJ: Erlbaum.—305

Siegler, R. S. (1991). *Children's thinking* (2d ed.). Englewood Cliffs, NJ: Prentice Hall. *An authoritative presentation of the major theories, and accompanying data, on the growth of cognition.*—117, 118

Sigel, I. E., Anderson, L. M., & Shapiro, H. (1966). Categorization behavior of lower- and middle-class Negro pre-school children: Differences in dealing with representation of familiar objects. *Journal of Negro Education, 35,* 218–229.—175

Silberman, C. E. (1970). *Crisis in the classroom.* New York: Random House. *A critique of American education; gave impetus to the "open classroom" movement.*—482, 485

Silberman, C. E. (Ed.). (1973). *The open classroom reader.* New York: Vintage.—487

Silver, E. (1991). *The reconceptualization of assessment in mathematics.* Paper presented at the annual meeting of the American Educational Research Association, Chicago.—629

Silverman, L. K. (1980, October-November). *How are gifted teachers different from other teachers?* Paper presented at the meetings of the National Association for Gifted Children, Denver.—155

Simmons, W. (1979). The effects of cultural salience of test materials on social class and ethnic differences in cognitive performance. *The Quarterly Newsletter of the Laboratory of Comparative Human Cognition, 1.* 43–47.—175

Skinner, B. F. (1953). *Science and human behavior.* New York: Macmillan. *The first brave statement of the ways in which operant conditioning can be used in solving many human problems, including those in education.*—233

Skinner, B. F. (1954). The science of learning and the art of teaching. *Harvard Educational Review, 24,* 86–97. *The paper that started the programmed-instruction movement.*—470

Skinner, B. F. (1957). *Verbal behavior.* New York: Appleton-Century-Crofts.—273

Skinner, B. F. (1968). *The technology of teaching.* Appleton-Century-Crofts. *A full treatment of the achievements and promises of operant conditioning for improving instruction.*—398

Skinner, B. F. (1973). The free and happy student. *Phi Delta Kappan, 55*(1), 13–16.—488

Skinner, B. F. (1987). *A statement on punishment.* Cambridge, MA: The Author, Harvard University.—248–249

Skodak, M., & Skeels, H. M. (1949). A final follow-up study of one hundred adopted children. *Journal of Genetic Psychology, 75,* 85–125.—66

Slavin, R. E. (1983). *Cooperative learning.* White Plains. NY: Longman. *A clear presentation of a technology that usually accomplishes many goals— academic and social. Written by one of the major theorists and developers of this method.*—443–446

Slavin, R. E. (1984). Students motivating students to excel: Cooperative incentives, cooperative tasks, and student achievement. *Elementary School Journal, 85,* 53–64.—345

Slavin, R. E. (1987). Mastery learning reconsidered. *Review of Educational Research, 57,* 175–213.—461, 462

Slavin, R. E. (1990). Mastery learning re-reconsidered. *Review of Educational Research, 60,* 300–302.—462

Slobin, D. I. (1970). *Suggested universals in the ontogenesis of grammar* (Working Paper No. 32). Berkeley: University of California Language-Behavior Research Laboratory.—128

Slobin, D. I. (1972). Seven questions about language development. In P. C. Dodwell (Ed.), *New horizons in psychology* (No. 2, pp. 197–215). Baltimore: Penguin.—130t

Smedslund, J. (1961). The acquisition of conservation of substance and weight in children. *Scandinavian Journal of Psychology, 2,* 1–10, 71–84, 85–87, 153–160, 203–210.—112

Smith, L. R., & Cotten, M. L. (1980). Effect of lesson vagueness and discontinuity on student achievement and attitudes. *Journal of Educational Psychology, 72,* 670–675.—410–411, 534

Smith, M. L. (1982). *How educators decide who is learning disabled.* Springfield, IL: Charles C Thomas.—205, 207

Smith, M. L. (1991). Put to the test: The effects of external testing on teachers. *Educational Researcher, 20 (5),* 8–11.—613–615

Smith, M. L., & Shepard, L. A. (1988). Kindergarten readiness and retention: A qualitative study of teachers' beliefs and practices. *American Educational Research Journal, 25,* 307–333.—661

Smith, M. P. (1972). He only does it to annoy . . . In S. B. Anderson (Ed.), *Sex differences and discrimination in education.* Worthington, OH: Charles A. Jones.—190

Smith, N., Greenlaw, M., & Scott, C. (1987, January). Making the literate environment equitable. *Reading Teacher,* 400–407.—194

Snell, M. E. (Ed.). (1978). *Systematic instruction of the moderately and severely handicapped.* Columbus, OH: Merrill.—209

Snow, R. E. (1977). Research on aptitude for learning. In L. S. Shulman (Ed.), *Review of research in education* (Vol. 4). Itasca, IL: F. E. Peacock.—218

Snow, R. E., & Yalow, E. (1982). Education and intelligence. In R. J. Sternberg (Ed.), *Handbook of human intelligence.* New York: Cambridge University Press.—101

Snyderman, M., & Rothman, S. (1987). Survey of expert opinion on intelligence and aptitude testing. *American Psychologist, 42,* 137–144.—52, 53, 67

Snygg, D. (1938). The relation between the intelligence of mothers and of their children living in foster homes. *Journal of Genetic Psychology, 52,* 401–406.—66, 67

Soar, R. S. (1966). *An integrative approach to classroom learning.* Philadelphia: College of Education, Temple University.—535, 544

Soar, R. S. (1973). *Final report: Follow-Through classroom process measurement and pupil growth, 1970–1971.* Gainesville: Institute for the Development of Human Resources, University of Florida.—535, 558, 559

Solnit, A. J. (1979). The adolescent's search for competence. *Children Today, 8*(6), 13–15, 40.—140

Sommer, R. (1967). Classroom ecology. *Journal of Applied Behavioral Science, 3,* 489–503.—427

Sontag, E. (Ed.). (1977). *Educational programming for the severely and profoundly handicapped.* Reston, VA: Council for Exceptional Children.—209

Spaulding, R. L. (1965). *Achievement, creativity, and self-concept correlates of teacher-pupil transactions in elementary schools.* Hempstead, NY: Hofstra University.—544

Speeth, K., & Margulies, S. (1969). Techniques for maintaining student motivation. *National Society for Programmed Instruction Journal, 8,* 24–27.—373

Spence, J. T., & Helmreich, R. L. (1978). *Masculinity and feminity.* Austin: University of Texas.—182, 187

Sperling, M. (1988). *I want to talk to each of you: Writing conference discourse and individualizing the process of learning to write.* Paper presented at the annual meeting of the American Educational Research Association. (ERIC Document Reproduction Service No. ED 299590).—458

Spielberg, C. D. (Ed.). (1966). *Anxiety and behavior.* New York: Academic Press.—159, 160

Squire, L. R. (1987). *Memory and brain.* New York: Oxford University Press.—280

Stader, E., Colyar, T., & Berliner, D. C. (1990). *Expert and novice teachers' ability to judge student understanding.* Paper presented at the meeting of the American Educational Research Association, Boston.—621

Stafford, R. E. (1972). Hereditary and environmental components of quantitative reasoning. *Review of Educational Research, 42,* 183–201.—184

Staines, J. W. (1956). Self-picture as a factor in the classroom. *British Journal of Psychology, 28,* 97–111.—158

Stallings, J. A., & Kaskowitz, D. (1974). *Follow-Through classroom observation evaluation, 1972–73.* Menlo Park, CA: Stanford Research Institute.—537, 558, 559

Stallings, J. A., & Keepes, B. D. (1970). *Student aptitudes and methods of teaching beginning reading: A predictive instrument for determining interaction patterns.* (Final Rep., OEG–9–70–0005, Project No. 9–1–099). Washington, DC: Department of Health, Education, and Welfare, Office of Education, Bureau of Research.—218

Stanford Achievement Test: 7th edition. (1986). New York: Harcourt Brace Jovanovich.—595 (fig.)

Starr, J. W. (1978). Discipline and corporal punishment in schools: A longitudinal study of the attitudes of a group of student and probationary teachers. *Research in Education, 19,* 67–75.—515

Stayrook, N. G., Corno, L., & Winne, P. H. (1978). Path analyses relating student perceptions of teacher behavior to student achievement. *Journal of Teacher Education, 29,* 51–56.—536

Stein, A. H. (1969). The influence of social reinforcement on the achievement of fourth-grade boys and girls. *Child Development, 40,* 727–736.—369

Stein, A. H. (1971). The effects of sex-role standards for achievement and sex-role preference on three determinants of achievement motivation. *Developmental Psychology, 4,* 219–231.—187

Stein, A. H., & Bailey, M. M. (1973). Achievement orientation in females. *Psychological Bulletin, 80,* 345–366.—187, 188

Stein, A. H., Pohly, S. R., & Mueller, E. (1971). The influence of masculine, feminine and neutral tasks on children's achievement behavior, expectancies of success, and attainment values. *Child Development, 42,* 195–207.—187

Stephan, W. G., & Rosenfield, D. (1979). Black self-rejection: Another look. *Journal of Educational Psychology, 71,* 708–716.—158

Stephens, T. M. (1977). *Teaching skills to children with learning and behavior disorders.* Columbus, OH: Merrill.—207

Sternberg, R. J. (1982). Reasoning, problem solving, and intelligence. In R. J. Sternberg (Ed.), *Handbook of human intelligence.* New York: Cambridge University Press.—74

Sternberg, R. J. (1985). Instrumental and componential approaches to the nature and training of intelligence. In S. F. Chipman, J. W. Segal, & R. Glaser (Eds.), *Thinking and learning skills* (Vol. 2). Hillsdale, NJ: Erlbaum.—74

Sternberg, R. J., Conway, B. E., Ketron, J. L., & Bernstein, M. (1981). People's conceptions of intelligence. *Journal of Personality and Social Psychology, 41,* 37–55. *How to find out what the man or woman in the street thinks intelligence is—and what that turns out to be.*—53

Sternberg, R. J., & Detterman, D. K. (Eds.). (1986). *What is intelligence?* Norwood, NJ: Ablex.—52

Stevenson, H. W., Lee, S. Y., & Stigler, J. W. (1986). Mathematics achievement of Chinese, Japanese, and American children. *Science, 231,* 693–699.—94

Stevenson, H. W., & Siegel, A. (1969). Effects of instruction and age on retention of filmed content. *Journal of Educational Psychology, 60,* 71–74.—413

Stewart, L. G., & White, M. A. (1976). Teacher comments, letter grades, and student performance: What do we really know? *Journal of Educational Psychology, 68,* 488–500.—369

Stewart, N. (1947). A.G.C.T. scores of army personnel groups by occupations. *Occupations, 26,* 5–41.—61

Stiggins, R. J. (1987). Design and development of performance assessments. *Educational and Psychological Measurement, 6 (3),* 33–42.—631

Stiggins, R. J., Backland, P. M., & Bridgeford, N. J. (1985). Avoiding bias in the assessment of communication skills. *Communication Education, 34,* 135–141.—632

Stiggins, R. J., Conklin, N. F., Green, K. R., and Brady, C. (in press). *Classroom Assessment: A Task Analysis.* White Plains, NY: Longman.—659

Stigler, J. W., Lee, S., & Stevenson, H. W. (1987). Mathematics classrooms in Japan, Taiwan, and the United States. *Child Development, 58,* 1272–1285.—560–561

Stipek, D. J. (1988). *Motivation to learn.* Englewood Cliffs, NJ: Prentice Hall. *A short but scholarly and practical guide to the field of motivation.*—353

Stodolsky, S. S., Ferguson, T. L., & Wimpelberg, K. (1981). The recitation persists, but what does it look like? *Journal of Curriculum Studies, 13,* 121–130.—495, 496, 498, 499 (fig.), 501*t*

Subkoviak, M. J. (1980). Decision-consistency approaches. In R. A. Berk (Ed.), *Criterion-referenced measurement: The state of the art.* Baltimore: Johns Hopkins University Press.—580

Sulzer-Azaroff, B. (1981). Issues and trends in behavior modification in the classroom. In S. W. Bijou & R. Ruiz (Eds.), *Behavior modification: Contributions to education.* Hillsdale, NJ: Erlbaum.—246

Sulzer-Azaroff, B., & Mayer, G. R. (1977). *Applying behavior analysis procedures with children and youth.* New York: Holt, Rinehart & Winston.—232, 246

Sulzer-Azaroff, B., & Mayer, G. R. (1986). *Achieving educational excellence.* New York: Holt, Rinehart & Winston. *One of the clearest applications of the technology of operant conditioning to contemporary school problems. A wide-ranging book based on a single theoretical position.*—211, 243

Suppes, P. (1966). The uses of computers in education. *Scientific American, 215*(3), 206–220.—473

Sutherland, M. (1981). *Sex bias in education.* Oxford: Basil Blackwell.—193

Svensson, A. (1971). *Relative achievement: School performance in relation to intelligence, sex, and home environment.* Stockholm: Almqvist & Wiksell.—183

Swanson, R. A., & Henderson, R. W. (1977). Effects of televised modeling and active participation on rule-governed question production among Native American preschool children. *Contemporary Educational Psychology, 2,* 345–352.—259

Sweezy, R. W. (1981). *Individual performance assessment: An approach to criterion-referenced test development.* Reston, VA: Reston.—580

Sykes, K. (1972). Print reading for visually handicapped children. *Education of the Visually Handicapped, 4,* 71–75.—214

Takanishi-Knowles, R. (1973). *Relationships among instructional group size, student engagement, and teacher strategies.* Unpublished doctoral dissertation, Stanford University, Stanford, CA.—427

Taylor, M., & Ortony, A. (1980). Rhetorical devices in black English: Some psycholinguistic and educational observations. *The Quarterly Newsletter of the Laboratory of Comparative Human Cognition, 2*(2), 4–6.—179

***Television and behavior: Ten years of scientific progress and implications for the eighties: Vol. 1. Summary report.* (1982).** Rockville, MD: National Institute of Mental Health.—262

Terman, L. M., assisted by others. (1925). Mental and physical traits of a thousand gifted children. In L. M. Terman (Ed.), *Genetic studies of genius* (Vol. 1). Stanford, CA: Stanford University Press.—216

Terwilliger, J. S. (1971). *Assigning grades to students.* Glenview, IL: Scott, Foresman.—662

Tharp, R. G., & Gallimore, R. (1988). *Rousing minds to life: Teaching, learning, and schooling in social context.* New York: Cambridge University Press.—553–555

Thistlethwaite, D. L., deHaan, H., & Kamenetzky, J. (1955). The effects of "directive" and "nondirective" communication procedures on attitudes. *Journal of Abnormal and Social Psychology, 51,* 107–118.—398

Thompson, E. (1960). An experimental investigation of the relative effectiveness of organizational structure in oral communication. *Southern Speech Journal, 26,* 59–69.—398–399

Thompson, L. (1951). *Personality and government: Findings and recommendations of the Indian Administration research.* Mexico: Ediciones del Instituto Indigenista Americano.—178

Thoresen, C. E. (1972). Behavioral humanism. In C. E. Thoresen (Ed.), *Behavior modification in education: Seventy-second yearbook of the National Society for the Study of Education* (Pt. 1, pp. 385–421). Chicago: University of Chicago Press.—252, 362

Thorndike, E. L. (1913). *Educational psychology,* Vol. 2: *The psychology of learning.* New York: Bureau of Publications, Teachers College, Columbia University. *Historically important in helping to silence the formal-discipline advocates, by one of the great men of the field.*—307

Thorndike, E. L. (1939). *Your city.* New York: Harcourt, Brace.—24

Thorndike, E. L., & Woodworth, R. S. (1901). The influence of improvement in one mental function upon the efficiency of other functions. *Psychological Review, 8,* 247–261, 384–395, 553–564.—307

Thorndike, R. L. (1963). *The concepts of over- and underachievement.* New York: Bureau of Publications, Teachers College, Columbia University.—330

Thyne, J. M. (1963). *The psychology of learning and techniques of teaching.* London: University of London Press.—407

Tieger, T. (1980). On the biological basis of sex differences in aggression. *Child Development, 51,* 943–983.—186

Tierney, R. J. (1985). Self-regulating learning from text: Teaching procedures. In A. Bergen & H. A. Robinson (Eds.), *Secondary school reading: What research reveals for classroom practice.* Urbana, IL: National Council of Teachers of English/National Council for Research in English.—312

Tobias, S. (1979). Anxiety research in educational psychology. *Journal of Educational Psychology, 71,* 573–582.—161

Tobias, S. (1989). Using computers to study consistency of cognitive processing of instruction. *Computers in Human Behavior, 5,* 107–118.—303

Tobin, J. J., Wu, D. Y. H., & Davidson, D. H. (1989). *Preschool in three cultures: Japan, China, and the United States.* New Haven: Yale University Press. *An exemplary cross-national comparison with an accompanying videotape. The societies are clearly seen to have different views of childhood and schooling.*—170

Tobin, K. G. (1987). The role of wait-time in higher-cognitive-level learning. *Review of Educational Research, 57,* 69–95.—542

Tobin, K. G., & Capie, W. (1982). Relationships between classroom process variables and middle-school science achievement. *Journal of Educational Psychology, 74,* 441–454.—542

Torrance, E. P. (1962). Developing creative thinking through school experience. In S. J. Parnes & H. P. Harding (Eds.), *A source book for creative thinking.* New York: Scribner.—153, 154

Torrance, E. P. (1967). The Minnesota studies of creative behavior: National and international extensions. *Journal of Creative Behavior, 1*(2), 137–154.—151

Torrance, E. P. (1986). Teaching creative and gifted learners. In M. C. Wittrock (Ed.), *Handbook of research on teaching* (3d ed., pp. 630–647.). New York: Macmillan.—156

Trachtenberg, D. (1974). Student tasks in text material: What cognitive skills do they tap? *Peabody Journal of Education, 52,* 54–57.—45

Trudewind, C., & Kohne, W. (1982). Bezugsnorm-Orientierung der Lehrer und motiventwicklung: Zusammenhange mit Schulleistung, Intelligenz und Merkmalen der Hauslichen Unwelt in der Grundschulzeit. In F. Reinberg (Ed.), *Bezugsnormen zur Schulleistrungsbewertung: Analyse und Invervoution.* Dusseldorf: Schwann.—346 (fig.)

Tryon, G. S. (1980). The measurement and treatment of test anxiety. *Review of Educational Research, 50,* 343–372.—161

Tuddenham, R. D., & McBride, P. (1959). The yielding experiment from the subject's point of view. *Journal of Personality, 27,* 259–271.—437

Turiel, E. (1966). An experimental test of the sequentiality of developmental stages in the child's moral judgments. *Journal of Personality and Social Psychology, 3,* 611–618.—146

Turiel, E. (1973). Stage transition in moral development. In R. M. W. Travers (Ed.), *Second handbook of research on teaching* (pp. 732–758). Chicago: Rand McNally.—144

Twyford, L. C., Jr. (1969). Educational communications media. In R. L. Ebel, V. H. Noll, & R. M. Bauer (Eds.), *Encyclopedia of educational research* (4th ed., pp. 367–380). New York: Macmillan.—413

Tyler, L. E. (1965). *The psychology of human differences* (3d ed.). New York: Appleton-Century-Crofts.—84

Tyler, R. W. (1934). *Constructing achievement tests.* Columbus: Ohio State University. *The pioneer treatment of the role of objectives in the construction of achievement tests, especially tests of complex kinds of achievement.*—277, 278 (fig.)

Tyler, R. W. (1964). Some persistent questions on the defining of objectives. In C. M. Lindvall (Ed.), *Defining educational objectives.* (pp. 77–83). Pittsburgh: University of Pittsburgh Press.—34

Tzeng, O. J. L. (1974). *The next-in-line effect on sentence memory.* Paper presented at the meetings of the American Educational Research Association, Chicago.—440

Underwood, B. J., & Schulz, R. W. (1960). *Meaningfulness and verbal learning.* Philadelphia: Lippincott.—281

U.S. Department of Education. (1989). *Eleventh annual report to Congress on the implementation of Public Law 99–142: The Education of the Handicapped Act.* Washington, DC: U.S. Government Printing Office.—200 (fig.)

U.S. General Accounting Office. (1987). *Bilingual education. A new look at the research evidence.* Washington, DC: Author.—133

U.S. Surgeon General. (1979). *Smoking and health: A report of the Surgeon General* (Stock No. 017–000–00218–0). Washington, DC: Superintendent of Documents, U.S. Government Printing Office.—27

Vandenburg, S. G., & Kuse, A. R. (1979). Space ability: A critical review of the sex-linked major gene hypothesis. In M. A. Wittig & A. C. Peterson (Eds.),

Sex-related differences in cognitive functioning. New York: Academic Press.—184

Van der Will, C. (1976).   The wording of spoken instructions to children and its effect on their performance of tasks. *Educational Studies, 2,* 193–199.—408

Van Riper, C. (1978).   *Speech correction: Principles and methods* (6th ed.). Englewood Cliffs, NJ: Prentice-Hall.—208

Varley, W. H., Levin, J. R., Severson, R. A., & Wolff, P. (1974).   Training imagery production in young children through motor involvement. *Journal of Educational Psychology, 66,* 262–266.—295

Verner, C., & Dickinson, G. (1967).   The lecture: An analysis and review of research. *Adult Education, 17*(2), 85–100.—390

Vernon, M. (1968).   Fifty years of research on the intelligence of deaf and hard of hearing children: A review of literature and discussion of complications. *Journal of Rehabilitation of the Deaf, 1,* 1–12.—213

Vygotsky, L. S. (1978).   *Mind in society: The development of higher psychological processes* (M. Cole, V. John-Steiner, S. Scribner, & E. Souberman, Eds. and Trans.). Cambridge: Harvard University Press.—122, 167, 181

Vygotsky, L. S. (1986).   *Thought and language.* Cambridge, MA: MIT Press. *Major work of the author whose insights are beginning to be recognized as important.*—123

Wade, S. E., Trathen, W., & Schraw, G. (1990).   An analysis of spontaneous study strategies. *Reading Research Quarterly, 25,* 147–166.—453–455, 456

Wagner, R. K., & Sternberg, R. J. (1984).   Alternative conceptions of intelligence and their implications for education. *Review of Educational Research, 54,* 179–224.—74

Wagner, R. K., & Sternberg, R. J. (1986).   Tacit knowledge and intelligence in the everyday world. In R. J. Sternberg & R. K. Wagner (Eds.), *Practical intelligence.* Cambridge, England: Cambridge University Press.—88

Wainer, H. (in press).   Understanding graphs and tables. *Educational Researcher.*—413

Walberg, H. J. (1969a).   Predicting class learning: An approach to the class as a social system. *American Educational Research Journal, 6,* 529–542.—534

Walberg, H. J. (1969b).   The social environment as a mediator of classroom learning. *Journal of Educational Psychology, 60,* 443–448.—534

Walberg, H. J. (1986).   Synthesis of research on teaching. In M. C. Wittrock (Ed.), *Handbook of research on teaching* (3d ed.). New York: Macmillan. *An organized collection of the results of many meta-analyses of research on teaching.*—332

Walberg, H. J. (1991).   Productive teaching and instruction: Assessing the knowledge base. In H. C. Waxman & H. J. Walberg (Eds.), *Effective teaching: Current research* (pp. 33–62). Berkeley, CA: McCutchan.—540

Walberg, H. J., & Anderson, G. J. (1968).   Classroom climate and individual learning. *Journal of Educational Psychology, 59,* 414–419.—534

Walberg, H. J., & Thomas, S. C. (1971).   *Characteristics of open education: Toward an operational definition* (Office of Education Title IV Contract No. OEC–1–7–062805–3936). Newton, MA: TDR Associations—486

Walker, D. F., & Schaffarzick, J. (1974).   Comparing curricula. *Review of Educational Research, 44,* 83–111.—589

Walker, J. T. (1982).   *Leave them laughing.* Sydney: Methuen.—265

Wallace, I., & Pear, J. J. (1977).   Self-control techniques of famous novelists. *Journal of Applied Behavior Analysis, 10,* 515–525.—265

Wallach, M. A., & Kogan, N. (1965).   *Modes of thinking in young children.* New York: Holt, Rinehart & Winston.—152

Waller, J. H. (1971).   Achievement and social mobility: Relationships among IQ score, education, and occupation in two generations. *Social Biology, 18,* 252–259.—84, 85 (fig.)

Walters, G. C., & Grusec, J. E. (1977).   *Punishment.* San Francisco: Freeman.—250

Ward, B. A. (1973).   *Minicourse 15: Organizing independent learning, intermediate level. Teacher's handbook.* New York: Macmillan.—459

Ward, B. A., Kelly, M. A., & Stenning, W. F. (1971).   *Minicourse 8: Organizing independent learning, primary level.* New York: Macmillan.—460

Ward, J. (1990).   "Think it possible that you might be mistaken:" A review of *The Burt Affair* by R. B. Joynson. *Educational Psychology, 10,* 255–267.—68

Weber, R. L. (1982).   *More random walks in science.* Bristol, England: Institute of Physics.—415

Wehman, P. (1981).   *Competitive employment: New horizons for severely disabled individuals.* Baltimore: Brookes.—210

Weigel, R. H., Wiser, P. L., & Cook, S. W. (1975).   The impact of cooperative learning experiences on cross-ethnic relations and attitudes. *Journal of Social Issues, 31,* 219–244.—442

Weiner, B. (Ed.). (1974). *Achievement motivation and attribution theory.* Morristown, NJ: General Learning Press.—341

Weiner, B. (1977). An attributional approach for educational psychology. In L. S. Shulman (Ed.), *Review of research in education* (Vol. 4). Itasca, IL: F. E. Peacock.—341

Weiner, B. (1986). *An attributional theory of motivation and emotion.* New York: Springer-Verlag.—338, 343

Weiner, B. (1992). Motivation. In M. Alkin (Ed.), *Encyclopedia of educational research* (6th ed.). New York: Macmillan.—352

Weiner, B., Graham, S., Taylor, S., & Meyer, W.-U. (1983). Social cognition in the classroom. *Educational Psychologist, 18,* 109–124.—342

Weiner, B., & Kukla, A. (1970). An attributional analysis of achievement motivation. *Journal of Personality and Social Psychology, 15,* 1–20.—336

Weiner, B., & Sierad, J. (1975). Misattribution for failure and the enhancement of achievement strivings. *Journal of Personality and Social Psychology, 31,* 415–421.—341

Weiss, J. (1980). Assessing nonconventional outcomes of schooling. In D. C. Berliner (Ed.), *Review of research in education* (Vol. 8). Washington, DC: American Educational Research Association.—599

Welwert, C. (1984). Read or listen? A survey of the comparative studies made during the years 1890–1980 concerning learning after auditory and visual presentation with an attempt to evaluate the results. *Didakometry, 69.* (School of Education, Malmo, Sweden)—386

Wendt, H. W. (1955). Motivation, effort and performance. In D. C. McClelland (Ed.), *Studies in motivation.* New York: Appleton-Century-Crofts.—336, 337 (fig.)

Wendt, P. R., & Butts, G. K. (1962). Audio-visual methods. *Review of Educational Research, 32,* 141–155.—413

Wesman, A. G. (1971). Writing the test item. In R. L. Thorndike (Ed.), *Educational measurement* (2d ed.). Washington, DC: American Council on Education. *Probably the most thorough treatment of the art of writing test items, especially its pitfalls and how to avoid them.*—645

Wessel, M. A. (1981). The pediatrician's perspective on corporal punishment. *Educational Comment/1981.* (College of Education and Allied Professions, University of Toledo, Toledo, OH)—515

Westbury, I. (1973). Conventional classrooms, "open" classrooms, and the technology of teaching. *Journal of Curriculum Studies, 5,* 199–221.—486, 502

Wheeler, L. R. (1942). A comparative study of the intelligence of East Tennessee mountain children. *Journal of Educational Psychology, 33,* 321–334.—85

White, M. A. (1974). Is recitation reinforcing? *Teachers College Record, 76,* 135–142.—500

Whitley, B. E., Jr., & Frieze, I. H. (1985). Children's causal attributions for success and failure in achievement settings: A meta-analysis. *Journal of Educational Psychology, 5,* 608–616.—339

Whitlock, C. (1966). Note on reading acquisition: An extension of laboratory principles. *Journal of Experimental Child Psychology, 3,* 83–85.—235

Whitmer, S. P. (1982, March). *A descriptive multimethod study of teacher judgment during the marking process.* Paper presented at the meetings of the American Educational Research Association, New York.—58

Whittaker, D. J. (1981). Attitudes towards corporal punishment amongst student teachers. *Durham & Newcastle Research Review, 9,* 13–21.—515

Why Asian students excel. (1986, August 3). *New York Times.*—94

Wiggins, G. (1989). A true test: Toward more authentic and equitable assessment. *Phi Delta Kappan, 70,* 703–713.—628, 629, 630t

Wiig, E. H. (1982). Communication disorders. In N. G. Haring (Ed.), *Exceptional children and youth* (3d ed.). Columbus, OH: Merrill.—209

Wildman, R. W., II, & Wildman, R. W. (1975). The generalization of behavior modification procedures: A review—with special emphasis on classroom application. *Psychology in the Schools, 12*(4), 432–448.—367

Willig, A. (1985). A meta-analysis of selected studies on the effectiveness of bilingual education. *Review of Educational Research, 55,* 269–317. *In a very politicized area, a researcher makes some sense out of the various aspects of bilingual education and decides in favor of it.*—134

Wilson, A. (1980). Structuring seminars: A technique to allow students to participate in the structuring of small group discussions. *Studies in Higher Education, 5,* 81–84.—426

Winne, P. H. (1979). Experiments relating teachers' use of higher cognitive questions to student achievement. *Review of Educational Research, 49,* 13–50.—541

Wittig, M. A., & Peterson, A. C. (1979). *Sex-related differences in cognitive functioning.* New York: Academic Press.—182

Wittrock, M. C. (1978). The cognitive movement in instruction. *Educational Psychologist, 13,* 15–29.—288

Wittrock, M. C. (1989). Generative processes of comprehension. *Educational Psychologist, 24,* 325–344. *A report on a series of studies with consistent results: When students have to create their own personal meaning they learn more. Learners must be cognitively active for maximum learning and retention.*—287

Wolf, M. M., Giles, D. K., & Hall, V. R. (1968). Experiments with token reinforcement in a remedial classroom. *Behavioral Research and Therapy, 6,* 51–64.—549

Wolf, R. M. (1964). The measurement of environments. In A. Anastasi (Ed.), *Testing problems in perspective: Twenty-fifth anniversary volume of topical readings from the Invitational Conference on Testing Problems* (pp. 491–503). Washington, DC: American Council on Education.—92–94

Wolf, R. M. (1979). Achievement in the United States. In H. J. Walberg (Ed.), *Educational environments and effects: Evaluation, policy, and productivity.* Berkeley, CA: McCutchan.—451

Women on Words and Images. (1972). *Dick and Jane as victims: Sex stereotyping in children's readers.* Princeton, NJ: Author, Central New Jersey Chapter of the National Organization for Women.—193

Wong, E. D. (1991). Beyond the question/nonquestion alternative in classroom discussion. *Journal of Educational Psychology, 83,* 159–162.—538

Wong, L. (1987). *Reaction to research findings: Is the feeling of obviousness warranted?* Unpublished doctoral dissertation, Stanford University, Stanford, CA.—11

Wood, B. S. (1976). *Children and communication: Verbal and nonverbal language development.* Englewood Cliffs, NJ: Prentice-Hall.—209

Wright, C. J., & Nuthall, G. (1970). Relationships between teacher behaviors and pupil achievement in three experimental elementary science lessons. *American Educational Research Journal, 7,* 477–491.—543, 544, 545, 550–551

Wyckoff, W. L. (1973). The effect of stimulus variation on learning from lecture. *Journal of Experimental Education, 41,* 85–90.—412

Yinger, R. J. (1980). A study of teacher planning. *Elementary School Journal, 80,* 107–127.—507–508

Youngs, R. C., Farmer, L., & Damm, F. (1970). The efficiency of selected instructional methods for developing independent learning. *Illinois School of Research, 6*(3), 5–15.—481

Ysseldyke, J. G., & Algozzine, B. (1990). *Introduction to special education* (2d ed.). Boston: Houghton Mifflin.—205

Zahorik, J. A. (1975). Teachers' planning models. *Educational Leadership, 33,* 134–139.—507

Zahorik, J. A. (1976). A task for curriculum research. *Educational Leadership, 34,* 487–489.—507

Zahorik, J. A. (1987). Reacting. In M. J. Dunkin (Ed.), *International encyclopedia of teaching and teacher education* (pp. 416–423). Oxford: Pergamon Press.—551

Zeigler, H. (1967). *The political life of American teachers.* Englewood Cliffs, NJ: Prentice-Hall.—432

Zellermayer, M., Salomon, G., Globerson, T., & Givon, H. (1991). Enhancing writing-related metacognitions through a computerized writing partner. *American Educational Research Journal, 28,* 373–391.—474

Zillig, M. (1928). Einstellung und Aussage. *Zeïtschrift für Psychologie, 106,* 58–106.—658

Zimmerman, B. J. (1989). A social cognitive view of self-regulated academic learning. *Journal of Educational Psychology, 81,* 329–339.—368

Zimmerman, B. J., & Kleefeld, C. F. (1977). Toward a theory of teaching: A social learning view. *Contemporary Educational Psychology, 2,* 158–171.—263

Zimmerman, B. J., & Ringle, J. (1981). Effects of model persistence and statements of confidence on children's self-efficacy and problem solving. *Journal of Educational Psychology, 73,* 485–493.—265

Zuckerman, H. (1977). *Scientific elite: Nobel laureates in the United States.* New York: Free Press.—267–268

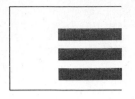

Subject Index